THE
JOYOUS WRITINGS OF
BARBARA
JOHNSON

The Inspirational Christian Library

THE
JOYOUS WRITINGS OF
BARBARA
JOHNSON

STICK A GERANIUM IN YOUR HAT
AND BE HAPPY!

SPLASHES OF JOY IN THE
CESSPOOLS OF LIFE

PACK UP YOUR GLOOMEES IN A GREAT BIG BOX,
THEN SIT ON THE LID AND LAUGH!

INSPIRATIONAL PRESS/NEW YORK

Contents

TO DAVID*

My son, who honors me by calling me his best friend. His experiences blend with mine to be a lighthouse for parents who are struggling to find some hope for their broken dreams.

*"There is hope for your future, says the Lord,
and your children shall come back
to their own country"* (Jer. 31:17, RSV).

---

* Called "Larry" in this book, as well as in *Where Does a Mother Go to Resign?* and *Fresh Elastic for Stretched-Out Moms.*

CONTENTS

---

* Ashleigh Brilliant, *Pot-Shots* No. 519, © Brilliant Enterprises 1974. Used by permission.

ACKNOWLEDGMENTS

My appreciation and thanks to the many people who have so graciously shared with me stories, poems, letters, and other materials that appear in this book. Bless you for the encouragement and joy you spread!

I have made diligent effort to locate the author and copyright ownership of all material I quote in this book; however, because I receive clippings, handwritten notes, church bulletins, etc. from friends and readers all over the world, I often have no way of identifying the original source. If any readers of this book know the correct source of items now designated "Source Unknown," I will appreciate hearing from you so corrections can be made and proper credit given.

Special acknowledgment and my sincere thanks also go to the following individuals and companies:

Ashleigh Brilliant for his permission to use Ashleigh Brilliant Epigrams, Pot-Shots, and Brilliant Thoughts (Brilliant Enterprises, 117 West Valerio St., Santa Barbara, CA 93101).

Nazarene Publishing House for permission to use "Tunnel Walking" by Robert E. Maner.

Tyndale House Publishers for permission to use poems from *Lord, I Keep Running Back to You; Lord, You Love to Say Yes;* and *Lord, It Keeps on Happening and Happening* by Ruth Harms Calkin.

Joyce Henning for permission to use the poem "He'll See Them Home."

Shannon Johnson, my daughter-in-love, for her sketches and creative suggestions that ultimately led to the drawings used in this book.

Minnie Lee Dear for permission to use her mother Pearl Waddell's poem, "I'm Fine."

—Barbara Johnson

PREFACE

Can you just "STICK A GERANIUM IN YOUR HAT" and be happy?

I know you can, no matter what happens. We all have to endure troubles in life. Sometimes we may go along for a while with just common irritations and then, WHAM! A big problem hits, and we have a real valley experience. But I believe that you grow in the valleys because that's where all the fertilizer is.

In my first book, *Where Does a Mother Go to Resign?* (Bethany Fellowship, Inc., 1979), I wrote about my own valley times: the terrible accident that left my husband blind and crippled for many months; the deaths of two sons, one in Vietnam and the other on a highway in the Yukon; and the homosexuality of another son who disappeared into the gay lifestyle for the better part of eleven years. I have learned to welcome the valley times because I have seen the growth in character that comes from them. And I have survived only by partaking of a steady diet of laughter, joy, and hope.

About four years ago, I was speaking at a Christian book-sellers function and decided to close my talk with a line from the new book I had just written entitled *Fresh Elastic for Stretched-Out Moms* (Fleming H. Revell, 1986). That line was: "Life isn't always what you want, but it's what you've got, so stick a geranium in your hat and be happy!" For some reason that thought clicked in the minds of my listeners, and they responded with a standing ovation, planting the seeds of another book to help hurting people. And here it is!

We can choose to gather to our hearts the thorns of disappointment, failure, loneliness, and dismay due to our present situation, or we can gather the flowers of God's grace, unbounding love, abiding presence, and unmatched joy. I choose to gather the flowers, and I hope you will, too. SO, FIND YOURSELF A GERANIUM AND STICK IT IN YOUR HAT! If this book helps you decide you want the flowers and not the thorns of life, I will have accomplished my purpose.

Joyfully,
Barbara Johnson

CHAPTER ONE

Pain Is Inevitable,
*But Misery Is Optional**

LOST
DOG with 3 legs,
blind in left eye, missing
right ear, tail broken and
recently castrated. Answers
to the name of "Lucky."†

After I spoke at a women's retreat recently, a darling gal rushed up to me saying, "Oh, Barb, you are just SO LUCKY! You have come through all your trials with so much joy and victory! Now you get to travel all over the country, be dressed up and meet so many famous people and enjoy being a celebrity. You have really got it all together now!"

I laughed and told the lady that I didn't believe there was any such thing as luck for Christians. Luck doesn't come into our lives, but a lot of other things do.

Look at it this way: One family out of 500,000 lost a son in Vietnam . . . we are one of those families. One family out of every 800 has a child killed by a drunk driver . . . we experienced that, too. Statistics say that one family out of every ten will have a homosexual child . . . we know all about that. And recently I became part of another set of statistics, namely

---

* The title of this chapter is an expression frequently used by Tim Hansel, but I've found it especially meaningful in my life.

† This notice once appeared on a bulletin board in a grocery store.

that out of every forty women over middle-age, one will develop adult-onset diabetes.

Diabetes—A New Experience for Me

This is something that is brand new in my life. Although it
is considered milder than juvenile-onset, it carries with it all
the life-threatening complications. I learned I had adult-onset
diabetes during a simple physical examination. Up to that
point, I had had no symptoms, no complaints, no warning
signs. My doctor was dead serious when he explained to me
the consequences of not following his orders, which seemed
ridiculous to me at first.

My orders were to avoid stress, get plenty of rest, restrict
intake of foods (eliminating all good stuff with sugar, of
course), eat several small meals a day at specific times, and
prick my finger daily to keep track of my blood glucose levels
(this lets me know if I'm maintaining good glucose control).
Then he finished by saying, "And because you're not the kind
to accept that you have a chronic, debilitating disease, you
must attend a support group for diabetic people."

"ME? ME ATTEND A SUPPORT GROUP? I *LEAD* a support
group. Why ever in the world would I *GO* to one?"

"Yes," he said, "otherwise you won't recognize the severity
of it and will neglect taking care of yourself!"

The following week found me dragging my feet as I entered
this room full of diabetic sufferers at a local hospital conference room. As I looked around, I saw about forty people, and
immediately I decided the doctor had selected the most devastated cases to present themselves that night, just for my benefit alone!

On my first visit I was considered a guest, so I didn't have
to say anything, just observe. That was good because what I
saw left me practically speechless anyway. One lady had gan-
grene and was to have her leg amputated soon. One man there
had no feeling in his legs or feet. Another lady was blind from
diabetes and also had other complications.

As the stories unfolded, it seemed that each one was more
horrible than the previous one. Every complication of diabetes

was described, and it seemed that of those present, they all had one or more of them to contend with. I could hardly wait to escape that meeting. What a hopeless group! Their future appeared bleak as they rehearsed the complications that could arise from this life-threatening disease.

The next week I was back in the doctor's office, pouring out to him how dreadful that diabetic support group was. "These people may need this, but I sure don't. Can't you tell me something GOOD to say tonight when it is my turn to share?"

"Well," he said, "having diabetes is like having carpenter ants in your body. You never know where they might attack . . . it could be the kidneys, the arteries, your vision, etc."

"That's hardly something encouraging that I could share!"

"Well, just pretend that the most upsetting relative you have has come to live with you for the rest of your life."

"That's another ZERO to share! But I have to speak at tonight's meeting, and I just have to say something positive to these poor, pitiful souls."

The doctor paused and then he smiled. "Well, knowing you, you'll think this is something good. One good thing about having diabetes is that you won't end up in a rest home because usually diabetics don't LIVE that long!"

"Oh, that's terrific news!" I said. "Who wants to end up in a rest home anyway? Besides, my husband, Bill, has just taken out some insurance with the American Association of Retired Persons which is supposed to cover any needs for a rest home. Now I can cancel my portion!"

I went home and joyfully instructed Bill to cancel my portion of that AARP rest home policy and then headed out for the hospital support group for the diabetics meeting.

There they sat, just as they had done the week before. No one had grown a new leg, and no miracles had happened since the last meeting. All of them just sat there in a circle, pouring out new complaints and new pains.

Finally it got to be my turn. I started out with my name and that I was only at this meeting because my doctor said I HAD to come to at least two meetings, but I wouldn't be back after this one.

"My doctor told me recently that I have adult-onset diabetes and warned me about all the complications that go along with it unless I take proper care of myself. And even then I have no guarantee I'll escape them. But I was back to see him today, and he gave me some really terrific news!"

Every face in the group sort of brightened up, and I continued, "The doctor told me I don't have to worry about winding up in a rest home because diabetics usually don't live that long!"

At this point, I could see that they were about to fall off their chairs, but I had to continue telling them how exciting it is for me to know that as a Christian I have an ENDLESS HOPE, not a HOPELESS END. It seemed that the Lord wrapped me in so much love for these folks that it just poured out of me. I told them that my exit from earth would be my grandest entrance in heaven and that earth has no sorrow heaven cannot heal. My joy is in knowing that my future is in God's hands and that heaven is closer to me than long life in some rest home.

There Is Only One Thing You Can Control

I said a lot more, but the main thrust was that I chose to look at what seemed *good* to me rather than to anticipate all the gruesome complications that can happen at some point. Afterwards, many in the group asked me questions about my ideas on life because, evidently, no one had shared anything encouraging with them before. I told them that pain is inevitable for all of us, but that we have an option as to how we react to the pain. It is no fun to suffer; in fact, it can be awful. We are all going to have pain, but *misery is optional.* We can decide how we will react to the pain that inevitably comes to us all.

Since learning that I have diabetes, I have read a dozen books and even watched some video tapes to learn all I could about how to cope with this chronic, debilitating disease. The most important thing I learned is that having a proper mental attitude works wonders. If you take care of yourself and do all the things that you must do to keep it in control so that it doesn't control you, you can live a happy, productive life.

I didn't want this disease, and I surely empathize with others who have endured it for many years, but I choose to do all I can to care for myself and enjoy each day that I am here. I constantly remind myself:

THE ONLY THING YOU CAN REALLY CONTROL
IN THIS LIFE IS YOUR OWN MENTAL ATTITUDE.

Recently I was in Sacramento speaking for a women's retreat, and a cheerful, perky gal in a wheelchair volunteered to help me at the book table. Her name was Mary Jane. She only had one leg, and I wondered if diabetes might have claimed the other one. But she just whirled around in that wheelchair, getting change and doing a fabulous job of handling customers who wanted to buy my books.

We talked later, and Mary Jane told me that her leg had been amputated because of cancer. Then she began to laugh and told me that for years her doctor had been after her to lose weight. He had put her on diets, which were always unsuccessful, and when she finally went in for the leg amputation, she said from the operating table, "Now you be sure to weigh the leg so that you can remove that amount of weight from my chart!"

What an attitude! Her pain is inevitable, but she chooses to make her option something *other* than misery!

So does a man I met at the La Habra post office. You'll be reading a lot about that place because it seems I spend a lot of my life there. My license plate says SPATULA, and the other day when I pulled in to park at the post office, I noticed the plate on the car next to me said: "2 BUM NEZ." I thought, *That's so cute — the guy probably has arthritis or something.*

As I tore around the car with my arms full of tapes and books to mail, I called out, "Oh, I just LOVE your license plate!" Suddenly I saw that he didn't have any legs! Talk about hoof-and-mouth disease! Someone was helping him out of the car, but he put me at ease by saying, "I'm glad you like it. My wife said I should get one that said, "NO LEGS," but I would rather have folks get a chuckle out of it like you did than have them feel sorry for me."

Bill and I See Life Differently

I love that man's attitude because it illustrates so beautifully how pain is inevitable, but misery is optional. We cannot escape having pain in this life, but our choice is in how we react to it. For years I've been trying to convince Bill, my darling but melancholy husband, that how you look at life can either bring a sparkle of joy or a handful of gloom.

Recently we had car trouble and had to be towed from San Diego to our home, a distance of nearly 100 miles at a cost of about one dollar per mile. I had never even been in a tow truck before, and it was really fun sitting up so high and looking down at all the little cars whirring by. Being up so high, I could see everything perfectly, even our car attached behind. But Bill didn't think it was fun at all. He didn't think it was an adventure. He didn't think there was anything cheery about it.

Trying to lift his dark and depressing mood, I chirped loudly, "But think of all the gasoline we are saving!" For me, it was a new, fun experience. We probably would never ride that far in a tow truck again, so why not enjoy ourselves since we had to be doing it anyway? But Bill didn't see it that way. We often view life differently, Bill seeing the glass half empty while I see it brim full and running over.

One thing I love about Bill is that he always lets me be myself. In chapter eight, I'll explain how God put our personalities together to balance each other and to be a smoothly working team. Bill's steady, organized ways do much to make our ministry a success!

Twenty Dollars for Two Maple Bars?

A few years back—before diabetes and *really* having to watch my diet—Bill and I decided to work on our mutual weight problem by walking. So, at night we would walk to the Baskin-Robbins ice cream shop to have an ice cream cone night cap. And in the mornings we would walk to the Yum Yum Donut shop for our usual hot coffee and warm maple bars. On one particular morning, we had made it to Yum Yum's in record time, and I reached in my sweater pocket for the twenty dollar bill I had brought along. Bill didn't have his wallet with him, and I had left my purse at home because heavy purses aren't much good on brisk walks.

We ordered our usual, and when the girl brought it, I plunked my twenty down on the counter. She took my money and disappeared to the back room to get cream and more napkins. When she returned, she asked for two dollars and fifty cents. She didn't speak very distinct English, but she made it clear she expected money. And I told her she had just picked up my twenty dollar bill when she had gone out back for more cream.

It didn't make any difference. All she could keep saying was that we owed her two dollars and fifty cents, and she didn't seem to "understand" about the strange disappearance of my twenty dollar bill! By this time, people were coming in the door and standing in line, all waiting to order their coffee and donuts. Bill was getting annoyed with all this fumbling around and tried to come to my aid. After all, he had *seen* the girl pick up the twenty dollar bill I'd laid down. So had another lady who had been sitting near by.

I thought, *Who do you call at a time like this?* Bill suggested cleaning out the cash register and PROVING she had taken our money. I also thought of calling the police but decided against it. They might not believe us, and we couldn't prove we put the money on the counter.

Very much embarrassed, we took the coffee and maple bars to a little table and sat down. I began planning on how we could leave if she still insisted we owed her money. We had no more money with us. And what if she called the police and said we couldn't pay her for what we ordered? Bill already had taken a bite out of his maple bar, and we couldn't return it . . .

I tried to appear unobtrusive, glancing at a newspaper lying on the seat next to me and reading the signs on the window, but Bill kept muttering loudly, saying things like, "This is the most expensive donut and coffee I've ever had—TWENTY DOLLARS FOR TWO MAPLE BARS AND COFFEE!"

We finished our maple bars and coffee and left without the girl trying to stop us. Bill kept yakking about it as we walked back home, wanting ME to call the main office of the Yum Yum Donut Shops and complain that they had taken our money. All the way back he fumed about paying twenty dollars for our small order. Suddenly I remembered that several years ago, in front of our church, I had FOUND a twenty dollar bill.

"Hey, Bill, remember when I found that twenty dollar bill a few years ago by our church?"

Bill didn't remember. But I told him, "Why not look at it this way? That was the same twenty dollar bill we lost today, so really we got the maple bars and coffee for FREE!"

Bill looked at me as if I were someone from outer space and continued being depressed about losing that much money. For a couple of weeks, his irritation over the whole episode left a heavy cloud over everything.

With his melancholy temperament, he harbored ill feelings. He didn't want to go back to the Yum Yum Donut Shop and preferred nourishing the idea that he had been done wrong. But I had decided I had more enjoyable things to do than worry about a lost twenty dollar bill, especially since, the way I looked at it, we really got the maple bars for free!

It Depends on How You Look at It

Now, I can't be sure of all the spiritual significance of the Yum Yum Donut Shop story, except to remember that the Apostle Paul also believed that having joy or misery all depends on how you look at it. His advice was, "Whatever is true, whatever is noble, whatever is right, whatever is pure, whatever is lovely, whatever is admirable—if anything is excellent or praiseworthy—think about such things" (Phil. 4:8, NIV). And that's exactly what I did about the twenty dollar bill. I thought our experience was praiseworthy, but Bill felt we had been gypped out of our money.

So, it is all in how we choose to look at the circumstances. We can look for the flowers or the weeds. We can see the bright side or look for the clouds. Remember:

YOU CAN BE AS HAPPY AS YOU DECIDE TO BE.

How you look at things really can make the difference in setting the mood for the day. I found the following little story (source unknown) and put it in my newsletter, *The Love Line*, to help people see how they can enjoy their day, their week, and their year, even in the midst of tragedy.

The day had started out rotten. I overslept and was late for work. Everything that happened at the office contributed to my nervous frenzy. By the time I reached the bus stop for my homeward trip, my stomach was one big knot.

As usual, the bus was late—and jammed. I had to stand in the aisle. As the lurching vehicle pulled me in all directions, my gloom deepened.

Then I heard a deep voice from up front boom, "Beautiful day, isn't it?" Because of the crowd I could not see the man, but I could hear him as he continued to comment on the spring scenery, calling attention to each approaching landmark. This church. That park. This cemetery. That firehouse. Soon all the passengers were gazing out the windows. The man's enthusiasm was so contagious I found myself smiling for the first time that day.

We reached my stop. Maneuvering toward the door, I got a look at our "guide": a plump figure with a black beard, wearing dark glasses and carrying a thin white cane. Incredible! He was blind!

I stepped off the bus and, suddenly, all my built-up tensions drained away. God in His wisdom had sent a blind man to help me see—see that, though there are times when things go wrong, when all seems dark and dreary, it is still a beautiful world. Humming a tune, I raced up the steps to my apartment. I couldn't wait to greet my husband with "Beautiful day, isn't it?"

You Can Always Get a Fresh Start

I think every day should be a beautiful day—a fresh start. When I speak in seminars and workshops, I often take along a box of FRESH START soap as a visual aid to emphasize this point. At home I use FRESH START to wash clothes and JOY to wash dishes. They both remind me that you can always find joy in a new beginning. When I wash clothes in the morning, I say, "Thank you, Lord, for a fresh start—a day that isn't even messed up yet and a new beginning." I can even enjoy doing the laundry because I think about getting a fresh start.

I've never met Patricia Liba, but something she wrote about "The New Day" sums up exactly how I feel:

> I woke up this morning to overcast skies, but the day was new . . . *a never-been-lived-before kind of day.* I took my shower and counted my blessings for the little things, like plenty of hot water and a brand new bar of soap. As I hummed an unrecognizable tune, I remembered how much I enjoyed and absorbed that old western movie last night, while munching on popcorn. I let my mind ramble further as I shampooed my hair and thought about our cozy, small, old home that contains just about every wonderful memory-maker ever known. No unpleasant memories here, although many of my possessions once belonged to now-gone loved ones. These knickknacks give my life fuller meaning and their comfort and continuity stay with me as I go about my daily chores. I smiled to myself and I shut the water off, glad that once dried off and dressed, I would be . . . stepping briskly and happily into my *never-been-lived-before* day.
>
> —Reprinted from *Sunshine Magazine*

I think of Pat's words every time I take a shower in the morning. I use Dove soap and think of how the Holy Spirit cleanses us and refreshes us, making us clean inside and out. I'm looking at a new day—a day that nobody has messed up yet. Nothing has happened, and it's a whole brand new day that I can enjoy. It's a day that hasn't been lived in, but I'm going to live it with gusto. I love the little sign on the desk of my friend who works at a mortuary:

ANY DAY ABOVE GROUND
IS A GOOD ONE!

I don't have all the answers to life, but I know Someone who does. I want to live as though Christ died yesterday, rose today, and is coming tomorrow.

Am I a Little Too Joyful?

Sometimes I meet people who think I'm a little too joyful—
that I'm ducking reality and ignoring the painful facts of life.
But I simply tell them I'm not ignoring the facts—I'm just
looking at them and trying to find joy, not misery.

We all know there are 365 days in a year, but I believe there
are only three days we should be concerned about dealing
with correctly. And two of those days we can do nothing
about—yesterday and tomorrow. Yesterday is a canceled
check, and tomorrow is a promissory note. But today is cash,
ready for us to spend in living, and that's why I say wake up
and rejoice and take advantage of the FRESH START. There
are no mistakes, nothing has happened, and nobody has
goofed it up—we've got today! We've got another chance!

Now if you can go through a few days like that, pretty soon
you've got a week and maybe even a month when you have
rejoiced over every new day and not worried about the past.
And if you're trusting in Christ, you surely don't have to
worry about the future. I like the Bible's advice to "Be beautiful inside, in your hearts, with the lasting charm of a gentle
and quiet spirit which is so precious to God" (1 Pet. 3:4, TLB).

That reminds me of a letter I got from a fantastic woman
who has been through one of the longest periods of suffering
I have ever known. She wrote a note to encourage me because
she knows my story is ongoing, just as hers is. In her note, she
said something I hope every reader of this book can grasp,
learn, remember, and recall on those days when you feel
drained and spent . . . completely washed out . . . when
you think you cannot go on another day . . . when you want
to resign and don't know where to go . . . when you really
want to hang it all up and forget the whole thing. On days like
that, remember this:

WE CANNOT LET OUR BURDENS
PARALYZE OUR PROGRESS.

How easy it is to just freeze with our finger on the panic
button, trapped in our grief and heartache, unable to help

anyone, even ourselves. So many of my phone calls reflect the paralysis that engulfs parents who are hurting when they first learn their kids are into drugs, the homosexual lifestyle, or some other mess. They are in the shock stage. The trauma is devastating. The hurt is such as they have never known. The pain is intense; they are fractured inside and think they will never be a complete person again. It is a "Humpty Dumpty" feeling, which they may have to learn to live with for a while.

Perhaps you, too, are going through this kind of experience. There are no pat answers, no simple ways to ease the pain, but *never let your burdens paralyze your progress.* Yes, you're hurting, along with hundreds and thousands of others who are hurting also. But progress will come to you as you reach out from under your load and try to lift the load of someone else. Try doing something for another person who also is straining with her burden. Love your way out of that paralyzed state, thaw the panic-button situation, and don't be immobilized any longer by your own burdens.

And that's why I'm writing this book. I've already referred to the tragedies that I believe give me the credentials to share with you. I tell that story in my first book, *Where Does a Mother Go to Resign?* (Bethany House, 1979). I'll repeat it in abbreviated form in the next two chapters, sharing some things that I didn't get into the first book, and giving some insights on what I've learned and keep learning as my husband, Bill, and I operate SPATULA, a special ministry designed to help scrape parents off the ceiling when they learn that they have a homosexual child or face some other broken dream in their family. The mailing list for our newsletter, *The Love Line,* that goes to these parents numbers in the thousands, and I also try to speak wherever I can—in person or on TV or radio—to help encourage parents who are in real pain because their kids have disappointed them.

Life Gives You No Time to Rehearse

Once when I was talking with Al Sanders on one of his "Vox Pop" radio broadcasts, he quoted something from Ashleigh Brilliant that I often say: "My life is a performance for which I was never given any chance to rehearse."* Then he asked, "Why do you say that?"

I told him this: "Suddenly life has happened. I didn't have any chance to prepare for the four tragedies that hit our family over a period of nine years. But I believe that when I talk to you now, I have credentials because I've been in the pits. I've been through the tragedies, but now I've got a lot of joy. I want to inject that joy and humor and hope into the people who are listening."

Every day is so precious, we have no time to waste. Some days may bring pain, but we always have a choice between misery and joy. The secret is to live one day at a time and to make the right choices as you go along. Ralph Waldo Emerson was a wise thinker, and one of the best pieces of advice he ever gave the world was this:

> Finish every day and be done with it. You have done what you could. Some blunders and absurdities no doubt have crept in; forget them as soon as you can. Tomorrow is a new day; begin it well and serenely and with too high a spirit to be cumbered with your old nonsense. This day is all that is good and fair. It is too dear, with its hopes and invitations, to waste a moment on yesterdays.

A few weeks ago I was chatting on the phone with Dr. Walter Martin about some problems I was having getting books sent to Canada where I was to speak at a Bible conference. I had been in his Bible class for years, and he had written the introduction to my first book, *Where Does a Mother Go to Resign?* Over the years his tapes have also been such an encouragement to me. He gave me some pointers about how to solve the book-shipment problem, and then, since I knew he had diabetes, I shared with him that I, too, had been diagnosed as having diabetes. When I joked about our probably never having to end up in a rest home, he laughed and said, "That being the case, perhaps I should sell my interest in a rest home back East." We laughed some more, and I told him about this very book, which I was in the process of writing.

---

* Ashleigh Brilliant, *Pot-Shots* No. 1318, © Brilliant Enterprises 1977. Used by permission.

Ten days after our phone conversation, Dr. Walter Martin was singing praises around the throne of God. A sudden, unexplained heart attack and he was gone! Life is so fragile for all of us. How important to make decisions that count for eternity! Eternity is waiting for all of us, but if we can accept the pain that comes in this life and choose to react positively, we can avoid misery. We always have the option to choose JOY!

Extra Thoughts to Take Along

THE PIT

A man fell into a pit and couldn't get himself out.

A SUBJECTIVE person came along and said:
  "I feel for you, down there."

An OBJECTIVE person came along and said:
  "It's logical that someone would fall down there."

A PHARISEE said:
  "Only bad people fall into a pit."

A MATHEMATICIAN
  calculated how he fell into the pit.

A NEWS REPORTER
  wanted the exclusive story on his pit.

A FUNDAMENTALIST said:
  "You deserve your pit."

An I.R.S. man
  asked if he was paying taxes on the pit.

A SELF-PITYING person said:
  "You haven't seen anything until you've seen MY PIT!"

A CHARISMATIC said:
  "Just confess that you're not in a pit."

An OPTIMIST said:
  "Things could be worse."

A PESSIMIST said:
  "Things will get worse!"

JESUS, seeing the man, took him by the hand and LIFTED HIM OUT of the pit.

—Source Unknown

* * * * * *

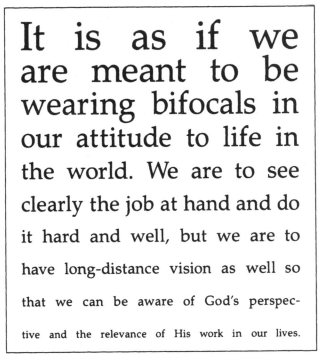

It is as if we are meant to be wearing bifocals in our attitude to life in the world. We are to see clearly the job at hand and do it hard and well, but we are to have long-distance vision as well so that we can be aware of God's perspective and the relevance of His work in our lives.

—From an Ophthalmologist's Newsletter

* * * * * *

RESOLUTIONS FOR AVOIDING MISERY

Choose to love—rather than hate
Choose to smile—rather than frown
Choose to build—rather than destroy
Choose to persevere—rather than quit
Choose to praise—rather than gossip
Choose to heal—rather than wound
Choose to give—rather than grasp
Choose to act—rather than delay
Choose to forgive—rather than curse
Choose to pray—rather than despair.

—Source Unknown

* * * * * *

DON'T FORGET

Life is about 10 percent how you make it . . .
And 90 percent how you take it.

CHAPTER TWO

I Can Handle Any Crisis—
I'm a Mother

Most of us mothers don't feel we deserve all the flowery verses and accolades that come to us on Mother's Day, but we know that this day is meaningful to our families. In the month of May, *The Love Line* newsletter is dedicated to moms, reminding them that:

> IF IT WAS GOING TO BE EASY TO RAISE KIDS,
> IT NEVER WOULD HAVE STARTED
> WITH SOMETHING CALLED LABOR.
>
> —Source Unknown

But that's what motherhood is—a labor of love. One of my favorite stories (and I have no idea where it came from originally) talks about how a mother's love outlasts everything. It seems an angel slipped out of heaven and spent the day roaming around the earth. As the sun was setting, he decided he wanted to take along some mementos of his visit. He noticed some lovely roses in a flower garden, plucked the rarest and most beautiful, and made a bouquet to take back to heaven.

Looking on a bit farther, he saw a beautiful little baby smiling into its mother's face. The baby's smile was even prettier than the bouquet of roses, so he took that, too. He was about to leave when he saw the mother's love pouring out like a gushing river toward the little baby in the cradle, and he said to himself, "Oh, that mother's love is the prettiest thing I have seen on earth; I will carry that, too."

He winged his way back to heaven, but just outside the pearly gates he decided to examine his mementos to see how well they had made the trip. The flowers had withered, the baby's smile had faded, but the mother's love was still there in all its warmth and beauty. He discarded the withered flowers and the faded smile, gathered all the hosts of heaven around him, and said, "Here's the only thing I found on earth that would keep its beauty all the way to heaven—it is a mother's love."

I like that story because it symbolizes so much of what being a mom has been like for me. The roses and the baby's smile remind me of a little poem I once heard that talks about "Saying It with Flowers":

> A rose can say I love you
> Orchids can enthrall
> But a weed bouquet in a chubby fist
> Oh my, that says it all!

Those chubby fists full of weeds and shy little smiles gave me some great Mother's Days, but later the bouquets and smiles faded. My love for my family had to absorb unbelievable pain and sorrow. Four tragedies hit us within a period of nine years, and any one of them could have been enough to sink the "Unsinkable Molly Brown."

"Your Husband Will Be a Vegetable"

The first blow came in 1966 when Bill and I were to be counselors for our church young people's group at a conference ground in the San Gabriel Mountains. Bill went on ahead that night, taking up supplies, and I planned to follow in my car after picking up a few last-minute items. Our two older boys, Steve and Tim, were going to the camp on the bus with their youth group, while Larry and Barney, our two younger boys, rode with me. So off we went on our great adventure.

The dark mountain road hadn't been used during the winter months, but it had been opened specifically for our church group to caravan up for a pre-Easter retreat. About ten miles from the conference grounds, I came upon a man sprawled in the middle of the road, covered with blood and glass. The only way I could tell it was Bill was by his clothes. I knew other cars would be coming along soon after me, so I left one of the children to stay with Bill in the road while I drove ten miles farther to camp to get to a telephone and call an ambulance.

It took almost two hours to get Bill to a hospital, but somehow he lived despite head injuries that left part of his brain exposed. Apparently Bill's car had hit some debris in the road and flipped over.

The events of the next couple of days are blurred for me, but I do remember a neurosurgeon and ophthalmologist calling me to their office to explain Bill's condition. The cranial nerves had been damaged, his vision was gone, and he was having seizures called "traumatic epilepsy." It was their opinion that he would never be able to function again within the family unit because he would be like a vegetable—without vision and without memory.

I couldn't believe it. Two days before we had been a happy family with four nice sons and no problems that I knew of. Now I was suddenly responsible for caring for four boys— two teen-agers and two under twelve.

When Bill was released from our local hospital, he couldn't see and didn't respond to any of us. In fact, he hardly moved, and it seemed the doctors had been right—he would be like a vegetable.

I knew I had to initiate getting some financial help, so I called in a friend to come and stay with Bill while I went out to get us on any available programs. First, I went to the office of Aid for the Blind; they gave Bill a free white cane. That was a start. Then I began seeking help in earnest from the Veterans Administration because Bill had been a lieutenant commander in the Navy and would be eligible for benefits. I was told that he would have to be examined by their medical staff to determine his level of disability.

A few days later, I brought Bill in with me. When the Veterans Administration medical committee examined him and his medical records, they agreed with the other doctors that he could never function normally again. They told me that as soon as a bed opened up in the Sawtelle Veterans Hospital, he would be qualified to live there. I didn't tell them that that wasn't what I had in mind at all.

Next I contacted the Social Security office to initiate disability payments for Bill, as well as aid for our four boys and myself. After making more visits to the Veterans Administration and Social Security to finalize payments, I also filed insurance claims because Bill had been ruled as permanently disabled. Because we had a CalVet loan, the mortgage on the house was completely taken care of. And our life insurance policy, which had a clause covering bodily injury, paid Bill $20,000 for his loss of vision—$10,000 for each eye. As far as the insurance company was concerned, Bill would be blind for life, and he was due the full amount.

All this took time and energy. It was a challenge just learning how to get on or collect from these agencies. Just as I finished obtaining help from the Veterans Administration, Social Security Disability, Aid to the Blind, and our insurance policies . . . GOD HEALED HIM! It wasn't an immediate healing, but during all those months while I was out trying to find financial help, Bill slowly regained his strength, and his sight miraculously returned, as well as his mental faculties. One of the first signs that something good was happening was that Bill started asking me questions like, "Who are you? Do you work here?"

Bill's recovery was so complete that he started to consider going back to work. Here I had all these lovely checks flowing in regularly, and now I had to figure out a way to GET OFF all these programs! There were moments when I wondered why God couldn't have healed Bill *before* I had done all that work. If you think it's hard getting ON these programs, you should try getting OFF! You don't just call the Veterans Administration and say, "Hello, remember my husband—the one you ruled as unrehabilitatable? Well, he is no longer blind, his brain damage is gone, he is suffering no more seizures, and he is going back to work as an engineer."

The Veterans Administration told me to bring Bill back to their offices and their doctors would decide whether or not he was to be taken off disability. Our doctor went with us, and when Bill was examined by Veterans Administration doctors, they could hardly believe he was the same patient they had declared unrehabilitatable just a year before. Our doctor, a vibrant Christian man, tried to explain that Bill's restoration had been God's touch on his life, something not easily understood by those who have not experienced God's healing hand.

One agency that didn't give Bill clearance was the Department of Motor Vehicles. It seems they take a dim view of giving you back your driver's license when you've been blind and had brain damage, seizures, and the like. When Bill went back to work, I had to drive him both ways every day because no one at the DMV wanted to give him a driver's road test so he could get a license.

Bill wasn't able to get his driver's license reinstated for many months and, while driving him was a chore, our lives were beginning to seem more normal. We felt that God is the one who specializes in taking broken bodies and fractured minds and putting them back together again. The word *restore* means "to pop back into place," and God had, indeed, brought restoration in those two years since the accident in 1966.

And Then Steve Marched Off to Vietnam

While Bill was mending, the Vietnam War shifted into high gear and our second son, Steve, who was seventeen at the time and a senior in high school, got restless. Many of his buddies had already joined the Marines, and he wanted to follow them. He disliked studying and school was a pain to him. With reluctance, I signed the papers that allowed him to enter the U.S. Marines just a few months before his eighteenth birthday. Steve was a Christian, and that was my comfort as he went off to training. When he enlisted, we thought the Vietnam thing was winding down, but by the time he finished basic training, it was full-blown, and he told us he would be shipped to Vietnam in March 1968.

I remember driving alone with Steve to Camp Pendleton the day he left. It was St. Patrick's Day, and we stopped for lunch at a place that was all decorated for the holiday. Normally, I would have enjoyed all the frivolity, but I was quiet and without much laughter.

We were early in arriving, so we had time to drive up a steep road that leads to a fabulous church in San Clemente, near Camp Pendleton. It has a spectacular view of the ocean, and although it was a dismal day with low clouds and fog, I have some indelible memories of our standing there by the church, looking out at the thrashing ocean below the cliffs. We prayed together there by the church, and then we slowly made the final lap of our trip to the Marine base.

In my mind, I have a memory video of Steve swinging his green Marine duffel bag over his shoulder . . . turning and waving . . . and then disappearing beyond the chain link gates of Camp Pendleton.

His frequent letters from Vietnam reflected the spiritual growth that had surfaced in his life. When you are a Christian and your buddies are dropping all around you in battle, all you have left is your faith in God.

Although he was killed on July 28, 1968, it was not until three days later that a car marked "U.S. Marines" drove up to our home. Two young Marines in full dress uniforms came to the door to tell us that Steve and his entire platoon had been wiped out in a battle near Da Nang.

When a loved one is in a dangerous situation, as Steve was, you live with constant apprehension and fear, but somehow, when it finally happens, it is like a "lifting"—that something is over. Indeed, life was over for Steve.

About ten days later, a call came from a mortuary near us, and a man's voice said, "Mrs. Johnson, you'll have to come up here and identify Steven's body because whenever a person dies in a foreign country, the law says that the body has to be identified."

Because Bill wasn't even driving a car yet, I decided he should be spared this gruesome situation, and I went by myself to the mortuary on a 100-degree-plus day in August.

I was ushered into a viewing room by a little man dressed in a dark suit, who stood waiting as I looked into the hermetically sealed box and tried to determine if the brown bloated face before me belonged to my son. He had lain facedown in a rice paddy for two days before being found. All they showed was the top half—I couldn't even be sure there was anything left of him below the belt. The little man kept standing there, and finally I decided that it must be Steve. I signed the little paper that said, in effect, "This boy belongs to this box."

As I walked out of that mortuary, I thought, *By now we've surely had the cup of suffering. Bill is back to normal—well, almost. He still watches old John Wayne movies over and over and doesn't think he has seen them before, and he forgets birthdays and anniversaries . . . but I guess lots of men do that . . . and now we've lost this beautiful son who is our deposit in heaven.*

Steven's memorial service included the congregation singing "Safe in the Arms of Jesus," which was the song our church sang when he left to go to Vietnam. We had a little brochure printed with Steve's picture on the front, the message from his memorial service inside, and the plan of salvation on the back. And we began to share with other families who had lost sons in Vietnam. It was possible to obtain names from *The Los Angeles Times,* which printed a list each day of young men killed in action in Vietnam. We sent Steve's brochure to these families, feeling it was an opportunity to share our conviction that, as Christians, we have an endless hope because we know Jesus Christ.

Tim Called from the Yukon—Collect

The next five years went by quickly. The war in Vietnam finally ended, and we began to have closure in our healing from the loss of Steven.

Tim, our oldest son, was twenty-three. He had finished college and then graduated from the Los Angeles Police Academy in June 1973. He and his friend, Ron, had decided to take an extended vacation, so they drove to Alaska, where they planned to stay a few weeks, make a little money doing some temporary summer work, and then return home in early August to get ready to carry out their fall schedules.

I must tell you that, although Tim was a handsome and darling young man, he wasn't what I would call a lot of fun. That he worked during college at Rose Hills Mortuary tells you an awful lot. His idea of fun—and this was the epitome of fun for Tim—was to bring home the bows from mortuary bouquets and decorate our two dogs and cat with them. These bows had messages like, "May he rest in peace," or "God bless Grandpa Hiram." Whenever I came home and found the family pets all decked out in funeral ribbons, I knew Tim was "having fun" again.

After Tim arrived in Alaska, he wrote about his new friends and also mentioned that he had been baptized. This sort of hurt my feelings because he had already been baptized in our church, and I thought we had good water there, but I sensed some new spiritual dimensions in Tim's letters, unlike the boy we had known at home.

On August 1, 1973, I got a collect call from Tim. Now, I have always enjoyed having a new month. I change the sheets, take a bath, have my hair done, and we do something special to have FUN on the first of every new month. Of course, I do this at other times, too, but I always make the first a special celebration.

Tim's first question was, "What are you doing, Mom, to celebrate the first of the month today?"

My quick response was, "Well, I was just HOPING for a collect call from you."

Tim went on to say, "Ron and I are on the way home. We should be there in about five days, and I can't wait to tell you what the Lord has done in my life. I've got a sparkle in my eye and a spring in my step, and I know the Lord is going to use my story all over."

I couldn't help but notice that Tim had an air of excitement in his voice; it was different from the conservative, well-modulated tone which was so familiar to me—one which seldom had shown much enthusiasm about anything. How exciting to think he would be home in five days to share with us all what had happened to change a quiet, sedate young man of twenty-three into an exciting, turned-on Christian.

Tim's call came around noon, and after we hung up, I started thinking of all of my efforts to get him entrenched in Christian activities. Once I had even bribed him with a new set of tires to get him to go to a Campus Crusade conference. But no matter what we did, Tim never took notes or seemed to act interested. He would just go with the flow, but would never get turned-on or excited . . . until NOW!

That night at dinner I was telling Bill and the other two boys, Larry and Barney, about Tim's phone call a few hours earlier. We were all laughing and enjoying what Tim had said, when the telephone rang. It was an officer of the Royal Canadian Mounted Police calling from White Horse, Yukon. It was hard to hear everything he was saying, but as the words came over the static-filled line, they came out like this: DRUNK BOYS IN A THREE-TON TRUCK . . . CROSSED THE CENTER LINE . . . HIT TIM'S LITTLE VOLKSWAGEN HEAD ON . . . TIM AND HIS FRIEND, RON, WERE KILLED . . . INSTRUCTIONS NEEDED FROM YOU AS TO HOW YOU WANT BURIAL PLANS MADE.

Tim and Ron had been immediately ushered into the presence of God! Stunned, I thought, *But this can't BE! I was just talking to him a few hours ago, and he was on the way home to share his story with us. He was to be home in five days! This can't be! I already have ONE deposit in heaven. I don't need TWO! Tim is our firstborn, a special gift. It just isn't FAIR!*

I lashed out at how this could happen to us . . . *again!* Hadn't we had enough? How could God let this happen when Tim was so thrilled about coming home to tell us of his exciting spiritual experience?

A few hours later, we got a call from the pastor of the church in Alaska where Tim had been attending during the summer. He said, "We're not going to let those boys' story die in the Yukon. We want to bring some folks down to share what really happened in their lives."

I thanked him and told him I would let him know the date of Tim's memorial service. Grief-stricken as I was, his offer to share with us was comforting. Later at the memorial service he told what had changed this dull, conservative boy into a sparkling, shining personality so turned-on to spiritual things. Tim had rededicated his life to the Lord and his friend Ron had become a Christian.

Our local newspaper published the story about the accident, including pictures with the heading: "TWO BOYS KILLED BY DRUNK DRIVER ON THE ALASKA HIGHWAY." The very next day some darling young girls dropped by to tell us how shocked they were to read of the accident. They brought along letters Tim had written to them, which they had just received. Evidently, the day before he had started for home, Tim had written to several girls he used to go with, as well as some other friends, and told them of his spiritual experience. His letter to one girl said, "Please forgive me for being such a creep. . . ." Any mother would wonder what that meant. Apparently, Tim wasn't as boring as I thought he was.

Another Call from the Mortuary

It took over a week to get Tim's body shipped down from the Yukon, and as we were preparing to have a memorial service, I received a phone call from the very same mortuary that had called five years before to the very day. The man's voice said, "Mrs. Johnson, I've never had to do this before, that is, call the same family twice, but you'll have to come up here and identify Tim's body since he was killed in a foreign country."

As I put down the phone, I remembered that Tim had been killed in the Yukon. Where was the Yukon, anyway? I had heard about Sergeant Preston and his sled dogs in the Yukon, but where actually was it? I looked at a map and saw that the Yukon is one of the territories that belongs to Canada and that, indeed, it was part of a foreign country.

I had made this trip to the mortuary five years before and thought then it would be a once-in-a-lifetime ordeal. Now I was driving there again on a hot day in August to identify another boy in another box. As I stood there in the same viewing room, jumbled thoughts raced through my mind: *This is the same dumb carpeting they had five years ago, and the same dumb wallpaper, and I am standing here next to this same little man in the dark suit, looking at ANOTHER boy in a box. I can't BELIEVE this is happening all over again!*

It all seemed the same and so familiar, as if it had happened to me in another life, or in a dream! I wondered if my whole life would involve coming to this same mortuary every five years to look at boys in boxes. When you have been hit by a truck while sitting in the front seat of a Volkswagen, there isn't a whole lot left. You look at what they show you in the plain pine box, and then you sign another little paper saying this boy is your son, Tim. But in no way does he look like the son you have had for twenty-three years.

Walking out of the mortuary that day, I could smell the fresh-cut grass and hear the crows cawing in the trees nearby. Suddenly I looked up and in the blue sky was an image of Tim's smiling face. All around him it was bright gold and white, and he was saying to me, "Don't cry, Mom, because I'm not there. I am rejoicing around the throne of God."

It was as if God had wrapped me in his special comfort blanket of love that day. I've never had anything like that happen to me before or since, but I think God knew I needed that special sparkle just then to remind me that He still loves me, that I am His child, and that He never leaves us in the midst of our pain.

We had the memorial service for the boys, and many of Tim's classmates from the Police Academy came and responded to the gospel message. Ron's parents had also accepted the Lord earlier that week. Later, articles about Tim and Ron appeared in several Christian magazines. The heading of a story in *Christian Life* said, "THEIR DEATH WAS ONLY A BEGINNING."

We began to see that, although they never made it home to share personally, Tim had been right: God was using their story all over the world to bring others to Him.

Barb, You're a Pro at This

A local pastor visited us a few days after Tim's memorial service. He knew about our previous loss with Steve and came to bring some words of comfort. His opening remark when I greeted him at the door was: "I'm not a bit worried about you, Barb, because you're a pro at this!"

A pro at what? A pro at losing another child? He probably meant that my inner strength would come from the Lord and

I would get through it, but what he said came out uncaring and unhelpful, so lacking in understanding.

In some ways, losing Tim was more difficult than losing Steve. We had some time to prepare ourselves for Steve's passing. We knew for many months he was in a danger zone and the shadow of death was always on all of us. When it happened, it was a terrific shock, but still somewhat of a relief because the terrible apprehension was over.

In many ways, Steve's death was like having a loved one die after a long time of suffering with something like cancer or AIDS. Then you have some measure of time to prepare for it, and you have already dumped part of your cup of grief during those months. By the time of the actual death, it is like a lifting from the time of suffering, and you can begin to have closure.

But in Tim's case, there was no warning of impending disaster, no signal of distress. It was only his bright, happy voice saying he would be home in five days and then, WHACK! It was all over! One moment we were anticipating his arrival with excitement, and the next we learned he was in the presence of God. It had happened so quickly that there had been no preparation, not even a thought that his life would be snuffed out.

We had many wonderful Christian friends who came to visit us and tried to be comforting. They said things like, "Isn't it wonderful that Tim is with the Lord?" Well, yes, it was wonderful, but I wanted him HOME WITH US!

Or, they would say, "How good it is that you have two other children left," and I would nod, that, yes, that was good, but I wanted TIM! I would agree on the surface with people who were quoting Scriptures to me and wanting to make themselves feel better by having me zip up my anger and distress quickly. Inside, however, I wanted to escape from all of them and their nice little platitudes. I wanted to open—to lance—the big abscess inside me. I knew the verses they were quoting and I believed them, but the raw edges of my heart were still bleeding too much. I needed to grieve.

To escape some of my "Ivory soap" Christian friends, I would drive alone at night to a dump a few miles away. I would park there and just sob, and sometimes even scream, to let out my pain. I would tell God how angry I was with these people for telling me how glad I should be that Tim was in heaven. I also told God how angry I was at Him for taking one so special and precious to me. This was my way of venting emotions that HAD to be released. God doesn't say to grieve not; instead, His Word says, ". . . that you may not grieve as others do who have no hope" (1 Thes. 4:13, RSV).

Looking back, I can see how Romans 8:28 and other verses that were quoted to me *are* all true. God *is* faithful, but the timing of these reminders was all wrong. Nice little plastic spiritual phrases don't help people unlock their grief. It is better to just put your arm around a grieving person and say, "I love you—God loves you." Beyond that, it might be best to just shove a sock in your mouth and keep quiet. Don't try to reason with people in grief to persuade them to accept their loss. When a believer dies, it IS wonderful to know that person is with God, but at the moment when those who are left behind are bruised and bleeding, the simple truth is this:

WHEN GRIEF IS THE FRESHEST,
WORDS SHOULD BE THE FEWEST.

For a couple of weeks, I went to the dump nightly to rid myself of my grief. In recent years, the dump has been closed at night because so many people were getting mugged, but I believe God protected me when I was making my trips. By going there to grieve, I was able to come back to face my Christian friends who were spouting little spiritual platitudes that didn't work for me.

How to Dump Your Cup of Grief

Recently I met a lady who sells clothing in a department store. She told me that she had experienced the loss of a child and she couldn't work or wait on people because the tears kept coming all the time. She was a Christian and yet she hadn't been able to stop grieving. I shared with her a little plan that could help her "accelerate" her emotions:

"Get some sad music tapes, the saddest you can find," I told her. "Make sure everyone is out of the house, then go to the bedroom, unplug the phone, turn on the sad music, flop on the bed and just SOB. Set a timer for thirty minutes and during that time cry and pound the pillow. Let out your feelings—VENTILATE. If you're angry at God, that's OK. He won't say, 'Off to hell with YOU.' He still loves you. But get those deep hurts out through the avenue of tears. Do that every day for thirty days and every day set your timer for one minute less. By the time thirty days have passed, you will have DUMPED a lot of your cup of grief."

Not long after I talked to her, the lady called me and said she had been taking my advice for only a week, and already she felt a lot better. She was to the point to where she could get through a whole day without the tears coming continually.

If you are experiencing difficulty in breaking open that deep abscess you have inside, perhaps this simple plan may help shorten your time of grief. There is no set amount of time to grieve that is considered proper or spiritual. But whatever time you need, "accelerating your emotions" may help you drain some of that pain and begin the road to recovery. The important thing is to have a closure time on your pain. Keep Psalm 84:5–7 ever in mind:

> Happy are those who are strong in the Lord, who want above all else to follow your steps. When they walk through the Valley of Weeping, it will become a place of springs where pools of blessing and refreshment collect after rains! They will grow constantly in strength and each of them is invited to meet with the Lord . . ." (TLB).

After Tim's memorial service in August, what helped me through the next few months was my continuing to try to help other people who had lost children. Now our ministry expanded beyond parents of Vietnam casualties, and we started talking with mothers and fathers who had lost their children in auto accidents or in other ways. I began speaking to parents' groups, telling them that the pain of losing two sons is incredible, but God's comfort blanket of love is still sufficient. I even got to the place where I could say that I was grateful for *two deposits in heaven*. We had been through dark times, and we had survived! What I didn't know was that total blackness was yet ahead of us.

Extra Thoughts to Take Along

Making the decision to have a child is momentous—it is to decide forever to have your heart go walking around outside your body.

—Elizabeth Stone, *Village Voice*

* * * * * *

THE WORLD'S GREATEST NEED

A little more kindness and a little less greed;
A little more giving and a little less need;
A little more smile and a little less frown;
A little less kicking a man when he's down;
A little more "we" and a little less "I";
A little more laughs and a little less cry;
A little more flowers on the pathway of life;
And fewer on graves at the end of the strife.

—C. Austin Miles
"A Little More and Less"*

* * * * * *

You *tolerate* my trivia,
laugh at my lunacy
and *care* when I cry.
That's what I call TLC.

—Source Unknown

MORNING WILL COME

Brokenhearted . . .
How can I bear the pain?
So many plans . . . permanently interrupted.
So many dreams . . . shattered.
Hopes . . . dashed.
All gone.
Why?
Why this?
Why us? Why me?
Helplessness . . . hopelessness . . .
Life will never be the same again.
Is it even worth living?
Where are you, God?

I'm right here beside you, my child.
Even though you may not feel my presence,
I'm holding you close under the shadow of my wings.
I will walk with you through this dark night.

Do not shrink from weeping.
I gave you tears for emotional release.
Don't try to hide your grief.
Let it become for you a source of healing,
A process of restoration,
For I have planned it so.
Those who mourn shall be blessed.
I'll be holding on to you,
Even when you feel you can't hold on to me.

Seek my face, child of mine.
Receive my promise, impossible as it may seem now,
That joy will come in the morning.
It may take much time,
But I will heal your broken heart.
I know the night seems endless,
But MORNING WILL COME.
I have promised.

—From the *Haven of Rest Newsletter*

*   *   *   *   *   *

HELP ME TO REMEMBER, LORD,
THAT NOTHING WILL HAPPEN
TODAY THAT YOU AND I CAN'T
HANDLE TOGETHER.

—Source Unknown

*   *   *   *   *

A SOFT PILLOW FOR TIRED HEARTS

And we know that in all things God works
for the good of those who love him,
who have been called according to his purpose.

—Romans 8:28, NIV

CHAPTER THREE

It's Always Darkest Just before It Goes Totally Black

EXPERIENCE *is what you get*
when you didn't get
what you wanted.

—Source Unknown

"Why me . . . why did this happen to me?"

Has anyone gotten all the way through life without asking that question at least once or twice? (For some of us, maybe twice a day!)

"Why me? Why us? Why did two young boys get taken from our family?" I asked all those questions quietly in my heart for the next two years, even as I continued going out to speak and share comfort and hope with other parents. I wanted to believe that life would get better from here on. After all, we had two sons left—Larry, twenty, and Barney, seventeen. We had much to be thankful for.

"God Has His Hand on This Boy . . ."

Larry graduated from a local two-year junior college, Friday, June 13, 1975, and it was one of the proudest nights of my life. Larry had been president of his class and president of the school choir. He had been voted the most outstanding student and had offers of several scholarships. He had also just returned from Russia where he traveled with a Christian singing group.

The pastor of one of the leading churches in Southern California was commencement speaker that night, and he also presented Larry with the Outstanding Student Award. To close the ceremonies, which were held outdoors in the college stadium, Larry led the entire audience in singing "The Battle Hymn of the Republic."

The commencement speaker talked with us afterwards and commented on all of Larry's honors by saying, "I hope you have a car with a big trunk to carry home all this glory!" I said that all we had was a Chevy, and we all laughed. Then the speaker added, "I've spoken with your son, and I know that God has His hand on this boy and will use him in a wonderful way."

Bill and I were absolutely thrilled with his words about Larry. We took all the ribbons, cups, and awards home to display on our mantle. How proud we were of Larry and of his accomplishments!

The next day I planned to pick up my sister and her husband who had been in Hawaii and were going to stop in our area for just twenty-four hours en route home to Minnesota. We wanted to make it a special event since it was the first time we had seen them since Tim's death.

We had it all arranged. I would pick them up at the L.A. airport, take them to Anaheim where we would all be staying at a motel near Disneyland, and then we would all go to the big bicentennial celebration at Disneyland that evening and enjoy the first presentation of the "Main Street Electrical Parade." Then we would stay in Anaheim, have some time together on Sunday, which was also Father's Day, and eat dinner at Knott's Berry Farm before they had to catch their plane.

Everything was in order for a fantastic time. What I didn't know was that this would be the most devastating day of my life!

As I headed out the door for the airport, someone telephoned, wanting to borrow Larry's big red Basic Youth Conflicts notebook. I went to his room and, as I lifted it out of his drawer, I saw a stack of homosexual magazines, pictures, and other stuff that I knew nothing about. There were also cassette tapes and letters from other young men. Why would Larry HAVE this? Could it be a research project at school? No, school was all over now.

I began to shake inside, but I told myself, "You have to get to the airport . . . you can't fall apart right now. There must be some logical answer as to WHY he has this stuff in his drawer."

I didn't have time to think, or question, and I couldn't collapse—at least not right now. How could we have a homosexual child? I didn't know anyone who had one, I didn't want one, and surely this could not be! Bill and I had a ministry going to help hurting parents, but not THIS kind of hurt! It would be easier to kill him and kill myself rather than face this!

I quickly grabbed two arm loads of the "stuff" and threw it in the trunk of my car. I couldn't bear to have it in my home. Last night my car trunk had been full of glory, and now it was full of garbage! I hastily wrote a note to Larry, telling him to meet us as planned at the Disneyland flagpole at 8:00 P.M. that evening. Then I added that I had found the "stuff" and that I had it with me, just in case he might be looking for it.

My hands were shaking, my heart was pounding, and suddenly I felt as if I had an elephant on my chest. In the note I also told Larry that I loved him and God loved him and that if he would PLEASE help me get through the weekend with these relatives, then we would fix it on Monday! I had always believed that God and mothers can fix anything.

Driving to the airport, I began to feel all the symptoms of panic—shortness of breath, heaving inside, and throbbing in my head. It felt as if someone had shoved a shag rug down my throat and I was gagging on it. My eyes were so full of tears I could hardly see to drive. Then my teeth seemed to start to itch! Evidently the nerve endings around my mouth were responding to the stress, but I just HAD to hold together until the relatives left the next day.

I got to the airport just in time to meet Janet and Mel as they came off the plane. Her first words were, "Boy, you look terrible. Are you sick?"

I said, "Of course not; it was just something I couldn't swallow." (Couldn't swallow was right!)

They had already been to baggage claim, and I saw that Janet had two pieces of purple luggage. Now, I knew nothing about homosexuality and even less about lesbianism, but I had heard somewhere that lesbians like purple. A crazy thought hit me: *MY SISTER IS A LESBIAN! SHE HAS PURPLE LUGGAGE! She works for the Billy Graham Association, is married to a minister, and she has PURPLE luggage! My own sister must be a lesbian because of this purple luggage!*

I Didn't Dare Open the Trunk!

When we got to my car, I became frantic trying to think of how I could avoid opening my car trunk. All of Larry's homosexual "stuff" was in there, and I had not bothered to cover it up with a blanket. Mel and Janet had brought some pineapples from Hawaii, as well as some of those dreadful leis that smell like funerals, and somehow I scrunched them and their belongings in the backseat without opening the trunk. We started for Anaheim and the motel, and I prayed I could ignore my panic symptoms and somehow stay on the road.

My mind was so shattered from finding out about Larry that it seemed as if the whole world was crashing around me. If my own son, whom I had loved and raised for twenty years, was a homosexual and my sister was a lesbian, what was left to believe in? I had heard of people who live in "la-la land," and I was definitely on the way there myself. I felt as if I had been on another planet and had just come back to visit the world. I wanted to go back to where I had come from, but there was no place to escape the weirdness of it all.

As we drove along the freeway, the crazy thoughts would not leave my tortured mind. My brother-in-law pointed out the Big "A" on the Angels' Stadium, and all I could think of was, *Oh, they're all homosexuals, they're all homosexuals!* It seemed to me that the shades had gone up and everyone had become homosexual.

We got to the motel where Janet and Mel changed into more comfortable clothes, and then we crossed the street to Disneyland. It was a special weekend, with the bicentennial celebration, the first night of the Main Street Electrical Parade scheduled, and it was also Flag Day. Instead of the usual A–B–C–D–E coupon books Disneyland uses for tickets, we were all given a red, white, and blue headband with a big feather sticking out of it. On the headband were the words "I'M A YANKEE DOODLE DANDY" in bold, bright letters. You couldn't escape wearing the headband because it was your ticket to the park that evening.

So, there I was, trying to act normal in Disneyland with what seemed like fifty thousand people around me all wearing "I'M A YANKEE DOODLE DANDY" feathered headbands. And all the while I kept wondering if everyone I saw was a homosexual!

As 8:00 P.M. drew near, we went over to the flagpole, and Bill went off to buy popcorn. Bill is loving and dependable, but it seems that any time there is a crisis, he is off buying popcorn. I tell him that when he dies, I'm going to have inscribed on his tombstone, "Bill is not here, he's out buying popcorn."

Janet, Mel, and I greeted Larry as he walked up. The last time we had all been together was at Tim's funeral, so they were really glad to see him. I wasn't sure I was, but I knew I couldn't throw up or anything—not just yet.

Then Tinker Bell Flew across the Sky!

So we all stood there at the flagpole, with a sea of Yankee Doodle humanity flowing by. Just then, one of Disneyland's special attractions came sailing across the sky. It was the Tinker Bell Fairy (suspended on a wire, of course) loudly hailing the Main Street Electrical Parade, scheduled to start in a few minutes. That only set my mind off again—the whole world was full of this homosexual stuff! Even the Tinker Bell Fairy!

Just then Janet said, "It's so crowded and hot here, I think Mel and I will go see Mr. Lincoln." The Mr. Lincoln display was only a few feet away, and so I said, "Go ahead. Larry and I have seen it many times, so go ahead." I was desperate to have a few minutes to talk with Larry and implore him to help me get through the weekend until Mel and Janet left on the plane Sunday afternoon.

And now Larry and I were alone in front of the flagpole at Disneyland with fifty thousand people surrounding us. We were both wearing the little headbands with the feathers saying, "I'M A YANKEE DOODLE DANDY." And the first thing Larry said was, "I'm a homosexual, or maybe I'm a bi-sexual."

I didn't know what to say. A bi-sexual? The word homosexual was in the Bible, but bi-sexual I'd never heard—it sounded like sex twice a month. While I was trying to figure that out, a lady came by, pushing a stroller with her chubby child in it. The stroller rammed into my foot, and a sharp edge dug into my leg and it started to bleed.

I thought, *Oh, how merciful God is. I won't have to kill him tomorrow. I won't even have to kill myself because I'm going to bleed to death right here.* I kept thinking of 1 Corinthians 10:13: God had made a way of escape so that I could bear all this. I was just going to hemorrhage right here and die right in front of the "Lost Children" sign at the Disneyland flagpole with fifty thousand people going by, all wearing headbands announcing "I'M A YANKEE DOODLE DANDY."

How wonderful—it was almost euphoric! I wouldn't have to worry about killing myself or killing him, or doing anything, and nobody would ever know. But THEN I realized that my car trunk was still full of homosexual magazines, and I couldn't die now because my husband would find all that and think they were mine. About then, Larry said he didn't feel well, that he wanted to get out of there. I thought to myself, *You're sick . . . but I'm dying! Yes, why don't you just go home, and we'll fix it tomorrow. God and mothers can fix anything . . . can't they?*

Mel and Janet emerged out of the crowd and greeted Larry enthusiastically, but all Larry could say was that he didn't feel too good because he was tired after rehearsing all day with a Christian singing group! After a few moments of polite chitchat, he excused himself and left.

Just a minute or two later, Bill returned with his popcorn, and my younger son, Barney, and his friend stopped by for a few minutes and then left because they were bored with the whole thing and wanted to head home to watch the motorcycle races on TV. (When you live as close to Disneyland as we do, it's no big deal.)

So Mel, Janet, Bill, and I wandered around Disneyland and

I kept looking at everyone and thinking that the whole world was homosexual. I saw Mickey Mouse and Minnie Mouse, and I was sure they were homosexual, too. It was as if everyone had a big "H" stamped on his forehead.

"He Can't Be; He's a Christian"

We went back to the motel for the night, and while Bill slept, I wept, moaned, and groaned in a pillow. It felt as if a bull were goring me inside. About 4:30 A.M. on Sunday, which was Father's Day, my husband finally woke up saying, "What's the matter with you?"

I gasped, "I think I'm having a heart attack. I don't know what you call it, but I think I'm dying. I can't breathe, and I'm choking. It feels as if I've got a rug in my throat and my teeth itch."

Bill said, "Well, I thought you were acting strange last night. I know something is wrong. What is it?"

"Well, I'm glad you noticed! Last night I just found out that Larry is a hooomooooo . . ." I could hardly say the words . . . "a homosexual."

Bill was aghast. "He CAN'T be; he's a Christian!"

"Well, that's what I thought. But he is. You should see what I have in my car trunk. Or maybe he's a bi-sexual, that's what he told me."

Hearing that Larry might be bi-sexual shocked Bill more than anything else. He bolted out of bed and started putting his clothes on. I said, "It's 4:30 in the morning; where are you going?"

"Why, I'm going HOME to fix him," said Bill, and he was gone.

So I lay there gasping and choking, wondering how I'd ever get through this. My husband was driving twenty-five miles back to our house to "fix his kid," and I thought, *Well, I'll just be dead when he comes back. That's all, I'll just be dead; I just can't live through this. I'll be dead when he comes back.*

About then my sister, hearing the ruckus, knocked on our door, came in, and asked anxiously, "What's wrong? Why did Bill leave?"

All I could think of was, "He went home to shave." What

else was I going to say? We had checked into a motel, paid good money, and where would my husband go at 4:30 in the morning?

"No, I know something is wrong. You had a fight with Bill, didn't you?"

If only she had been right—that would have been no problem at all! Instead, I had no choice, I would have to start Father's Day at 4:30 in the morning telling my sister that my son is a homosexual.

I stumbled out to my car and brought in a whole arm load of the homosexual magazines and threw them on the bed. Then I said, "Your *nephew* (I couldn't say 'my son') is a homosexual."

She sputtered, "He CAN'T be; he's a Christian."

There we stood, the daughters of a minister, both having led very sheltered lives while growing up. We stared at all the pictures of naked men and all the rest of that terrible stuff. We had never seen anything pornographic before. About as close as we had come to pornography was the men's underwear section of the Montgomery Ward's catalogue.

And as we stood there, frozen in shock, poring over all that garbage, in walked my brother-in-law, a very proper, godly man. He questioned what was going on because he could hear me sobbing and crying, and he thought perhaps Janet and I were having some sort of fight. And then he saw the pictures on the bed. Janet explained, "This stuff belongs to Larry—he's a homosexual."

And Mel's instant response was, "Why, he CAN'T be; he's a Christian!"

When Bill came back, we were all still in the room, looking at the magazines in bewilderment with no idea what to say. All Bill offered was, "I talked to Larry. There's nothing really wrong with him. You're just too emotional about this. It's just a phase. All kids go through a phase, and this is just a phase."

Oh, I wanted to believe that, but I knew Bill was wrong. He didn't even know what a bi-sexual was, so how did he know what was really wrong with Larry? Later, we went to church and on to Father's Day dinner at Knott's Berry Farm. It is all a blur to me, but I finally got Mel and Janet to the plane, and they went back to Minneapolis, where I was sure nobody ever had homosexual problems.

Tears blinded me as I drove home alone from the airport. Bill had taken his car and driven over to give Father's Day presents to his dad, and when I got home I found Larry there. We stood in the living room toe to toe, and it quickly escalated into a full-scale confrontation. I was sobbing bitterly and spouting Bible verses. He began to cry, too, and our conversation went in vicious circles.

I was so hysterical I could hardly make sense. Larry was exploding with anger because he had been exposed. (Later on he told me he never would have told us if I hadn't found the stuff.) I begged him to sit down and tell me how all this could be! Instead, he said violent and vicious things to me in the heat of his anger and used words I had never heard before or since from him.

I couldn't bear his accusations and obscenities. Instantly my hand shot upward and I slapped Larry's face hard. He grabbed my shoulders and pushed me full force against a grandfather clock. This was unbelievable! I was having a physical confrontation with this darling son who was the light of our home for twenty years! After shoving me against the clock, he fled to his room and slammed the door.

I heard him sobbing in his room, but my anger, denial, and guilt all kept me from going in to comfort him. COMFORT HIM? When HE was destroying our family?

In my desperate effort to make him respond, I had uttered threats and unloving things like, "I would rather have you be DEAD than be a homosexual!" At that moment I loved Larry, but I hated that part of him. I wanted to hug him, but I wanted to kill him—I was a kaleidoscope of emotional shock. It would be later that I learned that parents say all kinds of unreal things to their kids when they learn they are homosexual. In my own emotional frenzy, all I could do was quote Bible verses about homosexuality. And all the while I was also denying that this could really be happening to us.

Other parents have told me the same thing. When they learn of their child's homosexuality, they want to take them out of their will, take away the car, or do whatever they can do to control them. But that doesn't work. You just can't do it that way. This is something I had to learn. And it wasn't easy.

Devastating despair overwhelmed me, and I flung myself on my bed and sobbed for hours. Larry didn't come out of his room the rest of the day . . . no supper was fixed . . . I didn't answer the phone. I just lay there on my bed, hoping and praying that tomorrow I could find some answers. I would go to the Hot Line in Anaheim. Surely THEY would tell me how to fix this kid!

On Monday morning I went to a Hot Line organization that was supposed to offer help to homosexuals, but first I needed some help for me—someone to tell me I would get through this alive. I went in and blurted out, "I just found out that my son is a homosexual, and I want to talk to a mother who can help me."

And they said, "Well, we don't have any mothers, but we have two ex-homosexuals you can talk to."

Exasperated, I sputtered, "Forget it! I *have* one of those— that's why I'm here!"

I just turned around, stomped out and slammed the door. I didn't want to talk to any kind of homosexual, ex- or other- wise. I wanted to talk to a mother who had been through what I was going through and who could tell me I wasn't going to die. As I got in the car, I thought, *Lord, if I ever get through this—if I don't die or end up in a home for the bewildered—I promise that I'll start some kind of group to help parents who have this kind of terrible thing happen to them.* (We promise a lot when we think we're going to die anyway.)

And Then, a Final Zinger

When I got back home, one more shock awaited me. Larry's room was totally empty. I had been gone only an hour and a half, but in that time he had cleaned out everything and left. Out in the hall two little plaques hung side by side. One said, "TO THE MOST WONDERFUL FATHER OF THE YEAR." Larry had given that to Bill just the day before. The other one said, "TO THE MOST WONDERFUL MOTHER OF THE YEAR," and he'd given that to me just a month before on Mother's Day. Now he was gone, and all we had were the two plaques telling us how wonderful we were.

I called Bill at work and told him Larry was gone and that he'd taken the little Volkswagen that was registered to me because the insurance was in my name. Bill said he was sure Larry would be back, but I wondered where he would go.

I didn't know what to do. Should I go down to the DMV and tell them that my kid had taken off with a Volkswagen registered to me? Should I cancel the insurance on the car? I just didn't know what to tell people, and I wasn't sure I would survive.

How I did survive is recorded in a daily log that I included in *Where Does a Mother Go to Resign?* During the next few months, I stayed home, languishing in my bedroom, counting the roses on the wallpaper. I couldn't stand seeing anyone, and even going to the grocery store brought waves of panic. If I saw cartons of milk labeled "HOMOGENIZED," I would immediately think that even the milk had something homosexual in it.

As hard as losing Steve and then Tim was, at least I could count them as deposits in heaven. But now my third son had disappeared into the gay lifestyle, and I had no idea where he was or if I'd ever see him again.

And I couldn't tell any of my Christian friends what had happened. I felt too guilty, and besides, how could most Christians understand something as unreal as this?

So I just hid away in my bedroom, not wanting to see anyone, doing no cooking or cleaning, and very little eating. Bill put up some get-well cards on the mantel, so if anyone did come by, they might say, "Poor Barbara is still recovering from the loss of her two sons" and tend to ignore the disarray and clutter.

Bill just ate popcorn for most of that first year after Larry left. Fortunately, Barney, our younger son, worked at Taco Bell, so at least he had something to eat. Taco Bell wrappers started piling up all over the house along with the popcorn, which got spilled in strange places.

From the Pits to the Couch

Eventually, Bill insisted that I get help for my depression. I chose to see Dr. Wells, a psychologist who also happened to be a personal friend. On my first visit he shocked me by saying, "Don't blame yourself for this . . . we all have to make choices . . . it is a very black picture for you to accept. In my professional experience, I have had little success in changing the orientation of homosexuals. If and when Larry does contact you, don't talk to him about change."

"What do you mean, don't talk about change?" I sputtered. "Of course we're going to talk about change—we can't have THIS." I went on to berate Dr. Wells with Bible verses. How could he be a Christian and say God couldn't change Larry? I quoted him Scripture about how God changes *all things*, but Dr. Wells was unmoved as he patiently listened to my arguments. He seemed to understand I couldn't accept what he was telling me—at least at that time. After all, I wanted to fix Larry—as soon as possible.

To get some additional help, I began writing to top evangelical leaders around the country, asking for their counsel. In a few days I began getting their replies, which contained Scripture passages condemning homosexuality, prayer cloths and bottles of oil. I even got one suggestion to send his shorts to a certain address where they would be prayed for and his demon cast out. I didn't know where Larry was, and I sure didn't know where his shorts were!

Almost weekly, Dr. Wells and I continued our dialogue. One day, after Larry had been gone eleven months, Dr. Wells told me, "Well, if Larry has been gone eleven months, very possibly he will never come home again. He has probably found his emotional support in the gay lifestyle."

This really put me on a downer, and I went into a zombielike trance! Dr. Wells decided he'd better call Bill. I remember him saying, "She's in severe depression. We should commit her to a place where she can get twenty-four hour professional care because she's exhibiting suicidal feelings."

Bill is Swedish and somewhat stingy. I suppose *frugal* would be a kinder word, but stingy is more accurate. Bill's answer was, "Well, if my insurance will cover her, she can go. But if it costs any money, I think she can stay home—she's not vicious or anything."

And so those were my options. If Bill's insurance covered me, I could go make baskets at the home for the bewildered, and if it didn't pay, I could stay home and count the roses on the wallpaper.

Dr. Wells Was Right about Suicide

A day or two later as Bill was leaving for work, he told me that when he got home that night, he'd know if his insurance would cover me. After he left, I climbed in the car and started driving. I couldn't go on like this. I wasn't functioning as a wife, or a mother. I wasn't anything.

I'm just like a zombie or a zero with the rim rubbed out—I'm nothing, I thought. *I just can't believe that God would let all this happen to me and still really love me.*

I knew about a big viaduct on Ball Road going to Disneyland, and I thought I would just drive the car right off that viaduct, be killed, and all my troubles would be over. But as I started up the viaduct, I got to thinking, *What if I'm just maimed and then I'll be crippled and making baskets for the rest of my life?*

By the time I got to the top of the viaduct, I was sure I didn't want to kill myself, and then I said, "I can't believe it, Lord, but I've gotten to this point where I actually want to drive my car off a viaduct and kill myself. I'm taking a hammer out of my imagination, and I'm going to nail that kid to the Cross because I can't handle this any more. I'm tired of this elephant on my chest, my teeth itching, and this rug in my throat. This has been going on for eleven months, and I thought I gave it all to You long ago. But this time I'm saying that I'm really nailing him to the Cross, I'm giving him to You, and if he never comes home and I never see him again, *whatever, Lord, whatever happens*, I'm nailing that kid to the Cross and giving him to YOU!"

"Whatever, Lord," Was the Key

When I said those words, "Whatever, Lord," it seemed to release a million little sparkles inside me. The shag rug came out of my throat, my teeth stopped itching, and the elephant got off my chest for the first time in eleven months. All I'd said was, "Whatever, Lord," instead of my usual, "Why *me*? Why *my* kid? Why is my life such a mess? Why me?" All the heaviness was GONE!

For me, saying, "Whatever, Lord," was like Job saying, "Though he slay me, yet will I trust him" (Job 13:15, KJV). I turned that car around, and for the first time in eleven months I could take a deep breath. I sang all the way home—"The King Is Coming" and "Come On Down, Lord Jesus." I hadn't sung for eleven months, but that day I sang all the way home.

I called Bill, and I was so excited that I talked fast. So Bill had a hard time making sense of my flood of words.

"Where have you been?" he questioned.

"Well, I went down toward Disneyland and I was going to kill myself by driving off the viaduct, but instead I said, 'Whatever, Lord,' and nailed him to the Cross."

"You *WHAT*?" Bill demanded.

"I nailed him to the Cross," and I'm sure Bill was thinking, *I should have put her in the home for the bewildered yesterday. I've waited too long.*

"Don't go anywhere, stay there, I'm coming right home," and he hung up. I tried to tell him that he didn't have to come home, that I was fine, but he raced home anyway and sat me down for some answers. My babbling had him envisioning our kid nailed somehow on the 57 freeway! Just a few years before, Bill had been the one with brain damage, but now he reasoned gently with me as if he were my father or a counselor. I went through the whole thing again, and finally he seemed to understand that I'd been able to let Larry go and give the whole problem to God.

Very relieved he said, "I just can't believe what's happened, but I'll tell you one thing. I'm glad you're better because my insurance didn't cover you anyway."

The Prodigal Returns—Temporarily

The next day I started cleaning the house—for the first time in eleven months. Can you imagine what it was like? Popcorn kernels and Taco Bell wrappers everywhere. I got out giant

Hefty trash bags, put on some Christian records, and as I was singing my way through the trash, the phone rang.

It was Larry.

"Mom, I'm at In-N-Out Hamburgers, and I want to bring you one. What do you want on it?"

If Larry had called the day before, I would have said, "You little creep, don't you know they're ready to put me in the home for the bewildered?" But instead, I just said, "Oh, Honey, you come on home—anything is fine."

I knew that Larry was just testing the water to see if it was safe to come back. A little while later, in he walked and we ate hamburgers together. Because he was nervous, I didn't ask him many questions, but I did find out he was going to school at U.C.L.A. and living alone. He had gotten along fine during the past eleven months, and I didn't press him for a lot more information than that.

We talked and shared for quite a while, and then he left. But he came back the next week to talk to Bill and his brother, Barney. He kept coming back weekends and seemed glad to be with us. Every time we saw him, we'd talk mostly about surface things. I didn't want to delve into anything about homosexuality—I just wanted our relationship to be restored.

Larry continued to stay in close contact by coming over on weekends and calling us often. The next year he was best man at Barney's wedding, and the following June he graduated with honors from U.C.L.A. As glad as I was when he reconnected with the family, I still had a sense of doubt and foreboding. I walked on eggs, fearing that I'd say the wrong thing, cause a big explosion, and estrange him from us again.

But Larry wasn't the same kid anymore. He looked different, sounded different. We couldn't talk about anything spiritual. All we ever talked about were surface things. It seemed as if he had arrived from another planet, but I kept telling myself everything would be all right. I just wanted to put all the bad days behind us and not talk about it, but I eventually learned it wasn't behind us at all.

Early in 1979, a publisher contacted me and asked me if I would write my story. They didn't know much about Larry, but they knew what had happened to our two other boys.

I asked Larry, "How would you feel if I wrote all about this in a book?"

Larry said he didn't care, but I believe that he really didn't think I could do it anyway. I told the publisher I had never written anything, but one of the editors said, "Well, the Holy Spirit will propel it."

And that's exactly what happened. The book poured out of me in eight weeks, and I took it right up to the time when Larry had come back home. It was published in the fall of 1979, and the reaction surprised everyone, especially me. I started getting phone calls, inquiries, and requests to be on radio and television. A major book distributor picked up *Where Does a Mother Go to Resign?* and it was soon on their racks in airports and supermarkets all over the country.

How SPATULA Got Started

I was thrilled with the response to *Where Does a Mother Go to Resign?* because it provided an excellent tool for SPATULA, the new ministry for parents of homosexuals which we started in 1977. I had been volunteering at a Hot Line to give help to other parents, especially mothers, and I kept getting requests to begin some kind of support group that could meet weekly in my area. When some friends at the Hot Line asked me what I needed in order to work with parents, I replied that I needed about one hundred SPATULAS to scrape them off the ceiling. It was their suggestion that we call my parents' group "SPATULA," since scraping them off the walls and ceilings was what I was doing.

The name stuck, and I began meeting every Thursday night with a group of women, each of whom was welcomed into the group officially by receiving a large, red, plastic spatula. Our goal at SPATULA is to provide a cushion of intensive care for mothers who are on the ceiling after learning about their homosexual children. The first SPATULA group was so successful, others sprang up in other major cities around the country and *Christian Life* magazine ran a story. I was thankful that God helped me keep the promise I'd made two years earlier when I stormed out of the Hot Line office that couldn't give me any help.

"I'm Going to Disown My Whole Family!"

While things were going well with SPATULA, our relationship with Larry was deteriorating. After *Where Does a Mother Go to Resign?* came out, I didn't hear from him for a while. Then he came over to see me, angry and agitated. He brought along his Bible as well as his big red Basic Youth Conflicts notebook. He had always loved Basic Youth material and always said he believed it was the only way to live. That day he threw the Bible and the notebook down and said, "I don't want any part of this . . . you can have it all . . . it's not part of my life anymore . . . I'm doing my own thing!"

My response was total shock and disbelief. He walked out before I could even say much of anything to him. I didn't hear from him for several weeks, and then just after the New Year he called, sounding irate. He said, "How do you think I feel when I see that book at the airport and in Piggly Wiggly markets? Everywhere I see that book. I turn on TV and there you are . . . I turn on the radio and you're even on the radio . . ."

I was surprised and reminded Larry, "Well, you said I could write it . . ."

"Yeah, I suppose I did. But I never thought you could do it —such a dreary story, and who would read it anyway?"

"Apparently lots of people are reading it and getting lots of help . . ."

"Well, I don't like it. I have a lover in my life now, and I'm going to change my name and disown the family. I never want to see any of you again."

I gasped when he used the word *lover*. He didn't say, "I'm living with somebody," he said emphatically, "I have a lover," and it just blew me away. The conversation got pretty tense after that, but somehow I kept myself together. I realized then that we had already lost him, long ago. Nonetheless, all I could feel for him was love.

I recall saying, "Larry, homosexuality is not God's best for anybody, and I want God's best for you. I can't change your life, but there are two things I can do for you—love you and pray for you. And until they close the casket on my head and put a lily in my hand, I'm going to do just that. Just remember —we love you unconditionally, and the porch light is always on for you."

Larry was unmoved by my words, and he hung up in anger, letting me know that we definitely would not hear from him EVER again. Well, that wasn't quite true. We did hear from him again when an official form arrived in the mail saying that he had changed his name and had disowned us. Now my vow of "Whatever, Lord . . ." had come back to challenge me. Did I mean what I promised God back there on the viaduct on Ball Road three years ago, or didn't I?

The rest of this book comes out of the ideas and philosophies that came to mold my life as I spent over six long years never hearing from Larry. During those years, I learned the value of laughter, how to deal with guilt feelings, and how to stay calm when hysteria would well up within. Above all, I learned the meaning of hope. And it's hope I want to talk about next.

Extra Thoughts to Take Along

THE PORCH LIGHT

"Mother, why is the porch light on?"
   My son, it shines for you
Through the weary hours before the dawn
   As I wait the long night through.
My thoughts go back to the bygone days
   To my innocent little child;
Dear God! how quickly his baby ways
   Have been by the world defiled.

"Mother, how long will the porch light burn?"
   Dear son, until you come home,
For my aching heart will forever yearn
   Till your feet no longer roam.

My fervent, pleading, unceasing prayer
   Is for God to protect my son,
And I hear His answer, "My child, I care"
   As I murmur, "Thy will be done."

"Mother, is God's light burning still?"
   Oh, son! He loves you yet!
To draw you close is our Father's will,
   To rest without care or fret.
And God in His mercy will set you free
   To serve Him in peace and joy;
To be the man that He made you to be,
   My son, my beloved boy.

                     —Source Unknown

*   *   *   *   *   *

WHEN LIFE GETS HARD

There comes a time in everyone's life when trouble and difficulties seem to gang up. When this happens—when life gets hard—what is the creative way to handle things?

FIRST: Don't try to do it all yourself. Do not struggle and fret. Do not strain and complain. Do all you can about things and then put everything into God's hands, trusting Him to bring it out right. You can depend upon God. He will not fail you. Let go and let God.

SECOND: Pray for guidance and believe that direction is *now* being given you. Believe this guidance can be trusted. Depend upon it, for it won't fail you.

THIRD: Pray for and practice a calm attitude. Disturbing things will remain disturbing as long as you are disturbed. But when you become peaceful, conditions will iron themselves out. You cannot think creatively when your mind is upset. Remember: upset minds upset; peaceful minds "peacefulize."

FOURTH: Saturate your consciousness with faith, the creative faith that things will turn out right. Say aloud every day several times: "Thou wilt keep him in perfect peace, whose mind is stayed on thee" [Isa. 26:3, KJV]. "In quietness and in confidence shall be your strength" [Isa. 30:15, KJV]. "Peace I give unto you: not as the world giveth, give I unto you. Let not your heart be troubled, neither let it be afraid" [John 14:27, KJV].

FIFTH: Remind yourself of one great truth: hard experiences *will* pass away. They *will* yield. They *can* be changed. So just hold on, with God's help.

SIXTH: There is always a light in the darkness. Believe that. Look for that light. The light is the love of God. "Thy word is a lamp unto my feet, and a light unto my path" [Psa. 119:105, KJV]. Go ahead into the darkness unafraid.

SEVENTH: Ask the Lord to release your own creative ingenuity, your own strength and wisdom, which taken together can, for a fact, handle any problem successfully.

EIGHTH: Never forget that God cares for you, that He loves you. He wants to help you. Turn to Him, and gratefully accept His help.

NINTH: Remember that all human beings experience troubles similar to your own. Many years ago a graduating class gave a stone bench to their university on which were graven these words: "To those who sit here sorrowing or rejoicing: greetings. So also did we in our time."

TENTH: Finally, hold on to this great promise: "God is our refuge and strength, a very present help in trouble." And this is the truth. God will see you through, and a brighter day will dawn for you.

—Source Unknown

CHAPTER FOUR

I Feel So Much Better
Now That I've Given Up Hope*

Life is easier than you think—
All you have to do is:
Accept the impossible,
Do without the indispensable,
Bear the intolerable
and
Be able to smile at anything.

—Source Unknown

When we received that official notarized form saying Larry
had disowned us and changed his name, I couldn't help but
think of what the Bible says to Christians who are facing black
times: "Consider it pure joy, my brothers, whenever you face
trials of many kinds, because you know that the testing of
your faith develops perseverance. Perseverance must finish
its work so that you may be mature and complete, not lacking
anything" (James 1:2–4, NIV).

The first time Larry left, I thought I had learned something
about perseverance. Now that he was gone again—this time
apparently for good—I saw that God still had some trials in
mind to help me grow and mature. Growing is a lifetime job,
and we grow most when we're down in the valleys, where the
fertilizer is.

---

* For the title of this chapter I am indebted to Ashleigh Brilliant, *Pot-Shots* No.
519, © Brilliant Enterprises 1974. Used by permission.

While I was talking with a friend, she got a telephone call bringing some disturbing news. Instead of panic, her response was, "Well, here we GROW again!" She was right. We can *go* through painful trials or we can *grow* through them.

One of the best descriptions I've ever heard of how it feels to experience an ongoing trial came from a lady who was feeling desperate and undone. There just was no light in sight at the end of her tunnel. She told me, "I feel like I've been living in a parenthesis since I learned about my son. I keep trying to move the parenthesis, and it keeps stretching out, and I am *still* in this horrible parenthesis in my life!"

My Parenthesis Had Never Ended

Fortunately, when Larry left that second time, I was better prepared for my parenthesis—a time of trial and struggle that can be brief or seemingly endless. Actually, Larry's bitter reaction to *Where Does a Mother Go to Resign?* wasn't a new parenthesis at all. His angry exit from our lives only forced me to realize that the problem which began for me on that night at the flagpole on Disneyland's Main Street had really never gone away. The story was just continuing with a new chapter.

When Larry returned after his first absence of eleven months, I thought everything was "okay" and so did Bill. Larry's "phase" was over, and we just didn't talk about it. How wrong we were.

But now here I was, locked in another measurement of time and, until God chose to remove the ends of the parenthesis, I would have to live in another vacuum. Some people might call it a pit or a cave, but whatever you choose to call it, it's a contained situation. You can't go back and wish it were only a day ago or even two years ago. And you can't jump ahead—out of the pit into a happy, carefree time. Until God kicks the ends out of your parenthesis, you have to handle today, today.

This doesn't mean you ignore or negate God's promises and instructions. But you may have to settle for not being sure you understand what's going on—at least at the moment.

I love the cartoon caption that says, "Mother said there'd be days like this . . . she failed to mention that they could go on for months at a time."

One thing that helps is not to deny you're in the process. If you hurt, admit it. As one bumper snicker* advises:

WHEN YOU'RE DOWN AND OUT
LIFT UP YOUR HEAD AND SHOUT . . .
"I'M DOWN AND OUT!"

That's the first step in handling your parenthesis. The next step is to realize that whatever the problem is, *it won't last forever.* I was talking to a gal who has some real problems, and she told me her favorite Scripture verse is, "And it came to pass . . ." I looked at her rather quizzically and she laughed and added, "Just think, all this could have come to STAY!"

Pain Has a "Passing Through" Stage

Since every parenthesis has come to pass, you have to go through a "passing through" stage. It's okay to admit you're suffering and hurting, and you might even be angry with God. But then you go on to make the most of this particular time frame. As the passage from James reminds us, it's a chance to grow. So give it all you've got, and see what you can learn from this pain.

All the promises of God are there, and they're real, and they're true, but right now you're bleeding, you're raw and hurting, and you have to hang on to those promises even if they don't seem to work for you at the moment. As you go through the pain, it will lessen. The pain will flatten out and dilute itself, and then you can look back and realize how far you've come. You can start living with the parenthesis behind you! There may be occasional dips back into the pits, but you know you are getting out of that parenthetical period.

---

*As you probably have already noticed, I like collecting quips, sayings, and bumper stickers, which I prefer to call "bumper snickers" because they often provide so much humor.

Every time you feel closed in, or like you are smothering in a tight little box with the lid nailed down, imagine you are stepping over that horrid little parenthesis. You *are* going to get over this, and when you do climb over it and then look back, you will realize you've reached new gains and new values. You have completed a segment of growth as a person.

If any of God's prophets knew what it was like to go through a parenthesis, it had to be Jeremiah. In fact, you could say his entire life was one parenthesis after the other. And yet God told him, "For I know the plans I have for you . . . they are plans for good and not for evil, to give you a future and a hope" (Jer. 29:11, TLB).

I have come to love that verse because hope makes all the difference. Learning to relinquish Larry completely to God enabled me to face another (actually the same) parenthesis and know I could get through. I had said "Whatever, Lord," and I had meant it!

After Larry left, the SPATULA ministry began to take off. I'd share on television and radio shows, or I would speak in churches and conferences and people would ask, "Well, how is your son now?" And I would have to say, "Well, he's disowned us. He's changed his name, and he says he never wants to see us again."

That wasn't real hopeful news to share, but it was true at the time. All I had to hang on to was a love for God and a love for Larry and all those parents who had suffered the loss of a child or, worse, the pain of having a child reject their values and opt for a different lifestyle that leaves God out.

Real Hope Comes Out of Hopelessness

I identify with the woman described in the following poem from Ruth Graham's book *Sitting by My Laughing Fire*:

> She waited for the call
> that never came; searched every mail
> for a letter, or a note,
> or card,
> that bore his name;

and on her knees
at night
and on her feet
all day, she stormed Heaven's Gate
in his behalf;
she plead for him
in Heaven's high court.
"Be still and wait,'
the word He gave;
and so she knew
He would
do in, and for,
and with him,
that which she never could. Doubts ignored,
she went about her chores
with joy;
knowing, though spurned,
His word was true.
The prodigal had not returned
but God was God,
and there was work to do.*

For me, that describes hope. Hope is the essential ingredient to make it through life. It is the anchor of the soul. The
Lord is good to those who hope in Him. If your hope is gone, it
can be rekindled. You can regain hope—you can refocus your
view and wait on the Lord to renew your strength.

The title of this chapter may be puzzling you. How can you
feel better if you've given up hope? What it means is, once you
give up hope in all your *own* efforts and quit depending on
your *own* strength, that's when you can start to have REAL
HOPE in what God can do!

Think of your life, with all the mistakes, sins, and woes of
the past, like the tangles in a ball of yarn. It's such a mess
that you could never begin to straighten it out. It is such a
comfort to drop the tangles of life into God's hands, and then
LEAVE THEM THERE. If there is one message I want to
share with you, it is to place your child, your spouse, your
friend, whomever it might be, in God's hands and *release* the

---

load to Him. God alone can untangle the threads of our lives. WHAT A JOY AND COMFORT IT CAN BE TO DROP ALL THE TANGLES OF LIFE INTO GOD'S HANDS AND THEN SIMPLY LEAVE THEM THERE! That's what hope is all about.

Hope Is Not Dodging Reality

We just can't go through life pretending that griefs don't happen, and acting like the hurt and pain aren't really there. Faith is knowing that troubles do exist, but it is also the trust to know that they're not going to last forever and that you will feel better.

Hope is the essential ingredient to make it through life! It is the anchor of the soul. But you say your hope is gone? Don't worry, it *can* be rekindled. The Lord is good to those who hope in Him.

You can regain hope; you can refocus your view and wait on the Lord to renew your strength. Those without Christ may see only a hopeless end, but the Christian rejoices in an *endless hope.*

How Do You Define "Hope"?

Sometimes it's hard to explain hope—just what is hope, anyway? The cutest illustration of hope I've found is about a little boy who was standing at the foot of the escalator in a big department store, intently watching the handrail. He never took his eyes off the handrail as the escalator kept going around and around. A salesperson saw him and finally asked him if he was lost. The little fellow replied, "Nope. I'm just waiting for my chewing gum to come back."

If your face is in the dust, if you are in a wringer situation, be like the little boy waiting for his chewing gum to come back. Stand firm, be patient, and trust God. Then get busy with your life . . . there is work to do.

I like the note one mother sent me that simply said:

Dear Barb (and Gopher Bill): Like the sundial, this year I am only going to count the sunny hours! I don't know where we are—I don't need to know. It's all in His hands. How much safer could it be?

Her words remind me that nothing touches me that has not passed through the hands of my heavenly Father, NOTHING. Whatever occurs, God has sovereignly surveyed and approved. We may not know why (we may never know why), but we do know our pain is no accident to Him who guides our lives. He is, in no way, surprised by it all. Before it ever touches us, it passes through Him.

The Painful Art of Tunnel Walking

To come out of the darkness into the sunshine, it helps to remember you're in a tunnel, not a cave.

You will get through this if you just hang in there and keep on *walking through that tunnel.* I have a special friend named Peggy who often shares cards and thoughts with me, and one of the best she sent was this:

DARK MOMENTS ARE SHORT CORRIDORS
LEADING TO SUNLIT ROOMS!

One of the best pieces of advice on how to walk through your corridor or tunnel was written by Robert Maner, an evangelist who lives in Georgia. Several years ago in an article entitled "Tunnel Walking" in *Herald of Holiness,* he mentions terrible tragedies that can happen to any of us—a wife learns that her husband is leaving her for another woman; the doctor gives the dreaded news that you have terminal cancer; an unmarried teenage daughter says the shocking words, "Mom, I'm pregnant"; the State Patrol calls saying your son was killed "while driving under the influence."

All of these tragedies happen every day, and Christians are not exempt. When these things happen, there seems to be no light at the end of the tunnel. I know that feeling. You can hear Romans 8:28 quoted again and again, but it's still all dark— there is no light anywhere.

You can feel guilt, anger, bitterness, and depression all at once. You keep asking yourself, "Where did I fail? What did I do wrong?" As Robert Maner says, "Dreary days and nights seem to melt together in a meaningless twilight zone." He goes on to say that although you can't change what happened, there are some things that can help. You are a child of God, and that means you have certain rights, privileges, and resources. He writes:

Jesus will walk with you down your long dark tunnel. At first even His presence may seem far away. But if you look, and feel, He is there. Right by your side you can feel Him standing there. Suppose you had to walk this path alone? But you don't—He is actually there. You can talk with Him. Share your bitterness, your anger, your guilt. Tell Him how depressed you are. Tell how afraid of the darkness you are. Tell Him how lonely you are.

He provides courage in that dark tunnel life has forced you to walk. . . .

While you may see no light at the end of your tunnel, you never know when the tunnel will curve. And right around that curve may burst the light of a great new day. You cannot see it from where you are now, but it is there.

Then, too, every tunnel ends someplace. Otherwise it would just be a cave. And life is definitely not a cave for the Christian. Jesus verified that by His resurrection. Listen closely and you may hear His voice bidding you to quicken your pace.

I remember a time of tunnel walking years ago. The darkness was suffocating—so dense I could feel it. No light at the end of my tunnel could be seen. I prayed—or tried to—but I couldn't seem to get through the ceiling. Sleep was impossible, so I went outside and walked around in the night. When I looked up, the stars were all there. Not one was missing. I thought surely there would not be one left, but I was wrong. And the God who put them there was also right where He had always been. The next morning the sun rose just as it had always done. The birds were singing, too. Not even they failed me. The day came when the tunnel took a sudden and unexpected turn. There was light—lots of light. There were answers to prayer, too. It didn't happen overnight, but it did happen.

Your tunnel will have light at its end, faithful Christian. Just keep walking.*

The "Perfect Answers" Don't Work

One way to get through your tunnel is to remember nobody's life is perfect, even though commercials and TV shows like to claim it's possible. My friend, Lynda, was looking really sharp, and I told her so. She remarked that she had bought a new bra, and the name of it was "NOBODY'S PERFECT!" That reminded me of how many of us have to live in situations where nothing and nobody is perfect—not even halfway perfect at times.

It's easy to expect too much from people, or from products that are advertised as "The perfect answer." I was in a car wash recently, and while I was paying my bill, I saw a counter display selling little bottles called "New Car Smell." On the label was a picture of a spanking new car wrapped with a big bow on it, and without bothering to take a sample sniff, I just bought a bottle, figuring I could stand a new car smell in my '77 Volvo.

When I got home, I sprayed it around inside the car and almost got sick from the aroma that seemed to be a combination of old oil, tar, and bananas. If a new car ever did smell like THAT, the owner would surely think something was wrong.

I also remember some years back when stores carried unpopped popcorn that came in colors. The kernels were bright red, green, purple, and orange. I bought some, thinking that when it popped, we would have some truly colorful popcorn. We stood around and watched it popping, only to learn that it came out snow white as usual. The colors we anticipated never did show up.

Advertisements have a way of building our expectations, but we learn reality the hard way. No spray will make an old car smell new, and colored popcorn always comes out white. Yet, something inside of us keeps us willing to believe those ads.

---

*Robert E. Maner, 'Tunnel Walking,' from *Herald of Holiness*. Nazarene Publishing House. Used by permission.

Maybe we're always hoping for that miracle, and that's why we always try something new to see if it does what somebody says it will, to see if we can find the perfect solution.

Life Can Turn Upside Down

But nothing is perfect. We have to live in a world that is not perfect with people who are full of quirks and in homes that have imperfections. I have a friend who saved and scrimped to buy some expensive wallpaper for her son's bedroom. It finally arrived after being special-ordered, and she brought it home and put it away, planning to hang it as soon as she found the time.

Her husband discovered the wallpaper and, while she was out shopping for the day, he decided to surprise her by hanging it himself. So he worked all day, papering the entire bedroom with the lovely new paper, which was supposed to show colorful balloons with the strings hanging down. He made only one mistake: he hung all the paper UPSIDE DOWN, and the strings were all pointing up the wall like slithering snakes instead of hanging down gracefully as intended.

When my friend returned, she was shocked, but it was all done and couldn't be changed. So, she and her husband simply learned to live with the upside down wallpaper and adjusted to seeing the strings going up. She had wanted it to be just perfect, but it had come out exactly opposite of what she had planned. Learning to live with upside down situations is not always easy, but it is part of life because we all face living with imperfect situations.

We have a clock in our car that is always one hour off from October to April when the time changes. The mechanism that changes the dial is broken, and during those months I have to keep remembering that the clock in our car is one hour ahead of life. I have to keep adjusting my time and schedule according to a clock that is one hour off, and perhaps this is teaching me something. Some things in life are NEVER what they should be and you have to adjust. Being willing to adjust to something less than perfect is a sign of acceptance.

One heart-broken parent, whose child had disappointed her terribly, finally came to terms with her trials. One of the things that helped her was this little poem:

ACCEPTANCE

Acceptance is the answer to all my problems today.
When I am disturbed, it is because I find some
    person, place, thing, or situation—
Some fact of my life—unacceptable to me, and
    I can find no serenity until I accept that
    person, place, thing, or situation as being exactly
    the way it is supposed to be at this moment,
Nothing, absolutely nothing happens in
    God's world by mistake.
Unless I accept life completely on life's terms,
    I cannot be happy.
I need to concentrate not so much on what needs to
    be changed in the world as on what needs to
    be changed in me and in my attitudes.

                        —Source Unknown

I got a letter from a dear lady who admitted she had no offering to send for the SPATULA ministry, but her love and prayers are with us. She said:

My husband has not worked in four years since his legs were both amputated from an accident. My son is in contact with us now, thanks to SPATULA, and he has moved near us to help with the farming. I have recovered from my surgery for breast cancer, and thank the Lord for that. However, the eye problem I told you about has increased so much the doctors tell me that I will lose all my sight within a few months. But I am thankful my husband can read to me when I go blind, and he will interpret all the cartoons and jokes for me so we can laugh together when your newsletter comes each month. I have laughed more over your newsletter than all the smiles I could muster since these trials came to us. How I praise the Lord for SPATULA and the laughter it brings to me, along with the encouragement to hang on when everything looks so black.

In her pain, facing problems that would leave many people distraught, this lady still has reason to hope!

God Uses Troubles to Sweeten Us

Life is never perfect, but Jesus is. And He takes the imperfections—the broken pieces and the messes—and turns them into hope. Remember, no matter what you're going through, it didn't come to stay, it came to pass. You may be living in a parenthesis, but whatever you're going through, it won't last forever.

Not long ago Bill and I were driving through Palm Springs, the famous desert resort community. We came upon a roadside stand, and the sign said, "DESERT SWEETENED GRAPE-FRUIT." I thought, *That's the way it is with all of us when we go through a desert experience—when we're out there in the barren and dry wastes, not seeming to receive any encouragement from anybody. That's the time God uses to sweeten us as we learn to give our problem completely to Him.*

There are several steps we all go through when we try to give a problem completely to God. You take your first step when life rises up to knock you flat—you CHURN. You feel as if your insides are full of knives, chopping you up in a grinder. There is no other way to describe the devastation you feel when you're churning inside.

Your next step is to BURN. That's right, you want to kill your child, and then you want to kill yourself. You are so full of red hot anger and the anguish of frustration that your temper is out of control. You literally feel as if you're burning inside.

In your third step, you YEARN. Oh, you want so much for things to change! You just ache inside for things to be as they were before you knew about this. You yearn for the happy past, and this stage often lasts the longest of all.

But then you take your next step, which is to LEARN. You talk with others, maybe you find a support group, and you learn that you're in a long growth process. You become more understanding and compassionate. Spiritual values you learned in the past will suddenly become *real* to you. You will learn a great deal about unconditional love and reaching out to help others. The wonderful result is that you relieve your own pain.

And, finally, you take your last step—you TURN. You learn to turn the problem over to the Lord completely by saying, "Whatever, Lord! Whatever You bring into my life, You are big enough to get me through it." Now you can relinquish your heaviness to God, knowing that He is in control. He loves your child more than you do, and He has not rejected your child because of whatever is in his or her life. When you nail your problem to the foot of the Cross and say you have deposited that problem with the Lord and truly mean it, then you will be relieved of your crushing burden.

But now comes the really difficult part. Just because you've come through all those steps does not mean that you will not go back to churning, burning, and yearning on certain days. But each time you will stay in those stages for a shorter and shorter period. And you will be able to spend more of your days in turning it all over to God. In 1 Peter 5:7 we are told to cast our cares upon Him. That means to deposit your cares, just as you deposit money in a bank, and leave them there. So many parents write or call me and ask, "How can we give our kids to God and find some relief for this devastation we feel?" I believe, from my own struggling, that the answers are in the stages of relinquishment I describe above.

CHURN awhile . . . BURN for a time . . . YEARN for as long as it takes to move on . . . LEARN as much as you can . . . and then TURN it all over to the One who cares for you. Don't fret if you think you are not progressing or even when suddenly, for no reason, you find yourself back at square one. You may find yourself churning, just as you did at the beginning. That is normal and very typical of grief. Never forget this is a grief process, and you have to work your way through the shattering of your life.

Right now you have a broken dream. It may not always be so, but for now it is, and you have to accept it. But believe me . . .

healing does come. The mending process takes time, but you are making a long journey to becoming whole again, and you have *a door of hope ahead!* I love the way one woman signed an Easter card she sent me: "FROM AN EASTER PERSON LIVING IN A GOOD FRIDAY WORLD." Even in the midst of this messy old world, we can rejoice because we know our future—and our hope—is in Him!

Extra Thoughts to Take Along

Only some of us learn by other people's mistakes;
the rest of us have to be the other people.

* * * * * *

When you're lonely,
. . . we wish you LOVE.

When you're down,
. . . we wish you JOY.

When you're troubled,
. . . we wish you PEACE.

When things look empty,
. . . we wish you HOPE.

—Source Unknown

* * * * * *

TRUE UNDERSTANDING

We do not understand:
Joy . . . until we face sorrow
Faith . . . until it is tested
Peace . . . until faced with conflict
Trust . . . until we are betrayed
Love . . . until it is lost
Hope . . . until confronted with doubts.

—Source Unknown

* * * * * *

WHAT LIGHT?
I'M STILL LOOKING FOR THE TUNNEL!

* * * * * *

HOPE MAKES A DIFFERENCE

Hope looks for the good in people instead of harping on the worst in them.

Hope opens doors where despair closes them.

Hope discovers what can be done instead of grumbling about what cannot be done.

Hope draws its power from a deep trust in God and the basic goodness of mankind.

Hope "lights a candle" instead of "cursing the darkness."

Hope regards problems, small or large, as opportunities.

Hope cherishes no illusions, nor does it yield to cynicism.

—Source Unknown

* * * * * *

Thank You, dear God
For all You have given me
For all You have taken away from me
For all You have left me.

—Source Unknown

* * * * * *

TAKE YOUR BROKEN DREAMS
TO JESUS!

CHAPTER FIVE

One Laugh = 3 Tbsp. Oat Bran

BE GRATEFUL . . .

> *for husbands who attack small repair jobs around the house. They usually make them big enough to call in professionals.*
>
> *for children who put away their things and clean up after themselves. They're such a joy you hate to see them go home to their own parents.*

—Source Unknown

This chapter is "just for fun," but for a good reason. If I have learned anything through life's trials, it is this: *"A merry heart doeth good like a medicine"* (Prov. 17:22, KJV).

A good cry is a wet-wash, but a hearty laugh gives you a dry cleaning. A good laugh is worth a hundred groans any time in any market. *He who laughs, lasts* because:

LAUGHTER IS THE SUN THAT DRIVES WINTER FROM THE HUMAN FACE.

If you can learn to laugh in spite of the circumstances that surround you, you will enrich others, enrich yourself and, more than that, you will LAST!

Laughing Is Like Jogging on the Inside

Doctors and physical fitness experts tell us that laughter is just plain good for your health. One expert, who travels around staging workshops on how to be fit, says healthy people laugh 100 to 400 times a day.

And I read about one medical doctor who calls laughter "internal jogging." He says that hearty laughter has a beneficial effect on most of your body's major systems—and it's a lot more fun than calisthenics. Laughing 100 times a day works the heart as much as exercising for ten minutes on a rowing machine. When I speak, I invite my listeners to try "jogging on the inside"—having some good, long laughs in spite of the pain or frustrations in life.

One bumper snicker I saw became the title for this chapter: ONE LAUGH = 3 TBSP. OF OAT BRAN

You undoubtedly know all about oat bran, the new "wonder food" that has proven to be effective in lowering cholesterol levels. Dr. James W. Anderson, who is Professor of Medicine at the University of Kentucky, and a specialist in diabetes, bought a hundred-pound sack of oat bran and began using it in his own diet. In just five weeks, his cholesterol level dropped 110 points, or 38 percent!*

I'm not sure if laughter can lower cholesterol, but it's definitely healthy. And besides, laughter is a lot more appealing than eating oat bran, which I have found to be close to sawdust. Nonetheless, Bill and I have our oat bran almost daily. It helps diabetics control their blood sugar and also just plain reduces risk of heart attack.

Have you ever thought of how many days we waste if we don't learn to laugh? Someone said, "The most wasted of days is that in which one has not laughed." There are so many books out on how to love your family, how to succeed in marriage, how to get thin, how to get rich, how to cope, how to survive an earthquake, what to do when teen-agers run away from home, but nothing on how to learn to laugh. How often parents are told to "zip up your child and give the entire container to the Lord because there is no way out of this." But

---

* Josleen Wilson, *The Oat Bran Way* (New York: Berkley Brooks, 1989), p. 71, 72.

parents need to hear God can take them through whatever they're facing. And learning to laugh can make the journey so much more comfortable!

Try a Laugh Break—It Works!

I read one article that says the best thing to do when feeling overwhelmed is to take a "laugh break." If you're all worn out and feeling defeated, take time out to laugh. It can actually rejuvenate you.

In one psychological study, sixty people were divided into three groups and given equal puzzles to solve. All three groups failed the first set of puzzles. Then the researchers gave Groups One and Two some easier tests, like rearranging scrambled letters into words. Both groups did almost as poorly on this as they had on the first batch of really difficult puzzles.

Before taking the same scrambled letter test, however, Group Three was allowed to have a "laugh break." They got their chuckles out of reading a group of ten cartoons to see which ones were the funniest; then they took the scrambled letter test and scored well. The point is, humor can actually alter your mood. Humor made it easier for Group Three to get motivated. Their laugh break helped them overcome their earlier frustration and do a better job!

My Joy Box Grew into a Joy Room

The best way that I've learned to laugh is to pursue joy and actually collect it. My books and newsletters often mention my Joy Room, a 60' x 10' space attached to my home which is full of things to make me and my guests smile, chuckle, and even guffaw. My Joy Room started out as a Joy Box—a shoe box covered with some brightly colored paper—in which I put things that made me laugh. When I was going through the really terrible times and doing my own share of tunnel walking, I looked for things like cards, poems, and even Scripture verses that made me smile or laugh. In a way, *The Love Line* newsletter is simply how I share all my joy with other people. If you want to get on my mailing list, it's easy!

In the first years of our SPATULA ministry, I'd go out to speak, and if I'd talk about watermelons, people would send me watermelon potholders with cute little sayings. If I talked about balloons, I got balloon potholders. In no time at all, my Joy Box was brim full and overflowing, and we had to do something else. So much joy was coming back to me in the mail, I told Bill we had to build a room on the side of our home, and that's just what we did. Today on every inch of the walls, we have plaques, pictures, dolls, and gimmicks—all kinds of happy stuff all over the place.

One of my favorite occupants of my Joy Room is a little lady in a basket, with a sign that says, "DON'T PICK ON ME, I'M A BASKET CASE ALREADY." People have also sent me all kinds of dolls and stuffed animals. A foot-high Bugs Bunny sits on a carrot that's at least a foot and a half long. He's very precious to me because he was made especially for me by a mother whose son died of AIDS. She came through the death of her boy beautifully, and because of what's happened in her life, she's reaching out to other mothers who are going through the same kind of pain. She attends our SPATULA support group every month. She loves to talk or write to other mothers to encourage them.

I used to have a little blue sandman with cute red feet, a little package of sand in his hand and wearing a little hat to help him go to sleep. He was called Sleepy Sam, and I gave him to Al Sanders, host of the "Vox Pop" radio program because Al told me he seems to always need a nap in the afternoons lately. Because we are the same age, I like to remind Al that you're over the hill when you spell relief N–A–P.

Another favorite in my Joy Room is a big, beautiful doll made by a Roman Catholic nun. About eight feet long, with stretched-out arms and stretched-out legs, the doll is so realistic that she fooled a United Parcel man who came by one day. Instead of his usual loud knock on the door, he tapped very quietly. He said, "I didn't want to wake up the lady." I used to take this doll along on speaking engagements. I'd put her in the back seat, and it often looked like somebody was riding with me. Sometimes I would jokingly tell people I kept her in the backseat so I could ride the Diamond Lane.*

Love Gifts Fill My Joy Room

In addition to all the handmade love gifts that decorate every inch of my Joy Room, I get a lot of poems and sayings from our SPATULA family. One I especially like is called "Home Rules." It was taken from a church bulletin and the original source is unknown to me.

> If you sleep on it . . . make it up.
> If you wear it . . . hang it up.
> If you eat out of it . . . put it in the sink.
> If you step on it . . . wipe it off.
> If you open it . . . close it.
> If you empty it . . . fill it up.
> If it rings . . .answer it.
> If it howls . . . feed it.
> If it cries . . . love it.

One of the occupants of my Joy Room reminds me that sometimes you need to have tough love for your children. He's a little porcupine who actually looks more like a groundhog, but he reminds me that when you love your kids, they may send back responses as hurtful as porcupine quills. That's what happened when Larry disowned us and changed his name, saying he never wanted to see us again. But all the time he was gone, we kept loving him unconditionally.

Parents must remember they can't change anybody. Billy Graham's wife, Ruth, says, "It's my job to love Billy and God's job to make him good." I've adapted that idea, and I say it's my job to love my kids, and it's God's job to touch their lives.

As someone said, we spend the first three years of a child's life teaching him to walk and talk and the next fifteen teaching him to sit down and be quiet! But, ultimately, there are

---

* In California, the "Diamond Lane" is reserved for two or more people who are commuting together in the same car.

only two things you can do for your kids—love them and pray for them. So I keep my little porcupine in my Joy Room to remind me that, even though our kids may send back quills—that is, they may do or say things that sting and hurt, it's our job to love them with unconditional love, not "sloppy agape," but with a tough love that has some edges on it.

The Joy of a Serendipity

Sometimes I don't find joy; it finds me. It's just plain fun to go around speaking for women's groups in churches, conferences, luncheons—all kinds of places where women invite me in to share with them. Their creativity is astounding. Sometimes the room is decorated with little spatulas hanging down from the ceiling. Sometimes each table has a "Joy Box" centerpiece. After I wrote *Fresh Elastic for Stretched-Out Moms*, I'd go to luncheons that featured posters with limp rag dolls representing "stretched-out" mothers. In one case, a lady had set up a rag doll going through a real old-fashioned washing machine wringer! I always come away from these meetings feeling I've received more than I have given.

Recently, I was speaking somewhere and was told that I would be introduced by a lady who had never introduced anyone before. This dear gal practiced and practiced and even made a little tape of her introduction, which she played for me ahead of time to make sure she had everything right. That night she came with a new hairdo and in a new dress, complete with a corsage. The big moment arrived and she got up and said, "We're so glad to have Barbara Johnson with us. She's written a book and in that book there is a chapter called . . ." Her face got white and I could tell she had forgotten her whole speech, but she continued bravely, ". . . there is a chapter called 'Stick a Geranium in Your Cranium!'"

I laughed so hard I could hardly begin my speech, but then I thought, *"How appropriate!"* She was trying to describe a chapter in *Fresh Elastic for Stretched-Out Moms* called, "Stick a Geranium in Your Hat," which talks about using laughter and humor to make it through the nights and days that seem so endless when tragedy and pain occur. I've always liked the idea of facing problems by looking for the flowers, not the weeds. That's why *Stick a Geranium in Your Hat and Be Happy* became the title of this book. Maybe it isn't always quite that simple, but finding happiness and joy has to start somewhere, and I know it starts with a positive attitude.

Look for Joy—It's Everywhere!

We can learn to look for laughter and joy in the many ordinary places where we go. When I go to our La Habra post office in the morning, the cement on the sidewalk outside is just plain blah gray. But if I go in the afternoon, when the sun hits it, the cement sparkles with a million transient diamonds! So, I usually go in the afternoon, looking for the joy that can bounce off that cement right into my life, to remind me of the sparkles all around us, if we are willing to look for them.

But I repeat, you have to LOOK for the joy. Look for the light of God that is hitting your life, and you will find sparkles you didn't know were there. Recently, a darling young mom who has four kids, all under six, called me and wanted me to come over and do some counseling with her. I said, "Four kids under six . . . would you like me to bring a baby sitter, or something?"

"Oh, no," she said, "I have a perfect solution. It'll be no problem at all."

I thought to myself that this would be interesting. I wondered what she was going to do to keep four kids under six occupied while we tried to have a meaningful chat.

I went over to her house, and we went out into the backyard. Then she took two handfuls of pennies and threw them into a large patch of ivy growing on the hill. Then she gave each of her four kids a plastic baggie and told them to look for pennies in the ivy.

What a terrific idea! We had an hour of no interruptions. And, for all I know, she does the penny exercise every time she needs some time to concentrate or talk with someone. Anyway, it's a wonderful idea because her kids are learning how to look for joy as they search for the pennies in the ivy.

Try Doing Something Truly Outrageous

I read somewhere that one way you can put more laughs into your life is to do something just plain outrageous. How long has it been since you have done something really GOOFY? Intentionally, I mean. Like jogging in triangles? Or driving in circles in a parking lot just for fun? Or going to the market wearing your wig inside out? I had gone quite awhile without enjoying some goofy fun, so Marilyn (my partner in crazy fun) and I decided to do something about it. We knew of a pastor who had been having some tremendous family problems and who was feeling down and depressed. He had said to me, "What I REALLY need is a visitation from the angels!"

Well, that was all we needed. The next day Marilyn and I went by our church, where we slipped into the baptismal room unnoticed and "borrowed" two long, full-flowing, baptismal robes. We drove over to our friend's home and stopped to don the robes about a block from his house. A mailman walking by nearly dropped his pouch when he saw two

women get out of a Volvo and toss on these white robes with heavy weights in the bottom that sort of clinked as we walked.

When my husband, Bill, heard about our fun, he thought it was sacrilegious and unspiritual. His main concern was "Did you get the robes returned to the church?" But our pastor friend thought it was great. He got up in church and told everyone about these two women who came to give him a "visitation from the angels."

Laughing's More Fun with Someone Else

One thing about laughing, it's hard to do alone. You usually need somebody else to watch, listen to, or react to in some way. We can't do it all alone, whether it's laughing or anything else worthwhile. We need other people in our lives. We need other people to help carry the load. Sometimes I tell people to read the following story to their families so they can all laugh together. I don't know the original source, but it illustrates beautifully that you "can't do it alone." When one man was asked to fill out a group insurance form explaining the many injuries on which he was making a claim, this is what he said:

> I am writing in response to your request concerning Block No. 1 on the insurance form which asked for the cause of injuries, wherein I put "Trying to do the job alone." You said you needed more information, so I trust that the following will be sufficient.
>
> I am a bricklayer by trade, and on the day of injuries, I was working alone, laying brick around the top of a four-story building, when I realized that I had about five hundred pounds of brick left over. Rather than carry the bricks down by hand, I decided to put them in a barrel and lower them by pulley, which was fastened to the top of the building. I secured the end of the rope at ground level and went up to the top of the building and loaded the bricks into the barrel and flung the barrel out with the bricks in it. Then I went down and untied the rope, holding it securely to insure the slow descent of the barrel.
>
> As you will note on Block No. 6 of the insurance form, I weigh 150 pounds. Due to the shock of being jerked off the

ground so swiftly, I lost my presence of mind and forgot to let go of the rope. Between the second and third floors, I met the barrel coming down. This accounts for the bruises and lacerations on my upper body. Regaining my presence of mind, again I held tightly to the rope and proceeded rapidly up the side of the building, not stopping until my right hand was jammed in the pulley. This accounts for my broken thumb.

Despite the pain, I retained my presence of mind and held tightly to the rope. At approximately the same time, however, the barrel of bricks hit the ground and the bottom fell out of the barrel. Devoid of the weight of the bricks, the barrel now weighed about fifty pounds. I refer you again to Block No. 6 and my weight. As you would guess, I began a rapid descent. In the vicinity of the second floor, I met the barrel coming up. This explains the injuries to my legs and lower body. Slowed only slightly, I continued my descent, landing on the pile of bricks. Fortunately, my back was only sprained and the internal injuries were minimal. I'm sorry to report, however, that at this point I again lost my presence of mind and let go of the rope. As you can imagine, the empty barrel crashed down on me.

I trust this answers your concern. Please know that I am finished with trying to do the job alone.

Life Goes On—So, Laugh!

Robert Frost said he could sum up everything he learned about life in three words: "IT GOES ON!" I believe that's, oh, so true. The human spirit can survive pain, loss, death, taxes, and even wet panty hose and life goes on . . . and on and on. My encouraging word to all those I meet is "develop a sense of humor to carry you through these days. Without one, you are doomed to despair. With one, you can survive and actually enjoy the trip."

Years ago my Joy Box pulled me through the rough days when I had nothing else going for me. I felt all alone in that dark pit. I didn't know then that others had been through it and had *made it*. Collecting the poems, cartoons, verses, and all kinds of paraphernalia and knickknacks was a way to MAKE myself look for joyful things. It brought me from where I *was* to where I *am* now. I can look back and remember it, but I'm not there anymore. It came to pass; it didn't come to stay.

So my word to you today is: *Get yourself a Joy Box.* Just decorate a shoe box, and start today to collect things that are fun, cute, inspiring. When you start collecting joy, you'll find that it's like a magnet. At first a shoe box may be big enough, but soon you'll have to enlarge it to a basket. Then you'll need a barrel, and before you know it, you may have to add a room to your house, just the way we did in order to have space for all that joy.

One thing I treasure in my Joy Room is a wooden plaque on the wall with the name BARBARA on it. Printed below that name is its meaning: "COMING WITH JOY." I'm so thankful to everyone who has made God's love abundant and running over (see 1 Thess. 3:12). So many have sent me care and love and turned my Joy Room into a haven where people can come to kick back, put it in neutral, and just learn to smile again. Some people who come to see me have not smiled or laughed for months, but sitting in the Joy Room is a form of therapy. Even the grandfather clock seems to chime its message, "I love you, friend, so very much!"

I feel I have earned the Joy Room. I've come back from the Black Pit—back into life again.

I was talking with a lady once and said: "I wonder if there is any place in the Bible where it says that Jesus laughed."

She said, "I don't know where it says that in the Bible, but I do know that Jesus sure fixed it so *we* could!"

And I thought, *She's so right. God fixed it by having Jesus die on the cross and then raising Him from the dead. He fixed it so we could have laughter and joy, so we could look up and say, "Thank you, Lord, for what You've given us —salvation and eternal life."* And we can laugh—I genuinely believe we can laugh and be joyful Christians because of what He has done on Calvary for us.

Extra Thoughts to Take Along

If there were ever a man who knew sorrow, it would be Job, and yet in his story you find this promise from the Lord, if you trust in Him and put it all in His hands:

HE WILL FILL YOUR MOUTH WITH LAUGHTER
AND YOUR LIPS WITH SHOUTS OF JOY.

—Job 8:21, NIV

* * * * * *

Sometimes I Think
I Understand Everything
Then I Regain Consciousness

—Ashleigh Brilliant
Pot-Shots No. 423
© Brilliant Enterprises 1973

* * * * * *

DON'T TAKE LIFE SO SERIOUSLY—
YOU'LL NEVER
GET OUT OF IT ALIVE.

—Source Unknown

CHAPTER SIX

Guilt—The Gift
That Keeps on Giving

Lord,
There are countless things in my life
That are inexcusable.
There are things unaccountable
And things unexplainable.
There are things irrefutable
And things irresponsible.
But it comes to me with unutterable relief
That because of Your amazing love
Nothing in my life is unforgivable.

—Ruth Harms Calkin*

Whenever I talk to parents who have been shattered by the news that a daughter is pregnant out of wedlock or a son has opted for the gay lifestyle, I usually turn to two favorite tools: a bottle of "Guilt Away" and a windshield wiper. I actually have a spray bottle with "Guilt Away" on the label. This much needed "product" was invented by two young men who were nursing hangovers while on a sailing trip. They decided that they needed a modern way to get rid of guilt, so when they got back home they founded their own laboratory and started

---

* "Beautiful Fact" from *Lord, I Keep Running Back to You* by Ruth Harms Calkin, Pomona, Calif., © 1979. Used by permission. All rights reserved.

putting out eight-ounce bottles of rose water labeled "Guilt Away" for sale in stores across America.

With all that pain and guilt floating around out there, they expected to sell at least a million bottles the first year, and I'm sure they reached their goal. But, unfortunately, a squirt of "Guilt Away" doesn't take care of guilt. The reason I hold up my bottle is to get people thinking about the *real* way to spray away guilt—with 1 John 1:9, which says: "If we confess our sins, he is faithful and just to forgive us our sins, and to cleanse us from all unrighteousness" (KJV).

Erma Bombeck says guilt is "the gift that keeps on giving," and that's so true. Too many of us—whether moms or kids—can relate to the thought I saw expressed on a sign not long ago:

MY MOTHER WAS
THE TRAVEL AGENT FOR GUILT TRIPS.*

That's why I also carry a windshield wiper when I speak—to use as a reminder that we have to wipe away the past. You can't beat yourself over the head for mistakes you've made (or you think you've made). Maybe you've had alcoholic parents or been a victim of incest. All kinds of things happen to us to cause pain and guilt, but we don't have to carry this "gift" around with us. We can say, "Lord, wipe that thought or memory from my mind. Help me think of things that are good, pure, and lovely [Phil. 4:8] as You renew my mind from within [Rom. 12:2]."

God Had a Problem Child, Too!

Parents are always asking, "Where did I go wrong?" I tell them that God was a perfect parent, and look at the big mess He had with Adam! Who are we to think that we can be parents and not have big problems with our kids, too? While I was on a radio show, a pastor called in and told me he had a

---

* © 1987 Remarkable Things, Long Beach, CA. Used by permission of Larry Thomas.

woman in his congregation whose son was a homosexual. The woman was extremely distraught, and he was wondering what he could tell her. I told him this:

> The first thing you can say to her is that she's not to blame. Help her to not play the blame game. God was a perfect parent, and look at the mess He had with Adam. So try to get her to see that her son's homosexuality is not her fault—she hasn't done *anything* to contribute to that. Removing the blame is the first thing that you can do, and then help her to reach out with unconditional love to her son.

For many years, psychologists have argued about what really shapes the personality: the genes or the environment. How a child is brought up by his or her parents is important, but recent studies show that the genes play a major role. Some experts believe good parents can have rotten kids and lousy parents can have super kids. Often, there is no clear connection between the way kids are parented and the way they turn out.

I run into many parents who are wracked with guilt, asking: "What did we do wrong?" when their kids seem to go haywire. It helps to tell them that much of the latest psychological research concludes that parents really can't take too much of the credit or the blame for the way their kids turn out.

I'm not trying to get parents completely off the hook of being responsible fathers and mothers who should do the best job they can of rearing their children. God makes it clear that we should "Train up a child in the way he should go: and when he is old he will not depart from it" (Prov. 22:6, KJV). But what these psychiatrists are saying should bring some guilt relief to parents who feel they have failed completely. A lot of what our children grow up to be and do is *not our fault!* Our job is to love them, and then leave the final results up to God!

One of SPATULA's major expenses is its telephone bill. I get and make calls all over the country from parents who need help. Countless times I get calls from mothers who have gone completely *"bananas"* over the action of their kids. I can relate to them with empathy because I've been there. All of us get over those panic feelings at different times, and I was pleased to get the following letter from a mother who tells so clearly how she faced her panic and guilt and moved back into reality:

> I got so weary after two years of waking up at 2:00 A.M. with pains in my stomach. I knew if I kept it up, I would be completely ruined. So, I "had it out" with God. I pointed out to Him that Carol is *His* more than she is mine, and that He loves her more than I do.
>
> I said, "God, *You* should take care of her. You know how to reach her where I cannot." At that time I laid down my burden and *left* it. I no longer have any guilt, for I know I was the best mother I knew how to be. I probably made lots of mistakes, but no one could ever say I didn't CARE. . . . This is my philosophy, and it has worked to get me through this terrible depression of knowing my daughter was a lesbian. Perhaps it will help some other mother who is where I was a year ago.

The Lady with Hamster Hair

Mothers go into all sorts of emotional responses when they have learned that their child is into sinful behavior of one kind or another. When I learned about Larry's homosexuality, I was flooded with guilt as well as physical symptoms like "an elephant on my chest," a "shag rug in my throat," and "itchy teeth." I ran onto one mother who completely lost all of her hair within a week of learning her son was gay. I met her at a meeting, and when she pulled off the little scarf she was wearing on her head, there were only some fine, downy patches of sparse hair, sort of like the hair on a hamster.

I tried to give her some help, reminding her that the way our kids turn out is really not under our control. I must admit, however, that I felt relieved when she put the scarf back on her head and covered up her unsightly scalp. I had no idea if she could ever grow her hair back, but recently I got a call and a cheery voice said, "Remember the lady you met with the hamster hair?"

Actually, I vaguely remembered the lady, but I could never forget that hamster hair. "Well," she continued, "I want you to know that my hair has grown out, full and thick, and today I got myself an Afro!" That was terrific news! Hair can grow out, stomach pains can stop, and hearts can be mended, although it is often a longer process to mend hearts than to grow a head of hair.

Part of our SPATULA ministry is helping people learn to live with a heartache because changes are seldom in sight and long-term anxieties sometimes last indefinitely. That's why I always welcome testimonies from parents who have learned that they can trust God with all of life's problems and heartaches. We can all face tomorrow as long as we have complete trust in Him.

I hung up the phone after talking with my friend and thanked God that her Afro was a sign of restoration, of new growth, of something springing up where it was barren before. So take heart. You may have had panic signs of your own, but I'll bet you never had "hamster hair," did you? So there's always something to be thankful for. You could have become bald from all that trauma!

During a question and answer session at one conference, a woman asked me how she could help her husband let go of the guilt for the way their teen-age son was acting. I told her we all had to let go of guilt in our lives because none of us is perfect. None of us has been exactly the right kind of parent.

What the lady could do was try to enlarge her husband's vision and let him know that God has forgiven him for his mistakes in not dealing with his boy properly. To help anyone who is dealing with guilt, you must encourage him or her to deposit that guilt in God's care and ask forgiveness. Point them to a verse like Psalms 32:1 (the following is from *The Living Bible, Paraphrased*):

WHAT HAPPINESS FOR THOSE WHOSE
GUILT HAS BEEN FORGIVEN!
WHAT JOY WHEN SINS ARE COVERED OVER!
WHAT RELIEF FOR THOSE WHO HAVE CONFESSED
THEIR SINS AND GOD HAS CLEARED THEIR RECORD.

Once a person asks forgiveness and says, "Lord, I made a mess, forgive me," then he or she can get on with life. The important thing is that *you don't have to live in all that guilt.* I think we just have to say we did the best we could with what we knew. From there on, the results are up to God. If you have a failure of the crop, that's up to God, too. And as you give it to God and learn to relinquish it to Him, then you don't have to keep whipping yourself with all the remembered sins. You can get rid of the guilt, which we all want to do.

One Mom Kept Calling—at 3:00 A.M.

It's funny how some of us hang onto our guilt. I had one mother who kept calling me at 3:00 A.M. because she just didn't know why Ted was a homosexual. She lived on the East Coast and she'd often call me at 6:00 in the morning (3:00 my time). She was always crying, saying, "Oh, I don't know why Ted is a homosexual."

I didn't know why, either, but she seemed to have to talk to someone, even though it was 3:00 in the morning on the West Coast. So I'd let her talk, and talk, and talk.

Bill said, "Why don't you tell her it's three hours difference so she won't keep calling at 3:00 in the morning?"

But she never seemed to be able to get that straight. Finally, she made one more call at 3:00 in the morning, saying, "Oh,

I'm just so happy. I found out why Ted is a homosexual. It's because he's the one of the five kids that I didn't breast feed."

I told her that was good news, but I thought to myself, *Oh, good, now that you've found THAT out, you can begin to work on your life and your marriage and quit calling me at 3:00 in the morning.*

This poor mother had to hang it all on SOMETHING, and as soon as she knew that was why, then she could get on with her life. She had been going on a little rat wheel, but once she could get off, she could look ahead to something else. I knew that breast feeding or lack of it was not the right answer to Ted's homosexuality, but if she wanted to hang it on that for the moment, I'd let her. She needed something to help her stabilize and get on with her life. Then I was able to get her to see how she could put her problem in God's hands. Oh, yes, she doesn't call at 3:00 in the morning anymore.

Barney Was Our Lovable Little Imp

We never quite know how our kids will turn out. When my boys were growing up, I might have said that Barney, our youngest, would bring us the most grief. His real name is Dean, but when he was little he used to love the song "Barney Google, with the Goo Goo Googly Eyes," which he played continuously on our player piano. So, we nicknamed him Barney, and it stuck.

I talked about Barney in *Where Does a Mother Go to Resign?*:

. . . how I brought him home from the hospital on Christmas morning, all snug in a bright red Christmas stocking, which the hospital provided for all babies going home on Christmas;

. . . how he and another little boy painted our neighbor's porch black when he was six;

. . . how when he was nine he shut down the entire Market Basket supermarket when he dropped a dime in the checkout line and it rolled through a crack into the gear mechanism that shorted out the entire store!

. . . and how at age ten, while I was holding down a part-time job, he would alter the lists of chores I left for him and his

brothers to do after school and sign them with my special
trademark by putting on lipstick and blotting it on the notes,
just as I always did. Because he laboriously typed the notes
and then "signed" them with a lipstick kiss, his brothers and I
never suspected until the day Larry complained that he had a
list that was so long he couldn't possibly do it all. That's when
I checked and learned about Barney's forgery scheme.

Fortunately, Barney was a charmer and that helped us put
up with all his shenanigans. When he hit high school, I
thought we might have some real problems, particularly with
losing two of his brothers. He was ten when Steven died in
Vietnam, and when Tim died, he was fifteen.

I think Tim's death was the hardest for him to take because
he was very close to Tim. I doubt that I was much help to him
at that time. I probably wasn't any help at all because I spent
so much time crying at the dump, trying to work out my own
grief. Frankly, I didn't really worry about him. He seemed to
handle it all pretty well, and besides he had turned into a
Pillsbury-all-purpose type kid. Anything was fine. He'd eat
anything. Do anything we asked—no problem—except for
the traffic tickets.

Before Barney was eighteen, I had to go to court with him
twenty-two times for traffic tickets. A few of them were for
speeding, but most of them were dumb little tickets that he'd
get for not having the right equipment on his dirt bike. So, we
kept going to court in Pomona, which meant spending most of
the day there. We would go up in the morning and sit there,
and sit there, have lunch, then go back and sit there some
more, waiting our turn.

Finally, we would talk to a commissioner, and he would say,
"Now you're not going to do this again, are you? You have a
nice mother who comes up here with you, but next time we're
going to take your license or impose a fine."

Barney would flash his charming smile and say, "Yes, sir, I'll
never do it again!"

Well, Barney would soon get *another* ticket, and we'd go in
and see *another* commissioner. Fortunately, we never seemed
to see the same man twice in a row, so Barney never did lose
his license—he never even got fined. Whenever I see Barney

now, I tell him he owes me a two-week vacation for all that time I spent going with him to court. He's married now, and his lovely wife, Shannon, played a big part in bringing him to a total commitment to Christ. They have two lovely daughters, Kandee and Tiffany. Their home is truly dedicated to the Lord, who has done wonderful things for them and through them.

My "No U-Turn" Caper

Recently, any guilt I felt over Barney's antics when he was younger boomeranged in my face when I made one of my daily runs down to the La Habra Post Office, which is right next to the La Habra Police Station. As I came out of the post office, I noted a big sign that said, "No U-turn," but because I was in a hurry, I just made a beautiful, sweeping U-turn to get myself back in the right direction as quickly as possible.

I hadn't gotten half a block when a police car came up behind me, siren blaring and red light flashing. A lot of high school kids were going by, and so there I sat in my car as they pointed and chanted, "YEAH! YEAH! YEAH! YEAH! YEAH!" when the police officer walked up, pulling off his gloves. I hadn't had a ticket in years, but I remembered that's just how they do it. They stand there and just pull off their gloves, one finger at a time while you sit there and perspire (gently, of course). He finally got them off and said, "Didn't you see the 'No U-Turn' sign?"

I told him, of course, I'd seen it, but I didn't think "they really meant it."

The officer was not impressed, so while the high school kids kept staring and snickering, he stood there writing up a ticket. All the time I just wanted to get out of there. Finally, I took the ticket, stuck it in my glove compartment, and pulled away from the curb. I got about two blocks down the street, and suddenly I heard a siren again. There in my rear view mirror was a police car with the big red light going around.

I thought, *My goodness, I've only gone two blocks, what have I done?* I pulled over again and up came the same officer, pulling off those gloves, one finger at a time. Then he asked, "Do you have the original ticket I gave you?" I reached in the glove compartment and gave him what he had given me.

"No," he said, "don't you have the original?"

"Am I supposed to get more than one?" I asked. "That's all I have—that's all you gave me."

"Well, I have to have the original," was all he would say. He looked around in the backseat of my car where I had all my SPATULA stuff and finally decided I didn't have his original. So he told me to have a nice day and let me go. I put the copy back in the glove compartment and drove off. I wasn't going to tell anybody about this ticket, especially Bill, because he doesn't ever get them, and this was the first one I'd gotten in years. I didn't know what I was going to do about the ticket. I thought I might go to AAA and they could help me somehow.

Several days went by, and I knew it was about time to think about doing something about that ticket. Then in the mail came a letter addressed to my husband, "Mr. William H. Johnson," from the La Habra Police Department. The letter said, "Dear Mr. Johnson: You can disregard the ticket that you got for making the U-turn in La Habra because the original was lost."

When Bill saw that letter, he became practically paranoid.

"What's this? I didn't get any ticket. How come I'm getting this? MY NAME IS ON THIS!"

Bill knew he hadn't gotten a ticket. But I let him stew awhile. Why should I relieve his guilt? Then I finally told him, "It's not your ticket, it's my ticket."

All he could say was, "You deserve it; you're always doing that."

He heaped all this guilt on me, which I knew he'd do, and that's why I didn't want to tell him at first. I got a little ruffled and said, "If we all got what we deserved, we all deserve to go to hell, but it's only by the grace of God that any of us escape."

That profound bit of theology quieted him down a little, but it didn't do a whole lot for my guilt feelings, so that week I went out and bought a big box of See's candy and took it down to the police station. I didn't want to tell them who I was, because it's like getting shot at and missed when you get a ticket and then the police lose it! But if I gave them my name, who knows? They could look it up and perhaps find my ticket. So, I just laid the candy on the counter and said, "Have a happy day," and left.

When I got home, I thought I'd call Barney and tell him what happened. After twenty-two tickets of his own, he might be interested.

I got Barney on the phone and told him the whole story— about getting the ticket for the U-turn and how the letter had come saying they had lost the original so I could ignore the ticket completely.

"How could that be?" Barney wondered. "I've had twenty-two and they didn't throw any of my tickets away."

I couldn't resist—I just had to say it: "Well, Barney, if you really LIVE right . . ."

Barney just laughed, but there's a little postscript to this story. Not long afterward, we were leaving on a trip by car and stopped by his home. We went in and tried to say some hurried good-byes to Barney, Shannon, and their little girls, but just before we left, Barney said, "Oh, you can't go yet. We want to pray for you."

So, this big, 6'2" kid of ours grabbed our hands, pulled us all into a little circle, and prayed for our safety on the trip! I am sure he and his little family have prayed for us often— probably daily—but somehow, to stand in that circle of six people and have my baby son praying for us really brought the message home to me. We had come full circle. All the years of praying for our kids . . . having them dedicated to the Lord . . . teaching, training, loving, caring . . . watching them break our hearts and then seeing their growth and how the pattern of God's weaving in their lives comes out . . . all this has paid off! As somebody said, "Kids are not a short-term loan, they are a LONG-TERM INVESTMENT!"

Barney Taught Me Something about Guilt

I used to think I'd have to be nice to Barney because he would be the one who would pick out my rest home, but now that I have diabetes and am probably not going to need one, I don't have to be so nice!

One thing Barney has taught me is that condemnation only heaps up more guilt. When Bill and I learned of Larry's homosexuality, Barney told us that he had known about it for quite some time. But being the nonjudgmental type, he had said nothing. "Live and let live" was his approach, and when I look back, I can see the wisdom in that.

But I was trapped into being a mother, a parent who was supposed to uphold her standards. I couldn't accept a homosexual son. I would rather see him dead first! I became a guilt-ridden Christian, sure that I had made some bad mistakes that caused Larry to be the way he was. And then I made an even bigger mistake by rejecting him and judging him. But when I said, "Whatever, Lord," as I drove up that viaduct to commit suicide, I not only relinquished Larry to God, I handed over all my guilt as well and knew real forgiveness for the first time in eleven months.

I relinquished it ALL to God—Larry, my own failures, and whatever the future might bring. I was able to reach out and accept God's cleansing forgiveness and stand clean before the Lord! Many parents suffer needlessly because they do not deal with their guilt and receive the freedom to live *guilt free*. I found a little card that I display on the wall in my Joy Room:

> Dear God
> I have sinned
> Against Heaven
> And against You.
> I am no longer worthy to be called Your child.
>
> *Child, I know . . . I know . . .*
> *But My Son*
> *Is forever worthy*
> *To be called Your Savior.*

—Ruth Harms Calkin*

That card tells me that God believes I am worth loving— so are you. We are worth loving, even with our sins, even

---

* "Forever Worthy" from *Lord, You Love to Say Yes* by Ruth Harms Calkin, Pomona, Calif., © 1976. Used by permission. All rights reserved.

with that which is degrading to look at about ourselves. Even with our faults. Even with the shameful past. Even with our rebellion.

The Good News is that you can stop nailing yourself to a cross because Jesus was nailed to a cross for you. If you accept His forgiveness, you can live a guilt-free life from here on out.

Over four hundred years before Christ, a Greek poet said: "Even God cannot change the past." In a way, he was right. What has happened has happened, and there is no going back and changing it. But in another way, he was, oh, so wrong. God changed the past when He sent His Son to die on the Cross for our sins. That provided the only possible way your sinful past and mine could be erased. And that's why 1 John 1:9 makes sense. That's why you can keep coming to God, asking forgiveness. Whenever we sin, we have an advocate with the Father—His Son, Jesus Christ (see 1 John 2:1).

We Are All Treasures in His Hand

The opal is a beautiful stone, but when it lies in a jeweler's case, it's cold and lusterless, with no life in it. But let the jeweler pick it up in his hand and the warmth of his touch brings out the brilliant hues and colors. Likewise, when we hold the Lord at arm's length and refuse to let Him work in our lives, there is no brilliance, no color, no depth to living. But when we allow the touch of the Master's hand, His love warms us and we know we are jewels for His kingdom. Until then we are hidden treasures.

You may have seen the picture of the little boy saying, "I know I'm SOMEBODY . . . cause GOD don't make no JUNK!" That little boy has a better understanding of God's love and forgiveness than many adult parents do. Their self-esteem has been destroyed because of something that's gone wrong in the family. Guilt has destroyed their self-esteem, and they feel worthless. I know that feeling—I felt it for eleven months without relief, and I still feel it occasionally when I momentarily forget I am very special to God.

One of the most fun gifts I have ever received for my Joy Room is a shiny Red Plate on which is engraved: "You are special today!" You may have heard of these Red Plates. They come from a custom among Early American families. When someone deserves special praise or attention, that person will be served dinner on the Red Plate.

What a great idea for giving honor to a special person with a visible reminder of your love. But the best thing about the Red Plate is that it reminds me that I am special today to God, even if it isn't my birthday, or Mother's Day, or any other holiday. God loves me every day, and *I am always special to Him.*

I take no more heavy guilt trips, because Jesus has wiped my slate clean. He cannot see my sin because it is covered by His blood. He gave me a white robe of righteousness, which is kept clean by a special detergent called FORGIVENESS. Because Christ is in me, I have the hope of glory, and because of Him I deserve this special plate *every day of my life.* Anyone who comes to visit me and my Joy Room will see my Red Plate proudly displayed for all to see. I admire it often, just to make up for all the years when I didn't have it to remind me how special I am to God.

How I wish I could reach out to everyone—parents as well as their rebelling children—and give each one a shiny Red Plate like I have. I want to remind you of how special you are to me and to God—you are a very important SOMEBODY in His sight. Life is too short to be paralyzed by guilt, so accept His forgiveness and go forward with your life, determined to do your best.

Extra Thoughts to Take Along

RELAX

If we weren't meant to keep starting over . . .
would God have granted us Monday?

—From a Bumper Sticker

*　*　*　*　*　*

GOOD HOUSEKEEPING

Lord, it is not the dirt and clutter in plain sight
that nag at me.
It's that hidden dirt . . . you know, behind the
refrigerator, in the closets, under the bed.
Dirt that no one sees or knows about but me.

It's the same way with my life, God.
It's those hidden sins that I can't keep up with . . . those
petty little grievances, the grudges, the resentments,
the unspoken harsh feelings, the superior attitudes.
Thoughts and feelings that no one else knows about but
me . . . and You, God.
Help me, Father, to clean my heart as I would my home.
Take away all dust and cobwebs of pride, ill feelings and
prejudice.
The dirt behind my refrigerator will never hurt anyone.
The dirt in my heart will.

—Source Unknown

* * * * * *

TO GET A FRESH START, DO THESE EIGHT THINGS:

1. Be born again.

2. Accept God's forgiveness.

3. Freely forgive others.

4. Learn all you can from your mistakes.

5. Turn your weakness into your strong point.

6. Accept what you cannot change, and with God's help, turn
it into something beautiful.

7. Put the past behind you.

8. Get up and begin again.

—Source Unknown

* * * * * *

GOD'S "GUILT AWAY" PROMISE

"Therefore, there is now no condemnation for those who are in Christ Jesus . . ." (Rom. 8:1, NIV).

CHAPTER SEVEN

One Day I Shall Burst My Buds of Calm and Blossom into Hysteria

Life generally looks better in the morning.
It's just that morning takes so long to get here!

The problem with stress is that it comes at you from every direction, anytime, anywhere. I was in Texas to speak at a huge banquet, and as I started toward the podium, one lady grabbed my arm and said, "Don't step back too far because there's a hole in the carpet and you're liable to catch your heel in it."

Okay, I would be sure not to do that. I continued toward the platform when another lady, who had arranged all the flowers, whispered, "Don't push on the podium. The flowers may fall over!" That sounded a little like the guy at the book table earlier in the evening who had told me, "Don't lean too hard when you sign your books because the table collapses very easily."

By the time I got to the "danger zone" known as the podium, I was already pretty well stressed-out for the evening. But just before I began to speak, I saw the maintenance man headed my way, bringing me a glass of water. *How nice!* I thought. *At last something positive.* But as he placed the glass on the podium, he delivered the *coup de grace:* "Be careful—the last speaker we had spilled her water into the microphone and almost electrocuted herself."

Somehow I continued with my talk and, fortunately, my heel never caught in the carpet, the flowers didn't fall off the podium, and I never even touched the water, so we all had a good time anyway.

When Real Stress Is a Constant Companion

Of course, THAT kind of stress is nothing to the kind I hear about in letter after letter from totally stressed-out moms and other stretched-out folks who write to me every month. They are going through *real* stress, and I always include one or two letters in *The Love Line* newsletter each month, just to let readers gauge their own progress in getting out of the pit. I empathize with these letter writers because I've been an occupant of the pit myself, and I know that it helps to read about how others are going through the same kind of emotional struggle. It all doesn't seem so unreal when you hear about someone else who has stress for a constant companion. One woman wrote to say:

Dear Barbara and Co-Workers:

As always, I enjoy your newsletters thoroughly—don't know how you come up with so much new material every month. I know God is with you every day, for you to keep on hanging in there with such hope and prayer for us hurting parents. It's been five years for me, and some days I think I can't live through another. I still live in constant prayer and hope for a change. I still cry at the very thought of this happening in my family, and I will never, never understand. I don't think any of my family suspects—at least they don't let on. I dream of moving far, far away where nobody but God would know.

Another mom agonized:

These times have been horrible, and I sometimes wonder if there will ever be any relief. At the present time I am feeling numb and I cry over the dumbest things. Maybe it will not take so long, but I will keep praying. . . .

Still another letter I got simply said: "Help! Please help! My son came out of the closet and put me in it!"

One mother sent a desperate plea that put *me* under stress:

Please send us tapes for guilt ridden parents (us).

My husband is on the verge of a nervous breakdown, and I'm a close second.

Please be selective in your choice of tapes—my husband doesn't need any more condemnation nor do I right now. Although I'm more prepared than he.

My son is homosexual, and we still have one daughter at home who doesn't know yet.

We need help and right now. You are our only hope.

"Bad Stress" Is My Specialty

These letters come from women who are under what the medical experts would call "distress," or bad stress. There is another kind of stress, called "eustress"—the good kind of stress we all need to have just enough pressure and adrenalin flowing to help us get things done and enjoy life. But my mail bag is full of "bad stress"—the kind that can rip you apart if you let it suck you in. As one definition puts it, "stress is that confusion created when one's mind overrides the body's desire to choke the living daylights out of some jerk who desperately needs it."

I had a bad stress day myself recently when I took out a nice, new, shiny, powerful vacuum cleaner that I had just purchased. Having wielded my dependable old model for thirty years or more, I thought I knew all about vacuums and didn't bother to study the directions on operating the new one. Instead, I attached the power nozzle to the machine, already anticipating the whir of power as my new vacuum would perform for me.

Of course, I should have been suspicious when I saw a dial that indicated whether the dirt to be picked up was "FINE, MEDIUM, or COARSE." Fine dirt, I assumed, would be like silt or sand, and with my sandbox days long since faded into yesterday, I knew I could skip that setting.

But what about "medium" dirt? That might be raisins, cookie crumbles, or anything ordinary shoes might bring in. And "coarse" dirt? That could be peach pits, dirt clods, or stray Legos the grandchildren leave behind. Making a quick tour of the house, I found no collection of marbles or Tinker Toys lying loose, so I felt it was safe to set the dial on "medium dirt." Somehow I felt a little smug and proud, being able to set MY vacuum for medium dirt rather than coarse.

The indicator was set, the machine was plugged in, the bag was securely closed. I clicked the "on" button, and that began my day of disaster!

Within a few minutes, the long pedicels from a hanging plant which I had been coaxing along for several months disappeared into the machine, along with pieces of dirt clods, and green vines that had been attached. One entire side of the foliage on my plant was gone—sucked into the mouth of my hungry monster!

Before I could recover, my new extra-long telephone cord made a whirring noise as it disappeared and wrapped itself in tangles inside my voracious vacuum. I managed to disentangle the cord, but noted that chunks of the rubber covering were now missing, the holes making a regular pattern like huge teeth had clamped down on it.

And, of course, Bill should have known better than to leave his shoe in plain sight of the vacuum. In a few seconds, the tongue of the shoe was sucked up as well as the shoelace! Oh, well, I reasoned, the shoes were old and should have been discarded anyhow. But right after the shoe episode, my eyes grew wide with horror as the new Sony adaptor cord for Bill's stereo headphone set wrapped itself noisily into the vacuum brushes.

So far, my plant had been eaten, the telephone cord had been mutilated, Bill's shoes were declared unfit, and now his Sony adaptor was almost completely destroyed. If only we had a dog, I could blame the disappearance of the adaptor cord on a teething puppy. I wondered how long it would be before he noticed his adaptor cord was gone (completely eaten by the vacuum, except for the plastic head whose size alone saved it from being sucked into the nozzle as well).

Being the melancholy perfectionistic type that he is, Bill soon missed his Sony adaptor cord and began checking all the electrical outlets, thinking he might have misplaced it. Finally, my conscience forced me to break my silence.

Shamefully I had to admit my POWER vacuum had sucked up his precious Sony cord and that I had immediately ordered another one (which would take several weeks to arrive).

We're ALL Like My Vacuum

I learned a lot that day. It's funny how the wording on a little plastic dial can inspire your thoughts. But we're all like vacuum cleaners, really. We all suck up a certain amount of dirt along the way. I wonder if people who absorb only "fine dirt" get special recognition? What about "medium dirt" and "coarse dirt"? Every one of us must fit into some category on that dial because it's impossible to walk through life without getting soiled. There's filth everywhere—even on TV and in gossip, idle chatter. And what about our consumer culture, which makes materialism and greed sound like the only way to live? My new vacuum cleaner prompted me to sift through my own life, looking at areas where various degrees of dirt needed cleaning out.

I discovered that part of that dirt was stress. And I realized that being too busy and rushing about doing more than God wants me to do is dirt that I shouldn't be carrying.

The day following the rampage of my vacuum monster, I heard the gardener outside using his tools to keep our grounds clear of debris. But instead of *sucking up* the dirt, he was *blowing it away*. As he moved along the walkways, his blower whisked away anything in its path, and I was reminded of a book I had just finished reading, *Blow Away the Black Clouds* by Florence Littauer. It's a terrific book on dealing with depression. And one of the things that makes it so terrific is that it DOESN'T depress you!

I thought about my power vacuum and how we can spend our lives sucking in the dirt, absorbing it, taking it up, and putting it in a neat little bag to be disposed of later. But with that method, you're always collecting more and more. The gardener had a better approach. He simply blew all the dirt away and left a clean path where he walked. All the crevices and walkways were clean, and he didn't have the added worry of what was fine, medium, or coarse, either.

Are You Absorbing Too Much Stress?

I think there is a real application here to how we live. We can absorb and soak up a lot of crud and collect a lot of misery. We can hold on to the pains that are bound to come, almost cherishing them. We also do this with depression and other crummy stuff. We can cling to this until our bag is full, and then we may dump it—usually on somebody else.

Or we have the option of blowing all that negative thinking away—the criticisms and grudges, the self-depreciation that leads to compulsive behavior designed to please others. We can ask God to remove it completely, replacing darkness with His light, sweeping us clean of unforgiveness, bitterness, greed, and social ambition. He can make a springlike freshness in our hearts if we will know and practice the presence of the Holy Spirit.

Where are you today? Are you going through life sucking up grudges and grievances that turn into pressure and stress as you remember all the wrongs done to you? Are you carrying around other bagfuls of dirt from old sin areas? We often have the mistaken idea that stress is something other people and outside forces cause in our lives. Stress can be caused by external factors, but very often *we cause our own stress.* We can let God blow away our stress—get it out of our path, out of our lives. Then we can stand clean before Him with the assurance that He can keep us from losing our minds. Not only that, but He can help us renew our minds daily.

You Can't Control It All

Something that helped me cope with my stress instead of continuing to collect it along with a lot of other mental barnacles was realizing that *If there is no control, there is no responsibility.*

Dr. Harold Greenwald has co-authored a book called *The Happy Person.* He believes there are at least six realities in life that we can't change and we must accept. Getting older is one of them. Getting old is inevitable, but according to Dr. Greenwald, if you consider the alternative, it is a process you can learn to enjoy. (More on that in chapter 9.)

Also, there are always things in life that will not be fair. And there will be some people who won't like you no matter how kind, good-natured, and charming you might be.

You must keep in mind that life is a constant struggle. Some people think that if they can just get over the particular hump or through the particular tunnel in which they are struggling now, that everything will be smooth sailing from then on. That just won't happen. Better to see life as a series of problems that are opportunities to learn and grow, and then you won't get nearly as stressed out when the struggles come.

Above all, remember that you can't change people. That was a hard one for me because I always wanted to change Larry. But I had to let Larry do his own changing, with God as his motivator and power source. Once I stopped trying to change him, most of the stress went out of our relationship.

Use Laughter to Cope with Stress

With all its pain and problems, life is no joke, but as I explained in chapter 5, learning to laugh can help you cope. I agree completely with the professor of psychology who believes laughter is the best way to relieve stress and get yourself in a new frame of mind. In an Associated Press release (I don't know the date), Dr. Robert Leone of United States International University says, "When you're laughing your attention is focused. You can't do anything else. Everything else, whether it's depression or stress, stops." Dr. Leone also says a good laugh can cleanse your emotional state and make you feel better about going on. He lists all kinds of ways to put a little more laughter in your life:

1.   Try listening to a humorous record by one of your favorite comedians, or go see a funny movie. It's a temporary lift, but just the release of laughter will make you feel better.

2.   Try expanding your activities. For example, maybe you never sing in the car because you don't want people next to you on the freeway thinking you're weird. Try it sometime, and then you can chuckle over the funny looks you get.

3.   Quit making excuses for why you aren't happy. "At some point," says Dr. Leone, "you have to take responsibility

for your own happiness. People . . . settle for 60 or 70 percent happiness, but they could be a lot happier."

Singing Can Work Wonders, Too

I mentioned above that singing in the car might produce some weird looks and a few laughs, but there are even better reasons to sing. I often sing as I ride my exercycle, take showers, or do housework. The experts say you can live longer with a song in your heart. In one case, doctors put twenty professional opera singers, ages twenty-eight to sixty-five, through eight minutes of rigorous breathing exercises. Every singer did it in a breeze, but a group of forty nonsingers *under forty years old* struggled to finish the test and their heart rates soared.

Psychiatrists sometimes urge their patients to sing away tension and anxiety. When you sing, you get rid of energy, and this can take your mind off your troubles, spark pleasant memories, and ease physical tension. Try singing in the shower to get ready to face the day or singing in the car, especially when traffic is bumper to bumper. Pick songs that are inspiring and motivating. For me, hymns and gospel songs do that the best. Some of my favorite are "Amazing Grace" and "When Answers Aren't Enough, There is Jesus." And I also like the chorus that says: "In moments like these, I sing out a love song . . . I sing out a love song to Jesus."

How to Survive the Rat Race

One of the major causes for stress in daily life is PRESSURE. Recently I met Tim Hansel, author of a great book on dealing with pain called *Ya Gotta Keep Dancin'*. We were both invited to speak at the same conference, and I got a chuckle when Tim said, "I'll bet both our schedules are somewhere to the left of WHOOPEE!" That reminded me of one of my favorite bumper snickers:

> JUST WHEN YOU THOUGHT
> YOU WERE WINNING THE RAT RACE
> ALONG COME FASTER RATS.

We all have to run the "rat race." The trick is to try not to drop out of the race, but to pace ourselves so we can LAST. I've learned to be thankful for my diabetes because it has forced me to avoid stress and eat properly. I look at it as a positive thing—something that's good news instead of bad.

God's Advice for Defeating Depression

It's important to deal with stress because it can easily turn into depression. In fact, I once read an article that said depression is often caused by *not learning how to deal with the stresses in your life.* Women especially have to be on guard because their personalities tend to make them more prone to depression than men.

From my own experience, I agree. Almost every week I talk to depressed mothers who feel like the bull's eye on the dart board of life. Many of them just want to curl up and find a hole to hide in (which is what I did the first time Larry left for the gay life). But I urge them to try to keep busy, to keep going. And I also tell them to be patient. It takes time to get over depression, but it does end. It doesn't come to stay; like much of the other pain and hassle in life, it comes to PASS.

I found a wonderful paraphrase of 1 Corinthians 13. It can be a real help, particularly if you're feeling down and depressed. Try reading this paraphrase aloud every morning and evening, and the realization of God's love will start seeping into your life to blow away your black clouds:

BECAUSE GOD LOVES ME
(Based on 1 Corinthians 13:4–8)

Because God loves me, He is slow to lose patience with me.

Because God loves me, He takes the circumstances of my life and uses them in a constructive way for my growth.

Because God loves me, He is for me. He wants to see me mature and develop in His love.

Because God loves me, He does not send down His wrath on every little mistake I make, of which there are many.

Because God loves me, He does not keep score of all my sins and then beat me over the head with them whenever He gets the chance.

Because God loves me, He is deeply grieved when I do not walk in the ways that please Him because He sees this as evidence that I don't trust Him and love Him as I should.

Because God loves me, He keeps on trusting me when at times I don't even trust myself.

Because God loves me, He never says there is no hope for me: rather, He patiently works with me, loves me, and disciplines me in such a way that it is hard for me to understand the depth of His concern for me.

Because God loves me, He never forsakes me even though many of my friends might.

Because God loves me He stands with me when I have reached the rock bottom of despair, when I see the real me and compare that with His righteousness, holiness, beauty, and love. It is at a moment like this that I can really believe that God loves me.

Yes, the greatest of all gifts is God's perfect love!

—Source Unknown

Stress Is in the Eye of the Beholder

I learned from personal experience that one person's "stress" is another person's minor irritation. I can still remember when I was going through my black tunnel of despair and a lady called me to tell me her problem. It seemed that she had "fat pads" on her knees. My own heart was so raw and bleeding that it was all I could do to listen patiently to her complaints. But to her, the fat pads were an all-consuming problem, and she had to talk to someone about them.

Another woman wrote to me about a similar situation which she experienced, saying that she had gotten so frustrated she let off a little steam, which she later regretted. She writes:

Once a lady in my class asked for prayer because her husband would not pick up his socks. I said (and I am ashamed of it), "Would you like to trade places with me? I have a bad heart, a retarded son, and an alcoholic husband given to sporadic violence. I have an illegitimate grandson. A man my husband fired threw a Molotov cocktail into a warehouse we had just filled with roofing materials on credit, causing the second largest fire (our city) ever had. We had no insurance. After three years of struggling to pay for the burned stock, the recession forced us into bankruptcy.

And people tell me to lose weight when we are living on beans and potatoes."

I was immediately ashamed because the lady had all she could handle with the sock problem, and playing "Can You Top This?" gives the Lord no glory. I have learned a lot over the years, usually too late.

How true! We do learn a lot over the years and often it seems to be too late, but it's never too late to face stress and hassles with a positive attitude. Something can always be done to straighten life out, no matter how full of twists and snares it gets.

Under Stress at a Rescue Mission

I still say the most positive thing you can do about stress is to learn to laugh. Recently, I was invited to speak at the Los Angeles Rescue Mission on Skid Row. That was stress in itself because this isn't my usual audience. Bill had come with me, and because he had a bad cold, he sat up on the platform behind me nipping at a little bottle of cough medicine. Of course, it looked as if he were nipping at something else!

As I was trying to get into my talk, I noticed one man in the front row who had his hat pulled way down around his ears. Just then, one of the Mission workers came down the aisle with a long pole. It was almost twenty feet in length and had some kind of gripping device on the end. He reached the pole clear across the front row and snatched the man's hat, plucking it right off his head, then turned and walked out. The Union Rescue Mission has strict rules—no listening to speakers with your hat on, but I guess they had no rule about throwing speakers for a loop by reaching across the row with a twenty-foot pole and plucking off hats. Nobody seemed to notice, though. Everybody just kept listening to my story, which was at a very serious point. And all the while Bill kept sitting behind me, nipping away at his cough syrup.

At a moment like that, you have to decide, "How am I going to react to this?" Well, I just answered my own question. "Hey, this is too ridiculous to cry about, so I might as well laugh." And that's just what I did. The stress drained away, and I got through the talk okay.

On the Way—Not Yet Arrived

But even with all the ways I cope with stress, there are still little incidents that remind me I haven't completely arrived. It has been several years since that night at the flagpole in Disneyland, and while I have come far, I have not yet arrived. I still struggle with shocked feelings and flashbacks that bring tears. The strangest things can trigger me. For example, once I was in a local travel bureau looking at vacation folders. Suddenly my eye caught the following words on the front of a cruise ship folder: IS CRUISING REALLY FOR ME?

Before I knew anything about homosexuality, those words would have been no threat, but now that I had been "educated" in gay jargon, I knew that "cruising" doesn't always mean enjoying oneself on a luxury liner. Suddenly, all the old feelings of shock rushed back. My chest began to feel heavy, my throat got dry, my stomach felt like peach pits were churning around scraping the inside raw. Suddenly, I was back in the turmoil of that first day when I learned about Larry's homosexuality. Insane as it might sound, once again everyone looked gay to me.

I share this incident to help you understand that you will have yo-yo experiences. You may think you are making progress and then WHAM! you see one folder in a travel bureau (or something else), and you are right back to square one! The simplest things can trigger those feelings all over again. You feel you are getting some control over the crying and the outbursts, and then for the slightest reason you come unglued, and you feel as if the bottom has dropped out.

But when stress like this hits, remember you're in a long, tough process. We all take a couple of steps forward and then take a step back once in a while. But there *is* healing and there are *gains.* This, too, will pass, but oh, so slowly!

The setting of one of my favorite cartoons is also a travel bureau. A lady is standing at a counter, talking to her travel agent who obviously has just asked, "Where would you like to go?" Her answer: "Some place where troubles melt like lemon drops away above the chimney tops."

I love that. That's just where you and I would like to go, too, but unfortunately, we have to cope with life as it is. I am with all of you out there who are still fractured. I understand the yo-yo syndrome and what stress can do to keep you on it. Through years of struggle, my mind has learned a lot, but emotionally I am still fragile and need God's glue to keep my mind centered on Him.

When stress closes in, your best move is to turn to the Lord. ". . . take a new grip with your tired hands, stand firm on your shaky legs . . ." (Heb. 12:12, TLB). And, laugh as much as possible. It will keep stress under control, and it also accelerates the healing of your fractured mind!

Extra Thoughts to Take Along

OF ALL THE THINGS I'VE LOST,
IT'S MY MIND I MISS THE MOST!

*　*　*　*　*　*

If only I could get that wonderful feeling
of accomplishment
without having to accomplish anything.

—Ashleigh Brilliant

Pot-Shots No. 431
© Brilliant Enterprises 1973

*　*　*　*　*　*

TODAY IS THE TOMORROW
YOU WORRIED ABOUT YESTERDAY,
AND ALL IS WELL.

*   *   *   *   *   *

THE TIME IS NOW

Lord,
I see with startling clarity
That life is never long enough
To put You off
Until tomorrow.
The things that are before
Are all too soon behind.
I can never pick up
The years I've put down.
If I intend
To walk with You tomorrow
I must start today.

—Ruth Harms Calkin*

*   *   *   *   *   *

I DON'T KNOW THE ANSWERS,
BUT I KNOW SOMEONE WHO DOES.

*   *   *   *   *   *

---

* "The Time Is Now" from *Lord, You Love to Say Yes* by Ruth Harms Calkin, Pomona, Calif., © 1976. Used by permission. All rights reserved.

NEW BEGINNING

O God,
What shall I do?
I am at the total end
Of myself.

Wonderful, dear child!
Now start your new beginning
With Me.

—Ruth Harms Calkin*

* "New Beginning" from *Lord, It Keeps Happening . . . and Happening* by Ruth Harms Calkin, Pomona, Calif., © 1984. Used by permission. All rights reserved.

CHAPTER EIGHT

I Married Mr. Wumphee

My husband and I are very different people, a fact you have no doubt already observed. They say opposites attract, and in our case it seemed to happen on our first date. We started the evening with different partners (I had set him up with a girl-friend), and by the time we came home, Bill was with me and my friend was with the guy I had started out with.

When Bill and I got married, I didn't know anything about temperaments. I didn't realize that being talkative, emotional, demonstrative, enthusiastic, cheerful, and bubbling over with a good sense of humor meant that I was basically SANGUINE. And I'm sure that Bill, who is deep and thoughtful, analytical, serious, sensitive to others, and conscientious, had no idea that he was pure MELANCHOLY.*

All I knew was that Bill seemed steady, calm, faithful, and devoted. Something in me responded to that. Intuitively, I knew I needed someone like Bill to balance my own tendency to be too excited, all helter-skelter, and disorganized. And I think Bill sensed he needed me to offset his tendency to take

---

* The best description of temperaments I've heard and seen comes from Florence Littauer, who has published a set of cassette tapes on temperaments, as well as the book, *Personality Plus* (Old Tappan: Fleming H. Revell, 1983).

life too seriously. So we got married and learned that, while opposites attract, they also must *adjust* to each other. The only real point of this chapter (except to tell you some funny stories about Bill) is this: *You have to learn to accept people as they are (especially husbands)*.

I'll never expect Bill to be as happy and bubbling with enthusiasm over things as I am, and he has finally decided I'll never be as orderly, methodical, and organized as he is.

So, we have spent several decades adjusting to each other and building a strong marriage based on acceptance. Bill is really a great guy, he's just terrific, but I've had to learn that with his melancholy temperament he's what I call a "sinker"— not a "stinker" but a *SINKER*. Let me give you an example. Recently we had a beautiful smog-free day, which is getting pretty rare in Southern California. The sky was azure blue, and the clouds were fleecy white. I looked up and said, "Wow, it looks as if God vacuumed the sky."

Bill looked up and said, "Yeah, but He'll probably dump the vacuum bag tomorrow."

Bill doesn't see a glass just half empty; he sees all the smudges and water spots, too. Order and precision are all-important to him. He wants the checkbook to balance, and he likes his sandwiches made so that the bumps on the bread fit together perfectly. Sometimes I like to tease him by trimming off the edges of the bread so he never knows if the bumps matched or not. These things are important to him.

The other day he got a new key ring and spent almost an hour putting all the keys on the ring so they would all face the "right" way. He says he can't use my key ring because I have them jumbled every which way.

Stapled Socks Are Safe Socks

Bill's idea of real fun is stapling his socks together when he puts them in the wash so they won't get separated. He started doing this when our boys were growing up, so his socks wouldn't get mixed up with any of theirs. Being the type who would never staple anything together, I tried to rationalize it by remembering that Bill had been in the Navy; and besides, he's an only child, and they're all a little strange, anyhow.

I mentioned Bill's stapled socks at a conference somewhere, and, afterward, one gal came up and told me her husband not only stapled his socks, but he marked them "1" and "2" so that he didn't get his big toe in the wrong sock!

I Laughed 'Til I Dried

One thing I must be constantly aware of is that what is funny to me is often not funny to Bill. Awhile back I was in Atlanta to do some speaking, and afterward I hurried to the airport to catch my plane for home. I had already checked my luggage and was sitting in the waiting area expecting to board in a few minutes when the loudspeaker said, "All DC–10 flights have been shut down for at least three days." I went up to the counter and was told that my flight was a DC–10; therefore, I wasn't going anywhere for a while.

I called Bill and told him I wasn't coming home, that they were going to put us all up in a hotel, and we'd be there for two or three days. Bill suggested that I just relax and enjoy the chance to rest, but I reminded him that it would be hard to relax without any luggage.

They shuttled us over to a hotel near the airport, and I checked into my room. Because I was going to be there two or three days, I did what any sensible woman would do—I washed my panty hose, washed my slip, washed my face, and got ready to go to bed. I had *nothing* with me. My luggage had already gone to California (I hoped), and that was it.

Just as I finished washing my panty hose and slip and they were drip drying in the bathroom, I got a phone call. It was the airline saying, "If you can be here in twenty minutes, there is a flight leaving. But if you don't get that flight, there is nothing out of here for three days. It will be the only flight going out of here to California."

"Hold that plane, I'll *be* there to make the flight!" I shrieked. Then I saw my dripping wet panty hose and slip. I quickly rolled them in a towel and tried to get as much water out as I could, but it really didn't do much good. If you've ever tried to get wet panty hose on a dry fat body, believe me, it's not easy!

And then there was my slip. That didn't go on very well, either.

Somehow I managed to wiggle into the panty hose and slip, but that meant that my feet were soaking wet and I had to try to get them into my black suede heels. I dashed downstairs, dripping puddles everywhere, and grabbed a taxi. He got me to the airport in record time, and then I ran down the long concourse to the plane, dripping all the way. I made it to the gate just as they were closing up and getting ready to pull away. And, of course, when I sat in my seat, I left another big wet mark because I was still soaking wet.

When I got home, I told Bill the story, and he just cringed. He was humiliated to think that I might have left a wet spot on the plane seat. I told him, "The seat wasn't much of a problem; you should have seen all the water I dripped down the concourse to the gate!"

I had chuckled all the way home on that flight. I thought the whole thing was really funny, but Bill just found it embarrassing.

His and Hers Peanut Butter Jars

One thing that drives Bill crazy is a "messy" peanut butter jar. He doesn't like me to plunge into the peanut butter with my knife and make a big mess. He thinks peanut butter should be smooth, and when he gets to the bottom of the jar, he likes to scrape every bit of peanut butter up until the jar is so clean, it looks as if it's been scrubbed. THAT makes him really happy.

Sometimes he'll go out to the kitchen to make a sandwich and bellow, "Who has been in the peanut butter?"

Since there's nobody living there but the two of us, he knows the answer. Who else would be in the peanut butter but me? Then he makes me feel so guilty because I plunged into the peanut butter jar too deep and messed things up.

I finally solved all this by buying a big jar of peanut butter for him and a big jar for me. Now I just plunge in any old way I want to!

I have lots of women come up to me after I speak and say, "I think my husband must be your husband's brother, or at least a distant cousin. He's just like that." Maybe your husband is, too. You see roses; he sees thorns. You see God vacuuming the sky; he sees God dumping the vacuum bag. You're planning the next party, and he's worrying about all the trash the party will make; in fact, he worries about all the trash in the whole world, plus the shortage of water, the national debt, and any number of other serious matters. And the bottom line is he *likes* to worry about all that stuff!

How Bill Became "Mr. Wumphee"

Somehow our marriage has always worked because I simply tell myself, "That's the way Bill is and that's what he's going to be." And I'm sure he says the same about me.

Years ago he started calling me "Cumphee." I decided to come up with a nickname for him and finally settled on "Wumphee." People sometimes ask me what Wumphee means, and I say I'm not sure. Do pet names for your husband really have to MEAN anything? All I can say is, "He's just a Wumphee—and I like to have him around!"

A couple of years ago, I got my personalized S–P–A–T–U–L–A license plate, which caused any number of comments. Once I parked in an improper place (probably while hurrying into the La Habra Post Office) and someone called out: "Mrs. SPATOOLA! You can't park there!"

I was having so much fun with my S–P–A–T–U–L–A license plate, I decided that Bill needed his own personal plate, too. And I had the perfect name for that plate: W–U–M–P–H–E–E. We both drive Oldsmobiles. Mine is a late model, and Bill's is a 1974 Delta 88, which he picked up when an elderly man in our mobile home park died and his widow didn't need the car any more. It was in immaculate shape and took regular gas, which appealed to Bill no end because he wouldn't have to fool around with smog certification.

Whenever you want to order a personalized plate, you have to check to be sure someone else doesn't have that name already. So I went down to the Department of Motor Vehicles and got out their giant book, which lists all the personalized plates in California. As I sat there in the DMV office, lifting the heavy plasticized pages, which couldn't be ripped or torn and which were permanently marked, I came across names like S–T–R–E–I–S–A–N–D, S–I–N–A–T–R–A, and S–E–L–L–E–C–K. And then I saw the name S–P–A–T–U–L–A (my car). And then it hit me. Just as S–P–A–T–U–L–A is in the giant permanent DMV book, my name, Barbara Johnson, is in the Lamb's Book of Life and can't *ever* be erased!

It was like God wrapped me in His warm comfort blanket to assure me that I was His child . . . that my name was *forever* in His Book. It cannot be torn out . . . it cannot be defaced. Once you are born into God's family, you are permanently His. There are no abortions in God's Kingdom. When you are born into His river of life, you may get off into some eddy or into a little tide pool. But you are still in the river, and God always considers you His own property.

If you've ever been to the DMV, you know that it's a place without many sparkles, but that day God brought me a special sparkle, and I was so excited at the prospect of my name in His eternal Book that I nearly went up to Glory right then and there!

As you may have guessed, nobody else had a WUMPHEE for his personalized plate, so I ordered it. Then I dashed home and excitedly told Bill the whole story. I shared how blessed I was when I saw SPATULA in the DMV book and realized that my name—and his—are written in the Lamb's Book of Life. But Bill just gave me a blank look and didn't get excited at all.

When the plates arrived, Bill did put them on his Delta 88, but without much comment. I thought my present was a bust, but then one day, not long after, he called me and said, "I'll be late getting home because I'm going to get Wumphee some new shoes."

"What do you mean?" I wanted to know. "You don't need a new pair of shoes."

"No—I mean the car—I'm going to get new tires for my car. Wumphee needs new shoes!"

Now, for Bill, this was pretty lively as far as putting humor into one's life. Of course, I laughed and told him how funny that was. It seems that after getting the new plates for his car, Bill had pulled into this certain station where he buys all his gas, tires, and other things for the car. When the attendants spotted his license plate, they started calling Bill "Mr.

Wumphee." From then on it was natural to start calling his car "Wumphee" and to talk about buying it things like shoes.

He also covers Wumphee up from time to time with a car cover, and when he does, he talks about "putting Wumphee's coat on," just as you would for a person.

It's Hard for Men to Cope with Feelings

During those eleven months when I was counting roses on my bedroom wallpaper, weeping continually, and feeling so little self-esteem I started thinking about suicide, I became a burden that Bill didn't quite know how to handle. Frankly, he was not a lot of help to me, and of course, I was of no help to him. For a long time after we discovered that Larry was a homosexual, Bill kept saying, "It's a phase—just a phase." Farther down the line, he realized it was more than just a phase, and then he said, "The pendulum will swing." I wasn't sure what that meant, but now that our estrangement is over and we have a good relationship with Larry, he says, "The pendulum has swung." And that was about the extent of Bill's insight.

As I travel around the country speaking, I talk to many gals who ask me how Bill helped me during my times of depression. I have to tell them that, in my experience, men are not a lot of help because they don't have the emotional makeup to experience the depth of emotional pain women do. A man will hurt, but often he has no way of expressing this or letting it out. Most men don't seem to have the ability to empathize with the kind of problems their wives go through. They love their wives, and they want to help, but they just don't seem to know how to say the right things. While I was doing my tunnel walking, Bill didn't know what to say, so he did the next best thing: he took care of a lot of little chores that I detest and dislike.

For example, he kept my car clean and filled with gas all the time. He organized my kitchen cupboards and lined all the kitchen drawers with heavy vinyl linoleum. He organized my audio tapes for me so that I could find them quickly, and he built special shelves in my office to organize other materials. He helped me in so many small ways, not with WORDS, but with ACTIONS—anything to help me feel my life was in order while my mind was in turmoil over homosexuals, especially during those first months.

Of all the calls I get on the telephone, I'd say 99 percent are from Christian mothers who have problems. They want to talk to anybody who can help them. In many cases, their husbands are engineers or some other kind of cognitive, unemotional type. Engineers handle numbers and mechanical things very well because all that fits together very neatly. But when they have a kid who doesn't fit into their puzzle, they don't know what to do. They just can't handle it. So men tend to go off and do their own thing. They lose themselves in their job because they just don't know how to communicate with their wives at the emotional level.

I'm not saying that men can't communicate at all. It's possible that some husbands can give a wife spiritual help and even a certain amount of "good, practical advice," but there is an emotional level that few men can understand when it comes to a woman's feelings. God just didn't make them that way. And a wife only frustrates herself when she tries to get her husband to feel what she wants him to feel emotionally when he just isn't on that wave length.

What almost always happens is that the woman feels isolated and alone. She and her husband have this "problem child," but she gave birth to the situation—the problem came out of her body. And, believe me, it *is* a problem to understand how homosexuality fits into a Christian family.

Usually when the husband feels guilty, he blames someone else. In the case of a homosexual child, that someone else is almost always the wife. His wife feels guilty, too, but she usually blames herself, and they're both caught in the "blame game."

As a rule, men cannot face the emotional failure of having produced the problem. They generally refuse to even talk about it. What happens then is that the husband is usually able to move on and do his thing, but the woman is stuck in her awful hole of depression. And because she can't open up and talk, it all remains a secret and tends to make her all the more ill. I often say, "Openness is to wholeness as secrets are to sickness."

In our case, Bill just didn't feel the guilt that I felt, or at least he wasn't admitting it. And he didn't seem to have the same desire to get Larry back and work everything out. He didn't have any of those feelings, and that's why he was able to say it was all "just a phase" and be able to live with that.

It's no wonder that a lot of women I know feel as if they live in a vacuum. They are home alone all day in their "empty nest." The kids are gone, and their husbands are out working, playing pool, or maybe just stapling their socks in the next room. This kind of woman has no one to talk to. No wonder she watches soap operas and talk shows. She's starving for any kind of emotional input because she's not getting any from her husband.

Often, this kind of syndrome causes big trouble in the marriage. The wife wants to talk about why she has all these feelings, and the husband doesn't want to hear why she has all these problems. He'd rather go work with his computer or change the oil in the car. I believe that's why experiencing tragedies, such as having a child die or having a child disappear into the gay lifestyle, often wrecks a marriage and causes it to wind up on the rocks of the divorce court.

So, what can a woman do when she faces this kind of horrible black pit—a tunnel with no light anywhere? My counsel to women in this predicament is to FACE FACTS. Your husband is not going to change and become different. He is set in a kind of cement—a hardening of the attitudes, so to speak. First, you have to decide you will quit trying to change him. *Accept him* for what he is, and quit blaming him for not being able to give you the emotional help you need.

Second, you need to *find alternative ways* to get that emotional help. Develop three or four avenues through which you can get your emotional needs satisfied. For example, try tape cassettes or good books—they can really be good friends. Best of all, however, are women friends—someone you can talk to. My best advice is to locate a sister or friend going through the same pain and just talk it out—*drain the pain together.*

Not until I had my "whatever, Lord" breakthrough about Larry was I able to fully understand that there are areas where Bill just won't change. No matter how emotional or distraught I get, his melancholy characteristics will always be there. So that's why I say a wife must learn to adapt. Sometimes it's a simple solution, like buying another peanut butter jar. But no matter what you do, a sense of humor is vital. Keeping a sense of humor will save many sinking marriages.

The Case of the Lost Motel

Once you learn to adapt, you can appreciate your husband's good qualities. I certainly appreciate Bill's. Maybe I really know what "Wumphee" means after all. Maybe it's my way of saying that Bill is kind and caring and dependable. He often travels with me, which helps no end to keep me from getting lost because I'm not the greatest when it comes to directions. But as long as Bill's around, I never worry; he just gets me there.

On one recent speaking trip, we drove up to Felton,

California, a little town near the Mount Herman Conference Center, which is about fifty miles south of San Francisco near the Pacific Coast. One of Felton's major features is a big intersection with one road going to San Jose, one to San Francisco, and another to Stockton. We also found a river and some train tracks.

Bill had just had his wisdom teeth pulled and was under strict orders from the doctor to keep ice packs on his mouth to prevent any possible hemorrhaging. That meant we couldn't stay up at a speaker's cabin on the conference grounds because there wasn't any easy access to a steady supply of ice.

So, instead, we checked into a little motel near the river where he could get crushed ice and maybe some popsicles to help keep his sore gums cold. We got a room with a little refrigerator and got Bill all settled in with plenty of ice, but we never did find any popsicles.

It was late afternoon by then, and Bill decided to take me up the road to the Mount Herman Conference grounds where I was to speak that evening—a "dry run," as he called it. We made that run twice, and I felt pretty confident that I could drive the five miles to the conference grounds alone that evening.

When I left around 7:00 P.M., it was still light, and as I drove to the conference grounds, I thought, *This is no problem at all.* I had a great time talking to over three hundred women that evening. By the time I left to go back to the motel, it was just after 9:00; the sun had gone down, and suddenly the road was dark and not at all as familiar as it had been when I had driven up.

When I got down the hill to Felton, I came to the big intersection and didn't know which road to take. I saw one sign, "Stockton" and that didn't look right. Then I looked the other way and there was "San Jose"—no, that wasn't it, either. Finally, I had to try something, so I turned and started down a road that I hoped was right. After a few miles I came to a sign that said, "Scotts Valley." I thought, *We never came through here. This isn't the right road, either! What was the name of that motel, anyway?* I had forgotten; in fact, I wasn't sure I had actually ever seen a name on the place—it was sort of old and run-down.

So, I fumbled in my purse for the motel key and frantically inspected it, only to see, "P. O. Box 6, Felton, CA." By now I was getting pretty desperate. What *was* the name of that motel? I just didn't know!

As I came back into beautiful downtown Felton, it was getting close to eleven o'clock, and the sidewalks had definitely rolled up. Up ahead there was a bar with its neon sign blinking brightly on the otherwise dark street. I was so desperate I went in and blurted out: "I left my husband in a motel, and now I can't find it."

"What's the name of it?" the bartender grunted, looking at me a little strangely.

"Well, I don't know. All my key says is P. O. Box 6."

"Where are you from, lady?" was his next question.

By now I was almost choking and was sure that the man thought I was a little crazy. I managed to sputter, "I'm not from around here; I'm from Southern California. And I left him there because he just had his wisdom teeth out, and he needed to be near some ice. Now I can't find where I left him. But I do know there was a river and some railroad tracks and a health food store across the street because we went over there to see if we could find him some ice."

"You might try Highway 9," the bartender said, and he pointed me in the right direction. When I got back to my car, I was glad the bartender hadn't come outside to give me directions. There on the front seat was LONG LENA—my big stretched-out doll. If the bartender had seen LENA, he would have known for sure I had escaped from a local "home for the bewildered."

I drove out Highway 9, or whatever it was, with huge redwood trees looming on both sides of the road, my headlights piercing through the pitch-black darkness. As I came around a curve, I saw someone standing in the road, waving his hands. At first I couldn't make him out, and I thought I had better zoom on by because what kind of guy tries to wave down women in cars at eleven o'clock at night on dark roads? But then I saw it was Bill! He was just standing there, matter-of-factly, waiting for me! As I pulled up and rolled down the window, he said, "I just *knew* you'd have trouble."

Relieved to hear his voice, I asked, "How long have you been standing out here?"

"Well, quite awhile. You were supposed to be through speaking at 9:00, and now it's *only* 11:30!"

I looked over and there was the motel—but no sign on it anywhere. It wasn't my fault! How was I supposed to know the name of the motel when it was nowhere to be seen?

Bill wasn't upset, just relieved that I had finally gotten back. Since that little episode, he bought me a gadget that is a combination compass and directional finder so I can better tell if I'm going north or south, or left or right. How thankful I am that I have someone in my life who cares that much for me— to stand out on a dark road for over two hours waiting to flag me down because he "just knew" I'd have trouble finding my way back.

But that's Bill; he enjoys taking care of me and watching out for me. Sometimes when I go out speaking and he's not with me, I come home with my trunk full of stuff I've tossed in every old way. He gets a lot of pleasure out of saying, "Oh, what a mess you have," and then he organizes all of the books, facing them the right way, and gets everything in exact order and categorical—that's important, to have it in categories. He enjoys grumbling about it at first and muttering things about how I throw stuff all in a heap. Then, when it is all organized, he'll say, "Now your trunk is ready to go on the next trip."

I Don't Dare Leave Home without Him

When I have to fly out of town alone to speak, Bill usually takes me out to the airport to be sure I get my luggage checked correctly and get on the right flight. He also has to check the "Joy Box" items that I take along, as well as my boxes of books. Bill usually does all that and he's very good at it. But on a trip recently, I didn't have my melancholy husband with me; I had Lynda, who is every bit as sanguine as I am.

So there we were at the Ontario Airport, just talking away, having fun. The plane was supposed to leave at 12:50, but we were there early and had *plenty* of time. All of a sudden we looked up, and it seemed as if there was nobody left in the airport. I said, "Lynda, where has everybody gone?" It was 12:55! We had been sitting there laughing and talking and hadn't heard anyone announce the plane or anything. We ran down the ramp and there was the plane, almost ready to pull out. They had already made the last call. So we frantically dashed for the door and just made it, lugging all our carry-on stuff and wondering where all that time had gone.

Later, I called Bill and admitted, "I sure missed you today. I nearly didn't make the plane."

He chuckled and started chiding me, "Well, if you would pay attention to what you're doing, you'd be OK. If I could have been there, that wouldn't have happened."

So I told him that that just made me appreciate him all the more, and I'd never try to catch another plane without him. "When you're along," I said gratefully, "I can just sit and relax, and you'll get me on the right plane on time."

Why We Make a Great Team

A couple years ago when Bill retired, he became the official "gopher" for SPATULA. Even though he's a competent mechanical engineer, Bill loves doing the menial, mundane tasks. It's important that things be done right. Together we make a great team, and we even sign *The Love Line* newsletter together—"Barb and Gopher Bill."

I once got a letter from a darling SPATULANDER who was eighty-two years old:

Dear Barbara and Gopher Bill:

As I write your names, I'm thinking I wouldn't let Bill call himself "Gopher!" So, I stopped to look in the dictionary and found it is a sort of ground squirrel—ugh. The next thing I learned is that Minnesota is named the Gopher State. Now *that* is coming up a little.

Then as I read on, I found a gopher is a zealously eager person—an errand boy, assistant, or the like! The humorous spelling for this is "go for." And lo and behold, the name fits him to a "T." Now it makes sense. He is a *Gentleman* Gopher and a *Glorified* Gopher. He is also a *Generous* Gopher because he went overboard on the matter of accessories for your stationary bike—a helmet even! I'm so glad you are "saddled" with such a nice Guy!

So am I! We *are* different people, but that's what makes us tick. I create and initiate and flutter around, while Bill follows through, organizes, and keeps me pointed in the right direction. We each have our own gifts, and because we accept those gifts, they work together to help and encourage a whole lot of other people. I can't say it better than Bill did recently when I invited him (Mr. Wumphee) to the platform to share as I was closing my talk to a large group of women in Arizona. Here's what he said:

It always amazes me to see what the Lord has done in our ministry together . . . how He's put the two of us together and has come out with what we have. But the thing I've learned more than anything else is that the Lord has given each of us certain spiritual gifts, and it always surprises me to see the things my wife has in the way of gifts—being able to communicate and counsel and talk and write. I appreciate being able to come along with her. The Lord has been able to put the two of us together, so that we complement each other and not subtract from each other.

And that just about says it all. I married a Wumphee; he married a Cumphee, and we wouldn't trade for anyone else!

Extra Thoughts to Take Along

What's so remarkable about love at first sight? It's when people have been looking at each other for years that it becomes remarkable!

—Anonymous

*   *   *   *   *   *

A perfect wife is one who doesn't expect a perfect husband.

—Anonymous

*   *   *   *   *   *

The ages of woman:
    In her infancy she needs love and care.
    In her childhood she wants fun.
    In her twenties she wants romance.
    In her thirties she wants admiration.
    In her forties she wants sympathy.
    In her fifties she wants cash.

*   *   *   *   *   *

There are no perfect marriages for the simple reason there are no perfect people, and no one person can satisfy *all of* one's needs.

—Cecil Osborne
From *The Art of Understanding Your Mate*

CHAPTER NINE

Wrinkles Are God's Little Way of Saying . . . "I'm Stepping on Your Face"

You really know you're getting old when
you bend over to tie your shoes, and you wonder
what else you can do while you're down there.

—Source Unknown

For two hours I had been doing the talk show, and I had told my radio host and all the people who had called in just about everything I knew. We were almost out of time when the host turned to me and said, "Barbara, we have just two minutes left—if you could say one thing to encourage all the people who are listening, what would you say?"

I felt a twinge of panic. I wasn't sure I could even think of my name, and I had already said everything I knew—I couldn't even think of a Scripture verse. I glanced into the little Joy Box I take with me when I'm interviewed to see if there was anything left among my props that might give our radio audience some encouragement. Then I gleefully found one bumper snicker that I hadn't used, and I said, "Well, there is one thing I would like to tell everyone, and it's this: 'LIFE IS HARD, AND THEN YOU DIE.'"

The shocked host of the show looked at me as if I had lost every marble I had.

"Well . . . uh . . . Barbara . . . maybe you could tell us in a few seconds why you think that's encouraging . . . " he stammered.

I could tell my host was thinking, *"What is she going to do NOW?"* I wasn't sure either, but I plunged in.

"What I mean is, our EXIT from this life is our GRANDEST ENTRANCE up there. This life isn't it! There is pain and suffering . . . but those who want to name it and claim it are looking in the wrong place because there is nothing here to name and claim! *This isn't it!*

"This life is hard. There are all kinds of pain, there are all kinds of problems—AIDS, divorce, crime, disease . . . sin. Life is hard, and some of the people listening know how hard it can be. But I like what my little granddaughter told me: 'Grandma, you shouldn't say life is hard and then you die; you should say life is hard and then you GET TO DIE.'

"I really believe that's good news for Christians. We have an ENDLESS HOPE, not a HOPELESS END and, while life is hard, someday we will die, which isn't really bad—it simply means we'll leave this life and go to be with our Lord and Savior, and what could be better than that?

"That's why I believe in rapture practice . . . I go out in the backyard and jump up and down, practicing for the rapture, because one day we'll soon be *out* of here. I love that song, 'I'll Fly Away,' because I know my future is so secure with Him. This life holds no charm for me . . . my deposits are in heaven, just waiting for me to come! What a day it will be when we cast our crowns at His feet. This life is just a veil of tears, but earth has no sorrow that heaven cannot heal. Life is hard and tough, but it is only temporary . . . this life is only a vapor, but eternity is FOREVER!"

When we finished the interview, the lights were flashing on the call-in board. It seems that dozens of people wanted to talk to the lady who thought it was so glorious to die!

Billy's Book Was Encouraging, Not Depressing

From time to time I meet people who think it's depressing to hear that "Life is hard and then you die." But I don't think so. We're all getting older, and we're all going to die, unless the Lord comes first. Why not face it positively, instead of avoiding it and looking on it as the ultimate evil?

I was on a plane the other day reading Billy Graham's book *Facing Death and the Life Hereafter* (Word, 1987). The person in the seat next to me said, "Oh, what an awful book you're reading—how depressing."

I just laughed and said, "It's not depressing, it's exciting. It's a wonderful book."

"Do you have cancer or something?" my seat mate wanted to know.

I explained that we all have a life-threatening disease. We're all going to die because we're on our way out of here and it's a one-way trip. For a Christian, it's a pilgrimage, and I believe Billy Graham's book on death is one of the most encouraging I've ever read. He tells why Christians can face death with joy, not gloom. We're all going down the road very fast. You don't have to look very far in the obituaries to see that people are going every day. And if they are without the Lord, they have nothing. But with the Lord, they have eternity, eons and eons, to be with Him.

Facing death is really the ultimate triumph for a Christian. Perhaps you have a disease, and you don't recover. If God doesn't heal you physically, He heals you spiritually, and you spend eternity with Him.

As far as I'm concerned, whatever problems we're going through, we can think of them as temporary. As I said earlier, our troubles didn't come to stay; they are going to pass. And that helps you cope, whether it's cancer or problems in your marriage or problems with your children. Whatever it is, it's all temporary. And what's up ahead is going to be glorious because of the hope we have as Christians.

That's why I laugh at getting older and overweight. You can try to fight it off—and I try along with the rest of you, but the bottom line is, it won't matter. As the bumper snicker says:

EAT RIGHT, STAY FIT
DIE ANYWAY

I often hear that old cliché, "Women don't get older—they get better!" The question I always ask is, "BETTER THAN WHAT?"

Recently I was in a big department store looking for a night cream, and the salesclerk (she looked about fourteen to me) showed me something new called "MILLENNIUM." That sounded sort of spiritual, so I asked her what it meant. She said it had a special ingredient that made OLD skin become YOUNG!

And I thought to myself that it probably takes one thousand years to do it! The companies keep coming out with products that claim magical powers. My friend, Joyce, sent away for some marvelous stuff advertised on TV called "DREAM AWAY." You were to take these pills at night, dream away your fat, and wake up slim in the morning! The advertisement was enticing, but the product was a total failure—as you might guess.

We can hope for a miracle, but there is no simple, quick way to be young, thin, and lovely. As the years zoom by, you begin to think you're in a war to keep your mind together, your body functioning, your teeth in, your hair on, and your weight off. It can really be a chore. It's a lot like trying to hold a beach ball under water . . . sooner or later something pops up or out! My favorite excuse is, "I used to be Snow White . . . but I drifted!"

I Don't Belong with "Old" People!

They say that inside every old person is a younger person wondering what happened, and that's exactly how I feel much of the time. Bill and I live in a mobile home park and many of our neighbors are retired folk. That means a lot of the people are elderly, and I often think, *I don't belong here . . . there are OLD people living here.*

Not long ago Bill and I came across the following item on a child's view of retirement (original source unknown). It seems that following Christmas break, the teacher asked her young pupils how they spent their holidays. One small boy replied as follows:

We always spent Christmas with Grandpa and Grandma. They used to live here in a big brick house, but Grandpa got retarded and they moved to Florida. They live in a place with a lot of retarded people. They live in tin huts. They ride big three-wheel tricycles. They go to a big building they call a wrecked hall. But if it was wrecked it is fixed now. They play games there and do exercises, but they don't do them very well. There is a swimming pool, and they go to it and just stand there in the water with their hats on. I guess they don't know how to swim. My Grandma used to bake cookies and stuff, but I guess she forgot how. Nobody cooks there, they all go to fast food restaurants. As you come into the park there is a doll house with a man sitting in it. He watches all day, so they can't get out without him seeing them. They wear badges with their names on them. I guess they don't know who they are. My Grandma said Grandpa worked hard all his life and earned his retardment. I wish they would move back home, but I guess the man in the doll house won't let them out.

The other day I spoke at a retirement home for women, where most of the audience used walkers and wore hearing aids. Some even slept through my presentation! I shared with them and included a little humor like: "Wrinkles are God's little way of saying, 'I'm stepping on your face,'" and another one I really like:

GOD MADE WRINKLES TO SHOW
WHERE SMILES HAVE BEEN.

When I finished, a lovely little old lady came up to the front and said, "Mrs. Johnson, I loved your talk about wrinkles, and I want to give you something for your Joy Box. . . ." And then she handed me a little, blue aerosol can that said, "WRINKLE FREE—Spray Your Wrinkles Away."

I went along with her just for fun and told her that I couldn't wait to get home to try it. But, of course, when I read the rest of the label, I found it was for cotton, linen, and silk—not skin.

There is not a whole lot you can do about wrinkles, although women, especially, keep trying with face lifts, skin peels, night creams, and all the rest of it. I have a friend who's fifty years old, but she tells people she's sixty because she really looks *great* for sixty, but *awful* for fifty!

If You Don't Mind, Age Doesn't Matter

They say age is just a matter of mind; if you don't mind, it doesn't matter. Trouble is, a lot of people *do* mind. They are comforted by articles with headlines like: "LIFE GETS BET-TER WHEN WOMEN HIT MIDDLE AGE." According to a study by one specialist, middle-aged women have become more confident, independent, and organized—better able to cope with life. This researcher said, "Although we didn't find that life begins at forty for women, we did find that as they get nearer to middle-age, they are more complete human beings."

I suppose there's some truth to the man's findings. What a lot of us would like to tell him, however, is that life begins at forty, all right . . . it begins to deteriorate!

Women are under incredible pressure to stay looking young and beautiful. Sad to say, they learn that youth is that brief time between buying training bras and wearing surgical stockings. I often say that I'm living somewhere between estrogen and death, but somebody corrected me once and told me to say I'm living somewhere between the Blue Lagoon and Golden Pond.

There are all kinds of ways to tell you're getting older. For example:

- Everything hurts, and what doesn't hurt, doesn't work.

- Your back goes out more often than you do.

- Dialing long distance tires you out.

And, do you know why women over fifty years old don't have babies? Because they'd put them down and forget where they left them!

The Power of Making Memories

Some of our best days have been spent with our children, and I'm sure you can say the same thing. I believe a true serendipity of getting older is looking back to the times when our kids gave us so much fun—and maybe a few fits along the way.

Once when speaking to a group, I included a section in my talk about "building laughter in your walls" by making a special effort to have memorable good times with your family. A young woman came up afterward and said: "I read your book about today's experiences being tomorrow's memories. When I finished it, I told the kids, 'We're going to make some memories!' I took all kinds of pictures of my kids and put them in scrapbooks, and we even made some videos."

After describing how she made many wonderful memories, she told me about an incident with her son:

"My son, Jimmy, is seven, and one day he came home from school and said, 'Oh, I don't have any homework to do—I'm going skateboarding, then I'm going to watch TV, and I'm just going to have fun because tonight I don't have any homework.'"

This mom told me she was happy for her son, and let him go skateboarding. After dinner he watched all the TV he wanted, and about 9:00 he went up to bed. She and her husband watched TV until around 11:00 and were just getting ready to turn it off and go to bed themselves. She was congratulating herself on having everything ready for the next day, but as she looked up the stairs, there was little Jimmy, a forlorn figure in his jammies. Jimmy said, pleadingly, "I just remembered—I have to have a salt map of Venezuela for tomorrow."

Now, almost all parents know "salt maps" are what teachers like to assign their pupils so they can drive mothers crazy. After all, it's mom who usually winds up helping the kid get his salt map together. So there they were, at eleven o'clock at night. Little Jimmy had spent the evening skateboarding, watching TV, and having a great time and NOW it was salt-map time.

Mom said, "Get the salt, get the flour. Now, where's Venezuela?" And so they tore around getting all the stuff together. "Where's the blue paint? Where's the green paint?" Her husband, of course, had gone up to bed. It was not *his* problem. He was sound asleep, dreaming of Bermuda, not Venezuela.

Little Jimmy manfully tried to help. He sat there, struggling to stay awake as he drew his version of Venezuela, while Mom scurried around the kitchen, making exasperated sounds. Finally he looked up and tearfully said, "Mom, are we making a memory now?"

As exasperated as that mom was that night, she'll never forget the salt map of Venezuela and those precious words by her little guy. And it will be a priceless memory, one that she wouldn't trade for anything. As you get older, memories are like gold. They become more valuable than a lot of antiques and other "things" that you collect. I love the following insight on memories. Somebody sent it to me from a church bulletin. I think it makes a memorable point:

> As we go through life, each of us is taking a notebook of memories, whether we put our notes on paper, or only on the pages of the mind. As we write, it is important that we note down some little things each day for that time when those notes may be our highest joy. So note the day the lilacs bloomed, the day your little son picked a dandelion for you, the day the bluebirds found the house you made for them. In this age of bigness, the big things will crush us if we forget the words of One who said to consider the lilies of the field, and be not anxious.

I'm Awfully Well, for the Shape I'm In

Of course, we do everything we can to fight off old age, but it's a losing battle. Nonetheless, we like to think we can still handle it, that we're in pretty good shape, considering. As one poet put it:

I'm Fine

There is nothing whatever the matter with me.
I'm just as healthy as can be
I have arthritis in both my knees
And when I talk I talk with a wheeze.
My pulse is weak, and my blood is thin,
But I'm awfully well for the shape I'm in.
My teeth eventually have to come out,
And my diet—I hate to think about!
I am overweight and I can't get thin,
but I'm awfully well for the shape I'm in.
I think my liver is out of whack,
And a terrible pain is in my back.
My hearing is poor, my sight is dim.

Most everything seems to be out of trim,
but I'm awfully well for the shape I'm in.
I have arch support for both my feet,
or I wouldn't be able to go on the street.
Sleeplessness I have, night after night,
and in the morning I'm just a sight.
My memory's failing,
My head's in a spin.
I'm practically living on aspirin,
but I'm awfully well for the shape I'm in.
The moral is, as the tale we unfold
That for you and me who are growing old,
It's better to say "I'm fine" with a grin,
Than to let them know the shape we're in.

Pearl Waddell

I wasn't always into exercise. I used to agree with the bumper snicker that says:

EVERY TIME I THINK ABOUT EXERCISE,
I LIE DOWN 'TIL THE THOUGHT GOES AWAY.

That's not true anymore. A few years ago, Bill bought me a marvelous indoor exercise bike and installed it in my Joy Room next to my television set and near my Kermit the Frog telephone. He even found me an old helmet out in the garage and suggested I wear it while riding my bike!

So I donned the helmet and pedaled happily away, but eventually it got pretty boring, just pedaling and going nowhere and seeing no one. So I figured out a way that would bring me closer to everyone in my SPATULA family, and I could do it all from my own bike in my Joy Room. I decided I would bicycle across the United States and never leave home while doing it. Some people would think it was crazy, but it was just plain fun for me.

First, I got a big colored map of the United States and hung it up right in front of my bike, where I could see it as I rode. Then I got some push pins and every time I covered 25 miles on the bike, I'd move the pin accordingly. At the rate of ten to sometimes fifteen miles a day, it took me four months to get from L.A. to Denver.

I keep my zip-coded list of friends near the bike, and when I get to a particular city, I look to see who lives there. And then

I pray for those people and their particular problems and ask God to be especially close to them that day—to wrap them in His comfort blanket of love and let them feel His presence all day long.

I actually covered every state in the Union that way, even Alaska! When I knew I was in a state where the weather is cold, I'd put on ear muffs and a scarf, just to keep in the spirit of the whole thing. And if I was down in Florida, or maybe in Hawaii, I'd sip some iced tea as I pedaled along.

Some people listen to tapes as they ride, others watch TV, and some even try to read. Those schemes are all fine, but I think I've hit on the best idea of all—something that has put zing into my prayer life. As I "rode across the country," I prayed specifically for everyone in my SPATULA family, and that way I strengthened my own spiritual life as I strengthened my heart and lungs.

Did I slim down any? Not much (I'm really a perfect 10 you know; I just keep it covered with fat so it won't get scratched), but my love for all those I'm trying to help grew stronger as I pedaled across the miles. Currently, I'm on my second tour of the U.S., just coming into Kankakee, Illinois. To spur me on, I keep a bumper snicker on the wall that reminds me:

BRAIN CELLS COME AND BRAIN CELLS GO,
BUT FAT CELLS LIVE FOREVER!

The Moment of Driver's License Truth

Not long ago, I had to renew my driver's license, and when the new one came, I was pleasantly surprised. Compared to my picture on the one of four years ago, I had IMPROVED! The explanation wasn't difficult. Four years before I was so tight in the wringer and so far off in zombieland, and what one of my friends calls "the twilight zone," any picture of me had to reflect the shock I was in from coping with my family's problems.

Perhaps you've known the embarrassment of pulling out your driver's license for identification and watching the person stare at the picture and then at you. That person is wondering, Is *this really you?* Of course, you stumble around explaining why your driver's license picture failed to show all your "true beauty." That's the typical experience, but in my case I had looked so bad on the prior license that the new one was actually flattering. That was a day that made my heart smile indeed!

Applying for that new driver's license did remind me, however, of the changes the years can bring. The typical driver's license application has spaces where you fill in your eye color, hair color, weight, etc. Isn't it strange that women leave their weight the same as it was when they originally got their driver's license at the age of sixteen? And why is it that some men have a license they got years ago that says, "Hair: Brown," when their hair has long since disappeared and they're totally bald?

Tell me, have you ever seen a driver's license that had accurate information? What about people who have one brown eye and one blue one?—there is no space for that on the driver's license. Or how about women who have "convertible tops"; that is, they change the color of their hair so often, only their hairdresser knows for sure, and some weeks *she's* wondering.

Yes, the years can bring many changes, and it is often said that, as we grow older, we develop something called "hardening of the attitudes." There is no space on a driver's license for filling in the condition of one's attitudes. But all you have to do is get out on the freeways, and you'll quickly learn that a lot of people have become hardened, and then some!

I don't want that said of me. In fact, the following poem by an anonymous poet is my daily prayer.

ON GETTING OLDER

Lord, Thou knowest me better than I know myself,
that I am growing older and will someday be old.
Keep me from getting talkative, and particularly
from the fatal habit of thinking I must say something
on every subject and on every occasion.
Release me from craving to try to straighten out
everybody's affairs.

Keep my mind free from the recital of endless details,
and give me wings to get to the point.
I ask for grace enough to listen to the tales of others;
help me to endure them with patience, but seal my lips
on my own aches and pains. They are increasing and
my love of rehearsing them is increasing as the years go by.
Teach me the glorious lesson that occasionally it is
possible that I may be mistaken.

Keep me reasonably sweet; I do not want to be a saint—
some of them are so hard to live with—but a sour old
woman or man is one of the crowning works of the devil.

Make me thoughtful, but not moody; helpful, but not
bossy. With my vast store of wisdom, it seems a pity
not to use it all; but Thou knowest, Lord, that I want
a few friends at the end.

A "few friends at the end" is all you can really hope for.
Obviously, your best friend should be the Lord, but you do
want some others, too. In recent years, a lot of books have
been written about friendship—how to find friends, how to
be a friend, and while I haven't written any books on friendship myself, I do think I know the secret. You'll find out what
it is in the next chapter.

Extra Thoughts to Take Along

AGE IS NOT IMPORTANT—
UNLESS YOU'RE A CHEESE.

—From a Bumper Sticker

*   *   *   *   *   *

I think that the life cycle is all backwards. You should die
first, get it out of the way, then live twenty years in an old age
home. You get kicked out when you're too young, you get a
gold watch, you go to work. You work forty years until you're
young enough to enjoy your retirement.

You go to college . . . until you're ready for high school.
You go to grade school, you become a little kid, you play, you
have no responsibilities, you become a little baby, you go back
into the womb, you spend your last nine months floating, and
you finish off as a gleam in somebody's eye.

—Bob Benson

*   *   *   *   *   *

EAT DESSERT FIRST!
AFTER ALL, LIFE IS UNCERTAIN.

—From a Bumper Sticker

*   *   *   *   *   *

REFLECTIONS ON AGING

Remember, old folks are worth a fortune, with silver in their hair, gold in their teeth, stones in their kidneys, lead in their feet, and gas in their stomachs.

I have become a little older now and a few changes have come into my life. Frankly, I have become quite a frivolous old gal. I am seeing five gentlemen every day. As soon as I wake up, WILL POWER helps me get out of bed. Then I go down the hall and see JOHN.

Next, CHARLIE HORSE comes along and takes a lot of my time and attention. When he leaves ARTHUR RITIS shows up and stays the rest of the day. He doesn't like to stay in one place very long, so he takes me from joint to joint.

After such a busy day, I'm really tired and glad to relax with BEN GAY.

What a life! The preacher came to visit me the other day. He said, at my age, I should be thinking about "the hereafter."

I told him, "Oh, I do, all the time. No matter where I am—in the parlor, upstairs, in the kitchen or down in the basement—I ask myself, "NOW, WHAT AM I HERE AFTER?"

—Source Unknown

*   *   *   *   *   *

YOU DON'T STOP LAUGHING BECAUSE YOU GROW OLD,
YOU GROW OLD BECAUSE YOU STOP LAUGHING.

—From a Bumper Sticker

*   *   *   *   *   *

Some people, no matter how old they get,
never lose their beauty—they merely
move it from their faces into their hearts.

—Source Unknown

*   *   *   *   *   *

WORK FOR THE LORD. THE PAY ISN'T MUCH,
BUT HIS RETIREMENT PLAN IS OUT OF THIS WORLD.

—Source Unknown

*   *   *   *   *   *

For I am convinced that nothing can ever separate us from
his love. Death can't, and life can't. The angels won't, and all
the powers of hell itself cannot keep God's love away. Our
fears for today, our worries about tomorrow, or where we
are—high above the sky, or in the deepest ocean—nothing
will ever be able to separate us from the love of God demonstrated by our Lord Jesus Christ when he died for us.

—Romans 8:38, 39, TLB

CHAPTER TEN

I Don't Recall Asking for Any of This

Encouraging thought for the week:
Eat a live toad the first thing in
the morning, and nothing worse can
happen to you the rest of the day!

—Source Unknown

I often get "encouraging thoughts" from my good friend, Mary Lou, and one of her timeliest contributions came on a day when trying to help so many people who are down in the pit almost had me down there, too. I opened the envelope and here was a cartoon of a bewildered-looking woman tied hand and foot, lying on the railroad tracks. The cutline said: "I don't recall asking for any of this!" As I chuckled, I thought: *That's right! I didn't ASK for any of this, but it's what I've GOT, so I'll just take my own advice and stick a geranium in my hat and be happy!*

That little envelope from Mary Lou didn't contain anything expensive, profound, or "deep," but nonetheless, it picked me up and refreshed me for the rest of the day. I think that's the secret to being a real friend—to always be looking for ways to encourage and refresh others. Proverbs 11:25 has so much wisdom. Here's how it reads in the New International Version:

HE WHO REFRESHES OTHERS
WILL HIMSELF BE REFRESHED.

155

As you refresh others, you relieve your own pain. You may be going through a painful time right now or trying to get over a tremendous loss. If so, try "refreshing or watering" another person's life, and as you encourage that person, you will find that your own pain is lessened.

As I said in the first chapter of this book, pain is inevitable. The trick is to find ways to not let it turn into misery. So when someone sends a note, a card, or a clipping, or gives me a call that boosts my spirits, it prompts me to think of ways that I can refresh and encourage others in return. My question is always, "How can I help you flatten out the pain in your life? How can I help you be encouraged?" We can't remove each other's pain, but we can dilute it. That's what I believe our SPATULA ministry is all about—helping people live with the pain that is inevitable, bringing them some encouragement, joy, and even a few smiles to wash that pain away.

My Favorite Bible Character

Al Sanders, the host of "Vox Pop" radio, asked me a most thought-provoking question: "As you look over God's Word, the Bible, who would you like to be like?"

My answer was that I wanted to be like Onesiphorus, the man of whom Paul said: "May the Lord show mercy to the household of Onesiphorus, because he often refreshed me and was not ashamed of my chains" (2 Tim. 1:16, NIV). I have to admit that Onesiphorus is a somewhat obscure character. He's only mentioned once in the entire Bible, and his name sounds like a disease, to boot! But when I get to heaven, I'm going to look him up and tell him I've spent a great part of my life trying to be like him.

The Living Bible paraphrase of 2 Timothy 1:16 says Onesiphorus' visits revived Paul "like a breath of fresh air." There Paul was, awaiting execution. Everyone but Luke had deserted him. Then Onesiphorus, his old friend from Ephesus, searched everywhere for him and finally found him in chains and brought him refreshment.

"Refresh" literally means "to brace up, to revive by fresh air, to cool again." The Bible doesn't say what Onesiphorus did to refresh Paul, but just the fact that he took the time to find Paul was refreshing in itself. And Onesiphorus wasn't ashamed of Paul's chains. He encouraged Paul when he was weary and lonely by letting him know there was still someone who cared.

A Refreshing Note

I listen regularly to two radio programs—"Focus on the Family" by Dr. James Dobson and "Insight for Living" by Chuck Swindoll. And I have gotten so much refreshment and encouragement from their excellent insights.

Awhile back, Chuck Swindoll did an entire radio message on a man called Epaphroditus, and as I listened to his tape, he kept saying that Epaphroditus was the man who came to "refresh" Paul in prison. Now, Chuck Swindoll is one of the most knowledgeable students of the Bible anywhere, but I realized he had Epaphroditus mixed up with Onesiphorus! I had just done a little study of obscure Bible characters, and Onesiphorus was one of the men I studied. Epaphroditus did come to see Paul in prison and brought him a gift from the Philippian church (see Phil. 2:25–30). But 2 Timothy 1:16 clearly says that Onesiphorus was the man who found and *refreshed him* with his visits.

So, I just couldn't resist writing Chuck a note saying, "I heard your whole message on Epaphroditus, and he wasn't the man who came to refresh Paul—that was Onesiphorus." I sent off the note with feelings of trepidation—after all who was I to question Chuck Swindoll on something from Scripture?

Shortly thereafter, I got a letter from Chuck saying:

Dear Barbara:

Thanks for getting in touch.

You are right—it WAS Onesiphorus, not Epaphroditus. Easy to get those guys mixed up. Just goes to show us how obscure they really were. . . .

Warmly and gratefully,
Chuck Swindoll

One of America's greatest Bible teachers was honest enough to admit he had goofed, and he *thanked* me for my correction! Now, *that* was really refreshing! "A generous man will prosper; he who refreshes others will himself be refreshed" (Prov. 11:25, NIV). Chuck's gracious response not only refreshed me, but it inspired me to try even harder to walk in Onesiphorus' footsteps—to be a refreshing person, investing my life in others, knowing that as we refresh others, we ourselves are refreshed.

Caring or Clacking Christians?

I heard Chuck Swindoll share another refreshing thought on one of his broadcasts. He said that Christians can be like a sack of marbles—unfeeling, unloving, just *clacking* against each other as they go through life. Or, they can be *caring* people—like a sack of grapes pressing together to provide a soft, loving place to cushion and comfort each other from the hard crushes of life. There is no question what Onesiphorus was. The next time you talk to someone who's hurting and needing some comfort, decide who you'd rather be: a soft, comfortable grape, part of God's refreshing vineyard, or a hard, clacking marble, oblivious to those who are being crushed right before your eyes.

Shannon, my "daughter-in-love," heard me talk about caring and clacking Christians at a meeting and went home and drew the little cartoon strip on this page. It originally appeared in *The Love Line* newsletter, and I believe it illustrates the point better than any words ever could.

The clacking-versus-caring illustration reminds me of something Louis Paul Lehman once wrote in the Calvary Church bulletin in Grand Rapids, Michigan, where he was pastor for many years:

> Touch someone with a warm word. Warm someone with a genuine smile. Comfort another as you've been comforted (2 Cor. 1:4). Stand by one who is standing alone. The "sympathizing tear" and the echoing laughter can each warm a cold day. Warmth, as a song, is of such character that you cannot give it without enjoying it yourself.

The body of Christ is intended to warm those who are cold. As James said, we just can't tell people, "Go, I wish you well; keep warm and well fed" (James 2:16, NIV). We need to do something about their needs, whether they're physical or emotional.

What a Week It Had Been!

Have you ever had a year, a week, or a day when you just couldn't take one more small, insignificant irritation? I had one of those days recently when I was trying to get ready to go speak at a retreat in the mountains. The water softener was out of salt, so no suds in my bath. I got a run in the last pair of stockings in the drawer, and the phone was ringing with calls from hurting people who took longer than usual to counsel. And then there were a lot of requests in the daily mail that had to be taken care of before I could leave town.

I know there are lots of bigger problems in the world, but mine had piled up and had started to get me down. All that morning I kept looking for just a little encouragement, some small *lift* to make the day less hectic. I even made a tour of my Joy Room and tried to remember previous joys, but that day it seemed as if finding joy was not going to be easy to do.

I hurried down to the supermarket to stock up on a few things I would need for the trip. Naturally, I got a *dumb* basket with the wheels that go in different directions. As I made my way to the checkout counter, I felt forsaken once again because the space for customers with under ten items was closed. I would have easily qualified for the fast check-out line, but now I had to pick from two other checkout lines loaded with women who looked as if they were shopping for the U.S. Army.

"Please, Lord!" I prayed, "I need just a LITTLE encouragement today. Can't something happen to let me know You care about all the heaviness that has settled upon me?"

Just then, a young man stepped into an empty checkout stand next to the one where I was in line and said, "*Young lady, I'll be glad to check you out over here!*"

I looked around and saw no one, so I knew he was talking to me. Maybe it was the *young lady* part that lifted my spirits. But mostly I think it was knowing I wasn't forsaken. I believe he opened that line *just for me,* so I could whisk past all those other women with full baskets. What a simple way to be reminded of God's continual care. Joy may not always be easy to find. Sometimes diamonds are hidden in places where we can't always see their sparkle, but we have to keep on looking for them just the same.

That day at the supermarket, I was dejected and depressed and frustrated because it looked as if I would have to wait forever to get checked out of the store with just a few items, and I just didn't have time to wait that long. But the next moment I was happy, delighted, and encouraged because I was *first* in line. Not much else seemed to go right for me that entire week, but on that day at the supermarket, a little sparkle of God's care wrapped me in His love.

And a few days later, as I leafed through a magazine, a little cartoon with the words "Color me happy when I'm the first one in line" jumped out at me! It was a picture of a woman pushing a shopping cart. God was reminding me of the joy I had experienced a few days before. And I felt His comfort blanket around me all over again! I truly believe God cares for us in even the *smallest* ways so that we may have JOY abundantly!

People are hurting in so many ways, and there seems to be so many *joyless* people. Even those of us who have the deep, abiding joy that only the Lord can give sometimes sag under the weight of all of life's garbage. So whenever you see a

grocery cart, let it remind you that, even in small ways, God can reveal His care to you. Then you, too, can be as ecstatic as I was when you realize there'll be those times when you are the FIRST (and only) one in line!

Ever Feel Like Don Quixote?

Remember Don Quixote, the positive thinker who spent much of his life jousting with windmills? Maybe you know what it's like to feel that you are completely absorbed in fighting windmills every day of your life, sort of like chipping away at a concrete wall with a straw. I had a day like that recently, but, when the mail arrived, there was a tape from a pastor in Ohio whom I didn't even know. I put it in the recorder and listened to his message, which was on "hanging in there" and pressing on. He talked about a lot of things, and then asked some tough questions:

Why should we keep trying . . . why should we stand up against the stream of life? Why should we work to love the unlovely? Why should we never give up, even when we fail? Why should we keep on hanging in there when no one seems to appreciate our effort, and so few seem to even *know* the sacrifices our work causes us? Why should we encourage the downtrodden, those persons who have been defeated again and again . . . why should we never give up on a wayward child? Why should we keep on hanging on? WHY? WHY?

And I was wondering what he would say. Yes, *why?* It would be much easier to just give it all up and sit and rest awhile. Then came his answer, victory ringing in his voice. And what he said made my heart leap with rejoicing:

Because, someday *"the Lord himself will come down from heaven, with a loud command, with the voice of the archangel and with the trumpet call of God, and the dead in Christ will rise first. After that, we who are still alive and are left will be caught up with them in the clouds to meet the Lord in the air. And so we will be with the Lord forever. Therefore encourage each other with these words"* (1 Thess. 4:16–18, NIV).

What a hope! What a victory! What faith for living! What a way to dispel the doubts and heaviness in life! What a motivation to excel in all we do and to keep on hanging on! And what a reason to keep on loving and encouraging others. Someone sent me this in a note, and I just love it!

Love is the one treasure that multiplies by division. It is the one gift that grows bigger the more you take from it. It is the one business in which it pays to be an absolute spendthrift. You can give it away, throw it away, empty your pockets, shake the basket, turn the glass upside down, and tomorrow you will have more than ever.

I heard of the owner of a small, crossroads store who was appointed the local postmaster. But six months after his appointment, not one piece of mail had left the village. When concerned postal officials from Washington investigated, the local postmaster explained, "Well, it's simple; the bag ain't full yet."

Sometimes we Christians are like that. We think our bag has to be full before we can share love and encouragement with others. Your bag doesn't have to be full to share your blessing with others. You don't have to be wealthy to give a portion of your time, your talent, or your resources to help someone less fortunate. If your bag isn't full, it doesn't matter. Use what you have to enrich the lives of others, and you will soon find your own cup running over with joy.

There have been so many "daughters of encouragement" in my life who have brought in meals, typed endless papers, made phone calls, or just said to me, "Come to our place and just relax and be refreshed." I am everlastingly grateful for the many loyal friends who have been an encouragement to me in the SPATULA ministry, which is extremely demanding both physically and emotionally.

The Prisoners Blew Me Kisses!

I had a truly precious day a few months ago when I was invited to speak at Sybil Brand—a large prison for women in the Los Angeles area. When I was a kid, I often went with my dad when he preached in the local jails, and I would sing for the inmates. But that was years ago, and my first reaction to the Sybil Brand chaplain's invitation was, "I don't want to go speak at a prison. How can I relate to those women? I don't know anybody in prison . . . I've never been in prison . . . I don't want to go."

But Chaplain Lelia Mrotzek persisted and kept saying, "Your message will be useful."

Finally, I decided God was trying to tell me something, so I agreed to go. But when we arrived at the place, my negative feelings all came back. In a maximum security prison, they check *everything* . . . you can't take anything with you, just yourself. I brought along my helpful friend, Lynda, to give me support and encouragement, and after I heard the instructions from the chaplain just before going up front to speak, I decided I needed all the encouragement I could get! Chaplain Mrotzek said: "When you're on the platform speaking, pretend there is an invisible wall between you and the inmates.

You can't motion to the women, wave, touch them, or do anything to evoke a response."

Then she continued, "The first ten rows of women are dressed in light blue—they're not dangerous. The next ten to fifteen rows are medium blue, and they are in here for more serious crimes. The last twenty rows are in dark blue. They're the lifers and long-time inmates with big problems. But don't worry, there are guards with guns on each end of the rows so nobody can get up on the platform and bother you."

It was so comforting to hear that there were guards with guns to control all these inmates, especially the ones who "weren't very dangerous." But I went ahead with my talk and told my whole story—about Bill and Steven and Tim and Larry. As I came to the end, there were tears in the eyes of many of the women, and it looked as if I'd get through the whole thing without breaking any of the chaplain's rules. But somehow I forgot where I was and used one of my favorite comments on motherhood: "Being a mother is like getting a life sentence in prison with no hope of parole!"

I practically stopped in mid-sentence, realizing that I had probably said the wrong thing! But the gals just hooted and howled, and their response spurred me on to make another boo-boo.

I asked the women, "How many of you like to watch soap operas?" They all shot their hands up and I heard cries of, "Yes! I do!" I could see the guards starting to shuffle nervously and rest their hands on their gun handles, but I plunged on anyway:

"It's wonderful for you to own up to it. When I speak in churches and ask Christian women if they watch soap operas, none of them will admit it. That's why you're here, because you're so honest!"

With that, the women really started to howl. They laughed and clapped, and I could see that I was doing just what the chaplain had warned me not to do. I definitely had evoked a response. I could see the guards looking more and more concerned, and the chaplain in the back, sort of holding her head, but I could also see the women were really with me. So I kept going and told them that a friend of mine, who was addicted to soap operas, had come across this little piece a few years back, and I thought they'd like to hear it:

AS THE WORLD TURNS, being one of THE YOUNG AND RESTLESS, I spent THE DAYS OF OUR LIVES in a SEARCH FOR TOMORROW that brought me to THE EDGE OF NIGHT. I was headed for ANOTHER WORLD. After winding up in GENERAL HOSPITAL and being cared for by THE DOCTORS, Jesus Christ, THE GUIDING LIGHT, broke through my SECRET STORM. Lovingly He said, "I have rescued you from FALCON CREST: Now share in My DYNASTY, and be one of ALL MY CHILDREN . . . and I will give you ONE LIFE TO LIVE."

By the time I finished, I could just feel the excitement in the air, but then I remembered the chaplain's rules and thought, *Oh, I've done it all wrong . . . I've said the wrong things . . . I shouldn't have mentioned life sentences and no parole. I shouldn't have asked them to raise their hands . . . this is awful . . . I never want to come here again . . . why did I come? Lord, I shouldn't have come. Why did You make me come?*

I was standing there, feeling as if I were a complete failure, when the girls all stood up and started to file out. But as they passed by me, each one BLEW ME A KISS! What exciting encouragement to me! I hadn't wanted to come and talk in a women's prison. I'd said, "I can't help these women," but my story had encouraged them, and they had refreshed me as well.

The chaplain walked up, and I fully expected to be admonished for what had happened, but instead she said excitedly, "We've never had such a demonstration of love from these women for anybody."

A couple of days later, in the mail came a note from Chaplain Lelia Mrotzek:

Dear Barbara:

Boy—have I been busy! Not because I was behind, but because of the wonderful response from the service. That is such a wonderful way to be busy! Many rededicated their lives. I had one girl come today to say she was so encouraged and felt so comfortable there. She probably hadn't had much peace in her life. She said, "I'll be there again this Sunday." Hope she's not too disappointed when I preach! The deputies have come and shared how blessed they were, also. See . . . miracles still do happen . . . even the deputies listened!

Several of the girls also wrote me afterward, and I sent them some follow-up material. I thought again about how I'd dragged my feet about going to speak in a prison and then how I'd wished I had never agreed to come. I just hadn't believed I could accomplish much among such "hardened criminals." But God softened their hearts, and because they received encouragement, so did I. In a small way, I had been an Onesiphorus, bringing encouragement into a dark prison where refreshment is as scarce as a smiling face.

How to Be an Onesiphorus

Living like Onesiphorus isn't always easy, but it always pays. In an article on Onesiphorus in *Discipleship Journal* (1986, no. 35), Stephen S. Hopper, a pastor from Grass Valley, California, describes what it takes to be an effective "minister of refreshment." For one thing, you need genuine, *continuing* concern for others. Onesiphorus didn't make just one visit to Paul in prison; he came back again and again. In other words, he followed up. Lots of people say, "Now, if there's anything I can do, just call." Of course, the person who's hurting usually doesn't call, and all too often the one who offered help doesn't check back, either. If you want to be an Onesiphorus, you don't wait for friends in need to call—you call them!

To be an Onesiphorus, you have to be persistent. Onesiphorus searched hard for Paul until he found him (see 2 Tim. 1:17). He didn't wait until he had some free time or until he was "in the neighborhood." He kept going the extra mile until he could bring refreshment and encouragement.

Opportunities to refresh and encourage others are everywhere. Surely you know someone who is . . .

- In an unfamiliar situation, like a new job, or possibly away at school.
- Tired and weary of it all.
- Lonely, and wondering if anybody cares any more.
- Experiencing disappointment or discouragement.

- Uncertain of the future because of poor health, job setbacks, or any number of other reasons.

- Under tremendous stress, pressure, or pain.

If someone's name or face flashes to mind, stop right now and make plans about how you will be Onesiphorus for that person in the next few days, or maybe the next few minutes.

I get lots of letters that tell me it's worth it. One of the most special ones said:

> Dear Barb,
>
> I just had to share with you how God used your September newsletter to minister to me. September 29 my doctor called to tell me, very unexpectedly, that the mole he had removed was malignant. I had a rare, high-risk melanoma and would need more surgery. I hung up the phone, sat down at the kitchen table, and there on top of the stack of unopened mail was the September Spatula newsletter. My eyes fell on the cartoon of the lady tied to the railroad tracks with "I don't recall asking for any of this." I burst out laughing, and turned my face to my heavenly Father and said, "Lord, how true!" What a wonderful sense of timing and humor the Lord has. That little cartoon made a tense moment bearable.
>
> I had not asked God for the daily heartache that our 2 (out of 4) rebellious children have caused—but His sustaining grace has been sufficient for each day. I had not asked Him for our (4½ year old) cerebral palsy grandson that we are raising— but God made him a precious, loving sunbeam who's taught me much of His loving heart. And I had not asked God for this cancer, but I knew He was going to go through this experience with me—and He has. The doctor "got it all," the skin graft took, and I'm mending daily without fear of the future.
>
> Thanks for your ministry that meets us in a variety of needs where we are hurting and brings smiles to our hearts.

It's true that none of us can recall that we've asked for what life has brought us. But we can reach out to others and encourage them in the midst of whatever seems to be bearing down on them (or what has already run over them!). And as we do, we will *always* be encouraged as well.

One of God's Proverbs says: "Anxiety in a man's heart weighs him down, but a good word makes him glad" (Prov. 12:25, RSV). After years of helping me encourage others, God finally sent "that good word," and I'll share what it was in the next—and last—chapter.

Extra Thoughts to Take Along

THE MINISTRY OF LETTERS

Lord, sometimes I think
I can't strike another typewriter key.
I can't write another paragraph or word.
I can't even put a period
At the end of a sentence.
I look at the fat bundle
Of unanswered letters
And it all seems so futile
So time-consuming, so unending.
I can't think or concentrate.
What I write seems empty, lifeless.
I struggle to keep my thoughts coherent.
Yet, I know I must keep on.
I have committed myself
To a ministry of writing—
Writing letters!

And often, God, when I begin to question
My personal commitment
You send me a ray of hope . . .
A personal rainbow.
Someone stops me to say
"Ten years ago, when I needed it most
You sent me a letter of encouragement.
I've read it a hundred times.
It's worn and tear-stained
But I'll treasure it forever."

Lord, I don't even remember writing.
It's been so long.
But it doesn't matter.

I see again the value of ministry
And so I'll continue.
But first, Lord
I must put a period after the sentence
I so wearily wrote just an hour ago.

—Ruth Harms Calkin*

*   *   *   *   *   *

OATMEAL DAYS

It's not always the red-flag crisis days that are hardest to take. It's the "oatmeal days." The ordinary, "zero" days of little or no consequence. The ho-hum days filled with nothing of any particular interest. Colorless. Uninteresting. Unfascinating. Unspectacular. And unfun. The days everyone deals with.

We cope. We wend our way through the tangle of tedious activity and sandpaper people scattered through our day and get no applause, because coping is expected.

Not so during the red-flag crisis times. People tend to rally behind us with loving support. We're lifted above the crisis and enabled beyond human comprehension at times.

On oatmeal days, after a crisis has peaked, it may seem as if friends have forsaken us, as if God doesn't care. But the reality will be that life has merely pushed us and our friends one step further in the Christian growth-walk.

The God of the crisis times is the God of the oatmeal days, too. Because He said He is. Because He keeps His promises—always. Because we can't get along without Him. And because we wouldn't want to if we could.

—Source Unknown

*   *   *   *   *

HUGS

It's wondrous what a hug can do
A hug can cheer you when you're blue
A hug can say "I love you so"
Or "Gee, I hate to see you go."
A hug is "Welcome back again"
And "Great to see you, where've you been?"
A hug can smooth a small child's pain
And bring a rainbow after rain.
The hug: There's just no doubt about it
We scarcely could survive without it.
A hug delights and warms and charms—
It must be why God gave us arms.
Hugs are great for Fathers and Mothers,
Sweet for sisters, swell for brothers
And chances are your favorite aunts
Love them more than potted plants.
Kittens crave them, puppies love them,
Heads of State are not above them.
A hug can break the language barrier
And make your travels so much merrier.
No need to fret about your store of them
The more you give the more there's more of 'em,
So stretch those arms without delay
And give someone a hug today!

—Dean Walley

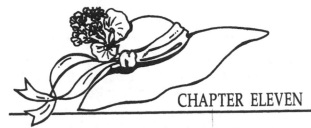

CHAPTER ELEVEN

My Future's So Bright
I Gotta Wear Shades

". . . when dreams come true at last,
there is life and joy."

—Proverbs 13:12, TLB

It was an extra busy Monday, early in May 1986. I had spent the prior weekend speaking at a three-day women's conference sponsored by Campus Crusade in Arrowhead Springs, California. Now I was back home, hurriedly getting ready to leave again almost immediately for an extended trip to Minnesota, where I would speak at the Billy Graham Evangelistic Association chapel, plus several Mother's Day banquets in churches in the Minneapolis area.

The trip meant being gone for Mother's Day, but that didn't seem to matter a great deal. Barney and his family were going to drop by before we left to wish me a happy Mother's Day, and Larry . . . well, Larry hadn't called for five Mother's Days in a row. He had been gone without a word or trace since January 1980, so I was getting used to it—or so I thought.

And then, as I was packing and going over notes of talks I would give to parents on how we all have to give our kids to God and leave the results up to Him because God never gives the score on a life until the game is over, the telephone rang!

It was Larry! The voice I had longed to hear for so many years said, "I want to come over and give you a Mother's Day present."

What a shock! I froze with apprehension! My first thought was, *Why now? Why does he want to bring me a present? I bet he's going to tell me he's going to marry his lover . . . or that he has AIDS.*

I just didn't know what to say, so I stammered, "Well, Larry, I don't know, I'm so busy getting ready to leave for a big trip . . . lots of speaking engagements . . . not sure we've got time . . . just a minute, let me talk to Dad . . ."

When I look back on this conversation, I can see the irony, but at that moment, I was confused, stalling for time. For six years I had been speaking to groups all over the country, telling parents to hang in there, that God would bring their wayward children back from the "far country," and now *my own son* was finally on the line, and I was telling him I was TOO BUSY to see him, because I was leaving to go speak about having hope and joy when your kids disappoint you!

I put my hand over the receiver and said to Bill, "It's Larry! He wants to come over and give me a Mother's Day present. I'm not sure I should let him come . . . what if he wants to tell us he's marrying his lover . . . or something even worse?"

Mr. Wumphee just looked at me and said unhesitatingly, "You have him come home!"

I could see Bill wasn't going to do anything to get me off the hook, so trying my best to sound light and happy, I told Larry, "Okay . . . you can come over."

The next hour seemed to drag by. Larry had said he was about fifty miles away, but I kept wondering if he would really come. And then I would wonder if it were all a bad dream. I could talk a good game to other parents, but now it was my turn to see if I could really cut the mustard! It was all too good (or maybe bad) to be true!

When the doorbell rang, I almost jumped. How could he be here that SOON? I opened the door, and there was Larry, standing tall, with a clear-eyed look I hadn't seen for eleven years. But he had no present in his hand, and my heart sank. He had come to give me some kind of news for a gift, and what would that news be? Would it leave me counting roses on the wallpaper again? I invited him in, cautiously, with only a perfunctory little hug—wondering if I should remark about the absent present. As we sat down in the living room, I could see big tears in his eyes, and then I heard his words:

"I want you to forgive me for the eleven years of pain I have caused you. Last week I went to an advanced seminar for Basic Youth Conflicts, and I . . . I rededicated my life to the Lord. I took all the evidence of the old life, the pictures and everything else to do with the lifestyle—everything—I took it to a fireplace and, while the whole thing was burning, I felt this complete release for the first time in eleven years. I'm released from that bondage I was in, and God has really cleansed me. Now I can stand clean before the Lord."

What a glorious Mother's Day present! A gift wrapped in LOVE!

And then Larry gave us a little bonus with news about the young man he had been living with. The night after Larry got his life right with the Lord, his friend went forward at the Basic Youth seminar and received Christ as Savior.

This young man was a brand new Christian and my son had rededicated his life to the Lord! We sat there for a long time and just hugged each other. He had asked for our forgiveness, and we needed his forgiveness as well for our failures to understand his hurts. We were overjoyed to have him back again, and that day a restoration began in our family that is continuing even now.

Joy Washed over Me

Larry stayed for over two hours, and we laughed and cried and hugged and shared. For years I had been talking about having joy and how joy is like God living in the marrow of your bones. Now, joy was washing over me in huge waves! All the verses I had been quoting to other parents now sang praises in my own heart.

"*Hope deferred makes the heart sick; but when dreams come true at last, there is life and joy*" (Prov. 13:12, TLB). Hope had been deferred for me for eleven years. Ever since that night at the flagpole at Disneyland in 1975, I had hoped and prayed, but my heart had been heavy. I had found joy where I could; I had refused to let misery overwhelm me, but now I felt life and joy in every cell of my body.

"'. . . there is hope for your future,' declares the Lord. 'Your children will return to their own land'" (Jer. 31:17, NIV). For eleven years, I had hoped and prayed that Larry would return to the Lord. Promises like this one were the only thing that gave me any real hope. And now he had "come back to his own land" after wandering in the gay lifestyle.

"I will . . . transform her Valley of Troubles into a Door of Hope" (Hos. 2:15, TLB). God had not only transformed my "valley of troubles" into a door of hope—He had thrown open wide that door and Larry had walked through it back into our lives!

"And you can . . . be very sure that God will rescue the children of the godly" (Prov. 11:21, TLB). What a promise for Christians who realize their righteousness or godliness comes only through believing in Jesus Christ! God had rescued my child. Our fractured relationship was being healed.

We left the next day for Minneapolis, where we planned to stay with my sister, Janet, and her husband, Mel, who is a radio minister and evangelist there. I was sure I could have flown there with my own wings, but Bill convinced me we should take a jet. I told Bill not to tell them about Larry's return because I wanted to save it for a surprise when I spoke at a banquet scheduled at their church that next evening. But when we arrived and Janet picked us up at the airport, Bill couldn't contain himself and blurted out, "Barb has a secret, but she's not going to tell you until later."

Of course, Janet wouldn't quit until she wheedled it out of me. And when I told her Larry had returned and asked for forgiveness, she wept with joy. Mel's reaction was to excitedly schedule me to be on his radio broadcast the next morning so he could have a scoop before I told about Larry at the banquet.

The next night at the banquet, which had a Mother's Day theme, I shared about Larry's return and the total peace and joy that Bill and I had for the first time since our long, eleven-year parenthesis of pain began in 1975. I explained that after Larry had returned the first time, we had lived in a sort of vacuum, not really mentioning his problem and "assuming" everything was all right. Before he left the second time, he had thrown the Bible in our faces and disowned us. Now, after a total of eleven years, God had kicked the end out of our parenthesis, and we were free!

The reaction to my news was dramatic—lots of tears, smiles, and even applause. Every mom in the room identified with my joy, and one mother, who had wanted to die after recently learning that her son was gay, got up and shared how she now had new hope because of what had happened with Larry.

Faith Is My Distant Cousin

I spoke several more times that Mother's Day weekend before returning home and setting off again to encourage some SPATULA cluster groups in the Seattle area with our wonderful news. *The Love Line* newsletter for July 1986 was a special one, dedicated to sharing the news of Larry's return.

Larry even contributed to that newsletter. He wrote all of our SPATULA friends and said:

> My mother has told me of the countless people who have prayed for me these many years. Praise God for His faithfulness!
>
> I'm sure many of you wonder what it was that brought such a change in my life. All I can say, briefly, is that when I attended a Basic Youth Seminar, taught by Bill Gothard, I discovered the victory that we have in Christ and the power to be free from moral impurity and bitterness.
>
> There have been many changes for me these past weeks since I rededicated my life to Christ. I can only say that I am truly thankful that God, in His mercy, has forgiven me and I look forward to being of service to Him.

That issue of *The Love Line* also included a congratulatory note penned personally by Dr. James Dobson a couple of months before. As you can see, he got so excited, he ran out of space:

50 E. Foothill Blvd., Arcadia, CA 91006 • (818) 445-1579

May 24, 86

Hey Barb

CONGRATULATIONS!

We share your wonderful news with thankful hearts

Jim

Dedicated to the Preservation of the Home • James C. Dobson, Ph.D., President

That newsletter generated a large amount of mail as many SPATULANDERS wrote to express their joy for me. But while all this speaking and writing about Larry's return was going on, I had a reaction that left me with the old doubts and fears. What if Larry suddenly slipped back into the old lifestyle? After all, there was so much residue from all those years of living in rebellion and sin. How long does it take to have a renewing of the mind? I just didn't know.

When Jim Dobson called and invited me to be on his "Focus on the Family" radio show to talk about Larry, I hesitated at first. I wondered if I was ready to go on national radio or television and share all this with the "whole world." Perhaps I should wait until some time had elapsed—to be sure Larry was really out of the gay lifestyle for good.

Larry had returned, and I was overjoyed that he had asked forgiveness and that being forgiven was so important to him. That was crucial in my mind because I knew God would work from that foundation. It would take time to know for sure if his contrition and tears would last. I guess I'm not a woman of a lot of faith. For me joy and hope go together; they're sisters. But faith is sort of a distant cousin for me. I've been told I have the gift of joy, but faith hasn't been my gift, so I borrow it from others who have plenty to spare.

Larry and I Made a Tape Together

But as the weeks went by, my fears subsided, and I agreed to go on Dr. Dobson's program in October. Just before doing the "Focus on the Family" broadcast, I made a tape with Larry to share with just the SPATULA family. We met in his apartment, high above sprawling downtown Los Angeles, and shared our thoughts about what had happened and how we felt now that he had been back for several months.

On that tape he shared what had brought about his change. Obviously, guilt had dogged his footsteps for eleven years, and he had longed to have his relationship to us restored. Then he attended an Advanced Basic Youth Conflicts Seminar led by Bill Gothard, and all of the principles and values he had so violently rejected eleven years ago had taken root in a new and wonderful way. As Larry said, "God either gives us the grace to overcome these things, or we become embittered. And I think Basic Youth Conflicts taught me how to overcome that bitterness and be able to enjoy the grace of God again."

Larry also talked about how important it was to ask his parents' forgiveness. He learned a very important principle: "If you can't respond to your parents properly, you can't respond to other people properly."

We also shared a great deal about our failures—his and mine. If there is anything the homosexual child needs when his parents learn of his orientation, it's unconditional love. But unconditional love is very hard to give in those first moments of being totally devastated and emotionally overwrought.

Larry quoted a Psalm that promises: "The Lord is near to those who have a broken heart,/And saves such as have a contrite spirit" (Ps. 34:18, NKJV). And then he said, "We all have failures, in whatever area is in our lives, but it really is important that we understand we must acknowledge those failures to the people whom we have failed and try to bring about restoration in our lives. . . . That's the miracle of the power that Christ gives us . . . to be able to transform failures into victories."

As our interview went on, I told Larry how wonderful it is to start out the day and know the past is over and that he doesn't have to live in bondage to the unhappy memories of the past and I don't have to, either.

"That's because we've been able to forgive each other," Larry replied. "Forgiveness is a very powerful thing—the ability to forgive and the ability to be forgiven. When someone comes to you and says, 'I was wrong in what I did to you, will you forgive me?' that's a very powerful thing . . . because it releases a burden of guilt. . . . What holds people back from doing that is their own pride, their own inability to say, 'I made a mistake, I was wrong.' Now, a lot of parents don't want to do that, but when a child sees the parent not willing to admit his mistakes, what makes you think the child would want to admit his own?"

As we talked, Larry recalled how our own relationship had been strained to the point of total destruction when I first learned of his homosexuality. "Some of the things that you said were terrible," he remembered. "Reckless words, like a piercing sword."

I remembered those devastating moments, too. On that shocking Sunday afternoon, I had said I would have preferred Larry's being dead to his being gay. That's why I tell people to shove a sock in their mouth and not to say anything for six months, or they'll say the wrong thing because they're in such a state of panic—completely unglued.

As Larry and I continued our discussion, I asked him what a parent should do if a child calls to say he has AIDS—how should parents deal with this? His answer pointed toward the only real hope anyone has in this fallen world. He said:

"Parents should remember that they're Christians, and that we do worship a God of deliverance, not of death. God wants to supernaturally reveal Himself to the world, and the only way He can do that is through Christians—through the people who love Him and worship Him. We live in terrifying times, but as Christians we have power over death and over sin, just as Christ did."

As we closed our interview, I asked Larry what the future held for him. He had gotten his life right before God and planned to serve the Lord. What did he think God had in mind for his life? He answered:

"All I know is that if I purpose in my heart to be loving in everything I do, the Lord will open up those things for me, and I'm confident in that. I know that as long as I'm in His Word and doing what He feels is right, and I'm joyful and thankful for everything that He has given to me, I don't have to fear the future."

That interview with Larry "made my heart smile," and I was able to do the radio program with Dr. James Dobson a few days later with confident joy. At one point I said to Dr. Dobson and the radio audience: "We're on this journey to becoming whole; the ones that are farther down the road can reach back and pull the other ones along. That's how it's supposed to be."

He interrupted me and asked, "Do you mean to tell me there may come a day when a parent could reach out and help somebody else?"

"I guarantee that," I told the radio listeners. "After a few months of walking in this tunnel, you're going to see a light at the other end, and it won't be another train coming. That light is going to be God's love and God's light on you, and as you go through this and you begin to heal, those raw edges are going to be healed by God's love and you're going to reach back and find another person who is where you are now. That's the whole purpose of this ministry—being able to pull the ones up that are in that deep tunnel and pull them through. We've seen it happen hundreds of times!"

New Joy Gave Us New Energy

Larry's return, not only to us but more importantly to the Lord, spurred us on to continue working with even more diligence to help pull parents through their long, dark tunnel of despair. Their letters continued to pour in, and one mom's words particularly grabbed my heart because she told of not *one* son who had declared he was homosexual, but *two*:

Dear Barb:

When my two sons (twins) told me two months ago that they were homosexual, I wanted to die. Really die! I considered suicide but was too chicken. I was sad, angry, and hurt, and so very confused. Where had we gone wrong? We had sent them to Christian schools. They went to church, had good Christian friends. What had happened? The only thing I could think of was to call a friend long distance. I did just that, and thank God, I did. She told me she was sending a book. About three days later it arrived: *Where Does a Mother Go to Resign?*

My head was like stone. I could not concentrate to read it. My wonderful husband began to read it to me. As he began to read, I realized I was not alone.

That book saved my life. Every feeling you expressed I was feeling at that time. I began slowly to come alive. Our sons were hurting, also. We began talking openly about the problem. I loved them so very much. We all cried together. They are *special* young men, and I feel our Lord has something great in store for them.

I know now, as you said, the only two things we can do is pray for them and love them. . . . Yes, there are still difficult days but I'm learning to put things in Jesus' hands. . . . Keep up the great work!

In twelve years of helping parents, I had never heard from anyone who had twins who were gay. This mother's pain was double, but she was climbing out of her pit by using two of the most important principles any parent needs when a child goes into the gay lifestyle, alcoholism, drug addiction, sexual perversion, and any number of other terrible problems that can afflict a family. These concepts almost sound contradictory, but in reality they work together to bring about change and healing.

- Love your child unconditionally.

- Let your child go—release him to God's care.

I would like to meet the mother of the prodigal son. I wonder where she was when her son was slopping the hogs and living in the pigpen. (She probably was in a home for the bewildered.) What was she doing when they were preparing the feast for his homecoming?

Unconditional Love Is Not "Sloppy Agape"

I'm often asked during interviews and talk shows just HOW can a parent show "unconditional love." One lady wondered if it meant just loving everyone and "letting them do their own thing." My answer was that that would be "sloppy agape" love that had no real substance or toughness. The point is, we may not always love what our children are doing—their lifestyle and values—*but we love them!*

Unconditional love does not mean that you cannot have rules concerning what your child can or cannot do within the family. I don't believe Scripture teaches that we should let the sin of one person destroy everyone else. For example, if the child is coming in drunk or on drugs, you can't let that disrupt the rest of the family. Recently, I picked up a saying that I like a great deal:

THE MAIN THING IS TO KEEP
THE MAIN THING THE MAIN THING.

When your child is in trouble, the main thing is to keep your relationship to God and your spouse and the others in your family solid while you continue to reach out to the one who's wandering. You have to say, "Hey, I love you, but I love you so much that I can't let you destroy the family. You're going to have to find another place. We'll help you."

If possible, get your child out on his own if he's over eighteen and able to hold a job. Support and love your child in every legitimate way you can, but do not support the sin that has him in its grasp. You want your child to know that home is a loving, warm, comfortable place, but it is not an incubator for immature behavior. Don't fur-line the pigpen for your child when he should be on his own.

If your child is younger (under eighteen), remember that you are still in charge of your home. You can still make the rules, and I repeat, you can have rules for your home and still have unconditional love for a rebellious child. You can set limits, lock doors, and throw out stuff that you don't want there. You don't have to have someone in your home doing things there that you don't want them to be doing and scattering all that pain and all that sin all over the house.

All this advice sounds simple, but I realize it is not easy to practice. The trick is to be firm in holding to your standards but at the same time to show your child unconditional love and compassion. In my experience, I found that unconditional love comes only out of constant prayer. "Praying about it" is often held out as the great Christian answer to everything, as if God will magically solve all problems if we just say our prayers often enough. I don't believe that, but I do believe prayer is the foundation to answering whatever is tearing and ripping at your family. I often quote this little poem to moms—and they understand. It may sound "sentimental," but I believe it contains a great theological truth:

MOTHER'S COVERS

When you were small
And just a touch away,
I covered you with blankets

Against the cool night air.
But now that you are tall
And out of reach,
I fold my hands
And cover you with prayer.

—Dona Maddux Cooper

Never Stop Loving Your Child

The late Joseph Bayly, who wrote many fine Christian books and articles over his long career, once shared his heart about the "rebel" in his own family. He had one boy out of a total of five children who decided to rebel over a four- or five-year period from the late teens to early twenties. After one year at Bible college, he declared his independence, cut all roots, and hitch-hiked across the country to live his own life on the West Coast.

With his son living half a continent away, Joseph Bayly became depressed, but his wife, Mary Lou, said, "We must pray all the more. *We're* not in San Diego with our son, but God is."

What is prayer but turning to God? And nothing can turn a parent to God more quickly than a wayward child. After all, when a child rebels and is utterly out of control, where else *can* you turn? And it's times like that when you have the chance to grow in faith. I have to admit, however, that I'm better at hope and joy than I am at faith.

Joseph Bayly also posed a very thought-provoking question: "Does faith really mean much unless it is tested, unless it is exercised in the darkness?" To answer his own question, he refers to Hebrews 11:1: "Now faith is the substance of things hoped for, the evidence of things not seen" (NKJV).

Bayly goes on to say that God does not disown you or me when we rebel against Him. Rather "He always is there, waiting with outstretched arms for us to return. He is the waiting Father." Likewise, "we must be waiting parents, with arms and love extended. Even if years of disappointment and anxiety pass in the meantime."

To Love Your Child—Let Go

It sounds confusing to some parents, but to unconditionally love your child, *no matter what,* you also have to LET THAT CHILD GO. How can you love your child and let him go at the same time? The answer: *Give him to God!*

Parents ask me over and over: "How can I give my child to God?" I explain how I did it that day I said, "Whatever, Lord . . ." but many parents are in such an emotional turmoil they need some kind of illustration to help. I found such an illustration recently, something that can perhaps help you mentally give your child to God's care.

Picture in your mind that you are placing your daughter or son in a gift box. Then wrap the box with lovely paper and a ribbon. Next, imagine the glorious throne of God which is at the top of a long flight of stairs. Picture yourself walking up those stairs, carrying your lovely gift-wrapped package.

Put your package down at the feet of Jesus, who is sitting on the throne. Wait there as He bends down, picks up the package, and puts it on His lap. Then He will remove the wrappings, take off the lid, and lift your child out.

Watch as Jesus wraps the child in His loving arms and holds him close. After you see Jesus holding him, you walk back down the stairs, pausing part way down to look back to reassure yourself that Jesus still has your child in His arms. Then you continue down the stairs, thanking God for taking control.

You have given your prodigal to God. He or she is no longer in your hands. Now you are ready to ask God to do whatever is necessary to help your child. You may have to see circumstances that may seem to tear you apart, but God will undertake to reach your rebel, often in very dramatic ways. Whenever you are tempted to take control again, you must practice this little thought exercise. Remember the specific time when you presented your child as a gift to the Lord, and He received him in faithful love.

I'm not saying this will be easy. The old cliché says, "Let go and let God," but letting go is always the hardest part. Once we let go, then it's easier to let God do what He's ready to do.

During those years when Larry was gone, particularly his

second absence, I would speak to various groups, and people would ask, "How is your family *now?*"

I would reply, "Well, my two sons haven't risen from the dead and my third son is still out there in the gay life."

"Well, how can you be so happy and have such joy?" people wanted to know.

And my answer was always the same: "It's because I've given it to the Lord. I've said, 'Whatever, Lord.' I've relinquished it to the Lord, and I've got a life to get busy with living."

Conviction from God Makes the Difference

If we're going "to let go and let God," we must fear less and trust in Christ more. I'm often asked if homosexuals can completely change. Many Christians believe homosexuality is like any other sin—that it's a matter of choice and all the homosexual has to do is "get right with God" and his orientation will become heterosexual.

Over the past years, I have met hundreds of homosexual young men, many of whom are Christians. I love these kids and believe that most of them don't want their homosexual feelings. They didn't ask for this. I don't think anybody would ask to be a homosexual because there is so much animosity and rejection. But for some reason that even the experts don't understand, something has happened at the core of their personality.

Although no one really knows what causes homosexuality, many believe this phenomenon could be brought about by any number of things. However, to suggest that there might be various causes for homosexuality does not mean that the Christian can approve of homosexual behavior.

It's not wrong to have homosexual feelings; the wrong comes in *acting out* the homosexual lifestyle. There are those who have homosexual feelings, but they don't ever act on them. They live their lives, realizing they have a very vulnerable area with which they're always going to have to struggle— just as we all have areas of our lives where we are more vulnerable than others. But I believe God will give us all, even the homosexual, the grace to live a clean life and to stand clean before the Lord.

Most of the homosexuals that I'm talking about have had Christian parents who tried to raise them right, and those parents just don't understand what happened. I don't understand, either. As we read in the book of Deuteronomy, "The secret things belong to the Lord" (Deut. 29:29, RSV). Most of these young men would never have chosen homosexuality, but for some reason, something got scrambled and didn't come out as it should have—something like a flower that didn't open. Instead of opening correctly, their sexuality became inverted. No one is at fault; it just happened.

With some good counseling and with love from their parents, their family, and their church, I believe homosexuals can live a clean life without acting out their orientation. However, a shift in behavior may depend on the person's motivation and the depth of his commitment to the gay lifestyle.

We know that the homosexual lifestyle is a real entrenching behavior. But we can't put God in a box and say He has to heal everybody in a certain way. You can't say that a person is only effective as a Christian when he's married and has a family. I just know that God has touched my son's life. He's clean before the Lord, and it's exciting to see what God is going to do in his life. And whatever happens, we know that it has to be God's touch in his life. Healing always has to be of God. It has to be God's touch in any area, whether it's alcohol, drugs, or whatever. Condemnation will not bring change. It is only conviction from God that brings a shift in behavior.

Why the Future Is So Bright

The title of this chapter comes from a bumper sticker that a friend found and sent me because it reminded her of me. But what it reminds me of is what Larry said when we made that tape together in 1986. His exact words were, "I don't have any fear for the future." I don't, either, because the future is now bright with God's hope and love.

You may be thinking, *"That's fine for you, Barbara—your child is back and living a clean life, but mine is still out there,*

wandering alone in a lifestyle that can destroy him." I understand. That's why I wrote yet another book, to let you know THERE IS HOPE.

God can take your trouble and change it into treasure. Your sorrow can be exchanged for joy, not just a momentary smile, but a deep new joy. It will be a bubbling experience of new hope that brings brightness to your eyes and a song to your heart. In the midst of the darkness, you will learn lessons you might never have learned in the day. We all have seen dreams turn to ashes—ugly things, hopeless and heartbreaking—but beauty for ashes is God's exchange.

Tears and sorrow come, but each time God will be there to remind you that He cares. Romans 8:28 means that God causes all things in our lives to work together for good. Flowers can even grow on dung hills, and compost makes great gardens. God is offering Himself to you daily, and the rate of exchange is fixed. It is your sins for His forgiveness, your tragedy and hurt for His balm of healing, and your sorrow for His joy.

Give God the pain and sorrow; give Him the guilt you feel. Tears and heartaches come to us all. They are part of living, but Jesus Christ can ease the heartache.

Remember, you are not alone; many are in God's waiting room for what seems like forever, learning lessons, suffering pain, and growing. But the fertilizer that helps us grow is in those valleys, not on the mountaintops.

The iron crown of suffering precedes the golden crown of glory. So give your child to God and then focus on getting your own life together. Also keep in mind that *you are not responsible for what you cannot control* and that God has only called you to be *faithful.* He did not call you to be *successful!*

Real genuine healing is a process. It takes a long, long time for the deep hurts to be resolved. Sometimes it seems that they will be with us forever, but understanding them helps dissipate their pain.

Life isn't always what you want, but it's what you've got; so, with God's help, CHOOSE TO BE HAPPY—and He will see you and your loved ones home safe at last!

A Final Thought to Take Along

HE'LL SEE THEM HOME

Don't despair so of your children,
    God will bring them to the fold—
Because He died to save them,
    They're special to the Lord.
He knows how much you love them,
    He loves them even more.
As long as you hold on in prayer,
    He'll not close the door.
Even now He sees your tears,
    And He whispers tenderly,
Of love that conquered all—
    That all men might be free.

So lay them at His altar,
    Let go and leave them there—
God will be faithful to your trust,

He won't withhold His care.
His hand will ever nurture,
    No matter where they roam—
And He won't be satisfied
    'Til He sees them safely home!

—Joyce Henning

This book is dedicated to my OLDER and THINNER sister, Janet, who has fondly called me "Punk" for as long as I can remember. Her best quality is her tender heart. When our kids were small, Janet and I took them to see the movie *The Adventures of Tom Sawyer* at a drive-in theater. It was much too violent for her. When Tom's Aunt Polly thumped him on the head with her thimble for being mischievous, Janet made us leave. But she has always been there for me, as she has for so many others. She cries easily (but always appropriately), and she will surely cry when she reads this excerpt from Carey Martin's essay, "What Is a Sister?" which is especially true for her:

> A sister is one of the most precious people in the story of your life. Together, you have shared some of the most special moments two people have ever shared. A sister is a perspective on the past, and she's a million favorite memories that will always last. A sister is a photograph that is one of your most treasured possessions. She's a note that arrives on a special day, and when there's news to share, she's the first one you want to call. A sister is a reminder of the blessings that come from closeness.
>
> A sister is a confidante and a counselor. She's a dear and wonderful friend, and—in certain ways—something like a twin. She's a hand within your hand; she's so often the only one who understands.
>
> What is a sister? She's someone more special than words; someone beautiful and unique. And in so many ways, there is no one who is loved so dearly.

Contents

Acknowledgments

I gratefully extend appreciation and thanks to the many people who have so graciously shared with me the stories, poems, letters, and other materials that appear in this book. You have provided some of the biggest splashes of joy in my life!

Diligent effort has been made to locate the author and copyright ownership of all material quoted in this book. However, because I receive clippings, handwritten notes, church bulletins, etc., from friends and readers all over the world, there often is no way of identifying the original source. Many of the anecdotes and tidbits used in this book are combinations of materials from different sources, and the letters I share have been changed and/or combined so that the writers' identities are protected. If any readers know the correct source of the items now designated as "Source unknown," I would appreciate hearing from you so corrections can be made in later printings and proper credit can be given.

Special acknowledgment and my sincere thanks also go to the following individuals and companies for these materials:

Ashleigh Brilliant for permission to use Ashleigh Brilliant *Pot-Shots* and *Brilliant Thoughts* (Brilliant Enterprises, 117 West Valerio St., Santa Barbara, California 93101).

The Russ Postcard cartoon feature by Dana Summers, included in chapter 1. Used by permission.

Introduction
"Barb, I Need a Splash of Your Joy . . ."

Not long ago I paid a visit to Focus on the Family to tape a radio interview with Dr. James Dobson, the founder and president. While we sat in his office, sharing our latest experiences, I sensed that he wasn't in his usual "up" kind of mood. There was a definite heaviness in his voice that wasn't typical of him.

I knew Dr. Dobson had been serving on the Attorney General's Commission on Pornography and that for over a year he had been spending one week every month traveling to various cities throughout the United States to study the problem. He had even received threatening letters and phone calls for taking part in the program, and it was obvious that all those months of stress had been a drain on him, physically as well as emotionally.

Sensing Dr. Dobson's downcast mood, I offered to come back at another time. "Then we could do the interview when you are feeling more refreshed and ready to go . . . ," I suggested.

Dr. Dobson just looked at me and said, "Barb, if there EVER were a time that I needed a splash of your joy, it's today!"

We went ahead with the interview and it came out much better than any of us had hoped. Later, I thought about what he had said.

Someday, I told myself, I'd like to write a book that would have refreshing words that could help others find "splashes of joy," no matter what situation they find themselves in. So, in a way, I owe part of the title for this book to Dr. Dobson, who tossed off that phrase, "splash of joy" so easily, never thinking it would become part of a book designed to inject some joy and hope into a joyless, hopeless world.

So now you know where the first part of the title came from, but what about the rest of it? Some of my friends told me that using a word like "cesspools" in a title would sound too graphic, and I listened carefully to what they were saying. But the more I continued to hear from folks out there who are in pain of every imaginable description, the more I realized that that's exactly where they are—in one kind of slimy cesspool or another.

Most of us can think about times when we've been "in the cesspool"; many of you are there right now. Almost everyone needs a splash of joy to get through the mess, to get cleaned off and get sweetened up—refreshed and ready to go again.

For several years I used the phrase "In His Grip" when autographing books requested at conferences or by mail. But to be honest, that got tiresome because of having to go back and dot all those *i*'s. Since I sign hundreds of books, I decided I wanted something that would be meaningful, but without so many places where I would have to dot some *i*'s or cross some *t*'s.

Finally, I came upon the perfect word. JOYFULLY says it all. In JOYFULLY there is nothing to dot or cross—it just flows out. It's a word that is a little "splash of joy" for me because it gives me the perfect trademark for every book that I autograph. JOYFULLY simply means "full of joy." What a blessing to have found one little word that I can make my own. It says what I feel, simply and completely, and it is the key to the way I live my life.

That's what this book is all about—living life joyfully. I want to bring you splashes of joy, whether you feel you're in a slimy cesspool or just a dirty mudhole that is causing you stress and frustration. Because of my books and Spatula Ministries, I get a lot of feedback that turns into splashes of joy for me. One dear woman wrote this darling note:

God uses you like an antiseptic on wounds to bring healing to the Body of Christ.

Thanks ♡

Another good friend wrote to say that so many people are hoping to hear words of encouragement as they ". . . search for a way out of the tunnel of despair, the slough of despond, the quagmire of panic, the quicksand of hopelessness . . . and all those kinds of places. God is using you to help people through."

Letters like that give back to me splashes of joy, as do comments made by women after they hear me as a retreat speaker. We gather in a circle after I spend three days telling them everything I know (actually, it takes less than three days, but I repeat myself a lot). Then I offer them the opportunity to talk about how they feel. Almost everyone shares and can hardly wait to get her turn. Those are times when the splashes of joy become little tidal waves that wash over me as I am reminded of Proverbs 11:25—as you refresh others, you, yourself, will be refreshed.

So I guess I'm writing this book for myself as much as for you. We both need splashes of joy, so let's go find some!

Joyfully,

Barbara Johnson

Smile! It Kills Time Between Disasters

Life is what you make it,
until something comes along and makes it worse.

When I opened the package, I should have known that THESE pantyhose would be "different." But somehow I just didn't get suspicious, even when they came wrapped as a gift just before April Fools' Day, given to me by a friend who was working in the novelty shop at Knott's Berry Farm. When I took them out of the box, they looked like any other pantyhose and I thought, *How nice of Alice to send these. I can always use another pair.*

Just two days later—on April 1—I decided to wear the new pantyhose while speaking nearby to a large group of women at a church brunch. When I pulled on the pantyhose that morning, I guess I should have realized something was a bit strange because they came clear up to my ARMPITS! Bill even commented, "What have you got on? It looks like a SA-RONG!"

I just ignored my "tell-it-like-it-is" husband and hurriedly finished dressing. *Obviously, Alice bought the wrong size, I told myself, but there's nothing to be done about it now because I don't*

have time to change . . . I've got to be at the church in twenty min-
utes . . .

The program went nicely, but as I got up to speak, I felt something beginning to creep up on me. I had on a V-neck dress
and, looking down, I was horrified to see something brown
inching its way right up out of my neckline! The brown stuff
just kept coming, and soon it seemed to be like some kind of
muff around my throat. Then I realized what was going on.
Those pantyhose Alice had given me were made of material
that *really* stretched. (I learned later they were 100 percent
SPANDEX!) My new pantyhose had actually begun to "grow
north"—straight up over my head! I could have tied them at
the top in a bow!

What to do? There was no way to shove the pantyhose down
my dress without making a big bulge in the wrong place. Besides, I was in front of five hundred women, with no privacy
to do anything. I decided to stop and tell the crowd that I ha
a friend who knows I love the first of each month—especially
April Fools' Day. She must have thought it would be great fun
to give me a pair of "unique" pantyhose—the kind that could
creep up clear around my neck!

Once the women understood that my problem was my
pantyhose and not some strange growth caused by spores from
outer space, they all began laughing and enjoying my embarrassment along with me. Not many speakers get to finish a
presentation with a brown muff that appears magically from
out of their dress. It was a first for my audience, and it was
DEFINITELY a first for me. But we all had a good time because I chose not to get flustered. Instead, I enjoyed making
the best of the situation.

When you look at all the pain and problems in the world,
creeping pantyhose isn't exactly a 7.2 on the Richter scale of human suffering. It does, however, illustrate the fact that there is
something about joy and laughter that is engaging and even
therapeutic, especially when things aren't going very well. The
overwhelming response to a recent book I did—*So, Stick a Gera-*
nium in Your Hat and Be Happy—is hard to explain, unless you

take into account the tremendous need so many folks have for some kind of relief, something to bring a smile or chuckle into a life that, as one letter said, "doesn't have any sparkles right now."

The following paragraphs offer just a peek into my post office box, which is the landing place for up to several dozen letters a day, almost always from women who are in, or just crawled out of, one of the slippery cesspools of life. Pain has MANY faces, and the universal cure is laughter—not because we try to deny the truth, but because we have learned to face it, absorb it, and smile through it.

From New York:

How I wish I could meet you face to face and speak with you. Sometimes I feel like no one understands my pain. My husband and I also lost two children. Donna, a beautiful young lady, turned to a life of prostitution and in November '84 she was murdered at the age of 22. We never did see her in her coffin—they shipped her home sealed.

A few months later, Jerry, age 27 contracted AIDS because of his gay lifestyle, and at age 28 he went home to be with

Jesus. . . . When our children died, everyone kept telling us to rejoice. We tried to, and in the interim I denied the reality of my grief and now I'm unable to cry, so the only emotion that comes from me is anger . . . I am so uptight right now I feel like a pressure cooker about to explode. I spend a lot of time with the Lord in prayer . . . the only time I get any relief from my terrible anxiety. . . .

Please pray for me. I'm a mess who's waiting for God to make something beautiful. He truly is the Rock that is higher than myself, and I continually run to Him, sometimes pleading for strength to make it through the next moment. . . .

From Colorado:

I found out last week that my son is HIV positive and has been ill a lot this winter. He called last Sunday night. Only God knows my pain and my son's fright.

Today I don't feel like I can hang on to God, so I'm letting God hang on to me, my son and my husband. . . .

From California:

It was just one year ago that our daughter had her diving accident and went to be with the Lord. We still miss her so much, but knowing where she is makes it easier to bear. . . .

From Alabama:

My life fell apart four years ago. We had a wonderful life, prosperous, one son, one daughter, beautiful home, health, etc. Our daughter announced her lesbianism at the start of her senior year in school.

Nine months later, my husband left me and our son without one word of warning (after 22 years together). I found out he was having an affair with a woman at his job. . . .

But my faith in God has never been stronger . . . and I still have my sense of humor! I know that God is in control, even though my life seems to be so out of control.

From Oregon:

It is Christmas morning with all the snow and the wonderful music of this happy season. I have just finished reading your book for the umpteenth time and as I type this I am smiling.

I do not smile often, but I am learning to laugh again. You see, my sister, Jean, died of cancer, my dear, dear husband shot himself in our bedroom, my father died of cancer, I lost my job after several years and then in July of last year I was rear-ended in an auto accident. I still cannot work full time, but I have gone back to school.

In the middle of the night I wake up with such desolation, fear, and the purely personal feeling of WHY? In the midst of all this I think I have truly found God again. I also know in my heart He has wonderful things planned for me. I just must find the faith to wait until He is ready to show me the path that I must follow.

From Nevada:

A year ago I lost my 21-year-old son by suicide. It has been a truly lost year for me and my family. A friend recently sent me a copy of your book, *Stick a Geranium in Your Hat and Be Happy*. The book helped me in many ways. I wanted you to know. I think it will also help some of the members of my support group.

From Missouri:

While I have not experienced any of your devastating losses and heartaches, I've had my own—my divorce after 19 years of what I thought was a good marriage; my oldest daughter living with her boyfriend, marrying him, and now, after four and a half years, facing divorce; my other daughter becoming pregnant at 17, getting married, having a beautiful baby boy, getting divorced, and remarried all in less that a year's time. But the beauty of it all was that God was with me through each experience. He not only shared my burdens, but sent others to help share the burdens and pain, too.

PAIN IS INEVITABLE BUT <u>MISERY IS OPTIONAL</u>!!! Thanks again.

How to Find Joy in the Midst of It All

These excerpts from my mail are just the tip of an iceberg infinitely bigger than the one that sank the Titanic. I have enough letters like this to fill this book—and several more like it. Thousands of us want to know how to find some splashes of joy—and, eventually, how to climb out of the cesspool and back to happier places.

I've been there in the dark, dank, lonely cesspool, and somehow—with God's loving help—I have managed to climb out. Still, seldom a day goes by that I'm not reminded of that cesspool; sometimes, I find myself teetering on the edge, ready to slide back in again. I don't have any magic pills or formulas, but FINDING JOY IN THE MIDST OF MISERY always works for me, and I know it can work for you, too.

Rubbish Removal for the Mind

Over the years I have learned some strategies for finding splashes of joy when life turns into a cesspool. Actually, *strategies* is not quite the right word. I leave the technical stuff to my husband, Bill, the engineer in the family. I prefer to share my *ways to live*—simple things that work for me, and they are all tied to one of my favorite verses:

> Fix your thoughts on what is true and good and right.
>   Think about things that are pure and lovely,
> And dwell on the fine, good things in others.
>   Think about all you can praise God for
>   And be glad about it.
>   Philippians 4:8, TLB

I call Philippians 4:8 my "rubbish removal service." It's the verse I use to dump the garbage from my mind and get rid of useless, rotting, noxious junk so I can replace it with things that are nourishing, fresh, and healthy. A lot has been written on "positive thinking," but Paul scooped everybody two thousand years ago with Philippians 4:8, which he wrote in prison, chained to a Roman guard, waiting to be executed.

In a JOY-*LESS* place, in JOY-*LESS* circumstances, Paul was JOY-*FULL* because he knew that the difference between splashes of joy and the cesspool often depends on how you want to look at what is happening to you and around you.

Not long ago I began noticing how the household products I use suggest the importance of one's attitude. For example, I like to use FRESH START laundry soap because it reminds me that Christians can have a fresh start. First John 1:9 promises us that if we confess our sins we are cleansed from all unrighteousness. That means that the past is a canceled check, tomorrow is a promissory note, and today is CASH. "Thank You, Lord," I pray in the morning, "for a new day that isn't even messed up yet—a fresh start. Thank you for a whole day full of exciting things . . . new experiences . . . new challenges."

I also use JOY detergent on my dishes, and while I appreciate the "lemon-fresh smell," I like the idea of finding joy in new beginnings even better. Joy is the land of beginning again for every Christian. Joy is having God live in the marrow of your bones. Happiness depends on what is going on around us, but joy bubbles up from deep within because of what God does for us. Happiness is elusive and can be wiped out in a second, but abiding joy from the Lord is like a deep river down in your heart that just keeps flowing.

Thinking about those two products helped me so much I started collecting more and more names, like ZEST, CHEER, GLAD, and PRAISE, to name just a few of several dozens that I have found. Then, just for fun, a friend of mine put them together in a little imaginary story which I have started sharing at conferences and seminars. It goes like this:

AN OPERA FULL OF SOAP
(AND OTHER THINGS)

As a young Christian mother, I loved living my life in mental IVORY palaces. It was NEVER DULL as I sought to raise my children with INTENSIVE CARE because I always had my godly husband to CARESS at night.

My Christian life was full of ZEST. There was so much to PRAISE God for. My own walk with the Lord started when I saw the DAWN, confessed my sins, and they VANISHed. I stood FAULTLESS before the Lord. Another JOY was that my children had PLEDGEd their lives to Christ. A final PERK was that my husband seemed to have a BOLD witness for the Lord. I thought I'd live like this until I went to GLORY, but lo and BEHOLD the TIDE turned.

First, my husband, who had been MR. CLEAN to me, said he needed a change and WISKed himself off with another woman. This was no BREEZE to me. Then a week later my middle son DIALed me on the phone and told me he was gay. All I could do was SHOUT.

I DASHed to my church for help, but my SOS call did nothing for my hurt PRIDE, and I fell into a depression. I began to GAIN a lot of weight. I was in such a pit that I stopped going to church and completely lost my SPARKLE.

Then an old friend called me. She was as good as GOLD. I told her my life was no JUBILEE. She said it didn't matter, and that her life wasn't SPIC AND SPAN, either. She said that if we shared together and put on the SHIELD of faith, we could get a FRESH START. We did—we prayed and talked together and got the spiritual SOFTSCRUB on the inside until we felt KLEAN 'N' SHINEd. My eyes began to have a TWINKLE again.

I'm GLAD my life worked out as it did because I've learned to live in a CLING FREE sort of way. I don't expect my family to be PERFECT for my own happiness. Sometimes I fail and my mind gets EZily OFF the track, but then I pray and the Holy Spirit comes in and RENUZIT. I anticipate that blessed LIFT-OFF when Jesus comes to take me to GLORY. Until then, I'm going to SNUGGLE up to the Word, and serve God.

The best part of my little household-products tale concerns putting on the SHIELD of faith and getting a FRESH START by SNUGGLE-ing up to the Word and serving God. I heard somewhere that the average woman spends fourteen years of her life doing household chores. Her husband may retire, but the typical woman keeps right on working—scrubbing, polishing, and using many of the products mentioned above. I started thinking about how we spend all that time cleaning and wondered if there wouldn't be some way to make the time more productive. What can we do with those fourteen years we're spending with our hands in the sink, our heads in the toilet, and our minds who knows where? Surely there has to be a way to get our minds off grime, rust, and stains and center it on what is good, pure, and lovely.

Scripture Memorization Made Easy

One of the best approaches to making household chores more inspiring comes from my daughter-in-love, Shannon, who is married to my son, Barney. She types out Bible verses that apply to the name of the product she is using (for example, verses on JOY) and then tapes them right on the back of the bottle. When she uses GLORY floor wax, she types out verses on glory and tapes them on the back of the container. She does this with all kinds of products, then she memorizes the verses as she does her household chores. When these verses are committed to memory, she peels them off the various containers and replaces them with more verses that apply to that same product.

It is amazing how many Scriptures come to mind when you think about words like PRAISE, SHOUT, BEHOLD, etc. Sometimes the verses seem to jump right out at you, and before you realize it you are bringing your thoughts into captivity, as it says in 2 Corinthians 10:5.

How much we need the balance and control that a reservoir of Scripture can bring into our lives! I used to sing a little chorus in Sunday school: "Thy word have I hid in my heart that I might not sin against Thee . . . that I might not sin . . . that I might not sin . . . that I might not sin against Thee." I

learned that little song when I was about six years old, and
those words (from Ps. 119:11) are still clearly imprinted in my
memory.

When I was growing up, a little cardboard plaque hung in
our dining room. It had blue and gold letters that said, "Let
the words of my mouth, and the meditation of my heart, be
acceptable in thy sight, O LORD, my strength, and my redeemer"
(Ps. 19:14, KJV). That plaque is a frozen frame in my video of
memories, and I can still see the words, which are part of my
reservoir of Scripture.

We know that Scripture SHOULD be put to memory, but
getting time to do it is something else. Putting verses on the
backs of household products is a simple, easy way to make your
chores less boring, and at the same time you are filling your mind
with edifying thoughts from God, Himself. It works for Shannon and it works for me. I now make it a habit to be on the
lookout for verses that are brought to mind by products I use.

For example, while walking through a local department store
this week, I passed the cosmetic counter and saw a jar of face
cream called ETERNAL and immediately John 3:16 came to
mind. Right next to that were perfumes called PROMISE and
REMEMBRANCE. Automatically, I began thinking of verses
that would go with these fragrances. Second Peter 1:4 talks
about God's "great and precious promises" (NIV) through which
we can escape the world's corruption. There are many promises in Scripture, and you can pick the ones you like the best.
One of my favorites is Romans 8:28, and I also like Psalm 34:19
(NIV): "A righteous man may have many troubles, but the LORD
delivers him from them all."

As for REMEMBRANCE, it suggests many wonderful passages, particularly Christ's words at the first communion, "This
is my body, given for you; do this in remembrance of Me" (Luke
22:19, NIV). And in John 14:26, Jesus talked about the Holy Spirit,
how He would teach His disciples all things and "bring to your
remembrance all things that I said to you" (NKJV).

After seeing a product called PROMISE at a cosmetic counter,
I was reminded that PROMISE is also the name of a marga-

rine. So, whether you're in a department store or in a super-market, all kinds of name brands can jump out to remind you to fix your thoughts on what is true, good, right, and lovely. What better way to do that than to commit the Word of God to memory as you clean, scrub, and shop?

Every Morning You Have a Choice

How we use the time God gives us is our choice every day. We can live as though Christ died yesterday, rose today, and is coming tomorrow, or we can live as though Christ died, pe-riod. We can count blessings, or we can count calamities. We can count blessings, or we can count life's blows and burdens. It's our choice.

All the FANTASTIC household products that make life so much easier today remind me of some instructions an Appala-chian grandmother gave a new bride years ago concerning how to wash clothes. You might want to copy it and stick it up over your automatic washer and dryer. Then, every time you're tempted to have a pity party because life isn't so perfect, you can read it and remember that life is *always a choice*.

WASHDAY, 1916

1. Bild fire in backyard to heet kettle of rain water.
2. Set tubs so smoke won't blow in eyes if wind is pert.
3. Shave one hold cake lie soap in bilin water.
4. Sort things, make three piles, 1 pile white, 1 pile colored, 1 pile work britches and rags.
5. Stir flour in cold water to smooth, then thin down with bilin water.
6. Rub dirty spots on board, scrub hard, then bile. Rub col-ored, don't bile, just rinch in starch.
7. Take white things out of kettle with broomstick handle, then rinch and starch.
8. Hang old rags on fince.
9. Spread tee towels on grass.
10. Pore rinch water in flower bed.

11. Scrub porch with hot soapy water.
12. Turn tubs upside down.
13. Go put on fresh dress, smooth hair with side combs, brew cup of tea, sit and rest and rock a spell, and count blessings.

I like her advice. What I get out of her words is that you have to make some choices before the blessings are there to count. The following poem is from a Wichita, Kansas, church newsletter. I have no idea who wrote it, but whoever did understood the power of attitude.

WE CHOOSE . . .

We choose how we shall live;
courageously or in cowardice,
honorably or dishonorably,
with purpose or in drift.
We decide what is important
and what is trivial in life.
We decide that what makes us significant
is either what we do or refuse to do . . .
WE DECIDE.
WE CHOOSE.
And as we decide and as we choose,
so our lives are formed . . .

"But, Barb," people ask me, "how can I make the choice to be positive when life is so negative?" Remember Philippians 4:8. You will be joyful if you want to think that way. Or you will be sad and depressed if you so choose. As someone said:

AN OPTIMIST LOOKS AT AN OYSTER
AND EXPECTS TO FIND A PEARL.
A PESSIMIST LOOKS AT AN OYSTER
AND EXPECTS PTOMAINE POISONING.

Pessimism seems to be in fashion lately. With all the bad news that you can tune in any time between 4:00 and 11:00 P.M., people may think you've gone "Looney Tunes" if you're optimistic. The truth, however, according to some psychologists, is that optimism is a much more effective way to live. One of the best uses of optimism is for fighting depression, that overwhelming feeling of helplessness or hopelessness that you get when you experience a loss, a failure, or a heavy disappointment. I love the bumper "snicker" that says:

A PESSIMIST IS SOMEONE WHO FEELS BAD
WHEN SHE FEELS GOOD
FOR FEAR SHE WILL FEEL WORSE
WHEN SHE FEELS BETTER.

On the other hand, optimism helps turn life around. The experts say that optimistic people achieve more in life, enjoy better health, age more comfortably, and live longer than pessimists. I like that, especially the part about "aging more comfortably."[1]

Set Your Automatic Pilot on "Optimistic"

It's good to hear that a pessimist can learn to be an optimist (I've been trying to tell Bill that for years). The best way to start learning to be an optimist is to change the way you think, especially how you explain to yourself the reasons why things happen and why life unfolds the way it does.

Pessimists tend to think negatively without realizing it. It's almost as if they are on some kind of negative automatic pilot. One example I love to use is the difference in how Bill and I look at things—even the weather. On one of the rare, smog-free, glorious days we have in Southern California, I looked up at the azure blue sky and the fleecy white clouds and said, "Wow, it looks as if God vacuumed the sky."

Bill looked up at the same sky and said, "Yeah, but He'll probably dump the vacuum bag tomorrow."

To put all that another way, an optimist would invent the airplane. If Bill had his choice, he would invent the parachute.

You see, the pessimist thinks he's taking a chance while the optimist feels he is grasping a great opportunity. If you are the type who might be looking for rain when there isn't a cloud in the sky, try to *become alert to your automatic thoughts.* Start being aware of the negative things you say about yourself, others, and life. When you realize you're talking negatively, just tell yourself to STOP. Set your mind's automatic pilot on "optimistic," and repeat Philippians 4:8 as a prayer—something like this:

> Lord, whenever I hear or read rumors, gossip, or just plain lies, help me fix my thoughts on what is true, good, and right. Help me tune out what is negative and suggestive and tune in what is pure and lovely.
>
> When I get irritated with others and start finding fault, help me dwell on the fine things in them. Help me forget about their faults and remember their strengths.
>
> And when I start feeling sorry for myself, help me remember all the reasons why I should praise You. Remind me of all the blessings You bring into my life to make me happy.

Smile—It Increases Your Face Value

Smiles are everywhere if you just take the trouble to look. There can even be a smile in how a book title gets garbled in a person's mind. I've had a lot of good examples of that with my last book (I call it *Geranium* for short). For instance, a woman from California who heard me on the radio got the title wrong *twice* in the same letter:

> I enjoyed the program you graced with your gift of gab. I don't read books but I might enjoy "Feather in My Hat" or whatever. I need a laugh in life and I know a few other people can say the same. . . .
>
> Hope you don't mind my long note just to order your book. I called the station and was advised "Flower in My Hat" would be an uplift.

As far as I'm concerned, it doesn't matter—feathers, flowers, or geraniums—just so I can give folks like this an uplift. One of my favorite optimistic poems is this:

> Life is easier than you think.
> All you have to do is:
> Accept the impossible,
> Do without the indispensable,
> Bear the intolerable,
> and
> Be able to smile at anything.
> Source unknown

To be able to "smile at anything"—that's the key. Not only does smiling kill time between disasters, but it also helps your attitude, and we all have to work hard to avoid hardening of the attitudes!

Dr. Charles Swindoll, pastor of the Evangelical Free Church of Fullerton, California, is one of the most optimistic, "up" people I have ever met. He always has a smile and loves to laugh. He is a living, breathing example of the power of attitude. He writes:

> The longer I live, the more I realize the impact of attitude on life. Attitude, to me, is more important than facts. It is more important than the past, than education, than money, than circumstances, than failures, than successes, than what other people think or say or do. It is more important than appearance, giftedness, or skill. It will make or break a company . . . a church . . . a home. The remarkable thing is we have a choice every day regarding the attitude we will embrace for that day. We cannot change our past . . . we cannot change the fact that people will act in a certain way. We cannot change the inevitable. The only thing we can do is play on the one string we have, and that is our attitude. . . .[2]

Play on your one string as optimistically as you can. Make the best of it, even when you get the worst of it—and never forget that every day holds the possibility of miracles. As an unknown poet said:

FRESH NEW DAY

If you awake and see the sunrise
Bathing earth in red and gold,
As you gaze you'll somehow find
It brings a washing of the soul.
It fills one with anticipation
To start the day with such a sight.
God is so very good to give
A fresh new day, giftwrapped so bright!

Source unknown

Splish/Splash . . .

OPTIMISM IS HAVING THREE TEEN-AGE SONS AND ONLY ONE CAR.

*　*　*　*　*　*

VALUES

So often folks have wondered why
God has placed on earth
The storms, the tears, the raging seas—
Destroyers of all worth.
But if it weren't for angry skies,
The torrents, and dismay,
How could we realize the worth
Of a sunny, cloudless day?

Source unknown

*　*　*　*　*　*

A PESSIMIST HAS NO STARTER, AN OPTIMIST HAS NO BRAKES.

*　*　*　*　*　*

IN THE LONG RUN, PESSIMISTS MAY BE PROVEN RIGHT,
BUT THE OPTIMIST HAS A BETTER TIME ON THE TRIP.

*　*　*　*　*　*

Cheery-O!

If you smile the day will be cheery,
   If you smile the day will be bright.
If you think good thoughts you'll be happy,
   And everything will work out just right.
So don't let a frown turn you sour,
   Don't let bad thoughts make you blue.
Just always remember, think positively,
   For how you feel is up to you!
                    Susan L. Wiener

*　*　*　*　*　*

LOOKING ON THE BRIGHT SIDE OF LIFE
WILL NEVER CAUSE EYESTRAIN.

*　*　*　*　*　*

Most of us miss out on life's big prizes.
   The Pulitzer.
   The Heisman.
   Oscars.
But we're all eligible for life's small pleasures.
   A pat on the back.
   A kiss behind the ear.
   A four-pound bass.
   A full moon.
   An empty parking space.
   A crackling fire.
   A great meal.
   A glorious sunset.
Enjoy life's tiny delights.
There are plenty for all of us.
                    Source unknown

*　*　*　*　*　*

FAITH IS PUTTING ALL YOUR EGGS IN GOD'S BASKET
AND COUNTING YOUR BLESSINGS
BEFORE THEY'VE HATCHED.

*   *   *   *   *   *

A SMILE IS A WRINKLE
THAT SHOULDN'T BE REMOVED.

*   *   *   *   *   *

A SMILE IS THE LIGHTING SYSTEM OF THE FACE
AND THE HEATING SYSTEM OF THE HEART.

*   *   *   *   *   *

A SMILE IS A LIGHT IN THE WINDOW OF YOUR FACE
THAT SHOWS THAT YOUR HEART IS AT HOME.

*   *   *   *   *   *

When you talk, do not say harmful things. But say what people need—words that will help others become stronger. (Eph. 4:29, NCV)

How to Lay Down Your Agonies and Pick Up Your Credentials

You have to face the music
before you can lead the band.

Smiling between disasters is a good start in finding splashes of joy, but surviving in the cesspool—and eventually climbing out—takes the ability to deal with pain and grief. Nothing comes into our lives by accident; and no matter how bad it makes you feel, it didn't come to stay—it came to pass!

The hard part is dealing with being alive while waiting for whatever it is to pass. When pain and grief capsize your life, it sometimes seems that all you can do is sink. Sometimes the pain comes through the finality of death. The following are just a few excerpts of the many letters I receive from people whose lives have been shattered by loss:

> One month and one week ago today our oldest child, Jeff, age eleven, collapsed in sudden death due to myocarditis (a nonsymptomatic disease of the heart muscle caused by a virus). We are having tremendous support from our church here and from neighbors and co-workers, but my world is shattered. My heart is torn in half. One half is grateful that he knew the

221

Lord . . . he is safe and happy in heaven with Jesus. But the human half of my heart longs for Jeff. . . . I walked the four miles to the cemetery and back this morning. I sat by Jeff's grave and cried and prayed and remembered.

*　*　*　*　*　*

Last summer while purchasing a book, I saw *So Stick a Geranium in Your Hat and Be Happy*. I was still in shock after my daughter's murder, a period of my life that is still a total blur. I thought, "Why not?" and bought it. That night I read it and laughed for one of the few times since Melanie's kidnapping and torture-killing by a couple of idiots who thought themselves to be high priests in a cult.

Your pain was not the exact replica of our pain, but pain for mothers is universal when it comes to the death of a child.

Another mother wrote to tell of having one daughter who developed cystic fibrosis and became so ill she was confined to a wheelchair. While this mother and her husband did all they could to make life happy for their daughter, she died at age fifteen. They tried for another child, and a year later a second daughter was born. Then, two years later, a surprise package came—a third little girl. Then the roller coaster took another plunge. "We were doing okay in life until March," the mother wrote. "Then SIDS [Sudden Infant Death Syndrome] hit our family and we lost our new daughter in her sleep. Life seems too hard."

When letters like these arrive—and they keep coming all the time—it helps me understand why I went through my own cesspools of pain. Those terrible times helped me earn the credentials that now enable me to help others deal with their pain as I continue to deal with my own troubles and the bittersweet memories that are like embedded shrapnel deep in my heart.

You see, memories are always there, a permanent part of our lives, and unless we can deal with them, they will continue to cause pain and grief that will cripple us. That's why it's important to make all the good memories we can *while* we can. Then when the bitter things happen, there will be enough sweet memories to absorb the shock and put a coating of love around the shrapnel, blunting its sharp edges.

When I look at my own tragedies, I realize they all involve the men in my life—the men I love the most. I have told thousands of people, in person and in print, about four of these tragedies: the devastating accident that almost left my husband blind and comatose, like a vegetable; the violent deaths of two of my four sons; and finally, the discovery that another son is gay.

All of this happened in a period of nine years, ripping apart the happy family that Bill and I had established together. I believe, however, that I started learning about how to deal with pain and bittersweet memories earlier in life. When I was twelve, my father was taken from us one night, quickly and silently, the way a heart attack often strikes.

"I'll Bring You Some Black Jack Gum"

My dad was the Associate Pastor of the Calvary Undenominational Church in Grand Rapids, Michigan, serving with the Senior Pastor, Dr. M. R. DeHaan. I'll never forget the night Daddy left for a board meeting at the church. It was still early in the evening and my mother, sister, and I were listening to the old Horace Heidt radio program, "A Pot of Gold," featuring calls to homes across America picked in random fashion from the phone book. As we sat there listening, we were waiting for the phone to ring, thinking it might be our call for the $1,000 Pot of Gold.

A call did come before the program was over, but the caller wasn't Horace Heidt. It was my dad, who told my mother he wasn't feeling too well, but he had taken some Tums and was still planning to attend the meeting. Then he got me on the phone and asked, "What can I bring you when I come home tonight?"

"I'd like some Black Jack gum," I said instantly.

My father laughed because he knew how much I loved Black Jack gum. I not only loved the licorice taste, but I had fun getting it smeared over my teeth and making it look as if some of my teeth were missing.

Once, while riding in the car with my parents, they came up behind a truck and wanted to pass, but the trucker wouldn't let us. He seemed to enjoy teasing me as I looked out the window at him. As usual, I was chewing a big wad of Black Jack gum and I decided to coat my teeth with it and give him a big "smile." I guess it startled him so much he decided to let my father go on by; as we went on down the road I could see him laughing at my black, "toothless" grin.

My father hung up, chuckling after promising he would bring me some Black Jack gum. Then he went back to his meeting and we went back to listening to "Pot of Gold."

When the program ended (and once again we hadn't received the lucky call) my sister and I went off to bed and later my mother did, as well. About midnight there was a knock at our door. It was Dr. DeHaan and a deacon from church. "I'm sorry," he said. "Your husband had one crushing chest pain and then it was over! There was nothing we could do for him."

I can still remember Dr. DeHaan's voice from down in the hallway telling my mother that Daddy was dead. The rest of the night is a blur in my memory now, except for two other sounds: my mother making the phone calls to relatives, and the mourning doves chirping in the trees about 3:00 or 4:00 A.M. They made such an ominous, lonely sound . . .

The Memories Kept Flooding Back

Sleep wouldn't come that night. I thought of my dad and how much he loved me. One thing that came to my mind was that whenever I got an earache, my dad would go out and buy a cigar, even though he never smoked. One of the old-fashioned remedies for earache was to blow cigar smoke into the ear to relieve the pain. My dad would practically make himself sick smoking that cigar and blowing smoke in my ear. And even now, when I see a man with a cigar, I remember Dad puffing on one while he held me and gently blew smoke in my ear.

I have all kinds of memories of my dad. Some of our best fun happened in the car. Often I'd ride with him and he'd drill me on Bible verses. He taught a Scripture memorization class on Saturday mornings at church, and he decided it would be good for me to learn all the verses perfectly as well, including the "addresses." And so wherever I went with him in the car he'd rehearse me on quoting the verse and then giving the reference.

Whenever we drove out to see my grandmother, who lived some twenty miles away in the country, we'd take a road that had big dips. And I mean really BIG DIPS. My dad knew how I loved to go over those dips in the car. While my mother didn't care for the game at all, he'd tell me to sit down on the floor by the backseat, which accentuated the feeling of going over the dips. We'd zoom over the road and I'd laugh and he'd laugh with me. Coming back from Grandma's we'd do it again, until we were both laughing so hard we were almost hysterical.

Recently, when I was back in Michigan, I had occasion to go over that same road, but today it's a nice smooth freeway with no dips at all. In my mind, however, the dips will always be there, and I'll always remember how my dad would take all the time in the world to go over those dips, back and forth, just so we could laugh and make memories that would last a lifetime.

Those memories flashed through my mind that night my dad died, and I lay in the darkness, crying and wondering what would happen to us. The next morning, after they had taken my father's body to the mortuary, someone came by to drop off the clothes he had been wearing when he died. In his pocket were several packs of Black Jack gum he had bought—just for me.

They Put Daddy in the Sun Room

When my dad died in 1940, it was the custom to bring the body back to the home after it had been prepared by the mortuary and placed in the casket. Then friends would come to visit, bring food, sit around and talk, and show their care and concern before the actual funeral.

We had what we called a "sun room" at our house, and I remember that it was there we put Daddy. I remember hearing Mother say, "Daddy always liked that room," and I thought, *as if it matters now.*

Up until that time I had never seen a dead person—I was only twelve. I didn't want to touch him or kiss him. All I could do was look at his cold, still body. It was my first encounter with the stark reality of death.

My mother said I had to get a new dress for the funeral, and I still remember the navy blue, print dress she picked out for me. Because I had sung with my dad a lot in church, Mom asked me to pick out the songs to be sung at his funeral. I chose "Under His Wings" and "Constantly Abiding," staid old hymns he had liked. I don't hear those hymns much today, but occasionally I'll be in a church that uses older hymnals and they will be sung. Then my mind will flash back fifty years as the words of those old songs bring back the memories.

Even as I write about my father's death, the memories are still there, pieces of shrapnel embedded in my heart. They are not "haunting memories"; instead, they're bittersweet because the pain has been dulled and flattened out with time. What makes it possible to bear the painful part of the memories are the sweet memories that have surrounded the shrapnel with love. That's why I call them "bittersweet."

No More Tragedy Until . . .

While my father's death was a tremendous blow to our family and my mother had to struggle over the next several years, I grew up and went through high school and college with no more tragedy. I got out of college and married Bill after meeting him on a blind date. If it's true that opposites attract, then Bill and I were destined to get married because we were, and still are, TOTAL opposites.

Bill had an excellent job in mechanical engineering, and God also blessed us with four sons, a comfortable home, a growing church, a swimming pool, two cats, and a dog. The years were sprinkled with normal stresses until 1966, when things started happening that turned our lives into a nightmare.*

On the night we left for our church retreat where we were to be counselors for the young people, Bill had gone on ahead of me, taking the food and other supplies. About twenty minutes later, I followed in our other car with all the children.

As I drove up the dark, curving, mountain road, I came upon a heap of a man lying on the roadway, covered with blood and glass. The only way I could tell it was Bill was by his clothing. The road had not been used all winter, and evidently he had hit some debris left behind by a construction crew.

Quickly, I jumped out of the car and, after making sure Bill was alive, I knew I had to get help fast. I left one of the older boys with him there on the road and drove ten miles to get to a telephone to call an ambulance. When it came, I rode with Bill to the hospital, leaving the children with friends from the church. Then I waited all night to get some word about his prognosis.

About 6:00 A.M. I went home alone and walked into an empty house. There was no Bill, no kids. I had no idea what I would do if he didn't make it. What if he did live but his brain was so damaged it couldn't work? Our lives had been clicking along very smoothly and now, suddenly, our family had gone from click to CLUNK. Nothing fit. Nothing worked. Nothing clicked any more.

Two days later the neurosurgeon and ophthalmologist gave me their verdict. Bill was blind and was having continual seizures from severe brain damage. They said his condition was "unrehabilitatable," a word I was to hear many times over the next few months. Because Bill was a veteran, the doctors advised me to have him admitted to Sawtelle Veterans Hospital because he would never fit into a family unit again. Bill, they

---

*The tragedies discussed in this chapter are described in further detail in two other books, *Where Does A Mother Go to Resign?* (Minneapolis: Bethany House Publishers, 1979), and *So, Stick a Geranium in Your Hat and Be Happy* (Dallas: Word Publishing, 1990).

said, would be a vegetable because of his irreversible brain damage, and he had five years to live, at most.

It turned out that it would be several months before a bed opened up at Sawtelle; so, after several weeks in intensive care, we brought Bill home to try and manage there. He was blind and he didn't know us; his memory was gone. I was able to locate someone to stay with Bill while I went out to apply for Social Security, his veteran's pension, disability, and Aid to the Blind. I even got Bill a white cane and a whole stack of records to listen to.

It was a slow process. Many people were praying, but there were plenty of nights when I wondered what would happen to all of us. How could I raise four sons and take care of Bill, too? He had always been in control—had always been such a perfectionistic person about handling the details of life. Now my strong, strapping husband had been reduced to a helpless invalid.

Then, after I managed to get Bill on all the various programs and enough money coming in to pay expenses, God healed him! He regained his sight, and his mind started to function. He finally recognized who we were, and some psychological therapy restored a great deal of his memory.

Where There's Smoke, There Should Be Smell

Even though Bill was slowly getting better, it was necessary to have someone there all the time for absolute safety. I learned this one day when I popped out to the supermarket for a few minutes to grab some groceries, thinking it would be safe enough to leave Bill alone that long.

What I didn't realize was that the accident had destroyed Bill's sense of smell. When I drove back up to the house, the roof was in flames! Dashing in, I found Bill there in the back bedroom, lying peacefully in his back brace, seemingly content with life.

"I've got to call the fire department," I shouted. "The house is on fire!"

"What?" Bill said. "I don't smell any smoke . . ."

The fire department came in just a few minutes and managed to extinguish the roof before the house went up in flames. They determined that somehow a bird had picked up a lighted cigarette somewhere and deposited it under one of our wood shingles. By the time I had gotten back from the market, the roof was ablaze.

As I looked at Bill lying there in his back brace, without sight or smell, I thought back to when he had been whole and our lives had been whole, as well. Because he had been a pilot during World War II, he enjoyed watching old war movies. He loved to see the planes and hear the roar of the engines.

Popcorn was Bill's favorite. One day while we were at Knott's Berry Farm he stopped in one of the shops and bought a giant earthenware bowl that looked big enough to be a bathtub for one of the kids. Bill loved to make popcorn on Friday nights and fill that bowl to the brim; then we'd all sit there eating it together, watching television.

Sweet memories like those helped me get through the first bitter years following Bill's injuries. I honestly can't remember doing a lot of grieving during those months following Bill's accident. I experienced a lot of anguish, frustration, and pressure, but I was really too busy to grieve. I kept praying that, somehow, Bill would recover, even though specialists had said he was unrehabilitatable.

You can imagine our sheer joy as we watched God do miracles before our eyes. Bill's vision returned, and he was even able to go back to work as an engineer. Our family's ship had been practically capsized by a hurricane, but God had righted things and we were getting back in balance. Of course, Bill was still a bit strange, but I didn't mind. He is an only child and they are all a little bit different anyway!

The Pain Had Just Begun

Actually, the pain I had experienced up until then was only a taste of what lay ahead. In the next five years I would lose two of my sons, one to enemy fire in Vietnam and another to a drunk driver whose three-ton truck would swerve across the center line on the Alaska Highway in the Yukon Territory. Each boy's death was different, yet each was the same.

During his senior year of high school, seventeen-year-old Steve became bored and restless. He was a Christian, but he started running with friends that we knew were into drugs and drinking. In the fall of 1967, he continued to pressure Bill and me to sign papers allowing him to join the marines because several of his friends had already gone in.

Neither Bill nor I was sold on the idea, but we were encouraged by news reports that seemed to be saying the Vietnam conflict was decelerating. Realizing that he could join on his own on his eighteenth birthday in December, I went down in October and signed the papers that made it possible for Steve to become a U.S. Marine.

Steve went off to boot camp, filled with fantasies of excitement and adventure, but within a few weeks he changed his mind. His letters began telling us the marines weren't as great as he had thought and he had doubts about being a marine after all.

A few weeks after Christmas that year, the Vietnam War burst into new levels of conflict. One bittersweet memory, forever a "freeze frame" in my mind, is Steven, with duffel bag over his shoulder, turning to wave to me before disappearing beyond the chain-link gates of Camp Pendleton as he left for Vietnam.

It was St. Patrick's Day, March 17, 1968, and it was the last time I was to see him alive. Five months later I would have to go identify his swollen, bloated body, which had turned a sickly brown from lying face down for two days in a rice paddy before being found. Leaving the mortuary, I knew this was no dream; this was REALITY. My grief was overwhelming, but over the following weeks and months I was able to accept what had happened by recalling bittersweet memories of Steve and how much fun we had enjoyed together. Those memories helped me get through the first stage of my loss.

The Hearse Came Complete with Shovel and Spade

Steve and I used to find many things we could laugh about. Maybe it was because we both had the same warped sense of humor. One time he and I were driving home from church, and we went by a car lot where a big, black Cadillac hearse was for sale for $350.

"Wow!" Steve exclaimed. "Look at that hearse—wouldn't it be great to have something like that?"

Steve hadn't had his driver's license too long, and I'm sure he never dreamed that I would consider buying the hearse. We stopped and talked to the salesman and learned that the car had been brought to California from Minnesota. The interior was a beautiful purple velvet. There was even a compartment near the back, and inside it was a shovel *and* a spade!

It was obvious Steve really wanted that hearse. Bill had already driven home from church with our other boys, and I decided to make a snap decision. I wrote out a check for $350 and bought the hearse. Steve could hardly contain himself as he drove it home.

When we got there, Bill could hardly contain himself, either—but not out of great glee. It took some fast talking to get him to let Steve keep the hearse. We really couldn't afford it at the time because Bill was still in recovery from his accident; but "anything for fun"—and the hearse was a lot of fun, indeed.

Steve's friends were enthralled with the hearse. They wanted to sit in it, drive it, and try out the shovel and spade. It only got six miles to the gallon, but being a good businessman, Steve managed to make a few dollars by renting it to some of his buddies for Halloween. They decorated it and had a great time driving it up and down, "haunting" the boulevard. I still have photos of Halloween night, as well as pictures of Steve and his friends heading for the beach in his hearse, with surfboards hanging out the back!

Bittersweet memories like that helped me get through our loss of Steve, as did sharing with other families who had lost sons in Vietnam. Using a list of names printed in the daily paper, we contacted families who had lost their sons in the war and started sharing our hope and faith with them.

Eventually, I began to tell myself that surely we had had our cup of suffering. Bill had recovered from what doctors called hopeless injuries. While his memory wasn't too good (he would still watch old John Wayne movies over and over, not realizing he had seen them before), he was functioning at work and was pretty well back to normal. Steve had been killed in Vietnam and was our deposit in heaven. Now we could go on with our lives. But as one saying puts it,

> LIFE IS WHAT HAPPENS
> AFTER YOU MAKE OTHER PLANS.

What would happen next was so unbelievable it was unthinkable. Violent death would take our Tim at a time when he was experiencing an excitement about spiritual things that he had never known before and when all of a productive life seemed ahead of him.

Tim's Sense of Humor Was "Different"

Ironically, many memories of Tim also include a hearse—not the one we bought for Steve, but a pink one he drove for his employer, a mortuary. Our first-born son was a serious, conscientious kid who wasn't into fun quite as much as the rest of us. His idea of something hilarious was to bring home bows from the funeral bouquets and decorate one of our dogs or our cat with "REST IN PEACE," or "GOD BLESS GRANDPA HIRAM."

When I spoke in the Northwest recently and told about Tim bringing home the BOWS from the mortuary to decorate the dog and cat, a darling little old lady came up afterward and said, "Mrs. Johnson, I feel so bad to think your son brought home the BONES from the mortuary." I tried to reassure her that Tim had never brought home any bones—only BOWS.

Tim would sometimes stop at home while on duty and have lunch, leaving the hearse (with one of its latest occupants) parked in the driveway. One day he took his little brother, Barney, to the mortuary. Making sure no one was around, Tim let Barney climb into an empty casket in one of the viewing rooms—just to see what it felt like. Then (just for fun) he shut the lid!

Barney let out a yelp and Tim opened the lid in a few seconds—after he had a good laugh, of course.

The next day Barney went to school and during sharing time he told his class what had happened. Barney's teacher listened to his incredible tale and later phoned me to say, "Mrs. Johnson, I don't like to tell you this, but I'm afraid Barney is starting to tell lies. He's coming up with stories that just *can't* be true!"

When she told me what Barney had said, I reassured her that Barney wasn't lying and that my college-age son just had a "different" sense of humor. But I'm not sure I totally convinced her.

Although he lacked what I call a "fun personality," Tim had no trouble attracting the young ladies. Tall and handsome, he always had several girlfriends; they would often come over for a swim in our pool. Another "freeze frame" tucked away in my memory is a giant inner tube floating in our pool with no one in sight. Tim and his girlfriend would be inside the inner tube, but it was so huge I couldn't see them. So, every now and then, I would go out to the pool just to check on them.

Tim's Last Call—a Bittersweet Memory

My most bittersweet memory of Tim was the last conversation I had with him—on the day he was killed. He was calling from Whitehorse, Yukon Territory (collect, of course), to tell me he and his friend, Ron, were heading home after spending the summer working and making friends in a church they particularly liked. What struck me most was Tim's voice. Instead of the calm, unexcited tone he usually had, he was bubbling with enthusiasm because of what God had been doing in his life.

"Mom, I've got a sparkle in my eye and a spring in my step," he said. "I don't have time to tell you about it now, but God's going to use my story all over! I'll see you in five days!"

But it wasn't to be. A few hours later, as we sat at dinner talking about Tim's call, the phone rang and a Royal Canadian Mounted Police officer told me my son and his friend were dead. Their little Volkswagen had been crushed by a three-ton truck with a drunken driver at the wheel.

The wounds of grief that had only partially healed from Steve's death five years before were now ripped open again and deeper than ever. I thought I had accepted Steve's death. He was our one deposit in heaven. Why did God need TWO?

Ten days later, I made my second trip up to the mortuary to identify another dead boy in a box. This trip was as unreal as the first. The mortician had called and said, "Mrs. Johnson, this is the first time I have ever had to call THE SAME FAMILY twice, but you'll have to come up here and identify Tim's body because he was killed in a foreign country."

Because Bill still wasn't getting around much, I drove alone to the mortuary. Incredibly, it had been just five years to that VERY DAY that I'd gone to identify Steve's body— also killed in a foreign country. It had been a hot day in August five years before when I had driven up this same road. Now, on another hot August day, I was even driving the same car (we don't change cars that often) to go look at ANOTHER boy in a box. I simply could not accept it. How could this be happening AGAIN? It was like a dream—no, a nightmare!

The memorial service for Tim and his friend glorified God in many ways as several of Tim's friends and classmates came to Christ. Christian magazines, including *Christian Life,* picked up the story and ran headlines like "THEIR DEATH WAS ONLY A BEGINNING."

I was thankful for all the good that came out of our tragedy, but it really didn't dilute the pain. I thought I had learned something about dealing with grief with Steven's death, but Tim's death showed me that grief is a stern schoolmaster, and you always have to learn how to deal with it on your own. There is no course you can take, no book you can read, no video you can watch. You are your own video, moving slowly across the screen, feeling your way through your part in a tragic drama. At times like that, you wish your life were like a VCR and you could FAST FORWARD through the parts you don't want to live through.

We All Grieve Differently

As I worked through the death of two sons, I developed some guidelines for dealing with grief. I learned these guidelines by trial and error—mostly error because my eyes were blinded with tears.

While there are certain stages of grief that everyone goes through, no two of us pass through these stages at the same pace or in the same way. When a loved one dies, the first stage of grief includes SHOCK, particularly if the death was not anticipated.

In Steve's case, he was in the midst of a war and we were aware that he could be taken at any moment because he was in a red-hot danger zone. When the news about Steve came, it was not nearly the shock that we experienced when we got that phone call telling us Tim had been killed in a car crash on the very day we were so excitedly anticipating his homecoming.

When the call came about Tim, I remember screaming through the house, "This CANNOT be . . . I just talked to him a couple of hours ago . . . He was on his way HOME!"

I could not believe that Tim was actually gone, crushed to death by a drunken driver. It simply could not BE. It had to be a nightmare or my imagination.

Shock is God's way of cushioning those He loves against tragedy. Going into shock gives you time to absorb what has happened so you can try to adjust to the news.

When Shock Wears Off, Pain Begins

Grief is to the emotions what surgery is to the body. Once the anesthetic of shock wears off, the PAIN can be intense. How long that pain lasts is different in each person's case. There is no time limit. Also, the grieving person must understand:

GRIEF CANNOT BE DRY CLEANED AWAY;
IT MUST BE WASHED IN TEARS.

In Spatula Ministries we deal for the most part with grief-stricken mothers, but we also deal with a certain number of dads. I'm glad to see that our society is becoming more permissive about thinking it's okay for a man to cry. I have a friend who told me about her son—a mature, married man who was the father of three children of his own. The day he heard on the radio that President John F. Kennedy had been shot to death, this grown man fled to his mother's house, burst through the door, buried his head on her shoulder, and sobbed like a child.

For this man, coming home to his mother and weeping symbolized comfort, warmth, and security—all the things little children get from their mommies. This big, strong six-footer wanted to cry openly and relieve himself from the inner pain and shock. And where else could he go but HOME, where there was security, where tears were understood without any questions?

If you're grieving, perhaps you will get the most help from those who are comfortable with their own tears, as well as yours. Tears are the lowest common denominator of humanity. As Helmuth Pleaser has said, "More forcefully than any other expression or emotion, the crying of our fellow man grips and makes us partners of his moment, often without even knowing why."

God reads the heart, and He understands the language of tears. You can find many wonderful verses about tears and weeping in the Psalms. For example, David wrote, "Record my lament; list my tears on your scroll—are they not in your record?" (Ps. 56:8, NIV).

A possible translation for this verse says that the psalmist asks God to put his tears in God's bottle, or wineskin. It is as if he knows that his tears will be precious to God, that God will preserve them, honor them, and eventually heal them.

It's Okay to Grieve

Some Christians make the mistake of thinking that grief isn't a "good testimony." They are on the ceiling, climbing the wall, or prostrate before the Lord in their grief, but they feel guilty about it. I agree with the writer who said: "Grief is not a sign of weakness, but a tribute to the loved one and a healthy response to our heartache. Avoiding grief postpones recovery. Clinging to grief prolongs pain. Neither approach helps us heal."[1]

That's good advice, but unfortunately, some well-meaning Christian friends can subtly imply that "grieving is *not* okay." When Tim died, people dropped by and tried to say all the right things, such as, "How wonderful it is that Tim is now with the Lord." Someone else mentioned that it was "good that you still have two children left." While I appreciated the intentions of these remarks, they didn't comfort me at all—they only worsened my wounds that were already more raw and bleeding.

Yes, I knew it was wonderful that Tim was with the Lord, but I wanted Tim home with us—with me, his mother, who had borne him, raised him, and loved him. As for having two sons left, yes, that was good also; but I wanted Tim, too! Now he was our second deposit in heaven, and I was wondering how much God would demand of us. Was Larry or Barney NEXT? But I really couldn't tell my friends these things because they wouldn't understand.

Grief Will Make You Angry

Recently, a mother wrote to me about her only son, Jeff, who was killed in an accident over four years ago. She had heard I was writing another book and she said:

> If, in your new book, you could help those in grief over los-
> ing a child. We still need help. It's like one day you cope and
> the next day you can't. If you could please tell us how you and
> Bill have coped after losing two sons. Do you ever get angry at
> God? Do you want to punch out people? Do people bug you?
> It's hard to see other families with their loved ones. I get re-
> sentful. I want to believe and yet doubts come in. To love God
> is sometimes hard. People say busy hands will help, but, Barb,
> sometimes you have to put your hands down—and then you
> cry. I have a good husband and two lovely daughters. I want to
> help them, but I seem lost.

In addition to shock and pain, another natural reaction to the death of a loved one is ANGER, particularly if death strikes from out of the blue, without any warning, and for what seems to be no reason. When my shock turned into pain over Tim's death, anger immediately welled up within me. Because my "Ivory-soap" Christian friends didn't seem to understand me, I would get in the car late at night and drive to a dump a few miles from our house. There I could grieve in private, without having to dodge their "Bible bullets."

Today that dump has gates, and no parking is allowed there at night because the police fear that someone could be mugged, or worse. But in 1973, the dump was open, and I would park there and just sob my heart out. Sometimes I would scream to let God know how I felt. I told God how angry I was with folks who kept telling me that I should be glad Tim is with Him. And I also told God how angry I was because Tim had been taken. "WHY, Lord?" I would ask. "Tim was so precious, so special, and he had just renewed his faith in YOU! What glory could it bring to have him DIE?"

When I share my story of going to the dump to grieve, and even to rant and rave at God, many parents tell me that they feel somewhat relieved because I have admitted that I was so MAD at God for losing my sons. I tell them that it is okay to express these emotions and it is okay to be mad at God. When we scream in agony and rage at Him through our grief, He doesn't say, "Off to hell with you, Sister!" Instead, He patiently loves us . . . carries us . . . wraps His blanket of tenderness around us while we are balking, hissing, and rebelling in every way.

You see, God gave us our ability to have emotions. They are part of our lives, and they are normal. Anger, wrath, wanting to kill someone (even yourself), and flailing away at God for letting this happen to you—these are all normal emotional feelings that aren't necessarily a final commentary on your spiritual condition. The Bible says that we should be slow to become angry and that anger does not bring about the righteous life that God desires (see James 1:19, 20); but it seems to me that this passage is talking about the kind of anger that comes out of pride, bitterness, and carrying a grudge.

Anger that comes out of pain and grief is a normal response to deep hurt. This kind of hurt is the same whether or not you are a Christian. If your leg is amputated, it hurts—no matter what your spiritual values may be. It is vital to understand that having emotional pain is okay, but *you must not leave it there inside yourself.* You must find ways to ventilate your feelings, and then healing can begin because:

OPENNESS IS TO WHOLENESS
AS SECRETS ARE TO SICKNESS.

You are only as sick as your secrets. All of us experience a kaleidoscope of emotions and they are all useful when they are directed in healthy ways. That includes anger. We can learn to drain our anger by releasing it. Then we feel better and can start to pick up the broken fragments of our lives. It's better to vent your anger at God than at other family members or your friends. God can take it, but your human loved ones may not be able to accept what you are saying.

So, if you are angry, let it out. Go into your room, pound on your pillow, and DRAIN SOME OF THOSE EMOTIONS. You may even want to sob without trying to stifle the sounds (more on this in chapter 3). You will find that as you ventilate your anger, you will dilute it, and eventually it won't be there any more. By ventilating it, you get your feelings out; then you can begin a cleansing of your heart and the slow process of mending. As you replace angry feelings with tenderness and forgiveness, you will experience healing.

The most important thing is to DRAIN YOUR PAIN, release your anger much as a safety valve releases steam. I love the "tantrum mat" that appears on page 241. I've included it in my *Love Line* newsletter, along with the directions for how to throw a tantrum. Obviously, it's just for fun, but it still carries a very deep truth. You need to let out your pain. As for "persisting symptoms" and seeing a Christian counselor, that's a possibility. I had those symptoms, myself, and in the next chapter I'll share that experience with you.

Grief Comes to Pass; It Doesn't Stay

You will get better and pass into the RECOVERY stage. Widowed twice herself, Ida Fisher, co-author of *The Widow's Guide to Life*, says three T's are essential to recovering from the loss of a loved one:

TEARS, TALK, AND TIME[2]

As true inner-healing takes place, all that is left is an emotional scar as a reminder of what happened. The dawn of hope will break over the darkness of grief. You can talk about the loved one who's gone and begin to cherish the memories instead of having the memories tear out your insides. Instead of feeling like embedded shrapnel, the bittersweet memories will be marinated in love. And soon you will be able to reach out to others who are in pain.

TANTRUM MAT

Directions: —
When the need for throwing a tantrum
is felt, place both feet on the space
provided and jump rapidly up and
down. Incoherent screaming is
also permissible. If symptoms
persist, see your nearest
psychiatrist — You MAY be a nut.

After Steve's death, we started helping other parents who had lost sons in Vietnam. When Tim died, the ministry expanded beyond the parents of casualties from Vietnam; soon I was sharing with parents who had lost children in auto accidents or other tragedies. Grief had changed me, but it had not destroyed me. God had held me up and brought me through the dark tunnel. As the psalmist put it, He was indeed "my hiding place from every storm of life" (Ps. 32:7, TLB).

When dealing with parents who are grieving, I explain that the recovery stage begins when you wake up one morning without that overwhelming urge to go back to bed and pull up the covers. It does happen; the heavy mantle of grief that has been weighing you down is lifted. You will actually be able to hear music again. The birds will be singing, the sun will be shining, you will realize that God has brought you through. You have survived, and you can lay down your agonies and pick up your credentials.

Following Tim's death, I had opportunities to speak to many groups of parents. I told them that losing two sons had brought incredible pain but that the pain was easing and I could actually feel God's comforting blanket of love around me. I could finally accept having *two* deposits in heaven.

Having gone through shock, pain, anger, and recovery twice, I had begun to learn about dealing with the grief caused by losing loved ones. We are to hold loosely to all that we have, realizing it is all so temporary. Our possessions—even our children—are all loaned to us. God can pluck the flowers for His garden whenever He chooses. We are only the caretakers. Sometimes it gives a better perspective if we can accept that everything we have is only on loan anyway.

But I still had more to learn. Life has a way of dealing new, even harder, blows. That's the way it was for me. One very important lesson still lay ahead.

Splish/Splash . . .

> You are His gem—
> Tested, shining and sparkling.
> You have survived the winds of adversity . . .
> You are a WINNER!
> You are an OVERCOMER!
> YOU HAVE CREDENTIALS!
>
> Source unknown

* * * * * *

Trouble is not a sign of inadequacy, stupidity or inferiority, but rather an inescapable part of life—proof that you are a card-carrying member of the human race.

Ann Landers[3]

* * * * * *

I will . . . transform her Valley of Troubles into a Door of Hope. (Hos. 2:15, TLB)

We Must Understand That It Is Not Always Necessary to Understand

Can this really be my life,
or has there been some mistake?
Ashleigh Brilliant[1]

As hard as it was to lose two sons, eventually there was a closure in their deaths and that closure became my ally. But it took time to reach that point. For weeks, the "Why me's?" still rang in my mind—especially after Tim was killed. "Why me?" is a natural part of grief. Read this letter one man wrote to God after he learned his son was born blind:

> God, You seem very far from me right now. I really don't feel like praying to You at all. But then, again, maybe I'm afraid of what I'm going to say. All my life I've carefully chosen my words when I prayed. I wanted to impress You with my sincerity and goodness. But today I'm very angry, the angriest I've ever been with You. You know how much I have wanted a baby. I prayed that the baby would be born healthy. Well, God, he is blind. HE'S BLIND! How can I ever again believe that You are a loving God? What infuriates me more is that my neighbor, an

atheist, has four strapping kids. It isn't fair, God. I do blame
You for this loss.

We need to give our anger to God. Job, after losing his family in a violent storm, hurled his anger at God, but God
understood. The Bible tells us we should grieve, but not as those
who grieve without hope. Yes, we DO blame God for some of
our losses. We should not feel guilty telling Him we are angry,
but as our anger cools we can learn a valuable lesson about a
monstrous myth—that faith in God is an insurance policy with
the feature clause being God's protection from severe blows.
We forget we are living in a broken world with broken lives,
broken hearts, broken dreams. What a spiritual flaw it is to
think that becoming a Christian gives us immunity from this
pain.

Some things we will never understand. Some losses will
never make sense to us, but in time and in God's economy we
can see that Romans 8:28 is true and does work. All things DO
work together for good for those who love God.

We have biblical principles to live by and wise friends to
give us counsel, yet we cannot always find an answer to all
the pain. Some of us will die, never knowing the "Why?" of
our lives. We will have to be content realizing, "The secret
things belong to the LORD . . ." (Deut. 29:29, NIV).

Does God Ever Have to Say, "Oops"?

We may never know the answer to the puzzling questions
of life, but does it matter? Do we stop praying because our
prayers were not answered as we wanted? In our case, we
asked God to bring Tim safely home from his trip to Alaska,
trusting that God would give him the "journey mercies" that
we asked for. Within a few hours of our prayers, our son was
smashed to death. Did this encourage our desire to pray? No.
Did it make us think, *What is the use of it all anyway?* Of course
it did. Why bother to pray when it did no good? He was killed

even though we asked for his safety. Were we mad at God? Certainly. How unfair, how cruel, how crushing.

But lying deep beneath all of these feelings was our underlying faith that God makes no mistakes—that He never has to say, "Oops!" God didn't cause that drunken driver to cross the center line. Despite all of our questions and our bitter grief, however, we still knew, deep down, that nothing ever happens to us that God doesn't know about. God still loved us, and He was there for us in our grief, in our pain—and in our anger.

Tim was taken at a time when he was closer to God than he had been in his entire life. While we were grieving for Tim, a pastor visited us to tell us that the Scriptures say God plucks the flowers for His garden when they are most beautiful. At first I didn't want to hear it, but later that thought came to be a comfort to me.

And eventually the "Why me's?" stopped and the healing comfort of closure began. Yes, Tim was gone; yes, I missed him terribly. But slowly I worked through the grief of losing a second son and arrived at a kind of plateau where I could say, "Surely, two deposits in heaven is enough."

But there was still more to learn. In many ways, dealing with the deaths of two sons was my undergraduate course in grief. In the advanced course, I learned that there are not only different *stages* to grief; there are different *kinds* of grief. And I learned that even death does not necessarily bring the worst kind of pain.

I Earned a Ph.D. in Pain

My postgraduate course in grief began the day I accidentally came upon homosexual pornography in Larry's dresser drawer.* Ironically, I made this discovery the morning after

---

* For more complete accounts of my struggles with discovering my son's homosexuality, see *So, Stick a Geranium in Your Hat and Be Happy* (Dallas: Word Publishing, 1990), chapters 3 and 11, and *Where Does a Mother Go to Resign?* (Minneapolis: Bethany House Publishers, 1979).

we had attended our twenty-year-old son's junior-college graduation exercises and watched him receive numerous awards, including Outstanding Student. One of the leading clergymen in California was the commencement speaker and he told us after the ceremonies, "God has His hand on this boy, and will use him in a special way."

When I found the homosexual material, as well as explicit letters written to Larry and sent to a post office box, I couldn't believe that all this garbage belonged to my son. Perhaps it was all for some kind of research project at school—the trouble was, school was over!

I was in shock as I drove to the airport to meet a plane carrying my sister and her husband, who were coming in for a special weekend celebration with our family. We were to be together for the first time since Tim's death.

I threw all of the pictures and letters into the trunk of my car and headed for the airport, sobbing and shaking in disbelief. My chest felt like an elephant was standing on it. I was churning inside, and the sounds coming out of my mouth were strange, choking sobs I had never heard before. It felt like a bull was goring me or a knife was being twisted violently back and forth in my heart.

All the way to the airport—almost an hour's drive—I groaned and wanted to throw up. I felt as if a shag rug had been shoved down my throat. At the same time, my teeth started to itch. My drive to the airport was awful, but it helped me let out some of the pain I was feeling inwardly, and that enabled me to get through the next few hours. Later that evening, I heard from Larry's own lips that he was, indeed, homosexual—or "maybe bisexual" (whatever that was. Homosexuality was in the Bible, but "bisexual"? I thought maybe it was someone who had sex twice a month. Why would he say THAT?)

My shock turned to anger and rage, and the next day Larry and I had a literal knock-down, drag-out confrontation in our living room. I screamed every Bible verse and word of condemnation I knew. He shouted back with every rebellious obscenity he could think of (many of which I had never heard before).

The following day Larry left in a fit of anger and did not come back or even contact us for almost a year. Then my rage soon turned to grief—my old, familiar tormenter—and the "Why me?" questions came back louder than ever. Folks asked me which was harder, losing two sons to death, or losing a boy into the gay lifestyle! As devastating as it was to bury two sons, it was even worse knowing another son was out there somewhere in a life so displeasing to God.

With Steve and Tim there had been grief, but there had also been closure. Good-byes were said, services were held, testimonies to God's glory were given, and graves were sealed. The raw edges of grief could heal because "it was over."

But in Larry's case, it was different. I was to be introduced to what so many parents have endured—long-term, continual grief.

Larry wasn't dead (although it might have been less hurtful that way). With the deaths of Steve and Tim had come support, friends dropping by, not always saying the right thing but at least saying SOMETHING to try to give comfort.

But who could I tell about Larry? Guilt turned me into a recluse. I dropped out of sight and stayed in my bedroom most of the time, counting the roses on my wallpaper and dwelling on bittersweet memories of how it used to be while Larry, who was in many ways the "apple of our eye," was growing up.

Larry and I Always Loved to Laugh

Larry had been so musically talented, so caring, and always eager to have a laugh. When he was ten he was in a church Christmas program and was assigned to sing a solo, "While Shepherds Watched Their Flocks by Night." I helped Larry practice the song and sometimes he'd get silly and start using other words: "While shepherds washed their socks by night all seated on the ground, the angel of the Lord came down and said, 'Will you wash mine?'"

We were kidding around one day and Larry kept singing it the wrong way, just to get me laughing. Finally I said, "I'll give you five dollars if you get up in the program and sing it that way."

Larry laughed and said he wouldn't, of course, but on the night of the program he changed his mind—without telling us! He got out there in front of all the people and sure enough he started singing, "While shepherds washed their socks by night . . ."

He kept right on going with all the rest of the wrong words; but instead of being shocked the audience got tickled, and soon, everybody was laughing and clapping. Oh, yes, I did pay him the five dollars; the fun we had was worth it!

There were lots of other memories, too. We bought a player piano, and Larry loved to put on a honky-tonk tune and run his hands up and down the keyboard as if he were playing the song. I could recall talking to a repairman in our living room while Larry was at the piano. From where we stood, it looked to the repairman as though Larry were really playing up a storm. "Boy, that kid can really play!" said the repair man as he went on his way. As the door closed behind him, Larry and I dissolved in laughter.

As a teen-ager, Larry worked at In 'n' Out Burger, and he'd come home after the late-night shift with hamburgers for the two of us. We would sit together, watch Johnny Carson, eat hamburgers, and laugh. Larry had such a contagious, rippling laugh I'd have to tell him to be quiet or he'd wake up everyone.

And there was his little red Volkswagen with a wind-up key welded on the back. I'd chuckle every time I saw him drive off for school or work.

After Larry left and didn't contact us, I kept searching and hoping. Every time I saw a Volkswagen Bug, I'd look for the wind-up key, but I never spotted Larry's car.

Living in the Shadows of Hope and Fear

As my anger about Larry turned into depression, the pain became intense. Pain usually has a physical cause, but it can also come out of deep mental or emotional hurts. In many ways, physical pain is easier to bear. But when you suffer emotional pain, you live in the alternating shadows of hope and fear. You hope you can get through this quickly and then you fear it will never end. While we always wish for a quick solution to our pain, we have to face the reality that there is no quick solution. When the hurt is deep and great, there is seldom an instant cure.

Pain goes on because the problem goes on. It might be betrayal by a spouse or a life-long friend; it might be injury from a serious accident that leaves you crippled or handicapped in some way. It could be some chronic problem in the family, like drug abuse, mental illness, or having a retarded child. And it can be, as it was in my case, a rebellious child who has broken your heart.

My mail comes predominantly from parents with long-lasting or chronic grief. One couple wrote to tell me about how they learned their thirty-year-old, talented, Christian, college-graduate, "never-gave-us-a-bit-of-trouble" son was a homosexual and had been exposed to the HIV virus. The mother's letter said, in part:

> I do not know how to describe how we felt then or even now because it is never the same for long. PAIN, anger, PAIN, guilt, PAIN, despair, PAIN, shame, PAIN, denial, PAIN, confusion, PAIN, loss, PAIN, fear, PAIN, numbness, and then it would begin all over again. My husband and I cried, prayed, talked, and hung on to each other. Each one trying to comfort the other when one was lower than the other. How could this be happening to us?

Just a few months later, this same mom and dad were numbed by another announcement. This time they learned that their twenty-seven-year-old, Christian, equally talented, college-graduate, "never-gave-us-a-bit-of-trouble" daughter

ALSO was a homosexual, but wasn't involved in a relationship at the time.

Since telling their parents that they are gay, both children have moved several hundred miles away but remained in contact. They both say that they have never felt any differently, that they have always been interested in only their same sex. They also say that they want to find a partner and develop a relationship that is as happy as their parents' marriage. The mother's letter continues:

> So here we are at an impasse, too afraid and ashamed to tell [anyone] and dying inside because it is a very heavy burden. We know the Lord as our Savior and believe that all things work together for good to them that love Him and are called according to His purpose. So why are we having so much trouble turning this whole mess over to Him? We agonize over what we must have done wrong to have both of our children turn out this way. I apologize for being so incoherent, but sometimes the pain is like a knife and I'm sure I will not survive—and I'm not so sure I even want to.

A letter like this shows that the term *heartbroken* is more than just a metaphor. In the nineteenth century, some physicians believed that severe grief could somehow damage the heart and even bring on death. One doctor wrote, "Dissection of persons who have died shows congestion in and inflammation of the heart with rupture of its auricles and ventricles."[2]

Today, many doctors would agree that grief can literally break your heart. And the letters I get verify it. The goal of Spatula Ministries is found in Isaiah 61:1: "to bind up the brokenhearted . . ."(KJV).

Obviously, my broken heart didn't kill me, but it gave me the same feeling that so many other mothers have described—pain in the chest, as though a knife were being twisted around.

One mother told me that she had learned to live with that knife in her chest by avoiding weddings, showers, or any other festivities that reminded her of the son who had discarded his family. That way, the knife didn't turn and twist as much. It was still there, but it was not destroying her.

When you are in pain like this, depression is ever present, or at least never far away. You need strength to just get through each day. "Why me?" becomes your favorite question. You know it's the wrong question to ask, but you can't help it.

Whoever coined the phrase "misery loves company" was right—to a point. Anyone in long-term pain and grief—caused by a wayward child, for example—is often drawn to others, especially other parents who have the same problem. That's why Spatula Ministries' support groups keep getting new members constantly. Parents sharing the same pain can identify with each other, opening up the abscesses, draining the pain by talking with others who understand because they are having the same feelings. It may not ease our pain to know that someone else hurts worse, but it does help to know that God measures our strength and allows us a heavy burden to stretch and strengthen us a day at a time.

One of the main splashes of joy I receive when I go out to share my story is when women come up afterward and say, "Wow, after hearing YOUR story, I don't have any problems at ALL." Isn't it fabulous how God can take the fractured pieces of a life and use them to bless others? We trust that the stories in this book will brighten many dark corners and plant seeds of hope where there is defeat. There IS a door of hope, you know, and you not only can find that door, but you can walk confidently through it with a smile or even a chuckle when you get to the other side.

Pain Can Isolate You

But finding others who can support you in your grief is not always easy, and sometimes you don't even want to find anyone, especially when tragedy first strikes. You can slip into such deep misery and depression, especially at the beginning, that you cut yourself off from all contacts. Pain can isolate you from friends, and even family, and that is exactly what happened to me. Right after learning about Larry, my heartache was so deep and so personal that I was unable to share it with others. I was just too sick and bruised, so I guarded my feelings and remained in my own prison of isolation.

I have heard of a method of prison-camp torture called "the cement sack." The cement sack is a concrete cubicle only big enough for a person to stand in during solitary confinement. In a real sense, I put myself in my own cement sack of anguish and misery. Misery is optional and at that time I chose misery of the worst kind.

After Bill would leave for work, I would stay alone in the back bedroom, counting the roses on the wallpaper and then breaking into periodic sobbing that sometimes took the form of wailing—the uttermost symbol of human agony. I had done a lot of crying over Steve and Tim, but the weeping I did over Larry was different. Normal crying is centered in the throat, but what I was doing came more out of my chest, where all the pain seemed to be located.

Without realizing it, I developed a "technique" to let out my grief. I now share this technique with others who are suffering this same kind of pain. I tell folks to lie across a pillow, face down (because this takes away restrictions in the chest and throat) and then let go—sob your heart out. In this position you can let the sobbing energy emerge more easily. Sobbing is as violent a release of physical energy as vomiting. Some parents who are in grief think that if they ever start this kind of sobbing, they won't be able to stop, but that is not true. When we realize that sobbing can be a tremendous release, and we know that our feelings are acceptable to God, we can channel our energy into getting rid of unresolved grief. Some psychologists suggest that grieving people *schedule* a sobbing time each day to help release their grief. Without knowing it, I suppose that was what I was doing before the "experts" discovered it.

While my periods of sobbing helped me release the huge reservoirs of pent-up grief, they did not prevent me from becoming depressed. Finally, Bill sent me to a psychologist who was of some help, but I continued in my depression because I couldn't apply what he was advising me to do. He tried to explain that he had had very little success in changing the orientation of homosexuals and that if Larry ever did contact me, I shouldn't try to talk to him about changing. I simply couldn't accept this idea. I knew that God could change all things, and I knew He could fix Larry if only I prayed hard enough.

My dialogue with the psychologist went on for months, but my depression grew worse. The day Dr. Wells told me that, because Larry had been gone almost a year, he might never come back, I went into such severe depression that he recommended to Bill that I be put in Parkside West, the psychiatric facility in our area.

Bill told Dr. Wells that he wasn't sure his insurance would cover me and, unless it did, we would tough it out at home, since I wasn't "really vicious or anything."

Just as the end of my rope was fraying, I learned one more key lesson about grief: I learned to REALLY let go, to relinquish the source of my grief TOTALLY to God.

That lesson came the next day, when I drove up to a high viaduct near Disneyland, planning to turn the wheel hard, go over the rail, and plunge fifty feet to what I hoped would be death. But as I neared the top, I realized two things:

1. Dropping fifty feet in a car might not do the whole job. I could wind up maimed, making baskets in the home for the bewildered.

2. I was TIRED. I was tired of the suffering and pain, tired of all the bittersweet memories, tired of the churning about Larry. Above all, I was tired of saying I was "giving him to God," but then in reality taking him back again and carrying the burden, myself. I was weary of being a shell of myself, unable to be rid of the heaviness in my heart.

It was then that I decided to "nail Larry to the Cross," and in my imagination, that's exactly what I did. I took out a hammer and I nailed him to the Cross as I prayed this prayer of relinquishment: "I can't handle this any more, Lord . . . I'm giving him to You, and if he never comes home and I never see him again, *whatever, Lord,* whatever happens, I'm nailing him to the Cross and giving him to You!"

I'm not really sure what happened or why, but I believe that the key words were, "Whatever, Lord." There was something about finally surrendering to God and telling Him that WHAT-EVER happened, whatever He decided to do or not do, it was all right with me. I was too tired to fight and struggle and churn any longer. I would accept whatever He chose to send my way.

When I said, "Whatever, Lord," it released a million little splashes of joy deep inside of me. My teeth stopped itching, the shag rug in my throat disappeared, the elephant that had been sitting on my chest for nearly a year was gone, and so was that knife twisting there close to my heart. I turned my car around and drove home to begin life again.

I realize that what happened for me is not necessarily what happens for everyone else. There is nothing magical or su-per-spiritual about saying "Whatever, Lord." The key, however, is to relinquish whatever is causing your pain. This is particularly true if it is a loved one who is leading a rebellious life. When I said, "Whatever, Lord," I was identifying with Job, who said, "Though He slay me, yet will I trust Him . . ." (Job 13:15, NKJV). Because I felt I had lost everything—except my mind, and that was slowly going, too—I came to the place where I could say, "Whatever, Lord," instead of, "Why me?"

That was the key. I personally surrendered my hopes . . . my plans . . . my life . . . MY SON. I realized I was powerless to fix him, to bring him back, or to change him. Only God's touch on Larry's life could do any of that. As Scripture says, God is the One who removes the heart of stone and puts a heart of flesh in its place.[3] I finally understood that all I could do was *let him go*—turn him over to God and let Him work in Larry's life.

Try Giving Your Gift Box to Jesus

I am well aware that it may be hard to picture how you are to let go and give your child or other loved one to God. "Nailing him (or her) to the Cross" may not work for you as it worked for me that day I was on the verge of suicide. One way of looking at it is picturing in your mind that you are putting your loved one into a gift box. Then, in your mind's eye, wrap the box with lovely paper and ribbon.

Next, picture a long flight of stairs. At the top is the throne of God, with Jesus sitting on it. Imagine yourself climbing up these stairs, carrying your beautifully wrapped package. When you get to the top, put it at Jesus' feet and wait until He bends down to pick up the package and place it on His lap. Picture Jesus opening your package and taking your loved one in His arms to hold him or her close.

You must be sure that Jesus has your loved one in His grip, and you must believe that He will *never* let go. You have given your loved one to Jesus. He will take over. Now comes the crucial moment. When you've given your gift to Jesus, turn

around. Then walk back down the stairs. Halfway down, you may want to pause and see that your loved one is safe in Jesus' arms. You may want to hear in your mind's ear Jesus saying, "No one will ever take this precious one out of My hands and I will never let him go."

As you continue walking down the stairs, thank God for taking control. Then, hear yourself praying: *Lord, that settles it. I have given (name) to You and have taken my hands off. Do Your work in (his or her) life as you see fit.*

I believe this kind of exercise works with relinquishing any loved one, whether it is a child in open rebellion, someone who has made bad choices and mistakes, or someone who is a victim of a chronic disease or crippling injury. The point is, once you go through this mental exercise and pray this prayer, you do not have to feel as though everything now depends on you. Whenever you are tempted to take control again, you must practice this little thought exercise and remember that definite time when you presented your loved one as a gift to the Lord and He received him or her with His tender, everlasting love.

The simple sketch on page 258 could be copied and placed in a prominent place to continually remind you that you have given your loved one to God. He or she is safe in the arms of Jesus and you can go on about the tasks that Jesus wants you to do, instead of trying to carry burdens that are too big.

Eternal Perspective Makes All the Difference

One reason I like the mental exercise of placing a loved one in Jesus' hands is that it focuses on the ETERNAL PERSPEC-TIVE that we need if we are to cope with disappointment and heartache. There is no better way out of the cesspool than the rope of eternal perspective—knowing that "THIS ISN'T IT." What is happening is only temporary, and it will pass. Having eternal perspective means keeping your rear-view mirror small and narrow and your windshield big and wide so that you can see farther down the road and look forward to what the future holds. True, you can't see the immediate future—tomorrow, next month, or even a few years from now. *But you do know you will be a winner in the end.*

I have never been much for the "name-it-and-claim-it" approach. Who really wants or needs this? Our eternal promise is so big and so glorious and full of blinding brightness that the dismal present fades in comparison. The present is a small glimpse of what life is really all about. The future is the big picture. And as we endure temporary heartaches, we will get a much clearer perception and realize:

> THE IRON CROWN OF SUFFERING
> PRECEDES THE GOLDEN CROWN OF GLORY.

Several years ago, my daughter-in-love, Shannon, drew a sketch like the one on page 258. Since that time, Bill has printed up thousands of these little sheets to be sent out to people served by Spatula Ministries. I tell the gals to put this little sign on their refrigerators or some other prominent place to remind them to always say, "WHATEVER, LORD!"

Since we started sending out these little signs, I've had about forty different women send me this same phrase done on glasses, napkins, and in needlepoint—just about any form you can think of. When I visit the homes of women who are part of our Spatula Ministries family, I often find the sheet tacked on their bulletin boards or framed and hanging on a wall.

She Changed But Her Kid Didn't

Recently a lady came up to me after a conference and handed me an envelope with a note and a twenty-dollar bill inside. The note said:

> When you were here around five years ago, my daughter
> had left her husband and two kids and declared she was a

lesbian. You talked to me and gave me your book. I was to send you the money for it.

Out of anger, because my daughter didn't change, I didn't send it. My daughter still hasn't changed, but I have. I've given it all to God and left it there. Here is the money for the book.

Love in Christ,
Sally

I love this lady's letter, not because she finally paid for the book, but because she saw that it is *our* job to love folks and it is *God's* job to change them. Parents naturally want to bring about immediate changes in their kids' lives, but God didn't command us to change them., He only commanded us to LOVE them. It is God who makes the changes in ANY of us.

Lots of parents have what some psychologists call the "rescue fantasy." They want to rearrange their children's lives and provide the happy ending, but that is not what God has told us to do. The very best we can do, other than listening to hurting folks and weeping with them, is to point to the only One who can really help bring healing. I often tell parents to remember to say:

I DIDN'T CAUSE IT,
I CANNOT CONTROL IT,
NOR CAN I CURE IT.

But God can! We have two choices when we are faced with suffering and tragedy: We can withdraw and become bitter, growing old before our time and dying inwardly, or we can reach out to God and grow inwardly. We have God's promise that it will happen and "there hath not failed one word of all His good promise . . ." (1 Kings 8:56, KJV).

Love Is the Glue That Mends Broken Hearts

The road to recovery is not a straight, upward climb. But you begin by realizing that you must understand that *it is not always necessary to understand everything.* Sometimes it will be a case of three steps forward and one step back. Or sometimes hope will reign in the morning only to be overcome by despair before sundown. Various emotions, like anger, depression, longing, and bitterness may chase each other through your mind, making it impossible to think logically or make sound decisions.

Each day becomes a new challenge to live without dropping back into that cesspool of shocked helplessness. You can be at peace for a few days and then suddenly the loneliness and emptiness will come rushing back. Perhaps you will look at the calendar and see that it is the birthday of your wayward daughter. Or perhaps you will see someone on the street who strongly resembles the child over whom you are grieving. That happened with me. I would be in a shopping mall and see a young man in the distance who had on a sport shirt exactly like one Larry owned. Just seeing that shirt would send waves of heartache through me. My strength would evaporate, and for the moment I would be defeated and dissolve in tears.

Sometimes your recovery period will be like a roller coaster with many highs and lows. At times you'll want to scream because you think the bottom is dropping out, that the heart-stopping plunge will never end, that you are totally out of control. But then you will feel the pain subsiding and the wound will start to heal and life will become a bit brighter because now you have a glimmer of hope. And once you have THAT, you are on your way, because hope is tough to kill.

As the saying goes, "Hope springs eternal." We hope even when all hope is supposed to be gone. We hope long after everyone else has given up. Hope can live with virtually no reinforcement. Hope can mend your broken heart—if you give God ALL the pieces.

We can face whatever comes once we have relinquished our lives and the lives of our loved ones to Him. He is the God we can trust for strength each day (see Deut. 33:25). He is the One with all the love and understanding, who has a clear and eternal purpose for us. We can trust God with all our problems, all our heartaches, and especially with all our long-term anxieties. Every morning as we wake ourselves up with a splash of joy we can say, "WHATEVER, LORD!"

Splish/Splash . . .

THE RAIN FALLS ON THE JUST AND ALSO ON THE UNJUST,
BUT CHIEFLY ON THE JUST,
BECAUSE THE UNJUST STEALS THE JUST'S UMBRELLA.

*   *   *   *   *   *

CHANGE IS A PROCESS, NOT AN EVENT.

*   *   *   *   *   *

WE ARE ALWAYS IN THE FORGE, OR ON THE ANVIL;
BY TRIALS GOD IS SHAPING US FOR HIGHER THINGS.

*   *   *   *   *   *

WHATEVER YOU WANT, LORD . . .

W — Whoever You put in, or take out of my life . . .
H — However You want things to end up . . . only You see the big picture.
A — As much as I can take, Lord . . . You know me best because
T — Time is nothing to You . . . help me to be patient.
E — Everything is in Your hands . . . Help me to let go.
V — Victory comes with You as my Guide.
E — Eternity with You will be worth it all!
R — Restoration is mine through You.

*   *   *   *   *   *

TAKE YOUR BROKEN DREAMS TO JESUS!

The Lord lifts the fallen and those bent beneath their loads.
(Ps. 145:14, TLB)

Wherever I Go, There I Am

If I have inside of me the stuff to make cocoons, maybe the stuff of butterflies is there, too.
Trina Paulus[1]

There's something about falling into a cesspool that just doesn't do much to improve your self-image. When disappointment and rejection invade our lives, they often rob us of our self-esteem as well. Many folks write to tell me what it's like to have your self-esteem flushed right down the toilet. They seldom use the terms "self-image" and "self-esteem," but that's what their letters are telling us.

One mother of an adult daughter and son wrote to say that first her daughter proclaimed her homosexuality by moving in with a woman friend who had a little boy. Neither this mother or her husband could accept their daughter's choice of lifestyle and they wrote letters to tell her they loved her and she would always be welcome in their home, but the rest of her "family" would not. The daughter responded by saying she appreciated the letters, but that she would not be seeing much of her parents and regretted that they would miss out on enjoying her family, especially the new "grandson." And no, she would not be home for Christmas.

Sensing a certain reserve in their son, they asked him what he thought of his sister's decision. That's when he told them that he, too, was gay. The mother's letter said, in part:

> Barbara, *I do want to resign as a mother.* I am ready to go be with Jesus. I DON'T WANT MY ONLY SON AND MY ONLY DAUGHTER TO BE GAY! . . . I want to have grandchildren; I want us to be a "normal" American family. I don't want this guilt, pain, shame and heartache. I don't want this little town to whisper and gossip about my children. I don't want my husband's eyes to flash pain and guilt when he is trying to be strong for me. . . .
>
> People have often counted on my faith, my interest and caring and yes—good spirits—to help them. I am a piano and voice teacher, and my 40 students are friends as well as students. Now I feel like a "zombie" in the studio. I sing in the choir and as a soloist in other groups. I feel like a fraud . . . I am 54 and I wonder what it was all for. What did my life accomplish? I have never felt so worthless or helpless.

Another mother, from Arizona, wrote to say it had been over a year since their youngest daughter's letter had arrived, announcing, "What I need to tell you is that I am a lesbian. There it is. Now where do I go from here?" The mother's letter continued:

> Our lives will never be the same. I feel I lost self-esteem and have to work to overcome this feeling of being lethargic. I am on an antidepressant, but it's a constant struggle to get work done.

That feeling of lethargy also overwhelms a woman who is a columnist for her local newspaper. Her husband had died and she had also lost a sister who had suffered painfully with Alzheimer's disease for eighteen years. Then a son was divorced and his two children suffered horribly from the results. Her letter said:

I used to speak to women on beauty and how to bring out your best. I need to do something, but my batteries are dead. I wail. Pray. Feel totally alone. I have no immediate family. Friends—yes—but still s-o-o-o alone.

Where do I go from here? I am a writer. My columns help people, but nothing is helping me.

Letters like these aren't unusual; they are typical of so many that come in all the time. When your self-esteem lies in tatters, you feel like saying:

> I USED TO BE APATHETIC.
> NOW I JUST DON'T CARE!

Self-Esteem Is Like a Three-Legged Stool

We all have a mental picture of ourselves. That picture is our self-image, and we will act in harmony with what we see in that mental self-portrait.[2] Another way to describe self-esteem is that it is simply how you feel about yourself. Do you like or dislike yourself? So much of the grief I hear about is the kind that can make a person dislike herself. It can make her feel worthless, helpless, and cut adrift, belonging nowhere.

A helpful way to look at what your self-esteem does for you is to picture a three-legged stool, with each leg representing a major feeling you have about yourself:

1. I belong.
2. I am worthwhile.
3. I am capable.[3]

To belong is to feel wanted, loved, cared for, accepted. One woman wrote to me to tell me what it feels like *not* to belong:

I'm 40 years old, with nine kids. My husband ran off with another woman four years ago when I was one month pregnant with my three-year-old *twins*. I've got no emotional support from my family . . . my older children avoid me because I suffer from panic attacks. I can't drive my car. I don't leave my home because I'm afraid I will have a panic attack and can't get back.

They think I've already lost my mind, but I know if I don't get some help soon I <u>will</u> lose my mind.
HELP!

Most of us have felt like this gal at some time or another. When I first learned that homosexuality was part of our family, I felt like an alien from another planet. I could not relate to anyone, and no one was relating to me. My feelings of self-worth were totally squashed. But there have been other times, maybe not so serious and occasionally even comical, when my self-esteem has been bruised more than a little bit.

When my first book, *Where Does a Mother Go to Resign?* came out, I was totally unfamiliar with being an author. I really didn't know what to do when folks would come up, hug me, thank me, and ask me to sign their book with "something just for them." Was I supposed to put in a Bible verse or just their name and my name? Was I supposed to add some spiritual thoughts? Being an author left me a little bewildered.

The book had been out only a few weeks when I stopped at a huge Christian bookstore in Orange County, California to make several purchases. As I looked through different books, I noticed that the authors had signed them on the flyleaf. Since so many authors live in the Orange County area, I assumed that when they had visited that store, they had just signed their own books so buyers could have a personally autographed copy.

Then I came upon a big stack of MY book, all lined up on a rack marked "New Books Just Published." I took out my handy pen and started writing my name in the flyleaf of the books. As I happily signed my name, I just relished the idea of thinking how surprised buyers would be to buy the book and then discover it had already been autographed!

Suddenly, a tall, serious-looking young man put his hand on my shoulder and said in a stern voice, "Lady, we don't allow people to deface our books here!"

I looked at the young man and thought of how I could respond. Should I get out my driver's license to prove who I was? Should I just scribble all over one of the books in defiance? Or maybe I would just slink out without a word of explanation. I felt so unworthy at that moment. After all, the book was just off the press, and if I had a big altercation with a Christian bookstore over "defacing" its merchandise, where would it all end?

I decided to just get out of there, and I did so without telling the young man who I was. I guess I thought that would only make it worse! Anyway, I knew I didn't belong there at that moment because I just wasn't ACCEPTABLE.

To feel worthwhile, or worthy, is to feel that you count, that you are doing the right thing, not the wrong thing, that you are a good person, not a bad one. One gal's letter describes what it's like to be made to feel worthless:

> As a family with a homosexual daughter, we have had a flood of emotions. . . . We live in a small farming community

where there are three churches and everyone knows everyone else's business. In fact, everyone is just about related one way or another. I suppose you can guess what happened when we found out that Cindy was living a homosexual lifestyle!

We had an evangelist in our church and he made this statement: "Any time a child becomes a homosexual, let me repeat, ANYTIME, whether male or female, it is ALWAYS the fault of the mother." This is just what I needed, on top of everything else.

The evangelist's unfortunate (and totally untrue) words did this mom untold damage. I wrote back and told her that her daughter's problem was NOT HER FAULT. One of my biggest tasks is to assure parents that when their children have a problem or decide to go astray, they do not have to feel guilty. (I'll say more on this in chapter 8.)

And to feel capable means that you know you can do it— you're up to whatever life may bring. You know you have the strength. You have confidence. A mother, whose son appears to have "married" his gay lover and now wears a ring in his nose as well as several in his ear, wrote to tell me her world was crumbling and everything was out of control:

> I don't think it could hurt any worse if he put on spike shoes and ground me into the ground—or put a knife in me and twisted it. . . . Barbara, please say something to help me get a grip on things again. I thought I was doing well and was helping others in the same situation. But now I feel I am sinking again.

My counsel to this mother was that, while her son was not behaving like an adult, he still was one and he had to make his own choices. As parents, we cannot always change the behavior of our kids, especially when they're adults. Also, we cannot let the sin of one child disturb the entire family. Her son had made some bad choices, but WHEN THERE IS NO CONTROL, THERE IS NO RESPONSIBILITY. She was not to blame for her son's behavior; what she needed to do was resist sliding back down into a cesspool of defeat.

I prayed with this mom and we asked God to help her get through this temporary setback. Now she was off balance and deeply hurt, but she would get through it. She wouldn't always feel this way if she would only hang on to that "rope of hope."

I believe that in cases like this there is a phrase that applies:

HURT PEOPLE HURT PEOPLE.

This mother's son was hurting inside, and he was striking out, wanting to hurt someone else, which is typical. If we remember that people who are hurt often strike out, in turn, to hurt others, it will help us to show compassion. Condemnation will not work. The only way anyone changes is through conviction, which comes from inside.

Think Highly of Yourself—But Not Too Highly

One of the best verses I've ever seen on self-esteem is Romans 12:3 (NIV): "Do not think of yourself more highly than you ought, but rather think of yourself with sober judgment, in accordance with the measure of faith God has given you." Some Christians believe this verse says we should not be concerned about high self-esteem, that we shouldn't think highly of ourselves at all, that we should put ourselves down to be lowly and humble enough for Jesus to accept us. But if we look again at Romans 12:3, we see that it does *not* say, "Never think highly of yourself—that's sinful." What it *does* say is, "Think highly of yourself—have self-respect—but don't get conceited or egotistical."

As Josh McDowell puts it, "In other words, we should be realistic and biblical in our opinions of ourselves. . . . We are to develop a healthy self-image, or self-evaluation that coincides with what God says about us. . . ." He continues:

A HEALTHY SELF-IMAGE IS SEEING YOURSELF
AS GOD SEES YOU—NO MORE AND NO LESS.[4]

So, no matter what has happened, no matter how badly one of your children has strayed or rebelled, no matter how badly your spouse or other family members or friends have treated you, you are *still God's child*, made in His image and *very precious* to Him. You are a son or daughter of the King—you are royalty. Someone sent in the following poem, which says it very well:

> When the *child* of God
> Looks into the *Word* of God
> And sees the *Son* of God
> He is *changed* by the *Spirit* of God
> In the *image* of God
> For the *glory* of God.

One of my favorite bumper "snickers" says, "Life is hard and then you die." Actually, that's the GOOD news because when Christians die, life's struggles are over and we go to be with the Lord. But the reason so many people have low (unhealthy) self-esteem is that "life is hard and you have to live it anyway." As Ashleigh Brilliant says,

IT'S EASY TO COME AND GO;
THE HARD THING IS TO REMAIN.[5]

But remaining is what life is all about. And you'll never raise your self-image if you blame circumstances or other people for your feelings. For example, some of us blame our low self-images on our parents, and it's true that mothers and fathers can do more to destroy (or build) a child's self-esteem than anyone. My husband, Bill, knows something about that.

Bill Became an Ace Anyhow

Bill and I went to a communication seminar given by Norman Wright a few years ago and one of our assignments was, "Write down something you remember that your father said to praise you or a good thing he said about you."

I dashed off several memories I had of when my dad had encouraged me, but Bill sat there with nothing on his page. I knew what he was thinking. He had come from a very rigid family and was the only child. His father, particularly, never showed much emotion or did anything to encourage him.

When World War II hit, Bill went into the navy to become a flier. His father told him he would NEVER make it in the navy as a flier, but Bill made it and then some. During the war, he became an "ace." According to government policy, an ace is any flier who shoots down more than six enemy planes, and Bill shot down seven. He was decorated with the Distinguished Flying Cross twice. He also was awarded two air medals, the Purple Heart, and the Presidential Unit Citation for Bravery.

In spite of all the achievements and honors Bill won, not once did his father ever admit he was wrong about his son or even congratulate him for his admirable record as a U.S. Navy flier.

So it was no wonder that Bill had to sit and think for several minutes before coming up with something his father had ever said to fill his emotional tank. Finally, just before we were to begin discussing what we all had written, Bill put this down:

> One time when I was about five, I was riding in the backseat of the car and my father and my uncle were in the front. My uncle's hat flew out of the open window and he turned around and started blaming me for tossing out his hat. But my father said, "Billy didn't throw your hat out the window."

This was the ONLY thing Bill could remember that his father had ever said to defend him or say anything remotely positive about him. But the good thing about all this is that, despite never getting any encouragement from his father, Bill didn't let that defeat him. He didn't allow that to destroy his self-esteem. He went on and made a tremendous success of his life. Somehow he knew he was worthwhile and capable. That made it possible for him to succeed.

The truth is, each one of us is special—a unique product made by God, and, as the well-known saying goes:

GOD DON'T MAKE NO JUNK.

He Isn't Finished with Any of Us Yet

God not only made you special, He's still working on you and in you to will and to do His good pleasure. He isn't finished with you yet.

When my son, Larry, was in college, a teacher gave his psychology class the following assignment: "Stand nude before a full-length mirror. Make a self-evaluation of what is seen."

In response, Larry turned in an essay that said, in part:

> This particular assignment created a problem for me. To submit myself to this assignment would violate my own personal convictions. I have dedicated my body to the Lord Jesus Christ and upon doing this am unable to follow the exact assignment. I have kept in mind your goal of self-evaluation and would like to share what I have learned about myself. . . .
>
> I consider God as my maker. He is the artist working on my life, and is more concerned with my inward qualities, building into me an enduring structure. Others are passers-by who do not realize the intentions or abilities of the Creator in my life's pattern. Therefore, it is not my place to judge God's unfinished work because of one very vital fact, GOD IS NOT FINISHED WITH ME YET!
>
> It is one thing to be descriptive, another to be judgmental. I feel the information you asked for would be both. In describ-

ing myself as assigned, I would be using others' standards as to my height, bulkiness, and conformation. . . .

I have found that I form a NEGATIVE self-image by accepting the values of people around me, but a POSITIVE and accurate self-image develops when I comprehend the values which God places on my appearance, abilities, parentage, and environment. Opinions of others create inferiority, insecurity, and rejection. However, because I have confidence in God's principles and design, I understand and joyfully accept the values He places on my life, because I can see what can happen to a vessel God is shaping for His own use. . . .

You asked me to tell you what was done to discover myself. I did two things. I began with a personal relationship with God. I accepted His plan and purpose for my life. I let God take charge of the design, and thanked Him for His workmanship thus far. I realized that God was not finished with me yet, and I began to have a new confidence and expectation for what He will do for the future.

Now I can thank God for His constant love toward me, and His Son who died for me that I may live—and mostly for the knowledge that my life is being constantly molded by Him into an object of use. God is the potter and I am the clay. I am the product of His design and my life reflects His workmanship and HE IS NOT FINISHED WITH ME YET.

We're All on the Same Road

Even though he didn't complete the assignment as given, Larry still got a good grade on his paper. Perhaps his teacher realized that what Larry said about himself is true of all of us. God isn't finished with any of us yet. Yes, there is changing and shaping that He wants to do, but He does it because we belong to Him, we are of infinite worth to Him, and He sees tremendous potential in what we can do.

On a trip I made to Texas, Kentucky, and the state of Washington, it was terrific to meet so many gals who have become part of Spatula Ministries. Once again, I realized how we are all bonded together by heartaches and how God's love brings us the healing touch, drains the pain, and helps us move along on the road to becoming well.

While on that trip, I was on highway 395 in Spokane. I knew Barney and his family live in their new home on highway 395 in Nevada, several hundred miles south of where I was. I telephoned Barney and when he answered I said, "I'm up here on highway 395—we're both on the same road."

Barney laughed and said, "That's right. Only you're just a lot farther north—closer to heaven maybe?"

We had a good visit and some more laughs, and then I began thinking that this is really how life is. We are ALL on the same road. Some of us are just not where we were. We have moved on and have come through the rough places—"farther along," as the old song goes. We've all been brought together by God's redeeming love to be forgiven for our mistakes, cleansed, and then sent on down the road, sharing together as we go.

That's a splash of joy that should build anyone's self-esteem, but, as somebody said,

THERE'S NOTHING LIKE A LITTLE EXPERIENCE TO UPSET A THEORY.

It's all very well and good to know you're on the same road with everyone else, but what about feeling as if you've just been run over? Beautiful, capable, never-have-a-thing-go-wrong people have a way of doing that without even meaning to. Maybe, like me, you identify with the unknown woman who wrote the following:

HAVING A HARD DAY?

When I read about a woman who's totally together career-wise, I'm proud—and I go home and eat a carton of Cool Whip.

When I read about a woman who has a perfect relationship with a supportive, sensitive man—I go home and eat a carton of Cool Whip and scream.

When I read about a woman who has adorable, bilingual children and regular, open, loving chats with her mother—I write out my frustrations in M&Ms and eat them one paragraph at a time. This Ideal Woman seems too far out of reach; it's hopeless.

It may not be realistic to try to match some "ideal woman" who has gifts that you do not. (She also may have her own problems—far worse than yours!) What you want to do is develop your own potential while you let God do His work in you. Actually, you and God are a team. As Paul opened his letter to the Philippian church, he said, "I am sure that God who began the good work within you will keep right on helping you grow in his grace until his task within you is finally finished . . ." (Phil. 1:6, TLB).

Then Paul went on to say, "Continue to work out your salvation with fear and trembling, for it is God who works in you to will and to act according to his good purpose (Phil. 2:12, 13, NIV).

This verse is the key to healthy (not egotistical) self-esteem. Paul is saying we must make ourselves available instead of shrinking back or becoming a recluse as I did for almost a year when our son, Larry, walked out of our lives to pursue a gay lifestyle. When I finally told God, "Whatever, Lord!" I not only released Larry completely to Him, I also released the lonely burden I had been carrying all by myself all that time. I sang all the way home that day. It was the first time since Larry had gone that I felt assurance that God still loved me.

We Are Opals, Not Diamonds

"She's a diamond in the rough" is a familiar way of saying somebody has potential to become far more than she is right now. But I believe that we are much more like opals than diamonds. Did you know that an opal is made of desert dust, sand, and silica and owes its beauty not to its perfection but to a defect? The opal is a stone with a broken heart. It is full of minute fissures that allow air inside, and then the air refracts the light. As a result, the opal has such lovely hues that the stone is called "the lamp of fire" because the breath of the Lord is in it.

An opal will lose its luster if it is kept in a cold, dark place, but the luster is restored when it is held in a warm hand or when light shines on it.

In so many ways, we can compare the opal to ourselves. It is when we are warmed by God's love that we take on color and brilliance. It is when we are broken inside ourselves—through our defects—that we can give back the lovely hues of His light to others. It is then that the lamp of the temple can burn brightly within us and not flicker or go out.

Still, there will be times when we lose the luster in our lives and it is vital to know how to restore it. When silver or brass become tarnished, we get out the tarnish remover and do some rubbing. What can we do when we need to bring back the shine in our own lives? We can pause early in the day to seek God's guidance. We can count our blessings and name them one by one.

An attitude of gratitude rids our lives of the film of frustration, the rust of resentment, and the varnish of vanity—all destroyers of self-esteem. When we count our blessings, we multiply harmony and good feelings, and the lamp's flame burns higher once again.

Without God's touch in our lives—His work in us to will and to do His good pleasure—there is no sparkle or scant joy. But when we allow Him to work within us—when we feel His hand upon us—we are no longer hidden treasures; we become sparkling jewels that beautify His kingdom.

Up, Up, and Away!

It's easy to talk about having a good self-esteem when life is soaking you with plenty of splashes of joy, but when you are in the cesspool of low self-esteem, it's different. I've been there and I know. Getting out of that cesspool seems impossible. The sides seem too "slickery" and slimy. But you can do it if you are willing to try and at the same time have faith that God is doing His work in you. Here are some ideas that can pull you up, out of the cesspool. They are simple ideas, but they are like ropes to help you climb up the slippery sides and make it back to seeing yourself as God sees you, no more and no less.

There is always something new you can learn. I'm not talking about nuclear physics or computer science (unless that's what you really want to do). I'm talking about simpler things, like learning new words or maybe reading up on faraway exotic places. Because I travel a lot, I like looking for unusual names of towns across the country. Lately I've developed my own "Joy Map" of the United States, which shows only the names of towns that are positive, fun, and uplifting. I'll tell you more about that in chapter 7.

The point is, the better informed you are, the more vital you will be, not only to others but to yourself. And as you become more aware of others, your self-esteem is bound to rise.

Learn what builds your confidence and take advantage of it. Remember one of the three legs of self-esteem? It's the idea that "I am capable—I can handle this."

You can find confidence in strange places—at the cosmetic counter with a new shade of mascara or lipstick, at the beauty parlor with a new hairdo or permanent, or at the clothing store where you can find a new dress or sweater.

Sometimes, when I feel a need for an injection of confidence, I pull out an old shoebox that I have kept for years. It is my original "Joy Box" and inside it are notes, letters, and greeting cards sent by special friends, some of whom have gone on to Glory. Every time I read through the cards and letters I get a lift. It is as if my special friends are talking to me. We all need others who can nurture us, enrich us, and remind us that we are valuable to them as friends, too.

I call my several special friends my "nurturing ones." Everybody should have four or five nurturers they can call. As you share with them, you can tell from their very tone of voice that you are being cared for, that your life is being enriched. It may be their gentle laughter or some subtle way of reminding you how much they care. A phone call to one of my special nurturing ones restores my confidence as much as anything I know.

Spend your time with others who pick you up and don't put you down. Find friends who accept you for who you are, instead of cutting you down to size to make themselves feel larger. If your spouse or your children put you down, let them know firmly but lovingly that you won't accept it. If your mother (or mother-in-law) is driving you toward the home for the bewildered, spend reasonable amounts of time with her, but don't let her control your life.

Emphasize your strengths and stay away from your weaknesses. Everybody does something well, even if it's as simple as crossword puzzles, Scrabble, or tying a scarf with just the right touch. If Mother Nature cheated you in certain parts of the looks department, emphasize the things that she did a better job on. It might be your hair, your eyes, your smile, or your ability to be kind and caring. Develop your specialty and use it every day. As you concentrate on your strengths you will have less time to dwell on your weaknesses.

One of the strengths I've developed is interviewing folks, which is a skill I didn't have some years ago when I began working as an intake receptionist at a counseling center. My responsibility was to interview potential counselees on the phone and make arrangements for their stay at the counseling center, which sometimes would last for many weeks. I would take down their histories and ascertain what crises they were in, how immediate their need might be, and if a spouse or other companion should accompany them.

One day a man called and sounded very disturbed, saying he wanted to bring his wife in for counseling right away. As I began to get the facts from him, he excitedly told me how impossible his wife was to reason with. When she had refused his suggestions to get help, he had shaved her head completely BALD! My shock was so great that I couldn't help muttering, "Well, we sure won't have any difficulty in recognizing HER, will we?"

It has taken time, but since that day I have learned to be more diplomatic. Now I really enjoy talking with people, drawing them out, and letting them share their feelings with me. All of which gives me good feelings about myself, as well.

The "I Am's" Are the Real You

One other thing you can do to build healthy self-esteem is become a student of what the Bible says about you. The following is a list of "I am" verses. Study one every day for two weeks and when you get through with the list, start over again—or find others! Soon these verses will become part of your very being, part of who you think you are and who you see when you gaze into the mirror:

I AM . . .

1. A child of God (Rom. 8:16).
2. Forgiven (Col. 1:13, 14).
3. Saved by grace through faith (Eph. 2:8).
4. Justified (Rom. 5:1).
5. A new creature (2 Cor. 5:17).
6. Led by the Spirit of God (Rom. 8:14).
7. Kept in safety wherever I go (Ps. 91:11).
8. Casting all my cares on Jesus (1 Pet. 5:7).
9. Doing all things through Christ who strengthens me (Phil. 4:13).
10. Bringing every thought into captivity (2 Cor. 10:5).
11. Being transformed by a renewed mind (Rom. 12:1, 2).
12. The righteousness of God in Christ (2 Cor. 5:21).
13. An imitator of Jesus (Eph. 5:1).
14. Filled with laughter and rejoicing (Job 8:21).

Recently I was at the NBC studios in Burbank, California to tape a television show on the role of women in today's society. I was escorted to the makeup room and left there alone for a few minutes. I sat in the makeup chair looking at a big mirror surrounded by those bright, merciless lights. All around the room were photos of movie stars of today and yesterday—Lana Turner, Ann Sheridan, Rita Hayworth, Loretta Young, and dozens more. But the focal point of the whole scene was the sign placed just above the mirror, which proclaimed in huge black letters:

> IF YOU WANT MAKE-UP, ASK ME.
> IF YOU WANT MIRACLES, ASK GOD.

When you're looking in the mirror at a time like that, it's always good to remember some of the "I am" verses.

Take a Risk—and Be Free!

Also remember that the key to climbing out of that cesspool of low self-esteem is willingness to take a risk. Actually, you *can* stay down in the cesspool and not take any risks at all. It's safer there, even if it isn't a pleasant place to be. On the other hand, you can dare to make things different. As Helen Keller said:

> LIFE IS EITHER A DARING ADVENTURE
> OR NOTHING.

I got a letter recently from a woman who has had all kinds of trouble with her sons who are now twenty-two and twenty years old. One of them left home when he was fourteen. She didn't hear from him for eight years and then received a call that he was in prison doing a twenty-five-year sentence for armed robbery. The other son is an alcoholic who has left his job, home, and belongings and has disappeared. A warrant has been issued for his arrest. In spite of all these cesspools, this mother writes:

> The years of my life have been miserable and self-defeating. But beneath it all I knew God was in charge and everything would ultimately be okay. Not pie in the sky, just simple truth. Because I grew up abused, I've had little self-esteem until these past three or four years. I have joy in me, and even in bitter times I could see humor and joy, but some around me thought me strange for that. With no personal strength (how could I be strong without the freedom of Jesus?) it added to my belief of being a wrong, weird person. But now I am free! How glorious to stand in the light, how safe. When I am afraid, I take slow, deep breaths and say, "I am safe in Jesus."

This mom has learned a crucial secret to preserving her tattered self-esteem:

PICK UP THE PIECES AND GO ON.

You can do this in all kinds of situations: when real tragedy strikes or in lighter moments, when you need to turn a minor disaster into a serendipity. I was speaking for a large women's group at a big hotel in Texas, and it seemed that problems were coming from every direction. The adjoining room had a banquet going on with lots of singing and loud music with drums. The microphone I was using kept cutting out every now and then, and to add to the problem, the air conditioning was inadequate for such a large room. To top it off, the chairs were the kind you could sit in for only twenty-five minutes without wanting to escape.

As I tried to compete with the loud music and the microphone malfunction, I hurried through my story in half the time it usually takes and had to leave out many of the details that would normally pull it all together.

Afterward, I made my way to the powder room and, while I was using the facilities, three gals who had heard my talk came bursting in. They were just bubbling over with words like, "Oh, wasn't that GREAT!" "Did you ever laugh and cry at the same time and feel so GOOD about it?" "Boy, I sure wouldn't have missed today for ANYTHING! I haven't been so encouraged and blessed in ages!"

I wanted to come out and hug all three of them, but instead I decided it would be best to remain unseen until they left. They would never know how their words had buoyed me up. Proverbs says, "Anxious hearts are very heavy but a word of encouragement does wonders!"[6] How true, especially when it is an OVERHEARD word, which really wasn't meant for your ears!

I felt renewed. I felt restored. My trip had been worthwhile after all because some people—at least three of them, anyway—were helped and refreshed. And in return, their encouraging words had glued together my broken pieces and I could go on.

That's always the key—*pick up the pieces and keep going*, even when it seems that the whole world is against you. It really isn't, you know. As one psychiatrist said to his patient: "The whole world isn't against you; there are millions of people who don't care one way or another."

But those who really love you care. And above all, God cares. We all have fractures in our lives. Sometimes they are physical, sometimes emotional, and sometimes mental. But we know that God can heal those fractured places, and He can glue together the fragments that are cracked and split and make us whole. Knowing that He cares is the secret of good self-esteem—seeing yourself as God sees you, no more and no less.

Splish/Splash . . .

SOME THINGS NEVER CHANGE . . .
LIKE THE TASTE OF POSTAGE-STAMP GLUE.

* * * * * *

BE GOOD TO YOU

Be yourself—truthfully.
Accept yourself—gratefully.
Value yourself—joyfully.
Forgive yourself—completely.
Treat yourself—generously.
Balance yourself—harmoniously.
Bless yourself—abundantly.
Trust yourself—confidently.
Love yourself—wholeheartedly.
Empower yourself—prayerfully.
Give yourself—enthusiastically.
Express yourself—radiantly.

                                        Source unknown

*   *   *   *   *   *

MOST PEOPLE ARE WILLING TO CHANGE,
NOT BECAUSE THEY SEE THE LIGHT,
BUT BECAUSE THEY FEEL THE HEAT!

*   *   *   *   *   *

Dear Christ, I would give
You every key of the little house that
You know as me.
The porch has been Yours,
And You've walked all through
The open rooms that the world can view.
But today, O Christ, I would have You go
To the secret rooms that I've treasured so.
They are hidden and small and set apart;
But I want You to own this house—my heart.

                                        Source unknown

*   *   *   *   *   *

HAVE CHARACTER!
Don't BE one!

*   *   *   *   *   *

CHEER UP!
TOMORROW WILL BE DIFFERENT . . .
NOT BETTER, JUST DIFFERENT!

*   *   *   *   *   *

But why is man important to you?
    Why do you take care of human beings?
You made man a littler lower than the angels.
    And You crowned him with glory and honor.
                    Ps. 8:4, 5, NCV

S.D.D.D.
(Same Doo-Doo, Different Day)

Don't lose your head in the battle . . . you won't have
any place to put your helmet.

A recurring theme in many of the letters I receive is STRESS, the daily wear and tear that comes from just being alive. I love the quip about the lady who goes for a drive whenever things get too stressful—she is now twenty-six hundred miles from home.

One thing my mail reminds me of is that we all have different lives, different cesspools, and different kinds of stress. A reader in the Northwest wrote this candid response after reading *So, Stick a Geranium in Your Hat and Be Happy:*

> I am sorry that your two older sons were killed. I can only imagine how difficult that must be. I pray that I never have to know that particular anguish.
>
> However, I must take issue with your reaction when you found out that your third son was a homosexual. My first reaction was "Lighten up, Lady!" That's basically how I felt after finishing the book, too.
>
> So your son is gay. Big deal. Has he robbed anybody? My son has. Has he been arrested for breaking and entering? My

son has. Has he been on drugs and/or alcohol? My son has. Has he killed anybody? My son has. An accident, but the boy is still dead, and my son went to jail for it. All this before he was 17.

This woman went on to talk a little about the stress she's been experiencing the last two years. Her husband was diagnosed with renal-cell cancer, which had also spread to his lungs. Then their fourteen-year-old daughter told them she was pregnant and wanted to place the baby for adoption.

Later in the fall, her husband had his left kidney removed, and their son, who had been paroled to a state group home,

lost his job. When her husband was in the hospital for his operation, she had to drive 150 miles each way to see him. Later, when he was able to go back to work, they both had to drive 100 miles round trip to work each day to their jobs.

Their son found another job, but then lost it and moved home with them, where his car was stolen and wrecked, and then he wrecked a replacement his parents bought for him. He also ran up $850 on their gasoline credit card in one month. On the good-news side, the treatment for her husband's cancer "seemed to be working," her daughter's baby was born, and her son got another job. But the stress continued; she wrote:

> My dear, *that* was stress. Stress is also having the doctor tell you that if the experimental treatment for cancer that your husband is undergoing doesn't work, there is nothing else to try. Stress is having your 20-year-old son call you in the middle of the night because he's out of work and out of money. Stress is facing the possibility of going on alone without enough money to meet the bills. Stress is not having enough to pay the bills, even after Don is home and back to work. Stress is seeing your first grandchild once for two minutes, and being afraid to hold him for fear you wouldn't be able to let go.

I appreciate this gal's letter because she tells it like it is. I called her to say that I understood and we had a good talk. She says things are better now, but her stress goes on. That's what causes the wear and tear, the constant, never-ending crises. As somebody said,

THESE DAYS
IT TAKES NERVES OF STEEL
JUST TO BE NEUROTIC.

Every day we live out the proof that stress is HERE, a fact of life, and we must learn to cope with it. You may have seen the cartoon that shows Ziggy driving by a highway sign reading:

HARSH REALITIES NEXT 2,500 MILES.

Actually, the harsh realities last a lot longer than that. The sign could read:

HARSH REALITIES FOR THE REST OF THE TRIP.

How Do You Handle Stress?

Karol Jackowski, author of *Ten Fun Things to Do Before You Die,* suggests that taking a long, hot-tub bubble bath is a great way to escape reality. She writes: "Because we are not God, the more we exceed our limits, the more we need to escape. Too much limitlessness is plain too much: overwhelming overload. Enough is enough is enough. No one knows better than you when you've reached or gone past your limit. So, when enough is definitely enough, find a place to escape reality and don't come back until you have to."[1]

Two Main Approaches to Stress

Readers of our *Love Line* newsletter and other folks who hear me speak constantly send me ideas that work for them when handling stress. As I sort through them all, there seem to be two main approaches to dealing with stress:

1. DO SOMETHING. Be efficient, set priorities, use time wisely, etc.

2. DO NOTHING. Relax, escape, let go, let God.

Sometimes it really helps to *take action* to relieve your stress. I can recall years ago when my mother used to come from Michigan to California for visits and while she was here she would try to do things that she thought would help me.

One of her favorite tasks was rearranging all my cupboards. Because I am left-handed, my mother always decided every-thing was in the wrong place. So she would switch the kitchen all around to make it handy for right-handed people—like herself. When she got my kitchen organized, she asked if she could work in the yard. Unfortunately for Mom, the yard was in good shape, but Bill thought of a way to keep her busy because she was driving him a little bonkers, too.

Before Bill would leave for work early in the morning, he would be out there in the yard, shaking our two trees and causing the leaves to fall. I suppose the neighbors wondered what Bill was doing at 7:00 A.M., shaking the trees in our back-yard. I'm not sure that we ever told them he was just trying to give his mother-in-law something to do—rake up the leaves—so she could feel "helpful" by making herself useful.

Mom never stopped trying to help. Ironically, when people try to help, they often cause more stress than if they hadn't bothered. In her case, this was, oh, so true. During one of her visits, Barney, who was quite young at the time, had a dreadful cold and cough. Mom offered to stay home with him while we went to church and I gave her some medicated, *non-rubbing* Musterole to put on his chest. Like most mothers, she felt she knew all about taking care of children, and she neglected to heed my advice and my clear instructions that this was the *non-rubbing* kind of Musterole.

She went ahead and massaged it right into Barney, rubbing around and around his face, ears, chest, and throat. When we got home from church, Barney's face was swollen, his eyes were puffy, his ears burned a bright red, and his chest was on fire. At least she hadn't put on an old-fashioned mustard plaster on him to "hold in the heat." Mom had good intentions—she just didn't always listen to instructions.

Cat Food Salad and Stress

Another good way to cope with stress is to be flexible. When you think about it, a lot of stress is caused just because folks can't change their plans, can't take less than they had planned to, can't do less than they had planned to do, etc.

But sometimes, stress causes you to change your plans because you really don't have any choice.

Some years ago, we had a Swedish girl who came to live with us. Helga had relatives here, but they loaned her to us to help with the housework while she learned English. Helga stayed with us for almost a year and during that time we enjoyed taking her around California and showing her the sights. Helga was slowly learning to speak some English but hadn't mastered READING it yet.

One day I was planning on having about twenty gals over for a shower/luncheon to honor one girl who was getting married. While I went out shopping for decorations, I left Helga at home making up the tuna salad that would be the main dish for our luncheon. Helga loved to make special creations out of radishes by making them into rosebuds. She was also skilled at turning celery and carrots into fancy shapes. The plan was for Helga to make a bed of lettuce, radish rosebuds, carrot and celery curls, and then top it off with a big scoop of tuna fish mixed with hard-boiled eggs and garnished with olives.

As I came through the door with the decorations, I was overwhelmed by a terrible smell that seemed to permeate the entire house. I went into the kitchen and there on the counter were all of the luncheon salad plates, beautifully assembled, and ready to serve. But the fishy odor was overwhelming!

I picked up one of the salads, took a strong whiff, and then realized what had happened. Quickly, I opened the cupboard where we kept the trash, and there were at least a dozen empty cans that had once held CAT food. I should have realized that Helga could easily mix up cat food with tuna fish. After all, the cat-food can had a picture of a little fish on it and it was natural enough for Helga, who couldn't read English, to think that she had the right can. Helga was so proud of how lovely her salad plates looked with the radish rosebuds and the carrot and celery curls, all sprouting around each scoop of cat food. She had worked hard to make everything special, but the fishy SMELL was enough to knock your socks off!! I was reminded

---

TWENTY ACTIVE WAYS TO COPE WITH STRESS

Following are twenty ways to cope with stress that involve taking decisive action, doing something to deal with whatever may be causing stress in your life.

Get up fifteen minutes earlier . . . Prepare for the morning the night before . . . Set appointments ahead . . . Make duplicate keys . . . Always make copies of important papers . . . Repair anything that doesn't work properly . . . Ask for help with the jobs you dislike . . . Have goals for yourself . . . Stop a bad habit . . . Ask someone to be your "vent partner" . . . Do it today . . . Plant a tree . . . Feed the birds . . . Stand up and stretch . . . Memorize a joke . . . Exercise every day . . . Learn the words to a new song . . . Get to work early . . . Clean out one closet . . . Write a note to a faraway friend.[2]

---

of a sign I saw at a fish market: "Our fish are so fresh, it makes you wanna *smack 'em!*"

With twenty women due to arrive in just a few minutes, you might say, I was under STRESS. I decided the only thing to do was to take everyone out to lunch at a cafeteria while we left all the windows open to air out the house. We would come back later for the shower festivities, hoping that most of the smell would be gone.

It all worked out pretty well. We could still smell cat food as the guest of honor opened her shower gifts, but we all had a hearty laugh about the mixup. Without a doubt, it was a shower we'll all remember, and it reinforced for me the importance of being flexible under stress.

Diabetes—Sword of Damocles

There are lots of ways to cope with stress. Above are twenty different tips for dealing with stress ACTIVELY by doing

---

TWENTY RELAXING WAYS TO DEAL WITH STRESS

Following are twenty ways to deal with stress that can help you relax and try to "go with the flow" rather than getting tense or upright.

Tickle a baby . . . Pet a friendly dog or cat . . . Don't know all the answers . . . Look for the silver lining . . . Say something nice to someone . . . Teach a kid to fly a kite . . . Walk in the rain . . . Schedule play time into every day . . . Take a bubble bath . . . Read a poem . . . Listen to a symphony . . . Play patty cake with a toddler . . . Take a different route to work . . . Remember that stress is an attitude . . . Remember you always have options . . . Have a support network of people, places, and things . . . Quit trying to "fix" other people . . . Get enough sleep . . . Talk less and listen more . . . Relax, take each day at a time, you have the rest of your life to live.[3]

---

something, or taking care of something. Above are twenty EASY-GOING ways to deal with stress by slowing down and taking time for things that are relaxing and restful.

As I cope with my latest "stress companion"—diabetes—I find myself trying to balance action by taking time to slow down. There is a lot of stress in just HAVING diabetes, a relatively unfamiliar disease to the general public because only about five million people are affected. When I was diagnosed with adult-onset diabetes a few years ago, I asked my doctor, "Is there any way to fix it?"

"No, you'll have it forever."

"You mean there's no cure?"

"No," said my doctor, "and in all probability it will get worse. Your pancreas is pooped out and isn't working any more. You'll have to change your whole lifestyle to adjust to this."

"Adjusting" to diabetes means continually balancing out your diet, doing proper exercise, and "avoiding stress." You have to poke a hole in your finger five or six times a day to monitor your blood sugar. You get up in the morning and your first thought is, *Time to prick my finger and check my blood sugar.*

You have to keep careful track of what you eat, and if you eat the wrong thing today, you'd better be sure you don't do it again tomorrow! You have to keep your blood sugar regulated all the time and hopefully you will avoid some of the severe complications of diabetes.

Diabetes is like the sword of Damocles dangling above your head. Blindness, amputations, kidney problems, or neuropathy (lack of feeling in the feet) are just a few of the possible problems it can cause.

This poem by Ernest Lowe vividly describes what it's like to have diabetes:

> To be told
> your cells are unhealthy,
> your capillaries . . . even your blood . . .
>   well, maybe not unhealthy,
> just abnormal.
> To be told you will most likely
> live a few years less
> and maybe you shouldn't have a kid,
> in fact—if you get a bad doc—
> maybe you should be sterilized.
>
> To be told you have to get under control
> while people ask you
>   "Why are you so controlling?"
>
> To be told you can live just like normal
> people if you will just watch your blood
> sugar, food, salt consumption, exercise, urine,
> schedule, feet, and stress,

24 hours a day,
7 days a week,
365 days a year . . .
That's what it's like
to be told you're diabetic!

Now then,
what can I tell myself?
They're talking statistics
and I'm living life,
my life like no other.

I tell myself
I make choices and sure I'm in
control, with every choice I make,
even the ones they call wrong.

I tell myself
this so-called burden
is also a gift to remind me
how precious each day can be—
the gift of knowing I'll live till I die.

That's what it's like to remember
I'm human.[4]

Scripture Washes Away Life's Doo-Doo

Just knowing you have diabetes is stressful. You are always wondering, did I eat enough grams of THIS? Did I avoid enough grams of THAT?

I've often smiled over my doctor's advice to "avoid stress." Any emotional hassle, such as an accident or an argument, and your blood sugar shoots way up. For the diabetic, this can cause complications.

So I try to avoid controversial things and just concentrate on helping people. But there is no way to get away from the stress of Spatula Ministries. The phone rings constantly, mail is always arriving, and new voices are pouring out their fresh heartbreaks. Fortunately, talking on the phone doesn't seem that stressful, maybe because the other person is doing most of the talking and crying while I am just listening.

Our monthly Spatula Ministries meetings do cause a lot of stress, however. When fifty to sixty people are sitting in one room letting out their anger, hurt, and anguish, it can get stressful, believe me! Then there are the "after-meeting" conversations that sometimes take hours. Sometimes folks ask how *I* get replenished. They want to know what I do to have my emotional tank filled.

One of my favorite ways to renew my spirit is to take a warm bubblebath with my tape player nearby so I can listen to my favorite Christian music or the reading of Scripture. The combination of water and music is therapy for me. I also have several videos featuring beautiful scenery with a narrator reading passages like Isaiah 26:3 (TLB): "He will keep in perfect peace all those who trust in Him, whose thoughts turn often to the Lord!"

My tapes and videos allow Scripture to come in and cleanse me after living in the daily doo-doo of life. We need to be renewed and refreshed, and I find that Scripture is like water washing over me. I feel as though I've had a spiritual bath that cleanses my mind and soul, and I'm reminded of a verse in Ezekiel where God says: "I will sprinkle clean water on you, and you will be clean; I will cleanse you from all your impurities. . . ."[5]

The other night I sat in a restaurant parking lot until 2:00 A.M. helping a young man dying of AIDS plan his funeral. It was too difficult for his parents, but he needed to talk about it. Although listening to him was stressful, I came home feeling honored because he wanted me to help make plans for what he knew was coming.

Afterward, I came home, and as I watched a Scripture video, I felt God's Word replenishing my joy.

When speaking for women's groups, I say, "You may think you have it all together, but then something will come along to remind you that you NEVER have it all together, no matter how old, no matter how much experience you have. The older you get, the more you realize that you get one wall up and the other wall falls down. If it's not a physical problem, it'll be emotional or mental. The point is that *you have to accept what life hands you.* You'll never have all the walls up at the same time— at least not on this earth anyway."

We live in a broken world. That's why Proverbs 3:5, 6 makes so much sense:

> TRUST IN THE LORD WITH ALL YOUR HEART,
> AND LEAN NOT ON YOUR OWN UNDERSTANDING;
> IN ALL YOUR WAYS ACKNOWLEDGE HIM,
> AND HE SHALL DIRECT YOUR PATHS. (NKJV)

The stress will always be there, but God will always be there, too, and that gives you the edge!

Splish/Splash . . .

> WORRY IS WASTING TODAY'S TIME
> TO CLUTTER UP TOMORROW'S OPPORTUNITIES
> WITH YESTERDAY'S TROUBLES.

*   *   *   *   *   *

> THERE WILL BE NO CRISIS NEXT WEEK.
> MY SCHEDULE IS ALREADY FULL.

*   *   *   *   *   *

> THE PEOPLE WHO TELL YOU NEVER TO LET LITTLE THINGS
> WORRY YOU HAVE NEVER TRIED SLEEPING IN THE SAME
> ROOM WITH A MOSQUITO.

*   *   *   *   *   *

> IF YOU TREAT EVERY SITUATION
> AS A LIFE-AND-DEATH MATTER,
> YOU WILL DIE A LOT OF TIMES.

* * * * * *

WE CRUCIFY OURSELVES BETWEEN TWO THIEVES:
REGRET FOR YESTERDAY
AND FEAR OF WHAT TOMORROW MAY BRING.

* * * * * *

NOTHING IS IMPOSSIBLE
TO THE PEOPLE
WHO DON'T HAVE TO
DO IT THEMSELVES.

* * * * * *

I'M NOT GOING TO WORRY
UNLESS THE ANIMALS START LINING UP
TWO BY TWO FOR THE NEXT SPACE SHUTTLE!

* * * * * *

How often we look upon God as our last and feeblest
resource. We go to Him because we have nowhere else to go.
And then we learn that the storms of life have driven us, not
upon the rocks, but into the desired haven.

George MacDonald

* * * * * *

THINGS WILL PROBABLY COME OUT ALL RIGHT,
BUT SOMETIMES IT TAKES STRONG NERVES
JUST TO WATCH.

* * * * * *

FAITH MAKES
THE UPLOOK GOOD,
THE OUTLOOK BRIGHT,
THE INLOOK FAVORABLE,
AND THE FUTURE GLORIOUS.

* * * * * *

Don't worry about anything; instead, pray about everything; tell God your needs and don't forget to thank him for his answers. (Phil. 4:6, TLB)

Laugh and the World Laughs with You . . . Cry and You Simply Get Wet!

Nothing beats fun.

Dear Barbara,

I received your book as a Mother's Day gift. I haven't read a book in years, but this one is so good I couldn't put it down. I also haven't laughed in about seven years. I thought I forgot how.

* * * * * *

Dear Barbara and Gopher Bill,

I am single, never married, no children, but your answers to dealing with some of your problems were a real encouragement to me. I really enjoyed the humor in your book. Laughter really is a pick-me-up.

* * * * * *

Dear Spatula Ministries,

I've been living a shaky life . . . grief, pain . . . all jumbled up inside. I felt like I couldn't share because so much had happened . . . I felt like a Christian "freak." I found your book at

303

the grocery store. I've laughed like I haven't for three years. I've also wept until the grief felt gone. Thank you for sharing and giving me a glimpse of hope.

* * * * * *

Dear Barbara,

I needed your words the day I read them for the laughter that parts of the book triggered. There truly is NOTHING like a deep, gut-stirring, tear-streaming laugh. I thank you!

* * * * * *

These letters are all reflections on what God said long ago: "A happy heart is like good medicine. But a broken spirit drains your strength" (Prov. 17:22, NCV). Recently I had the opportunity to share my story at a retreat, and afterward the gals filled out an evaluation of what they liked about the weekend. As I looked over a copy of my "report card," one phrase kept popping up: "I loved the humor and the chance to laugh." Everywhere I go there is the same response. Folks do love to laugh, and when you think about what laughter can do, it's easy to see why.

A Good Laugh Is the Best Medicine

Someone said the best doctors in the world are Dr. Diet, Dr. Quiet, and Dr. Merryman. Laughter actually produces positive physiological results. For example, it exercises the lungs and stimulates the circulatory system. When you laugh, your body is revitalized by what could be called internal massage. Laughter, as somebody said, is like jogging on the inside.

Because laughter is therapeutic, hospitals are developing "laughter programs" and doctors are actually "prescribing" mirth as a way to get well. At Johns Hopkins Hospital, they show "Candid Camera," "The Three Stooges," and other comedy films on closed-circuit television. Down in Texas at one Catholic hospital, the nuns tell funny stories to patients on a daily basis to help them feel better.[1]

In his book, *Anatomy of an Illness as Perceived by the Patient: Reflections on Healing and Regeneration,* Norman Cousins told about his battle with an incurable and excruciatingly painful disease. His body's collagen, the fibrous material holding his cells together, was deteriorating, and he was, in his own words, "becoming unstuck." Gravel-like substances under his skin produced nodules on his body and he was having difficulty moving his neck, hands, arms, fingers, and legs. Doctors put the odds for his recovery at five hundred to one.

With his doctor's approval, Cousins decided to treat himself by eating healthy food, taking vitamins, particularly vitamin C, and undergoing what he called "laugh therapy." Because he wasn't sure the other patients in the hospital were ready for his new approach, he checked out of the hospital and into a hotel room, bringing along a lot of "Candid Camera" clips, Marx brothers movies, and cartoons—anything that might make him laugh. He watched all these again and again and after a while he developed a formula. If he laughed hard for ten minutes straight, he would have two hours of painlessness. Cousins amazed doctors by eventually recovering.[2]

How Laughing Controls Pain

The experts say that laughter helps control pain in four ways: (1) by distracting attention, (2) by reducing tension, (3) by changing expectations, and (4) by increasing the production of endorphins, the body's natural pain killers.[3]

When you laugh, it takes your mind off the pain and actually creates a degree of anesthesia. You don't feel the pain as much because your attention is elsewhere.

All of us are familiar with how anxiety, worry, and stress can cause tension in the head and the neck muscles; the result is often another Excedrin headache. Laughter reduces muscle tension and has even been known to have the same effect on a headache as aspirin or other pain relievers.

Another thing about laughter is its ability to change your expectations, or, in other words, change your attitude. In a way, laughter is like a shock absorber that eases the blows of life.

Dr. David Bresler, director of the UCLA Pain Control Unit, says that pain is the most common, expensive, and disabling disorder in the United States, but that you can eliminate a great deal of pain by simply changing your mind. "Almost always, people who have chronic pain are also depressed," says Dr. Bresler. "It's not just their lower back that hurts, their life hurts and they have places that hurt in their lower back."[4]

In other words, our general attitude toward life is directly related to our sensitivity to pain. Laughter and humor are related to a positive outlook and a will to live.

Laughter could be called a tranquilizer with no side effects. When you laugh, the pituitary gland releases those endorphins mentioned earlier, which are "chemical cousins" of drugs like heroin and morphine.[5] The more you laugh, the more the level of endorphins in the brain increases and the more your perception of pain decreases. Laughter causes your body to literally produce its own anesthetic.

Not only is laughter healing, it helps keep you in shape and able to fight off disease. One Stanford professor discovered that laughter is like good exercise—equal to running, swimming, or rowing. Dr. William Fry's research showed that laughter increases the heart rate, improves circulation, and works the muscles of the face and stomach. Dr. Fry learned that if he spent ten seconds doing hard belly laughing, it would raise his heart rate to the same level he would reach in ten minutes of rowing (a very strenuous exercise). Thus, he estimates that if you laugh one hundred times a day, it will have the same training effect as a ten-minute workout on a rowing machine.[6]

Laughter Is Good for Your Soul

Laughter is not only good for the body, it's good for the soul. Psychologically, the ability to see humor in a situation is as important as the laughter, itself. A sense of humor can help you overlook the unattractive, tolerate the unpleasant, cope with the unexpected, and smile through the unbearable. A genuine sense of humor is the pole that adds balance to our steps as we walk the tightrope of life. And, if we happen to fall into one of life's inevitable cesspools, a healthy sense of humor can help us cope. I like the saying:

> OUR FIVE SENSES ARE INCOMPLETE
> WITHOUT THE SIXTH—A SENSE OF HUMOR.

Having a sense of humor doesn't mean that you go around laughing at everything. A person with a sense of humor doesn't make jokes out of life; she only sees the ones that are already there. In other words, you can see the funny side along with the serious side.

My friend, Marilyn Meberg, who is a conference speaker as well as a family counselor, says that many of us take ourselves too seriously. We worry about always looking good, correct, and dignified. The result is that we miss out on a lot of fun.

Speaking at one weekend conference, Marilyn said, "There are things that will happen to you that cause you to feel you have lost control. But if you can laugh at yourself and the circumstances, you've regained control. Circumstances will not control you if you turn them around and make something funny out of them. My suggestion to you is that there are many, many times in your daily experience when you can turn your situation around and laugh. Laugh at the situation. Laugh at yourself. When you do, you're in charge instead of it being in charge of you."[7]

That reminds me of something else that's well worth remembering:

HAPPY IS THE WOMAN WHO CAN LAUGH AT HERSELF;
SHE WILL NEVER CEASE TO BE AMUSED.

I believe that if we can divide our problems into those that can be solved quickly and those that cannot, we will have come a long way toward relaxing when confronted with things that we cannot change. Humor is God's weapon against worry, anxiety, and fear. Remember that:

FEAR IS THE DARKROOM
WHERE NEGATIVES ARE DEVELOPED.

Job said with subtle wisdom, "For the thing I greatly feared has come upon me, and what I dreaded has happened. . . ."[8] Negative thoughts give birth to negative ordeals, and positive thoughts yield positive experiences. Laughing people can survive and land on their feet. Those who cannot laugh will stay in the cesspool of despair.

As somebody said, your day goes the way the corners of your mouth turn. Life is like a mirror. If we frown at it, it frowns back. If we smile, it returns the greeting. Every Christmas I like to remember that the best Yuletide decoration is being wreathed in smiles.

Laughter helps us love one another. In his best-selling book, *Loving Each Other*, Leo Buscaglia said: "A bond of love is easy to find in an environment of joy. When we laugh together, we bypass reason and logic as the clown does. We speak a universal language. We feel closer to one another."[9]

Glad and happy sharing creates *koinonia*—a Greek word that means "loving fellowship." By contrast, sad, depressing conversations are counterproductive. Who of us has not watched tensions dissolve in the presence of love and humor? We see this happen continually in our Spatula meetings. Deep pain is present. Abscesses are festering with anguish and pain, waiting to be opened and drained. Sometimes the depressing stories can become almost overwhelming, but then somebody will say something humorous and it will pick up the mood of everyone there. We all feel lifted above the pain we are bearing together.

For example, at a recent meeting of our Spatula chapter, a grief-stricken father was sharing about his son, who had decided to become a girl. He was going to be taking his son to dinner and his son had already let him know that he would be coming "in drag," that is, dressed as a woman.

Heartbroken, with tears in his eyes, the father said, "I don't know what to do. How can I handle this?"

There were about fifty people in the room, but you could hear a pin drop. Finally, the silence became so unbearable I decided somebody had to say something; so, to lighten up the situation, I suggested, "Maybe you could wear your wife's clothes and your son would feel more comfortable."

There was a moment of stunned silence. Then somebody started to laugh, and pretty soon we were all laughing, including the father. Humor had stepped in to save the situation when logic or good, practical advice wouldn't have helped a great deal. Besides, there is no "good, practical advice" in such an impossible situation.

There are many reasons to laugh, so go ahead. Since it takes forty-three muscles to frown but only seventeen muscles to smile, why not conserve energy? Keep this in mind:

> AN OPTIMIST LAUGHS TO FORGET;
> THE PESSIMIST FORGETS TO LAUGH.

Here's another thought that may help you keep things in perspective:

> There are two days in every week about which we should not worry, two days which should be kept free from fear and apprehension.
>
> One of the two days is YESTERDAY, with its mistakes and cares, its faults and blunders, its aches and pains. Yesterday has passed forever beyond our control. All the money in the world cannot bring back yesterday. We cannot undo a single act we performed. We cannot erase a single word we said. Yesterday is gone.

The other day we should not worry about is TOMORROW, with its possible adversities, its burden, its large promise and poor performance. Tomorrow is also beyond our immediate control. Tomorrow's sun will rise, either in splendor or behind a mask of clouds—but it *will* rise. Until it does, we have no stake in tomorrow, for it is yet unborn.

This leaves only one day—TODAY—anyone can fight the battles of just one day. It is only when you and I add the burdens of those two awful eternities—yesterday and tomorrow—that we break down.

It is not the experience of today that drives us mad—it is remorse or bitterness for something which happened yesterday and the dread of what tomorrow may bring.

Let us, therefore, live but one day at a time.

Source unknown

MOTORCYCLE COWASOCKY

Just a reminder that we are all udderly flawed !

And, I might add, let's live it with smiles on our faces!

It's funny what becomes funny to us. When you think about it, we really laugh about serious things: money, family, parents, children, sex—even death. (Perhaps you have heard of the funeral director who signed all his letters, "Eventually yours.") Life is full of tensions, stress, and grim realities. When we need a break now and then, how do we spell relief?

L-A-U-G-H

As somebody said, laughter is the cheapest luxury we have. It clears up the blood, expands the chest, electrifies the nerves, clears away the cobwebs from the brain, and gives the whole system a good cleansing. I really believe laughter is the sweetest music that ever greeted the human ear, and I also believe God loves to hear our laughter.

Out of the Mouths of Babes

I'm continually receiving stories, jokes, clippings, and quips, and one of the most popular categories is children. Kids cause their share of pain and worry, but they're also good for laughs (fortunately for them!).

I ran across a story (I don't know who wrote it) about some children who started dropping coins into a wishing well, whispering aloud their wishes.

"I wish I had a puppy," said one.

"I wish I had a race car," said another.

A boy about ten years of age walked up and looked thoughtfully into the well. Then, grudgingly, he tossed in his coin and muttered, "I wish I had a magnet."

President Lyndon Johnson used to tell a story about a little boy who wanted some money very badly because his daddy had died and his mother was having a hard time making ends meet. The boy wrote a letter to God, asking for a hundred dollars to help his mama. He mailed the letter and it wound up on the Postmaster General's desk. The gentleman was so touched he slipped a twenty-dollar bill into an envelope and mailed it back to the youngster. Two weeks later, another letter to God from the little boy wound up on the Postmaster General's desk. It said, "Much obliged for all you've done, but the next time, please don't route it through Washington because they deducted eighty dollars."[10]

Another one of my favorites comes from a mother who has four grown children. One is living with a girl and they aren't married, another is an alcoholic, a third is on drugs, and the youngest is gay. She told me, "Barb, I should never have had kids. I should have had RABBITS. At least THAT way I would have gotten one good meal out of the deal."

Goofs Are Always Good for a Laugh

It's fun to collect funny sayings and improper uses of words, sometimes called malapropisms. One list I found included these samples:

- If you can't do it right, do it yourself.
- Arrogance is bliss.
- Abstinence makes the heart grow fonder.
- No news travels fast.
- Every clown has a silver lining.
- Run it up the flag pole and see who sits on it.
- Am I my brother's beeper?
- No man can serve two masters with one stone.
- Rome wasn't burned in a day.
- It's on the fork of my tongue.
- Take it with a grain of truth.
- That's the frosting on the gravy.
- People who live in glass houses shouldn't throw sour grapes.[11]

But one of my all-time favorites about goofs is an old story that has made the rounds, especially among newspaper publishers and editors who have to live with an irritating fact of life called the typographical error. We've all seen typos in newspapers, but here is an example of how an error got into the classified section of a small-town daily, and the more they tried to correct it, the more disastrous it became:

(Monday) FOR SALE—R. D. Jones has one sewing machine for sale. Phone 555–0707 after 7 P.M. and ask for Mrs. Kelly who lives with him cheap.

(Tuesday) NOTICE—We regret having erred in R. D. Jones's ad yesterday. It should have read: One sewing machine for sale. Cheap: 555–0707 and ask for Mrs. Kelly who lives with him after 7 P.M.

(Wednesday) NOTICE—R.D. Jones has informed us that he has received several annoying telephone calls because of the error we made in his classified ad yesterday. His ad stands corrected as follows: FOR SALE—R. D. Jones has one sewing machine for sale. Cheap. Phone 555–0707 and ask for Mrs. Kelly who loves with him.

(Thursday) NOTICE—I, R. D. Jones, have NO sewing machine for sale. I SMASHED IT. Don't call 555–0707, as the telephone has been disconnected. I have NOT been carrying on with Mrs. Kelly. Until yesterday she was my housekeeper, but she quit.[12]

Laughs from the Book of Parables

The Bible may be the world's best seller, but it isn't necessarily always the world's best-studied book. People get biblical knowledge mixed up, as this story shows:

A freshman entering Bible college was asked what part of the Bible he liked best.

"Well, I like the New Testament best," he answered.

"What book do you like in the New Testament?" the interviewer wanted to know.

"Oh, by far, I like the Book of Parables best," the freshman replied.

"Would you kindly relate one of those parables to me?" the interviewer asked.

The freshman complied, saying, "Once upon a time, a man went down from Jerusalem to Jericho and fell among thieves. And the thorns grew up and choked that man. And he went on and met the Queen of Sheba and she gave that man a thousand talents of gold and silver and a hundred changes of raiment. And he got in his chariot and drove furiously, and as he was driving under a big tree his hair got caught in a limb and left him hanging there.

"And he hung there many days and many nights and the ravens brought him food to eat and water to drink. And one night while he was hanging there asleep, his wife, Delilah, came along and cut off his hair. And he dropped and fell on stony ground. And it began to rain, and it rained forty days and forty nights. And he hid himself in a cave. And he went out and met a man and said, 'Come and take supper with me in my cave.' But the man answered, 'I cannot for I have married a wife.' And the cave-dweller went out into the highways and byways and compelled people to come in.

"And he went on and came to Jericho and he saw Queen Jezebel sitting high up in a window and when she saw him she laughed. And he said, 'Throw her down.' He said, 'Throw her down' again. And they threw her down seventy times seven. And of the fragments they picked up twelve baskets. And now, what I want to know is, Whose wife will she be on the day of resurrection?"

Source unknown

The hapless freshman's biblical confusion might make us smile; and it might remind some of us of how we've gotten certain biblical concepts a little twisted around ourselves. But on occasion I like to balance this kind of church humor with something I found while traveling in Nevada not too long ago.

High on a hill above Reno stands a large church called the Reno Christian Fellowship. Like a beacon, it overlooks all the gaudy, brilliantly flashing casino signs in the streets below. From this pinnacle, you can view the entire city and then see the twinkling lights fade off into the desert beyond.

Goal: Educators & spiritual mentors

Missionaries work to develop strong leaders that can take over the responsibilities of a ministry in their own countries.

Why?

Jagga Juh-ER-uh

Gupta GOOP-tuh

Seukuman S Eu Kuh mahn

B / the communal & successful & outstanding national leaders

Ilt 2 Tim 2:30 on board

pg 304

Prov 17:22

My daughter-in-love, Shannon, had been to this church, and when I told her I was speaking there, she told me to be sure to see the sign posted as you start down the driveway to leave the church.

When I finished speaking and we were preparing to leave the parking lot, I suddenly remembered and said to Bill, "We must be sure to look for the sign Shannon told us about." As we started down the driveway that would take us to the road leading into Reno, there it was in large letters:

YOU ARE NOW ENTERING THE MISSION FIELD!

Reading that sign gave me goose bumps because its meaning reaches far beyond the Reno city limits. WHEREVER we live—THAT is our mission field!

When Life Gets Out of Control—Laugh

Marilyn Meberg tells a story that beautifully illustrates how we may be facing circumstances that seem to be controlling us. It describes how we can regain control by finding something to giggle about that gives us strength to get through the moment. It's not that we try to giggle away grief or death, but it is true that we can sometimes alleviate a measure of pain by finding something to laugh at for the moment.

Marilyn's mother died recently and prior to her death she requested that her body be cremated rather than having the usual funeral with people gazing upon her corpse and saying things like, "Oh, doesn't she look NATURAL!"

Marilyn did exactly as her mother asked and her body was cremated. Later, the mortuary called and asked Marilyn to come in and claim her mother's ashes. She and her husband, Ken, drove down to the mortuary and, while he waited in the car, she went inside. A man handed her a container about the size of a shoe box telling her, "Here are the cremains."

The box had her mother's name on it, the date of her birth, and the day she died. Carrying it gave Marilyn an eerie feeling.

Everything she had known of her mother in her earthly state was now supposedly shifting around in this little box.

She went out the door of the mortuary and walked toward the car, where she could see Ken looking at her from the front seat. Marilyn's husband had always adored her mother and she could tell he felt awkward about what she was carrying. So did Marilyn. And she had other feelings, too—pain, hurt, grief. The whole thing was becoming too grim and too hard to deal with.

Marilyn opened the car door, saw the look on Ken's face, and simultaneously assessed her own feelings. She felt a strong need to "lighten the moment," so she decided to put the cremains box on the backseat. As she did so, she leaned over warmly and said, "Mom, do you need a seatbelt?"

"MARILYN!" was all her husband could say, but Marilyn didn't mind. She had been hearing him say that for years whenever she did anything a little off the wall, which was pretty often.

Nonetheless, her concern about a seatbelt for Mom did the trick for the moment and lifted their spirits just a bit. She recalls, "It wasn't that I was being irreverent about my mother, or her cremains. It was just for those few seconds I needed to lighten the moment and feel that I had a measure of control rather than having the circumstances control me."[13]

Humor can lighten the grim, painful, and frustrating moments of life, as well as the times when no hope is in sight. The apostle Paul faced plenty of moments that were grim, painful, frustrating, and even hopeless. Yet he wrote: "We rejoice in the hope of the glory of God" (Rom. 5:2, NIV).

I believe laughter is like a needle and thread. Deftly used, it can patch up just about everything. That's why I urge folks to keep a joy box for mementos, greeting cards, clippings, and little knickknacks of every imaginable description, all of which can bring a smile or even a chuckle, especially when you're feeling discouraged. Years ago my joy box grew into a JOY ROOM that now takes up half of the mobile home where we live. Whenever I enter my Joy Room, I not only find smiles, I find hope.

On the back of the main door to the Joy Room is a huge sign with my favorite motto: "WHATEVER, LORD!" Beneath the sign sits a doll that looks like a little old lady, and she asks, "Dear God, if I give all my love away, can I have a refill?"

On a shelf nearby sits a darling little alarm clock/music box that can be set to wake you up to such tunes as, "It's a Small, Small World"; "Heigh Ho, Heigh Ho, It's Off to Work We Go"; "Zippity Do Dah"; and "Super-Cali-Fragil-Istic-Expi-Ali-Docious." Wouldn't every mom love to have one of these little clocks to help get her kids up for school?

A few feet away sits a little monkey on a perch, and when you turn the handle, his tail goes up and down and he makes funny noises. His sign says: "WELCOME TO THE NUT HOUSE."

A lot of friends send me sayings and mottoes done in cross-stitch. One of my favorites has two darling little bears surrounding the phrase, "Love Makes Life More Bearable."

Since *So, Stick a Geranium In Your Hat and Be Happy* came out, almost every time I speak at a banquet, I seem to pick up another geranium hat. I now have twenty-one of them on display in my Joy Room, reminding me of friends across the country.

My Joy Room walls are filled with many other signs, mottoes, and plaques. A few of my favorites include:

LIFE IS TOO IMPORTANT TO BE TAKEN SERIOUSLY.

*   *   *   *   *   *

I am wonderful, marvelous, extra-special, unique, first-rate, exceptional, outrageous, surprising, superlative—and, above all—HUMBLE.

*   *   *   *   *   *

MID-LIFE CRISIS:
WHEN MORTGAGE PAYMENTS AND THE TUITION BILL
EQUAL MORE THAN YOU MAKE.

*   *   *   *   *   *

THINGS ARE LOOKING UP . . .
I'M NOW ONLY TWO WEEKS BEHIND.

*   *   *   *   *   *

Another plaque that I especially like is a Scripture verse carved in wood by Bob Davies, my good friend at Love in Action:

> In the fear of the Lord, one has strong confidence, and His children will have a refuge.
>
> Proverbs 14:26, RSV

I also love the miniature wagon that sits in one corner with a sign painted on its side: "Lord, I need a push!" Another favorite is a hot-water bottle shaped like a woolly lamb. When filled he becomes fat and fluffy.

Almost everything in my Joy Room has been sent to me by someone. One special note mounted on the wall comes from a group of people in the Midwest who are all parents of homosexual children. They call themselves "The Humpty-Dumpties," and they sent me a poem that expresses perfectly the spirit of my Joy Room because it offers a smile along with a reminder of the hope we have through faith in God:

> GOOD MORNING, HUMPTY DUMPTY, SIR,
> HOW AMAZING, YOU'RE STILL HERE!
> BY LEGEND YOU WERE SHATTERED,
> HOW COHESIVE YOU APPEAR.
>
> HUMPTY JUMPED, AND SAID WITH A SMILE,
> "THE TALE OF HORSES AND MEN

WASN'T THE END! THE KING HIMSELF,
PUT ME TOGETHER AGAIN!"

Keep Working On It

I opened this chapter with some comments from people who wrote to tell me how much they appreciate humor. Here is one more letter from a gal who really understands why nothing beats fun:

> You don't know me from Adam, but I feel I know you as a dear friend who helped me through an incredible crisis.
> Three weeks ago I had a mammogram. One day later I had a lumpectomy. Two weeks ago I had a mastectomy. Forty-eight hours later I was told the cancer had spread to the nodes. On that particular night (I was still in the hospital), I took a sleeping pill. Didn't work. I picked up the book my youngest daughter had brought in for me at the hospital. Your book. I read it through the night. I cried with you and laughed (especially at the pantyhose) with you. Whenever I feel I'm going into a downer I pick up your book again.
> Following your advice I've tried to come up with (something) funny each day. Yesterday's was:
> "I'll only go bra shopping if they'll give me 50 percent off."
> Pretty corny, really, but I'm working on it.

A lot of funny things ARE corny, but keep working on it, because laughter can always be heard further than weeping. Always—and I mean always—TAKE TIME TO LAUGH. It is the music of the soul!

Splish/Splash . . .

THERE IS HOPE FOR ANYONE WHO CAN LOOK IN A MIRROR
AND LAUGH AT WHAT HE SEES.

*　　*　　*　　*　　*　　*

ONE THING YOU CAN SAY FOR KIDS, AT LEAST THEY
DON'T BORE YOU WITH CUTE THINGS THEIR PARENTS
SAID.[14]

* * * * * *

Phyllis Diller says life is tough: "Did you ever look in a mirror and wonder how your pantyhose got so wrinkled . . . and
then remember you weren't wearing any?"[15]

* * * * * *

HUMOR IS THE HOLE
THAT LETS THE SAWDUST
OUT OF A STUFFED SHIRT.

* * * * * *

Do you know how you can tell if you are co-dependent?
When you are dying, you see someone else's life pass before
your eyes!

* * * * * *

The trouble with owning your own home is that, no matter
where you sit, it seems you're looking at something you should
be doing.[16]

* * * * * *

LITTLE BOY'S PRAYER

Dear God, take care of my family, take care of the whole
world. And please, God, take care of Yourself, or we're all sunk.

* * * * * *

A CONFUSED MOTHER WRITING TO HER SON . . .

Dear Son,

Just a few lines to let you know that I'm still alive. I'm writing this letter slowly because I know you cannot read fast. You won't know the house when you come home—we've moved.

About your father—he has a lovely new job. He has five hundred men under him. He is cutting the grass at the cemetery.

There was a washing machine in the new house when we moved in, but it isn't working very good. Last week I put fourteen shirts into it, pulled the chain, and I haven't seen the shirts since.

Your sister, Mary, had a baby this morning. I haven't found out whether it's a boy or a girl, so I don't know whether you're a aunt or an uncle.

Your Uncle Dick drowned last week in a vat of whiskey in the Dublin Brewery. Some of his workmates dived in to save him, but he fought them off bravely. We cremated his body and it took three days to put out the fire.

Your father didn't have much to drink at Christmas. I put a bottle of castor oil in his pint of beer—it kept him going 'til New Year's Day.

I went to the doctor on Thursday and your father came with me. The doctor put a small tube into my mouth and told me to keep it shut for ten minutes. Your father offered to buy it from him.

It only rained twice last week. First for three days, and then for four days. Monday it was so windy that one of our chickens laid the same egg four times.

We had a letter yesterday from the undertaker. He said if the last installment wasn't paid on your grandmother within five days, up she comes.

> Much love,
> Mother

P.S. I was going to send you ten dollars, but I had already sealed the envelope.

*   *   *   *   *   *

HE WHO LAUGHS LAST
PROBABLY INTENDED TO TELL THE STORY HIMSELF.

*   *   *   *   *   *

. . . the cheerful heart has a continual feast. (Prov. 15:15, NIV)

How Can I Be Over the Hill
When I Never Even Got to the Top?

*You're young only once
but you can be immature forever[1]*

Wherever I go, women agree that two of their least favorite subjects are AGING and DIETING. My advice is to not let either one steal your joy. I decided a long time ago to stop fretting over increasing years and extra pounds and relish each day instead.

That doesn't mean I ignore healthy eating, nor does it mean that I seldom exercise. Before having diabetes made exercise a must for me, I was not a real enthusiast about working out. My idea of exercise was a good, brisk sit, or maybe wrestling with the cellophane wrapper on a Twinkie.

To paraphrase the bumper "snicker," every time I thought about exercise, I would lie down until the thought went away. Or Bill and I would ride our bikes—right down to the corner doughnut shop in the morning for coffee and maple bars.

In *So, Stick A Geranium in Your Hat and Be Happy*, I told about Bill buying me a fabulous Schwinn indoor bicycle and setting it up in our Joy Room, where I am well equipped to utilize my time and never feel bored as I ride my new bike. If I want to read, there is a book stand mounted on the handle bars. If I want to talk on the phone, my Kermit the Frog telephone is within easy reach. If I want to watch a certain TV program, a small television set is on a table nearby. If I don't want to do any of those things, I just might want to enjoy all the fun stuff that is in my Joy Room as I pedal away. My exercise bike is a cool, clean, and classy way to do what I'm supposed to be doing --being active and exercising.

While I sometimes do all the things mentioned above, my favorite pastime is putting some zing into my prayer life. I have a big map of the United States posted on a wall in front of my bike, and as I ride I make imaginary trips from one town to another, visiting Spatula friends who have written me. Every time I reach a town from which I have received a letter, I pray for the letter writers, asking God to be a help and comfort to them that day.

Lately, my daughter-in-love, Shannon, has drawn me a NEW map of the United States, which I call my "Joy Map." The distinctive feature about this map is that it has actual towns whose names suggest joy, laughter, or something pleasant. I have this map mounted on the wall next to the other one, and now, from time to time, I travel from Bliss to Ecstasy, from Utopia to Sublime, from Yum Yum to Comfort, or from Bountiful to Prosperity. As I visit towns like this in my imagination, it is no trick at all to cover long distances in a single ride. It's really fun to start at Happy, Texas, and wind up in Joyful, Mississippi!

The Beach Ball Keeps Bobbing Back Up

Keeping weight down is a constant struggle for so many of us. Fighting the battle of the bulges is like holding a beach ball under water all your life. If you relax for just one minute, POW! Up it goes. Then it's a big struggle to get that ball back under the water again.

It seems that most of the time you're being forced to eat like a rabbit. After all, when you take all the fat, sugar, salt, and starch out of life, what's left except stuff that's high in tasteless fiber?

So, I have a lot of empathy for folks who struggle with weight and dieting. I know what it's like to struggle with wanting to eat and not being able to. The other day I ran across an old recording by the late Victor Buono, which included the following prayer by the tortured dieter:

> Lord, my soul is ripped with riot,
> Incited by my wicked diet.
> "We are what we eat," said a wise old man.
> Lord, if that's true, I'm a garbage can.
> I want to rise on Judgment Day, that's plain,
> But at my present weight I'll need a crane.
> So grant me strength that I may not fall
> Into the clutches of cholesterol.
> May my flesh with carrot curls be sated,
> That my soul may be polyunsaturated.
> And show me the light that I may bear witness
> To the President's Council on Physical Fitness.
> And oleo margarine I'll never mutter
> For the road to hell is spread with butter.
> And cream is cursed, and cake is awful,
> And Satan is hiding in every waffle.
> Mephistopheles lurks in provolone,
> The devil is in each slice of bologna.
> Beelzebub is a chocolate drop
> And Lucifer is a lollypop.
> Give me this day, my daily slice
> But cut it thin and toast it twice.
> I beg upon my dimpled knees,
> Deliver me from Ju Jubees
> And when my days of trial are done
> And my war with malted milks is won
> Let me stand with the saints in heaven
> In a shining robe, size thirty-seven!
> I can do it, Lord, if You'll show to me

The virtues of lettuce and celery
If You'll teach me the evil of mayonnaise
The sinfulness of hollandaise
And pasta Milanese
And potatoes à la Lyonnaise,
And crisp fried chicken from the South.
Lord, if You love me, SHUT MY MOUTH![2]

Calories That DON'T Count

When you're dieting, there is nothing easier than rationalizing why it might be okay to eat "just one" and then a few more, even though you know the stuff is loaded with grams of fat and tons of calories. In my own collection of dieter's rationalizations is the following list of "calories that don't count."

   1. **Food on Foot.** All food eaten while standing has no calories. Exactly why is not clear, but the current theory relates to gravity. The calories apparently bypass the stomach flowing directly down the legs, and through the soles of the feet into the floor, like electricity. Walking appears to accelerate this process, so that an ice cream bar or hot dog eaten at the state fair actually has a calorie deficit.
   2. **TV Food.** Anything eaten in front of the TV has no calories. This may have something to do with radiation leakage, which negates not only the calories in the food but all recollections of having eaten it.
   3. **Uneven Edges.** Pies and cakes should be cut neatly, in even wedges or slices. If not, the responsibility falls on the person putting them away to "straighten up the edges" by slicing away the offending irregularities, which have no calories when eaten.
   4. **Balanced Food.** If you drink a diet soda with a candy bar, they cancel each other out.
   5. **Left-Handed Food.** If you have a glass of punch in your right hand, anything eaten with the other hand has no calories. Several principles are at work here. First of all, you're probably standing up at a wedding reception (see Food on Foot). Then

there's the electronic field: A wet glass in one hand forms a negative charge to reverse the polarity of the calories attracted to the other hand. It's not quite known how it works, but it's reversible if you're left-handed.

6. Food for Medicinal Purposes. Food used for medicinal purposes NEVER counts. This includes hot chocolate, malted milk, toast, and Sara Lee cheesecake.

7. Whipped Cream, Sour Cream, Butter. These all act as a poultice that actually "draws out" the calories when placed on any food, leaving them calorie-free. Afterward, you can eat the poultice, too, as all calories are neutralized by it.

8. Food on Toothpicks. Sausage, mini-franks, cheese, and crackers are all fattening UNLESS impaled on frilled toothpicks. The insertion of a sharp object allows the calories to leak out the bottom.

9. Children's Food. Anything produced, purchased, or intended for minors is calorie-free when eaten by adults. This category covers a wide range, beginning with a spoonful of baby-food custard, consumed for demonstration purposes, up to and including cookies baked to send to college.

10. Charitable Foods. Girl Scout cookies, bake-sale cakes, ice-cream socials, and church strawberry festivals all have a religious dispensation from calories.

11. Custom-Made Food. Anything somebody makes "just for you" must be eaten regardless of the calories, because to do otherwise would be uncaring and insensitive. Your kind intentions will not go unrewarded.[3]

Dieting May Be Bad for Your Health

Like thousands of others, I've lost weight but always seem to find it again. Medical experts call it the "yo-yo syndrome" and I've had my share of those ups and downs. I keep dreaming of my slim, girlish figure, which is now carefully hidden under a lot of padding. That's why my all-time favorite cartoon is the one on the following page.

A lot of "fluffy" folks must have been encouraged when *Time* magazine came out with an article saying that much of the di-

eting that's been going on in recent years can be downright unhealthy. It said going through cycles of losing weight and then gaining it back can actually shorten your life. The famous Framingham Heart Study revealed that yo-yo dieters have a 70 percent higher risk of dying from heart disease than folks who are overweight but stay at a fairly steady level. The researchers concluded that the stress involved in losing and gaining weight back may increase your blood pressure and cholesterol levels, and that's why there is more danger of heart disease.[4]

The *Time* article didn't say that everyone should stop diet-ing, period. But what a lot of people need to do is set more realistic goals and not try to be the slim, sylph-like figures that are continually displayed on television. In 1990 the federal gov-ernment came out with new tables listing healthy weights for men and women that allow for a range of thirty pounds or more at each height, and up to a sixteen-pound gain after you reach age thirty-five. Another statistic, released by the Calorie Con-trol Council, says that the number of dieters in the United States has dropped from 65 million in 1986 to 48 million in 1991.[5]

My friend, Lynda, read about a fabulous idea for weight control. Doctors give you a balloon to swallow and then it is inflated in your stomach. Because the balloon keeps your stomach feeling "full," you don't want to eat and, of course, you lose weight. However, there is one STRING attached— literally! It is tied to the balloon and then extends back up the esophagus and hangs out the nose! (It seems the string is im-portant in case the balloon breaks or there is some other emergency.)

Lynda and I began brainstorming on what we would do if we swallowed one of these balloons and had the string hang-ing out of our nose. What if one of our grandchildren decided to pull on it? Or what if it got caught in our toothbrushes?

Then we got a brilliant idea. Why not tie a brightly colored bead on the end of the string and let it dangle there, making a fashion statement? When you became tired of that, you could try stuffing the string up your nose out of sight, but then it would undoubtedly itch and eventually you'd sneeze and out the string would pop! If you were having trouble getting con-versation started at some get-together that bead would surely do the trick!

The balloon idea sounded glorious except for that stupid string. Too bad. Lynda and I finally decided it was another miracle cure down the tube, or maybe you'd have to say up the nose. Whatever, we decided to skip on swallowing a bal-loon and keep on wrestling with the beach ball as best we can.

All We Need Is Maturity

One reason we like to laugh at our struggles with weight is because it's better than crying. After all, if we were "disciplined and mature," we could fight off these childish desires to eat too much of what isn't very good for us. I'm all for being mature, but the trouble is, the word suggests sainthood.

If you're mature, you're patient and willing to forego instant gratification, even when it is a carton labeled "Håagen Dazs."

If you are mature, you can persevere, no matter how tough things get or how discouraged you might be.

If you're mature, you can handle frustration, discomfort, failure, and all other kinds of unpleasantness.

Humble people are mature. They are able to say, "I was wrong," and when they're right they don't have to say, "I told you so."

When you're mature, you can make decisions and then even follow through on them. And, of course, being mature means being dependable, keeping your word, and not bailing out with alibis.[6]

Maturity means growing up—and growing up is always optional. On the other hand, growing old is *not* optional—it's mandatory. It just happens whether you're ready for it or not. As Ashleigh Brilliant says:

NOTHING IS MORE QUIET
THAN THE SOUND OF HAIR GOING GREY.[7]

Been to a Reunion Lately?

Because readers of the *Love Line* know I like to collect funny sayings and poems about aging, they are constantly telephoning or sending clippings in the mail. Today a lady called me and said she had just seen the following sign on a crematorium in, of all places, Palm Springs, California:

WE'RE HOT FOR YOUR BODY.

I've put together this commentary on aging, compiled from several sources:

> The material in dresses is so skimpy now, especially around the hips and waist, that it is almost impossible to reach one's shoelaces. And the sizes don't run the way they used to. The 12s and 14s are so much smaller.
>
> Even people are changing. They are so much younger than they used to be when I was their age. On the other hand, people my own age are so much older than I am.
>
> I ran into an old classmate the other day, and she has aged so much that she didn't recognize me.
>
> I got to thinking about the poor dear while I was combing my hair this morning, and in so doing I glanced at my own reflection. Really now, they don't even make good mirrors like they used to.

Another way to be reminded of the passing years is to go to a class reunion. You undoubtedly have been to one of these traumatic events, which are gatherings where you come to the conclusion that most of the people your own age are a lot older than you are. Another definition of a reunion is an event, "where everyone gets together to see who is falling apart."

I've never been to any kind of reunion—high school or college—but the other day I had the next best thing. While speaking at a conference I ran into two gentlemen who were in school with me over forty years ago. They were kind enough to say they recognized ME, but I must admit I could barely recognized THEM. It reminded me of how men are supposed to have three basic hair styles: parted, unparted, and departed. When I saw their bald pates, I was also reminded of the reason why men don't have to have facelifts: If they wait long enough, their face will grow right up through their hair!

Class reunions are times when nothing helps you recognize your old classmates as much as their nametags. It's such fun to come across pictures of myself when I was a young girl.

Somehow that sweet, young, high-school face seems more familiar to me than how I look now. I can still remember being so thin that I had to drink Ovaltine to gain weight. All I can say is, it sure did work!

For All Those Born "Before"

A sure sign that you're getting up there is that you can remember back when things were different—a LOT different! I often share the following list with audiences at retreats and other programs. It's something I've put together from several sources—and it often grows as soon as I've shared it because someone will suggest another difference I can add:

WHAT A DIFFERENCE FIFTY YEARS MAKES!

We were before the pill and the population explosion. We were before TV, penicillin, polio shots, antibiotics, and frisbees, before frozen food, nylon, dacron, Xerox, or Kinsey. We were before radar, fluorescent lights, credit cards, and ballpoint pens. For us, time-sharing meant togetherness, not computers or condominiums; a chip meant a piece of wood; hardware meant hardware; and software—well, software wasn't even a word.

In our time, closets were for clothes, not for coming out of, and being gay meant you were happy and carefree. In those days bunnies were small rabbits and rabbits were not Volkswagens.

We were before Batman, Rudolph the Red-Nosed Reindeer, and Snoopy. Before DDT and vitamin pills, disposable diapers, Jeeps, and the Jefferson nickel. We preceded Scotch tape, the Grand Coulee Dam, M&Ms, automatic transmissions, and Lincoln Continentals.

When we were in school, pizzas, Cheerios, frozen orange juice, instant coffee, and McDonald's were unheard-of. We thought fast food was what you ate during Lent.

We were before FM radio, tape recorders, electric typewriters, word processors, electronic music, digital clocks, and disco dancing.

We were before pantyhose and drip-dry clothes, before ice makers and dishwashers, clothes dryers, freezers, and electric blankets, before Hawaii and Alaska became states.

We were before Leonard Bernstein, yogurt, Ann Landers, plastics, hair spray, the forty-hour week, the minimum wage. We got married first and then lived together afterward. How quaint can you be?

In our day, grass was mowed, Coke was something you drank, and pot was something you cooked in.

We were before coin-operated vending machines, jet planes, helicopters, and interstate highways. In 1935 "made in Japan" meant junk, and the term "making out" referred to how you did on an exam.

We had fountain pens with bottles of real ink. We had stockings made of real silk with seams up the back that were never straight. We had saddle shoes and cars with rumble seats. We had corner ice-cream parlors with little tables and wire-back chairs where we had a choice of three flavors.

I have become unstuck in time, and in the springtime of my senility, I am a misfit. I don't like to jog. I don't know how to pump my own gas. My legs are white and my stockings are brown when the opposite is the style. I'm not into veggies or yoga or punk. My idea of a good time is to walk with a man, not jog with a Walkman.

I seek silence in a day when silence is as rare as a Gutenberg Bible. The man I live with is my husband and, after forty-two years, he's still the same one. How embarrassing!

Grandma Ain't What She Used to Be

For many of us older folks, grandchildren come with the territory. Somebody said:

JUST WHEN A WOMAN THINKS HER WORK IS DONE . . .
SHE BECOMES A GRANDMOTHER.

Actually, my two granddaughters, Kandee and Tiffany, are more fun than work.

When Kandee was about five years old, I took her with me while speaking at a conference. During song time, all of the words to the songs were displayed on a big screen, and when I looked out in the audience, I saw little Kandee singing lustily as if she could read every word to every song. I knew (or at least I thought) that Kandee couldn't read yet and later I asked her how she knew all the words to the songs. "Oh, Grandma Barb," Kandee said excitedly, "I don't know any of them. I just sing 'watermelon-peanut butter' and it all comes out right!"

When Tiffany was six, she saw me on television, talking about one of my favorite bumper stickers: LIFE IS HARD AND THEN YOU DIE. When I got back, Tiffany was still there and she told me politely but firmly, "Grandma Barb, what you ought to say is, 'Life is hard, and then you GET to die and be with Jesus!'" I took Tiffany's advice and have been saying it that way ever since.

I like being a grandmother, but I try not to become too "grandmotherly." This poem sums it up pretty well for me:

THE VERSATILE AGE

The old rocking chair is empty today
Grandma is no longer in it.
She is off in her car to her office or shop
And buzzes around every minute.

You won't see her trundling off early to bed
From her place in a warm chimney nook.
Her typewriter clickety-clacks through the night
For Grandma is writing a book.

Grandma ne'er takes a backward look
To slow her steady advancing
She won't tend the babies for you anymore
For Grandma is taking up dancing.

Source unknown

Growing Old with Mr. Wumphee

The other day I saw a cartoon picturing a wife sitting at one end of the sofa reading a magazine while her hubby slumped on the other end, fast asleep. The wife said: "Carl, if we're going to grow old together, you're going to have to slow up and wait for me."

That made me smile for two reasons: It was cute and I'm glad I don't have to say something like that to Bill. I'd say we're growing old together at just about an equal pace, even though I'm the sanguine and Mr. Wumphee is the pure melancholy. (In case you're wondering why I call Bill Mr. Wumphee, years ago he gave me the nickname "Cumphee." I needed a nickname for him and I came up with Wumphee, which doesn't mean anything, but at least it rhymes with Cumphee!)

I like dashing around, getting excited, and having FUN, while Bill is more dignified and deliberate about life. You can imagine his chagrin one night when we got into an elevator near the top floor of a big, new, fancy hotel, and I decided it might be fun to stop at every floor on the way down—to see if each one had the same decor, I guess. So I ran my finger down the panel, touching EVERY NUMBER!

Sure enough, the elevator obeyed my programming and stopped at EVERY FLOOR. People would get on and wonder what in the world was happening as the elevator stopped at every floor, the doors would open, and no one would get on— or off.

Bill sort of scrunched back in the corner and pretended he wasn't with me. No one knew I had done it, of course, so I acted as perplexed as the rest of them. "Wonder what's wrong with the system?" I said loudly. "You would think a brand new hotel could do better than THIS!" Everybody on board probably thought they just hadn't ironed out all the bugs yet. I wasn't about to tell them anything DIFFERENT!

We made twenty-two stops in all before we got to the lobby. It was a special memory for me, but a nightmare for Bill. Even now, when we get on an elevator where there are lots and lots of buttons, he starts to groan when I make a gesture as if I'm going to make one big SWIPE down the panel and repeat what happened that night. I'm only joking, of course, because I AM trying to become more mature as I get older.

Poor Bill. He doesn't think a lot of my crazy antics are much fun at all. His idea of a good time is getting the bumps on the bread matched when he makes sandwiches, or putting all the glasses in the cupboard according to correct size. He also likes categorizing the Spatula Ministries' bills each month in separate folders.

Just last Sunday we went over to a neighbor's house and Bill immediately noticed the telephone cord was all kinked up. So he spent fifteen minutes getting it totally straightened out and smooth again. Bill quickly spotted the messy cord because he's always straightening out ours. After I've been on the phone all day, it can get pretty twisted—and me along with it!

Bill is usually much better at remembering things and details than I am. He keeps track of the Spatula checking account and always balances the checkbook to the penny. In contrast, I handle our personal checking account, and if I come within a twenty-dollar difference from the bank statement, I feel I did great!

Bill may be a master at details, but tact and diplomacy aren't two of his strong points. One day I put on a new dress because I was going out to tape a TV program. Just before I left for the studio, I asked him if I looked okay. Bill said, "You look real nice and MATRONLY!"

Now, I know I AM a matron, but I don't want to be told I LOOK like one! I went back in the bedroom, changed into something else, and vowed never to wear the "matronly" dress again. Bill will probably never know how much that observation cost him. He made the remark innocently enough, I guess, because to him matronly means dignified or conservative, but to ME it means I'm ready for support hose.

Could Rubber Peanuts Be THAT Delicious?

Usually I have been the practical joker in the family, but every now and then Bill gets into the act, too, sometimes without realizing it. Several years ago—when Bill's mom was still

MY STAIR TREADS HAVE

STARTED TO WEAR OUT

HADLEY ROBERTSON

SO I'VE PLACED A RAISIN IN
THE MIDDLE OF EACH AS A
REMINDER TO USE THE
OUTSIDE EDGES FOR AWHILE.

alive—he would often drive over to spend the day with her and his dad. Because she loved all kinds of nuts, I would send along a casserole or some other dish made with nuts. Sometimes I'd just send a dish of assorted nuts for Grandma to nibble on.

It was around April Fools' Day and Bill was headed over to see his mom, so I decided to have some fun. I found a small package of RUBBER peanuts and sprinkled them in with the dish of mixed nuts I was sending over. I thought it would be cute to have Grandma try one of the rubber peanuts and get a chuckle out of the joke I had played on her.

I waited all day for Bill to come back home to tell me what happened when Grandma tried the rubber peanuts. He walked in and put the empty dish on the table and I asked, "Where are all the rubber peanuts? What did your mom say when she tried one?"

"I don't know," Bill said.

"What do you mean you don't know? All the rubber peanuts are GONE!"

"Well," said Bill, "I'm not sure what happened. I gave Mom the bowl and Dad and I went out grocery shopping. When we came back, the bowl was empty!"

"You mean she ate ALL the peanuts?" I asked in dismay.

Bill just sort of smiled and said, "When I asked her what she had done with the rubber peanuts, she just said, 'What rubber peanuts?'"

I know some of these crazy stories I tell are pretty hard to believe sometimes. But I promise you I am not making this up! And if you think about it, it is conceivable that Grandma had eaten the rubber peanuts without even noticing. After all, she was eighty-seven at the time and still had all her own teeth. She always ate everything I sent over eagerly and with gusto. Anyway, Grandma lived almost ten more years, so the rubber peanuts couldn't have been the cause of her passing!

Mr. Wumphee usually accompanies me on my out-of-town speaking trips. Recently we were in Spokane and somebody called Bill up on the stage to say a few words. Bill claims that he hates to do that, but he always seems to have a great time, and so does the audience.

. On that particular occasion, he said, "I have only one observation to make. I think that when you're married, you should be best friends, and that's why I'm happy to wear this 'Best Friends' button." And then he held up a button he had gotten at the conference with a picture of BOTH of us on it. So, while we're very different, we're very good for each other. We don't mind getting older, because we each have a best friend to do it with!

Plenty of Growing Up Left to Do

I'm still hoping to figure out what I want to be when I grow up. Every now and then I ask myself, *How could I have possibly come so far and still have so far to go?* A good goal—and I invite you to make it your goal, too—is to be what this poem calls a "mid-life grownup":

> We aren't as self-centered as we used to be.
> We're not as judgmental—or just plain dumb.
> Adulthood has come, and it brings
> (Along with deepening laugh lines)
> Some sweet compensations.
>
> We aren't as self-righteous as we used to be.
> We've learned to tell the real from the tinsel and fluff.
> Growing up is tough, but it brings
> (Along with receding gum lines)
> Some sweet compensations.
>
> We aren't as self-pitying as we used to be.
> We know what we like—in work, in play.
> There's still more growing ahead. May it bring
> (Along with a softened jaw line)
> Some sweet compensations.
>
> Source unknown

One of my favorite actresses is Angela Lansbury, who has made "Murder, She Wrote" almost a way of life for thousands of people across the country. I heard Angela interviewed on "Donahue" recently, and one woman in the audience said that her mother would not even answer the phone during the hour that "Murder, She Wrote" was broadcasting.

As I sat there admiring how Angela conducted herself on the "Donahue" show, I thought, *Angela Lansbury is my idea of what I want to be when I get to be her age.* But then I realized I AM her age—along with Shirley Temple, Mickey Mouse, and Erma Bombeck!

Be Childlike, Not Childish

To be honest, I suppose I'm more interested in becoming more childlike than becoming more mature. Note that I said child*like,* not child*ish.* Almost ten years ago I wrote a page for the September issue of our *Love Line* newsletter and said:

> Well, the kids are all starting school and most of us who are mothers at the age between estrogen and death don't have to think about back-to-school sales or packing lunches with "ants-on-a-log" (celery stuffed with peanut butter and raisins sprinkled on top). September brings to my mind kids and how I won't be one again or have one again. But I know there is still a child IN ME who helps me rediscover the sense of wonder and spontaneity that so many grownups lose along the way. I would like to share some thoughts about ways to KEEP that child in us alive!
>
> They say when you turn 40 life begins . . . but it begins to DISINTEGRATE! When you turn FIFTY, you really are in the stage between estrogen and death, and we are continually reminded that it takes more time and energy to just HOLD THE LINE! So what if the aging process happens . . . it hits EVERYONE! One neat thing is IT ISN'T YOUR FAULT! How wonderful to know that this situation isn't something we did to have it come on us! No blame-game here!

When I counsel mothers who are still "in the twilight zone," I encourage them to inject some humor in their lives. Our youth may be lost or fading, but by letting ourselves be a child again, we can tap into a boundless fountain within us. So learn to laugh. Kids laugh out of sheer joy . . . no big reason. Quit taking yourself so seriously. Do some fun things just because you want to be impulsive and adventurous. If your life is so planned out you can't be flexible, you have forgotten how to be like a child. We know that "hardening of the attitudes" is a SURE sign of advancing age.

So hang loose in every area you can. Listen to that long-lost child and catch the small, simple blessing, often fleeting. Remember the sweetness of Indian Summer, the sharp fragrance of orange peel so reminiscent of Christmas, the surprise in children's eyes as they see the silvery sparkle on a frosty morning.

Reflect on shared joys and rewarding friendships. Remember the sapphire sky and the sunset's afterglow? To see and appreciate these things is like seeing the world through the eyes of a child. BE A CHILD AGAIN! Let yourself recapture that childlike essence. It's wonderful to be CHILDLIKE, just don't confuse it with being CHILDISH. There IS a difference.

Almost ten years after writing those words, I find them to be even truer than ever. As Bonnie Prudden says:

YOU CAN'T TURN BACK THE CLOCK,
BUT YOU CAN WIND IT UP AGAIN.

For me, being childlike means accepting the age spots, wrinkles, and other outward signs of aging with as much grace and style as possible. After all, it's better to be over the hill than under it!

As for the battle of the bulge, KEEP AT IT BECAUSE HELP IS ON THE WAY. According to the experts, an anti-fat pill is in the works. It will be a few more years before it is available, but they are trying to develop ways to fool the brain into thinking the body is fatter than it really is. Somehow, this pill will tell you that your body has had enough food and you won't be craving that midnight or midday snack. Can you imagine what it would be like to be able to take your anti-fat pill each day? And why not? They have pills for just about any other ailment or condition.

So keep pushing that beach ball down. In a couple of years it may be gone forever!

Splish/Splash . . .

> I SWAM 10 LAPS
> I RAN 3 MILES
> I BIKED 7 MILES . . .
> IT'S BEEN A GOOD YEAR!

*   *   *   *   *   *

Probably the only great thing about pantyhose is that every time you wash them they go back to their original shape. I look at that puckered, starved, withered six inches of nylon and feel reborn. God has given me a second chance to pack it in.

*   *   *   *   *   *

> YOU ARE WHAT YOU EAT
> SO I EAT ONLY RICH FOOD.

*   *   *   *   *   *

When short hemlines came back in fashion, a woman dug an old miniskirt out of her closet. She tried it on, but couldn't figure out what to do with the other leg.

*   *   *   *   *   *

> THE EASIEST WAY TO GET A HEALTHY BODY
> IS TO MARRY ONE.

*   *   *   *   *   *

I'M NOT RICH AND FAMOUS . . .
BUT I DO HAVE
PRICELESS GRANDCHILDREN.

*   *   *   *   *   *

What to Count

Don't count how many years you've spent,
Just count the good you've done;
The times you've lent a helping hand,
The friends that you have won.
Count your deeds of kindness,
The smiles, not the tears;
Count all the pleasures that you've had,
But never count the years!

Source unknown

*   *   *   *   *   *

MY MIND WORKS LIKE LIGHTNING . . .
ONE BRILLIANT FLASH AND THEN IT'S GONE AGAIN!

*   *   *   *   *   *

NEVER TRY TO GUESS YOUR WIFE'S SIZE. JUST BUY HER
ANYTHING MARKED "PETITE" AND HOLD ON TO THE
RECEIPT.

*   *   *   *   *   *

THERE IS NO BETTER EXERCISE FOR THE HEART
THAN REACHING DOWN AND LIFTING SOMEONE UP.

*   *   *   *   *   *

MY MEMORY IS EXCELLENT. THERE ARE ONLY THREE
THINGS I CAN'T REMEMBER. I CAN'T REMEMBER FACES,

I CAN'T REMEMBER NAMES, AND NOW I HAVE FORGOT-
TEN THE THIRD THING.

*   *   *   *   *   *

AVENGE YOURSELF:
LIVE LONG ENOUGH TO BE A PROBLEM
TO YOUR CHILDREN.

*   *   *   *   *   *

Even to your old age and gray hairs
    I am he, I am he who will sustain you.
I have made you and I will carry you;
    I will sustain you and I will rescue you.
                    Isa. 46:4, NIV

Motherhood Isn't for Wimps

Cleaning your house
while your kids are still growing,
is like shoveling the walk
before it stops snowing[1]

Every May, I dedicate our *Love Line* newsletter to moms because:

1. It's Mother's Day.
2. They deserve it.

At least once a year I think moms should be able to wake up and realize:

I'M NOT JUST A HOUSEWIFE,
I'M A DOMESTIC GODDESS![2]

I know a lot of mothers are opting for careers outside the home, but that doesn't do away with their "housewife" chores. I have worked off and on over the years, myself, but I always came home to the housewife work at the end of the day, which seldom made me feel like a domestic goddess. I ran across an article entitled, "Who Mothers Mothers?" That's a provocative question. It certainly isn't your husband. He has his own schedule and responsibilities. Some younger moms say their husbands are helping more at home, but they seem to be the minority. Even in the so-called "enlightened nineties," *the family still depends on Mom to make it tick.* I like the unknown poet's verse that describes a scene many moms are all too familiar with:

OF DETERGENT AND DETERMINATION

Some may climb Mount Everest
   in search of thrills galore,
But I scale peaks that rival it
   just past my laundry door:
Slopes of socks and underwear,
   sheer cliffs of shirts and pants—
Oh, yes, I live in mortal fear
   of a laundry avalanche!

Who mothers mothers? It certainly isn't the kids. THEY are the ones who get up every morning determined to prove that motherhood is definitely not for wimps.

Then who really mothers mothers? Other mothers, of course! Only a mom understands when another mom needs a break from car-pool crazies, a listening ear, or just the discretion to look the other way when the kids go temporarily insane at the supermarket check-out counter.

At Spatula, we try to put hurting moms in touch with other hurting moms so they can find comfort, help, growth—and IMPROVEMENT. Husbands are protectors and breadwinners, but they aren't always equipped to help when you're hurting. Often, it's best to find a solid Christian WOMAN friend to listen to you ventilate and release your pent-up emotions. Then you will find that you will begin to get WELL. You will be comforted. IT REALLY WORKS THIS WAY!

You Never Get Over Being a Mother

Where would we be without our kids? Maybe Maui? The Caribbean? Acapulco? For years I've collected quips on the "challenge" of motherhood (and fatherhood, too, for that matter). Here are just a few samples:

THE SECRET OF DEALING SUCCESSFULLY
WITH A CHILD IS NOT TO BE ITS PARENT.

*   *   *   *   *   *

THE JOY OF MOTHERHOOD:
WHAT A WOMAN EXPERIENCES WHEN ALL THE CHILDREN
ARE FINALLY IN BED.

*   *   *   *   *   *

A MOTHER OF THREE NOTORIOUSLY UNRULY KIDS
WAS ASKED, "IF YOU HAD IT TO DO ALL OVER AGAIN,
WOULD YOU HAVE CHILDREN?"
"YES," SHE REPLIED, "BUT NOT THE SAME ONES."

*   *   *   *   *   *

THE SMARTEST ADVICE ON RAISING CHILDREN
IS TO ENJOY THEM WHILE THEY ARE STILL ON YOUR SIDE.

*   *   *   *   *   *

JUST WHEN YOUR KIDS ARE FIT TO LIVE WITH
THEY'RE LIVING WITH SOMEONE ELSE.

*   *   *   *   *   *

Obviously, all these jokes and jibes about being a parent only cover up what everybody knows is true: Moms AREN'T wimps, but they ARE softies who will do ANYTHING for their children. You can get over a lot of things, but you never get over being a mother.

For example, my youngest son, Barney, who lives near Carson City, Nevada, with his wife, Shannon, and their

I try to take just one day at a time...

but lately several days have attacked me at once.

daughters, Kandee and Tiffany, flew down to Florida recently to get some training he would use in his curb and landscaping business. The day Barney left, a radio news flash said there was a heavy infestation of killer bees in Florida and I immediately remembered that Barney is allergic to bee stings. My first thought was, *I wonder if he remembered to take his bee-sting kit—the one he carries in his truck when he is out working. I bet he didn't take it with him.*

I could hardly wait to get to a phone to call Shannon to learn what happened. Shannon didn't answer, so I began praying, "Oh, Lord, protect him because if he gets stung and doesn't have the kit and doesn't get to a hospital—I mean—he could DIE! I realize You already know this, Lord, but You also know

I'm his mother and I can't help but remind You of these things now and then."

Here I was, praying about my thirty-two-year-old son who hadn't lived at home for fourteen years, and I was still worrying about whether or not he was carrying his bee-sting kit!

Finally, I just said, "God, You'll have to protect him and put Your arms around him because I can't. If he doesn't have the kit and gets stung . . . well, he can get to a hospital to be helped."

It turned out that Barney had not taken the kit with him, but he didn't get stung by a single bee. Did the Lord protect him because of my prayer? I'd like to think so—at least that I gave Him a little nudge. God understands that you never get over being a mother. You can't resign. There's no way out. You worry about your kids—and you worry about your kids some more. Having a child is like getting a life sentence in prison with no hope of parole. You are a mother until they put you in your grave.

Why Do Mothers Cry?

As a mom, I have shed my share of tears over my kids, just as you have. I love a column someone sent me on why mothers cry. According to the author, when he was a little boy he found his mother humming her favorite song, "An Irish Lullaby," while tears trickled down her cheeks.

"Why are you crying?" he asked his mom.
"Because I'm a mother," she told him.
"I don't understand," he said.
His mom just hugged him tightly and said, "You never will."
Later the boy asked his father why Mother seemed to cry for no reason.
"All mothers cry for no reason," was all his dad could say.
The little boy grew up, still wondering why mothers cry, so he finally put in a call to God and when he got Him on the line, God said, "You see, Stan, when I made mothers, they had to be special. I made their shoulders strong enough to carry the

weight of the world. I gave them the inner strength to endure childbirth and the rejection that eventually comes from their children.

"I gave them a hardiness that allows them to keep going when everyone else gives up, and to take care of their families through sickness and fatigue without complaining.

"I gave them the sensitivity to love their children under all circumstances, and no matter how badly they are hurt. This same sensitivity helps them to make a child's boo-boo feel better, and helps them share a son's teen-age anxieties.

"I gave them a tear to shed. It's theirs exclusively to use whenever it's needed. It's their only weakness. It's a tear for mankind."[3]

Here is another story about a mother's tears that one of my friends sent me:

There once was a procession of children marching in heaven. Each child held a lighted candle, and as they marched along they sang. Their faces shone with happiness. But one little girl stood all alone.

"Why don't you join us, little girl?" one happy child asked.

"I can't," she replied."Every time I light my candle, my mother puts it out with her tears."

The Pitfalls of Parenting

Two common pitfalls for a lot of parents, especially moms, are:

1. Being afraid to let them grow up, try things, stumble over a few rocks in the road.

2. Feeling guilty when their kids do stumble, have problems, rebel—or worse.

The first pitfall—wanting to make life perfectly smooth for our kids—is the "overparenting" syndrome, or what Erma Bombeck calls TMM (Too Much Mother). A mother should be like a blanket . . . keeping the children warm but not SMOTHERING them.

From the moment they can start toddling off on their own, our kids want to separate from us. At age two, they tell us, "I do it MYSELF." By the time they hit the teen-age years, kids are practically at war with their parents over what they think they can or can't do.

From the parents' point of view, kids think they're far more capable than they really are. Furthermore, if they'd just act more RESPONSIBLE, perhaps mothers wouldn't have to worry so much. Maybe you've heard some of the following, and probably you've even used one or two of them yourself:

THE WORLD ACCORDING TO PARENTS

- "Bring me the change."
- "Call us when you get there."
- "I hope I'm alive when your kids turn sixteen."
- "Stop whining and eat it, NOBODY LIVES FOREVER."
- "If you break your leg, don't come running to me."
- "You WILL have fun."
- "Do it to make your mother happy."
- "Wait until your dad gets home."

Source unknown

Just as the mother bird shoves her fledglings out of the nest and the mother bear boots her little cubs out of the den to start foraging for themselves, so we human moms need to let our kids strike out on their own. As one writer says, "We . . . cling to our children as if we are afraid to trust God with them!"[4]

I'm not suggesting that we start neglecting our kids—far from it. But I think we should start letting go of them a lot earlier. One way to make life *hard* for our kids is to make life too *soft* for them.

In chapter 3 I talked about letting go of Larry and finally being able to pray, "Whatever, Lord," when he had appeared to stray so far from God and the foundation we had given him.

children are a great comfort in your old age...
and they help you reach it faster too!

Children are a gift of the Lord ... Psa. 127:3

© 1989 Cedar Hill Studio

Even better, however, is for moms to pray, "Whatever, Lord," when their kids are little, realizing that, "God has a Will and a Way for our children, and the road ahead may be rough. He foreknew them just as he foreknew us. At some point God and child must meet and establish their own relationship."[5]

Guilt Quickly Turns into a Deep Cesspool

The other pitfall that turns into a cesspool for so many parents is guilt, the emotion Erma Bombeck calls the "gift that keeps on giving." A constant theme running through many letters I receive concerns the guilt and sense of failure parents feel when a child rebels and rejects the family's values. As one mother wrote to me:

> I know there are many hurting parents out there and we are not unique. We want to stand firm and be faithful, we want to be happy! We don't want to choose misery [but] we have failed.

Guilt becomes particularly overwhelming when parents hear their son or daughter say, "Mom, I'm gay—I have been almost since I can remember." A mother whose son grew up in the church and at one time attended a Christian college with a goal to work with young people in counseling against drugs wrote to say this after she learned he was gay:

> Barbara, I thought I knew the answers before it became *my son*. It's a secret I carry ashamedly; it hurts me so to have my only two children so far apart.
> How do these things happen? Why? What can I do? . . . I'm desperate . . . Help me to help my child!

Another mother wrote after talking to me on the phone about her son, whose homosexual lifestyle was affecting her two younger children, as well as the whole family. As heartbreaking as it was, she and her husband had to ask him to leave because of the damage he was doing in their home. They couldn't let the sins of one person destroy their whole family.

At first he was angry and she heard very little from him, but he did spend Christmas with the family and they got along fairly well, mainly because she and her husband didn't question or judge him. Their relationship is still strained, however, and she writes:

> What has been hard for my husband and me to understand is why he is so involved in this. We brought him up in the belief of God and salvation. My husband does not feel much now but anger and relief that he is out of the home, but I have to pray daily for God to give me the strength to trust Him. I placed my son in His arms, but yet I keep feeling anxious each day. I find myself checking the newspaper, or scanning the streets when I'm in the area where I think he might be.
> P.S. Any tips on how to not feel so guilty? Especially since we asked him to leave, I feel like a hypocrite, even though circumstances forced us to do so. But I feel so badly. One part of me wants to bring him home and take care of him.

Another mother wrote to tell me of her son's divorce and his moving back home, where he now lives with his parents and "drinks too much." His two little girls visit every other weekend. The mother's letter continued:

> He was raised in a Christian home and therefore I carried such guilt, knowing I had failed somewhere. God surely led me to that bookstore on a day when I needed to hear the words of joy found in your book . . . It has opened my eyes to so much. I know I must love him and let God change him. We parents feel that changing them is our job. It's not. It's God's.

This mom has gotten the message! It's our job to love our kids; it's God's job to bring conviction.

When a child strays away or adopts a destructive lifestyle, parents automatically ask, "What did I do wrong?"

"Nothing most other parents didn't do, too," I tell them. "Remember that God calls us to be faithful; He doesn't call us to be successful."

Parents can only do their best—no more, no less. Even what they do or don't do isn't the final cause of how their children turn out. For years the behavioral school of psychology said that the child's environment has the main influence on a child's development, but recently more psychologists are saying that genetics are the key factor. Since even the experts don't agree on this, perhaps it is a balance or blend of both.

The point is, parents don't have to accept the blame for their kids' choices. There is no need to wear a guilt quilt. Instead, wrap yourself in God's comfort blanket and remember two things:

1. IF THERE IS NO CONTROL
   THERE IS NO RESPONSIBILITY.
2. GOD HAS THE FINAL WORD
   ON WHAT HAPPENS TO YOUR CHILD.

Also remember that there is an abundance of God's grace for us all. Grace can cover even your shame and guilt, no matter how badly you feel.

Because we use and reuse a lot of cassette tapes, Bill bought me a fabulous invention called a tape eraser. You slip a tape in it, and when it comes out the tape is completely BLANK. Something inside completely erases the tape so it can be used again for new material.

This machine is only about as big as a tape, itself, and works like a charm. I pasted a little cartoon on the outside—a little girl asking, "Dear God, when You forgive, do You use an eraser?"

Sometimes I sit and erase hundreds of tapes for reuse, and I think of that wonderful land of beginning again where we are forgiven our sins and cleansed from all unrighteousness (1 John 1:9). Calvary covers ALL my past sins. Jesus took on all our guilt and wiped out all charges against us. Just as my little cassette tape eraser can cleanse a tape and make it fit for use like brand new, so can God cleanse my heart and make me fresh and clean.

And the most important thing is to remember that God's "tape eraser" is always ready when we fail or make mistakes. You may have heard the story of the minister who was entertaining some important Christian leaders. His wife had made a lovely, formal meal using her finest crystal, silver, and china. Their seven-year-old son was at the table, and as he reached for something he knocked over his water goblet. It was a tense, silent moment. The boy had fear written all over his face as he stared at his father, who was looking toward him intently.

Then the minister reached out and dumped his own goblet, splashing water all over the place as his son had done. Following suit, each guest did the same. It was as if they all understood that the father didn't want the son to feel guilty alone. He was willing to identify with his son at this embarrassing moment.

This homey little story is only a tiny glimpse of how grace works. Yet it helps us picture how God identifies with us in all our suffering and our failures. And as God identifies with us,

HE SPLASHES HIS GRACE ALL OVER US. There is more than enough for everyone.

Today's Experiences Are Tomorrow's Memories

Instead of smother-mothering your kids and then feeling guilty about their poor choices, take every opportunity to make good memories instead. Overmothering means focusing so tightly on the child that neither one of you has room to breathe. Making good memories calls for focusing on BOTH of you. You do things to make good memories for the child, but you also do things that make them for YOU.

In chapter 2, I described the bittersweet memories that occur when sorrow invades a family. But there are also the PLEASANT or FOND memories that remind you of dreams and plans and good times that are and always will be part of you. Remember:

> THE MEMORY IS A WONDERFUL TREASURE CHEST
> FOR THOSE WHO KNOW HOW TO PACK IT.

It's not surprising that so many middle-aged men, in particular, walked out of the movie *Field of Dreams* with tears in their eyes. The film, about a man who turns an Iowa cornfield into a baseball diamond complete with lights, touched a nerve across America because it reminded so many men of the days when they played baseball and perhaps dreamed of making it all the way to the majors.

For all of us, today's experiences are tomorrow's memories. In looking back over more than fifty years to things that happened when I was a small girl, the indelible memories are there, reminding me of who I am and where I came from.

I started singing when I was about three years old and, because my dad was a church music director, he gave me all kinds of opportunities. For example, Billy Sunday, the Billy Graham of that day, came to our town to preach. My dad stood me up on a chair so I could reach the microphone and sing during Billy Sunday's meetings, which were held in a big tent where the ground was covered with wood shavings and sawdust. When folks talk about the "sawdust trail" today, I know what that means because I was there. I can still smell those meetings in my memory whenever I'm around freshly cut lumber. And I still remember some of the songs I sang. One was:

> GOD CAN SEE EACH FALLING TEAR;
> HE SEES THE HEART THAT'S SAD AND DREAR.
> HE KNOWS THE PATH THAT'S FULL OF FEAR;
> DON'T GIVE UP FOR HE IS NEAR.

The audience would join with me to sing another song that went like this:

> Everybody happy, SAY AMEN!
> Everybody happy, SAY AMEN!
> Praise the Lord for what He's done,
> Praise the Lord for victories won,
> Everybody happy, SAY AMEN!

The audience would sing the first part of the line and I would chirp, "SAY AMEN!"—loudly and with much gusto, of course.

Some missionaries to China visited our church and taught me to sing a song to the tune of "Bringing in the Sheaves." What I thought I heard them teaching me sounded like this:

> Don you ting wah chee . . .
> Don you ting wah chee . . .
> Hi lo ling tum fi low,
> Don you ting wah chee.

Rattling off these words for the congregation usually got lots of applause. After all, here I was, a little kid, singing a song in Chinese—very impressive! A few years later, I sang the same thing for some REAL Chinese friends and they didn't understand a word I said!

My memories include my bedtime routine. I would sit on my dad's lap and he would rock me as we would listen to the "Amos and Andy" radio show together. It always ended at 7:30 and then I knew it was time for bed.

Sometimes my sister, who was eight years older than I was, would have to take care of me, and she would want me to go to bed earlier so she could get me out of her way. She would set the clock an hour or so AHEAD; but I always knew, until I heard the closing strains of "Amos and Andy," it wasn't time for bed, no matter how many times she moved the clock ahead!

Parents Are Writing a Lasting Record

Parents can write many things on the heart of a child, sometimes without realizing it. Often what you are as a parent—your integrity, your character—will make a memory your child will never forget.

When I was about ten years old, I found an advertisement somewhere that said if I could sell one hundred jars of Cloverine Salve I would earn a bicycle. Somehow I got my mother to order the 100 jars, anticipating how I would sell them all and get myself a BIKE. Cloverine Salve, according to the ad, was for everything—cows' udders, washing machines, sore cuts, squeaky door hinges, you name it. Today I guess it would be a cross between Vaseline and WD-40.

I can still remember going from door to door, pleading with folks to buy my Cloverine Salve. It was winter in Michigan and biting cold. The snow swirled around me as I trudged from house to house. I had packed several jars of the salve in a sack and just carrying it was burdensome. My galoshes were wet inside where the snow had spilled over the tops. My socks got wet and my feet were cold. And every time I got to a door I would have to remove my woolly mitten in order to push the doorbell. Soon my fingers were like icicles.

Despite all of my efforts to tell folks how useful the salve was, nobody wanted to buy it. If you have ever lived in a cold climate like Michigan and trudged through snow and slush with the biting cold piercing right through your clothes, you know how DETERMINED I was to sell that salve. But all I kept getting was "No, thank you"; then I'd pick up my sack and move on down the block to the next rejection, always hoping that I could earn the shiny bike shown in that advertisement.

I would come home after my "sales trips," totally discouraged because my sack of salve had not diminished. And our garage was still STACKED with boxes of Cloverine Salve. My longed-for bike seemed to be just a broken dream. I had managed to get rid of only a few jars by selling them to relatives who loved me anyway and felt sorry for me. But I was nowhere near selling them all, and that was the deal, if I was to get that new bike.

Just as I was about to give up, my dad came to my rescue. He had seen me come in so many times with teeth chattering, clothes sopping wet, face red and chapped from the biting cold. He knew it was an overwhelming task and that no one wanted the salve because it was the depression and no one had any extra money for things like that.

But as a caring dad, he wanted my dream to come true, so he purchased all the remaining jars of Cloverine Salve from me, saying, "Oh, we'll eventually use them all up." Thrilled to pieces, I watched him make out the money order to pay for the salve and then I ran to the corner mailbox to send it in.

For the next several weeks I waited with excited anticipation for a beautiful, shiny bike like the one pictured in the advertisement. I knew that soon I would be riding that bike, pedaling around the neighborhood with my hair blowing in the wind. I envisioned streamers coming from the handlebars and, of course, a nice loud jingling bell. What excitement . . . what anticipation for a little girl who at last would have her VERY OWN BIKE!

Finally, the bike did arrive in the mail. The only problem was, it was made of aluminum, about fifteen inches long and six inches high! It was nothing more than a TOY! My disappointment was twice as great as my anticipation had been and I started to cry bitterly. I had expected a nice, new, shiny, red bike with a bell and streamers—everything I had dreamed of. Instead, I had gotten a cheap toy that you could hold in two hands.

My dad saw my tear-streaked face and a few hours later he had me in the car and we went shopping for a new bright, shiny red bicycle. This was back when times were hard and people were hurting from the depression and luxuries like new bikes were not readily available. But we shopped and shopped and finally found that "just-right" bike.

I'm sure that Dad and Mom went without other things in order to get me that bike, which I treasured and rode for years. Once in a while I see an ad for Cloverine Salve—in some old farm catalog or on a poster in an antique shop. Then the memory of that day when my dad took me out to buy that new bike floods back and splashes me with joy.

The Things We Never Forget

When we look back at childhood, there are "things we will never forget." Some of the ideas I remember most fondly are:

1. The simple joys of picking wild violets or gathering hickory nuts with a grandparent.
2. Being ill, missing school, and getting strawberry ice cream.
3. The first time I slept in a tent.
4. Holidays with all the relatives joking, laughing, and eating.
5. Catching "lightning bugs" and putting them in a bottle.
6. Watching a favorite TV show with the family.

This morning I flipped on our television set and heard the nostalgic tune that was the theme song for the "Little Rascals" program from more than thirty years ago. I sat transfixed as I watched Spanky, Darla, and Alfalfa cavorting across the screen with their songs and antics. And I thought back to when I had heard boyish chuckles and outright belly laughs as my children had delighted in all the "Little Rascals'" mischief.

Watching that rerun was a special time, as the Rascals drove an old, beat-up car down a winding street and Alfalfa sang off key. I enjoyed that time alone, remembering all the fun we had had on Saturday mornings. Then I realized those original "Little Rascal" days were long gone for me. And those little boys who laughed so uproariously were gone from our family room, too.

Instead, now I sat alone with memories of the laughter we had built into the walls of our home and our hearts. I suppose I could have become morbid about it, but instead I began to think of Philippians 4:8 and how important it is to think on things that are pure and good and also happy. (I'm sure Paul meant to put "happy" in there some place.) And so I captured in my mind the rollicking fun of Saturday mornings as our boys were growing up. I could almost smell the cereal with bananas they would devour as they watched their favorite TV characters—and we laughed and laughed together.

The Memory of the Micro-Sweater

Today's experiences ARE tomorrow's memories, and I thank God I took time to make as many as possible. While Steve was still in high school, his girlfriend knitted him a beautiful light-green sweater, and when he came home with it, we all admired it because it was, indeed, lovely. He was so proud of that sweater, and he loved it more than anything else in his entire wardrobe.

But a day or two later, he came home from school all upset. He had spilled hot chocolate all over his sweater and was sure it was ruined. "Don't worry," I said, "I'll wash it for you and it will come out fine."

"Oh, no," he protested, "don't you touch it. You might SHRINK it!"

I just smiled at Steve's very explicit orders to leave his sweater alone, but after he left for school I did what any mother would do. I carefully washed the sweater, which came out looking as beautiful as ever. As I put it in his dresser drawer, a devious little thought crossed my mind. If there were only some way to make Steve think the sweater was ruined, and then have him find it clean and carefully folded and waiting in his drawer . . .

Later that day, as I was going to the market, I went by a store that sold Ken and Barbie dolls and all the accessories. Looking in the window, I was delighted to see a tiny, light-green sweater that perfectly matched Steve's in color, texture, and style! The only difference was that Steve's sweater was at least fifteen times larger! The tiny sweater in the window was the size of the palm of my hand and I knew I had to have it!

I went in and bought the micro-sweater and rushed home. With only a few minutes to spare before Steve was due home from school, I laid the tiny sweater on his bed. Then I went out to the kitchen to wait for Steve to come through the door. Sure enough, he was home in a few minutes, said his usual "Hi," and went right on by me to his room. I just kept humming and fixing dinner, but it didn't take long for Steve's howl of anguish to come down the hall.

"My sweater . . . it looks like a coaster! You RUINED it! I KNEW this would happen. You BOILED my sweater!"

I went to his room to see what all the ruckus was about (as if I didn't know). Desperately, Steve was trying to stretch the tiny sweater to make it larger, but it was no use. "Oh, yes," I said, "I tried to wash your sweater but I guess it must have shrunk . . . ."

I let Steve writhe in anxiety for a few more seconds and then started to laugh. "Steve, do you really think that I would hurt something that meant so much to you?" I asked as I calmly opened his dresser drawer. There was the puffy green sweater, looking brand new and quite a bit larger than the miniature he was holding!

Steven's look of sheer delight as he took the real sweater out of the drawer is a memory I'll always treasure. I can still see his quick smile and twinkling eyes and hear his voice saying, "Awww, I KNEW you wouldn't REALLY hurt my sweater."

Steve thought I HAD ruined his sweater, but he still enjoyed the joke. Maybe he was just so relieved that he still had his sweater—but anyway, he started to laugh, too.

We kept the little green sweater on display for awhile and every time we saw it, we had another good chuckle together.

After Steve was killed and I began speaking to women's groups, I would take the little green sweater with me and display it as I shared my story. On occasion I have mentioned that the little green sweater was getting worn out because I have shown it so many hundreds of times. At least five women have made me duplicates of the sweater—same color, same style—but I still have the original one, too, which brings back precious memories every time I speak and share this story.

Rockabye Barney on the Dryer Top

Recently I received a lovely cross-stitch, done by Barney's wife, Shannon, of the poem that appears on the next page.[6]

Shannon's cross-stitch not only thrilled me, but it stirred a lot of memories of that little boy I raised with love. The best memories are the ones that a mother treasures in her heart, the ones that no one knows about but her. One of my special memories of Barney is when he was a baby. He was born December 22 and I brought him home on Christmas morning in a big red stocking. Our special little gift developed colic and was constantly fussy, especially at night. I always said if Barney had been my FIRST, he definitely would have been my LAST.

Barney was the epitome of two of my favorite quips:

PEOPLE WHO SAY THEY SLEEP LIKE A BABY
USUALLY DON'T HAVE ONE.

L. J. Burke[7]

*   *   *   *   *   *

A PERFECT EXAMPLE OF MINORITY RULE
IS THE BABY IN THE HOUSE.

To get Barney to sleep, I would wrap him up tightly in a
baby blanket, place him in a wicker laundry basket, then set

To my mom-in-love, ♡

You are the mother I received on the day I wed your son.

I just want to thank you, Mom, for the things you have done.

You have given me a gracious man with whom I share my life.

You are his lovely mother and I his adoring wife.

You used to pat his little head, and now I hold his hand.

You raised with love a little boy... then gave to me a man.

from your daughter-in-love

the basket on top of the clothes dryer and turn it on. (Please note that I set him ON the dryer, not IN the dryer.) Only then would Barney stop crying as the vibration and noise of the dryer lulled him to sleep.

Then I would set the timer on the dryer for 58 minutes (if I let it go an hour, the buzzer would wake him up). Then I would set my own alarm for a few minutes less than that and get that much shut-eye, myself. When my alarm went off, I would have to get up and re-set the dryer, hoping Barney would sleep another fifty-eight minutes. During his first six or seven months of life, that was the only way I could get any sleep at night. If I didn't leave Barney on the dryer and keep resetting that timer every hour, he would wake up screaming—and so would I.

The dryer trick worked until Barney was about seven months old; then he learned how to crawl OUT of the laundry basket and OFF the machine. By then, however, his colic was somewhat relieved, so we were able to sleep through the night.

Countless times I'd rock him to sleep, myself, as I sang songs and made up stories. And it worked, as the rhythm of the rocking would soothe him and quiet him down.

There is something almost magical about rocking. It begins in the womb with the child rocking as the mother moves about. Most of us were rocked as children, and it seems we never outgrow our need to be rocked.

Rocking soothes and comforts. I believe every home needs a rocking chair for use by the kids as well as the grownups. Older folks, grieving over the loss of friends who die or move away, often find comfort in rocking. Yes, rocking appeals to just about every age. At the Polly's Pie Shop restaurant near where we live, the waiting area is lined with about twenty rocking chairs. Bill and I find it so enjoyable just to sit and rock that we almost hate to have our turn come to be seated for lunch.

Now Barney, that little guy I rocked for countless hours, has grown up into a broad-shouldered, muscular man, over six feet tall and weighing nearly 180 pounds. Not long ago I received a rare treat from my son—something I treasure very much. On his way home from that trip to Florida (without his bee-sting kit), Barney wrote me a letter:

> Mom, I always have wanted to write you, but never had enough time to sit down and do it! So, I'm on the plane back from Florida and able to do so. I really appreciate you and love you, and know you love me also. There have been times in my life when I probably should have done something different or could have gotten into something else, but I am where I am today and happy because of you and Dad, who have given me and the girls and Shannon the love and the will and encouragement to hang tough!
>
> I love you so much, and am so proud of you. I just don't get to tell you enough how thankful I am for you and Dad. After being in business for myself for the last 2 years and dealing with employees and where they have come from and how they've been brought up, I can really appreciate how fortunate I was to have Dad and you.
>
> Love,
Barney

As I finished Barney's letter, I had tears in my eyes, but I guess that's what motherhood is all about. As somebody said:

AT TIMES
KIDS CAN BE A PAIN IN THE NECK
WHEN THEY'RE NOT BEING A LUMP IN YOUR THROAT.

I'm glad I've had my share of both, and I hope you are, too!

Splish/Splash . . .

LITTLE GIRL'S ESSAY ON PARENTS:

The trouble with parents is that they are so old when we get them, it's hard to change their habits.

* * * * * *

A mom with little boy in tow met her pastor in the church hallway and said, "I was thinking of doing what *Hannah* did. As you will recall, she took her kid to the church and LEFT him there!"

* * * * * *

THE BEST WAY TO KEEP CHILDREN AT HOME
IS TO CREATE A PLEASANT ATMOSPHERE—
AND TO LET THE AIR OUT OF THEIR TIRES.

* * * * * *

Mother, talking to old college friend: "Remember, before I was married I had three theories about raising children? Well, now I have three children and no theories."

* * * * * *

RUN THE VACUUM OFTEN . . .
NOT TO CLEAN, BUT TO DROWN OUT THE KIDS.

* * * * * *

SCHOOL DAYS
CAN BE THE HAPPIEST DAYS OF YOUR LIFE . . .
PROVIDING THE CHILDREN ARE OLD ENOUGH TO GO.

* * * * * *

A SWEATER IS A GARMENT WORN BY A CHILD
WHEN HIS MOTHER FEELS CHILLY.

* * * * * *

YOU CAN GET CHILDREN
OFF YOUR LAP,
BUT YOU CAN NEVER GET THEM
OUT OF YOUR HEART.

* * * * * *

TO BE IN YOUR CHILDREN'S MEMORIES TOMORROW
YOU HAVE TO BE IN THEIR LIVES TODAY.

*   *   *   *   *   *

Don't keep on scolding and nagging your children, making
them angry and resentful. Rather, bring them up with the loving discipline the Lord himself approves, with suggestions and
godly advice. (Eph. 6:4, TLB)

Oh, Lord, Let My Words Be Tender and Sweet, for Tomorrow I May Have to Eat Them!

*There is only one thing more painful
than learning from experience,
and that is not learning from experience.*

As I continue working with families who are torn by misunderstanding and confusion, an observation by Ashleigh Brilliant keeps coming to mind:

> IF ONLY I COULD RELATE TO
> THE PEOPLE I'M RELATED TO.[1]

So many parents and their grown children are caught in the same trap. They wish they could be close to one another, but they are separated by a huge canyon of disagreement, hurt feelings, or resentments. They try to send words to each other across that canyon, but so often the words don't arrive, or if they do, they convey the wrong message and the canyon grows even wider.

I know how this feels, and something that happened on Easter Sunday vividly reminded me of how wonderful it is to communicate in a warm, nonjudgmental way. Larry came over for dinner, and later he left to drive to his condo, about an hour away. Two hours later I received a phone call: "Mom! You'll never believe what happened to me after I left your place!"

I could tell from Larry's voice that something was definitely not right and, like any mother, I immediately considered panic. What in the world could Larry mean? And then he continued, "I had to stop for gas just before I got on the freeway, and while I was pumping gas, the nozzle went crazy and wouldn't shut off. By the time I finally got it stopped, gas was everywhere—in my hair, my eyes, and all over the new sweater you gave me."

"My goodness!" was all I could say. "What did you do then?"

"I went in the men's room, took off the sweater, and decided it was ruined; I just threw it in the trash barrel. My pants were soaked with gas, but I couldn't throw them away. So were my shoes. I paid for the gas, got back in the car, and drove home. I was glad nobody threw a cigarette out his window into mine or I would have exploded, I was just SOAKED with gasoline. I'm going to take a bath and try to get this smell off of me, and it looks as if I will have to throw away the rest of my clothes."

I told Larry I was glad he wasn't hurt or anything like that, and thanked him for calling. But after we hung up, I began thinking about that sweater. It was one I bought at Knott's Berry Farm and I had given it to him for Christmas. It was all cotton, a beautiful maroon color, and he had really liked it. I hated the thought of Larry's sweater winding up in the gas-station trash barrel.

Taking a big plastic sack with me (having faith I would ultimately find the sweater), I started up Fullerton Road, the most direct route to the freeway Larry would take to go on home. I stopped at the first gas station I found, got out, dragged my plastic sack with me, and asked the attendant, "Did a young man come in here a couple of hours ago for gas and have it spill all over him?"

The attendant looked at me a little strangely and said, "Naw, lady, I don't think we've EVER had that happen . . ."

I went through the same procedure as I worked my way up Fullerton Road, stopping at seven gas stations in all. Finally, I got to the eighth and last station and decided, *This MUST be it,* because I could see the freeway just a block ahead. I got out of my car with my plastic sack in hand and asked the question that by now had become a broken record. But this time a darling young man said, "Oh, man! Did we ever! We were so SORRY about what happened. He was saturated with gas!"

"That was my son," I told him. "He tells me he threw his sweater in your men's-room trash container, and I've come to try to get it back."

Sure enough, when the young man checked the restroom for me, he came back with the sweater in the plastic bag, matted, soaked in gas, and very smelly. I thanked him profusely and drove back home. Even with the sweater tied up in the plastic sack, my car was permeated with the smell of gasoline. When Bill heard I'd found it, he said, "Well, just leave it outside and it will air out. For Pete's sake, don't bring it in the house that way."

So I spread it out on some lawn furniture and left it there overnight hoping that most of the odor would be gone by morning. Believe it or not (remember, we live in Southern California), that night it poured. I went out the next morning and there was the sweater, all soggy now, not only with gas but with rain water. I decided I couldn't possibly take it to the cleaners in that condition.

From Mom—With Love and Cologne

I wrung out as much moisture as I possibly could, and then proceeded to wash it at least three times in Woolite, plus three different fabric softeners. It came out soft, silky, almost WAXY smooth, and smelling perfectly fresh. Finding a nice box just the right size, I neatly folded the sweater, and for good measure tucked in several tissues well sprinkled with Bill's Royal Copenhagen aftershave and cologne. Now I was sure it would smell good when he opened it.

I thought how much fun it would have been if I had gotten the sweater to Larry on April 1, but the trouble was it was already April 1. There was still time to get to the UPS office though, and I sent it off, knowing he'd get it by April 2 at least. I could hardly wait until he called to tell me he had gotten back a sweater he never expected to see (or smell) again!

All week I kept waiting for Larry to call me about the sweater, but that call never came. It was now Friday, six days since I had found the sweater and cleaned it up. Before leaving to speak at a women's retreat in a valley just north of Los Angeles, I left a message on Larry's phone machine telling him that I would stop by on my way home on Sunday to take him to lunch at the Dorothy Chandler Pavilion near his condominium building.

That following Sunday I arrived in plenty of time and decided to go over to his condo to get him, so we could walk together to lunch. I rang the bell and Larry flung open the door. There he stood in all his maroon-sweater glory saying, "SMELL ME, MOM, SMELL ME!"

Lunch Stirred Bittersweet Memories

We talked about the sweater all through lunch. He just couldn't believe that I could ever find it and, after finding it, get the gas smell out.

It was a delightful time. We laughed together easily, and I was thankful life was so good for us right now. As we sat in the Music Center restaurant enjoying ourselves, I remembered being in this same building on October 21, 1975, and feeling heartbroken because Larry wouldn't even speak to me. When I had learned about his homosexuality in June of that year, my rage had clashed with his angry reaction. He had left home and disappeared into the gay lifestyle. I had disappeared into our bedroom to count the roses on our wallpaper and slip deeper into depression.

We didn't hear anything from Larry. Then, in October, I saw a story in the *Los Angeles Times* saying the choral group Larry sang with would be performing at the Music Center. Accompanied by my sister, I went that night to hear the group sing and quickly spotted the smiling son I hadn't seen or heard from for four months. I never took my eyes off of Larry during the entire first half of the program. He was a bit thinner, perhaps, but he looked wonderful.

Our seats were close to the front, and as the house lights came on for intermission, Larry looked into the audience and saw me. Our eyes locked for just a second or two and then the curtain closed. I could hardly wait for intermission to be over so I could see him again during the second half of the program. I was hoping we could go backstage after the performance to congratulate him, but when the curtain went up Larry was not there. The place where he was supposed to stand and perform was empty. Apparently, he had grabbed his clothes in the dressing room and bolted out of the Music Center because he didn't want to see me at all!

Having Larry be so close and then losing him again made my depression even worse. Eventually it led me to the brink of suicide (see chapter 3). Larry was gone with no word for almost another eight months, and then, the very day after I came out of my suicidal doldrums by deciding to "nail him to the Cross" and say, "Whatever, Lord," he called and came home. I was glad, but there was still a nagging feeling that said, *This is not the time for real joy*, and I was right.

Larry Decided to Disown Us

For the next three years, Larry stayed in touch while going to college at UCLA and living alone in an apartment near the campus. He would drop by and see us frequently, but we never talked about homosexuality. We just talked about surface things.

Then, in 1979, when my first book, *Where Does a Mother Go to Resign?* came out, Larry became sullen, unfriendly, and finally very angry. He let me know that he "had a lover," and while I did not go into a rage the way I had when I discovered his homosexuality, I was firm in saying that I didn't think homosexuality was God's best for anybody—especially my son. I would love him and pray for him. The porch light would always be on for him.

Larry did not listen. He hung up in anger, telling us that he was going to change his name and disown us because he never wanted to see us again. Sure enough, a few days later we received the official papers from the court that told us he had done just that. It was early in 1980. We would not hear from Larry for six years. I would go out to speak and share with other parents about how to handle pain and someone would ask, "How is your family doing now?"

My standard answer was: "Well, my two sons haven't risen from the dead, and I have a third son who has changed his name, disowned his family, told us he never wants to see us again, and has disappeared into the gay lifestyle. But who wants to hear a dreary story like that? I'm here to tell you not to give up hope, particularly when you're in a hopeless situation, because God only gives out the score on a life when the game is over—and the game isn't over YET with my kid."

One thing I have always stressed is that where there is no control, there is no responsibility. I couldn't change Larry. I couldn't fix him. I didn't even know where he WAS! But my joy lay in the fact that I knew I was living in a set of parentheses that would eventually be opened. Someday, one end of those parentheses would be kicked out and I would get on with my life. This whole thing hadn't come to stay; it was going to pass. I was living with a DEFERRED HOPE, but I knew it wouldn't be that way forever. As Proverbs says, "Hope deferred makes the heart sick; but when dreams come true at last, there is life and joy."[2]

I knew, even when trapped in those parentheses, that during a time of deferred hope, God still goes after the prodigal; God seeks out His own. He could end these parentheses any time He wanted to. I clung to the Proverb that says, "And you can also be very sure God will rescue the children of the godly."[3]

"Mom, I Want to Bring You a Mother's Day Present"

I went on like that until just before Mother's Day 1986. Eleven years had passed since that day I had learned the truth about Larry's homosexuality; then came a shocking phone call. It was Larry, who said he wanted to bring me a "Mother's Day present." I confess all kinds of thoughts flashed into my mind—most of them bad. Was he bringing home his lover to tell us they were going to get married? Even the unthinkable crossed my mind: AIDS!

Fear paralyzed me. What could Larry want to bring me after all this time—all this estrangement? Bill could tell I was talking to Larry, and, sensing my hesitation, he said, "Tell him to come home." I did, and within an hour Larry arrived. He was supposed to be bringing me a present, but there was no package in his hand. It turned out he didn't need a package. What he had to give us was far better.

Larry came in, sat down, and with big tears in his eyes he asked us to forgive him for the eleven years of pain he had caused us. He had attended a Bill Gothard Advanced Seminar and had felt such conviction he had gone home to burn all the evidence of the old lifestyle and become clean in God's sight. There had been real restoration to God in his life and now he wanted to be restored to us, as well!

The word "restore" means to "pop back in place," and surely this is exactly what was happening as we hugged him and clung together, thanking the Lord for healing the fracture we had lived with for so long.

Rebuilding a Relationship Takes Effort

After Larry returned, we began building our relationship completely anew, and we're still building it, learning more about each other all the time.

A lot of mail comes from parents who are trying to do the same thing. Once we get past the shock that comes when our children go off on a detour in life, one of our main concerns is how to relate to our son or daughter. We don't want to condone what they are doing, yet we don't want to condemn and judge either. After all, we are called to be witnesses, not judges.

Letters like the following are typical of people who are struggling to relate to their children:

> Our daughter, a junior at a Christian college, believes in the Lord and has a very caring heart, but has convinced herself that the Bible does not condemn her choice of lifestyle. We have told her that we love her and will always be here for her, but we do not agree with her on this issue. She seems to be getting in deeper and deeper and we need to know how to deal with all of this.

*   *   *   *   *   *

> Mother's Day of this year, our 25-year-old son, whose background is in and out of drugs and alcohol, told us he thought he was gay. . . . Our hearts are broken and the first reaction was—"If you choose this life, you're no longer a member of this family." Since then, there have been conversations—pleading—and I'm sure you know the rest.

As I answer these letters, I try to share some of the principles I learned during the eleven years that Larry was estranged from us, as well as the years that have elapsed since he gave up his former lifestyle and became clean before God. The rest of this chapter will outline these principles and how to use them.

1. Stuff a Sock in Your Mouth

When the shock, anger, and rage first grip you, stuff a sock in your mouth and keep it there for at least six months. No matter how badly you want to lash out with Scripture verses, sermons, name-calling, or worse, just shut up. Venting your anger on your child will not help. I know. One thing that Larry told me after he returned was how my initial rage had hurt him. "Some of the things that you said were terrible," Larry told me. "They were like piercing swords."

The title of this chapter sums it up pretty well: Be careful of using words that cut and slash because there may come a day when you have to eat them. It reminds me of a little prayer I found in some of the "joy mail" a friend sent to me:

> Dear Father,
> help me to bridle my tongue,
> so that on judgment day
> I will not be found guilty
> of assault with a deadly weapon.

2. When the Going Gets Tough, Use Tough Love

When a child chooses a lifestyle that is self-destructive, he or she needs your love more than ever, but what's needed is *tough love*, not sloppy *agape* or syrupy sentimentality. I don't mean that parents should become mean or uncaring. Tough love is different and is usually the most difficult thing a parent can ever try to demonstrate. Whatever you do, you must learn not to let this loved one manipulate you. He may use lying, stealing, threats, flattery—you name it—to trap you into playing his game and thereby controlling you. Don't let that happen by keeping the following points in mind:

• You must not feel responsible for your child's addiction. This only makes you feel angry, depressed, guilty, and even physically ill.

• Do not try to rescue your loved one. Let your loved one hurt as a result of his or her own personal choices and actions. Parents should remember that they can't fur-line the pigpen for their prodigal kids.

• Accept the fact that this will be a very hard time for you, especially if you can observe daily the self-destructive addiction of your loved one. Try to treat yourself as lovingly and nurturingly as possible. Do things that are fun and enriching for you.

• Find a group that will give you support and the reassurance that it's necessary for you to become detached from the problem. Keep your compassion at a distance. You can't save this person, even if you want to.

• Your loved one is a very dependent person—not just on his or her particular vulnerable area, but on you. This person needs you more than you need him. He is a denier and will not face his dependency. You must face the truth, though, even if he won't; change your own life to get stronger and not let him pull you down.

• If your child threatens to leave without your ever seeing him or her again, remember that this is the rebellion lashing out at you. Actually, he needs you more than he'll ever admit. Your happiness does not really depend on him. You can survive, even if the threat is carried out. Even if you don't know where he is or how he is doing, you have given him to God and God has His hand on your child now. You can expect the adult child to continue to deny the truth as long as he is committed to staying out of fellowship. Remember that down deep he knows the truth, no matter what he says or how he rationalizes his behavior when he feels he's being "unjustly attacked."

• Tough love is tough on everybody! It hurts as much as surgery! But it's every bit as necessary. Stop telling yourself, *He's suffering so much. I must help him.* If you continue to "help" him, you will be helping him make wrong choices. Tough love is letting him hurt enough to get appropriate help.

• Remember that people don't seek help if they don't hurt. Tough love means letting go—completely. It means minding your own business. It means letting him have the dignity to pick up the pieces of his life and not be an emotional cripple any more. And do not worry that tough love will make you a calloused, unfeeling person. What it does do is give you an objectivity, much like that of a doctor who can perform needed surgery in order to save a life.

• Understand that he can't get well overnight. Long years of habit are hard to shake. If he tries to make you feel guilty, it's because he's frightened and angry. He may well have a way with words and can be quite charming, so be careful lest he manipulate you. Don't be fooled by his bluster and arrogance; he is only a paper tiger. You can learn how to live beyond his problems and not accept the consequences of his behavior as your own. Life is too short to be living in a practice hell. You have your right to get *his* monkey off *your* back. You can't let the sin of one person destroy the whole family.

• Selfishness, immaturity, and irresponsibility are all manifested in a rebellious spirit. He believes he is the important one. Nothing is as important as that which helps him get momentarily puffed up to serve his delusions of grandeur. The sooner you let go of his problem and let him take responsibility for it, himself, the better chance there will be that he will treat you with more respect.

• He feels sorry for himself, so when you learn to say no to his pleas for pity, he may see you as abandoning him. That's okay. He needs to take responsibility for his own choices. If he sees you worrying, it only rewards his attention-seeking. Rescuing someone keeps that person dependent on you and preserves a neurotic relationship. Being a rescuer may make you feel comfortable for a time, but the person you are rescuing may grow to resent you later.

• The kind of assurance the wayward one needs—that he's desirable and lovable—can come only from deep inside him. It will come only when he is willing to face his problem and do something about it.

• Have courage. If you act just one time out of self-respect instead of fear, you will feel better inside than you have probably felt in years. When you accept the reality of your loved one's vulnerable area, several things will happen. You will start getting rid of your personal anger toward him. You will begin to detach yourself from his manipulation, and you will start planning your life for you. Without your having to say it, he will see that the problem is his, not yours. You will have found your serenity and he will have a chance to choose recovery for himself.[4]

Beware of the blame game! It can cause the sin of one person to practically destroy the entire family. The mother blames herself, and sometimes the father blames the mother—or he may decide to blame himself. Soon everyone is caught up in the "blame game," which is destructive to any family.

When Larry threatened to disown us (which he did) and change his name (which he also did), and then said he never wanted to see any of us again, all that was a dagger to my heart. But somehow I knew God would bring us through it. My mother's love for Larry never faltered, even as he drove that dagger deeper.

One thing that helped was that I had others who needed me. We had begun a ministry founded on Isaiah 61:1: "to bind up the brokenhearted. . . ." I couldn't let one child destroy my life, the rest of my family, and my faith in God. What Larry had done was a defeat, but it was only a TEMPORARY one. I had a choice. I could withdraw and become bitter or I could reach out to God with the knowledge that I would grow inwardly through all of this. I relied on 1 Kings 8:56 (KJV): "There hath not failed one word of all his good promise." I had God's promise that He loved me and He cared. As the psalmist says, "weeping may endure for a night, but joy cometh in the morning."[5]

As I put my trust in God, I began to realize my happiness really did not depend on what was happening in my son's life. God showed me that I could decorate my own life by helping others. The dawn does come. The sun does shine after the rain. There is peace after the storm. This poem came to mean a great deal:

> After a while you learn
>   That love doesn't mean leaning,
> That kisses aren't contracts, and presents aren't promises . . .
>   And you begin to accept defeats
>   With your head up and your eyes open,
> With the grace of a woman, not the grief of a child.
>   So you plant your own garden
>   And decorate your own soul,
> Instead of waiting for someone to bring you flowers.
>   And you learn that you can endure . . .
>   That you really are strong

> And you really do have worth,
> And that with every new tomorrow
>   Comes the dawn.
>
> Source unknown

Inside those long parentheses, while we waited with hope deferred, we prayed that God would do His work, according to His timetable, not ours, and that eventually Larry would make the choice to want to change his lifestyle. We knew we could not "fix" him or make any choices for him.

Now that Larry has been restored from his time of rebellion, God is using him in special ways. He works for the court system of Los Angeles and attends law school at night. Frequently, he talks with other young men who are struggling with their homosexual orientation and he is also a continual encouragement to me in Spatula Ministries. He is particularly helpful in doing research for my conference messages, as well as in preparation of the *Love Line* newsletter.

Larry is a real whiz with computers and he has access to all kinds of software. For example, if I need a Scripture verse, I just call Larry and he comes up with several that will fit. It is our goal to write a book together someday to share with other parents the principles of restoration through forgiveness and understanding that we have both learned through our years of estrangement.

So far in my list of guidelines, I've suggested that you "stuff a sock in your mouth" and use tough love to deal with your child's rebellion. Now I want to offer a third suggestion, one that applies to all parents and children:

3. Love Your Child Unconditionally

Not long after Larry left the gay lifestyle for good, we made a tape together that was sent out to the entire Spatula family.

Some of that tape appears in *So, Stick a Geranium in Your Hat and Be Happy*,[6] but I want to share some additional parts of it here, which may be helpful to parents who are trying to build a better relationship with wayward children.

BARBARA: What would you suggest to young people who have gone off into a life of homosexuality and completely broken with their parents, saying they don't want anything to do with them? How can the parents show unconditional love to a child who is rebellious?

LARRY: There is a great need for people to understand the importance of committing their lives to being kind and loving. When a person does that, then they become righteous. They're doing what God wants, and as I've said, life is a web of relationships. When people respond properly, when they give out a loving attitude, others have to respond to that. If someone is very hateful, others respond to that as well.

BARBARA: We call it a "porcupine" type of love—when you love your kids and they shoot back those porcupine quills and say those awful things to you. Yet you have to love them unconditionally. It's our job to love and it's God's job to work in their lives. Kids may respond with a lot of retorts and unloving things, but if parents can still love them unconditionally, then I think God's going to honor that.

LARRY: God says that we are responsible for five things: words, thoughts, actions, deeds, and attitudes. In studying wisdom in the Scriptures and trying to understand the mind of God, I've come to realize that the words that come out of my mouth are only a reflection of the attitude I have within me. So, if I have a loving and a caring attitude, my words will reflect that.

BARBARA: Loving unconditionally is so important, but it's hard if your child doesn't communicate with you. All the years we didn't have any communication from you were difficult. It's very hard to show love when somebody doesn't respond. How do you think that worked in the years that you weren't in touch with us?

LARRY: I think that's when the parent has to turn it all over to God. Scripture says, "The king's heart is in the hand of the LORD, / Like the rivers of water; / He turns it wherever He wishes."[7] This verse tells me God turns people's hearts wherever He wants them to go. You've just got to trust God in those kinds of situations and know that God will touch their hearts at the right time.

I believe that what Larry was saying is that no one can love unconditionally in his or her own strength. You must trust God to turn the heart of your wayward child (and to keep your heart turned the right way, as well). Unconditional love is a beautiful ideal that is far beyond human strength. We must trust God for grace and patience, especially when the porcupine quills are flying thick and fast. And we must learn to FORGIVE. This is perhaps the most important building block of any loving relationship, and Larry and I talked about that as well.

4. Be Willing to Ask—and Receive—Forgiveness

As our interview continued, I asked Larry how he felt during all those years he was away.

BARBARA: Did you always feel that we loved you?

LARRY: I felt that there was a lot of animosity, but there was a lot of love, too; so I would say there was a lot of good and bad. But that was a time when we were both afraid of what was happening. We didn't know how to respond. It was a very difficult time for both of us. Fortunately, we have been able to put those things aside and to know the basic core relationship that a parent and a child can have.

BARBARA: So many parents have tried to train their kids to do the right thing, but they go off and do their own thing. And so the parents feel guilt because they believe they have failed. It's hard to explain to parents that they are not responsible for their kids' choices.

LARRY: I think that when parents have a problem with a child, it's time for the parents to examine their hearts and minds. God is using those problems to highlight certain principles that have been neglected, and if parents neglect those principles then the whole family suffers for it.

BARBARA: I think one thing we're going to have to learn to do as parents is to zip up the past because we've all made mistakes. We have to say, "The past is over, yesterday is a canceled check, tomorrow is a promissory note, but today is cash. Today I haven't made any mistakes—yet. You can start out every day fresh and new to serve the Lord and how wonderful it is to start out every day and know the past is over. You don't have to live in bondage to things that were in the past that were unhappy for you, and I don't have to, either.

LARRY: That's because we've been able to forgive each other. Forgiveness is a very powerful thing—not only the ability to forgive, but the ability to be forgiven. When someone comes to you and says, "I was wrong in what I did to you; will you forgive me?" that's a very powerful thing because it releases a burden of guilt we carry because of whoever we have offended. But what holds people back from doing that is their own pride, their own inability to say, "I made a mistake, I was wrong." A lot of parents don't want to do that, and when the child sees the parent not willing to admit his mistakes, what makes you think the child would want to admit any mistakes?

BARBARA: In many cases parents need to ask their children to forgive them for their lack of love, but a lot of parents say, "Why should I ask forgiveness? What did I do? My kids went off into the gay life. I didn't do anything." But it's that attitude that's wrong and it won't help any kind of relationship. Parents should ask their child for forgiveness when they haven't shown understanding or love. That's the beginning of spiritual growth. Parents have to grow and change through all this as well as their children.

LARRY: Another important fact is that when a person is reacting so violently or so angrily, it's time for the other person—the parent—to examine his or her life to see what it is that brought this on. Is it an attitude of pride or an unbroken spirit? The parents should not look on themselves as authoritarians, but rather as friends of their grown children. And if they've offended them, the parents should go to the children and ask for their forgiveness. You'll find a lot of parents aren't willing to do that.

BARBARA: There's no perfect parent. After all, God had problems with Adam. We try to be perfect parents, but we're not and we fail.

LARRY: Everyone fails, but that's why Christ came. That's why we have the Bible and those principles to live by. We need to realize that we can admit our failures and be able to put them aside.

One of the key words Larry used in our interview is *friend.* Parents will move a long way toward building a better relationship with their adult children when they realize they must become more the friend and less the parental "authority." The following words by William Arthur Ward describe the kind of friends we want to be to our kids:

A FRIEND IS . . .

A friend is one who is not hard to find when you are penniless.

A friend is one who makes your grief less painful, your adversity more bearable.

A friend is one who joyfully sings with you when you are on the mountaintop, and silently walks beside you through the valley.

A friend is one with whom you are comfortable, to whom you are loyal, through whom you are blessed, and for whom you are grateful.

A friend is one who warms you by his presence, trusts you with his secrets, and remembers you in his prayers.

A friend is one who gives you a spark of assurance when you doubt your ability to fulfill your noblest aspiration, climb your special mountain, or reach your secret goal.

A friend is one who helps you bridge the gaps between loneliness and fellowship, frustration and confidence, despair and
hope, setbacks and success.

A friend is one who is available to you, understanding of
you, and patient with you. A friend is no less a gift from God
than is a talent; no less a treasure than life itself.

A friend is also someone who listens.

5. Listen More, Talk a Lot Less

The last line of the essay quoted above mentions listening,
one of the most powerful tools available for building good relationships with friends and loved ones. There is a lot of talk
about "communication" today, and it's true that we all need
to learn how to communicate better with each other. But communication can become just another buzz word that doesn't
mean much. On the other hand, listening is something specific
that any of us can do if we want to try. Most people think communicating means doing a lot of talking, but, in truth, I think
real communication begins when you start listening to the other
person. As James says, be QUICK to listen and SLOW to speak.[8]
A good definition of listening is this:

> ATTENTION WITH THE INTENTION
> TO UNDERSTAND THE OTHER PERSON.[9]

In his excellent book on communication, *Speaking from the
Heart*, Ken Durham writes:

> Christian listening is an act which communicates to another,
> "Right now, I am here for you. No one else, just you. I want to
> hear and understand what you have to say. I'm all yours." Lis-
> tening is allowing the other person to set the agenda for the
> conversation, seeking to clarify his point of view. Ultimately,
> listening is helping a person to understand himself better.[10]

The following poem sums up Christian listening very well:

LISTEN

When I ask you to listen to me
and you start giving advice
you have not done what I asked.

When I ask you to listen to me
and you begin to tell me why I shouldn't feel that way
you are trampling on my feelings.

When I ask you to listen to me
and you feel you have to do something to solve my problem
you have failed me, strange as that may seem.

So please listen and just hear me.
    And, if you want to talk,
    wait a minute for your turn;
    and I'll listen to you.

Source unknown

If you are having trouble communicating with your son or daughter . . . if you simply "can't talk about it" . . . maybe the best thing you can do is to invite your loved one to share feelings. Put away your desire to quote Scripture, give advice, or lecture. Two of my favorite mottoes are:

NOBODY CARES HOW MUCH YOU KNOW
UNLESS THEY KNOW HOW MUCH YOU CARE.

*   *   *   *   *   *

TALKING IS SHARING . . .
LISTENING IS CARING.

A lasting gift to a child, including grown children, is the gift of a parent's listening ear—and heart. Listen first and talk afterward. Then, instead of saying things that may bruise and cut, your words will be pleasant, like honey, sweet to the soul of your child[11] and healing to your relationship.

Splish/Splash . . .

SOME PEOPLE FIND FAULT
LIKE THERE WAS A REWARD FOR IT.

* * * * * *

TAKE A TIP FROM NATURE . . .
YOUR EARS AREN'T MADE TO SHUT,
BUT YOUR MOUTH IS.

* * * * * *

OPPORTUNITIES ARE OFTEN MISSED
BECAUSE WE ARE BROADCASTING
WHEN WE SHOULD BE LISTENING.

* * * * * *

NEVER WASTE YOUR PAIN!
Dear Lord . . .
   Please grant that I shall
   Never waste my pain; for . . .
   To fail without learning,
   To fall without getting up,
   To sin without overcoming,
   To be hurt without forgiving,
   To be discontent without improving,
   To be crushed without becoming more caring,
   To suffer without growing more sensitive,
   Makes of suffering a senseless, futile exercise,
   A tragic loss,
   And of pain,
   The greatest waste of all.

Dick Innes

* * * * * *

THE ONLY CONDITION FOR LOVING
IS TO LOVE WITHOUT CONDITIONS.

* * * * * *

Self-control means controlling the tongue! A quick retort can ruin everything. (Prov. 13:3, TLB)

We Are Easter People
Living in a Good Friday World

Due to the shortage of trained trumpeters,
the end of the world will be postponed three months.

Folks often ask me, "Barb, where do you get your joy?" That question always makes me think of the thirteenth verse of 1 Corinthians 13, the "love chapter": "And now these three remain: Faith, hope and love. But the greatest of these is love" (NIV).

With so many cesspools to fall into in life, we need a spring we can go to for splashes of joy—a spring full of living water that only Jesus provides.

Joy Begins with Faith

I love the line Tony Campolo uses—surely one of the greatest statements of faith ever written: "It's Friday, but Sunday's Comin'."

On that first Good Friday, Jesus' followers were in a real cesspool. Jesus had been nailed to a cross and now He was dead. Mary was distraught with grief. The disciples were scattered like frightened sheep. Pilate was confident he had washed his hands of the whole mess. Unbelievers were cynically saying that this so-called Messiah hadn't changed a thing. And worst of all, Satan was dancing around saying, "I won! I won!"

Yes, it was Friday, but then the temple veil split open like an overripe watermelon, rocks moved, tombs opened up, and the Roman centurion who had been sent to oversee the execution of some troublemaker wound up babbling, "This WAS the Son of God!"

And then came Sunday. Mary Magdalene and the other women came to Jesus' sealed and guarded tomb to find the stone rolled away and an angel in blazing white saying, "He is not here—He is risen!"

On Friday all had been darkness, despair, and grief. But NOW it was SUNDAY and the whole world had cause for joy greater than any known before or since.

Actually, we aren't Easter people living in a Good Friday world, we are RESURRECTION people.

As an unknown writer said:

> Resurrection says that absolutely nothing can separate me from the love of God. Not sin or my stupidity. Not the sinister or the selfish, not the senseless or the secular.

The foundation of all joy for Christians is that we can live as though Christ died yesterday, rose today, and is coming tomorrow. It starts here and it's for everyone, no strings, no admission fee, because we are saved by grace and grace alone. That's what Paul meant when he said we are saved by grace through faith (Eph. 2:8, 9). It doesn't have anything to do with what we can do. As I always say,

JUSTICE IS WHEN WE GET WHAT WE DESERVE.
MERCY IS WHEN WE DON'T GET WHAT WE DESERVE.
BUT GRACE IS WHEN WE GET WHAT WE DON'T DESERVE.

Grace is God's unmerited favor which is showered upon us. And that grace is FREE to all who ask for it. We begin by trusting Jesus Christ. That's it. He is our first experience of joy. And we continue to have splashes of joy as we learn to trust in Him alone.

But what about the times we slide back into that cesspool of despair? Has God forsaken us? We have questions and more questions. WHY? HOW? WHERE ARE YOU, LORD? As Ruth Harms Calkin writes:

> Lord, I ask more questions
> Than You ask.
> The ratio, I would suppose
> Is ten to one.
>
> I ask:
> Why do You permit this anguish?
> How long can I endure it?
> What possible purpose does it serve?
> Have You forgotten to be gracious?
> Have I wearied You?
> Have I offended You?
> Have You cast me off?
> Where did I miss Your guidance?
> When did I lose the way?
> Do You see my utter despair?
>
> You ask:
> *Are you trusting me?*[1]

Ruth Calkin's words remind me that there are 354 "fear nots" in the Bible—almost one for each day of the year. If we feed our faith, our doubts will starve to death. The feeblest knock of faith opens heaven's door because faith looks beyond the darkness of earth to the brightness of heaven.

Before he died, I heard my good friend Walter Martin tell about the time he and two agnostics were guests on the "Phil Donahue Show." Topics for the day included death, heaven, and the penalty for sin. As the program drew to a close, Phil Donahue went up to Dr. Martin in his familiar way and said, "Well, now, Doc, don't you think that when I get to the end of the road, God will put His arms around me and say, 'Aw, c'mon in, Phil!'?"

Dr. Martin flashed Phil Donahue a wide smile and responded, "Oh, Phil, He already did—two thousand years ago. He invited you to come on in THEN."

When I think about this story, it brings tears to my eyes as I realize how God made it possible for us to be assured of heaven because of His loving sacrifice for us. We have an open invitation with a heavenly R.S.V.P.

Walter Martin is now with the Lord, but his response to Phil Donahue that day is a splash of joy that still continues to encourage me. It gives me extra courage when I need it. It is so true: Our WORDS OF FAITH go on long after we are gone.

Joy Comes Out of Hope

One of the cleverest—and saddest—epitaphs I ever heard appears on the headstone of Mel Blanc, voice of so many famous cartoon characters, including Porky Pig and Elmer Fudd:

TH-TH-TH-THAT'S ALL, FOLKS!

I don't know what Mel Blanc personally believed about life after death, but this life ISN'T all, folks! There is, oh, so much more! We don't face a hopeless end because we have an endless hope! Our hope is in the FACT that, because of our faith, we are going UP. Somebody sent me these thoughts on the word UP, adapted from an essay by Frank Endicott:

WHAT'S UP?

We have a two-letter word we use constantly that may have more meanings than you would imagine. The word is UP.

It is easy to understand UP meaning toward the sky or toward the top of a list. But when we waken, why do we wake UP? At a meeting, why does a topic come UP, why do participants speak UP, and why are the officers UP for election? And why is it UP to the secretary to write UP a report?

Often the little word isn't needed, but we use it anyway. We brighten UP a room, polish UP the silver, lock UP the house, and fix UP the old car. At other times, it has special meanings. People stir UP trouble, line UP for tickets, work UP an appetite, think UP excuses, get tied UP in traffic. To be dressed is one thing, but to be dressed UP is special. It may be confusing, but a drain must be opened UP because it is stopped UP. We open UP a store in the morning and close it UP at night. We seem to be mixed UP about UP.

To be UP on the proper use of UP, look UP the word in your dictionary. In one desk-size dictionary UP takes UP half a page, and listed definitions add UP to about 40. If you are UP to it, you might try building UP a list of the many ways in which UP is used. It will take UP a lot of your time but, if you don't give UP, you may wind UP with a thousand.

Frank Endicott cleverly lists a lot of uses for the word UP, but he forgot two important ones. First, there are a lot of people who need to CHEER UP, and, second, one way or another, Christians are going UP—to heaven—to eternal life with Jesus. I like the picture of going UP in Psalm 90:10 (RSV) which says: "The years of our life are threescore and ten, or even by reason of strength, fourscore; yet their span is but toil and trouble; they are soon gone, and we fly away."

Can you believe it says we will FLY AWAY? I can't be sure that the psalmist was thinking of the Second Coming when he wrote those lines, but he pictures exactly what Paul says in 1 Thessalonians 4:16, 17 (NKJV):

> For the Lord Himself will descend from heaven with a shout, with the voice of an archangel, and with the trumpet of God. And the dead in Christ will rise first. Then we who are alive and remain shall be caught up together with them in the clouds to meet the Lord in the air. And thus we shall always be with the Lord.

That blessed hope of the Christian is all wrapped UP in the Second Coming. I often urge folks to get in plenty of "rapture practice" by going out in the backyard and jumping UP and down, just to limber UP for the big day when the trumpet sounds and we all go UP. As I like to say,

HE'S GONNA TOOT
AND WE'RE GONNA SCOOT!

I often mention rapture practice when I speak, and once an elderly lady came up afterward and asked, "Honey, when you do your rapture practice, do you do it on a trampoline or on the grass?"

I also love the letter from the lady who said she and her husband were planning to celebrate their fiftieth wedding anniversary by going up in a hot-air balloon. She said, "I'm going to stick a geranium in my hat and be happy and have a terrific pre-rapture joy ride!"

Sometimes I talk with folks who wonder WHEN Jesus is coming. Down through the years different people have "set the date," but they have forgotten one thing: The Bible never sets the date. Meanwhile, it's a Good Friday world, full of pain, guilt, and shame. AIDS stalks the earth, killing thousands, and it will take thousands more before a cure is found—if ever. I have found a plaque that I often give to AIDS victims to remind them and their families of the endless hope all believers have beyond this life. The picture shows Jesus taking someone into His arms and hugging him, and the words say:

WHEN I COME HOME TO HEAVEN

When I come home to Heaven
    How joyful it will be!
For on that day at last
    My risen Lord I'll see.

No greater happiness than
    To see Him face to face,

> To see the love in His eyes
>   And feel His warm embrace.
>
> I've done nothing to deserve
>   That perfect home above.
> It was given freely through
>   The grace of Jesus' love.
>
> Then why should earthly cares
>   Weigh down upon me so?
> They'll be a distant memory
>   When home at last I go.[2]

As I said in chapter 3, hope is hard to kill. In fact, it has saved the life of more than one person who felt hopeless. A note that came in the mail, and which I treasure very much, says:

> Thank you for your book . . . God really spoke to me through your words. I'm a sophomore medical student. Stress, anxiety and depression were my constant companions . . . suicide was never too far from my door. Now I have hope . . . Thank you.

Somebody said one of our greatest enemies is not disease—it's despair. One of our greatest friends is hope. And the reason we can have hope in this life is because of our hope in the life to come. I have always liked acrostics, and this one says it all about hope:

> He
> Offers
> Peace
> Eternal.

But the Greatest Joy Is Love

One of the happiest phrases in all of Scripture is tucked away in 1 John 4:8: "GOD IS LOVE." And I like to add, "GOD IS JOY." To know and feel God's love is to know the deep kind of abiding joy that you want to splash all over others.

Jesus reassured us that He would not leave us comfortless (see John 14:18). He did not promise endless days of ease, but rather love and growth as we travel over the bumps and wash-outs in life. He didn't say we would all ride in limos. We might make our trip in a beat-up station wagon, a pickup truck, on a bicycle, or even in a wheelchair. No matter how we travel, the important thing is feeling God's breath upon us. We need a quickening that lets us know God IS love and we can have fellowship with Him.

Sometimes it helps to get away alone in a lovely setting. It could be at the ocean with the waves crashing on the beach, or it might be while bobbing around in a sailboat, or just walking along a path and feeling the breeze blowing through the trees.

But God's love can happen ANYWHERE. Once it happened to me at the Department of Motor Vehicles office when I was selecting a personalized license plate for Bill. As I looked through the giant book of license-plate names that had already been used, I realized that my own name is written in another book that is much more important—the Lamb's Book of Life, and that I am forever a daughter of the King. God reminded me that I am His child. I am royalty! God's warm comfort blanket enfolded me with the assurance of His care. I felt His presence so strongly that I had tears in my eyes. The warm comforting feeling of His love splashed over me—EVEN AT THE DMV!

But the specific place really doesn't matter. Being marinated in God's love is what counts. It's your personal relationship with God that makes the difference and brings the joy from His fountain of life. Experience has taught me that only those who have gone from despair to hope can know what a refreshing fountain of life feels like. One of my favorite thoughts is:

GOD LOVES A DANGLING CHRISTIAN.

In other words, God wants the believer to be TOTALLY dependent on Him. And when you cry out to Him for help, His love is the rope that pulls you out of the cesspool to His refreshing fountain. Once you come to the fountain and have been splashed with God's joy, something happens. You realize that you aren't the only one who knows what a cesspool is like. Sometimes in our loneliness it is easy to think we are the only ones who have had to suffer, "just like this." But when God's love touches us during our suffering, we can see how shallow our caring for others has been.

C. S. Lewis has said that grief is like a long, winding valley, where any bend might reveal a totally new landscape. And when we come upon that beautiful new landscape, we have a clear vision of what it means to be a spirit lifter. Love is the greatest gift we have to give, and if we let Him, God will help us be sensitive to loneliness, grief, and pain wherever it exists—which is all around us.

God Always Needs More Pipe

Think of a gardener irrigating his garden. He is able to channel life-giving water to all areas except to one little dying plant way over in the corner. The gardener knows that if he had just one more piece of pipe he could run it over to that wilting plant and transform it with new life.

So it is with the Master Gardener. Because He chooses to minister through us, He needs many lengths of pipe to bless persons here, there, and all around. Perhaps in your area there is a drooping, wilting person who needs God's touch right now. Proverbs says, "Anxious hearts are very heavy, but a word of encouragement does wonders."[3]

We can be that extra piece of pipe through which He can channel His cheer, encouragement, and joy to those who need it. Christ, Himself, set the example of what it means to be a spirit-lifter. On the night before He died, during one of the darkest moments that He and His disciples had ever known in the three years that they had been together, He told them to "cheer up, for I have overcome the world."[4]

At Spatula Ministries we feel our usual way of being a pipeline is through answering letters and making phone calls, sometimes to very frantic, despairing people on the other end of the line. We also go out to speak all over the country, and once a month we conduct a support group for parents of gay children, which is a prototype for dozens of such groups all over the nation. But sometimes God asks us to run a very personal pipeline directly to someone who needs a special bit of TLC.

Greg's Mom Received His Suicide Tape

About 11:00 on a Saturday morning last year I got a frantic call from a mother who said, "My son, Greg, lives in La Habra and he just sent me a tape cassette saying he is HIV positive and is going to take his life. Would you go find him? We don't know who else to call."

As I talked with this mother, I learned that she and her husband had been on a trip and had gotten back to their home in Idaho sooner than expected. When they arrived back home, the tape was waiting, and she was sure her son had thought that by the time they were supposed to hear the tape several days later, he would have already taken his life.

Greg's mother gave me his address, and I left immediately to try to find him. His apartment was only about three miles from my home and I drove as fast as I could, thinking of the days that had elapsed since he had sent his mother the tape. What if it were too late?

I pulled up to an old apartment complex where this young man was supposed to be and discovered it had just been painted. The Spanish architecture was now garish shades of orchid and turquoise, and there were no numbers on any of the apartments because the painters had taken them down temporarily.

I went from door to door, asking everyone about a young man named Greg, but nobody there seemed to speak English and my Spanish is pretty much forgotten so I got no positive responses. I was beginning to think I had the wrong address when, on my way toward the front of the building, I saw one door ajar. Thinking perhaps it was the laundry room, I pushed it all the way open and looked inside. The tiny room was dark and dank, and smelled like cat dung. The only furniture was a long, skinny bed, a table, and a chair. Then, in the semi-darkness, I made out a tall, dark, emaciated young man who just sat there, staring into space.

"Are you Greg?" I asked.

Startled, the young man looked up at me and said, "Yes, but who are you?"

I told him who I was and that his mother had called me that morning and had wanted me to see him. "God really loves you, Greg," I said. "Whatever you've been into, God loves you and He'll forgive you. God won't turn His back on you. You may have strayed off, but I want you to know that Jesus died for your sins and still loves you and wants to welcome you back. Can I pray with you? Can I talk with you?"

I prayed with Greg and then we talked for almost an hour. He told me he couldn't believe anybody would care that much for him. He'd gone to a Christian college for awhile, and when students there learned that he was gay he would find notes taped on his door that said, "GET OUT, YOU FAGGOT!"

Finally he had left college and dropped totally into the gay lifestyle. But mental conviction hounded him because he knew it was wrong. He left Long Beach and moved to La Habra to make a fresh start and forsake all the sinful past. But just after taking his first step to restoration with God, he learned he had a full-blown case of AIDS.

Greg also told me that he had no money, hadn't eaten for days, and his car was about to be repossessed. He had planned to kill himself that very day by using sleeping pills, and to prove it, he held up a bottle full of them.

I reached into my purse and gave him all the cash I had with me—thirty-five dollars. Then I said, "Greg, I'm going out to get you some food and other stuff. Please don't do anything desperate while I'm gone. I'll be back soon."

Greg promised that he would wait for me, and I went home and told Bill the story. While Bill scraped up some money, I went out to the supermarket and bought some eggs, cheese, bread, and other groceries, as well as some vitamins. Then I hurried back to Greg's apartment. I had only been gone for an hour, but when I got there it was locked and there was no response to my knock on the door.

I found the apartment manager and said, "I need to get into this young man's apartment because I was here an hour ago and I need to put away some groceries."

"I don't know what's going on with him," the lady said. "He's lived here a week, but he's never been out of the apartment. Nobody ever comes to see him, and I saw his car being towed away about an hour ago."

The woman let me in, and when I opened Greg's refrigerator there was nothing in it but half a can of 7-Up. I put away the groceries. I left a note with my phone number that said, "Greg, I don't know where you are, but please call me as soon as you get back."

When I got home the phone was ringing and it was Greg! "I just can't believe that anybody would do this," he told me. "I'd gone out to get some groceries with the thirty-five dollars because I hadn't eaten anything all week. I just can't believe that God would really care about me."

The next day I took Greg up to a church in the Glendora area and got him involved in a support group for AIDS victims. They took him under their wing and worked out transportation so he could get up to the church for support-group meetings and Sunday services.

It turned out that Greg has a beautiful voice and he soon had a tremendous ministry at the church, singing for all kinds of events, including funerals of young men in his support group who died from AIDS.

Meanwhile, Greg continued living at the orchid and turquoise apartment house and went back to a job he had in an office two miles away. With his car repossessed, Greg faced walking that distance each day, but, fortunately, some friends provided him with a bike. For the next several months he used that to go back and forth to work. The route to Greg's office went right by our house and he would often stop by for a snack or just to visit on his way home. It was hot and smoggy, but Greg never complained. He considered himself fortunate to be able to ride the bike to work and back.

Just before Christmas Greg was transferred to a branch office about thirty miles from La Habra. The good news was that it was much closer to the church where he loved to be with new Christian friends after making a complete break with the old gay lifestyle. The bad news was that he had to move to a new place that was farther away from his job, and he was in desperate need of a car.

By this time we had really learned to love Greg and we were concerned about how he would manage with moving and getting back and forth to work. One day Bill came in and told me he had just had a revelation. Because Bill has very few revelations, I was all ears.

"I'm going to give Wumphee to Greg so that he can get moved and keep his job!" Bill said.

Earlier, I said that my nickname for Bill is "Wumphee." I also mentioned that I had gotten him personalized license plates for his 1974 Oldsmobile, a car that should have been a tuna boat—at least it's as big as one. Wumphee seemed to me to be the obvious choice for the license plates, so that's how his beloved car came to be nicknamed Wumphee, too. The only problem was that as soon as he bolted on the personalized plates, service-station attendants everywhere started calling Bill "Mr. Wumphee." He said it was bad enough having his wife call him that, but having to hear, "Have a nice day, Mr. Wumphee" every time he filled up was almost too much.

Despite all that, Bill loved Wumphee, so I knew that giving the car to Greg was no small gesture on his part. Not only that, but Bill cleaned out the car, filled Wumphee's giant tank with gas, and also put a case of oil in the trunk (Wumphee burns almost as much oil as gas).

All of this really surprised me because Bill is known for his Swedish frugality (i.e., being tight). As a final touch, we put a lot of nickels, dimes, and quarters in the ashtray so passengers would be encouraged not to smoke in the car, and Greg would have plenty of change for parking meters— or hamburgers.

The next time Greg came by, Bill handed him the car title for Wumphee. Not much for ceremony or sentimentality, all he said was, "Everything works. You don't need to do anything to Wumphee, just keep oil in him because he does burn a lot of oil."

We all celebrated on that joyful day. Bill got a splash of joy when he saw Greg's eyes light up over the car, and I felt so relieved that Greg's transportation problem was solved, and so simply! Just before Greg drove off tooting the horn, Bill mentioned that when Greg got his own license plates, he wanted back the personalized plates. Greg was more than happy to return them and now the WUMPHEE plates are proudly displayed in our joy room.

Greg Knows That God Is Real

Since that day when Greg's mother made her frantic phone call, she and her husband have kept in touch with him. They came down to help him get moved and while here they also attended a Spatula meeting and became strong supporters of the ministry. As I completed this chapter, Greg was coping with his illness and had the energy to work and minister with his musical ability in many different settings.

Not long after I found Greg on the verge of suicide, I contacted Marilyn Meberg, one of the teachers he had had at college. He remembered her fondly as someone who was a "bright spot" in his life at that time. I told Marilyn Greg's story and she was thrilled, because she was in the midst of prepar-

ing some new presentations on God's love and care—the way
He is a shepherd to all of His sheep. She wrote to him, and
she and Greg have agreed to share parts of their letters with
you:

Greg,
My heart breaks for the pain you've experienced from the
isolation and support you did not receive, and more than anything, the fear that God, too, had turned His back on you. How
unlike the nature of God to abandon us and yet, how prone we
are to think He probably feels toward us like others do. It knocks
my socks off that God should direct Barb to your door on the
very day when you most needed Him. I stumbled across an incredible couple of verses that fit your experience. Ezekiel 34:11,
12 says: "Behold, I Myself will search for My sheep and seek
them out. As a shepherd cares for his herd in the day when he
is among his scattered sheep, so I will care for My sheep and
will deliver them from all the places to which they were scattered on a cloudy and gloomy day."
Dear, dear Greg—God has searched you out, found you
among the "scattered" and draws you to Himself that you might
know you are esteemed and loved! Unfortunately, all too often
the "sheep" do not have the compassion and acceptance of the
Shepherd. We hurt each other inexcusably. Don't confuse their
actions with those of the Shepherd. There are no conditions from
Him, Greg—only believe in Him and receive Him. WHAT A
DEAL! God love you, Greg, and hold you close!
                                              Marilyn Meberg

Not long afterward, Marilyn received this letter from Greg:

Dear Mrs. Meberg,
Thank you for sharing Ezekiel 34. As I sit here just blown
over by the blessings that God has bestowed on this little wandering sheep, I'm overwhelmed. He has indeed searched for
me out of the places I've wandered, not just physical places but
those places in my heart that have wandered away from His
warmth and slowly gotten cold. I want to say a couple of things.
For the first time in my life I know that God is real. No more

looking at the menu and admiring the nice pictures of the food; my meal has come and I've tasted its fullness. I know that death is real, I've seen it in the eyes of my friend, Brent, and I know that one day I, too, am going too die. And I know that the Shepherd who gathered me unto Himself here will welcome me when I get on the other side.

For Christmas, Greg gave me a darling Erma Bombeck calendar and each day, as I tear off a sheet, I think of him and his wonderful sense of humor and the talents he is using so effectively for the Lord. On one occasion I gave him an assignment to look up a great many Scriptures for me to include in something I was doing for the *Love Line* newsletter. He diligently finished the task and brought the list to me. It represented hours of work, and Greg was so proud that he had accomplished all that I had asked of him because he wanted, in some way, to do something for us after what we had done for him. That is how the principle works:

> AS WE REFRESH OTHERS,
> WE, OURSELVES, ARE REFRESHED.

Take Time to Love

In sharing Greg's story, we see so many who are hurting because they are in one cesspool or another. If you have been touched with God's love, He wants you to take time to touch others. As the final line of a well-known poem puts it:

> TAKE TIME TO LOVE—IT'S GOD-LIKE.

There is no limit to the lives you might touch for the Master if you decide to become a pipeline for His love. You have probably read the following poem somewhere, sometime. It is very well known and it has been repeated in one form or another in many places. "The Old Violin" is included here because it states so clearly the message of this chapter:

'Twas battered and scarred, and the auctioneer
Thought it scarcely worth his while
To waste much time on the old violin,
But held it up with a smile.
"What am I bidden, good folks?" he cried.
"Who'll start the bidding for me?
A dollar, a dollar—now two, only two—
Two dollars, and who'll make it three?
Three dollars once, three dollars twice,
Going for three"—but no!
From the room far back a grey-haired man
Came forward and picked up the bow;
Then wiping the dust from the old violin,
And tightening up all the strings,
He played a melody pure and sweet;
As sweet as an angel sings.
The music ceased, and the auctioneer,
With a voice that was quiet and low,
Said, "What am I bid for the old violin?"
And he held it up with the bow.
"A thousand dollars—and who'll make it two?
Two thousand—and who'll make it three?
Three thousand once and three thousand twice—
And going and gone!" said he.
The people cheered but some of them cried,
"We do not quite understand—
What changed its worth?" The man replied:
"The touch of the master's hand!"

And many a man with life out of tune,
And battered and torn with sin,
Is auctioned cheap to a thoughtless crowd,
Much like the old violin . . .
But the Master comes, and the foolish crowd
Never can quite understand
The worth of a soul and the change that's wrought
By the Touch of the Master's Hand.

Myra Brooks Welch[5]

There are many ways to touch people for the Master. In other books, I've shared about wrapping a brick with gold-foil paper and giving it to folks as a gift.[6] It serves as a perfect doorstop and it's inexpensive and easy to make. I suggest that first you make one of these bricks for yourself. Get a used brick or buy a new one for a few cents at a builder's supply store. Find some bright shiny GOLD wrapping paper and wrap the brick carefully. Then put on a colorful bow and perhaps some cherries or berries or some other sprig of color.

Now you have a beautiful reminder that you are GOLD IN THE MAKING! The furnace of pain you have come through or are going through has made you as gold for the Master's use! You have been and are being refined, purified, tried—being made WORTHY!

Do you know, if all the gold in the whole world were melted down into a solid cube it would be about the size of an eight-room house? If you got possession of all that gold—billions of dollars' worth—you could not buy a friend, character, peace of mind, a clear conscience, or eternal life. Yet you are GOLD IN THE MAKING because of the trials you have come through. Now, THAT'S an exciting idea!

After you have your own shiny gold brick, nicely sitting by your door as a stopper, make another such brick for a good friend. Perhaps it is someone who has been a "gold brick" in your life and has refreshed and encouraged you, and they may be needing a lift of their own right now. Take your gift to this friend and tell her how she has refreshed and encouraged you. Tell her you want to thank her for how she has helped you through your own time of testing and that you want to remind her that she, too, is gold in the making.

Before long, you may be making many other gold bricks to share with other friends who are like gold in your life.

Something else I've been doing lately is wrapping up a small piece of wood about the size of a match box. I use bright, shiny paper, complete with ribbon, and send it to friends with the following message taped on the box:

> This is a special gift
> That you can never see
> The reason it's so special is
> It's just for you . . . from me.
> Whenever you are happy,
> Or even feeling blue,
> You only have to see this gift
> And know I think of you.
> You never can unwrap it,
> Please leave the ribbon tied . . .
> Just hold it close to your heart
> It's filled with LOVE inside.

Those are just a couple of ideas—nothing profound or expensive—but simple ways to reach out to touch someone for the Master and spread some splashes of joy in a cesspool world. You may prefer another approach, but the important thing is to do SOMETHING. As one lady's letter put it:

PRETEND YOU'RE A STAR
AND POKE A HOLE IN SOMEONE'S DARKNESS.

Larry Sends a Serendipity

As I was closing an interview with Dr. James Dobson on his "Focus on the Family" broadcast, he had some nice things to say about Spatula Ministries:

> Barbara, it's quite an act of compassion that you allow people that you don't even know to reach out to you with such misery. Most of us have such difficulties in our own lives we don't need anybody else's. And it's one thing to put your arm around a brother or sister at church who is hurting, someone that you've known through the years and try to help them; it's another thing to try to tell the whole world that you'll accept their problems— not only their problems, but their misery. You have done that through the years. I don't know many people like that. My hat is off to you. It doesn't have a geranium in it, but it's off to you. I really do appreciate who you are.

Slightly embarrassed, I was trying to tell Dr. Dobson I appreciated his kind words and his ready smile, but he interrupted me saying he had a surprise that would put a smile on MY face. "We have placed a phone call just a short time ago to Barbara's son—the one she has referred to a number of times," he told the radio audience. "He has a message that we want to leave with all of you."

Then I heard Larry's voice saying these unforgettable words:

> The eleven years of estrangement were difficult years for both my parents and me. And during that time it became very evident to me of the gripping power of bitterness and resentment that had engulfed our family. But now, however, we're all grateful for God's healing restoration.

> And if you've read my mother's book, *So, Stick a Geranium in Your Hat and Be Happy*, you'll know the details and the impact of her ministry on my situation and on those people who have been similarly situated. I'm thankful for you and all your listeners who have prayed for me and my family and can only offer this word of advice at this time:

> If we as Christians can purpose in our hearts to be kind and loving in all that we do and put away a condemning spirit and learn the fear of the Lord, then surely the light of Christ will be able to shine in our disbelieving world, and restoration and revival will take root in the lives of those that we touch on a daily basis.

To sit there and hear my darling son say those words after the long years of estrangement wasn't a mere splash of joy, IT WAS LIKE A TIDAL WAVE! As his mom, and more importantly now, AS HIS BEST FRIEND, all I can say is . . .

WHOOPEE!

Splish/Splash . . .

> HAPPINESS IS LIKE JAM:
> YOU CAN'T SPREAD IT WITHOUT

GETTING SOME ON YOURSELF.

*   *   *   *   *   *

WHEN GOD MEASURES A PERSON,
HE PUTS A TAPE AROUND THE HEART
INSTEAD OF THE HEAD.

*   *   *   *   *   *

HE LOVES EACH OF US,
AS IF THERE WERE ONLY ONE OF US.
St. Augustine

*   *   *   *   *   *

LOVE . . .

is the one treasure that multiplies by division: It is the one gift
that grows bigger the more you take from it. It is the one business in which it pays to be an absolute spendthrift; give it away,
throw it away, splash it over, empty your pockets, shake the
basket, turn the glass upside down, and tomorrow you will have
more than ever.

Source unknown

*   *   *   *   *   *

SALVATION
DON'T LEAVE EARTH WITHOUT IT!

*   *   *   *   *   *

GIVE LAVISHLY! LIVE ABUNDANTLY!

The more you give, the more you get—
The more you laugh, the less you fret—
The more you do unselfishly,

The more you live abundantly . . .
The more of everything you share,
The more you'll always have to spare—
The more you love, the more you'll find
That life is good and friends are kind . . .
For only what we give away
Enriches us from day to day.

Source unknown

*　*　*　*　*　*

THINGS BEYOND OUR SEEING
THINGS BEYOND OUR HEARING
THINGS BEYOND OUR IMAGINING
ALL PREPARED BY GOD
FOR THOSE WHO LOVE HIM.

*　*　*　*　*　*

And you can also be very sure that God will rescue the children of the godly. (Prov. 11:21, TLB)

Going Up with a Splash

Life is too short to eat brown bananas.

Recently I spoke at a conference held in a remote area of Nebraska. My cabin was perched just below a train trestle, and what a special quality that place had because of the trains that rumbled through at all hours of the day and night.

I spent a great part of the night awake, but it was fun because I was fascinated with the first far-off toots of a train's whistle as it came to a crossing. Then I'd picture it as it would approach, pass by, and speed on through the night. As I listened closely, I learned to distinguish one kind of locomotive from another, just by the sound of the air horn or the clacking of the engine.

As I kept hearing the passing of the trains, I would reminisce about those times when I was a little girl visiting my aunt who lived where you could hear the trains go by in the night. What warmth there was in those familiar sounds!

The only train I hear these days is the steam locomotive at Knott's Berry Farm! How fortunate I felt that night to be able to listen through the night to those clacking sounds as the trains rumbled across the trestle high above my head.

On the way to breakfast the next morning, I looked up at the trestle and thought about how railroad tracks, themselves, are a work of art. In the early morning and late afternoon, as the sun moved toward the horizon, the tops of the rails shone with an almost radiant brightness. The highly polished steel stood out from the dull, weathered appearance of the ties and the ballast.

How beautiful these brightly glowing ribbons of steel appeared in the golden light of the sun. I couldn't help but make the connection that train tracks are beautiful only after taking tremendous weight, stress, and pressure, all of which polish them to their high luster. And the same is true of so many people I know.

As we ate breakfast, many of the women were complaining and some asked how I could sleep with all those train noises going on. I said I didn't mind, and then I asked one lady how come it seemed that all the trains were going east. Her reply, "Because that's the way the engine is headed!"

I refrained from reminding her that I was the one who was supposed be telling the jokes! Instead, I kept thinking how glad I was to be able to enjoy sounds and reminders of faraway times—finding joy in the small things. After all, I could always sleep at other places or at home, but seldom would I have the excitement of being awake most of the night listening to the passing trains and having my memories stirred so pleasantly.

Sounds do trigger my memories, and so do smells. Each of us can probably think of particular odors that are reminiscent of happy times. For those of us who live where the smell of burning leaves is still allowed by law, there are memories of high-school pep rallies and Halloween pumpkins. Or think about smelling dried pine needles and you're back in the woods on your first campout.

The scent of rubbing alcohol will probably always cause a twinge in the pit of your stomach as you remember childhood shots or hospital backrubs.

The sweet, old-fashioned perfume of purple lilacs evokes the ghosts of childhood backyards with brick walls and dense shade trees.

The smell of damp wool will always make me recall wet mittens with icy cuffs, snowballs, and apple-cheeked kids coming in out of the sub-zero cold.

Our ears and noses can teach us as much about life as any book. That's why I love to hear trains and whistles, as well as smell fresh-brewed coffee, baby powder, new leather, and gentle rain on summer dust.

And, personally, I love the smell of gasoline as it is being pumped into the tank. Maybe it reminds me of those long, cross-country car trips with the kids' Crayolas melting as we crossed the hot desert, eager to reach the next pit stop.

No matter what month of the year it might be, there are smells in the air that can trigger memories and make you feel alive. As J. H. Roades said:

> DO MORE THAN EXIST . . . LIVE!
> DO MORE THAN TOUCH . . . FEEL!
> DO MORE THAN LOOK . . . SEE!
> DO MORE THAN HEAR . . . LISTEN!
> DO MORE THAN TALK . . . SAY SOMETHING!

To this I would add: Do more than just smell a fragrance . . . *enjoy* it. In fact, enjoy everything you can while you can.

When I was growing up in Michigan, we bought apples by the barrel and my mother always made sure that we ate them ALL, even the mealy, soft, brown ones at the bottom. When I married Bill, I thought I had escaped having to eat mealy, brown, overripe fruit, but I quickly learned that he was just like my mom, only his specialty was bananas.

When the boys were small, Bill made sure that they ate ALL the bananas, even the ones that had gotten soft and speckled with brown. It seemed as though we never did get to eat nice, fresh, yellow bananas; we always were finishing up the brown ones—unless I tossed them out when Bill was at work! Maybe that's why I always love a new month, because I toss out everything leftover or overripe and start with fresh produce all over again. In my opinion, life is too short to eat brown bananas. And that goes for apples, too!

And although I'm glad I don't have to do that any more, I'm also glad Mom made us eat old, mushy apples and Bill made us eat the brown bananas. It taught me a valuable lesson that is found in one of my favorite readings, "The Station," by Robert J. Hastings. He definitely did not believe in eating brown bananas!

Tucked away in our subconscious minds is an idyllic vision in which we see ourselves on a long journey that spans an entire continent. We're traveling by train and, from the windows, we drink in the passing scenes of cars on nearby highways, of children waving at crossings, of cattle grazing in distant pastures, of smoke pouring from power plants, of row upon row of cotton and corn and wheat, of flatlands and valleys, of city skylines and village halls.

But uppermost in our minds is our final destination—for at a certain hour and on a given day, our train will finally pull into the station with bells ringing, flags waving, and bands playing. And once that day comes, so many wonderful dreams will come true. So restlessly, we pace the aisles and count the miles, peering ahead, waiting, waiting, waiting for the station.

"Yes, when we reach the station, that will be it!" we promise ourselves. "When we're eighteen . . . win that promotion . . . put the last kid through college . . . buy that 450 SL Mercedes Benz . . . pay off the mortgage . . . have a nest egg for retirement."

From that day on we will all live happily ever after.

Sooner or later, however, we must realize there is no station in this life, no one earthly place to arrive at once and for all. The journey is the joy. The station is an illusion—it constantly outdistances us. Yesterday's a memory, tomorrow's a dream. Yesterday belongs to a history, tomorrow belongs to God. Yesterday's a fading sunset, tomorrow's a faint sunrise. Only today is there light enough to love and live.

So, gently close the door on yesterday and throw the key away. It isn't the burdens of today that drive men mad, but rather the regret over yesterday and the fear of tomorrow.

"Relish the moment" is a good motto, especially when coupled with Psalm 118:24, "This is the day which the Lord hath made; we will rejoice and be glad in it."

So stop pacing the aisles and counting the miles. Instead, swim more rivers, climb more mountains, kiss more babies, count more stars. Laugh more and cry less. Go barefoot oftener. Eat more ice cream. Ride more merry-go-rounds. Watch more sunsets. Life must be lived as we go along.[1]

Robert Hastings is right. There is no station you can get to in this life that will make any difference, so you might as well enjoy the trip. But there is a very important Station that will come eventually.

While I was speaking in Canada, we came to the end of the conference and, because everyone would be leaving immediately after the final message, an announcement was made to put on your traveling apparel—they called it "going-home clothes." I couldn't help but think about that. We are all pilgrims making our trip homeward.

From years before, I remembered an old song we used to sing in "rounds." One side of the church would sing, "I'm on the homeward trail . . . I'm on the homeward trail . . ." and the other side would come back with "Singing, singing, everybody singing, HOMEWARD BOUND!" This would go on for several rounds, until the last strains of the song would be soft and almost distant, fading as the song ended with "HOMEWARD BOUND."

Through faith in Christ, we are all homeward bound. As God gradually transfers our loved ones to heaven, we have more and more deposits there, and as 1 Corinthians 2:9 says, "Eye has not seen, nor ear heard, nor have entered into the heart of man the things which God has prepared for those who love Him" (NKJV). What bright hope is in those words. And if ever there were a time when we needed hope, it is NOW!

Romans 15:13 says, "May the God of hope fill you with all joy and peace as you trust in Him, so that you may overflow with hope by the power of the Holy Spirit" (NIV). For me, overflowing with hope means overflowing with splashes of joy. So, if we don't get to splash joy down HERE, we'll splash joy together up THERE.

IN OUR FATHER'S HOUSE ARE MANY MANSIONS . . .
I HOPE YOURS IS NEXT TO MINE!

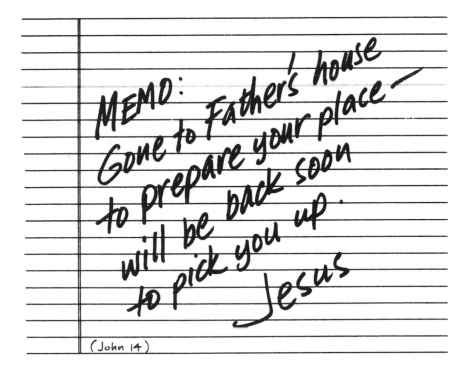

MEMO:
Gone to Father's house
to prepare your place —
will be back soon
to pick you up.
                    Jesus

(John 14)

Endnotes

Chapter 1 Smile! It Kills Time Between Disasters

1. For one psychologist's viewpoint, see "It Pays to Be an Optimist Even When Almost Everyone Is Pessimistic," an interview with Dr. Martin E. P. Seligman of the University of Pennsylvania, *Bottom Line Personal*, 12, no. 10 (30 May 1991): 1.
2. Charles R. Swindoll, *Strengthening Your Grip* (Waco, Texas: Word Books, Inc., 1982). Used by permission.

Chapter 2 How to Lay Down Your Agonies and Pick Up Your Credentials

1. "Twelve Steps in the Grief Process," from Theos National Headquarters, 1301 Clark Building, 717 Liberty Avenue, Pittsburgh, Pennsylvania 15222.
2. Ida Fisher, *The Widow's Guide to Life* (Long Beach, Calif.: Lane Con Press), quoted in *Horizons*, a bimonthly newsletter published by Secure Horizons (July/August 1991), 1.
3. Ann Landers, *The Ann Landers Encyclopedia, A to Z* (New York: Ballantine Books Edition, 1979), ix.

Chapter 3 We Must Understand That It Is Not Always Necessary to Understand

1. Ashleigh Brilliant, *Pot-Shots*, No. 954, © Brilliant Enterprises, 1976. Used by permission.
2. The doctor's name was Benjamin Russ, and his book was *Medical Inquiries and Observations Upon the Diseases of the Mind* © 1836. It is quoted in Colin Murray Parkes, *Bereavement, Studies in Grief in Adult Life* (New York: International Studies Press, 1973).
3. See Ezekiel 11:19.

Chapter 4 Wherever I Go, There I Am

1. Trina Paulus, quoted by Sue Monk Kidd, *When the Heart Waits* (New York: Harper & Row, 1990).
2. Josh McDowell, *Building Your Self-Image* (Wheaton, Ill.: Living Books, Tyndale House Publishers, Inc., 1988), 19, 20.
3. For more about these three "legs" of self-esteem, see Maurice Wagner, *The Sensation of Being Somebody* (Grand Rapids: Zondervan Publishing House, 1975), chapter 4. Wagner's book is an excellent discussion of how to build an adequate self-concept.
4. McDowell, *Building Your Self-Image*, 39–40.
5. Ashleigh Brilliant, *Pot-Shots*, No. 251, © Brilliant Enterprises, 1971.
6. Proverbs 12:25, TLB.

Chapter 5 S.D.D.D.D. (Same Doo-Doo,Different Day)

1. Karol A. Jackowski, *Ten Fun Things to Do Before You Die.* (Notre Dame, Ind.: Ave Maria Press, 1989).
2. Adapted from "101 Ways to Cope with Stress," Life Focus Center, 2255 Broadway Drive, Hattiesburg, Mississippi 39402.

3. Ibid.
4. Poem by Ernest Lowe used by permission.
5. Ezekiel 36:25, NIV.

Chapter 6 Laugh and the World Laughs with You . . . Cry and You Simply Get Wet

1. See Donald E. Demaray, *Laughter, Joy, and Healing* (Grand Rapids: Baker Book House, 1986), 25.
2. Norman Cousins, *Anatomy of an Illness as Perceived by the Patient* (New York: Norton, 1979).
3. Dr. Laurence Peter and Bill Dana, *The Laughter Prescription* (New York: Ballantine Books, 1982), 8.
4. Peter and Dana, *The Laughter Prescription*, 9.
5. Demaray, *Laughter, Joy, and Healing*, 29.
6. See "A Laugh a Day May Help Keep the Doctor Away," *Prevention*, 43, no. 6 (April–May 1991), 50, 51.
7. From a message presented in 1989 by Marilyn Meberg, Lake Avenue Congregational Church, Pasadena, California. Used by permission.
8. Job 3:25, NKJV.
9. Leo Buscaglia, *Loving Each Other* (New York: Holt Rinehart and Winston, 1984), 116.
10. This story is included on one of the tape recordings of the late President Lyndon Johnson at the LBJ Presidential Library in Austin, Texas.
11. From an unidentified page entitled, "Mute Points and Other Figurines of Speeches." Its source is unknown.
12. The original source of this story is unknown. I have checked with three different newspaper/press associations in California and New York. All knew of the story and reported having seen it used in different settings, but none knew the actual source.
13. From a message presented in 1989 by Marilyn Meberg, Lake Avenue Congregational Church, Pasadena, California. Used by permission.

14. *Reminisce,* 1, no. 1 (1991), 46.
15. Ibid.
16. Ibid.

Chapter 7 How Can I Be Over the Hill When I Never Even Got to the Top?

1. Remarkable Things, © 1988, Long Beach, California 90805. Used by permission.
2. I understand that Victor Buono died some years ago. I have no way of tracing the origin of this tape.
3. "Calories That Don't Count," Old Towne Press, 227 E. Chapman Avenue, Orange, California.
4. Anastasic Toufexis, "Forget About Losing Those Last Ten Pounds," *Time* (8 July 1991), 50.
5. Toufexis, *Time,* 51.
6. I am indebted to Ann Landers for some of these ideas on maturity.
7. Ashleigh Brilliant, *Pot-Shots,* No. 611, © Brilliant Enterprises. Used by permission.

Chapter 8 Motherhood Is Not for Wimps

1. Original source unknown. Quoted in *Phyllis Diller's Housekeeping Hints* (New York: Doubleday & Company, 1966).
2. Remarkable Things, © 1988, Long Beach, California 90805. Used by permission.
3. From a column by Stan Walwer, "Why Mother's Tough to Understand," Highlander Newspapers, City of Industry, California. Used by permission.
4. Sondra Johnson, "Praying for Adult Children," reprinted with permission from *The Breakthrough Intercessor* © Breakthrough, Inc., Lincoln, Virginia 22078.
5. Ibid.

6. Original cross-stitch design by Pat Carson, Sumter, South Carolina. The poet is unknown.
7. L. J. Burke, quoted in "Promises for Parents: Daily reminders that children are a gift from God," A *DayBrightener* product from Garborg's Heart 'n' Home, Bloomington, Minnesota. Used by permission.

Chapter 9 Oh, Lord, Let My Words Be Tender and Sweet for Tomorrow I May Have to Eat Them!

1. Ashleigh Brilliant, *Pot-Shots*, No. 129, © Brilliant Enterprises, 1984. Used by permission.
2. Proverbs 13:12, TLB.
3. Proverbs 11:21, TLB.
4. Adapted from Toby Rice Drews, *Getting Them Sober*, vol. 1 (Plainfield, N.J.: Haven Books, 1980).
5. Psalm 30:5, KJV.
6. Barbara Johnson, *So, Stick a Geranium in Your Hat and Be Happy* (Dallas: Word Publishing, 1990), 167ff.
7. Proverbs 21:1, NKJV.
8. See James 1:19.
9. Adapted from Ken Durham, *Speaking from the Heart* (Fort Worth: Sweet Publishing, 1986), 99.
10. Ibid.
11. See Proverbs 16:24.

Chapter 10 We Are Easter People Living in a Good Friday World

1. "Lord, I Ask More Questions," from *Tell Me Again, Lord, I Forget*, by Ruth Harms Calkin, Pomona, Calif., © 1974. Used by permission. All rights reserved.
2. "When I Come Home to Heaven," by Beth Stuckwisch © 1984. Used by permission of Dicksons, Inc., Seymour, Indiana.

3. Proverbs 12:25, TLB.

4. John 16:33, TLB.

5. Myra Brooks Welch, *The Touch of the Master's Hand*, (Elgin, Ill.: The Brethren Press, 1957).

6. See Barbara Johnson, *Fresh Elastic for Stretched-Out Moms* (Old Tappan, N. J.: Fleming H. Revell Co., 1986), 176–77.

Encore! Encore! Going Up With a Splash

1. Robert Hastings, "The Station," *A Penny's Worth of Minced Ham* (Carbondale, Ill., Southern Illinois University Press, 1986). Used by permission of Mr. Hastings.

I am so grateful to be able to dedicate this book to Andrew Johnston, my special friend, who so patiently sifted through hundreds of letters for me in preparing the material for this project. His encouragement and continual willingness to help were the special ingredients that allowed this book to be completed.

And not just completed, but finished with joy. Andrew and I laughed together over so many parts of this book, and we had so many chuckles over which letters to put in and which ones to leave out. If you find yourself laughing over anything in the following pages, it's very probable that Andrew and I laughed together over it too.

Andrew is in heaven now, and as I think of him, I can see him with his head thrown back and laughing as he found humor in even the small things.

Memories are so special to me . . . the legacy Andrew left to me in happy memories is priceless. His courage and devotion have been an inspiration to me, and in turn, they allowed this book to be written so that YOU, the reader, will be able to pack up your gloomees in that great big box, then sit on the lid . . . throw back your head . . . and laugh like crazy!

Contents

Acknowledgments

With sincere appreciation, I acknowledge the many people who have shared with me the letters, poems, clippings, articles, and other materials used in the writing of this book. Many of these materials came from supporters of Spatula Ministries, a nonprofit organization designed to peel devastated parents off the ceiling with a spatula of love and begin them on the road to recovery.

Diligent effort has been made to identify the author and copyright owner of all material quoted in this book. However, because so many unidentified clippings are sent to me from all over the world, it is sometimes impossible to locate the original source. I would be grateful if readers who know the correct source for items now labeled "Source unknown" would contact me so that proper credit can be given in future printings.

The letters used in this book are based on actual correspondence I've had with hurting parents, but most letters have been edited to protect the writers' identities. In a few special cases I have requested and received permission to use real names and facts, and I thank those writers for sharing so graciously.

Special acknowledgment and grateful thanks also go to the following individuals and companies for these materials:

Some information in chapter 2 is reprinted from GOOD GRIEF by Granger Westberg, copyright © 1962 Fortress Press. Used by permission of Augsburg Fortress.

Also in chapter 2 are letters as seen in a Dear Abby column by Abigail Van Buren. Copyright © 1992 UNIVERSAL PRESS SYNDICATE. Reprinted with permission. All rights reserved.

The cartoon in chapter 2, "I'm perfectly willing to compromise," is adapted from Ashleigh Brilliant Pot-Shot No. 2122. © Ashleigh Brilliant Enterprises, 1981. Used by permission. More information on Ashleigh Brilliant Pot-Shots may be obtained through Brilliant Enterprises, 117 W. Valerio, Santa Barbara, California 93101.

The "Sometimes I get so frustrated" baby-photo cartoon in chapter 3 is reprinted with permission of The C.M. Paula Company, 7773 School Road, Cincinnati, Ohio 45249-1590. The photo is used with permission of H. Armstrong Roberts, Inc.

The poem "When life drops a pooper," used in chapter 3 is from card number 015337 © Recycled Paper Products, Inc. All rights reserved. Original design by John Richard Allen. Reprinted by permission.

In chapter 5, Dennis the Menace ® is used by permission of Hank Ketcham and © by North America Syndicate.

Also in chapter 5, a portion of an Ann Landers column is reprinted. Permission has been granted by Ann Landers and Creators Syndicate.

The two cartoons used in chapter 7 are from greeting cards. The "Extra-Strength Deodorant" cartoon is from card number 068111 © Recycled Paper Products, Inc. All rights reserved. Original design by Kevin Pope. Reprinted by permission. The blow-drying porcupine is from card number 240047 © Pawprints. All rights reserved. Original design by Lynn Munsinger. Reprinted by permission.

Introduction

If It's Free, It's Advice;
If You Pay for It, It's Counseling;
If You Can Use Either One, It's a Miracle!

The radio call-in show was going well and I had already fielded several easy-to-handle questions—problems similar to those I had heard before and for which I could offer some practical suggestions that had worked with others.

Then a caller frantically reeled off an incredible barrage of pain and frustration. Her husband was alcoholic. Her son was gay, and her unmarried daughter had just uttered the words every mother fears: "Mom, I'm pregnant."

On top of all *this*, her house had burned, the contractor hired to rebuild it had co-mingled funds, and now creditors were coming from every direction, wanting their money *now*.

Somehow the poor woman managed to say all this in one breath while the talk-show host and I looked at each other in bewilderment. Then she finally stopped and waited for my answer. But I was dumbfounded. What could she do? Where could she go? To whom could she turn?

The pause grew into a pregnant silence. The talk-show host fidgeted as I frantically searched my mind for something that might help this poor woman. How could I possibly solve all her problems with a twenty- or thirty-second speech over the radio? Finally, I blurted out, "GOD ONLY KNOWS!"

There was a moment of shocked silence, then people in the studio audience started tittering. The talk-show host started chuckling, and then even the woman on the other end of the line had to laugh as she realized that my answer, not given flippantly but in real empathy, was true. Only God could know the answer to all those problems!

That's why I have always liked Deuteronomy 29:29, "The secret things belong to the LORD" (NIV). When we are at wit's-end corner, when life is a mystery that seems to have no answer—*only God knows*. Meanwhile, however, we have to cope, grapple, survive—yes, and triumph. That's what this book is about: finding answers when there don't seem to be any, adapting to situations that appear to be hopeless, and accepting people in your life—particularly your loved ones—when they are doing the totally unacceptable.

Can You Fix My Kid?

In fourteen years thousands of parents have come to Spatula Ministries with every conceivable kind of problem. On the first night they attend a Spatula support group, parents typically want to know, "How can I fix my kid?" Soon, however, they realize that isn't the question. The real questions are: "How can I fix myself?" "How can I help my spouse get through this?" "How can we keep our marriage strong so we can deal with what life has brought us?"

And as they continue to share—and to listen—they make some lifesaving discoveries:

They learn about the need to love their wayward children unconditionally. They learn that they can't change their children. *They can only change themselves.*

They also learn how to be rid of their guilt, how to forget the past and look toward a future that is bright with hope.

They learn how to get on with life, how to put their loved ones in God's care—in short, how to let go.

They learn that helping others is a tremendous benefit because, as I have said so often, when you refresh others, you yourself are refreshed.

And somewhere along the way, they learn to laugh again in spite of the painful memories or the ongoing cares. They finally realize they will feel better. It takes time, a great deal of time. It also takes many tears, and it takes a lot of talk—hours and hours of talk. But it does happen. They come in wounded, dazed, and troubled, but after a while they learn how to drain the abscess of pain and begin the healing process.

As I worked on this book, I searched for a word to describe all the STUFF that can happen to us. Words like *problems, troubles,* or *tragedies* just didn't cut it because they were too grim. But then I found it—gloomees. I think you'll admit it's hard to say "gloomees" without at least a hint of a smile.

I believe laughter is the best prescription for pain there is; that's why I titled this book *Pack Up Your Gloomees in a Great Big Box . . . Then Sit on the Lid and Laugh.*

When the gloomees close in, that's the time to see the humorous side of things, not to deny reality but to help make sense out of what is so UNREAL. And sometimes, as you will see in the following chapters, it gets very unreal indeed!

Your Letters Light Up the *Love Line*

Our local Spatula Ministries support group meets once a month in the Southern California area. Over the years, dozens of other branches of Spatula have sprung up and now the Spatula network of caring and love stretches across the country. But as important as our support groups are, they are only part of the total outreach. I spend hours on the telephone each month, talking to parents who may have no support group nearby. In addition, my husband (Gopher Bill) and I publish the *Love Line,* a monthly newsletter that provides help, inspiration, and laughs for thousands of other folks.

Besides the humor, one of the most popular features in the *Love Line* is the letters from parents. Some of these folks have just landed on the ceiling because of unthinkable problems and disaster, and they need a spatula of love to scrape them off and get them back down on their feet. Still others have been coping with pain for quite awhile. In some cases they are drowning, going down for the last time. But others are learning to tread water and even to dog paddle and they want to share their progress with the rest of the Spatula family. I'm often told, "The letters from the other parents are my favorite part of *Love Line*. Keep 'em coming!"

Because letters like these mean so much to folks who are hurting, I've made them a key feature of this book. Sometimes I share my answer to them; others I let speak for themselves with wisdom that is far better than mine. My only problem with sharing these letters is a lack of space; there are so many more I'd like to include.

As you read some of these letters you may want to say, "This *can't* be true! Somebody is putting Barbara on or she is just making this up!" It's possible that someone might write a letter full of fictional problems, but frankly I doubt it. As for making them up, I couldn't begin to imagine all these problems—I don't think anyone could.

Believe me, I don't have to make anything up! I find plenty of it every day in my mailbox or in the voices of those who call on the phone, frantically wanting to talk to someone who will "please listen."

I Don't Claim to Be an Ann or Abby

I hope you don't think this book is going to be Barbara's version of Dear Abby or Ann Landers. An advice columnist I am not! Frankly, I'm a better listener than I am a giver of advice and answers. In the final analysis, God is the only One who knows the answers to anyone's problems. But along the way, He has given us some principles that can and do work. By going through my own refining fire, I have learned a little bit about what helps people when they descend into the inferno of suffering and think there is no way out.

In the following chapters there will be times when I deal with questions one at a time and try to give specific suggestions that might help. In other cases, I may quote several letters and then give a broad answer that's based on my own experience or on input from knowledgeable people I trust. Oh, yes, I'll also be sharing many letters from parents who are coping and who want to help others find their way back to sanity. And behind every answer or suggestion stands the only One who can really help any of us. Truly, *God only knows.*

You should expect to be resistant to some of the answers you find here. You may read things here that you aren't prepared to accept. I wasn't prepared either. In fact, I still haven't found answers to a lot of things. When I learned of my son Larry's homosexuality, I went to a Christian counselor who told me at the very start, "I've had very little success in changing the sexual orientation of homosexuals." I didn't want to hear that. I wanted that doctor to tell me how to fix Larry—fast. Instead, it took months and then years—eleven years in fact—before anything happened. Larry wasn't "fixed," but his heart changed, and, more important, over those years *I* changed. God changed my heart of stone into a "heart of flesh." He gave me the ability to accept, adapt, understand, and, above all, to love unconditionally.

People who know my story ask me how I ever survived learning about Larry's homosexuality and then enduring the lonely estrangement that occurred because I lashed out at him with anger and even hatred. This happened *after* I'd already endured devastating injuries to my husband and the deaths of two sons just as they reached the threshold of adult life. All of these experiences squashed my heart, but out of that came a fragrance in my life that could never have happened without going through the crushing pain. One of my favorite bits of verse says it so well:

THERE IS NO OIL WITHOUT SQUEEZING THE OLIVES,
NO WINE WITHOUT PRESSING THE GRAPES,
NO FRAGRANCE WITHOUT CRUSHING THE FLOWERS,
AND NO REAL *JOY* WITHOUT SORROW.

How did I survive? I tried a lot of things and I learned a lot, mostly by trial and error. And I'm still learning. I try to steer away from the pat answer and the hollow formula. I also avoid the instant solution, the microwave maturity, the quick fix, the heavenly Band-Aid without surgery. That just isn't the way God works. As Jesus said in John 15:2, we need to be pruned, and pruning can be painful.

The bottom line, however, is exactly what I told that desperate lady who called the radio station that night wanting to know how to unravel the mysteries of a life that had overwhelmed her. *God only knows.* The secret things *do* belong to Him. When the gloomees try to strike us down, He always has the answer. And when we seek Him with all our hearts, the gloomees don't have a chance!

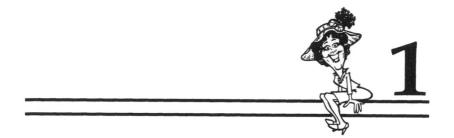

We're All in This Together . . .
You're Just in a Little Deeper

Welcome to the Real World

That lady who called the talk show with a life full of problems was one of many I meet all the time—in person, on the phone, or through the mail. While she had more than her share of setbacks, there are folks who experience even greater tragedy.

For example, one mom's recent letter also included a news clipping published several years ago describing her "all-American family," which included her husband, herself, and seven kids ranging in age from eight to nineteen. The article mentioned how both parents stressed spiritual values and how the father, while successful in his job, believed his family was even more important than his career. The article went on to describe the children as polite, bright, articulate, and outstanding students who wanted to please their parents by doing well in their studies. Sundays were family days—church, then dinner with the grandparents. One of the grandmothers was herself a former recipient of an "outstanding mother" award. And to top it off, every year the dad took the whole family on a vacation trip.[1]

Here, indeed, was an example of what a truly God-fearing model family should be like; but just two years after this article appeared in the local newspaper, their trials began. By the time the mother wrote to me, she listed the following blows to her all-American family:

The ninth-grade girl began needing help for depression. Her seventh-grade sister had been hospitalized five times for anorexia and almost died. A sophomore son away at college began to manifest clinical depression. (He ultimately committed suicide.) Another son had shown frightening signs of becoming addicted to alcohol. Finally, the youngest daughter had been diagnosed as having "bipolar disorder." Daily doses of lithium seemed to be helping stabilize her moods. The woman's letter continued:

> My faith has always been the most important thing in my life and my husband has always insisted on the importance of a sense of humor. You have the rare gift of combining both. May God continue to bless your efforts with your spatula of love!

I have a special empathy for these parents because my family, too, was going along in an all-American way before our roof fell in. I also appreciate this woman's emphasis on faith and a sense of humor. It is amazing how overwhelming pain and bitter disappointment bring out the need to laugh. Another mom who wrote to me described it like this:

> A friend gave me your book, *Stick a Geranium In Your Hat and Be Happy*. I read it and laughed out loud. That's something that has been missing from my life—laughter. It felt so good. I have a thirty-year-old daughter—she has been "in the world" since she was a teenager. She was baptized when she was eleven years old. Since her rebellion, there has been a marriage, a child, a divorce, and now a new child is on the

way even though she is not presently married. Drugs, illness, counseling, denial—you know the whole story. This new baby is due March 2. The father is a rock 'n' roll songwriter/house painter. Jesus help us!

Many people who write to me in pain reveal a positive attitude full of faith and trust even when they don't quite understand what's going on. It's as if they know they might as well let a smile be their umbrella—they're going to get soaked anyway. One woman said:

> I have been in a tunnel for a while. Our oldest daughter has three sons, a nine-year-old with leukemia, a seven-year-old with cerebral palsy, and the six-month-old has an appointment at children's hospital this month for tests to see what's wrong—he cannot hold his head up and has trouble seeing.
> We are all believers, but even God's own people travel through dark areas, don't we?

Another mother (I suppose 95 to 98 percent of my mail comes from wives and mothers) wrote to tell how she and her husband drove two and a half hours to where their son lived so they could take him out to dinner. He had already let them know he was gay, and they were devastated. When they got there, the father told his harried and very concerned-looking son, "Your mom was missing you so very much and she wanted to travel to see you to give you a hug."

What they thought might be a terrible encounter turned out to be a time when they could assure their son they loved him very much and that God loves him even more and wants only the best for his life. Their son hoped they could see his "friend" as a roommate—just like the ones he had back in college. They said, no, they still believed his lifestyle was wrong and they would never back down on that, but they would love him as much as they always did. The mother's letter went on to say:

> I don't know if I told you or not, but my oldest daughter had separated from her second husband and moved in with

us. Our second daughter is mentally retarded . . . and now
our youngest son is gay. I can't believe all of this has happened
to us . . . and in the meantime we buried a sister-in-law who
died of a long-time cancer battle. So it is really tough in our
lives at the present. . . .

In Tribulation There Can Still Be Hope

The above letters are only a taste of the thirty or so I receive
almost every day. All these hurting people could probably identify easily with King David, who also knew what it was like to
have life go sour:

> Save me, O God, for the waters are come up to my neck—
> they threaten my life. I sink in deep mire, where there is no
> foothold; I have come into deep waters, where the floods
> overwhelm me. I am weary with my crying; my throat is
> parched; my eyes fail with (hopefully) waiting for my God.
> (Ps. 69:1–3AMP)

I especially like the Amplified Bible translation of verse 3,
which speaks of how David waits "hopefully" for God to act.
Often we find ourselves hoping and waiting, and then hoping
and waiting some more. We experience the tough moments of
life, the moments when we have done all the appropriate
things: We have prayed, we have read the Word, we have taken
our stand, we have put on the armor of God. But nothing
changes. Circumstances remain the same. We have praised God
and rejoiced in the victory He's going to give us, but our depression remains.

In those moments we confess with David that the floodwa-
ters are overwhelming us and yet we still have hope. God will
act, won't He? Our hope may start to fade, and in those moments we must evaluate our faith with hard questions.

Do we have any faith at all?

Do we have enough faith?

Is what faith we have ineffective?

Or could it be that we don't know how to use our faith very well at all?

In times like these, you are in TRIBULATION, an English word taken from the Latin word *tribulum*, "a tool used to thresh grain." Tribulation doesn't refer to having just one blow come down upon you. The thought behind tribulation is that you have had one blow right after another. While you're going through these heavy blows, you may look at others who are enjoying a comforting relationship with the Lord and be tempted to tell them:

> PLEASE SPARE ME THE GHASTLY DETAILS
> OF YOUR HAPPINESS![2]
> —Ashleigh Brilliant Pot-Shot 1753 © 1980.

When people around us are rejoicing and praising God while we are struggling through deep mire and flood waters, we begin to wonder if something is the matter with us. We begin to feel like second-class Christians. And then the final straw comes if these people who are being blessed and who don't face the problems we do are quick to give us the glib answers: "Just praise the Lord . . . You are just not praising the Lord enough . . . What you need to do is take your stand . . . Just praise the Lord!"

When the flood waters of the cesspool have come up to your very soul, you don't need challenges; you need COMFORT. You need a friend to come alongside and say, "I am hurting with you . . . I am standing with you . . . I am weeping with you. I am undergirding you as best I can. Link your shield of faith with mine and somehow we will make it together."

When Pain Becomes a Permanent Guest

In these troubling times, God is stretching our faith. Twenty years ago Margaret Clarkson wrote a book entitled *Grace Grows Best in Winter*. Her goal was to show that one's trust and faith in God's grace and love grow in the icy, trying times when those cold winds come to chill the soul. As she put it, "the time

has arrived when you know that pain has come to you, not as
a temporary lodger, but as a permanent guest, perhaps even
as master of your house of life."[3] That's how one desperate
mother must have felt when she wrote to tell me:

> I look forward to your newsletters and read every word
> and want to continue getting them; but to tell you the truth,
> they really don't help much. [Some parents] talk about their
> children bringing home "friends"—and they have nice little
> chats? I think I would kill my son, his friends, and myself if
> he ever brought any of them home.
>
> My son was such a sweet, bright young man . . . He and
> his two brothers fussed a lot among themselves; they're all
> so different. But he was always smiling, always so full of joy,
> and so helpful. Old and young, men and women, EVERY-
> ONE liked him.
>
> Now he's girlish, effeminate. He isn't disrespectful, just
> not there. He won't talk. He isn't a part of our family . . .
> I don't think I can stand it a day, an hour longer. I don't sleep.
> Then I sleep forty-eight hours or more. I know what other
> people are going through—that doesn't change what I feel.
> Besides, I only talk about this one. I've lost two children to
> death. My daughter lives on the streets with a drug-crazed
> creep (she brought him here once). My sister-in-law, who I
> thought was one of my best friends, told me recently that she
> hated me the day her brother brought me home as his bride
> and had not changed her mind since (thirty years). . . .
>
> I don't want to be the kind of person everybody hates or
> who does everything wrong—I don't know how I can be
> such a failure in so many ways. That isn't all, but it's
> enough to say I'm not feeling sorry for myself for just one
> little item; it's for being overwhelmed and not knowing
> what to do, and for knowing I am this way and not likely to
> be any different, and for knowing my being this way isn't
> enough for my children or my family or my husband and
> his family. . . .
>
> I'm supposed to be old and wise and teaching younger
> women and others the ways of the Lord—and here my
> life's falling apart. Sorry—there's just no one else to talk to.

Everybody Has Two Big Questions

No matter what the pain and problems may be like, everybody is looking for the answers to two basic questions: WHY? and HOW? Folks who write to me often ask, "Why me?" "Why us?" "Why our family?" But just as often they also want to know, "How?" "How can I deal with this?" "How do I learn to live with pain?"

I don't have all the answers. Frankly, sometimes I'm not even sure I fully understand the questions. I wish I could always have something to say that would make everything all right right now, but I don't. I do know one thing, though:

> WHATEVER COMES TO ANY OF US
> IS SENT OR ALLOWED BY GOD.

To some people, that may make God sound weak, uncaring, or even sadistic, but when you're facing the real world it helps to remember that God is in control. He is still at work, even when we feel that our suffering will never end. Like the psalmist commanded, we must "hope . . . in God."[4]

Michael Malloy, director of Christian Counseling Services in Nashville, Tennessee, attended a seminar conducted by Dr. Larry Crabb, a Christian psychologist and author of many excellent books such as *Inside Out*. Malloy was intrigued when Dr. Crabb asked the group, "Do you use God to solve your problems? Or do you use your problems to find God?"

When we use God to solve our problems, we may try following biblical principles we've been told will solve everything. Unfortunately, we can do this and life still has a way of caving in. Then, when the principles don't seem to work, we are in danger of doubting God as well as our own faith. On the other hand, when we "use our problems to find God," we aren't looking for the quick fix or the instant solution; we are learning something about the "theology of suffering." Michael Malloy wrote:

Those who suffer well and keep a passion for God in the midst of their pain are often called saints. I think of two women in my life who had considerable influence—both grandmothers.

One, named Birdie, lost her first family, husband and ten-year-old daughter, in the '20s. She met my granddad about a dozen years later and married him after his divorce—when divorce was really not popular. She was "the other woman" but as I got older and spent time with her after my granddad died, I came to see the beauty of her spirit that overcame the loss of two families—one by death, the other by being shut out by most of our relatives.

The other lady was my Dad's mom, Martha, who lost her husband just before the fourth of July in 1925 in a farming accident. She remarried and had twins, one of whom was damaged at birth but lived until he was 24.

I recall Robert at Grandma's house when I was young. He had to be fed, diapered and seldom left his wheelchair. Grandma cared for him constantly. At other times I recall going with her to clean doctors' offices. When I was in college in nearby Stillwater she would spread a table of food fit for harvest hands on Sunday nights for me and my college roommates. She was always doing something for somebody. . . .

My grandmothers saw things many of us don't see about life. There is a "window" that opens to those who move into suffering in pursuit of God. None of us want to suffer. What we want is out of it—but when it comes we have a choice to let it take us to a high plain or to become cynical, bitter and disillusioned.[5]

When Michael Malloy talks about the "window" that opens to those who move into suffering in pursuit of God, I think of a favorite verse in Hosea where God speaks of transforming our valley of troubles into a "door of hope" (Hos. 2:15 KJV). In the face of any hopeless situation, hope is there, even if we don't feel it. God can take sour, bitter things in our lives and blend them into something that smells and tastes as sweet as honey.

Suffering Is Like Baking a Cake

I like to compare suffering to making a cake. No one sits down, gets out a box of baking powder, eats a big spoonful, and says, "Hmmm, that's good!" And you don't do that with a spoonful of shortening or raw eggs or flour, either. The tribulation and suffering in our lives can be compared with swallowing a spoonful of baking powder or shortening. By themselves these things are distasteful and they turn your stomach. But God takes all of these ingredients, stirs them up, and puts them in His own special oven. He knows just how long to let the cake bake; sometimes it stays in God's oven for YEARS. We get impatient and want to open the oven, thinking *Surely the cake must be done by now.* But not yet, no not yet. What really matters is that the cake is BAKING and the marvelous aroma is filling the house.

I find that people who trust God with their suffering have an invisible something, like the invisible aroma of a freshly baked cake, that draws people to them. As Paul put it, "all things [all the ingredients of pain and suffering] work together for good to them that love God" (Rom. 8:28 KJV).

When we believe that nothing comes to us except through our heavenly Father, then suffering begins to make a little sense to us—not much, I admit, but a little bit, and that's all God needs to work in our lives, just a mustard seed of faith. Then we can see that God is using our pain to work something in us that is redemptive. Every trial or broken relationship goes into God's oven and eventually we begin to "smell" like cake or fresh bread. Even our suffering counts for something!

God Has Plans for Each of Us

The apostle Paul knew something about suffering. He was beaten, whipped, stoned, and shipwrecked. He lived in danger from foes and friends alike, especially the false brothers who betrayed him. He went without sleep, food, and water. And on top of all this, he lay awake many nights agonizing for the churches he had founded, especially when they went astray and fell victim to false teachers. (See 2 Cor. 11:23–29.)

Despite all this, Paul could also say, "But thanks be to God, who always leads us in His triumph in Christ, and manifests through us the sweet aroma of the knowledge of Him in every place" (2 Cor. 2:14 NASB).

You see, God knows what He is doing with each of us. I believe that what He said to the Jews when they were in captivity also applies to believers today when we face "hopeless problems." Through Jeremiah God told them, "For I know the plans that I have for you, . . . plans for welfare and not for calamity to give you a future and a hope" (Jer. 29:11 NASB).

You may be in a tough situation, possibly a real calamity that seems more hopeless than any described in the letters included in this chapter. But if you are trusting God, the word calamity really doesn't apply because calamity, as defined in the dictionary, is "an uncontrolled disaster." And when you are trusting the Lord with your pain, nothing is out of control in your life. After God told the Jews He had plans for their welfare that would give them hope, He went on to say, "Then you will call upon Me and come and pray to Me, and I will listen to you. And you will seek Me and find Me, when you search for Me with all your heart" (Jer. 29:12–13 NASB).

In his editorial on suffering, Michael Malloy also said:

> **Knowing God is everything.** There is nothing more than Him, although throughout our lives we will be tempted to believe in a variety of "set of hoops" doctrines that we must jump through to see God. It ultimately comes down to believing what at this point we cannot see. But we have the assurance that when we have persevered long enough, we will see Him and know Him as He is. And you know what? I think that those who have endured suffering for a time get a sneak preview of the all that is to come.[6]

In this real and broken world we will have suffering, but it's comforting to know that Satan is not in charge. The Lord is faithful, and no matter how bad things get, He protects us from the evil one. We can rest assured that, while Satan is dangerous and deadly, he does not call the shots.

Satan cannot call the shots because he hasn't paid the price of admission. We don't belong to ourselves; we have been bought with the greatest price. Once we realize that, we can rise out of any pit we might fall into in this life. We know that ultimately nothing can harm us because we can always say:

MY ME DOES NOT BELONG TO ME.

Many people who write me feel powerless and over-whelmed, just like the lady who said her life was falling apart and she had no one to talk to. I know how she feels because I felt that way myself. And I know the trap she has fallen into because I fell into it too. We can get so caught up in trying to run on our own steam we forget to ask God to guard our hearts and give us power we do not have in ourselves.

As we cope with the real world, it helps to keep an eternal perspective, not one that can see no farther than today's pain. That's why one of my favorite sayings is:

THE IRON CROWN OF SUFFERING
PRECEDES THE GOLDEN CROWN OF GLORY.

In one of his best-selling books, humorist Robert Fulghum talks about the "Uh-Oh frame of mind." It's a perspective that lets us see life's catastrophes as momentary difficulties rather than horrendous tragedies. As Fulghum puts it, "When you see something as 'Uh-Oh,' you don't have to dial 9-1-1."

When we have the Uh-Oh philosophy of life, we welcome the surprises a day may bring, and instead of pressing the panic button we say, "Here we go again . . . back to the drawing board," and "Has anybody seen Plan B?" Fulghum sums it up by saying, "'Uh-Oh' is more than a momentary reaction to small problems. 'Uh-oh' is an attitude—a perspective on the universe. It is part of an equation that summarizes my view of the conditions of existence:

'Uh-Huh' + 'Oh-Wow' + 'Uh-Oh' + 'Oh, God' = 'Ah-Hah!'"[7]

Obviously, the most important part of Fulghum's equation is "Oh, God." If ever there was an "Uh-Oh" kind of guy, it was the apostle Paul, who said:

> That is why we never give up. Though our bodies are dying, our inner strength in the Lord is growing every day. These troubles and sufferings of ours are, after all, quite small and won't last very long. Yet this short time of distress will result in God's richest blessing upon us forever and ever! So we do not look at what we can see right now, the troubles all around us, but we look forward to the joys in heaven which we have not yet seen. The troubles will soon be over, but the joys to come will last forever. (2 Cor. 4:16–18 TLB)

The Fine Art of Burden Casting

No, I have no magic formulas for making pain go away, but I do recommend the following method for burden casting because it is based on Psalm 55:22: "Cast your burden upon the LORD, and He shall sustain you" (NASB). What I'm going to tell you may sound simplistic, but I know it works because it points you toward God Himself. Here's what you should do:

Think of the particular burden that is weighing you down. Now, in a few words, write your burden on a small piece of paper. (If you have more than one burden, write each one down on separate pieces of paper.)

Seal each burden in its own separate envelope. Then go to a place where you can be alone to pray. Get on your knees and, with both hands, lift up each envelope. Tell God your burdens as well as your fears and your doubts. Tell Him EVERYTHING about this burden because this is the last time you will be speaking of it in such detail.

As you do this, you may notice that you are crying and your arms may hurt as you lift up your burden. But hold that envelope up there until the pain in your arms is equal to the pain in your heart. Then drop your arms and say, "Lord, take it."

Now look at your watch or clock, and, on the outside of the envelope, write down the date and time that you gave your burden up, for example, "On June 10 at 4:00 P.M., I gave this burden to my heavenly Father and He took it."

Finally, put that envelope some place where you keep your treasured things. Perhaps that would be your Joy Box.*

Now you are ready to walk by faith because you know everything is okay. Of course, Satan will be quick to tell you everything is NOT okay, but hold on to Romans 1:17, which says, "The just shall live by faith" (KJV), not by listening to Satan or anyone else who wants to fill your mind with doubts and fears.

As you walk through each day, rely on the knowledge that God has your burden; you gave that burden to Him on such-and-such a date. And because you gave Him your burden, now you have hope. I see that hope every day in my mailbox. Not all of the letters I get are sad or full of pain. I get a bunch of letters from folks who are upbeat and full of hope because, in one way or another, they have cast their burdens on God. One woman wrote to say:

> I have been in a "parenthesis" for five years and cannot see the end, but I am focusing on Jesus Christ.

Another mother reminded me that I had published an earlier letter (in the *Love Line*) she had written about her daughter, who is an alcoholic. Now she was writing back to say:

> Well, I wanted to let you know some good news. With the help of our blessed Lord and lots of prayers, she is doing a

---

* I've described how to make a Joy Box in other books, including *Splashes of Joy in the Cesspools of Life,* and *Stick a Geranium in Your Hat and Be Happy,* and I touch on it again in chapter 7.

turn-around. She has stopped drinking (I believe) and has entered school to be a medical assistant. She is doing most excellent in her studies, and seems to be getting along much better with her husband and four small children. She seems to be finding herself at last and I am confident that this will last. But even if it does not last, it has been quite exciting to see her change, gain a little weight and get more control of her life—at this time at least.

So there is hope. Prayers do work. The Lord is Good.

While Spatula reaches out to people in every conceivable kind of mess, a large portion of our ministry deals with parents who have discovered that one—and sometimes more than one—of their children is gay. When one mother went through this kind of shock she got in touch with us and we sent her literature, prayed with her on the phone, and helped "peel her off the ceiling" with our spatula of love. Eventually, she wrote to tell us:

> Because of what I learned from you, I am able to not only love but also enjoy my son's company. What you shared made sense and I found it to be true. My husband and I have a good relationship with our son. When I first found out, I was in shock. Then depression came, followed by a suicide attempt and six weeks of psychiatric hospitalization.
>
> That was three and a half years ago. I chose to adopt your attitude, which I now know is God's attitude, and now I believe . . . God has used all of this for good as He promised in Romans 8:28.

So many parents who contact Spatula are estranged from their children in one way or another. It's a special joy for all of us when a mom can write something like this letter we received:

> I praise God that both of my children are strong Christians, though it hasn't always been so. There was a time when just the mention of God made my daughter angry and now she and I have long discussions about the love of God and how

we want to grow more like Him, along with many other God-centered topics.

My daughter knew I prayed continually for her. I made sure she had her tapes of Amy Grant that she had loved before she left the Lord. She loved Amy's voice and listened to the tapes "just for the music"—but, oh, how I prayed those words would hit their mark. They did and I praise God.

For about five years my daughter was a big part of the world. She could drink the guys under the table and I prayed, "Lord, make her sick." It didn't happen at once, but it did happen. To this day even a sip of wine makes her sick.

She told me after she was back with the Lord how much she loved us and was thankful for our prayers, but mostly that we never condemned her and that she knew she was always welcome and loved no matter what she did. Those words were the greatest gift she could have given me.

Hope Helps Us Live—and Die

The counselor who helped me when my life was so bleak once wrote to me to say that my ministry encourages people to survive their losses. And then he added:

> EVEN DYING PEOPLE DIE MORE GRACIOUSLY
> WHEN THEY HAVE HOPE,
> EITHER FOR RECOVERY OR FOR HEAVEN.

That's a good thought! In fact, it's burned into my memory, and I see its wisdom confirmed when I receive letters such as the following:

> In the first week of October, my twenty-year-old daughter and seven-and-a-half-month-old granddaughter were killed in an auto accident. They were victims of a drunk driver. My daughter was an unwed mother who dropped out of high school at seventeen and a half and left home. She had been living on government assistance for two and a half years.

It was very difficult for my husband, son, and me, but we did maintain contact with her and included her in family activities.

Until she became pregnant, she had been in church with us at least every other week. During the last year of her life, she had not attended church. Three months before she died I explained my concerns to our pastor. The pastor, after several attempts, did get our daughter to come to his office and talk to him. She talked with him in late September, repented of her sins, asked for forgiveness, and vowed to try to change her life. Ten days later, she and her daughter died. We look at the last few months of her life as a miracle!

I treasure this mother's letter because it reminds me of the power of hope. When the daughter turned to God in faith, it not only gave her hope, it also provided hope for her mother who, in just a few short days, would be left behind to struggle with the deaths of a child and a grandchild.

Hope means the most, perhaps, when we face the stark reality of death. Many people who telephone or write to me are coping with the death of loved ones. A precious child, wife, or husband is gone—totally GONE. Death is so FINAL. There are no instant replays or second chances. What can we do when we face death? How can we find strength to go on? How can we find closure for grief and pain?

In chapter 2 we will talk about these questions and how to find the kind of strength that can make all the difference.

Gloomee Busters

GOD SAID IT, I BELIEVE IT, AND THAT SETTLES IT.
(Then why doesn't it make sense?)

☐ ☐ ☐

I'D UNSCRAMBLE THE EGGS
IF YOU'D READ ME THE RECIPE BACKWARDS.

□ □ □

PRACTICAL GUIDE FOR SUCCESSFUL LIVING: PUT YOUR HEAD UNDER THE PILLOW AND SCREAM.

□ □ □

CHOICE, NOT CHANCE, DETERMINES DESTINY.

□ □ □

JUST FOR TODAY

JUST FOR TODAY I will try to live through this day only and not tackle my whole life problem at once. I can do something for twelve hours that would appall me if I felt that I had to keep it up for a lifetime.

JUST FOR TODAY I will be happy. This assumes to be true what Abraham Lincoln said, that, "Most folks are as happy as they make up their minds to be."

JUST FOR TODAY I will adjust myself to what is, and not try to adjust everything to my own desires. I will take my "luck" as it comes, and fit myself to it.

JUST FOR TODAY I will try to strengthen my mind. I will study. I will learn something useful. I will not be a mental loafer. I will read something that requires effort, thought and concentration.

JUST FOR TODAY I will exercise my soul in three ways: I will do somebody a good turn, and not get found out; if anybody knows of it, it will not count. I will do at least two things I don't want to do—just for exercise; I will not show anyone that my feelings are hurt; they may be hurt, but today I will not show it.

JUST FOR TODAY I will be agreeable. I will look as well as I can, dress becomingly, talk low, act courteously, criticize not one bit, not find fault with anything and not try to improve or regulate anybody except myself.

JUST FOR TODAY I will have a program. I may not follow it exactly, but I will have it. I will save myself from two pests: hurry and indecision.

JUST FOR TODAY I will have a quiet half hour all by myself, and relax. During this half hour, sometime, I will try to get a better perspective of my life.

JUST FOR TODAY I will be unafraid. Especially I will not be afraid to enjoy what is beautiful, and to believe that as I give to the world, so the world will give to me.

—Source unknown

Though no one can go back
and make a new start,
anyone can start from now
and make a brand new end.

—Carl Bard

I wish I had a box so big
That every grouch I'd pack,
And when I'd shut the lid I'd see
That none of them came back.

I'd lock it so securely
And I'd cast away the key
And then I'd throw the box into
The deepest, deepest sea.

And in its place I'd get a box,
The biggest I could find,
And fill it right up to the brim
With everything that's kind.

A box without a lock, of course,
And never any key;
For everything inside that box
Would then be offered free.

Smiles there'd be in plenty,
And twinkles for the eyes.
A face adorned with these would surely
Give a glad surprise.

And grateful words for joys received
I'd freely give away,
Thanksgiving songs to pass around
To cheer the dullest day.

The children would come running up
To share the good things found,
For the joys are so infectious
And there's enough to go around.

Oh, let us each begin to pack
Our grouches right away,
And open wide a box of praise
To brighten every day.
                    —Source unknown

GOD DOES NOT SEND US ANSWERS TO OUR SUFFERING.
INSTEAD, HE TAKES IT UPON HIMSELF.

But those who hope in the LORD
    will renew their strength.
They will soar on wings like eagles;
    they will run and not grow weary,
    they will walk and not be faint.
                    (Isa. 40:31 NIV)

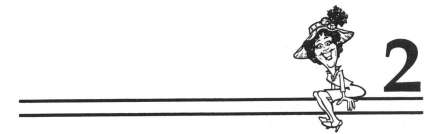

If You Can't Go Around It, Over It, or Through It, You Had Better Negotiate with It

Death is God's way of saying,"Your table is ready."[1]

The first time I saw the Ashleigh Brilliant quote that titles this chapter,[2] I couldn't help but think of how true his cryptic words are of the last great enemy—DEATH. As my good friend Marilyn Meberg says, "We're all marching relentlessly to the grave."

To stave off that "happy" thought, we try to use face-lifts, tummy tucks, hair coloring—anything to avoid the fact that age is taking its toll on us. We spend millions trying to deny what is happening to our bodies as we acquire various physical limitations. When our eyesight fails, we wear glasses. When our hearing goes, we adapt to hearing aids. And when our minds go . . . then we're REALLY in trouble!

Perhaps you know why women over fifty
don't have babies?
They would put them down somewhere
and forget where they left them.

Death stalks all of us, so we have to adapt the best ways we can to the new challenges that come with aging. But in many ways, dealing with the prospect of your own death is easier than facing the death of a loved one, particularly if the person you lose is young and has much of life yet to live.

There is a finality to death that is inescapable. You can't go around it, over it, or through it. All you can do is negotiate—not for a reversal that could bring your loved one back, because there is none. Instead, you plead for some kind of understanding, some way to make sense of it all as you try to get through it, allowing your grief to take its course and let the pain eventually drain away.

Death comes in many ways, but when you think about it, all those ways can be grouped into two categories—expected and unexpected. Terminal illness is probably the most common cause of expected death, but it's not the only one. In a way, we half anticipated the death of our son, Steven, from the moment he marched off to fight in Vietnam. We lived in fear from that day until four months later, when the Marine staff car drove up and two young men in full-dress uniforms came to our door. While the news that Steven had been killed in an ambush near Da Nang was a shock, it was not as total as the one that would come later.

Five years after we buried Steven, death visited our home again. During the winter and spring of 1973 our oldest son, Tim, who was twenty-three, went through training to become a Los Angeles County deputy sheriff. He also took an accelerated training course at the Los Angeles Police Academy. Although he completed all the training successfully, Tim chose not to enter law enforcement and decided he would go back to college that fall. For a change of pace, he and his friend, Ron, decided to spend the summer in Alaska, where they hoped to find work while they enjoyed seeing some new horizons.

Because he knew I loved to celebrate the first of every month, Tim called me (collect, of course) on August 1, 1973. He asked me what I was doing to celebrate the new month and, of course, I told him I was just WAITING for a collect call from him!

As we talked, Tim sounded excited about what had been happening at the church he and Ron had been attending throughout the summer. He said he would be home in just five days to tell us all about his experiences—especially what God had been doing "to put a sparkle in my eye and a spring in my step!" That didn't sound like my conservative, sedate son who had never showed much emotion or excitement about anything! I spent the rest of the afternoon thinking about how thrilling it would be to have him home in five days to share how God had become so real in his life.

At dinner a few hours later, I was telling Bill and our two younger boys, Larry and Barney, about Tim's phone call and we were all marveling at what he had said. Suddenly the phone rang again. Was it Tim wanting to tell me something else that couldn't wait until he got back? No, it was the Royal Canadian Mounted Police calling from Whitehorse, Yukon, to inform us that our son had been killed in a head-on collision with a drunk driver. That was a TOTAL SHOCK and I'll describe it in more detail later in this chapter as I deal with letters sent to me by folks who are coping with the same kind of unexpected blow that only death can deliver.

Grief Has Different Stages

One mother wrote to me and said, "I am reaching out to you because of your expertise in pain." Perhaps losing two sons in violent deaths should have made me an expert on this kind of pain. But I don't think anyone can really become an expert; you merely settle for being a survivor. There were plenty of times when I was ready to fold up and be admitted to the local Home for the Bewildered, but somehow God kept me going, always trying to find something positive, and even something humorous, to get me through the day.

Humor helps to combat my own grief and helps me accelerate the grief process for others. I love little quips and quotes and have collected hundreds of them over the years. Humor is not something to be used to make fun of a situation, only to make fun out of what seems to be a hopeless catastrophe. Folks need something that will help get them through the times when nothing seems to calm them, not even reminders of comfort from the Bible given by well-meaning Christian friends. It's not that these Scriptures aren't true; it's just that the pain is so intense you can't appreciate what the words are saying right at that moment. Later these Scripture verses can become very meaningful, but, ironically, there were times during my own sieges of grief that the following observation made a kind of crazy sense to me:

MAN CANNOT LIVE BY BREAD ALONE;
HE NEEDS PEANUT BUTTER, TOO.

I guess I try to be the eternal optimist. And you know the difference between an optimist and a pessimist, don't you?

An optimist is a person
who thinks he knows a friend
from whom he can borrow.
A pessimist is one who has tried.[3]

Of course I'm well aware that in those first hours and days after death strikes, you aren't ready to hear much of ANYTHING, whether it's inspiration from the Bible or somebody's attempt to make you smile. You can only struggle through these fresh stages of grief and hope that someday you may get to a place where you can smile and even laugh again. Many letters come from people who say, "I hadn't laughed in a number of years, but then I read your book. . . . "

There is nothing magical about my books. It's just that FINALLY these people have reached a stage in their grief where they can find something to smile about, where they can feel the first glimmer of joy after going through that long, dark tunnel they plunged into when death struck their family.

Through personal experience and dealing with grieving families, I've learned there are at least three stages to grief:

First, there is SHOCK, often accompanied by PANIC.

Second, there is SUFFERING, when you grieve and feel as if you want to die, yourself.

Finally, there is RECOVERY, when you wake up one morning without that overwhelming urge to go back to bed and just forget about living.

When death comes, there is no escaping this three-part process. Because we have families or close friends we truly care about, there is no way to avoid suffering; sooner or later, death pays a visit to every door. That's the bad news. But there is good news as well.

Grief doesn't have to be all bad; it can be something good. Grief is the healing mechanism God uses, particularly when we allow Him to enter into the process. One of the most valuable little books I've ever found on grief and the grief process is *Good Grief* written by Granger Westberg more than thirty years ago.[4]

Westberg points out that when the Bible says "Grieve not," it doesn't mean we're supposed to be like the Stoics, those Greek philosophers who never showed any emotion. Westberg believes the Bible sees grief as a normal and potentially creative process. He refers to the part of 1 Thessalonians 4:13 that says, "that you may not grieve as others do who have no hope" (RSV). Then he suggests this paraphrase: "Grieve, not as those who have no hope, but for goodness' sake, grieve when you have something worth grieving about!"[5]

In his little book, Westberg describes ten stages of grief. His first stage is like mine—SHOCK—which serves as a temporary anesthetic in response to hearing about some horrible tragedy, such as losing a twenty-year-old son in a blazing car crash. When we go into shock, we're making a temporary escape from reality. Sometimes shock lasts through the funeral of the loved one so that a surviving wife or mother, for example, might be praised for her "serene faith" because she seems almost radiant as she greets those who come by to pay their respects. In truth, she needs to be watched carefully and should be visited soon after the funeral when the serene exterior breaks down and she has to face what has really happened.

If we're to pass through the pain and suffering that come from a terrible tragedy, we must move on through the temporary escape mechanism of shock and into reality. Granger Westberg subscribes to the idea that, as soon as possible, we should help those people who are facing a heavy loss by letting them do as much for themselves as they can. We want to help them "get on with their grief work." Sometimes well-meaning relatives and friends try to do everything for the widow or the surviving parents. There are things that we can and should do, of course, but the sooner we let a person deal with immediate problems and make some decisions again, the better off that person will be.[6]

Many of the additional stages of grief in Westberg's outline fall under the stage I call SUFFERING. This is when our "grief work" starts in earnest—because grief definitely is hard work. When death takes our loved one, we need to express the strong emotions that well up inside. Bottling up our grief is the worst thing we can do. Looking "serene" at the funeral is not necessarily a sign that all is well. We may have a temporary period of "serenity," but then we realize how dreadful our loss is and there is an uncontrollable urge to "let it all out." According to the experts, nothing causes more stress than losing a loved one, particularly a spouse or a child. Crying it out makes all the sense in the world because, in addition to venting the emotional flood, it actually removes harmful chemicals that build up in the body due to the tremendous stress!

Men usually have a harder time showing grief than women because they are taught from boyhood that "big boys (and certainly men) don't cry." They are culturally conditioned to be "invulnerable," so they shut off feelings such as hurt, disappointment, sadness, and fear. When men face grief, they may explode in rage, run from their feelings, or simply bottle them up.

In one study of separated and divorced men and women, researchers found that men responded to emotional pain by "denying it, drinking, immersing themselves in work or dating, taking up risky pursuits such as sky diving, going completely and sometimes criminally out of control, or developing stress-related illnesses such as ulcers, colitis, and frequent vomiting."[7]

Women, on the other hand, cry much more easily and as a rule are less vulnerable to stress-produced diseases like ulcers and heart disease. In other books I've discussed my technique for shedding tears: Lying across a pillow, face down, takes away restrictions of the chest and throat and you can really sob your heart out and drain away the poison of the pain.

But while tears bring a lot of relief, they are no guarantee that you will be immune to another common stage of suffering—depression. I wasn't, and I know how it feels when God seems to be unreachable and uncaring. When tragedy strikes, we are sure no one has ever faced the same kind of grief we are facing. No one could possibly understand. These are some of the feelings I'll deal with in chapter 6; I know how devastating depression can be.

Physical symptoms of distress are also typical during periods of grief. We seem to feel ill or we sense that we have a "pain" somewhere, but it is more psychosomatic than real. This feeling of being ill or in pain means we haven't worked through some of the real problems related to our loss. Unless we can deal with these emotional problems we may remain ill, and going to the doctor to get prescriptions, shots, or other therapy won't help much.

These are just a few of the levels of grief and suffering we may go through when we face the sudden and unexpected death of a loved one. In the remainder of this chapter I'll share letters from folks who have struggled with this kind of loss. I have grouped their letters to try to deal with some of the more important questions that are bound to come up in the wake of the news that "Your son has just died in a car wreck," or "Your husband's body was found hanging in the garage—it looks like suicide."

The Hardest Death to Handle

Perhaps the hardest situation occurs when a loved one takes his or her own life. Added to the shock felt by those left behind are their questions—and often their guilt. Why? Was it my fault? Should I have seen it coming? Could I have helped in some way? Where is this loved one now? One mother wrote:

> My son completed suicide in October and I know that he believed in Jesus Christ as the Son of God. And I believe he is with the Lord, but a shadow of a doubt is always creeping in. . . . You know that Tim and Steven are with our Father in heaven. If only I had that 100 percent assurance. . . .

This mom wants to believe that her son is with the Lord, but she can't be 100 percent sure because the tiniest doubt keeps creeping in. Stated directly, her question is this:

Does a Christian who commits suicide lose his or her salvation?

This question comes in many forms. I'm writing this chapter in early spring, and since Christmas I've gotten letters from more than fifteen families who have experienced a loved one's suicide. They are looking for answers, comfort, and, above all, assurance that their loved one is "okay." Does God forgive even something like THIS?

After all, the Bible tells us that our bodies are God's temples and His Spirit dwells within us. We read the words that warn that God will destroy anyone who destroys His temple (see 1 Cor. 3:16–17). And there is also the issue of the suicide taking into his or her own hands something that is only God's prerogative. Moses quotes God as saying, "I put to death and I bring to life" (Deut. 32:39 NIV). And there is also that familiar reminder by the psalmist, "My times are in your hands" (Ps. 31:15 NIV). Other verses from the Scriptures could be quoted that seem to say it is possible to lose your salvation. (See, for example, 1 Cor. 10:12 or Heb. 6:4–6.)

On the other side of the argument, you can quote the words of Jesus from John 10:27–30 (NIV):

> My sheep listen to my voice; I know them, and they follow me. I give them eternal life, and they shall never perish; no one can snatch them out of my hand. My Father, who has given them to me, is greater than all; no one can snatch them out of my Father's hand. I and the Father are one.

I am not a theologian, so I can escape debates about eternal security. The scholars have argued that issue for hundreds of years and they aren't even close to unanimous agreement.

But when talking to the grieving survivors of suicide, I prefer to believe that even suicide doesn't negate a person's salvation. Salvation is a very individual matter and many factors enter in. Paul R. Van Gorder, a teacher with the Radio Bible Class program that originates in Grand Rapids, Michigan, has this to say about suicide and the possible loss of salvation:

> No, a Christian who is a suicide does not lose his salvation. . . . We must remind ourselves that salvation depends entirely upon the grace of God. No amount of human effort or self-worth can bring redemption. Once we have received it as a gift, we are not in danger of losing it for some unconfessed sin. . . . If that were the case, then it seems logical to assume that no one would reach heaven. All of us have sins we have forgotten about or never confessed. . . .
>
> We do not know what happens in a human mind that causes a person to take his own life. But we do know this: if that person was genuinely saved, he will "never perish." Though he may succeed in his suicide attempt, he will continue to have the gift of eternal life.[8]

After Mr. Van Gorder's thoughts were included in an issue of the *Love Line* newsletter a dear woman telephoned and said, "Do you know you just killed a lot of people in your newsletter because you said it's all right to commit suicide?"

Of course I told her I had no such intention and was only
trying to comfort people who were left behind to struggle with
the question of Why? From my knowledge of suicidal people,
they don't decide to do it based on thinking God will forgive
them. They are much too desperate to think that through to its
conclusion.

I know about that desperation because I came dangerously
close to that very state of mind, myself. When depression over
my son Larry's homosexuality (see chapter 6) became unbearable, I drove to the top of a viaduct where I intended to go over
the edge and end it all. But I was still thinking clearly enough
to have two things hold me back:

First, the training I had received while growing up caused
doubts in my mind about my eternal security if I killed myself.
I had been taught that you don't enter God's throne room
UNINVITED.

Second, I feared the attempt wouldn't kill me, only maim me,
and I'd be crippled, making baskets for the rest of my life in the
Home for the Bewildered.

Suicide is always a poor choice. It is like walking out of the
opera during the overture just because the conductor drops his
baton. Suicide is a permanent solution to a temporary problem.
The only trouble is, suicidal people don't see their misery as
temporary. They see their problem as overwhelming and believe suicide is the only way to end the pain.

But what about our original question? Does God send all
suicides to hell? Or, to put it the other way, do all suicides go to
heaven? As I said before, God only knows.

One mother's letter began:

> This is another one of those difficult letters, but I felt you
> would want to know. My son took his own life last week. He
> was still living in a homosexual relationship but having
> difficulties with it. I have no peace at this point, not knowing
> if he repented before his death, and not knowing where he is
> now. Except for this area of his life, he was such a fine, loving
> son. I find it hard to believe that with all the promises in the
> Bible and all the prayers offered for my son, a loving Father
> would not hear and answer. . . .

You cannot tell this darling mother who is grieving with such a loss that if she had prayed more or if she had only trusted God more her prayers would have been answered. You cannot glibly tell her she can move this mountain in her life "if only she has enough faith."

What you CAN tell her is that there are no pat answers for how God works in our lives. Many things have to be completely left to Him alone. Perhaps this is another of those secret things that will never be revealed to us (see Deut. 29:29).

So many parents write us with stories that have no happy endings . . . their child has taken his or her life, and it's over, final! In other cases the pain tortuously repeats itself. One mother wrote:

> My mother committed suicide when I was four. An uncle I was living with committed suicide when I was eleven. My son, at the age of twenty-three, kept up the family tradition by also committing suicide.

In another tragic case, a mother called and said that just a few days before, their teenage son had told them he was a homosexual. His father had ordered the boy from the house, and the very next day they found him hanging in the garage.

I also hear from many parents whose children are far from home and dying with AIDS. The parents don't know how to help, what to say, or what to do. This is happening more and more as the worldwide AIDS epidemic accelerates. We will address some of these concerns when we focus on homosexuality and AIDS in chapters 4 and 5.

For the hurting parents whose children have died through suicide or in other violent ways, we must all hold tight to the promise that God loves our children and He has provided a loving sacrifice for them. HIS BLOOD IS A COVERING FOR OUR CHILDREN . . . and the bottom line is that when you completely relinquish them to HIM, God is in charge and in complete control. Our loving Father loves them more than we do.

Remember that those who take their lives go to meet a just and loving God. Your loved one is in His hands. None of us live lives totally free from sin. We all make some very bad mistakes, but I still like the German proverb that says:

THOSE WHO LIVE IN THE LORD
NEVER SEE EACH OTHER FOR THE LAST TIME.[9]

In the face of suicide or any other unexplainable tragedy, I want to hold on to the comfort in that promise. But to do so FULLY there can be no grudges, no unfinished business, no lack of forgiveness when forgiveness is needed.

Suicide Must Be Forgiven

Those who are left behind after a suicide may feel angry with the one who has done this to himself or herself—and to them. Temporarily at least, they resent the loved one who has died by his or her own hand. Sometimes they feel ready to die, too. Considering this, they may think:

If I die, too, I'll forgive you.
If I live, we'll see!

There is a lot of truth in that little quip. The question we often ask ourselves is:

How can I forgive the one who committed suicide?

One dear mom wrote to tell me about the hundreds who attended her son's funeral following his suicide. Many of them were his teenage friends who were challenged by the youth minister to think about their purpose in life. This mom gets very lonely for her son because he had been so much fun—life with him had never been dull. He had won blue ribbons for his artwork and he also was an excellent musician.

Perhaps what she remembers most—scenes that are frozen in her mind—are memories of when her son was just a little fellow with a sweet smile and a certain way of tilting his head and making observations that only a mom could really appreciate. But this same mom also admitted a lot of ambivalent feelings:

> In January, my world was turned upside down and started spinning out of control when I was told that my beautiful talented son had committed suicide (one month before his sixteenth birthday). I remember saying over and over, NO, this can't be, I was going to pick him up from school in two hours. I was so numb I couldn't feel anything. When I was able to feel, it was guilt, anger, and being alone because no one knew the hurt that I was feeling.
>
> I couldn't find anyone to be mad at, so I got mad at myself and God. There were times I was mad at my son. He had so much to live for, how could he do this? But when I was mad at him, I would also feel guilty. I could never stay mad at him when he was alive. He knew just how to work dear ole Mom, so I never stayed mad for a long period of time.
>
> I miss him and still find myself wondering why, but I thank God for allowing me to be his mother for fifteen years. I know I wasn't a bad mother, only that God could take better care of him. My son may have the answers, but I don't think they will be important when I see him again.

We forgive a loved one for committing suicide in the same way we forgive anyone for doing anything wrong to us. This mom solved the forgiveness problem with her mother's heart. She couldn't stay mad at her son for very long, even after he had dealt her such a terrible blow. She still loved him so much, unconditionally, that she was able to make peace with it.

Moms Always Feel the Most Guilt

The same mother mentioned earlier in the chapter who was left with the shadow of a doubt concerning her son's salvation also admitted she struggles with guilt:

My son was an alcoholic and had been in treatment twice. This is always very hard for me to talk about. I attend another group called Survivors of Suicide. In those meetings, gradually in many cases it comes out that the loved one was addicted to drugs and/or alcohol. I believe this makes the death that much harder, as our relationship before their death was generally not a very good one. In addition to the usual guilt over the death, and especially suicide, those of us left have added guilt over not being able to control the alcohol and drug use. Especially when you are a mother. As you say, God and mothers are supposed to fix anything.

Who is more susceptible to feeling guilt than a mother? A mom is sure she is the one who should have fixed things or said something or done something that would have made all the difference. The mother quoted above feels guilty for not being able to control her son's use of alcohol and drugs.

One thing we moms need to understand is that we cannot control everything—particularly our children when they want to use drugs or alcohol. Those are choices they make, and we parents are not to blame.

In *Good Grief*, Granger Westberg says one stage of our grieving is feeling a sense of guilt about our loss. He doesn't mean normal guilt, which people often feel when they violate standards and values they know are right. What Westberg is talking about is "neurotic guilt" that is felt for no reason or that is completely out of proportion compared with how responsible you might be.

Neurotic guilt often grips us when we think about things we should have said to or done for the one who has died. Parents write about failing to talk with children the night before they died in an accident. Perhaps there was an argument and they weren't speaking. Perhaps the child got home late from a date and the parents had already gone to bed.

Other parents tell me they feel guilty about thoughts they had before a child was taken suddenly. Sometimes they weren't good thoughts, and they know the Lord isn't pleased with them. They know they "ought to feel guilty" for having those thoughts—and so they do.

It also helps to understand that everyone has neurotic feelings to some degree. I had my share when Steven and Tim died, but in each case the guilt washed over me for different reasons.

After Steve was killed in Vietnam, I kept thinking, *If only I hadn't gone down and signed those papers that allowed him to go into the Marines two months before his eighteenth birthday.* Yes, I could argue with myself and point out that he could have gone in anyway in two months and all I tried to do was keep him from grouching around the house because we wouldn't let him join the Marines with his friends.

And then, of course, I could argue the other way and tell myself if I had made him wait those two months until he was eighteen he probably wouldn't have been in that particular place and been caught in that particular ambush. Neurotic guilt causes lots of regrets, lots of "if onlys," and all we can do is look back and say that at the time, we did what we thought was best.

In Tim's case my memories would flash back to that last phone call. Part of what we had talked about was my offer to pay to have Tim's car shipped home from the Yukon rather than have him drive the Alaska Highway and spend five days on the road. Perhaps I made the offer because I had some kind of motherly premonition of disaster, but Tim just laughed and said, "Mom, there are no places to ship cars from up here. This is the Yukon!"

A week after that phone call I had to go to the same mortuary where I had identified the body of our son, Steve, five years before TO THE DAY. Steven had been shipped home by the government in a hermetically sealed casket. This time I went to the SAME viewing room to identify my son, Tim, whose body had been shipped home by the Canadian government in a pine box. As I looked at what was left of Tim, I went through all the "if onlys." If only I had INSISTED that he ship the car and fly home. If only I had been more positive about it. If only I had squashed the idea of that long drive home.

But then I had to return to reality and accept some facts. Tim was twenty-three when he died, old enough to know how to ship a car if he wanted to. The truth was that Tim had wanted the adventure of driving home. When his camera was found, we had his film developed and the last picture he had taken of himself was one on the bank of the Yukon River. He had wanted to make that trip.

One reason guilt feelings are so hard to sort out is that real guilt and neurotic guilt are often interwoven. Perhaps we did say things we shouldn't have said. Perhaps we did think thoughts we shouldn't have thought. Aren't those sins in God's eyes? Yes, but they can be confessed and forgiven, just like other sins. The point is, to carry a load of guilt around with you after a loved one is gone is wasted energy.

We have to let go of the loved ones who are taken from us, and we have to be free from our guilt at the same time. We must trust them to God because, no matter how much we may second-guess ourselves, we did all we could do at that time, and what was done (or not done) is a done deal—finished. If we feel we have in any way wronged the one who died, we confess it, accept God's cleansing forgiveness, and go on. It doesn't mean we stop our grief work, but it does free us to work on areas that need our attention.

To constantly carry a burden of guilt after we lose someone through death is to limit God's forgiving power when, in fact, God's forgiveness is unlimited. We must seize this truth and hang on to it. After all, when Jesus told Peter that he should forgive "seventy times seven" (Matt. 18:22 KJV), what Jesus was really saying was that we should forgive indefinitely. If God teaches us this standard, surely He holds the same standard for Himself.

Fear and Doubt Often Ask "Why?"

Fear and doubt are commonly mixed in with feelings of guilt after a loved one's death. Perhaps the first question many people ask when death strikes down a loved one is:

WHY did God let this happen?

A mother wrote to me about losing her manic-depressive middle son to suicide when he was thirty-two. He left behind a wife and two children who undoubtedly asked many questions beginning with "Why?" The mom's letter went on to say:

> I feel like a failure, yet I know I did my very best. I sure would like to talk with you. Your attitude is so great. I keep praying and have tried to put the children in His hands, but when my son committed suicide, I really became scared of God.

Why did He let this happen? We all loved Mark so much and his children miss and need him so much.

All this mother really wants to know is, "Why is there evil in the world?" I sure don't know, but God does. I do know that when Adam and Eve ate that piece of fruit in the garden, it had tremendous repercussions for all of us. We live in a fallen, broken world and NOTHING IS IDEAL. There are no guarantees that people won't get drunk, cross center lines, and kill us or our loved ones.

Yes, it's true that God could intervene. He could reach down and turn steering wheels, He could cause bullets to miss their mark, and He could foil suicide in any number of ways. Not only could He do these things, but in some cases He has done them. The question that is so hard to grapple with is: Why does God seem to intervene in one case but not in another? We don't know the answer to that question. We can only trust that God knows what is best and within His permissive will (not necessarily His directive or intentional will), what has happened has happened. Along with Job, all we can say is, "Though he slay me, yet will I hope in him" (Job 13:15 NIV).

Anger Is Always Part of Grief

When death takes someone we love, sooner or later we are bound to feel anger. In *Good Grief*, Granger Westberg points out that this anger often includes hostility and resentment. He admits that this doesn't sound very much like "good grief" because resentment and hostility are unhealthy emotions and they can do tremendous damage if we allow them to take over our thoughts.

At the same time, I've talked to many Christians who are angry over the death of a loved one but just can't admit it. They've been taught that anger is a sin, and instead of admitting their anger they speak of being "hurt," "shocked," and "devastated." Actually, though, they are very angry and wish they could lash out in all directions. When you're in the resentment/hostility stage, you're angry with the whole world.

. . . You're angry with the loved one who has committed suicide. As one widow wrote to me, "My husband had the nerve to hang himself on Christmas Eve."

. . . You're angry with doctors who either didn't do enough to save your loved one or who tried to help but your loved one died anyway.

. . . If a car crash has killed your loved one, you're angry with the other driver or you're angry with the police for letting drivers like this run around loose.

When Tim was killed, we learned that his little VW had been smashed to bits by a three-ton truck driven by a drunken sixteen-year-old. In those first days after the accident, I felt such WRATH that some drunk could cross over the center line and send two boys into eternity. Yes, I knew that, while their crushed bodies were left in that VW their spirits had been ushered immediately into God's presence, NEVERTHELESS, anger boiled up within me. How UNFAIR! How WRONG! Anger seethed within me and boiled up again and again like a volcano repeatedly erupting into clouds of ash and rivers of molten lava.

And a lot of my anger was directed straight toward God. For at least two weeks I drove to a nearby dump late at night where I could sob and sometimes scream out my rage. How could God do this to us AGAIN? Hadn't we had enough pain with Bill's accident and Steve's death in Vietnam? But NOW THIS! I had one deposit in heaven; I didn't NEED another one. Sure, I had two children left, but I wanted THIS ONE! How unfair could God be to make us bear another loss like this?

Fortunately, God doesn't reciprocate when we get angry with Him. Instead, He works quietly to bring about His will and whatever will ultimately glorify Him. The night of the accident the parents of Ron, the boy who died with Tim in the wreck, came to our house to learn what had happened and before they left they had placed their faith in Christ.

A day or so later, Tim's picture appeared in the local paper with a headline that said, " Two LOCAL BOYS KILLED ON THE ALASKA

HIGHWAY." In no time, several darling college girls began coming to our home to show me letters Tim had written to them the day before he started home. (I guess Tim wasn't as conservative as I had thought he was!) Tim's letters told the girls about his experiences that summer and how God had become real to him. These girls were eager to know more about the kind of God that could turn Tim on like that, and at least two of them accepted Christ right there in our home.

It was then that I began to see through my pain and grief and realize that the death of my son and his friend might be an end to their lives here on earth, but it was just the beginning of their work here. The next week we held a memorial service that was attended by nearly a thousand people, and later we heard still more reports of how others who had attended the service had been touched by the Savior. Many more people were brought to salvation when articles about the boys, with titles such as "Their Death Was Only a Beginning," appeared in various magazines and their story was told in a special segment of "The Unshackled" radio program.

Though my grief was still very real, I began to understand that, in God's economy, the timing of my son's death was right. My anger dissolved as I saw others accepting Christ because of Tim's testimony. You see, anger cannot reside with joy. The joy of seeing others come to the Lord because of Tim's death helped FLATTEN OUT that anger and allow a measure of JOY to replace it.

The Trip to Whitehorse Wasn't Easy

A month or so after Tim's memorial service, Bill and I traveled to the town of Whitehorse in the Yukon Territory to settle an insurance claim concerning the accident, and also to collect Tim's personal effects. When we arrived at the site where the crash had happened, the oil spill from Tim's little VW was still visible on the south-bound side of the road.

I thought of how Tim had trained with the sheriff's department and the Los Angeles Police Academy, how he had driven police vehicles and learned all about law enforcement and traffic. Yet here, out on an open stretch of the lonely Alaska Highway outside of Whitehorse, all that training hadn't helped when a three-ton truck had crossed the line and ended his life.

I wondered what Tim's last thought had been. Had he suffered? Had he called for help? We talked with the Mounties and they assured us that Tim's death had been immediate, which was at least a measure of relief. It helped to know that Tim had gone immediately into the presence of God with no time to hurt after he had been smashed by the truck.

To claim Tim's personal effects, we had to go with the Royal Canadian Mounted Police officer to an area where vehicles were impounded until final disposition was made of the case. After being hit by the truck, the little VW was a mass of crumpled metal. A yellow barrier tape fluttered around the car and a fierce guard dog was on duty (to protect the evidence, the officer told us). He helped us get past the dog and under the barrier tape. Then I reached into what was left of the backseat for Tim's camping gear and his Bible. I could see the blood splattered on the car seats and the windows, and all I could think was how grateful I was that Tim's death had been QUICK and he hadn't suffered.

Later I had a picture of the smashed VW enlarged, and I attached it to the back of a large picture of a happy, smiling Tim. Often, when I go out to share my story, I use these photos to demonstrate to my listeners what REALITY is. I show the pictures as a reminder of how quickly lives can be changed forever by a loved one's sudden death in faroff places like a rice paddy in Vietnam or a smashed little VW on a lonely highway in the Yukon.

Bill and I had to stay in Whitehorse for a few more days to wait for the train that would take us back to Skagway, where we would finally catch a boat back to the United States. Whitehorse is a small community, and we were treated very kindly by the local townspeople; they all knew about the tragic accident. The teenager who had driven the truck that had killed Tim and Ron was in the local jail. He had been so intoxicated it was two days before he knew what he had done.

But what about the boy's parents? The accident wasn't THEIR fault. We located them and asked if they would come to our hotel. We wanted to share with them our feelings about God's redemptive love for all of us, regardless of our choices. The boy's parents came, and they were lovely people, grief-stricken over what their son had done. Actually, I believe they were overwhelmed that we even wanted to talk with them. They were quiet and reserved at first; then we played a tape recording of Tim's memorial service for them and showed them letters we had received about how God had used Tim's story. As we talked, we saw their reserve melt into openness, and we were able to honestly love them and feel a rapport with them.

Our son was dead and now their son was in jail, facing the consequences of what he had done. WHOSE PAIN WAS WORSE? Can we measure such pain? A broken heart is a broken heart, whether it's caused by death in a fiery crash or by having a son who has to live all his life with the knowledge that his bad choices killed two young men. My heart hurt with compassion for those parents. In fact, as God filled us with compassion for them, it squeezed out any anger we may have still felt toward their son. Somehow we knew God was still in control of it all, and being angry over the Why? of it wasn't so important anymore.

Traveling to Whitehorse wasn't easy, but meeting those hurting parents and letting God's love flow through us to them in their dark hour of suffering made it all worthwhile.

Does the Pain Last Forever?

One of the most frequent questions I get is stated in many different forms, but essentially what people want to know is:

How long will my pain and grieving last?

I heard from one mother who had purchased *Stick a Geranium in Your Hat and Be Happy* to read strictly for enjoyment and inspiration. She had no pain or tragedy in her life when she bought the book. But that changed a few months later:

> My 19-year-old daughter was killed in an automobile accident. Because the police were unable to find any positive identification, my husband and I, like you, were forced to look at our child and say, "Yes, that's our daughter." So, I can honestly say I know how you feel.
>
> I'm reading your book again, but for a different reason. I know Terri is in a better place. I know she's free from pain and heartbreak and I know God will see us through this, but how long before the ache in my heart eases, or, as her brother Tim (he's 20) says, "How long before the empty feeling in my gut goes away?"
>
> I'm not really asking for answers. It just feels better to say this to someone who really knows how I feel.

Another mother wrote to say that reading *Geranium* made her laugh and cry at the same time. She had lost a son in his thirties when he died in an auto accident, and she had been trying to get her life back. But it had been "so very difficult," she said.

I understand those "How long?" questions. How long does the empty feeling stay in one's gut? How long does the void remain after a bright, happy, caring child is struck down by a disease in a twinkling? The only answer I have is that, for each of us:

THE PAIN LASTS AS LONG AS IT HAS TO.

We are all different, and we all grieve at our own rate.

This past year has been one of real loss for my friend, Delores, who lost a son to AIDS. Recently, on the one-year anniversary of his death, flowers were put on the church platform in Brent's memory and a tribute was given to him. After twelve months of grieving, those flowers and the tribute read by the pastor represented closure for Delores. The day after the church service she called me and said she had mourned enough; somehow the passing of the one-year mark was what she had needed. Now she was going to clean out her son's room and get rid of things she had previously been unable to part with.

Some people may find closure a few months after the loved one's death. Others need a year, and some take longer. For Delores, the flowers on the platform and the tribute from the pastor signified the turning point; she sensed it was time to zip up her grieving and get on with her life. No longer could she make her son's room a shrine where she kept his collections and other personal effects. She decided to clean it out, paint the walls, install new carpet, and add some new decorations. Closure had begun.

Recovery Begins with Hope and Joy

As we are able to let go of a loved one who has died, we move into the last part of our "grief work," the step Granger Westberg calls "struggling to affirm reality." This doesn't mean we become our old selves again. We will never be our old selves again. We come out of any kind of deep grief as different persons than we were before. We can come out stronger, kinder, and more understanding of the problems of others, or we can come out bitter and self-pitying, uninterested in others' problems because we have too many of our own.

One good definition of the word *affirm* is "to bear witness to." Bearing witness is an important part of our faith. In his work with hundreds of people who went through deep grief, Granger Westberg saw that the ones who coped best were those who had a deep faith; God and His love were very real to them. The person with real faith takes that faith seriously and practices it diligently, staying in training, so to speak, so he or she can be in shape to wrestle with whatever comes.

I read somewhere that the future has two handles. We can take hold of tomorrow by the handle of anxiety or by the handle of faith, and . . .

IF YOU GRASP TOMORROW WITH FAITH,
YOU KNOW THE HANDLE WON'T FALL OFF.

Scripture tells us that God will never test us beyond what we can bear (see 1 Cor. 10:13). I know Jesus talked about having faith that could move a mountain, but I doubt He asks for that kind of faith in a flippant or easy manner, especially when we are facing terrible agonies of grief and suffering caused by the death of loved ones. And keep in mind that Jesus also said even a mustard seed of faith can do a great deal. Think of it this way:

IF YOUR FAITH CANNOT MOVE MOUNTAINS
IT OUGHT TO AT LEAST BE ABLE TO CLIMB THEM.

And as we climb the very real mountains of pain, we can start looking for splashes of joy, even when joy seems impossible. A question many people ask me is:

Will I ever know joy and laughter again?

The fact is, joy will return if you are willing to look for it. One woman who had lost her husband wrote, "In the last couple of months I am truly experiencing that GOD REALLY DOES LOVE ME!" Then her letter continued:

> My husband died instantly with a massive heart attack four years ago at Christmas time when we were in Virginia visiting his mother. He was fifty-two and we had absolutely no warning. . . . it just happened and he was gone.
> Like you, I have been in the tunnel (for me it was a deep, dark, cold well that I couldn't get out of and it seemed that no one would help me) and I just wanted to die for a long time.
> The recovery road is very hard and takes a long time and a lot of hard work, work that I really didn't want to do. I never thought I would experience joy again BUT I AM! I even feel giddy at times with this wonderful feeling of love and joy that can only come from God. . . . I didn't think I would ever feel like this again and it is JUST WONDERFUL!

Philippians 4:13 Really Does Work

Personal experience has taught me that you can find joy in reality. Terrible things can happen. Loved ones can be plucked away in any number of tragic situations. Nonetheless, as we affirm our faith within reality, the Lord does help us. I have never received a more powerful example of how we can have joy despite the pain and grief than the following letter that came to me recently:

> Seven years ago my husband and two-year-old son were killed in a house fire. It was not an accident. It was a homicide and suicide due to an illness my husband had.
>
> I am left with two teenage daughters to raise by myself and need all the help and encouragement I can get. My girls are fourteen and fifteen years old. The last seven years have been difficult just trying to put our lives back together—we could not have done it without the Lord's help! All we are and all we have are from HIM!
>
> The verse I claim is Philippians 4:13: "I can do all things through Christ who strengthens me." This was the Scripture passage that hung in our living room and the only thing in that room that survived the fire. I know God left it there to remind me that no matter what happens to me or around me, God's Word will always remain firm.

This mother knows what hope is all about. A major part of coming out of the black tunnel of grief is hope. When we have done our grief work, hope gradually starts to dawn. The dark clouds start to break ever so slightly and the rays of the sunshine through in slender glimmers of light. What seems to be an endless time of grieving begins to run its course and recovery actually seems possible.

Granger Westberg believes that a true sign of hope is wanting to get back into things that we couldn't manage to do when we were still in the tunnel. Not only do we want to participate in old activities, but we want to try new things. As Westberg puts it, "Hope is finding out that life can become meaningful again."[10]

Hope Always Expects the Best

When biblical writers used the word "hope," they usually did not mean "wishing something were so." The biblical concept was more of a settled anticipation, a favorable and constant expectation. The Greek verb form for *hope* used in the New Testament frequently is related to the concept of trust. For example, in Titus 2:13, Christ is called "that blessed hope" (KJV).

When death strikes a family, it usually seems as if hope is exhausted. But hope can be rekindled. After the Babylonians sacked Jerusalem, the prophet Jeremiah wrote his book of Lamentations. In the early chapters he mourned the devastation of the once mighty city of God and the Lord's anger with His rebellious people. Jeremiah called himself a man who had seen affliction by the rod of God's wrath. He had been trampled in the dust and deprived of peace, become a laughingstock among his own people, and had "forgotten what prosperity is" (see Lamentations 3, especially vv. 1, 14, 16–18). But as Jeremiah remembered his bitter and galling afflictions and how his soul was so downcast, he went on to say, "Yet THIS I call to mind and therefore I have hope" (Lam. 3:21 NIV, emphasis added).

What was the "THIS" Jeremiah had in mind? You may recognize his next words, which inspired one of the great old hymns of the church, called "Great Is Thy Faithfulness":

> Because of the LORD's great love we are not consumed,
>   for his compassions never fail.
> They are new every morning;
>   great is your faithfulness. . . .
> The LORD is good to those whose hope is in him,
>   to the one who seeks him;
> it is good to wait quietly
>   for the salvation of the LORD. (Lam. 3:22–23, 25–26 NIV)

Even when we've landed with our faces in the dust, even when we are caught in a wringer, we can always have hope. And even when hope is lost, it can be regained; we can refocus our perspective. As we wait on the Lord, our strength will be renewed and so will our joy. In the Scriptures, hope and joy always go together. I like to say hope and joy are sisters.

Hope is God's holding power that gives a consistent flow of joy deep beneath the waves of trouble in the winds of sorrow. Hope invades the mind and heart with joy and gives us the deep confidence that we are God's forgiven children and that He will never let us go.

> THE SUREST MARK OF A CHRISTIAN
> IS NOT FAITH OR LOVE, BUT *JOY*.

We Found Hope in a Duffel Bag

About three months after Steve died in Vietnam, a large, dark green duffel bag arrived at our door. The return address was simply "U.S. Marines." Bill and I took it to a back bedroom and carefully opened it. Inside was Steve's gear—big Marine boots with the dried muck and mud still on them, mildewed fatigues, some books, and a Bible. Everything smelled of rot and mold. We almost choked as we went through it, partly from the stench but also from the emotions that swept over us.

There was also a camera and some trinkets. Then Bill opened Steve's wallet, all dry and crusty from the effects of heat and moisture. Steve had lain in that rice paddy three days before they had found him. And inside the wallet, all tattered and torn, was my last letter to him. The final page of that letter said, in part:

> I came to work early today to get this letter off to you and hope you can make it out as I am typing fast to get the message across. Usually I write letters to you with jokes or news about the kids and happenings around home . . . but today I felt a special need to reaffirm our faith in eternal life and being prepared to meet God. I particularly wanted to assure you that whether you are at home here in West Covina or over there in Vietnam, you are still SAFE in God's hands, and even if your life would be sacrificed for us in Vietnam, even THEN, Steve, you are safe in the arms of Jesus.

We all love you and miss you in a thousand ways. I think
of you pouring ice water from the fridge, and cutting watermelon and spitting the seeds all over the sink, and scraping
the trash barrels on the driveway as you dragged them out
each week for pick up. I keep hearing you out by the pool
with the kids, and enjoying the tube. Our thoughts are with
you daily and our prayers.

Somehow today, I wanted to get all this on paper to you to
think about, and to let you know we are proud and thankful
for you, especially for your faith in what we believe also,
because it seems to be so important now.

Even death, should it come to us, EITHER of us, or any of
us, that is, brings us just a step closer to God and to eternity,
because we have placed our faith in Jesus Christ. . . .

Somehow I think you understand me, just as I understand
you. I love you, just as your dad does, and so do the kids. We
miss you every day, hope you got the box OK, the one with
the Silly Putty especially. That was from Barney. He misses
you particularly, and remember you told him to hit a homer
for you. About the only homers he hits are in the front window of the house, I am sorry to say.

                              Take care, love always,
                                    Mom and Tribe

As usual, I had kissed my signature at the close of the letter,
and now the lipstick was all smeared and blurry, but that didn't
matter. Steve had read the letter and had kept it with him as he
went into battle, even though his instructions had been to burn
all his mail in case he was captured. Instead, Steve had stuck the
letter in his wallet, probably intending to burn it later. Or perhaps he deliberately kept it with him as a symbol of the hope he
had in Christ and of the family back home who loved him and
shared that hope with him. (Steve's buddy, Tom, who had escaped death because he was held back from patrol for other
duties, later paid us a visit and explained that my letter had
arrived the VERY MORNING of the ambush in which Steve
had been killed.)

Sitting there in that bedroom surrounded by Steve's smelly
Marine gear, I was reminded of Jeremiah's words in Lamentations. We, too, had been afflicted and filled with bitter herbs.

Our teeth had been broken on the gravel of grief. We had been trampled in the dust. Prosperity seemed like a forgotten word, and our souls were downcast.

But as I re-read the letter Steve had taken with him into his final battle, I realized that, despite all the pain, we still had an ENDLESS HOPE and with it ENDLESS JOY. The Lord's great love and compassion fail not. Truly, they are new every morning. Great is His faithfulness. Steve was our deposit in heaven. We could pick up the pieces of our lives and move on.

Gloomee Busters

HOPE MAKES A DIFFERENCE

Hope opens doors where despair closes them.
Hope draws its power from deeply trusting God and what He
    does to change people's lives.
Hope lights a candle instead of "cursing the darkness."
Hope regards problems, small or large, as opportunities.
Hope cherishes no illusions, but it does not yield to cynicism or
    despair.

                —Adapted. Source unknown

It is a great comfort to know
that God has His hands
on the steering wheel of the universe.

FAITH CAN MOVE MOUNTAINS,
BUT ONLY HARD WORK CAN PUT A TUNNEL
THROUGH.

WHEN YOUR DREAMS TURN TO DUST—VACUUM!

□　□　□

A farmer was taking his little boy to a distant place. While walking they came to a rickety bridge over a turbulent stream. The little boy became apprehensive. "Father, do you think it is safe to cross the stream?" he asked.

The father answered, "Son, I'll hold your hand." So the boy put his hand in his father's. With careful steps he walked by his father's side across the bridge. They made their way to their destination. That was in the daylight.

The night shadows were falling by the time they returned. As they walked, the lad said, "Father, what about that stream? What about that rickety old bridge? I'm frightened."

The big, powerful farmer reached down, took the little fellow in his arms, and said, "Now you just stay in my arms. You'll feel safe." As the farmer walked down the road with his precious burden, the little boy fell sound asleep.

The next morning the boy woke up, safe at home in his own bed. The sun was streaming through the window. He never even knew that he had been taken safely across the bridge and over the turbulent waters.

That is the death of a Christian.

—Source unknown

□　□　□

God saw that you were getting tired and a cure was not to be.

So he wrapped His arms around you and whispered, "Come with Me."

Golden heart stopped beating . . . hard-working hands at rest.

God broke our hearts to prove to us, He only takes the best.

—from a letter written to Spatula
by a mother who had lost her son

□　□　□

GOD
has not taken
them
from us;
He has hidden
them
in His heart
that they
may be closer
to ours.
—from a bookmark. Source unknown

☐ ☐ ☐

I will . . . transform her Valley of Troubles into a Door of Hope. (Hos. 2:15 TLB)

There's One Place
You Can Always Find Me . . .
At the Corner of Here and Now*

What's down in the well comes up in the bucket.

This poem caught my eye the other day when I was reading Dear Abby. It sums up life for a lot of us:

> Dear Abigail Van Buren: Please give me your advice:
> My job is gone, my shoes are worn, I live on beans and rice.
> The government won't help me; my state is going broke;
> My boy has been arrested (they caught him sniffing coke.)
> My wife has up and left me; my son resides in jail;
> The bank in which I own some stock will be the next to fail.
> My pants are getting shabby, and bagging at the knees;
> I can't afford a bar of soap to wash my BVD's.

---

* For the title of this chapter I am indebted to Ashleigh Brilliant for Pot-Shot No. 778, © 778 Ashleigh Brilliant Enterprises, 1975. Used by permission.

My daughter says she's pregnant, but doesn't know the guy;
My cotton's full of weevils and my cow is going dry.
My hens have all stopped laying—I can't afford their mash;
My checks are quickly bouncing, and the stores insist on cash.
I've lost my only savings on horses at the track;
The Klan is out to get me because my friends are black.
I asked the priest to help me, while making my confession;
He blamed it on the Protestants for causing this recession.
And so I turn to you, my friend, before I go to ruin;
My only source of good advice is Abigail Van Buren!
                                        —George

Not to be outdone, Abby succinctly replied:

Dear George:
Please do not appeal to me
To heal our sick economy.
It's plain to see we've lost our pants;
Now give the other guys a chance.[1]

Many of the things that happened to "George" have happened to people out there in Spatula Land—and a LOT more. Many of them write to me or call me to pour out their hearts, and some can even see a little humor in their situations. For example, I talked with one lady who later wrote back:

After I last spoke with you, everything was going along fine. I had a CAT scan and ultrasound prior to starting chemotherapy after my mastectomy and it has been discovered I have probably cancer of my right kidney, which is being removed next Monday. I would appreciate your prayers that it will be found to be benign! The good Lord delivered me to this world with two of most things. I seem to be going out with only one of everything! Fortunately, I had a CAT scan (actually an MRI) of my head and I don't need a transplant there. Any eccentricity is due to my English heritage and/or raising four children!

After reading *Geranium*, a woman, who sounds very much like a pleaser who's almost fed up, wrote to share her frustrations.

While she doesn't face cancer or surgery, she has remarried and now has several adult stepdaughters who make each day seem like a giant drip of Chinese water torture.

The stepdaughters always want her to baby-sit, and if she tries to say no, she is roundly criticized. They also come over quite often for dinner, but no one ever lifts a finger to help. This frustrated mother sums up her life by trying to see at least a glimmer of humor:

> I was almost ready to kill myself a couple of weeks ago and the Lord helped me. I tried talking to my husband but he can't see it . . . so I'll just keep praying for his eyes to be opened and for a holy boldness for him and myself. I do love these kids in spite of all this, though—most of the time. Ha! Ha!

Both of these women are trying to smile through their grief, but they are both facing long, hard roads that have different kinds of bumps. It reminds me of Francis Thompson, the English poet, who said:

> Grief is a matter of relativity:
>   The sorrow should be estimated by its proportion
>   to the sorrower;
> A gash is as painful to one as an amputation to
>   another.

Five Steps Through the Pain

Many—almost all—of the letters I receive share the pain, but then they go on to say things like: "We're trusting God . . ." "We've learned to give this over to the Lord . . ." "God is giving us strength for this . . ." I'm encouraged when I read these words about trusting God because, after all, *God only knows!*

In another book,[2] I've talked about traveling near Palm Springs, California, and coming upon a roadside stand with a sign that advertised "Desert-Sweetened Grapefruit." I've often shared the analogy that those of us who go through pain are like that. The bitter desert of grief sweetens us as we learn to give our problems completely to God. The grapefruit story includes my description of several steps that we go through when ongoing pain plasters us flat to the ceiling.

I'm repeating those steps here without apology. I guess I feel a bit like Robert Fulghum, who says he often repeats himself in the hope that sooner or later he just might say something right. Like Fulghum, I'm still wrestling with dilemmas that are "not easily resolved or easily dismissed. . . . Work-in-progress on a life-in-progress is what my writing is about. And some progress in the work is enough to keep it going."[3] So, here once again are my steps for dealing with pain:

FIRST, WE CHURN, a process I often liken to having your insides ground up in a meat grinder, or having a knife plunged into your chest.

SECOND, WE BURN as the shock wears away and the anger takes its place. We may want to kill someone—a child who has caused us unbelievable pain, a drunk driver who has killed a loved one, a spouse who has deserted us for another. Whether we're screaming in anger at the top of our lungs or silently gnashing our teeth, the burning within is a CONSUMING FIRE.

THIRD, WE YEARN for things to change. We look to the happy past, the good old days when life was good and God seemed close and our family gave us nothing but blessings. But now the good old days are gone, and while we know dwelling on the past is futile, we still do it anyway. The yearning stage can last longer than any other.

FOURTH, WE LEARN—a lot of things. We learn what we are really made of. We may learn from others, perhaps in a support group. We discover that we are in a process of long, slow growth. The spiritual values we've always taken for granted ("Oh, of course, I believe that . . .") have now become much more than nice theories. As pain makes us more compassionate and more loving, we find that our values are a real part of who we are, not something we'd like to be.

LAST, WE TURN our problems completely over to God. We finally see that we can do a lot of thinking, feeling, and talking, but only two words really help: "WHATEVER, LORD!" Whatever God allows in our lives, He will get us through it some how, some way. No matter how ridiculous life may be, we can hand it all to the One who is STILL in control. This is honest relinquishment, and because this learning to let go is so important, much of chapter 6 will be devoted to that subject.

One thing to understand about these five stages is that you don't go through them once and then say, "Whew! I'm glad THAT'S over!" No, you may go through many of these stages again and again. You can reach the fifth stage and believe you've turned it over to God and the very next day you can be back churning or burning or yearning. It happened to me. It still happens from time to time. But I find that I'm in those painful stages less often and for shorter times.

To Learn and Turn—ADAPT

The best stages to be in are LEARN and TURN. I want to learn what God has for me, and then I want to keep turning it all over to the One who cares for me far more than I could ever imagine.

For anyone with ongoing pain, my best advice falls somewhere between LEARNING and TURNING. The word I want to key in on in this chapter is ADAPT. I often hear the advice that we must "accept whatever life brings." We must accept our pain, our sorrow, our grief. Accepting others is always a good idea, but I resist the idea of resigning myself to accepting pain. Instead, I'd much rather ADAPT to the challenges that pain may bring.

Adaptability is one of the most important qualities for having a healthy life, even in the face of chronic disease and continual problems. Circumstances of our lives are constantly changing. Either we adapt to fit these new challenges or our well-being deteriorates.

Some years ago researchers did a study of infants who were laid next to a cold metal sheet that had been placed in their bassinets. Some of the babies turned away from the cold as soon as they felt it while others simply lay there touching the cold metal and crying. The adaptability and spirit of the first group— the ones who turned away from the cold metal—is similar to the spirit found in a group called Candlelighters that is made up of parents whose children have cancer. They support each other in adapting to the terrible circumstances surrounding their families. They have chosen to light a candle instead of cursing the darkness of ongoing pain and suffering.

One reason I am against mere acceptance of one's problems or limitations is that it leads to becoming "resigned to your fate"—just plain giving up hope. You become trapped in "if-only" thinking that prevents you from doing what you want to do and need to do.

Recently I saw a picture of an Indiana license plate bearing the "two forbidden words":

IF ONLY

Saying, "IF ONLY I had done this," "IF ONLY I had gone there," or "IF ONLY I had done that," can lead to all kinds of situations, most of them bad.

IF ONLY can fill your stomach with ulcers.

IF ONLY can give you high blood pressure.

IF ONLY can deprive you of fun in your profession.

IF ONLY can take the zing out of your marriage.

IF ONLY can depress you to the point of suicide.

You see, yesterday is gone forever and tomorrow may never come. TODAY IS IT! So give it your best shot, and at the end of the road you will be at the place of your choice instead of being haunted by IF ONLY, IF ONLY, IF ONLY. . . .

Wayward Children Can Drive You Up the Wall

My mail tells me that painful, ongoing situations, problems, diseases, and challenges are bad enough. Muttering "IF ONLY' will only make them worse. A million and one things can happen, and they often do. By far the greatest number of letters I get about ongoing pain come from parents of children who have caused them tremendous disappointment. In many cases children simply choose to rebel against all the values they've been taught. In other cases, they make poor choices that affect the whole family.

Strangely enough, adult children often blame their problems on their parents. So parents might as well grin and bear it. Someone sent me a little placard that sums up a BASIC AS-SUMPTION held by many (most?) adult children:

> I KNOW I AM RESPONSIBLE FOR MY LIFE
> AND MY DECISIONS.
> I KNOW IT IS IRRESPONSIBLE TO BLAME
> OTHERS FOR MY PROBLEMS.
> I ALSO KNOW THAT EVERYTHING WRONG
> IN MY LIFE
> IS MY PARENTS' FAULT.[4]

In the rest of this chapter, I'd like to share letters from folks whose children have caused them ongoing pain. Some are struggling, groping for answers. Others are learning how to take action and adapt to their situation.

What do you do when you raise a child to have Christian values and pour your life into teaching him or her the difference between right and wrong, and then have that same kid throw it all back in your face by growing up to follow a lifestyle totally different from what you have taught? In other words:

HOW DO YOU COPE WHEN THE APPLE OF YOUR EYE
BECOMES A BONE IN YOUR THROAT?

To watch helplessly as a darling child you have nurtured and loved goes off on a detour is one of the most frustrating emotional vacuums a parent can endure. Discouraged parents go through a kaleidoscope of emotions—anger, shame, hurt, feeling unappreciated and resentful—I know because I've been there.

These feelings can be caused by a runaway child or an adult child who drops into the gay lifestyle or a thousand other situations. Children can go astray of the law and be arrested or even jailed. Perhaps they are chronically dishonest, or heavy into the use of alcohol or drugs. They may be dabbling in satanism or another cult. Perhaps they have "disconnected" from the family or they may be still living at home at the age of twenty-nine, still expecting you to support them. They may have married into agnosticism or some kind of abusive situation. Or perhaps they are not married and just have a live-in partner.

When a child has gone morally or spiritually astray, it becomes a deep emotional injury to the parents. It is like having a knife thrust into your chest and having no way to remove it. You have to learn to live with that knife, to move carefully so it won't dig deeper and cause more pain than you already have.

Frequently I get letters from parents whose grown children have chosen to live in sexual immorality of some kind. Their questions could be summed up as follows:

How do I deal with their "shacking up," living together arrangements, pornography, etc.?

One mom has four sons who are "good boys," but her fifth—the oldest—is a "heartache and an embarrassment to our family." The real trouble started when he was in junior high and got in with the wrong crowd. She writes:

He began secretly listening to hard-rock tapes that he borrowed. He used headphones and was up in his room and we didn't know. He also began smoking marijuana. We were so dumb we didn't recognize the odor. He was always spraying Lysol in his room.

Throughout his teenage years he skipped school and got in minor trouble with the police (speeding, etc.). We sent him to a Christian school for grades eleven and twelve. Then we sent him to a Christian college. He was there three months and got expelled for drinking.

He now quits jobs (is unemployed at the moment) and has moved out of our home and into a trailer a few miles away.

He has recently moved a girl of about 19 or 20 into the trailer to live with him. He says she is pregnant and he has to "do the right thing" and let her live there. Her parents and other family members are all for this arrangement. When we ask him when the child is due, he keeps moving the due date up. We have not seen her so we do not know for sure. . . .

Our son doesn't think he is doing anything wrong. He says he asked God to forgive him, but he continues to live in sin. We have some communication with him, but not much.

How do we handle this? He wasn't raised like this. Even with all his trouble he went to church each Sunday until the last year. We prayed for God to help him for years and to send him a good Christian friend—but He never did. We are so confused. <u>PLEASE help us in any way you can!</u> I'm so depressed that this is affecting my entire life. I can't live like this. I don't know anyone else with this problem. I feel so guilty.

Wayward sons are hard enough, but wayward daughters can *really* tug at a mother's heart. One mom wrote to tell her daughter's story:

In high school we had a good relationship, if that means she told me nearly everything. But following my advice was another thing. I went through the worries of knowing she felt sex was a normal thing for two who are "in love"—and she has been in love many times. I did discuss birth control since my talk about abstinence was not being accepted. It was a relief when she graduated never having become pregnant!

But then I learned that while out with friends she had tried alcoholic beverages—becoming drunk a few times. So naturally, I was afraid every time she was with friends, especially when she was driving.

Speaking of driving—she bought a used car—it has been well used during the past two years: (1) Going too fast and skidded on gravel road, landed on its side in ditch, car roughed up—daughter OK. (2) Not paying attention, hit van in front who stopped suddenly—property damage only. (3) Pulled out in front of car—didn't see it—was hit on passenger side, car worse, daughter OK. Plus several more minor accidents. The Lord has sure had His hands full protecting this daughter—but He has continued to do so.

This mother's letter continued and mentioned that her daughter started staying out all night with friends, causing the mother to be unable to sleep. Confrontation led to the daughter's moving out and trying to live first with an ex-employer (male), and when that didn't work moving into a girlfriend's apartment. Currently the daughter is on good terms with her mother but causes her all kinds of grief by going from one boyfriend to another. The mother closed her letter by saying:

> Barbara, it seems it will never end. I thank God for giving me strength to make it through all this so far—and you've just heard a little of it.
> I love my daughter. We have so much fun together—but when she calls on the phone my heart is back up in my throat until I learn it isn't an emergency or crisis this time—she just called to say Hi!
> Thanks for being my sounding board. This has been therapeutic. It's the first time I've put it in writing!

This mom's letter is a good example of how emotional pain knits itself together in various degrees of intensity as we feel anger, disgust, fear, grief, embarrassment, shame, guilt, and hurt all at once. We all experience grief when there is a loss, such as a runaway child or a wayward child. The child may still stay in touch, as the daughter described in the letter above has done, but in some ways her communications are more disturbing than not bothering to call at all.

What this mom is really grieving for is the "loss" of her daughter in the sense that she has lost her daughter's personality and her spirit, and she just doesn't know her daughter any more. The little girl she brought up to know better has disappeared into an adult who seems bent on her own destruction.

The biggest perk for me in this mom's letter is that she thanks me for being her sounding board and speaks of how therapeutic putting it in writing has been. Lots of folks find relief in sharing their emotions by writing to me or talking with me on the phone. As they share, parents finally realize that when a child is off doing his or her own thing, they can't help by being distraught themselves. They realize they have to get their emotions under control by refusing to play the blame game.

Especially when dealing with wayward children, playing the blame game (blaming yourself for what they have decided to do) only leads to wallowing in guilt and self-pity. Guilt immobilizes you and makes you unable to be the kind of supporting parent your kids need. As for self-pity, you go in circles, centering more and more on yourself, which only increases your misery.

For parents who are feeling guilt and self-pity about what a child may be doing or has done, I have one important reminder:

WHERE THERE IS NO CONTROL
THERE IS NO RESPONSIBILITY.

Face it, your adult child is out of your control. That means your child is no longer your responsibility. When an adult child goes off the deep end of rebellion, a mother has to remember that she has had eighteen years to build in her values. If her child has gone against those values, it doesn't mean she has failed. She did her job, and what her son does with what she did is really his or her choice. Children are going to do their own things. But along with that, remember that God can pull their tails whenever He wants to. They may think they are in control, but their times are in HIS hands.

As for feeling guilty because she doesn't know anyone else with the problem, this Mom should realize that in today's society premarital sex and sleeping together before marriage are more the rule than the exception. So-called "living-together" arrangements are especially hard for parents who grew up in my generation. There were people who "slept around" and "shacked up" back when I was young, but today it is a completely different ball of wax. If a young man or woman can't see what's wrong with fornication, it's doubtful that the mother is going to convince him or her otherwise.

For this mom to accept guilt over her son's immoral conduct is only to play the futile blame game. When our kids stray from what they've been taught, we don't have to accept their way-wardness. Instead we can ADAPT, and the best way to adapt is to realize that we can't handle the situation for them. Our children must decide for themselves the kind of life they will live. We must realize that we have loved them, trained them, and taught them. Now it is time to let them go. (For more on letting go, see chapter 6.)

I often hear from parents who feel uncomfortable because Proverbs 22:6 hasn't seemed to work in their family. This verse says, "Train up a child in the way he should go, And when he is old he will not depart from it" (NKJV). Parents want to know, "If this verse is a promise to Christian parents, why has it failed in our case?" Or maybe the real point is that they believe they have failed, and that only makes them feel all the more guilty.

I used to ask the same question until I learned a little more about what the original Hebrew means. In my copy of the New American Standard Version a marginal note on Proverbs 22:6 says, "According to his way." Best-selling author and master Bible teacher Chuck Swindoll believes this means:

> God is not saying, "Bring up a child as *you* see him." But instead, he says, "If you want your child to be godly and wise, observe your child, be sensitive and alert so as to discover *his* way, and adapt your training accordingly."[5]

Right along with this interpretation is the way the Amplified Bible expands on Proverbs 22:6:

> Train up a child in the way he should go [and in keeping with his individual gift or bent], and when he is old he will not depart from it.

The "his own way" interpretation of Proverbs 22:6 isn't suggesting that you let your kid run amuck as he or she grows up. The overall teaching of Scripture clearly tells parents to give their children the best training and nurture they can (see, for example, Eph. 6:4). At the same time, if your kid goes off on a detour, it does not mean you have failed or that God's Word is null and void. It simply means that after you have done your best to train your children by respecting the kind of persons they are, they make their own choices and they are responsible for those choices.

I like the way one mother put it. She believes Proverbs 22:6 means, "Train up a child according to his own temperament, learning the best way he responds to you, to life and to God."[6] The principles in Proverbs 22:6 are sound, but they do not guarantee a charmed life for your kids.

You want to do your best to fill your children's reservoir with the right values, to give your children a built-in system for right and wrong. Then, when they make their own choices in life, it is your hope that their good, solid training will surface often, particularly if they get into deep water and find themselves floundering. It is then that they often remember what they have been taught. It's true that God's Word never returns void. Whatever we write on the hearts of our children is not erased by time and there is no question that early training is vital.

And there can be payoffs—wonderful payoffs. This past Mother's Day my youngest son, Barney, sent me a lovely plaque. I doubt that Barney was thinking about how this plaque beautifully sums up Proverbs 22:6, but I'd like to believe he was just trying to tell me something very special:

> MOTHERS HOLD THEIR CHILDREN'S HANDS
> FOR A WHILE . . .
> THEIR HEARTS FOREVER.

How Can You Love When Your Heart Is Breaking?

Loving our kids through the tough times is always our goal, but that doesn't make the pain any easier to bear. In fact, the pain can INCREASE. Parents write and ask me in one way or another:

How do I cope when my kids break my heart?

For example, I got a letter from a mother of "four wonderful sons" who told how she had lived the "best mother, best cook, best grandma" life for quite a while—and then it "all fell apart." One son ran them into bankruptcy but they forgave him and the many lies he had told. Three years later, however, he still won't talk to his parents. Two other sons married girls from families with totally different values from the Christian ones they'd been taught at home. Now the wives have forbidden their husbands to see the parents and have also refused to let the grandparents see their grandchildren. This brokenhearted mom and grandma writes:

> I just can't seem to find my life. . . . How do you block out memories of love, caring, up all night taking care of them when they were little? Den mother, Scout leader, birthdays, seeing their eyes light up on Christmas . . . I feel I'm in prison and I've done nothing. I can't get dressed. It's not fair. I keep asking, Why? The one son who stuck by us is so upset with his brothers and their wives that it has destroyed his feelings for them. So my family is nothing any more. I used to laugh, but I can't find me anymore. My life was my family. I feel like my life was for nothing.
>
> How can you repair a broken heart? . . . I don't know what tomorrow will bring. I pray a lot to God. How in God's name do I cope? Time, is that the answer? I'm running out . . . I don't want to hear one more person say, "It could be worse," or "You had no shoes, that man had no feet!" Your pain is "your pain." I just want it to go away. I knew an older woman once who, years ago, had electric shock treatments, and she couldn't remember her childhood and some of her family at the time. I thought, How terrible! But now I think I'd go for it.

It's obvious this mom can't accept what has happened, and I don't blame her. I wouldn't accept it either, but I would try in every way I could to ADAPT. After all, no matter what happens to us:

BROKEN HEARTS KEEP ON BEATING[7]

As this mother says, her pain is her pain. That's absolutely right. So often when we are in pain we want it to go away. We want God or somebody to fix things and take away our discomfort, but in many cases there is no way to escape it, and that is why we must learn to adapt, to live with that knife in our chest and keep it from twisting around too much.

Drugs and Alcohol Equal Lots of Pain

It's hard enough raising children and hoping they absorb the right values, but when drugs and alcohol are added to the equation, stress multiplies quickly. When kids go off the deep end with chemicals, it's hard to remain very positive. At a time like that, it's easy to define an optimist as "a person who hasn't been given all the facts yet." In fact, I've talked to parents who could easily find some dark humor in the quip:

WE SHOULD HAVE HAD RABBITS
INSTEAD OF KIDS . . .
AT LEAST WE WOULD HAVE GOTTEN
ONE GOOD MEAL OUT OF THE DEAL!

One dad wrote me twice to share the frustrations of having a son in drug rehabilitation; his letters said in part:

> I don't suppose you've had the opportunity to "guide" a child through a drug rehab program. . . . Our son has been going up and down . . . like a roller coaster. I recently was

asked by staff (in the rehab center) to witness one of his rebellious states—carrying around a chair like he was going to defend against lions (or swing it at somebody).

When I grabbed him by the sweatshirt and told him to drop it, all he could do was scream at me, "Let go of my shirt, man!" He then proceeded to rip off both pockets of my new shirt. Sure I was angry, but it was as though I was face to face with the demon inside him.

Later, he had to be restrained because he just "wants to be left alone." He seems destined to destroy himself—and only the intervention of God will prevent it.

Surely I ask, "When?" and I hear the answer, "In My time." I resign myself to accept that voice, hoping it is not a mirage. . . .

The family support group keeps encouraging us, things will get better. Sometimes I believe all the positive feedback for an entire 24-hour period, but the next day dawns and I've got to turn the pepper grinder again. Then I slide into the valley and find I'm believing only half of all the positive stuff only half the time. That means I'm only 25 percent positive that he'll get better or I'll feel less of a failure. . . .

P.S. I'm sorry for the mood swings, but what do you expect from a guy who just turned 40, reading a book written by a woman?

I admire this dad for reading my book to find some answers and for admitting he needs to find some direction in life. And I really enjoyed his "P.S." because in recent years a little book has come out entitled *Everything Men Know About Women*.[8] Inside, the pages are *completely blank!* So, for this dad to glean some insight from a woman's perspective is truly a compliment.

Putting kidding aside, however, I want him to know that, yes, things WILL get better, but perhaps they will get worse FIRST. He has to be prepared for the long haul with his son, and it *will* be like a roller coaster, not a smooth escalator. He can't glide effortlessly to euphoria. It will be up and down, and down and up, and sometimes he will be knocked off his pins trying to make sense out of what is happening. One thing is for sure:

THERE IS NO PLACE
FOR A MOTHER TO GO TO RESIGN!*

I want this dad to know there are no ex-parents. Once you have a child, it's like getting a life sentence in prison with no hope of parole! So here's how I would answer that dad:

Search out the positive. Cling to the hope that time will be your greatest ally, and be thankful you are a man and not a woman with more than just mood swings to complain about. You don't have to worry about PMS or hot flashes, which often afflict moms as they go through problems with a wayward child.

One day you'll look back at all this and laugh. Believe me, *trust* me; I see it happen all the time. Folks who think they will never get beyond the pits find out that one day they are back on top. They are back in balance and life goes on. I love your honesty and openness. Most men cannot show the transparency you have. But hang on to the fact that you *will* get through this and you *will* feel better!

When Your Kids Hurt, You Hurt

Sometimes parents endure ongoing pain, not because their kids have rebelled or rejected them, but because life has dealt their children a severe blow. For example, one of the most painful things parents can endure is to give a child in marriage and see that marriage disintegrate for any number of reasons.

In some cases, I get letters from mothers who have had three or four children wind up in divorce! Here's what one pastor's wife went through in an eighteen-month period:

November: I had a segmented mastectomy, chemotherapy for six months, 25 radiation treatments.
March: Youngest daughter divorced.
June: Oldest daughter divorced.

---

*Believe me, I know! (See Barbara Johnson, *Where Does a Mother Go to Resign?* [Minneapolis: Bethany House, 1979].)

July: Broken ankle—therapy for two months.
October: Third daughter divorced.
February: Next-to-oldest girl divorced after 15 years—
husband walked out for a 21-year-old.

This mom said she is coping, and that God has made the family stronger through all of this. Then she added:

> We know now more than ever that His grace is sufficient for any and all situations. (I think I could write a book sometimes. Ha!)

Another mother of three children, all in their thirties (six grandchildren), thought everyone was happily married, and then "things happened." Her letter continued:

> Our second daughter's husband went bankrupt in his construction company and became a drinker and a woman chaser, and they were divorced. At the same time our first daughter and her husband were having their second child and, three weeks after the son was born, he left her for her best friend. They were divorced three months after the second daughter's divorce. Both girls had been married twelve to sixteen years.
>
> It has been seven years of struggle both financially and mentally. We all live in the same small town. Two months ago our son and his wife (married sixteen years) separated. No divorce yet, but who knows. They have two children.
>
> Throughout all of this we have had the love and support of our church family and friends and the love of God and His promises that there is a way through our struggles, one day at a time.

Both of these moms are adapting to the devastation of multiple divorce as best they can. Like many other parents, they are looking for the best possible answers to questions like these:

How do we help our children through a divorce?
What part should we play?

Both of these mothers appear to be nonjudgmental. They are accepting their kids and adapting to the situation as best they can. In most cases, these are the first steps parents can take.

When a grown child's marriage ends in divorce, parents can be supportive but not patronizing. The same principle about every child making his or her own choices applies. Perhaps your son or daughter chose an individual you really didn't approve of. It will do no good now to criticize and say, "I told you so . . ."

The best thing to do is back off and let your children live their own lives. You may be tempted to step in, take over, and start parenting again, but avoid that at all costs. Instead, try to give them lots of emotional support because their self-esteem is probably at an all-time low.

Of course, you may need to help financially, and if the divorce has left your daughter a single mom, she may be looking to you for help with child care. Always keep in mind that you walk a very fine line. You are needed—sometimes desperately—but you must wait to be invited. When your kids ask for your help or advice, you can give it. Always keep in mind however:

ADVICE IS LIKE SNOW,
THE SOFTER IT FALLS, THE DEEPER IT SINKS.

The Pain Goes On and On and On . . .

Every day letters come from parents who are learning to cope with situations that once seemed overwhelming. One mother wrote to thank me for the message in *Geranium*, commenting that all her life she had been the serious member of the family and she appreciated the wit and humor in the book. Then she said:

> Although my situation is different (whose isn't?), I could definitely relate to your story. I am the mother of two sons, both alcohol-drug addicted for over 20 years. Recovery

entered my family a little over three years ago. I say recovery "entered" the family, as today the entire family is in recovery, including my husband and I from our co-dependency issues.

Another mom shared her deep concerns about her daughter, who has had problems with alcohol—and automobiles. The mother explained:

This week she was caught driving while her license was suspended. She wasn't drinking—the brake light on the car wasn't working so she was stopped. She isn't gay and definitely likes the opposite sex as she has a seven-year-old son and is divorced from her alcoholic ex-husband. But at one time she drank, being in this unlovely situation. (That was the reason for the suspended license in the first place.)

So tears are often near the surface. And along comes your *Love Line* and I read and cry and laugh—and like the poem says, "I find some work to do!"

The stories of ongoing pain I've shared in this chapter are truly only the tip of the proverbial iceberg. Just a sampling from my weekly mail reveals:

. . . a precious red-headed granddaughter born with only a third of her brain because of her mother's drug abuse.

. . . a mother struggling to help her oldest daughter, who has been psychologically ill for twenty years. Her daughter-in-law is a recovering manic depressive, another daughter is slowly conquering panic attacks, and still another daughter combats marriage problems but won't share any of her feelings with the family.

. . . a mentally retarded daughter who has had open heart surgery and part of her stomach removed. Her sister may have to have brain surgery, and the father in the family has been out of work most of the time recently.

. . . a fourteen-year-old boy who flipped his four-wheeler and spent thirty-three days in ICU only to be moved to a private room where he remained in a coma.

The Real World Is One Rough Place

Do you see why I believe "God only knows"? So often I would like to fix everything for these dear folks who write to tell me how life has welcomed them to the real world. I do my best to send them whatever help I can—tapes of messages I've given, suggested reading that might help them with their particular problem, or suggestions of organizations that might be able to give them experienced or professional help. But the bottom line is this:

TAKE YOUR BROKEN DREAMS TO JESUS . . .
ONLY HE KNOWS THE ANSWERS TO YOUR PROBLEMS.

Only as we turn to Him in faith will we feel His comforting hand on our lives. In most of these same letters that recount disasters great and small, folks often add their thoughts about faith and trust in God.

A neighbor was telling me recently how difficult it was to leave her daughter at college and how depressed she has been. She does not know any of the problems we are having with our son (you can share with so few people) but I was thinking of how wonderful it would be to be able to bring a child to college—to know where the child was and that her life had purpose and direction. There are some situations we cannot change—but we can change our attitudes about them. As long as there is life, there is hope and it is this which really keeps us going, especially in the midst of the trial. Like Daniel in the Old Testament, we have experienced the fire, but it has not consumed us. . . .

In these . . . I held the family together and supported my dear husband and children but *I* began coming totally "un-glued"! . . . the strain on my marriage, children, and my sanity multiplied. I hadn't taken care of ME! It never even crossed by mind! I couldn't function at home or work. My emotional strain turned into physical problems: chest pains, choking, insomnia. . . . Don't ask me why I picked up the phone and called you (someone I've never met) for advice. And over a distance of thousands of miles, God used you to guide me to the information I needed in my life!

We learned that we couldn't answer the questions and life went on anyway. God has been our only solid ground and at times I was angry at Him for the mess our lives were in. We are learning to cope and get on with life. Thank God for people who are willing to share their stories. I hope that by sharing our "endless hope" we can help others know that God can handle any problem. . . .

Knowing today that recovery is a process, I feel a newness of my spiritual faith in God and His Son Jesus. Only God can perform miracles; both my sons' sobriety is proof of that. The road back has been very rocky, but with God's help the rocks can become stepping stones. . . .

I read your book from cover to cover all night and in my diary copied down many of your quips. I cannot tell you how many times over the next few months God continued to use you in my life. You had been through phases I had not yet entered, but you gave me light along the way. I have now passed through some of these phases and have not only by God's grace been forgiven but have also forgiven my now-ex-husband and his fiancée, and the "others" who chose to be involved in our divorce. God had restored me into His joy, despite my circumstances. . . .

All of the above comments remind me of the old saying:

> WHAT'S DOWN IN THE WELL
> COMES UP IN THE BUCKET.

In other words, whatever reservoirs of strength and hope you have deep inside will come up when pain inevitably invades your life. One of the most dramatic examples I have ever heard of drawing on inner strength is this story that ran in *People Weekly* concerning a teenager who slipped and fell into a piece of spinning farm machinery that amputated both of his arms in just a few seconds:

He Tried to Keep His Blood Off Mom's Carpet

John Thompson, eighteen, was alone, doing chores on his family's sixteen-hundred-acre North Dakota farm when the accident happened. Realizing his arms were gone, he struggled to his feet and staggered back to the house where he used a stub of bone hanging out of what was left of one arm to open a screen door. Then he used his mouth to turn the doorknob and get into the house.

Somehow he got the phone off the hook and managed to dial his uncle's home a few miles away by holding a pen in his mouth. His seventeen-year-old cousin answered and he told her he needed an ambulance because "I'm bleeding very bad and I don't have any arms."

Then John hung up, went into the bathroom and crouched in the bathtub because he didn't want to stain his mother's carpet with his blood! Family members arrived a few minutes later and tried to help John keep his spirits up as they waited for the ambulance to arrive.

Through it all, John Thompson never lost consciousness or his sense of humor. When his aunt told him the ambulance would be there in a second, he quipped, "One thousand and one . . . well, it's not here."

When the ambulance crew hurried in to take John to the hospital, they were stunned by what they saw. They were also amazed when John reminded them to retrieve his arms, which were still lying near the power take-off mechanism that had ripped them off. He even directed them to garbage bags in the kitchen so they could pack the limbs in ice!

Miraculously, John's arteries had closed off as if a natural tourniquet had been applied; he was rushed to a medical facility twenty minutes away. A little later he was air-lifted to a trauma center where six microsurgery experts waited to reattach his limbs, one of which had been severed above the elbow and the other one torn off at the shoulder. The operation went well, but doctors were not sure about how much use John would regain of either arm. Afterward he faced at least five years of grueling physical therapy.

With his usual positive attitude, John was already trying to figure out what he'd be able to do with his hands and how he would finish high school. In talking about the accident, he said, "I'm grateful for everyone's prayers and everything, but anyone would have done what I did. You do what you have to do."[9]

Few people will ever have to face the incredible trauma John Thompson went through, but many of us face our own particular traumas, and what John says is as true for us as it was for him: "You do what you have to do." And as you do it, what's down in the well comes up in the bucket. That's why it's so crucial to be able to draw on reservoirs of inner strength that only God can provide. As the psalmist puts it:

HE TURNS A DESERT INTO POOLS OF WATER,
A PARCHED LAND INTO SPRINGS. . . .[10]

How much pain can we take? God only knows, but Jesus promises: "If anyone thirsts, let him come to Me and drink" (John 7:37 NKJV). He will provide the living water that will make all the difference.

> A little love, a little trust
> A soft impulse, a sudden dream,
> And life as dry as desert dust
> Is fresher than a mountain stream.[11]

In this chapter, we have touched on several "ordinary" ways kids can cause ongoing pain for their parents. Obviously, there are many others, but in chapter 4 I want to focus on one painful problem I used to think was extraordinary.

The day I discovered my own son was a homosexual, my world was shattered. Anger, rage, and homophobia were all part of my initial reaction. I felt I was the only one in all the world who had a homosexual child. I learned a great deal in the next few years, as Spatula Ministries was born. Now I know homosexuality is not as unheard-of as I thought it was back in 1975. It is our RESPONSE that makes it so unreal to deal with; that's what we will look at in the next chapter.

Gloomee Busters

> Life is like an ice cream cone:
> Just when you think you've got it licked—
> IT DRIPS ALL OVER YOU!

☐ ☐ ☐

IF AT FIRST YOU DON'T SUCCEED,
SEE IF THE LOSER GETS ANYTHING.

When life drops a pooper
That's unkind to our noses,
Use it for fertilizer;
It's your chance
To grow roses![12]

I DON'T MIND THE RAT RACE
BUT I COULD DO WITH A LITTLE MORE CHEESE.

The secret of dealing successfully with a child
is not to be its parent.

CAN YOU THANK ME FOR TRUSTING YOU
WITH THIS EXPERIENCE
EVEN IF I NEVER TELL YOU WHY?

Parents: People who bear infants,
bore teen-agers, and board newlyweds.

MONEY ISN'T EVERYTHING,
BUT IT SURE KEEPS THE KIDS IN TOUCH.

Climbing the Musical Scale

DO—Do not worry over things that may never happen, and even if they happen, worry will not help. Do count your blessings before you count cares.

RE—Radiate good will and a spirit of benevolence. Like laughter, it is infectious and makes yourself, as well as others, feel better.

ME—Mete kindness, understanding, tolerance, and forgiveness generously. You reap as you mete.

FA—Far-reaching are the therapeutic benefits of spiritual thinking. You become as you habitually think. Resentment, hatred, spite, envy, and vengeance pack radioactive fall-out that gnaws at your vitals. They are self-consuming.

SO—Sow the seeds of love, friendship, empathy, and helpfulness. These hardy seeds take root in the crustiest ground.

LA—Laugh at yourself now and then. He who can laugh at himself is less apt to be at war with himself. Laugh at yourself, even if you don't feel like laughing.

TI—Teach yourself awareness and appreciation of all the wonders of nature. Thank God daily for the precious gift of life. Genuine gratitude and discontent are never found together.

DO—Do not expect someone else to open the door to happiness for you. You must do it yourself. You alone have the key. Turn it.

—Source unknown

□ □ □

There are times when, regardless of the score,
just to be ALIVE is to be winning.
—Ashleigh Brilliant Pot-Shot 981 © 1976.

□ □ □

SOME DAYS YOU'RE THE BUG . . .
SOME DAYS, THE WINDSHIELD!

□ □ □

Blessed are the flexible
for they shall not be bent out of shape.

My grace is sufficient for you, for my power is made
perfect in weakness. (2 Cor. 12:9 NIV)

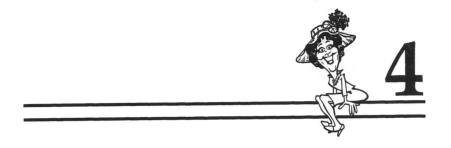

You're a WHAT?!?

What to Do When Your Favorite "Who" Becomes a "What"

With everything that is going on today, some sins look almost "acceptable" compared with other alternatives. I got a letter from one mother who received a disturbing call from her son. He told her he and his wife had separated, that it was all his fault, and that he had a "terrible problem."

The son asked his mother to call his wife, and when she did so, her daughter-in-law said, yes, it was true that her husband had had an affair and that it was possible that he might have given her a "terrible disease."

Because the daughter-in-law was so distraught, the phone conversation ended rather quickly and when the mother-in-law hung up she feared the worst. Could it be that her son was gay and he had given his wife AIDS? She had to wait three days before she was able to fly to the city where her son and his wife lived to get more details about the crisis. Her letter continued:

I let him talk without interrupting him until he came to the telling of his affair. I insisted he tell me who and when he told me, I said, "You mean with a GIRL?" He said, "Yes, of course!" My first words to come out were "Oh, I'm so GLAD!" He thought I had really flipped because he knew of my deep Christian beliefs about marriage and adultery. When I was able to explain about my terrible misunderstanding, he was horrified, but as we talked he finally said, "Well, Mother, now I know how to tell you bad news . . . just tell you something worse first, then you will be so relieved you won't be overcome by the bad news!"

As terrible as those three days of waiting and wondering were, this mom learned some lasting lessons. She grew in her faith as God helped her cope with the most difficult testing of her life. And through living in stark fear of AIDS for three days she now has tremendous compassion for all families who face this deadly situation. She said, "I'll never be the same person I was before this three-day trial."

I never learned the last chapter of this story. I'm not sure if the couple got back together, but I know this mom kept loving her son through it all. While her views on adultery didn't change one bit, she was able to see that, as bad as an affair can be, there could be things that are even more devastating.

She was waiting to hear the awful words, "I'm gay and I've tested HIV-positive," and when they didn't come, she heaved a great sigh of relief. But what happens when you do hear your son or daughter (or spouse) announce, "I'm homosexual . . . I have a lover . . . I'm moving out"? What *do* you do when your favorite "who" becomes a "what"?

When the Bomb Drops Out of the Closet

I've talked to many parents who say, "If only he had run off with some woman. I could handle *that*! But THIS?"

I don't judge these parents at all for giving one trauma more weight than another because I understand. I did it too.

When I discovered that my son, Larry, was a homosexual, the emotional effect was like the explosion of a hundred-kiloton bomb. And since starting Spatula Ministries more than fourteen years ago, I have talked to thousands of parents who have heard those same fateful words and their reaction has been just like mine was. It may not be rational or even Christian, but for most parents, on a scale of one to ten, hearing that their child is gay is a thirteen!

That's why we named our ministry "Spatula." As bad as so many things can be—losing a child through death, hearing the fateful word *cancer*, learning that your daughter's marriage is breaking up due to adultery, and on and on—there is something about the word *homosexual* that literally makes people hit the ceiling, and only a spatula of love can peel them off and help get them back down on their feet! Here are just a few samples of how parents reacted when they got the news:

> Our 34-year-old son, who has a wife and two children, told us in June that he was gay and he and his wife would be getting a divorce. We were both devastated. I am just now beginning to care if I live or die.

> I spoke with you for a few minutes when we heard of our lovely son Peter's lifestyle choice. Oh, how it hurts! One day I'm up, the other I'm down. Today is <u>BLACK</u> and I couldn't even go for my walk.

> My husband became so distraught that he wanted to kill our son, his friend, our younger son, me, and himself. He thought that would be the only "way out."

This past Monday my husband's and my world was destroyed. Our 19-year-old son told us he is a homosexual. What else do I need to say? We are Christians, have worked in the church, taught Sunday school for young people for 20 years. We're highly respected in the community. . . . What do we do now? I begin to rest in Jesus and then panic sweeps over me to drown me. The suffering of his father overwhelms me! The devil has struck at our most vulnerable point.

If you think I sound composed—I am today. I've waited two weeks after reading your book to find a day I could write instead of wanting to color or cut out paper dolls. My friend gave me pre-cut paper dolls, says she doesn't trust me with even the round-tip scissors! Good friends are hard to find!

My daughter came home for spring break and told me she is a lesbian. I lost it. I grabbed my Bible and begged and cried and screamed (something I have never done), threatened suicide, but nothing changed except that she turned completely away from me.

I can identify with all of these parental emotions—and more! After losing Steve and then Tim, I thought I had had my fill of the cup of suffering, but I was wrong. As bad as dealing with the deaths of two sons was, there were many things about those deaths that were easier than dealing with learning the truth about Larry.

Larry and I Had a "Perfect" Relationship

As my mind goes back to that incredible day in June 1975, I clearly remember the kaleidoscope of emotions that seemingly struck me all at once. Larry didn't come to me and admit he was a homosexual; instead I discovered it accidentally by finding homosexual material in a dresser drawer where I had gone innocently looking for a BIBLE STUDY BOOK for a friend of his. Accompanying the initial shock was total disbelief and even denial. How could this be? He had shared so much with us, particularly enjoying music with me and so many other fun things we had done together.

During high school, Larry had worked the night shift in a local In 'n' Out hamburger place, and after getting off work he would bring home hamburgers for both of us. He'd always come home smelling of onions and french fries and sometimes find me watching the Johnny Carson Show. He'd flop down on the big puffy chair next to the TV; then we'd eat the burgers and he'd share with me the funny things that had happened at work.

One night he described a really fat lady who rolled up to the drive-through and ordered fifteen hamburgers, fifteen orders of fries, and fifteen chocolate shakes! She was alone in her car and when she drove up to the window to pick up her order, Larry automatically asked the routine question, "Is this to eat HERE or to go?"

We had a good laugh about that story and many others. He'd tell me about his friends who came by to see him and other conversations about people we knew and enjoyed. It was our time to share, watching Johnny Carson, eating hamburgers, drinking Cokes, and laughing—always laughing.

Larry has a rippling laugh that is infectious—absolutely contagious—and VERY AUDIBLE. I was always afraid we would wake up Bill or Barney with our raucous laughter, but we did have FUN.

All through those years there wasn't even a hint from Larry about his struggle with homosexuality nor any kind of indication that this was part of his life. He had many opportunities to tell me when we sat there alone at night in the quiet of our darkened house, but he never said a word about his personal struggle.

As I thought back over some of our conversations, I remembered once that he wanted to know what I thought about eter-

nal security. I have always been persuaded that the believer is
secure in God's love, and out of my own reservoir of Scriptures
I told Larry why and how I knew this was true and how it applied to my own life, as well as his. After discovering that Larry
was gay, his questions about eternal security made a lot more
sense to me.

Another puzzle in June 1975 was the Mother of the Year
plaque Larry had given me only a month before on Mother's
Day. It told me what a wonderful mom I was and added some
other flowery phrases that come to mothers on special days. But
now, where had the darling son I thought I knew so well gone?
What had happened to the laughing, happy-spirited boy who
suddenly had a DARK SIDE I never knew before?

When I made my devastating discovery in Larry's dresser
drawer, there was no time to get answers to my frantic questions. Larry wasn't there and I was due at the airport in forty-
five minutes to pick up my sister, Janet, and her husband, who
were flying home from a vacation in Hawaii. We had all
planned to go to Disneyland that evening and then celebrate
Father's Day together before they continued their flight home
to Minnesota.

I'm not sure why, but I picked up all of the "stuff" I had discovered and threw it in the trunk of my car. I'm also not sure
why I wrote Larry a note that said:

> Larry, I found the magazines and stuff in the drawer and I
> have it all with me. I love you and God loves you, but this is
> so wrong. Can we just get through tonight and, after the
> relatives leave tomorrow, talk about it? Please meet us at the
> flagpole at Disneyland at 8:00 so we can enjoy the big bicen-
> tennial parade and fireworks with them anyway.

If I had wanted to keep things quiet until after my sister and
husband had left, it would have been better to have left the stuff
undisturbed in his dresser drawer. It would have been better to
just smile through it all, have a wonderful time at Disneyland
that evening, enjoy a great Father's Day, put them on the plane

with smiles, and THEN go back home to confront my son and tell him what I knew.

Nothing Made Sense—NOTHING

What I did instead made no sense, but then life wasn't making much sense right about then. As I drove at what seemed to me to be pell-mell speed to the airport, I felt all the symptoms of a panic attack: shortness of breath and a strong suspicion that an invisible elephant was sitting on my chest and a shag rug had somehow been stuffed down my throat. And for some crazy reason, my teeth itched!

Deep inside I felt pain, as if I were being gored by a bull. I had never been *gored* by a bull, but I was sure THIS is what it had to be like. Strange groaning sounds were coming out of my mouth, and I wondered if this was "only" a panic attack—or the beginnings of a heart attack.

What was going on? After all, I was no stranger to crises and shocking news. Nine years before I had picked up my half-dead husband on a dark mountain road with his head smashed open from an accident, and I'd held together as I went to call for help and then got him down that mountain road to the local hospital.

And just two years after that, death had come to our door for the first time when Steven had died—and I coped with that. Then five years later, death had paid a second visit with the phone call from the Yukon telling me Tim was dead. I hadn't felt any rugs in my throat or elephants on my chest THEN, so what was going on THIS time?

Was I having all these symptoms because I had a stack of homosexual magazines and letters written to my son in the trunk of my car? Should I dump them somewhere before meeting Janet and Mel at the airport? But how could I dump them without being seen? I had no sack to put them in. Besides, maybe it was illegal to have such material—maybe they were like drugs or something.

I knew nothing about homosexuality and I certainly had no way to cope with learning that my darling son was one. But worst of all, I felt so BETRAYED. How could Larry have kept this part of his life from us so completely? Why didn't he say something to me, especially since we had shared so much together?

My Son Had Always Been So Thoughtful

Thinking back to the night of Bill's accident, I recalled how Larry was only eleven at the time, yet he had been so mature and so steady. After I had called an ambulance for Bill, I left Larry up at the retreat center in the care of other people from our church. Then I hurried back to where I had found my husband and got there just in time to join him in the ambulance for the ride down the mountain to the hospital. Without any help or prompting from the adults present, Larry got on the phone and called our family doctor, our pastor, and his teacher at the Christian school he attended and told all of them what had happened. By the time the ambulance arrived at the hospital, all three of them were there waiting for us!

Larry had the presence of mind to do this telephoning while everyone else was praying and trying to figure out what to do. He was only eleven years old, but I really believe he had the gift of mercy even at that young age, and he knew how to use it.

And during the next two years, Larry was so caring and thoughtful as we battled with doctors' diagnoses that said my husband would be blind and a vegetable for the remainder of his life, which they estimated at only five years at best. More than anyone else, Larry had made it possible for me to get through that incredible time of adjustment. As I learned to be the nurse and total support for Bill, Larry helped me iron out life's wrinkles; he'd cheer me up when the stress hit me hard.

When I found out Larry was gay I asked, How could he BETRAY us like this? How could he have been living ANOTHER

LIFE that we knew nothing about? Had I been so busy with Bill's recovery that I had not looked for any signs? But then, why would I look for signs when everything appeared so normal?

Now I know that part of the reason for Larry's secrecy was that he was, as always, trying to be kind. In great pain himself, he wanted to spare us the pain of knowing what neither he nor we could understand.

All the time only feelings of anguish and betrayal flashed through my mind during that drive to the airport. But I also distinctly remember planning that I would somehow get through the weekend and then on Monday I would go about getting Larry's problem FIXED. After all, I thought, God and mothers can fix anything, and surely there was some kind of pill, injection, medication, or therapy that would FIX MY KID. Nothing was impossible for God and mothers!

Already I was anticipating my confrontation with Larry. I would tell him that he must either "turn or burn." Then he would recite 1 John 1:9 and it would all be over. He would STOP whatever he was doing and he would be cleansed. This terrible thing would be out of our lives and we could fit the pieces back together.

No, there was nothing that could not be FIXED, and certainly my confrontation with Larry would do just that, fix it, and this horrible nightmare would be over with, ONCE AND FOR ALL!

But while I tried to reassure myself about being able to fix Larry, I also thought about Scripture verses that talk about a "reprobate mind." Was a reprobate mind something you could have and then lose later? Did Larry have a reprobate mind because of the materials I had found in his room? What exactly WAS a reprobate mind?

Surely all the filth in my trunk could not be a part of the boy I loved so much. Who was this person who had this dark side in his life that had never surfaced before? Did God love him and forgive him? Could I love him and forgive him? Could things ever be the SAME again?

Parents of Gay Kids Can Get a Bit Confused

My questions piled up, one upon another. As I look back on that incredible day in 1975, I can see that panic, pain, and anxiety were mixed with ignorance, misunderstanding, and naiveté.

In 1975 I didn't know anyone who had a homosexual in the family, much less a homosexual child. It was such an UN-NATURAL thing! To run off with a girl would have been sinful, but at least that was a natural type of sin. This was abnormal—because it was something I knew nothing about.

That was 1975. Today I hardly know anyone who DOESN'T have a homosexual somewhere in the family. Since starting Spatula Ministries, I have gotten letters that show I'm not the first mother who thought her child could "just be fixed" somewhere. For example, one parent wrote:

> My daughter has just become a lesbian and she is in college. She has three weeks' vacation at Christmas and we wondered if she came to California during her school break if you could fix her up before school starts so she won't have to miss any school over this?

Since Spatula Ministries was begun more than fourteen years ago, I've been asked just about every kind of question by parents of gay children. Often they write or call while they are still coping with the initial shock of learning about their child. My own experience helps me sympathize when they sound a little confused and upset, and when they get words wrong and concepts twisted. Following are some excerpts from ACTUAL letters that have come in the mail, including one letter that began: "Dear Spatula MISERIES."

> I found out my son is a homosexual. He keeps asking why we are treating him like a leopard. What does he mean? We

have not even seen him for several weeks. What does he think we are doing . . . operating a zoo?

Ever since we learned our daughter was a homosexual my husband has been impudent. What should I do for his impudence?

My daughter wrote some letters to a friend and talks about being a lesbian. Isn't Lebanese what Danny Thomas is? What does that have to do with girls writing love letters to each other?

My husband told me that he is a homosectional. Where can he get help for sectionals?

I have tried for many months to know why my son could possibly be a homosexual. I finally realized that out of the five children he was the one I didn't breast feed. I am glad I have the answer now because this has disturbed me so much trying to figure out the cause of his problem.

Parents Ask the Hard Questions

Recently a lady wrote to tell me: "I read that sweating will keep boys from getting involved in homosexuality!" If only her information were correct, but I'm afraid sweat glands don't have a whole lot to do with it! Not only does my mail show me there is a lot of confusion about homosexuality, there is also a lot of real agony among parents who desperately want to know the answers to very real and tough questions. In the rest of this chapter, I want to deal with some of their most frequent queries:

> *My husband and I were actively involved with our son when he was young and spent much time with him. He has always seemed so happy and well-adjusted. He was involved in Boy Scouts and 4-H (all masculine activities). How can he be gay?*

This is quite possibly the most frequent question I receive. I often hear from parents who say their children accepted Christ when they were young and that they regularly attended a Bible-believing church as they grew up. They even went to a Bible college, yet these children turn out to be homosexuals. In fact, they often have their first homosexual experience at a Bible college! Parents ask this question in dozens of ways: "We tried to do everything right. We tried to bring our children up in the nurture and admonition of the Lord. So what went wrong and what can we do for our child now?"

As for "what went wrong?" no one is totally sure. Some say homosexuality is all the result of choice, but in all of my counseling experiences, I have never met a homosexual who *chose* his orientation (nor, for that matter, do I know any heterosexuals who have chosen their orientation). Recent studies indicate that sexual orientation probably has a genetic component. But even among those who believe that environmental factors are involved, most are quick to point out that such influences occur long before a child is old enough to "choose" such a thing.

I have talked with and read the opinions of a dozen or more Christian psychologists, psychotherapists, and counselors, and *none* of them agree on the cause of homosexuality. At this point, it is safe to say that no one can explain it completely. It may be that a multiplicity of reasons contribute to being homosexual. I've been learning about this for fifteen years and I still have more questions than answers. But I do know this: We are all living in a fallen world. *Nothing is ideal or perfect.*

GOD CALLS US TO BE FAITHFUL;
HE DID NOT PROMISE WE WOULD BE SUCCESSFUL.

I tell parents: You tried your best to be the parents God wanted you to be. Keep in mind that God was Adam's parent, and look what a mess he turned out to be! So who are you to expect you can do better than God? Just love your children, and believe that the reservoirs of Scripture and training they have will prompt them to get their hearts right with God. Pray that their decisions and choices of behavior will eventually be regulated by their commitment to the Lord, and trust that the Lord knows more than you do about the hard places in their lives.

As parents, our prayers should be that our kids will stand clean before the Lord. If they have a good biblical marriage, that is fine. If they remain unmarried, that is fine also. To be celibate is a lonely life, but there is a gift of celibacy. No one seems to want it, but it is a gift. The main point, however, is that parents cannot blame themselves for the actions of their children. Whatever choices your kids make, they must answer to God, not you.

□ □ □

How should we react to our son's announcement that he is gay? Doesn't the Bible teach that we should withdraw ourselves from anyone who is deliberately sinning?

There are verses that say we should not keep company with brethren who are indulging in sinful behavior (see 1 Cor. 5:11 and 2 Thess. 3:6) and I appreciate what those verses have to say in a corporate church-body setting, but I don't think they necessarily apply to family relationships. More to the point, I don't think we can pull a verse out here and there and hang all of our theology on that. The flow of God's message is God's redemptive love for all of us.

As for how these parents should respond to their son, I would suggest they consider some important factors. First, if the son is under eighteen, I do not ever advise turning him out on his own. Sending a teenager out on his own only throws him into the arms of the promiscuous lifestyle. I draw the line, though, at eighteen. If the son is older than eighteen and is practicing a promiscuous lifestyle rebelliously and with no concern for parents' feelings, then my advice about the best way to respond is this: Do what will be the MOST COMFORTABLE FOR YOU. Perhaps this would not be total "unconditional" love, but you cannot let the behavior of one person destroy your entire family. Tell your son you love him and will pray for him, but that to preserve your own sanity, you prefer not to be faced with this in your home.

Then help your son get settled in another place and show thoughtfulness by helping him stock the refrigerator with food and get other necessary items such as facial tissue, soap, bathroom tissue—*anything that reminds him of your unconditional love for him.* Many parents may feel their child is not worthy of their love, but then who *is* worthy of unconditional love?

Be aware that condemnation will not bring about any change in your son's lifestyle. It is only conviction from God that can cause a shift of behavior in ANY of us. Only God can take a heart of stone and make it a heart of flesh (see Ezek. 11:19).

□   □   □

Our homosexual son says he is the happiest he has ever been. How can he be so happy when he has been taught that this lifestyle is so wrong?

It seems that many children, boys in particular, go through a great deal of anguish as they grow up having emotions they feel are not right. They are so afraid someone will find out, and many of them struggle for years trying to live two sides of the coin. Then, when they are discovered or when they reveal that they have a homosexual orientation, they are RELIEVED because now they can be out in the open and not have to hide their struggle any more.

As for their being happy, that is hard to say. All I know is I have never met a Christian homosexual, man or woman, who told me he or she would *choose* to be gay. The complicated array of factors that contribute to homosexual feelings are so complex and interwoven that they cannot be explained in a few paragraphs. Many whole books try to explain them and fail to come up with conclusive answers.

As I was finishing this book, I noticed that for two days Ann Landers had devoted her column to the question, "Are you glad you are gay, or would you rather be straight?" According to Ann, responses came in thirty-to-one saying, "Yes, I'm glad I'm gay." But I repeat, in more than fifteen years of working with homosexuals of all ages, I have never met a homosexual Christian who said, "I'm glad I'm gay."

Ann Landers ran several letters from gays, some of which said they were glad about their orientation; but others said things like this: "Am I glad I'm gay? You've got to be crazy. I've been beaten up, spat on and discriminated against in the job market. Who would choose THIS?"

Another homosexual wrote Ann to say, "Am I glad I'm gay? My response is an unqualified *yes*. It's thrilling to know that there are people out there who would happily kill me because of my sexual orientation. I am delighted that the government discriminates against me at tax time when I can't file jointly. I'm ecstatic that I'm barred from serving my country in time of war. I'm overjoyed that all major religions reject my lifestyle. I love it that I could lose my job if the truth were known. Best of all, it's great to be viewed as an outcast by one's own family. This is what it means to be gay."[1]

Unfortunately, this gay person's letter, filled with bitter sarcasm, is all too true. Sometimes the persecution can be even worse for a Christian homosexual. A gay son may tell his parents he is "happy," but deep inside he is usually lonely and afraid. It is our job to love our children and to provide all the comfort we can as we assure them God still loves them. Christ's loving sacrifice has provided a way for all of us to be forgiven and accepted by the Lord.

□   □   □

Should I tell any of my friends that my child is gay?

Each family's situation is different, but a key principle is not to let your child muzzle you so you have to bear all the pain yourself while the child goes off blissfully to pursue his lifestyle. In a sense, when this happens the child has dumped all his pain on you. He has come OUT of the closet and put you IN!

In most cases, it is wise to tell the rest of the IMMEDIATE FAMILY what is happening. Tell them why you are hurting and what you are going through at this time. Otherwise, people may think you have cancer or you're getting a divorce because your emotions are in such obvious upheaval.

In referring to the "immediate family," I do not usually include grandparents. Telling grandparents is not always helpful because they may be much too old for this kind of shock. A lot would depend on their emotional strength and resiliency.

But the immediate family can bind together to pray for the loved one who has gone into this lifestyle and, above all, to show unconditional love toward him. If they are together in this, they will be more united and caring for each other than ever before.

If your homosexual child has instructed you not to tell anyone, tell your child that you need support too. After all, he has his own support system out there in the gay community and you need one also.

Obviously, you shouldn't advertise for support. It isn't wise to put an item in the church bulletin for prayer, for example. But you can select a few close friends you can trust. Most parents are usually able to find one or two other couples with whom they can open up and be honest about their feelings.

Also, it is best to tell your boss at work so that he understands why you may not be acting like your old self. Let the boss know you are going through a grief process that is every bit as real as the grief you would feel if your child had died.

The overall principle is to BE SELECTIVE and tell only those who you think will be supportive. Keep Ecclesiastes 4:10 in mind: "If one falls down, his friend can help him up. But pity the man who falls and has no one to help him up!" (NIV).

You are in for a long haul and you need to share your problem with a few who can encourage you spiritually. They may not know a lot about homosexuality. They may not have ever experienced this kind of thing themselves, but if they are compassionate people, they can give you a great deal of emotional nurturing.

The bottom line is this: *Do whatever it takes to make yourself more comfortable. Think of yourself, not specifically of what will help your child.* This may sound selfish, but I emphasize it for a good reason. You need all the support you can get right now. Your child will do his thing and leave you to pick up the pieces. Just be sure you don't fall apart as well. Do whatever will help you get your priorities in order to keep your home together.

PAMPER yourself during this time. There's a big knife stuck in your heart and you must do what you can to keep it from twisting and causing even more pain. Be selfish because you are the wounded one now. Anything you can do to help yourself, any way you can bring some comfort to yourself, is okay. You can reach out to help your child later, but right now you need warm support around you, SOME SUPPORT WITH SKIN ON. When you're going through a difficult time, you need a little pampering. But most of all, you need HOPE.

I treasure the following letter I received from Dr. Wells, the psychologist who counseled me through my first year of agony after learning about Larry. Several years after I got Spatula Ministries going, I sent Dr. Wells one of my books and some of the other materials I had developed for parents, and he wrote back and said:

> Your ministry seems clearly for parents of homosexuals. It encourages them to survive their losses. . . . For your parents of homosexuals, their hope is for recovery from their pain, even though their chief hope may be healing for their loved ones. Keep instilling hope. They are motivated. They will benefit from your service.

Don't expect the unmotivated to receive help. . . . Where there is no control there is no responsibility.

In these few words from Dr. Wells is a great deal of wisdom, but not all of his advice is easy to hear. Letting go of your gay child is the hardest part. When you see your child taking a detour in life that is leading him toward what you see as a cliff, it is so difficult not to want to intervene and stop him. But here is where you have to depend on the values that you have built into your child. You love your kid enough to put him in God's hands while you get on with your own life.

Whatever you do, don't let your child's behavior put you in the Home for the Bewildered, wringing your hands and saying, "What have I done?" Realize that you have done your best and then move on with your life. Have faith that you WILL GET THROUGH THIS. He or she is your child whom you love unconditionally, whatever he or she is doing. This child is in need of your love right now—and always.

□   □   □

The parents of our son's "friend" are very accepting of the gay lifestyle. Our son resents the fact that we cannot condone how he is living. We want him to continue to visit us, so what should we do?

What the parents of your son's friend do is their decision; they will live according to their values. The first thing to understand is that there is a big difference between accepting your gay son and his friend as persons who need your love, and accepting the gay lifestyle. Your son probably is involved with a young person similar to himself. Your best approach is to show God's love to both of them.

Perhaps you will be more comfortable at first if you meet with your son and his friend at a neutral place for lunch. But it will be even better when he can bring his friend to your home. The warm memories of home can help in the healing of your relationship with your son—much more so than the impersonal atmosphere in a restaurant.

Sometimes you have to weigh which alternative is most painful and try to do the less devastating thing. The estrangement of not seeing your son can be far more painful than accepting him *no matter what his situation is.* Neither choice offers a smooth road; we just have to decide for ourselves which one we can live with the easiest.

From fifteen years' experience, I have learned that parents who do have their child come home, even with his friend, get through all this the best. Your son's friend is probably a very nice person, just as your son is. What would Jesus do? I believe He would show unconditional love in this situation.

My friend, Anita, tells of having her gay son call and ask if he could drop by for the weekend. When she said, "Yes, of course," he dropped his little bombshell and let her know "WE'LL be by around six for dinner." Her son had never brought his friend home for dinner and at first Anita was not prepared for their first face-to-face meeting. Thoughts of her son in bed with this man kept popping into her mind, but then she somehow found the strength to see this young man in a different light. She writes:

> Some of my anger faded away; afterward, as I reviewed our conversation, I realized that I had handled it well, something I could not have done without the Lord's healing in my life. As years have passed, I have been able to leave my son in the hands of God. This gives me the peace that I need. I still have difficult times, but I am learning and growing.[2]

My gay daughter wants to come home for a few days this Christmas and bring her girlfriend with her. I can't stand to see them together. Should I allow them to share the same room? Should I make them sleep in separate rooms, or should I simply forbid them to come at all?

First, I believe you should open your home to your daughter and, yes, to her girlfriend as well. Do all you can to keep the communication channels OPEN. Reassure your daughter of your love and care. God is in charge of her and has not negated her because of her actions. Think of your daughter as needing love and direction. Your love is imperative to her right now while she is struggling with her identity crisis.

While I have never had to face the issue of having a child bring home a homosexual friend for the holidays, my own policy would be "Sleep in separate rooms." Tell your daughter that, while you love her with all your heart, you simply cannot accept the idea of her and her friend sleeping together under your roof. Tell her that while you love her very much, you do not condone her lifestyle and that you hope she understands how you feel. If she brought home a boyfriend you would still not put them in the same room either!

If your daughter decides to bring her friend for the holidays and stay in your home according to your conditions, trust God for strength when they walk in together. I believe He will give you the strength to love them both as people who need care, not condemnation.

What can I say when I am face to face with my son's "friend"?

Make friendly conversation, just as you would with any other person in your home. Reach out in Christian love to the friend as well as to your own son. Make your home a loving place and they will be comfortable with you. What would you have to gain by making them feel uncomfortable? This would change nothing.

Most parents tell me they like their son's (or daughter's) friend and have no difficulty showing hospitality once they get to know this person.

Our daughter wanted to have a party for her friends on the women's volleyball team at her college. We let her go ahead but then we were horrified to discover that the whole group is lesbian. My husband nearly had a heart attack when he was told that his daughter was one of them. Where can I get help for my daughter? Is it right that this is allowed in a state college?

First, get help for yourself and do not worry about your daughter right now. Remember what my counselor, Dr. Wells, advised in the letter quoted earlier: Don't expect the unmotivated to want help. The kind of help that's needed right now is for your husband and yourself. You cannot take your daughter someplace and get her FIXED. It is you who are bleeding inside, so get the help you need. Your daughter will do her thing and, until she wants some counsel, you are helpless to provide it for her.

As for what happens in a state college, there is nothing you can do about that. There are even Christian colleges where these kinds of relationships go on. For years we Christians have tried to sweep all of this under the rug, but now the rug has become so lumpy we have to deal with it. Be aware that you are going through a shock experience, *but you will get through it.*

We have learned that our son is homosexual and we are just sick. We have other, younger, children in the home. How can we keep this from them, or should we tell them?

In our experience we have found that it is best if the whole family is involved in getting through this. If children are very small they will not be able to understand, but any child older than seven or eight can comprehend when something is definitely wrong at home and they wonder what it could be.

If possible, get the whole family together to share what is happening. Let the younger children know you are going through a difficult time and that their older brother or sister is hurting just as much as the family is hurting. Nonetheless, *you will all still love him.* He is still part of the family. This is a time when the family must bind together because the healing process will be a long haul.

I know the Bible has many verses that can comfort hurting people, but what does it have to say to the parents of a homosexual? Please give me something I can cling to right now.

The Bible is RICH with verses to encourage hurting people, whether they have a homosexual child, a dead child, or a wandering mate. There aren't any "special" verses for parents of homosexuals. The best approach I know of is to get out your Bible and go through it to find verses that have a personal meaning for you, verses you can adapt to your own situation.

Look up subjects such as pain, disappointment, anxiety, and comfort in a concordance. You will find dozens of verses that you can cling to and, best of all, finding them yourself will be like finding buried treasure. The Word of God is rich with treasure, but it all lies in the eyes of the beholder. You need verses that are meaningful to you and that fit your problem. Finding them yourself will bring you through your despair faster than having to just absorb what someone else has already mined from the rich veins of God's Word.

For example, just to give you a start, here are references of verses on comfort from the Thompson Chain Reference Bible:

Psalm 35:5; 42:5; 103:13; 119:50; 138:7

Isaiah 46:4; 61:3; 63:9

Matthew 5:5

John 14:1

Romans 8:28

1 Thessalonians 3:7; 4:13

So get busy and make this a real project for yourself. When you find verses that are real treasures for you, memorize them. Or write them out on small cards and carry them with you. Also, try sticking verses on your bathroom mirror, or paste them on household products that you use often—such as your bottle of Joy or box of Cheer. In countless ways, you can make these verses a part of yourself. Soon you will begin to feel your anxiety lifting and God's peace descending on your heart.

Let God's Word speak to you. Write His Word on your heart, remembering that it not only helps you not to sin against Him, but it also brings light, and light is what *you* need right now. Get going and find that light! Then you can start to dispense it to others who are groping in the darkness.

I read in one of your books that I should show unconditional love toward my homosexual child. How can I do that when the Bible itself puts conditions on what we do with our lives?

The Bible does put conditions on our actions, but God never puts conditions on His love for us. There is a BIG difference. While I talk a lot about unconditional love, I'm well aware that for human beings to achieve TOTALLY unconditional love is impossible. But isn't that what being a parent is all about—attempting the impossible? Herbert Vander Lugt puts it this way:

> I know it's hard to show unconditional love when a son or daughter keeps hurting you and making you feel ashamed. But if you are a Christian, you have the responsibility to keep on loving them. And you can, through the power of the indwelling Holy Spirit. It will help to keep these two facts in mind: (1) We human beings are highly complex creatures—so complicated that we cannot understand everything about ourselves, let alone others. (2) All of us, the respectable as well as the wayward, are in continual need of God's grace and mercy.
>
> When dealing with a person who is rebelling against you and God, remember this: We are all alike in that we are complex creatures. We aren't just animals; we're moral beings in God's image. We possess a conscience, but we have been flawed by sin. We live in a universe that is both beautiful and

ugly. The beauty reflects God's goodness, and the ugly demonstrates the reality of sin and the curse.

Moreover, we often have ambivalent attitudes. Sometimes we want to fulfill our lower desires, and at other times we long to be better. We often do things we hadn't intended to do. Time and time again we regret something we did or said—even after we become Christians! How true in our experience are the words of Paul, "I have the desire to do what is good, but I cannot carry it out. For what I do is not the good I want to do; no, the evil I do not want to do— this I keep on doing. . . . . What a wretched man I am!" (Rom. 7:18, 19, 24 niv)[3]

Over the years, we have talked with hundreds of parents who are devastated by homosexuality in their families. Each situation varies, depending on background, economics, and family relationships. But there is always one common denominator: *Showing unconditional love toward the gay child accelerates healing of the relationship.*

Unconditional love is the anchor that every gay child needs for the stormy journey. When he knows his parents love him, it tells him God has not negated him either, but that God loves him wherever he is on the path. It is a long journey to wholeness, for both the parents and the child, so remember:

UNCONDITIONAL LOVE IS LOVING
WITHOUT CONDITIONS.

Behind the question about the "conditions" the Bible puts on our lives is another question that desperately needs clarifying, particularly in the Christian community:

Is homosexuality a sin?

At first glance, many Christians would say, "Of course it is." But others would say, "Homosexual behavior is a sin, but not homosexual orientation." Stephen Arterburn, founder and director of New Life Treatment Centers, puts it this way:

When you're talking about this, please never use the word "homosexuality" as sin, use the word "homosexual behavior." It's a very small thing, but if you want to have any kind of hope of dealing with people, I think you have to make that distinction between the two. . . .

Homosexuality is a definite preferential attraction, it's an erotic attraction to members of the same sex. Whether a person acts on that attraction is the key issue, I believe, in the eyes of God. . . .

I believe that a person who is experiencing the homosexual lifestyle, if they want to, can establish a life and a lifestyle outside of homosexuality that is very satisfying and enriching. In fact, many, although not all, can go on and have heterosexual relationships that are quite satisfying and get married.[4]

I'm just glad that I don't have to be the judge when it comes to understanding homosexuality. I don't think condemnation solves this problem. Only conviction from God can change any of our hearts. We can't just pull a few verses out here and quote them to that person; it has to be redemptive love that rescues any of us from the choices we make.

Choosing Your Response to "I'm Gay"

When your favorite "who" becomes a "what" you must choose how you will respond. There are two basic approaches:

1. The *wrong* approach is to banish your child from the family. Have nothing to do with him at all. Forbid him to ever visit your home, and let him know he's certainly not free to bring along any friends if he ever is allowed to come.

2. The *right* approach is to love your child unconditionally. Let him know he and his friend are welcome in your home under certain conditions and that, while you do not approve of his lifestyle, your love for him will never change or fade.

Over the years I have received many letters from parents at every stage of their journey through the nightmare of learning their child is homosexual. Some are ready to commit suicide, and others are full of hate, homophobia, and righteous wrath, quoting biblical proof texts about not having anything to do with sinners.

Other letters plead for help, wanting to know what to do and how to do it. And then there are letters from parents who have struggled with the shock, shame, and guilt but now understand. They have adapted to the situation and they have HOPE.

As one father described this hope he said "it's not hope that my son will change, but hope that grows from a confidence in what we've always experienced in our lives when we thought we knew what was best for us . . . the knowledge that God has a better idea."

This father's letter went on to tell how he and his wife had survived, not with a magic cure-all, but with several key means of support. At Spatula support group meetings they had the opportunity to pour out their hearts in a nonthreatening, nonjudgmental atmosphere. They learned they would survive, and they did!

In addition to their support group, they found many members of their immediate family who were comforting and understanding of the situation, so they didn't have to live a secret life. One of their biggest milestones came when they stopped focusing on straightening out their child and acknowledged that that was God's business. The father's letter continued:

> This is not to say we exulted in his circumstances. Rather, we reminded ourselves that God loved us unconditionally and He would have that be a model of our love toward our children.
>
> This was a major factor in the restoration of our relationship to our son. When he recognized that we were not preoccupied with straightening him out, he was able to let down his defenses and freely express his love toward us. Also it allowed him to freely share his hurts and fears with us . . . and for us to be a comfort to him. (It's funny how our stereotypes imagine a person totally given to sexual expres-

sion. The reality is that the fears and hurts of the homosexual are generally those that we ourselves experience. The burden of their homosexuality does, however, I believe, heighten their pain in relationship to what others might experience.)

Another insight came to us as we weighed the advice of well-meaning friends that we should distance ourselves from our child; that was the importance of a healthy parent-child relationship in the restoration of the child and the parent (yes, <u>both</u> need to be restored!). Never does a child need the love and security of his parents more than when in the throes of dealing with his homosexuality. Even a casual knowledge of the homosexual issue shows the vulnerability of the homosexual to the drug scene and suicide. What a terrible time to abandon your child, right at the time when he needs you most!

We still hurt, but less often than before. We are still afraid, but rarely. We are not naive. We know there will be pain down the road. But the good news is that God is in control (wasn't He always?). We have a deeper, more loving relationship with our child than before. We have new friends that we never had before, friends who love us with the full knowledge of our circumstances. We know the fulfillment that comes from reaching out to others with empathy and helping them get through a tough time. We look forward with anticipation to what God's plan is in our lives . . . ahead to how He will take this low point in our lives and turn it to blessings. We've moved from "Why me, Lord?" to "Thank You, Lord!"

"I Didn't Choose to Be This Way!"

The wife of a pastor who had served his denomination for well over a quarter of a century wrote an anonymous article in her denominational paper, telling of the shock she and her husband felt when they received a letter from their son saying he had struggled with homosexual feelings since the age of twelve. The letter came just two months before his graduation from a Christian college. There were long telephone calls, crying, and angry shouting, but not many answers. During one of their talks with their son, the mother asked him if he knew how much he had hurt them. His answer cut deep into her heart: "Do you know how much I've hurt all these years? I didn't choose to be this way."

From that moment, this mother—and dad—devoted themselves to unconditionally loving their son. They joined our Spatula support group and shared their story to let fellow Christians know how badly homosexuals need the right kind of love. In her article, this mother wrote:

> The homosexually oriented person needs more of the very thing we too often go out of our way to deny them. We must love as Jesus loves—unconditionally. This does not mean we endorse the homosexual lifestyle. . . .
>
> The second reason for opening my heart is to let other parents know that you can survive and find support in other Christian parents who hurt because of a child who is convinced he is gay.
>
> Were it not for us finding other parents who were willing to share their own journey, we would have died. They helped us to get beyond the searching for a reason for this happening to us (blaming ourselves proved to be a dead-end street) to asking how we could now become a part of a solution. We found that there is something we can do for our adult child— we can love him. In fact, that is really all we can do—but we must not fail to do it. Our motto has become: "FROM THIS MOMENT ON . . . LOVE!"[5]

From these parents, who both write of a journey that has brought them from despair to new levels of understanding, come two key pieces of advice for what to do when your favorite "who" has become a "what."

As the father quoted above said, acknowledge that God is in control. Pray that He will help you stop asking, "Why me, Lord?" and help you become able to start saying, "Thank You, Lord!"

And as the mom says, when it's all said and done, when all the opinions have been uttered, preached, shouted, and shared, there is only one thing we can do:

FROM THIS MOMENT ON . . . LOVE!

I think in closing this chapter the most helpful sentence I could share is what my son Larry said when he was interviewed recently on "Focus on the Family." It blankets the whole, wide area of how we can seek wisdom on this:

> If we as Christians can purpose in our hearts to be kind and loving in all that we do, put away a condemning spirit, and learn the fear of the Lord, then surely the light of Christ will be able to shine in our disbelieving world and restoration and revival will take root in the lives of those we touch on a daily basis.

Gloomee Busters

DON'T WORRY ABOUT THE WORLD ENDING TODAY
IT'S ALREADY TOMORROW IN AUSTRALIA.

You can't go back
and unscramble the eggs.

I CAN NO LONGER FACE LIFE
SO I HAVE DECIDED
TO GO THROUGH THE REST OF IT BACKWARDS.[6]

If my life resembles a garbage dump
it is up to me to sort it through,
turn over the soil, and plant flowers
to make use of all the natural fertilizer.

□ □ □

DON'T LET YOURSELF SUFFER NEEDLESSLY—
FIND A NEED TO SUFFER.[7]

BE STILL AND KNOW THAT I AM GOD.
Be still, MY MUSCLES, and know God's RELAXATION.
Be still, MY NERVES, and know God's REST.
Be still, MY HEART, and know God's QUIETNESS.
Be still, MY BODY, and know God's RENEWAL.
Be still, MY MIND, and know God's PEACE.

—See Psalm 46:10

Psalm 1

No matter where I am blown or pushed,
    I will flourish!
Those with less strength would wilt and die
    on the soil on which I now stand.
But because I DO love the Lord,
    I WILL SURVIVE AND IMPROVE!

Others might expect me to wither,
    But God expects me to bloom.
I will show them how tough I am—
    I will bloom—IN AND OUT OF SEASON.

—Source unknown

SELF-CONTROL INCLUDES MOUTH CONTROL.

Wayfarers

There is no permanent calamity
For any child of God;
Way stations all, at which we briefly stop
Upon our homeward road.

Our pain and grief are only travel stains
Which shall be wiped away,
Within the blessed warmth and light of home,
By God's own hand some day.
—Martha Snell Nicholson

Earth has no sorrow that heaven cannot heal.
—from the hymn "Come Ye Disconsolate"

JESUS

Whatever the question, He is the Answer.
John 14:6
Whatever the problem, He is the Solution.
Matthew 11:28, 29
Whatever the hurt, He is the Healer.
Luke 4:18
Whatever the bondage, He is the Liberator.
John 8:32
Whatever the burden, He is the Overcomer.
John 16:33
Whatever the need, He is the Supplier.
Matthew 7:7, 8
Whatever the sin, He is the Forgiver.
Psalm 103:2, 3

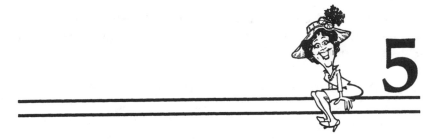

Life Is a Sexually Transmitted, Terminal Disease

Someone Jesus loves has AIDS[1]

AIDS.

Its frightening toll grows steadily until it looms on all our horizons like the scriptural pale horse whose rider, DEATH, is given the power to kill a fourth of the earth's population (or more).[2]

To give you an idea of how fast the plague of AIDS is spreading, realize that the first cases of AIDS in the United States were identified in 1981. AIDS occurred only as a trickle at first, but the total number of cases soon became a steady stream, exceeding 100,000 by July 1989.

Then, by late 1991—*just twenty-eight months later*—the stream became a torrent as 100,000 more victims learned they, too, had the terminal virus. Every year the death toll rises. In 1991 it reached 32,430.[3] A mother of four children, who has many family problems of her own, wrote to tell me she is well acquainted with the AIDS death toll. To her, it is more than just a number in the newspaper:

> I am an apartment manager of forty-eight units, 75 percent of which are occupied by gay tenants. I get along with people very well, but it breaks my heart to see this lifestyle, especially since I lost five tenants in the last year to AIDS. All I can do is pray for them and share with them my testimony of the Lord and how He has gotten me through my "tunnels."

AIDS is a particularly dangerous disease for homosexuals, but as almost everyone knows by now, AIDS plays no favorites. During that same twenty-eight-month period when AIDS cases reported in the U.S. doubled from 100,000 to 200,000, the number of people who contracted AIDS *heterosexually* increased 153 percent.[4] Among these cases was Magic Johnson, NBA superstar, who announced in November 1991 that he was HIV positive. Through numerous sexual contacts with different women, he had contracted the first stages of AIDS and now, even for one of the greatest athletes the world has ever seen, it is simply a matter of time.

If anything has changed the face of Spatula Ministries, it has been AIDS. I dealt with my first cases of AIDS in the early 1980s. There were just a few then, but now, like the national figures, my Spatula cases have skyrocketed also. What can be said to the sufferers of AIDS or to their parents? In many situations, parents have been plunged so deep into shock or rejection of their child they refuse to talk to a dying son or daughter. So I go instead and may find myself at 2 A.M., following a Spatula support-group meeting, helping a gaunt, hollow-eyed young man plan his funeral.

You may be thinking *how morbid!* But that's not necessarily true. Some of the most thrilling examples of faith in Christ I've seen have come out of helping folks deal with this dreaded foe called AIDS—what some Christians believe is God's judgment on homosexuals.

The Letter from Andrew

One darling young man named Andrew contracted AIDS and started coming, along with his precious family, to several of our Spatula meetings at the Crystal Cathedral. There's a piano in the room where we meet, and Andrew's mom and dad are gospel singers, as are Andrew and his sister. On several occasions, we asked the whole family to sing, and what a blessing they have been to everyone. One of their most encouraging songs was, "He Giveth More Grace When the Burdens Grow Greater." This special family was going through its own parentheses of grief, yet they ministered to all of us.

Later, a letter came from Andrew. My heart was touched by it and I knew it would touch the hearts of others, so I included it in an issue of the *Love Line*. For a young man in his twenties to write such an inspirational letter while facing certain death was unusual, and I know his letter will touch your life as it did mine:

> Dear Barbara,
>
> Next to the love I have for my beautiful Savior, my family comes first in my life. I read your "Love Line" tonight and couldn't sleep. All of the encouragement in those pages seems to come straight from the heart of God.
>
> As I read, I began to think like a parent (is that possible?) and about how much this ministry has done for my family. I thought the open wound caused by my venture into the homosexual lifestyle (ten years ago) would never heal.
>
> I'm sure you have heard before that "God answers prayer, but not always how we expect Him to." My family can say "Amen" to that.
>
> That open wound has been sewn with the glorious thread of God's love for His children. I can now sing—Jesus loves <u>even</u> me, and I <u>know</u> that He does! I am His child. I am not perfect; I still stumble; but . . . I am His, and He is mine!
>
> With AIDS in the picture I know that a difficult time may still be before us. But I can't help think . . . I could still be out there drowning. Just far enough from the lighthouse that I

couldn't be helped. Praise Jesus! I am safe in His arms, and if He desires to take me home—I desire to go! And for my family—as the song says, "To multiplied trials, His multiplied peace!"

Barbara, please pray that if the Lord desires to use me to touch lives, as He has with you—that I would not be blind to that opening door. (The Lord must be so used to my blindness, He may have to get someone to kick me through it.)

I love you so much, Barbara. God bless you richly in His work. You are in my prayers, as are the lives you are ministering to.

Love in Christ,
Andrew

Folks often ask:

Do victims of AIDS die lonely, bitter deaths with no hope at all?

I have many more letters and memories of late-night conversations that prove there is ALWAYS hope, even for the person with AIDS. In fact, AIDS victims almost always have an advantage spiritually. They know they don't have long and they quickly come to grips with who they are and what is going to happen.

Andrew's letter is a good example. It reflects the inner strength the Lord has given him as he faces the unknown. He wants to be used to touch other lives in whatever way God chooses while he is himself going through the deep waters. What a wonderful truth it is for us that EITHER way we are winners! If we are taken to be with Him we are OUT of all this pain and spend eternity with Jesus! If He chooses for us to stay here, we are building up treasures in heaven where nothing can corrupt. Without Jesus, we face a hopeless end. But with Him, we have an ENDLESS HOPE!

In the rest of this chapter, I want to share letters from AIDS victims as well as their parents. These letters show that, from the Christian perspective there is faith, hope, and love, but the greatest of these is always love—or maybe a better word is "compassion." AIDS has changed our lives forever and we must reach out to each other. As never before, we all realize we are marching relentlessly toward the grave. Truly, life IS a sexually transmitted, terminal disease.

Should the Prodigal Be Allowed to Come Home?

One of the typical situations I often hear about is the AIDS victim who wants to come home to his family, but one or both parents want nothing to do with him. Their question always revolves around:

Do we accept a child whose deliberately sinful lifestyle has caused him to get AIDS?

At Spatula we talk with many young men and women who have been estranged from their families after leaving home and getting involved in the gay lifestyle. Then, when AIDS rears its ugly head, their normal approach, like the prodigal son's, is to go home to be with the family, to reestablish the broken relationships. Typical of the letters we receive from parents facing this problem is the following:

> My son, after seven years, wants a reconciliation because now he has AIDS. I have seen and talked with him; however, his father does not want him to come home. There's been no change in his life, only now he wants us to accept him and be with him as his time comes. That makes it all the harder for those who have learned you have only two choices: (1) accept them and allow them to continue to be a part of your life when you feel so strongly about their sin, or (2) separate from them. Neither one offers a choice you are happy with, that's for sure.

I understand the pain involved in a choice like this. But what is more normal than to want to COME HOME? "Ye, who are

DENNIS THE MENACE

"I **HAD** TO COME HOME. 1 NEED SOMEBODY TO BE ON **MY** SIDE!"

weary, come home," isn't that the song we sing at church? Should the AIDS victim be allowed to come home? The best answer to this question is to ask yourself the question I mentioned in chapter 4:

WHAT WOULD JESUS DO?

Wouldn't He care for the sick and injured and the dying? Wouldn't He bring healing and comfort to those in distress for WHATEVER reason? Surely we are to love our kids no matter what. What better way could there be to show genuine Christian love than by opening our hearts to the AIDS victim, to bring him home, to care for him, making his last months as comfortable as possible? When AIDS devastates the family circle, it is time for everyone to come together to share in the pain. Out of that can come blessings far above anything we could ask or think.

When you have a dying son, you don't weigh the question of how he got that way, whether he chose his orientation, whether it was inherited or learned. You only know you have a son with very limited time to be with you. How vital it is to be sure that at some time he has accepted Christ as his Savior. Perhaps there has been no spiritual growth to this point, but *now* you have the opportunity to promote some spiritual growth in his life.

You will be his caretaker and caregiver and be able to provide all the warm, loving influences of the home. Perhaps you can enjoy Christian music or some videos together ; there are many other ways parents can influence a child. You have it all, but time is short. You can make up for the years he was estranged by concentrating on unconditional love right now.

Trust God to bring healing to his spirit, if not to his body. Then you will get comfort from the fact that you made his last days as comfortable as possible. And, like many parents I know, you may be able to say that your family will be restored one day in heaven. As someone has said:

CHRISTIANS NEVER SAY GOOD-BYE FOR THE LAST TIME.

No matter what your child has done, you love and accept him where he is and give him all the loving care he needs. The rest is up to God.

Another question that I often hear, especially among Christians, is:

Is AIDS a judgment of God on homosexuals?

Unfortunately, some Christians, even some pastors and Christian leaders, have said as much. There is more than one story like the one shared by Harold Ivan Smith in an article written for *Charisma* magazine. He described how a weeping woman called a minister and asked him if he conducted funerals for people who were not members of his church. The minister said, yes, he did, but he wanted to know if she was a member of any church and had she contacted her own pastor? The woman said, yes, she had, but that her son had died with AIDS. "And what did your pastor say?" the minister wanted to know.

The woman's voice broke, "Not only would he not conduct the funeral, he also did not want anything to do with us and said it would be a good time for me to move my membership."[5] In that same article, Smith mentioned a report on AIDS by then-Surgeon General C. Everett Koop, who made it clear that AIDS is not a homosexual disease. It is contracted by people of all races, male and female, homosexual and heterosexual. In short, AIDS plays no favorites.

Writing in *Christianity Today*, Philip Yancey weighs different views about the possibility that God has sent AIDS as a specifically targeted punishment against a certain group of people. He points out that many Christians doubt this is so:

> They see a grave danger in playing God or even interpreting history in His behalf. We can too easily come across as cranky or smug, not prophetic. "Vengeance is mine," God said, and whenever we mortals try to appropriate His vengeance, we tread on dangerous ground. Among the gays in my neighborhood, Christians' statements about the AIDS crisis have done little to encourage repentance. Judgment without love makes enemies, not converts.[6]

Yancey goes on to ask some obvious questions of those who see an apparent cause-and-effect link to behavior and sexual preference:

> What of victims who are not gay, such as a baby born to a mother infected through a blood transfusion? Are they tokens of God's judgment? And if a cure is suddenly found, will that signify an end to God's judgment? Theologians in Europe

expostulated for four centuries about God's message in the Great Plague: But it only took a little rat poison to silence all those anguished questions.[7]

Right along with the above question comes another that ponders the eternal destiny of people who may die of AIDS, particularly homosexuals:

Is it possible for someone who has died of AIDS to go to heaven?

My answer is, "You bet!" It's just as possible for someone to die of AIDS and go to heaven as it is for someone to die of cancer, alcoholism, heart disease, or any other ailment and go to heaven.

One young woman wrote concerning her uncle who died of AIDS, which he got as a result of his gay lifestyle. Her question was:

> Is it possible for my uncle to have been saved? He lived somewhat of a double life: Christian to our family but also a fairly wild gay lifestyle. I'm having a difficult time reconciling this in my mind, along with the guilt of not making an effort to confront him with the issue and witness to him. As far as I know, he never turned from the gay lifestyle, but died believing he was okay and that God accepted him just as he was.

Was this young woman's uncle saved? Perhaps I am beating the same drum, but God only knows. Everything depends on what he decided to do about Jesus Christ in his life. As I said in chapter 4, homosexual orientation is not a sin, but practicing homosexuality is. When this woman's uncle stands before God, the first question will not be, "Were you a homosexual?" The first question will be, "What did you do with my offer of salvation?"

Dealing with AIDS victims or their families when they don't believe anything is wrong with the homosexual lifestyle is a difficult issue. The question here seems to boil down to:

How can I show compassion without agreeing with the AIDS victim's homosexual lifestyle?

One letter came in from a social worker who works across the desk from a dear Christian friend whose ex-husband is dying from AIDS. She said:

> I've tried to be understanding and loving, but at the same time let her know where I stand. She has been able to completely forgive her husband, but she also totally accepts his lifestyle choice. She feels that he is a happier person because he has finally owned up to "what or who he is." Her children accept their dad's lover as their "uncle" or "our dad's special friend." Susan and her ex want the children to have a loving (normal?) relationship with their dad up until the end—which isn't far away because he's very sick. Susan and I work together all day, every day, and I want to be a comfort to her. Any advice you have, I'd appreciate.

So often we worry about letting people know where we stand—giving our Christian testimony—that we forget the real issue. No, his lifestyle is not God's best, but if she has accepted and forgiven her husband and accepts his lifestyle, then that is her way of dealing with it, and it is not up to us to criticize her for this. We all have various mechanisms for dealing with stress and, at this time, this is her way of dealing with the horror of AIDS.

Her ex-husband has AIDS, his time will be short, and it will soon be over. We would hope that she will care for him as a man who was her husband and is still the father of her children so that there will be no regrets when he is gone. The family needs all the support they can muster and being a friend to her is the best way of being a comfort. Facing death, whether by AIDS or any other horrible disease, is always difficult. Let the family do it in their own way without being critical of their method. Just get in there and show Christian love to her, as well as to those she loves in order to help her through this.

Many letters come from parents who have watched their son or daughter die an agonizing death from AIDS. Even if the stricken child accepts Christ (or comes back to the Lord), there still may be gnawing questions that linger for these parents:

How do I live with the regrets? How do I cope with the guilt? And what about the biggest question of all: WHY?

A letter came from a mother who watched for forty-three days as her son suffered an agonizing death from AIDS. He had been checked into the hospital for exploratory surgery, which revealed lymphoma all through his body. Later blood tests revealed the cause. Two days later he had respiratory failure and just before doctors put him on a breathing machine he told his parents he had AIDS. They never heard him speak another word because for the next forty-three days the breathing machine never stopped.

Two months before her son died, this mother had decided to give him to God and try to go on with her life as best she could. She wrote:

> I told the Lord, "I give up, Father. Mitch is Yours. Do whatever You have to so he will come back to You and live for You the rest of his life." I had prayed for him for years and years but never like that.
>
> Well, you see what happened! Yes, Mitch came back to the Lord on his death bed (and I am eternally thankful) but he sure didn't have any chance to live for God. I think the thing that probably hurts worse than any of it is that he could never talk to me. He was able to write a few things that are very precious to me, but most of it was clouded by the drugs he was given for pain.
>
> One minute I rejoice that God took him home out of all that misery as quickly as He did, and then I swing around and scream, "WHY? God, you could have healed him. You could have allowed him to at least talk to me!"
>
> The hurt, the pain, and feeling of being in a void plus a feeling that part of me is gone is still there but not as severe. But the questions are always in the back of my mind. I keep telling myself I did the best I could. It was a choice he made as an adult. Then I try to go on.

This mom is not only battling her grief, but irrational guilt as well (see chapter 3). She is letting this false guilt rob her of the joy of knowing that her son is with the Lord.

The first responsibility for any of us is to place our faith in God through His Son, Jesus, and then leave the rest up to Him. How He wants us to live for Him or how long is strictly God's business. If this mom and I could chat, I would say:

I know how it hurts that you couldn't talk to your boy in those final days as he struggled for life and breath. But there are many ways to communicate. Just knowing you were there, feeling the squeeze of your hand, told him how much you loved him. I always say that as parents we love our children BECAUSE, not ALTHOUGH. Our love for them doesn't change when we find they are rebelling against us or caught up in a sinful lifestyle that we cannot approve. In fact, the bond between us can be strengthened when we pour out our love to them. As we minister to them, our love for the Lord and for others grows even stronger.

Love is always the healing balm for all of us. Love covers everything, even the "Why?" I, too, have often asked God "Why?" *Why* did Steven have to be in that particular ambush? *Why* did Tim have to be on the same road with the drunk driver of the three-ton truck? But asking why is pointless and debilitating.

A better question (which is not easy to ask) is "To what end?" You are already headed in the right direction, and now you must ask, "To what end?" You say your pain is already lessening and it will continue to be more bearable as the days go by. Keep telling yourself you did the best you could. You are not responsible for your son's choices. This is the way out of the tunnel.

Testing HIV Positive Puts Everyone in Limbo

I get many letters from parents of adult children who have tested HIV positive. Now the sword of Damocles dangles over the family in earnest. It is only a matter of time until the dreaded diagnosis of AIDS will come. Parents, usually moms, write to share their shock, bewilderment, and fear:

> My son finally tested positive for the AIDS virus after refusing to consider it for years (he was healthy for five and a half years despite being HIV positive), and now I think maybe it was better we hid our heads. He's not at a stage of sharing much with me as yet—in fact, I feel like I'm on the receiving end of his anger. With a house full of company, foremost my mother, I've been putting on my happy face and praying for strength—for all of us.

> We've been absolutely shattered in the last two weeks, and being in a small, rural community, have no one to share our grief and sadness with because of obvious reasons. Our 35-year-old single son has tested HIV positive, and he admitted to us two weeks ago he was gay. He is the eldest of our three sons. He also has a severe blood disorder and either of his diseases will surely kill him sooner or later. . . . My middle son called and talked to me this week about working on a "positive" attitude. . . . Later I relayed all this to my husband and he said, "Well, we are positive all right. We are positive we are in one hell of a mess here!" Then, we had a laugh over that.
>
> We need help from somewhere. We both are normally very strong, but this is horrible.

> A friend of mine at work is homosexual and has AIDS. When he was young he gave his life to the Lord, but as a young man he turned to the gay lifestyle. A few months ago when he was ill, he learned that he had AIDS. He knew he was HIV positive, but figured it would be years before his T-cell count would go down. He was wrong. His mother, who lives in another state, does not know he is gay, let alone that he has AIDS. . . . My friend with AIDS does not have a lot of

friends at the moment and I have been the support person in his life—the person he can talk to. The friend he lived with for many years is expected to die because of AIDS in a few months, if not weeks.

When the HIV-positive verdict comes in, it is devastating for everyone, the victim as well as parents and friends. Now we wonder *Who can we tell? What do we do?*

First, we must realize that eventually the fact will be known and it is up to the person who is HIV positive to determine how much he wants known about his illness. So many things hang in the fire, such as insurance, job security, and other ramifications. The person who is afflicted must be the one to determine how much and WHO to tell.

For parents, this is a time to help alleviate uncertainties their stricken child may feel. Now is the time for unconditional love. You, the parents, along with your child, will be living for many months, perhaps years, in a sort of twilight zone. You will not know from day to day if "this is it." You never know what's coming or when—suffering, blindness, loss of memory, complete deterioration. Because you love your child, you want to smooth away as much pain as possible, giving him total support to assure him of your care throughout the entire ordeal.

The Role of Forgiveness

It is important that parents go through this thing together with their child. This is the time to resolve conflicts and mend relationships, to make up for any breaks that may have happened in the past.

Forgiveness plays such a big role . . . in fact, it may be the only real answer to accepting what is almost too painful to bear. Without forgiveness, there will be hardness of heart, and hard, brittle hearts break more easily. But God can turn the heart of stone into a heart of flesh (see Ezek. 11:19).

By caring for a dying person, *no matter why this person is sick*, we can best demonstrate Christian love. Perhaps physical healing will not occur, but spiritual and emotional healing can happen. A young man who was gay came to our Spatula meeting; he had just lost his companion to AIDS and he, himself, had just tested positive for HIV. This young man had no church background and commented, "I don't go to church and don't know anything about Christians except that they HATE homosexuals."

What a sad commentary—that we Christians should be known for our dislike or hatred of others, rather than for our love. Parents who care for a child with AIDS have an unusual burden to carry. They are not only losing their child, but they have a stigma attached to the family because of AIDS. Often they withdraw from the church and from their friends and become isolated and lonely. After all, having AIDS isn't something you put in your church bulletin.

Christians must open their lives to the hurts of others, and if we have any questions about how to react to the victim of AIDS, we only need repeat the question, "WHAT WOULD JESUS DO?" We know the answer, and it provides the best possible advice.

Fortunately, attitudes in the church and among Christians have been changing in recent days. I keep getting calls from people who want to know how to help. I like what was said in an editorial in the *Wesleyan Advocate* about how God's people can act toward the victim of AIDS:

1. The loved one must be committed to God.
2. God's help and guidance in prayer must be sought daily.
3. We must believe that healing can and will come—to one's mind and emotions, if not for the loved one and the disease.
4. Forgiveness must be asked of God and given to the sinful.
5. We must refuse to condemn, for Jesus did not and does not.
6. We must communicate hope at all times.

In brief, AIDS stands for

Aches   and Alienation,
Isolation and Incapacity,
Despair   and Death,
Suffering and Sadness.

The church has not always been at its best in the face of these new challenges. But I hope that can change as more and more frequently the opportunity will come to reach out to parents and other loved ones who suffer from the shock of these social and spiritual lapses among family members. The Christian's attitude must be characterized by

Acceptance of,
Interest in,
Dedication to, and
Support for the person who has fallen prey to one of sin's
    latest curses.

Condemnation, judgment, fear, and rejection will only make the afflicted one's plight worse. Comfort, empathy, faith, hope, love, and understanding will be welcomed by anyone who is going through such a valley of despair.[8]

AIDS Puts Faith to Its Ultimate Test

As I said in the opening of this chapter, not all the reports on AIDS are grim. I have received many letters from parents who are rejoicing because they have an endless hope; they don't just see a hopeless end. Here are just a few samples:

You see, as I shared with you last year, our beloved son was homosexual and also HIV positive since April 1990. I can now report that he has a resurrected body because in September 1991 he went home to be with our Lord. . . . For 16 days he lived on life-support systems, and he had dialysis five times. Twice we were told death was imminent, but he rallied each time. The doctors had told us we would have to unplug him. Praise God, we didn't have to do that as he just closed his eyes and went home to be with Jesus. . . .

It's been about six years now since we found out our son was gay. . . . I knew I had found a friend in you, Barbara, and you <u>called</u> me. That boggled my mind. We learned to love our son unconditionally, no matter what. So we have, and I'm glad. We have a wonderful relationship with him. It has really paid off—UNCONDITIONAL LOVE.

I eventually met his friend and Jesus helped me get through that. We became good friends, long distance, and now he is dying of AIDS. He has gotten quite bad and will have to be placed in an AIDS home. I can't explain my feelings. I have cried so much over the past couple of days. Today I called him and <u>he</u> (my son's friend) <u>comforted me.</u> He is a wonderful, sensitive young man who was brought up in a dysfunctional home by an alcoholic.

I just wanted you to know how helpful you have been over these past years. Thank you for reaching out to those of us who struggle with our feelings.

□ □ □

By absolute determination, many prayers, and God's grace, my son lasted until February. . . . Finally, one night my son asked to go to the hospital as he was having great difficulty breathing. For the first time, other than for an accident, he went in an ambulance. I rode with him and was quite aware that this would be our last trip to the hospital. . . . I stayed with him in his room, camping out, so to speak, until the fourth morning when he went to be with his Savior.

A very precious friend who was both an R.N. and a minister said he had rarely seen anyone go with such peace and grace. He assured me that my prayers had been answered. If it had not been for that death sentence, it is most unlikely my son would have heeded anyone who spoke to him of our Lord. Hallelujah! He waits for me in heaven and we will see each other once again.

Doctor Ralph Osborne, who formerly served on the staff of Hollywood Presbyterian Church with Dr. Lloyd Ogilvie, is a good friend and supporter of Spatula Ministries. Recently he shared with me (and Spatula Ministries) a letter from a highly respected professional friend who had been diagnosed with AIDS, but who had a burning heart much like that of the disciples who saw the risen Lord on the way to Emmaus in Luke 24.

It says so well what it means to have an endless hope in the face of a hopeless end, as far as this world is concerned.

Ralph asked if I might write something of my experience with God and His purpose in my life and the reality of my faith in Him.

I had been a Christian since the age of eight, but did not come into a vital relationship with Him until a year and a half ago. I entered into that relationship because I was tired of hating myself and being angry at God. What I discovered was that He was there all along but I had kept Him at arm's length because I never felt I was good or worthy enough to be accepted by Him. He took me as I was, and that fact allowed me to let God love me and I was able to love myself. That started me on an exciting journey. I can best describe it as an encounter with the Living Christ. I had an intellectual knowledge of Him and His attributes but had not come into a real relationship with Him.

Several months after my journey with God began, my faith was put to its ultimate test. I found out that I have AIDS. My worst fear in life was realized. Everything that I had ever hoped or worked for, all my dreams came screeching right to a halt in front of my eyes. I asked myself, "What do I do with this?" It didn't take me long to realize I was out of my league on this one! So, I put my life in God's hands again and said, "I am powerless over this. Your will is all that I have." Now, I listen to my doctors, do what they say, and give it all to God.

To me, this situation is a baptism of fire. It is going through the worst hell of your life but in the midst of that hell is an indescribable sweet joy, for you know that He is there with you in the midst of it all. It is the Divine Presence of the Living Christ.

I am learning many things about life and God in dealing with AIDS. One is that none of us has any guarantee for tomorrow in terms of physical life or death. I have quit living in the past or in the future. I try to embrace each day as a gift from God and discover what joy I might find in my work and those people around me. Having a disease like AIDS brings you face to face with your fear of death. As Christians, we should all have to face this fear. It is ultimately a very freeing experience.

I tell you all this, not that you will believe that everything in the Christian walk is rosy and easy, but that in the midst of great sorrow He is there. Whether it be the loss of a child, parent, or any loved one; the betrayal of a spouse, the loss of all possessions or a job, even in facing your physical death, He is there in full love and power. I would not have chosen AIDS for myself, but having this disease has been a very profound experience in that it has taken me to a depth with God that I might not have reached otherwise. I count the cost and it is sufficient.

God bless all of you.

Time Makes a Difference

I have often said:

> EVERYTHING—EVEN AIDS—COMES TO PASS, NOT TO STAY.

New proof of that came when I received a series of letters from a mom who, when her son was dying of AIDS, wrote to let me know that something I said in one of my books hadn't been that much help at all. A few months later she wrote back to explain that during the past year her husband had died of an aneurysm and her son had finally succumbed to AIDS as well. She did not feel that my story and hers had much in common because her story "did not have a happy ending." But a few months later she wrote again and said:

> After losing my son to AIDS last June, I have developed a philosophy about AIDS:
>
> I've learned to accept without agonizing or arguing . . . it happened.
> I've learned to forgive without forgetting . . . I can never approve.
> We who are "touched" by this dreadful disease suffer GREAT AND GRAVE risks when confiding in another human being. . . . Don't take the risk unless you (as well as the other person) can live with it.

There will be many who need support and understanding
. . . It is hard to find. This disease will touch us all in some way
or another. Keep your sense of reality when dealing with it.

I salute this mom. She is right. AIDS is touching us all, but at
the same time it is helping many of us touch one another in
ways we had never dreamed possible. Today I was making Bill
a sandwich for lunch and I started thinking that if we give
someone a piece of bread with butter, that's KINDNESS, but if
we put jelly or peanut butter on it, that is *LOVING* KINDNESS.
It reminded me that I always want to give to others and add
that gracious touch. How true this is of those who have AIDS.
Loving kindness is just what these kids need—that EXTRA
touch.

In his powerful personal story, *How Will I Tell My Mother?*
Jerry Arterburn shares what that extra touch was like for him
in the final days of his life:

In April 1987 I once again came down with pneumonia. No
one thought I could survive it. I was determined to live
through it, however, and once again I made a miraculous
recovery. At that point I began to work on this book, and my
life became somewhat more secluded. . . . For a while I lived
with Steve and his wife, Sandy, in Laguna Beach, California.
Then I went to stay with Terry, who has four kids and a saint
for a wife, Janette. It was beautiful in both locations. What an
inspiration to watch the whales in Laguna or the waterfalls
and greenery of Tennessee. God's world is so beautiful, and I
had never before fully taken the time to notice.

The Bible says God never sends us a problem we cannot
handle with His power. It also says He will provide comfort.
In both cases, the Scriptures have held true for me. I have
grown close to a sweet and loving Jesus and understand that
sickness and disease do not come from Him. Our God is there
to help us fight the evil forces. I have peace and comfort like I
have never felt before, even though I know AIDS continues to
ravage my immune system. I pray each night for all who have
been afflicted. I pray that God will comfort all of us and all
our families. God is a good God and a perfect God.

For me, during these difficult times of struggle, as each day grows darker, a new dawn draws closer. That closeness to the God I love gives me a superhuman peace and sensitivity that keeps me filled with hope for a new and better day.

> Sing, O heavens!
> Be joyful, O earth!
> And break out in singing, O mountains!
> For the Lord has comforted His people,
> And will have mercy on His afflicted.
>   —Isaiah 49:13[9]

Gloomee Busters

> Have you ever felt
>   that even though
> you're taking things
>   "one day at a time" . . .
> it's about twenty-four hours
>   more than you can take?

> Just when I was getting used to yesterday,
> along came today.[10]

> PEOPLE WITH TIME FOR OTHERS
> ARE HAPPY ALL AROUND THE CLOCK.

> Instead of giving someone the gate,
> try mending the fence.

MAKING WAVES ALMOST NEVER TURNS THE TIDE.

It doesn't take a dictionary
to learn the language of love.

The Bible teaches us the best way of living . . .
the noblest way of suffering . . .
the most comfortable way of dying.

□ □ □

The Harder Part

Inventing the artificial heart—
That was the easy part.

Who can splice a severed soul?
Who can invent a glue
   to mend a broken heart?
Can shattered minds
   be traded in for new,
Or egos rusted by despair
   be given body shop repair?

To find a cure for these
That are beyond prosthetic remedies
That is the harder part.

□ □ □

And God Said, "No"

I asked God to take away my pride and God said, "No." He
said it was not for Him to take away but for me to give up.

I asked God to make my handicapped child whole and God said, "No." He said the body is only temporary.

I asked God to grant me patience and God said, "No." He said patience is a by-product of tribulation. It isn't granted, it's earned.

I asked God to give me happiness and God said, "No." He said He gives His blessings. Happiness is up to me.

I asked God to spare me from pain and God said, "No." He said sufferings draw you apart from worldly cares and brings you closer to Him.

I asked God to make my spirit grow and God said, "No." He said I must grow on my own, but He will prune me to make me fruitful.

I asked God if He loved me and God said, "Yes." He gave His only Son who died for me and I will be in heaven someday because I believe.

I asked God to help me love others as much as He loves me and God said,

"Ah, finally you have the idea!"

—Source unknown

□   □   □

For I am convinced that nothing can ever separate us from his love. Death can't, and life can't. The angels won't, and all the powers of hell itself cannot keep God's love away. . . . Nothing will ever be able to separate us from the love of God demonstrated by our Lord Jesus Christ when he died for us. (Rom. 8:38–39 TLB)

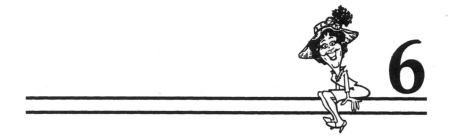

6

Where Do I Put My Hatred While I Say My Prayers?[1]

This life is a test. It is only a test. If it had been an actual life, you would have received further instructions on where to go and what to do.[2]

As I waited to speak following a recent luncheon, a friend seated on my left began describing how she had learned her husband of seventeen years was a homosexual. He had divorced her to live in the gay lifestyle with a young man in one of California's beach towns. Our hostess, who was seated on my right and was getting ready to introduce me, overheard the story. She leaned over and said very distinctly through clenched teeth, "IF I FOUND OUT MY HUSBAND WAS A HOMOSEXUAL, I WOULD SHOOT HIM AND TELL GOD HE DIED!"

I understand why that lady was so vehement. We are taught from childhood that anger and hatred are BAD emotions no "genuine" Christian should have. Yet, when devastating pain

---

[1] Ashleigh Brilliant Pot-Shot 585 © 1974.

hits, red-hot anger can well up from within us like lava spewing out of a volcano. We may refuse to admit we have these intense feelings but the more we try to deny them the more they can overwhelm us.

It's not easy to admit that hatred was ever a part of me, but it was. When I learned my son was gay my shock turned into boiling, raging anger that scalded both of us and left a scar that is still a visible reminder of how uncontrolled emotions can ruin a relationship.

My, What Lovely Purple Luggage

After discovering Larry's homosexual "stuff" in his dresser drawer, somehow I got through what I've come to call Black Saturday.* With the stuff in the trunk of my car, I managed to drive to the airport, pick up my sister, Janet, and her husband. I was in no condition to be with people, but I tried to keep from losing it. Unfortunately, the first thing I saw was Janet's two pieces of PURPLE luggage. Somewhere I had heard that lesbians love the color purple, and while I knew it was unreal, I couldn't stop thinking, *My own sister has purple luggage. She works for Billy Graham, her husband is a minister, and she's a lesbian!*

Trying to behave as if nothing was wrong, I muttered something about how pretty Janet's new luggage was, but then I realized I wouldn't dare open my car trunk because Larry's homosexual stuff was lying there, uncovered, ready to let the whole world know my secret. I hugged Janet and Mel and told them my trunk wouldn't open, so we shoved their luggage and a crate of pineapples they had brought from Hawaii into the backseat. Then I drove to a motel across from Disneyland, where we planned to spend the night after enjoying the special Disneyland bicentennial celebration being held that weekend.

---

* More complete accounts of "Black Saturday" may be found in *Stick a Geranium in Your Hat and Be Happy* (Dallas: Word, 1990), chapter 3, and in *Where Does a Mother Go to Resign?* (Minneapolis: Bethany Fellowship, 1979), chapter 1.

After we got settled in our rooms, we went over to the park to join fifty thousand other people in the bicentennial festivities. It was nearing 8 P.M., the time I had told Larry to meet us, so we waited at the flagpole on Main Street and in just a few minutes he walked up. Janet and Mel could tell something was really upsetting me, but they said nothing. They greeted Larry warmly, and we all talked for a few minutes. Then Janet and Mel excused themselves, saying they wanted to see the Mr. Lincoln exhibit.

Larry and I stood there by the flagpole looking into each other's eyes. Mine were full of panic; his were dark and full of apprehension. His first words were, "I'm a homosexual—or maybe I'm bisexual."

As fifty thousand people milled around us, I frantically tried to understand. *Bisexual? What was that? Sex twice a month? Why would he say that?* Bisexual was a foreign word to me, but I knew from the Bible what homosexual meant and when he used that word, it resounded in my ears like the crack of doom.

And it didn't help a bit when, at the very moment Larry expanded my vocabulary with his exotic new word, the Tinkerbell fairy came sailing through the sky above our heads, proclaiming loudly that the Main Street electrical parade was about to start! The thought flashed across my mind, *Now they're EVERYWHERE—even in the AIR!* Just then Janet and Mel came back and I tried to keep a stiff upper lip, but as somebody said, that only makes it very hard to smile.

Somehow I got through the entire evening without telling them about Larry. I finally had to the next morning, though, and they were as astounded as I was. Later, after having Father's Day dinner at Knott's Berry Farm, I took my sister and her husband to the plane. We didn't talk much—we just cried. What COULD we say? We hugged tearfully near the jetway and then they were gone. And there I was with my "problem."

Driving back from the airport, I tried to plan my next move. Bill had already talked to Larry alone early that morning and had returned to tell me, "It's just a phase." But I had an overwhelming feeling it was a lot more than that. Because Bill was going over to see his parents and drop off a Father's Day gift for his dad, I decided now would be a good time to have it out with Larry. We would get this whole thing settled once and for all. Surely he could be fixed. Surely God wouldn't allow this to happen to OUR family. There had to be some kind of medicine or pill that would fix Larry. I kept assuring myself that God and mothers can fix ANYTHING, even this.

How Could My Darling Son Betray Us?

No matter how hard I tried to block them, angry thoughts about how Larry had betrayed us kept flying into my mind. What had happened to the darling child who, at the age of three, would stand up before people and sing, "Hot-diggety-dog-diggety . . . oh, what you do to me . . . it's all so new to me . . . oh, what you do to me"? And as he sang, he would bounce to the words, making folks laugh at his antics. Was he gay THEN? Did all this happen suddenly? WHEN? What did I do to cause this? Surely it must have been my fault. Had I been too close to him? Did I enjoy him too much?

But, no, that couldn't be right. Larry had been full of life, with friends and activities of his own. It was just that he had made our home so ALIVE and FUN—he enhanced our family with his bubbly personality. And yet how could this be the same son who had collected all that pornography? Where did he get those letters from men in his drawer? Some of it was even addressed to our home! Had it come when I was gone? Had I just put it in his room without looking at what it was? And if I had looked, would I have known what it was anyhow?

That was probably it. There had been no reason to suspect. I didn't belong to any local chapters of the FBI (Family Bureau of Investigation). I had always honored Larry's privacy, as I did the other boys' concerning what they had in their rooms. But this must have been where I had been negligent—failing to check the mail he received, at least to look at the return address. Surely I had messed up somewhere to have this happen NOW!

After parking the car in the garage, I went in to face my son—the homosexual/bisexual who apparently had betrayed every bit of the Christian nurturing we had given him for twenty years. Larry was waiting for me, and at first neither one of us spoke. We each wanted the other one to start, and finally I did. I tried to be calm, but my anger quickly boiled up and soon I was lashing Larry with Bible verses, Christian self-righteousness, and a slap in the face. He retaliated with obscenities and a fierce stubbornness I had never seen before. Then came a shove that pushed me against the grandfather clock.

That day I heard words from my son that I had never heard before in my life, and he saw just how deeply homophobia can affect a frustrated mom who sees her whole world crumbling. I loved my son, but my hatred for what he was saying overshadowed that love. All that came through at the moment was disgust for him.

I'd Rather You Were Dead!

I realized Larry was sick—emotionally ill—and I knew I had to do all I could to get him some help. I was so upset that my desires to help him were blurred by my anger. At one point, I exploded, "I would rather have a son be DEAD than to be a homosexual!"

My words lashed Larry like a scourge, but all the time I thought I was doing the right Christian thing by reminding him that he was a believer and that he "knew what the Bible teaches." He had to know that "God can change anyone's life." And he was well aware that "God can cleanse us from any kind of sin and make us whole again."

But all my fervent pleas fell on deaf ears. Larry's facial expression was contorted and his eyes were dark and flashing. His look seemed to say, *It's no use, I can't talk to you. You don't understand.*

He was right. I didn't understand. I burst into tears again and fled to my own bedroom while Larry stormed into his room and slammed the door. Between my sobs, I could hear Larry crying as well. Even then my motherly instincts wanted to go and comfort him, but then my hatred flared up and I thought, *How can I comfort YOU when you're destroying our family?*

The next day Larry was gone. I found his room completely empty when I returned from a trip to a hot-line center in Anaheim, where I had gone to get some help. I wanted to find a mother who had been through my agony, but all they offered me was two ex-homosexuals. I told them forget it, I already HAD a homosexual, and if there wasn't a mother they could refer me to, I'd just go back home and try to cope by myself.

My Anger Turned into Depression

And that's what I did. A detailed account of how I tried to cope is found in *Where Does a Mother Go To Resign?* Finding Larry gone without leaving a note telling me where he was put me into a total funk. The anger that had raged the day before now turned inward to become depression.

Retreating into my bedroom, I spent most of my days and nights grieving. The wallpaper in the room had these wonderful pink and red roses that climbed up and over a trellis, and I lay in bed, counting the roses and imagining I was weaving them in and out of the trellis. When I got tired of this, I would look up at the ceiling at an air-conditioning vent and imagine myself threading roses through the grate.

I didn't spend all my time in the bedroom. On a couple of occasions I had to attend funerals of friends, where, strangely, I found some relief because at least there I could cry openly. No one thought I was weird because it was an "appropriate" time to shed tears.

And I'd also go out now and then to the grocery store, but even there this terrible curse that had descended on all of us followed me. Going through the dairy case I'd see the word "HOMOGENIZED" on a carton of milk and, irrational as it may sound, I'd think there was something HOMOSEXUAL inside.

But most of the time I was a recluse, staying in my bedroom where I could find comfort by sliding deep under my comfy quilt. I avoided contact with people, even my family. I didn't cook anything for an entire year. Bill lived on popcorn; Barney survived by working at Taco Bell.

But I didn't care. I just wanted to be alone and not have to accept any responsibility. I was wounded . . . the knife was shoved deep into my chest . . . and I just wanted to lie there quietly, so I wouldn't cause it to plunge in deeper.

My isolation was like a protective fog. I didn't have to see anyone or make sense of a conversation. No one confronted me and wanted to know what was wrong. Everyone who knew us felt I had still not recovered from the loss of two other sons. They had no idea of the REAL loss, because I couldn't and wouldn't tell anyone.

How to Know When You're Depressed

My homophobia kept me in a constant state of depression for almost a year. I've read quite a bit about depression and have learned that the word is used to describe everything from feeling blue to being seriously ill. Some experts believe depression is "more disabling than arthritis or heart disease—an illness [that,] in its severest form, drives 15 percent of its victims to commit suicide."[3]

In their excellent manual on the symptoms, causes, and cures of depression, *Happiness Is a Choice*, doctors Frank Minirth and Paul Meier list some 101 telltale traits and signs of the depressed person.[4] I doubt that I had all 101, but I had a lot of them!

Just a few of the signs of depression include feeling sad, bored, disappointed, lonely, lacking confidence, not liking yourself, afraid, angry, guilty. Those with depression have difficulty making decisions and they're frustrated with life. You feel desperate, as though you've lost your faith, and life is meaningless. You may think of suicide, and in some cases even make plans to do it.

While going through depression, you may get careless about how you look. You may move slowly and have drooping posture. Your face may sag. You may be easily irritated and want nothing to do with anyone, as communication with others becomes practically nonexistent.

Physical signs of depression include difficulty sleeping and, often, a major change in appetite or weight (I lost thirty pounds in less than three months). You also experience fatigue and total weariness. For the depressed person, life drains away all vitality, energy, and strength. Even breathing becomes a problem.

While spending almost a year in that bedroom counting all those roses, I experienced just about every symptom listed above. By the way, my final rose count was 1,597!

Dr. Wells Was Kind, But Candid

For a week or so after Larry left, I rode a roller coaster of emotions. Fortunately, however, I still had enough wherewithal to realize I had to get some help. But I didn't know where to go, and I didn't have anyone to talk to. Bill, sensing my desire to be totally alone, kept to himself. So I began writing things down to help myself keep in touch with some kind of reality. That helped me realize I was slipping into a box, actually an emotional coffin. I could see that no one else was going to peel me off the wall and put me back together.

Even though I was depressed, I never stopped praying. I decided to strike a deal with God: I would work as if everything depended on me, but I would realize that, in the long run, everything depended on Him.

And God honored the deal. He gave me the strength to get out of that coffin. It was my first small step toward getting well, but a long series of ups and downs lay ahead of me.

My depression drove me to see a Christian therapist named Dr. Wells. He was kind and professional, and he was also a personal friend for whom I had worked in the past as a secretary. But friend or not, he didn't pull any punches after I had talked and he had listened. Finally, when it was Dr. Wells's turn to talk, he told me what he thought about homosexuals from his years of experience.

According to Dr. Wells, I was no longer at the "mother level" with Larry. While I was still his parent, our relationship was really more on an adult-to-adult plane; therefore I should take no credit or responsibility for his choices.

"Well, I certainly don't want to take any of the credit," I said, "but I do feel responsibility to help him change."

Dr. Wells replied, "In my experience, I find that if they do make any change in lifestyle at all, it is their own decision and nobody else's."

I hated hearing that because the anger was still simmering inside me. With Bible verses for backup, I reminded Dr. Wells that all things can become new. Surely no Christian needed to be chained to a life that was so harmful. I wanted God to change Larry RIGHT NOW—yesterday, in fact.

What Was Larry DOING Out There?

All through that summer I continued my sessions with Dr. Wells, but my depression did not lift. I kept thinking about Larry being out there somewhere in what they called "the gay lifestyle." Was he hurt? Sick? Did he miss his family? How was he making a living?

My mind was a blender full of emotions that whirled around and around. I loved Larry. I hated Larry. I wanted to kill him. I wanted to kill myself. I wanted to bury him, and I wanted to bury myself.

I stayed on that roller coaster, sometimes feeling some improvement and then plunging back down again, mainly because I simply would not accept the idea that this thing had happened to our family and that Larry couldn't be fixed IMMEDIATELY.

As difficult as it was to have two sons die, neither tragedy put me in the deep depression that I experienced after learning about Larry. I continued to think it would be easier to have him dead than to be out there in the gay lifestyle, engaging in despicable acts with other men. In a very real sense, it is harder to let go of someone who is living a rebellious, destructive life than to let go of someone who has died. Somewhere I found the following observation that describes my feelings perfectly during those desolate months after Larry vanished:

> THE BLACK TARPAULIN OF DEPRESSION HIDES
> GOD'S SUNSHINE OF HOPE FROM OUR VIEW.

So I understand what people mean when they write to me and say, "I'm depressed," or "I've been in a depression for the last two years." My mail is full of pain, but it is also full of honesty:

> I'm presently battling intermittent depression and I know I can stick a geranium in my hat, dress up like a million dollars and smile until my face cracks, thereby fooling everyone around me, but happy I ain't. Pain I can handle. Misery I don't care for at all, but that's where I've been. We lost our daughter Cindy to ovarian cancer five months ago. We were with her throughout the L-O-N-G agonizing process until she died at her home. . . . I can handle death and loss, but the long agonizing process of dying hardly seems necessary and I admit to being angry at God for not intervening to either heal or take His child home sooner. Anyway, that's the basis for my depression.
>
> Let me tell you that your book really helped me and the strange thing is—you didn't tell me a single thing I don't already know and have used many times to counsel others.

☐ ☐ ☐

> Three days before our twenty-fourth wedding anniversary I came home from work to find a note on the desk that said he had moved out and intended to file for divorce. . . . Even though God was with me and gave me Scripture after Scripture to uphold me and embrace me and encourage me, the

pain was still more than I thought I could bear at times. . . .
In the last few weeks I have been really struggling with severe
depression and have been wondering what purpose my life
has. I'm very, very empty and dry; it's hard to even pray, and
when I do, I'm not sure what to pray for or even how to pray.
I am so very lonely. My oldest son is married and the youngest
one is away at college. There is no one to come home to at
night to share with, to be touched by. . . .

Thank you for the wonderful ministry. My husband has
been out of work for more than three years. I am at a point
where I don't know if I should murder him, make him move
out, or hang in there and keep praying. Cf course, your book
has encouraged me to do the latter. . . . I realized there was
no light at the end of my tunnel, consequently I made an
appointment for my husband to begin treatment with a
psychologist and he has finally admitted to his depression.

Although my problem doesn't have anything to do with
homosexuality, the pain that I suffer because of my children is
very much the same. The guilt, the whys? the how-comes?
etc., etc., etc.

I feel as though I know you and wanted you to know how
much you have helped me already. I need to keep your book
handy and use it often to get myself back on the right track. I
know depression is an awful thing and a waste of time and
energy. I really want to live a productive life, as I know that
nothing I say or do at this point will change anything with my
kids.

The bad news in these letters is that all of these people are
depressed to some degree, but the good news is that they are
trying to tell somebody how they feel. One of the first things I
learned from Dr. Wells is that as long as you are talking and
ventilating, you are not in danger of "losing touch with reality."

One of the first positive steps you can take to conquer depression is to refuse to be isolated. Get help from somebody! The depressed person who doesn't get help can be in danger of slipping permanently into La-La Land and confined forever in the Home for the Bewildered.

Throughout that summer and into the fall, I continued to see Dr. Wells regularly, but my ride on the depression roller coaster continued. I did get a real lift around mid-October when I accidentally learned that Larry was still with his choral group and would be singing at the Los Angeles Music Center. With a friend accompanying me, I went to the program with high hopes, but the evening turned into a disaster. Just before the intermission, Larry spotted me in the audience, and when the group came back on for the second part of the program, his place was empty! He had fled and I never got to speak to him at all.

That put me into another sickening downward spiral and a deep depression that lasted well past Christmas. The calendar changed from 1975 to 1976 and I began seeing Dr. Wells a little less. By the following spring, I was telling myself I was improving. At least I was showing my normally cheerful self to the world; but inside there was still plenty of churning, burning, and yearning going on. I was still very angry, still in a chronic, low-grade depression, even though I was hiding it in the few contacts I had with others.

Maybe I'll Just Swallow a Razor Blade

According to doctors Frank Minirth and Paul Meier, one of the signs of depression is the belief that MORNING is the worst part of the day.[5] Right around Mother's Day, mornings began looking extremely bad to me. I guess the thought of Mother's Day without Larry was more than I wanted to handle. One day I muttered to Bill, "I wish you used double-edged razor blades. Then I could swallow one in a piece of bread and it might kill me."

THAT got Bill's attention! He insisted that I see Dr. Wells IMMEDIATELY. I did as Bill asked, but it didn't gain the results he hoped for. When Dr. Wells reviewed my case and saw that Larry had been gone almost a year, he dropped a bomb that shattered my cheerful exterior into a million pieces:

"Well, if Larry has been gone this long," he said, "very possibly he will never come home again. He may have found permanent emotional support in the gay lifestyle."

I went home in a total "downer" mood and retreated to the back bedroom where I slipped into a zombie-like trance. I didn't even bother to count roses. Later that same day Dr. Wells called Bill and told him I was extremely depressed when I left his office and he suggested having me put in Parkside West, a very fine institution in our area that specializes in twenty-four-hour care for people who are suicidal.

Bill told Dr. Wells he wasn't sure his health insurance would cover something like that but that he'd check on it and call him back. Meanwhile, he thought I could stay at home because I "wasn't vicious or anything."

The next day as Bill was about to leave for work, he told me that he would make some calls that morning to learn if his insurance covered me or not. After he drove off, I sat there considering my options: if Bill's insurance covered me, I was headed for Looney Tunes haven. If it didn't cover me, I was supposed to stay home and count more roses on the wallpaper. Then the thought hit me: *Why toy with suicidal thoughts any longer? Why not go ahead and get it OVER with?*

I got in my car, backed out of the driveway, and started down the street, not knowing for sure where I was going. All I knew was I couldn't go on like this. I wasn't functioning as a wife. I wasn't a mother. I had shut out my friends. I felt like a zero with the rim rubbed out—a NOTHING. How could God say He loved me and let all this happen?

One Sharp Turn Would End It All

As I headed up a high viaduct, I fully intended to get to the top, turn the wheel sharply to the right and plunge my car to the freeway below. All my troubles would be over—or would they? After all, it was only a drop of probably fifty feet; perhaps it wouldn't be enough to finish the job. Maybe I'd just wind up maimed and crippled for life, sitting in a wheelchair, making baskets—with lots of roses, of course.

As I neared the top of the viaduct, I already knew I couldn't kill myself. But I also knew I had to do SOMETHING to get rid of this horrible burden I had carried for almost a year. I had given Larry to God many times over the past months, but I'd always taken him back again. I knew the Bible's instructions to cast our cares on Him because He cares for us (see 1 Pet. 5:7). This verse means that we should DEPOSIT our cares with God and *never pick them up again.* That was my problem. How could I "deposit Larry with God" once and for all?

As I came over the top of the viaduct, I thought of an answer. Perhaps I could take a hammer out of my imagination and just NAIL him to the foot of the cross. That would do it. I had to find some way to really deposit this horrible burden on the Lord and not keep carrying it around myself. If I nailed that burden down, I couldn't pick it up again. It was an appealing idea because, to be truthful, I was exhausted.

As I started down the other side of the viaduct, that's exactly what I did. In my mind, I took out a hammer and nails, and mentally nailed to the cross my burden of worry and anxiety over my son.

"Lord," I prayed, "this time I'm really giving Larry to You. By nailing him to the cross, I'm giving him to You once and for all. If he never comes home, it doesn't matter. If I never see him again, it doesn't matter. It's all in Your hands. WHATEVER, LORD—whatever happens, I'm nailing that kid to the cross and giving him to You!"

I've never been much for miracles—at least in my own life. I have the gift of joy but not of faith. (It's comforting to know that none of us is expected to have *every* gift.) So what happened next wasn't typical of me at all. It was as though those words, "Whatever, Lord," opened some hidden chambers inside. The heavy depressed feeling I had carried for so long evaporated. I felt a million tiny splashes of joy bubbling up inside me. I sang all the way home—the first singing I had done in a year—then ran into the house and telephoned Bill.

The excitement in my voice made him think I had totally lost it. I tried to explain about "nailing Larry to the cross," but after I made several attempts Bill finally told me not to call anybody else or to tell anyone ANYTHING. He was coming right home. Bill was the one with brain damage from the accident. He was the one who hadn't known anything for two years, and now HE was telling ME not to call anybody or talk to anybody until he got there.

Bill made it home in record time and I went over the whole thing once more, while he tried to see what had transformed me from a zombie back to a happy, joyous person. Eventually he seemed to understand that talking about "nailing Larry to the cross" was my way of saying that I had finally let go of Larry and given him ENTIRELY, TOTALLY, and COMPLETELY to God.

Bill was relieved. He had learned that day that his insurance wouldn't have covered me anyway.

Then the Phone Rang

The next day the miracle continued. For the first time in almost a year I felt like cleaning the house, and as I was vacuuming the phone rang. It was Larry wanting to know if he could come home to bring me a hamburger as he always used to do. If he had called the day before, I would have said, "You little creep, don't you know that they are ready to put me in the Home for the Bewildered?" But yesterday I had nailed Larry to the cross; today I was able to say, "Come on home, Honey." All I could feel for him was overwhelming love.

The next hour was a mixture of joy, apprehension, and curiosity. As Larry and I ate our hamburgers, I could see he was nervous, so I didn't ask him questions about his life or his lifestyle. He did tell me he was going to school at UCLA, working, and living alone. After a while, Larry left, promising he would be back to see us the next week. After he left, I sat there thinking, *Isn't this just like God? The minute I really let go of my son, he is returned to me.*

It turned out, however, that Larry wasn't really back. He stayed in touch with us for a couple of years and then he was gone again, this time with more anger than ever and more determination to live the gay lifestyle. But I felt at peace because I had finally learned what it means to let go of, or relinquish to God, the one you love.

In the rest of this chapter, I want to talk about relinquishment—and forgiveness. When you can say, "WHATEVER, LORD," and really mean it, depression loses its power to gnaw at your insides. When you let go, life no longer drains everything out of you. When I let go of Larry completely, my heartache turned to JOY.

What Does It Really Mean to "Let Go"?

One of the best things I've ever seen on the subject of relinquishment was done by some good friends in an organization called "Love in Action." The following is excerpted from an article by Bob Davies and Lori Torkelson who are happy to share these thoughts with people in pain:

One of the most frustrating pieces of advice one Christian can give another is to "just give your problems up to God." Most people aren't sure what "giving up" really means. Three basic dictionary definitions of "relinquishment" are:

1. To surrender a right
2. To put aside a plan
3. To loose one's hold on something or someone

This lays out what we're talking about in more concrete terms. The kind of relinquishment we're dealing with usually involves all three of these actions!

All of us in some way are involved in relinquishment. Daily we must make choices. Things that separate us from God must be given up. We can understand this when it concerns things, but when it comes to people, there is often confusion as to our Christian responsibility. Also, relinquishment is so difficult because it often involves someone we are closest to, just the last person we would want to let go of.

When God asks us to let go of someone close to us, the pain of letting go may feel like punishment—but it's NOT! Relinquishment is not the act of God removing from our lives someone we're sinfully attached to. Real "giving up" is a mature decision we make in response to God's request. Abraham saw his surrender of Isaac as an act of worship (Gen. 22:5). When God asks this of us, He is testing our loyalty, perfecting our ability to trust Him with that which is most precious to us. The fact that God requests us to relinquish someone is an encouraging sign that He knows we already have established a relationship of trust with Him. He doesn't ask us to relinquish above the level of our capacity.

Aspects of Relinquishment?

• Facing our limitations. Eventually we reach the point of acknowledging our own helplessness in relating to our loved one, realizing we've reached the limits of our human love and wisdom. We are ready to acknowledge our need to let God take over.

- Acknowledging God's ownership. Like Hannah, we realize that the person we love belongs to God—not to us. Though we may have been entrusted with a position of care and responsibility toward them, they ultimately belong to God and are His responsibility.

- Letting go of our expectations. We may have had many things we hoped would be fulfilled by the person we love: hopes that our children would marry and raise families, exciting plans for the future we made with our husband or wife when we married. And it's certainly not wrong for us to have these hopes! But part of relinquishment is coming to terms with the fact that these things may not happen. We surrender our expectations, realizing that God will still bring fulfillment to our lives, though maybe not in the way we had planned.[6]

To Find Complete Closure You Must Let Go

No matter what may be depressing you, *relinquishment is a key to getting well*. In chapter 2 we looked at dealing with the death of loved ones and the need for CLOSURE—completely letting go of the one who has died, letting the wounds of grief heal, and getting on with your life. I often hear from parents who have a very difficult time doing this. They want to know:

HOW can I let go of my loved one?

Some parents don't seem to want to let go. I got a long letter from a mom who had lost her "favorite son." She wrote to me at the end of the year, after losing her boy the previous spring in a fiery car crash. She admitted that some days she relived that horrible day and pleaded for her son to be "given back" to her. She knew this was foolish, but she couldn't help it.

She wrote about not being able to sleep without taking medication and how she wished she could dream of her son but the dreams never seemed to come. She wanted to see his handsome face and hear his giggle. He had always been an inspiration and the clown of the family. Everyone had a good time around her son. As she said, "He was our lifeline and we failed so many times to tell him."

This mother was also haunted by feelings of guilt because she was not able to spend much time with her son during the three or four weeks preceding his death. She had to be in another city spending time with her daughter and new grandson. When she did get back home, he was busy with college classes. The night before he died, he came in very late and even though the mother was up, he was tired and went immediately to bed. Not a word was spoken between them. She wrote:

> Oh, if I could go back to that night.
>
> The accident happened around 7:30 A.M. Friday morning. By the time we arrived at the scene, we couldn't see the vehicles for the black smoke. I can't believe I left the scene as I was asked to do by the State Police. I should have stayed til my son's body was removed from the scene. Another mistake I can't correct. . . .
>
> My youngest daughter, who is 14, says I do everything for my son. He is the only one I think about. Everything I do should have been done when he was alive. She asks when is her time with me, when she is dead also? I think her grief is as great as mine because she and my son were very close and a lot alike. . . .
>
> Barbara, I don't know what to do. I can't function as I did. I am consumed with trying to keep the memories of my son alive. He was never any trouble and asked for so little. If ever I had a perfect son, it was this boy. Why does God seem to call home the best? He was only 20 and trying so hard to educate himself and make us proud of him. We failed so many times to tell him that he didn't have to prove anything to us, and we were proud of him all the time. . . .
>
> You, yourself, know the suicidal thoughts that cross our path and how hard it is to quench the thoughts. I have a spouse, three daughters, and a grandson born one month before my son's death. I have plenty to be thankful for. But so many times I'm blinded to all of this because my boy is alone in heaven and needs his mama to be with him. I pray the Lord will come tonight!

I have deep concern for this mom, not only because she lost her only son, but because she simply can't seem to accept what she already knows—that he is in heaven with God and very happy there. He is content to wait for her, but she spends each day wanting him to be returned or wanting to join him.

When I contacted this mother, I gently tried to share with her that I know I have two boys in heaven, but they aren't alone at all. For one thing, they are with Jesus, and that is more than enough. They don't need me to be with them. They are rejoicing and happier than they ever were on earth.

As we try to find closure over the death of a loved one, perhaps we can ask God to give us a FROZEN PICTURE of that person in heaven. We can imagine the beauty of what God has prepared for those who love Him. We can take comfort in the Scripture's promise that "eye hath not seen, nor ear heard" what lies ahead for us (see 1 Cor. 2:9). We can have an image of our loved one in a glorious place where there is never-ending joy.

When Tim was killed and I had to go to the SAME viewing room with the SAME carpeting and the SAME wallpaper in the SAME mortuary and stand there next to the SAME mortician in the dark blue suit to identify ANOTHER boy in a box, the grief rolled over me in waves until I thought I would drown.

But when I walked out of that mortuary into the August heat, five years *to the day* after I had identified Steven's body, I had an experience that gave me the frozen picture of Tim that I needed. As I walked to the car, I could smell freshly cut grass and could hear crows cawing in the trees. Then I looked up and there in the sky was an image of Tim's smiling face! He was surrounded with a bright shining light and I heard him saying, "Don't cry, Mom, because I'm not there. I'm rejoicing around the throne of God."

As I said before, miraculous experiences aren't familiar to me. I had never had that happen before and haven't had one since, but perhaps God knew I needed something extra that would help me find closure after losing a second son in violent death.

Letting Go of the Living Is Harder

After reading *Stick A Geranium in Your Hat and Be Happy,* a mother wrote to share how her seventeen-year-old son, unable to handle the stress, turned to drugs after cancer had struck down her husband. The father of the family endured five years of hospitals, radiation, surgeries, and terrible pain as the bones in his back disintegrated and broke. The mother described what happened:

> Our 17-year-old son, who was a dream of a young man, a body builder, a fanatic about eating right and working out and couldn't stand cigarettes, within six months after my husband was hospitalized, was a drug addict. He freaked out. He became skinny and so pitiful. He fought—carried guns and knives. He stole from us. He quit school his senior year.
>
> I couldn't believe what I was seeing with my eyes, my husband dying slowly—no cure—and my son was killing himself with the drugs. Our home was like hell on earth. . . . It was like the devil himself had moved into our home—once a loving happy family, a Christian home. Was this real, was I dreaming? I'd go to my bedroom and beg God to let us have our other life back.

This mother and wife knew exactly what churning, burning, and yearning are all about. After her husband had been ill about eighteen months, the woman's mother began running into walls and was soon hospitalized and dying, herself. She was given radiation treatments and had to be fed and bathed. Thus, the woman had to endure a terminally ill husband, a terminally ill mother, and a teen-age son who was killing himself with drugs. On one occasion her son overdosed and, while being taken to the hospital, pleaded, "Mama, pray that I'm dying." He survived and now, in his mid-twenties, is "still fighting the demons of hell." Her letter continues:

> My son is getting better, but his anger is so great—it's a giant only God can deal with. As a mother I deal with it daily.

I've got to nail it to the cross and say "Whatever!" just as you did.

This precious mom's words apply to anyone who is facing ongoing grief, the kind that can drive you all the way to despair. Finally, when there is no recourse, no cure, and seemingly "no hope," you have to nail it all to the cross and say, "Whatever, Lord!" I was glad to see that this mother closed her letter with two verses of Scripture that give her the strength to go on:

> For I know the thoughts that I think toward you, says the LORD, thoughts of peace and not of evil, to give you a future and a hope. (Jer. 29:11 NKJV)

> For God has not given us a spirit of fear, but of power and of love and of a sound mind. (2 Tim. 1:7 NKJV)

Being Deserted Can Become a Living Death

Many letters come from depressed wives whose marriages have gone sour. Their husbands want to leave or perhaps have already deserted them. Their questions always come down to:

My husband has left me—how can I go on when life doesn't seem worth it?

There is something about the pain of being rejected, or even a spouse's threat to leave, that can drive the other marital partner to the brink of suicide. Following is a typical letter from a wife who's on that brink:

> I'm 31, with a 2 ½-year-old little boy, and my husband has filed for divorce. As a Christian I was told to let this ungodly man go. The church told me to leave him. I can't begin to tell you how painful this is. I don't know how to survive this! I want Jesus to take me home. Barbara, please pray for me. This life is now a living hell. I don't have money for proper legal

counsel, let alone for counseling for this guilt, pain, condemnation, I'm so-o-o sad. I feel so alone.

This man I married for life is now a monster and threatens to take my child away from me. I can't bear this anymore. What do I do? Can one be given more pain than one can bear? I've thought of taking my life but I love my son too much to do that—but I even question that at times. Sometimes I think I'll do it!

When the pain and depression become overwhelming, we can be plagued by thoughts of how wonderful it would be to "be free of all this." But as I said back in chapter 2, suicide is a permanent answer to a temporary problem. My advice to this deserted wife, and anyone in a similar situation, is this:

Yes, it is dark for you, but suicide is never the answer. The devastation it makes for loved ones cannot even be counted. Even though you feel as if you are in a bottomless pit, there is a way out. Your suffering will not last forever. You will work your way through the maze if you tackle each day counting on God to give you grace to make it through.

It is much easier to think about handling one day at a time and not the whole future at once. Put one foot in front of the other and plod through one day. Before long, you will have made it through a week and then a month. Soon you will have made it through several months, and you will see a bright light ahead that isn't just another train coming!

Instead, you will discover there is a lighthouse out there for you. That lighthouse is the Light of the world and He never changes or moves. He is always there to seek out His own. Only through Christ can you make your way through the heavy fog to safety. Christ is the lighthouse who will always help you get your bearings IF YOU LOOK FOR HIM.

One of my favorite verses is 1 Corinthians 10:13:

. . . God is faithful; he will not let you be tempted beyond what you can bear. But when you are tempted, he will also provide a way out so that you can stand up under it. (NIV)

In Scripture, the Greek word for "tempted" can also be translated "tested." The idea is that of going through a trial. Read 1 Corinthians 10:13 again, inserting the word "tested" for "tempted" and you can see why it's one of my favorite verses.

Is It Better to Have Loved—and Lost?

It's hard enough to have your husband leave you after years of marriage, but it's even more of a blow when it happens while you're still a bride. This wife wrote:

> I have been married for three months and three days. Well, a month ago my husband expressed to me that he made a mistake and no longer wanted to be married to me. It's not like we rushed into this. We've been together since high school, eight years in October. The last month I've been so hurt and confused I came close to killing myself and/or him.

The first thing this dear gal needs to do is become familiar with the laws of her state. She should contact an attorney who might advise her about the possibility of filing for an annulment. On the other hand, she says they had "been together since high school, eight years." If "together" means that they lived together, asking for an annulment might not work.

Even more important, however, is her emotional state. She should try to find a good counselor, someone at her church perhaps, who can guide her through these months of complete upheaval until she can get her balance again.

Also, she may need to contact a professional counselor who can provide her with psychological insight into her emotional needs as she grows through this rejection time.

Here is one other piece of advice. It may not be just what everyone wants to hear, but in this case I do think it contains some food for thought. Any time you get so depressed you are tempted to kill yourself, it's time to do some hard thinking. Someone once told me:

'TIS BETTER TO HAVE LOVED AND LOST—
MUCH BETTER!

I am sure there are many ex-wives and ex-husbands who may disagree with this idea, but it does provide another way of looking at the problem. Any time we have the opportunity to love someone else, we have a great privilege and a great responsibility. To have fulfilled our end of the responsibility is all God really asks.

Occasionally I hear from someone who planned a wedding but it never happened. For example, one disillusioned young woman wrote:

> I was supposed to get married in June, but it didn't happen. The wedding was postponed. Now we don't communicate at all. It's like a whole year of my life has been wiped out or didn't happen—it's still just so <u>unbelievable</u>. It's truly a living nightmare! It has not been easy trying to bounce back. Sometimes the life of a hermit looks very appealing.

I would answer this hurting young woman by saying I'm sure being jilted is no fun, but it can be one way to find God's best for you. The pain is intense for you now, but eventually you will heal. Later, you may even be able to appreciate this paraphrase of the idea I shared earlier:

IT'S BETTER TO HAVE LOVED AND LOST
THAN TO BE CHAINED TO A CHUMP FOR GOOD.

The one who left you behind may not be a chump, but it's obvious that he wasn't the one for you. Some place farther down the road you will look back at all this and be able to THANK GOD for sparing you from what could have been. Also, while it hurts now, remember that this experience can make you a wiser and more discerning person, better equipped to make choices.

Letting Go Always Includes Forgiveness

Many folks write to tell of how they were rejected, abused, and "treated like dirt." Their stories may differ, but the bottom line is that they want to know:

HOW can I forgive and forget what was done to me?

For example, I received a letter from a young woman who hinted at being sexually abused by her father, but she really spoke more of the mental abuse that parents can be guilty of as their children are growing up. This single mother wanted to know:

> What about parents who disappoint their children?
> I have been very disappointed in my father for many years. From . . . mental harassment, to physically beating us, for not standing up for his family, for always making me feel I was the one who was—and consequently still feel like—I am the one who is wrong.
> He had or implied to me (and by my mother's reactions appeared to have had) an extramarital affair. Treated my mother like second-hand merchandise, was never there to cheer me on at my softball or basketball games. Washed my mouth out with soap if I ever said a swear word, but used them liberally himself. Didn't go to church regularly, despised the idea of family devotions, and many other things that have all had an influence on who I am and how I respond to things in my life now.
> Gives me no verbal or monetary support as a single parent. Oh, I suppose I disappointed him by becoming pregnant. Would it have been better to have had an abortion and never said anything because I might have disappointed him? I have taken offense at your statements of children disappointing their parents. Maybe someday you may see that those disappointments were as a result of parents disappointing their children.

My word of encouragement to this young single mom is not to let "if only" eat her alive. It would be so easy for her to play the "if-only game": *If only* he had been there for her when she was growing up. *If only* he had treated her mother better. *If only* he had been a devoted Christian dad. And now that she struggles as a single parent, *if only* he could give her *any* kind of support, verbal or monetary.

But none of that is happening. No wonder this dear single mom takes offense at my statements about children disappointing their parents. In her case, *she* has been disappointed and the shoe is on the other foot! That doesn't make the shoe any easier to wear; in fact, it is probably more difficult.

This single mom can dwell on the past with her father's failures, but it will do no good. Life has dealt her a lousy hand but she has to decide how to play it out. As Robert Louis Stevenson said:

LIFE IS NOT A MATTER OF HOLDING GOOD CARDS, IT'S PLAYING A POOR HAND WELL.

It always comes back to the same thing: attitude. Your attitude can be so cemented into your life that you make your current problem an absolute that can never be changed. You dwell on it, saying, "I had lousy parents," or "I had a weak and neglectful father who was a hypocrite. I'm stuck and there is no way out . . ."

Or you can take the other view, which says *no problem has to be an absolute*. Everything can be studied, observed, applied, and evaluated. That's how we learn to adapt. Adapting is a continuing process because life is ever-changing. Challenges arise and detours loom up. Our goals have to change. The only healthy answer is to be flexible.

Recently a friend of mine came over to bring me several packages of bubble bath. She knew how much I delighted in having all this wonderfully luscious smelling stuff to revel in while taking a bath, but she had to say, "I am definitely a SHOWER person. I never could stand taking a bath, and in all my years I've only taken showers. If I go to visit someone and they don't have a shower, I can't wait to get home because I cannot adjust to taking a bath at my age."

A red flag went up in my mind. My friend can't adjust to something like taking an occasional bath? What was causing her to be so adamant? Was she experiencing hardening of the attitudes?

Just to make sure I wasn't being cemented into my own preferences, I deliberately took a SHOWER for the next few days, just to remind myself that we have to be adaptable, flexible, moldable—able to "go with the flow," as the kids say.

Becoming resigned to the fact that "life did me wrong in the past" is the path to feelings of hopelessness. Adaptability, however, provides hope that we will reach our destination at some point. If I could put my arms around the single mom whose father had been so neglectful, I would tell her this:

I know it hurts. You have been treated as no daughter should ever be treated, and your dad is continuing that dirty treatment by not giving you any kind of support. But don't just accept this as your fate. ADAPT. You are on a journey, just as I am. I've had to adapt many times and I want to tell you that as you learn to adapt you learn to enjoy and not just endure.

As we go through life, we all suffer emotional fractures. Yours happen to be very splintered, but you can learn from your past and you don't have to WASTE YOUR SORROWS. Be sure to love your own child and try to keep her emotional tank full to the brim. Loving your child will release some of the pain within you. It will help you forgive the one who hurt you. Remember that forgiveness is an incredibly healing force. It's like a salve smoothed on the places in your memory that are still stinging with pain.

Use this experience for the good so that you can instill in your daughter the emotional security that you were robbed of, yourself. You might try imagining God reaching down and wrapping YOU in a special comfort blanket and saying, "There, there, it's all going to be better."

When you are alone and in need of a lift, try singing songs to yourself, for example:

Father loves me, Father loves me,
Father loves me, Father loves me.

This simple phrase, repeated over and over to a rhythmic tune as though you're singing "Allelujah" will be a comforting reminder that YOU ARE LOVED. You are special. You will feel whole again.

To Let Go—Forgive

Ask any psychologist and he or she will tell you that many patients are depressed because they can't bring themselves to forgive. Someone they trusted has hurt them badly. They keep chewing on that hurt and never letting it heal. According to Lewis Smedes, author of *Forgive and Forget: Healing the Hurts We Don't Deserve*, you have three choices for handling unfair pain: (1) You can try to deny it and make believe it never happened. (2) You can try to get even, but as Smedes says, "getting even is a loser's game." (3) You can forgive, which is hardest by far, but it's the only healthy way to cope with the situation. Smedes wrote:

> Forgiving is love's toughest work. But you can make it easier if you don't confuse forgiving with forgetting. You do not have to forget in order to forgive. Besides, some things should never be forgotten, lest we let them happen again.[7]

To really forgive someone, Smedes advises us to go ahead and feel the pain. And when pain is undeserved, we tend to feel it even more deeply. At the same time, we may feel resentment, even hatred. We shouldn't be afraid of these feelings, but we shouldn't dwell on them either. These are the feelings that can lead straight into depression.

To begin to heal yourself, start seeing the person who hurt you as weak and needy. Don't excuse the person, but begin to try to understand. This brings you to what may be the most important step of all:

TO FORGIVE,
SURRENDER YOUR RIGHT TO GET EVEN.

One of the most creative ways to forgive I've ever seen comes from a woman whose letter said:

> I have strengthened my prayer life by weeding my flower bed. I used to have names on all the weeds and really would hoe, chop, and mutilate people who had frustrated me. Now my weeds are still named, but instead of chopping them, I gently pull them and pause and pray for them. I call it the love approach instead of the angry approach. I also have added to my list those who need extra encouragement through prayer and not just my "hit list."

You may want to try this mom's approach to weeding resentment, dislike, and even hatred out of your life. In addition, here are some more tips from Dr. Smedes:

> It helps to be concrete. Don't try to forgive someone for being what he or she is. Forgive people only for what they do. Forgive in verbs, not nouns, one thing at a time.
> And remember, forgiveness only works when you are ready. It's good to remember this when we want someone to forgive us. You'll forgive when you decide that you've had enough pain. . . .
> There is no easy way to forgive. Forgiving is a type of spiritual surgery. You slice out of your past a cancer that shouldn't be there. And surgery is never easy. In short, forgiveness reverses the flow of hurt pouring silently but painfully out of your past.[8]

Forgiving Yourself Can Be Hardest of All

Sometimes the hardest person to forgive is yourself. Recently I spoke to a Rotary Club and during my talk I emphasized that yesterday is a canceled check, tomorrow is a promissory note, and today is cash. I reminded them that we shouldn't crucify ourselves between two thieves, regret for yesterday and fear for tomorrow. I also quoted 1 John 1:9: "If we confess our sins, He is faithful and just to forgive us our sins and to cleanse us from all unrighteousness" (NKJV).

Afterward, a man of about forty-five came up to tell me how much the talk had meant to him. In fact, he said it had literally changed his life. At the age of nine, he had accidentally killed a fifteen-year-old friend, and he had carried that burden of guilt and inability to forgive himself right up to that very day. His guilt had destroyed his first marriage and now it was threatening to ruin a new relationship with a woman he wanted to marry. The only problem was, she had a fifteen-year-old son, the same age as the friend he had killed. Her son also had the *same first name* as his friend.

"I really can't explain it," he said, "but hearing you talk today helped me understand that I could forgive myself, that I can look ahead and find a light. I know the past is over and I don't need to whip myself any longer with my guilt."

That's the key—realizing that what has passed is in the past, and it won't do any good to whip yourself any longer.

On the day I "nailed Larry to the cross," I carried my heavy burden up on that viaduct, intent on killing myself, but I came down the other side free of the pain, the depression—and the hatred. Letting go of Larry also meant forgiving him for all the hurt he had caused. For months I had tried to tell myself that I had forgiven Larry, but all that time I had still been nursing the hurt. It festered deep inside until it drove me to the brink of suicide.

But at the moment I said, "Whatever, Lord," I not only forgave Larry, I forgave the whole world. In fact, I had been mad at God for almost a year. Now I decided to forgive Him too! And as I forgave, I felt forgiven! The joy flooded into my heart and a song came to my lips.

Perhaps we could argue about what comes first: forgiving or

letting go. Maybe you do them both at the same time. As the poet says:

> To let go doesn't mean to STOP CARING,
>   it means I can't DO IT for someone else. . . .
> To let go is not to try to CHANGE or BLAME another,
>   I can ONLY change myself. . . .
> To let go is not to JUDGE, but to allow another
>   to be a human being. . . .
> To let go is not to REGRET the past,
>   but to GROW and live for the future.
> To let go is to FEAR LESS,
>   trust in Christ more,
>   and freely give the love He's given to me.[9]

Gloomee Busters

> Every now and then, without warning,
>   each of us has a good day;
>   Please, Lord, it's my
>   turn today,
>   ain't it?
>
> Maybe tomorrow?
>   next Tuesday or Wednesday?
>   . . . half a day Thursday?
>   (8:30 to 9:15 Friday morning?)

EVEN IF IT BURNS A LITTLE BIT LOW AT TIMES,
THE SECRET OF LIFE IS
TO ALWAYS KEEP THE FLAME OF HOPE ALIVE.

Honest Hymn Singing

If I were entirely honest every time I sang a hymn or gospel song, here's how some of the old titles would come out:

I Surrender Some
Oh, How I Like Jesus
He's Quite a Bit to Me
Take My Life and Let Me Be
There Is Scattered Cloudiness in My Soul Today
Where He Leads Me, I Will Consider Following
Just As I Pretend to Be
When the Saints Go Sneaking In

—Source unknown

YOU ARE NOT WHAT YOU THINK, BUT WHAT YOU THINK, YOU ARE.

May those who love us, love us.
And those who don't love us,
May God turn their hearts.
And if He doesn't turn their hearts
May He turn their ankles,
So we will know them by their limping.

—Source unknown

RUB IT OUT, DON'T RUB IT IN.

Perhaps you have heard of the little boy who prayed, "Father, forgive us our trespasses, as we give it to those who trespass against us."

At least the little boy was being honest. It's just like many of us to want to lash back instead of love back!

It's human to want to pay back those who offend us; but it's God-like to forgive.

We don't forgive to be forgiven, but if we're forgiven by God, we will forgive others.

When we forgive others, we promise to do three things:

    (1) not to take it out on others,

    (2) not to talk about it to others,

    (3) and not to brood about it any more.

Let's rub it out, and not rub it in.

—Adapted. Source unknown

FAITH, HOPE, AND CHARITY . . . IF WE HAD MORE OF THE FIRST TWO, WE'D NEED LESS OF THE LAST.

The good Lord never gives you more than you can handle unless you die of something.

WHAT TO DO IN CASE OF EMERGENCY

1. Pick up your hat.
2. Grab your coat.
3. Leave your worries on the doorstep.
4. Direct your feet to the sunny side of the street.

What happiness for those whose guilt has been forgiven! What joys when sins are covered over! What relief for those who have confessed their sins and God has cleared their record! (Ps. 32:1 TLB)

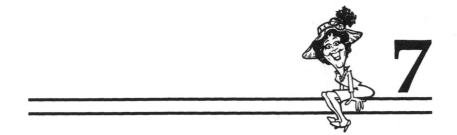

Pack Up Your Gloomees in a Great Big Box,
Then Sit on the Lid and Laugh!

If Noah had been truly wise,
he would have swatted those two flies.[1]

Collecting poems brings me almost as much joy as bumper snickers and one-liners. The other day I found a bit of verse that sums up my philosophy for dealing with life when pain and trouble bring on the GLOOMEES:

> Build for yourself a strong box,
>   Fashion each part with care;
> When it's strong as your hand can make it,
>   Put all your troubles there;
> Hide there all thought of your failures,
>   And each bitter cup that you quaff;
> Lock all your heartaches within it,
>   Then sit on the lid and laugh.

Tell no one else its contents,
    Never its secrets share;
When you've dropped in your care and worry
    Keep them forever there;
Hide them from sight so completely
    That the world will never dream half;
Fasten the strong box securely—
    Then sit on the lid and laugh.
                   —Bertha Adams Backus[2]

When Jell-O Ran Red on the Wall

Long before the four horsemen of pain descended on our home, I always enjoyed a good laugh and would do my best to turn problems into something we could all chuckle over. For example, there was the time I sometimes call "the Johnson kids and their crazy Jell-O caper."

One day I came home from shopping and heard all four of my boys out in the kitchen, shrieking with laughter. Tim was about sixteen at the time, Steve was fifteen, Larry was eleven, and Barney was eight. But Tim was the ringleader who was engineering the whole show.

I couldn't imagine what they were doing until I walked in and saw them sitting around the table, dipping tablespoons into a big bowl of red raspberry Jell-O with bananas in it. They were FLICKING big spoonfuls of the red gooey stuff against the white brick wall at the far end of the kitchen, and then watching it ooze down as the pieces of banana caught on the bricks.

Oh, what fun they were having, but I had to decide how to react: Faint? Scream? Spank? (KILL?) Here was an opportunity to make memories for life. This was a moment all of us would never forget, so I decided to make the most of it.

At least half of the big bowl of red Jell-O was still there, waiting to be eaten—or fired at the bricks. *The kids are going to have to clean all this up anyway,* I mused to myself. *So why not have some fun?*

Sitting down at the table next to Tim I asked, "Where's my spoon?"

Tim was so glad I was going to shoot the Jell-O instead of him that he grabbed a big cooking ladle and handed it to me. After all, why fool with mere tablespoons when you're trying to have fun? I loaded the giant ladle with a glob of red Jell-O and slung it against the brick wall. I started to laugh, got another load, and let it fly. I could see why the kids enjoyed Jell-O slinging so much.

At first they didn't know what to make of me, but then they got the message—especially when I told them between chuckles that they would have to clean it up anyway so we might as well all have a good time first.

So, there all five of us sat, firing red Jell-O at the bricks as fast as we could and laughing so hard we were almost hysterical. Soon the wall was a red dripping mess. There wasn't a white brick left anywhere.

I suppose some child-rearing experts could say I was modeling irresponsibility for my kids, but I don't think so. After we used up all the Jell-O, it took them almost two hours to scrub down the wall and clean up the floor. But the memories we all made that day were UNFORGETTABLE. Even now whenever Barney or Larry see Bill Cosby advertising Jell-O on TV, they remember the day Mom caught them firing raspberry missiles at the white brick wall and how she joined in on the fun.

Jell-O Memories Are Good for My Health

That Jell-O scene is a frozen picture in my mind and I still thaw it out now and then when life gets stressful. What better way to alleviate stress than to be aware of the humor in day-to-day living! For example:

You can get humor from your memories, as I do by thinking of the word *Jell-O,* but you can also be ready to laugh about even mundane things. Next time you see a sign in a cafeteria that says, "Shoes required to eat in cafeteria," ask the person you are with, "I wonder where the socks have to go to eat!"

Always be ready to laugh at yourself. Recently I traveled to Grand Rapids, Michigan, where I had been invited to hold a two-day conference in the very church where I had been a member as a child. Some generous folks loaned me a lovely new car to use while I was in town, and my sister, Janet, became the "official driver."

On at least two occasions while using the car, we had to stop to ask people on the street for directions, and both times we couldn't figure out how to get the car window open. Instead, we had to OPEN THE DOOR in order to talk to people. For some reason, we couldn't find the window-opener button. We pushed all the buttons on the dashboard, but only succeeded in turning on the radio, tape player, air conditioner, atmosphere control, etc. I remember telling Janet, "How dumb for a wonderful computerized car like this not to have a way to get the windows down!"

The next day we returned the car and I happened to mention to the owner, "This is a beautiful car, but how do you get the windows down?"

He pointed to a crank on the door and said, "You just turn the crank."

Janet and I looked at the side of the door, and there it was—the "old-fashioned" crank handle that *all* cars used to have a few years ago. For a second, we gasped with embarrassment. Then Janet looked at me and we began to laugh. How stupid could we be not to think that the car might have a crank on the door to roll down the windows? Somehow, all the other computer instruments, lights, and buttons on the dash had totally fooled us. For the rest of the day, we laughed at ourselves so much the tears often flowed down our cheeks. Obviously, neither one of us is "mechanically inclined."

Memorize Proverbs 17:22 and practice it often: "A cheerful heart is good medicine" (NIV). More and more medical researchers are actually admitting that there is a "physiology of happiness" that not only affects our hearts but the rest of our physical bodies as well, especially the immune system.

When tragedy strikes, many folks tend to become physically ill. For example, after losing a loved one they may let their minds become full of negative thoughts and the ensuing "chemical stew" inhibits the immune system, which leaves them much more susceptible to disease. On the other hand, when we can unload our troubled memories and find relief in laughter, our immune function improves.

Dr. Paul McGhee, a psychologist and president of The Laughter Remedy, has been conducting laughter research for twenty years. He was recently quoted in a newspaper as saying, "There really is something to this idea that one's frame of mind has an impact on the body's health system." McGhee went on to say that during the nineties we'll be hearing more and more about a whole new area that he calls "managing your mood for better health."[3]

Norman Cousins helped revolutionize the approach to getting well when he used old movies of the Marx Brothers and Laurel and Hardy to treat himself for a terminal disease. He wrote *The Anatomy of an Illness* to share what he had learned. During the following ten years, many in the medical community followed Cousins's lead. For example, Clemson University did a study of nursing-home patients who had watched "The Honeymooners" and other old comedies. Their aches and pains vanished and as a rule these "old folks" felt better.

In recent years, grants have been awarded to 125 hospitals, nursing homes, and other agencies to start humor programs for their patients. Specifically, here's what a little laughter can do for you:

Laughter helps you relax and unwind. Just try lifting anything heavy when you're enjoying a good belly laugh. You can't do it because your large muscles are totally relaxed. The only ones working are some muscles in your face and your abdomen.

Laughter strengthens the immune system. Research shows that when you have a really good laugh, the body produces more immunoglobulin A, the body's warrior against upper respiratory infections.

Laughter improves your circulation by increasing the heart rate and boosting the oxygen supply to the brain. This is part of what helps you relax and calm down.

Lynn Erdman, coordinator of nursing services in a large cancer treatment center, was quoted in the same article as McGhee. Of laughter, she said, "You feel like the burdens of the world have been lifted from you." At her hospital, Erdman likes to pass out prescriptions for laughter that warn patients of *"humoroids."* And what is the cure for humoroids? "A mild *laughsitive* each day."[4]

Laughter is a way to live an enriched life instead of just maintaining your existence, getting through each day somehow. Laughter is a key to finding pleasure and, when you have to endure mental and emotional pain, you need all the pleasure you can get. I'm not talking about being "lovers of pleasure rather than lovers of God" (2 Tim. 3:4 NIV), or "enjoying the fleeting pleasures of sin" (Heb. 11:25 TLB). Those verses describe the kind of hedonism that leaves God out, but there are unlimited legitimate pleasures you can enjoy by letting God in. For example:

. . . enjoying a tasty meal . . . listening to favorite music . . . watching the embers of a fire . . . marveling at the leaves turning color in the fall . . . AND SEEING THE HUMOR THAT IS ALL AROUND US.

All of these are pleasure-moments God wants us to enjoy, and we can do so if we learn to fine-tune the pleasure channels of our lives to His frequency. For me, the greatest pleasure comes from writing books and speaking to encourage downhearted people. My greatest satisfaction comes from telling SAD hearts how to become MERRY.

Chuck Swindoll, who loves to laugh as much, if not more, than anyone, wrote an excellent book called *Living on the Ragged Edge*, which is based on Ecclesiastes, King Solomon's observations about finding a meaningful life. If anyone knew the difference between seeking hollow pleasure and the right kind of pleasure, it was Solomon, who said:

> Go, eat your bread with joy,
> And drink your wine with a merry heart;
> For God has already accepted your works.

Let your garments always be white
And let your head lack no oil. . . .
Whatever your hand finds to do, do it with your might.
(Eccles. 9:7–8, 10 NKJV)

As Swindoll comments, God wants us to get on with life, not groan over the past. In other words:

HAVE A BLAST WHILE YOU LAST![5]

Olive Oil—and Pet Shampoo

Solomon's words in the verse above about letting our heads lack no oil took on special meaning for me not long ago. Bill and I were planning to leave Friday noon for a weekend conference near Denver, where I was to speak several times. I had made an appointment to have my hair done early Friday morning, giving us plenty of time to get to the airport. The night before, however, I had decided to give my hair my super home-conditioning treatment by saturating my scalp with heavy olive oil. Yes, I know you can buy oil treatments at the store, but I guess I'm a little frumpy (and also cheap!). After applying the oil, I wrapped my head in a towel and went to bed, confident that in the morning my hair would be sleek and glossy—after it was washed, of course.

Just as I was about to leave for the beauty shop early Friday morning, Judy, my hairdresser, called and said, "Barb, our power is out. We have NO hot water and NO hair dryers."

"But my hair and scalp are soaked with olive oil—I gave myself an oil treatment and I have to get it OUT!"

Judy suggested I find some shampoo that had coal tar in it, wash my hair thoroughly a couple of times, and then call her back to see if their electricity had been restored. I said, "Okay," but after hanging up I wondered, *Where will I find shampoo with coal tar in it at 7 A.M.?*

I rewrapped my oily head in a towel and dashed down to the 7-Eleven store on the corner where I found a shelf containing lots of plain shampoos, but none of the labels mentioned coal tar or pine tar. As I turned away from that shelf, my eye fell on a bottle of SARGENT'S PET SHAMPOO that was supposed to be good for getting rid of fleas on dogs. In bold letters the label read: "WITH PINE TAR." And farther down on the label, in smaller words, it also said, "Coal tar added, will kill lice."

"THAT'S IT!" I almost shouted aloud. "I've gotta have it!"

I dashed home and soaped up twice with the dog shampoo, rubbing it in "real good," just as Judy had instructed. Then I called her, only to learn that the electric power was still out. My appointment was down the drain, so to speak. What to do now? I was on my own, equipped only with dog shampoo and NO HAIR DRYER. Because I have my hair done weekly at the shop, I never had use for one.

Then I remembered our good old Electrolux vacuum cleaner, the same vacuum with the super suction power I've described in a prior book. I dragged the vacuum out of the closet, plugged it in, and reversed the suction to turn it into a mighty blower. Then I lay down on the rug, hoping the warm air would do the drying job.

Eventually, my hair did dry but I had two problems: (1) Now I smelled like tar or naphtha or whatever it is they put in pet shampoo, and (2) Instead of looking shiny and glossy, my well-blown hair made me look like a porcupine caught in a high wind.

There was also one other problem. Time was running out. We would have to leave within minutes to make the plane.

WHAT WAS I TO DO? I could tie a turban around my head and possibly try to get my hair done in Denver before I had to speak, but that wasn't likely since the schedule didn't really allow for it. Then I remembered a special box out in my Joy Room where I keep assorted toys for the grandkids when they come to visit. In that box was an old beat-up blonde wig that the kids love to wear to play dress-up. The crown of the wig had been thinned and refashioned by a puppy somewhere along the way, and it was full of cracker crumbs and Crayola wrappings my grandchildren had dropped in the toy box. I shook it out thoroughly and pulled it down on my head, shoving my hair up under the wig and pulling out a few strands through the holes in the crown. My hair was dark brown and the wig was ash-blonde, but no matter. By this time, I was DESPERATE.

Bill was calling me, so there was no more time to make any improvements. I grabbed my purse and dashed out to the car where he was waiting. During all the time I had been going through my hair crisis, he had been completely oblivious to any problem. He had been chatting with a neighbor, packing, taking out the trash, adjusting the thermostat—lost in his world of details and completely unaware of my near-frantic condition. As I got in the car, I checked myself out in the visor mirror and almost cried as I saw the frayed, chewed-up ash-blonde wig with wisps of my own dark hair peeking out at the sides and at the crown.

"What's the matter?" Bill asked as we turned onto the freeway.

Almost tearfully I explained what had happened and how pathetic I looked for the trip. But Bill continued driving in his same unjangled way. Glancing at my hair, he just smiled and said, "You don't look any different to me!"

Laughter Is in Nation-Wide Demand

According to my mail, a lot of people are looking for joy and laughter. Here are a few of their comments:

> I pray for more joy in my attitude that I can laugh more and enjoy life more. I tend to be too serious, so your book has been a breath of fresh air.

☐   ☐   ☐

> We have lost a six-year-old daughter with leukemia and know from experience some of the pain and grief you write about. It certainly has given us the credentials to help others in similar situations. It took eight years to work through our experience before we could talk about it to each other. Thank God we stuck together rather than separate as so many couples do when situations so hard come into their life.
>
> There is a great need in our area for people to find some joy in life. People have bottled up the springs of joy and God forbid if they should laugh at anything silly, let alone let anyone know that humor does have a place in life.

☐   ☐   ☐

Parents with broken dreams, broken families, and broken hearts need a special touch as often as possible. God is using you and your ministry to give us "joy-aid."

I just finished reading your book and received a tremendous blessing. I'm reminded each day to look for a laugh as I'm a very serious negative individual and realize God has deliverance that can glorify Himself in being a help to others.

I did receive a copy of your book and began reading it when I really was in need of a lift. But I recommend the publisher put on the following label:

WARNING
For women with bladder weakness,
wearing your DEPENDS is recommended.

Your book came at a very needy time in my life as I had just lost my husband very suddenly after 31 years. . . . I was having a very difficult time handling my loss and trying to be brave for my children, making decisions alone, living alone, going to bed alone, waking up alone, living the life of a marble rolling around on the linoleum, no direction, just existing. Then I started your book and realized I sure had nothing to kick about. I had 31 good and wonderful years with very few bumps in the road. I had always used humor in my life to ride over the bumps, but humor had left me, and your book and lessons helped me to get it back.

These letters are only a sampling of the mail I get from folks who haven't laughed in months or even years. A basic question many people have is:

Will I ever laugh again? How long does this intense pain last?

One of my favorite bumper snickers says, "Pain is inevitable, but misery is optional." (In fact, I like it so much I used it on the cover of my book, *Stick a Geranium in Your Hat and Be Happy*.) But sometimes, when you're in pain because of a loss or someone is driving you to the Home for the Bewildered, you think misery is NOT optional. You may feel as if you will NEVER be normal again.

A heavy mantle of grief will enclose you in the thick fog of despair, but shedding tears, talking, and the passing of time will work wonders. One morning you will wake up and realize suddenly that you're not thinking about your pain. You will actually be able to hear the birds sing or see a fluffy white cloud drift across the sky. One day you will have that glimmer of hope and begin to realize there is something more to life than your SPECIFIC PROBLEM.

To put it another way, the night of grief will end, and, as Psalm 30:5 promises:

JOY COMES IN THE MORNING.

The intense pain will ease up, flatten out, and not be so encompassing. I cannot give any specific time as to how long anyone's pain will last. It depends on what you are doing to accelerate yourself through your grieving period. All kinds of resources are within your reach: helpful audio and video tapes, support groups, recovery systems, or just opening your heart to a trusted friend.

Keep in mind that, while tears and talking help, *time is your most trusted friend*. Scar tissue may remain from the hurt you suffer, but your deep wounds will heal. One way to get through this is to keep telling yourself:

ONE DAY I'LL LOOK BACK ON ALL
THIS AND LAUGH.

EXTRA-STRENGTH DEODORANT

Sometimes life is the pits.

If you think that sounds crazy, I understand. I believed that I would never laugh again, much less be able to tell audiences about the experiences our family went through, and be able to do it with humor. For example, I've found many a laugh in my ignorance of homosexuality and now as I retell stories of how I learned about Larry, I put in plenty of examples that make audiences chuckle.

For example, in 1975, who knew what *bisexual* meant? I sure didn't. I had to learn the hard way that it doesn't mean having sex twice a month! Another good laugh always comes out of my sister's purple luggage and my naive (totally erroneous) fear that Janet was a lesbian because lesbians supposedly love the color purple. In truth, lesbians like all kinds of colors, depending on personal taste.

Several months after my "Whatever, Lord" experience and Larry's return, I visited Janet in Minneapolis, where I confessed my "purple paranoia" problem with her luggage. I was glad when Janet laughed harder than anyone at my story. These days I like to tell folks that purple is the color of royalty, and I love purple myself because I'm a daughter of the KING!

Over the years my story, which began with the utter devastation that struck four times in nine years, has been turned into an account sprinkled with humor and joy, but it didn't happen overnight. I hope it shows people how, as we look back, we can poke fun at ourselves and see humor even in tragic moments. We can see how God can use the fractures in our lives to bring restoration to others. That is why I appreciate the way God has taken the painful episodes in my life and used them to infuse others with the joy He has given me.

Will you ever laugh again? OF COURSE you will! You will feel better. You will smile and eventually laugh out loud. Hang in there. Tomorrow could bring that shining moment—in fact, it might even happen TODAY!

Parents Need All the Laughs They Can Get

Because I deal with so many hurting parents, I'm always

looking for something to help them see the funny side of life. Believe me, if you've ever been a parent, you know you can use all the laughs you can get!

Somebody sent me the following instructions on "How to Eat Like a Child" and, as so often happens, no source was given. But whoever wrote the following directions knew something about kids and how to laugh at being a parent. (Even if you've never had a kid, you have probably seen one eating somewhere, so don't skip this because you'll miss some good chuckles.)

PEAS: Mash into thin sheet on plate. Press back of fork into peas, hold fork vertically, prongs up, and lick off peas.

MASHED POTATOES: Pat mashed potatoes flat on top. Dig several little depressions. Think of them as ponds or pools. Fill pools with gravy. With your fork, sculpt rivers between them. Decorate with peas. Do not eat. Alternate method: Make a large hole in center of mashed potatoes. Pour in ketchup. Stir until potatoes turn pink. Eat as you would peas.

SANDWICH: Leave the crusts. If your mother says you have to eat them because that's the best part, stuff them into your pocket or between the cushions of the couch.

SPAGHETTI: Wind too many strands on fork and make sure at least two strands dangle down. Open mouth wide and stuff in spaghetti; suck noisily to inhale dangling strands. Clean plate, ask for seconds, and eat only half. When carrying plate to kitchen, hold tilted so that remaining spaghetti slides onto the floor.

ICE CREAM CONE: Ask for double scoop. Knock the top scoop off while walking out the door of the ice cream parlor. Cry. Lick remaining scoop slowly so that ice cream melts down outside of the cone and over your hand. Stop licking when ice cream is even with top of cone. Eat a hole in bottom of cone and suck the rest of ice cream out the bottom. When only cone remains with ice cream coating the inside, leave on car dashboard.

SPINACH: Divide into little piles. Rearrange into new piles. After five or six maneuvers, sit back and say you are full.

CHOCOLATE CHIP COOKIES: Half-sit, half-lie on bed, propped up by pillow. Read a book. Place cookies next to you on sheet so that crumbs get in bed. As you eat the cookies, remove each chocolate chip and place it on your stomach. When all cookies are consumed, eat chips one by one, allowing two per page.

MILK SHAKE: Bite off one end of paper covering straw. Blow through straw to shoot paper across the table. Place straw in shake and suck. When shake just reaches your mouth, place a finger over top of straw—the pressure will keep the shake in straw. Lift straw out of shake, put bottom end in mouth, release finger, and swallow. Do this until straw is squashed so you can't suck through it. Ask for another. This time shoot paper at the waitress when she isn't looking. Sip your shake casually—you are just minding your own business—until there is about an inch of shake remaining. Then blow through straw until bubbles rise to top of glass. When your father says he's had just about enough, get a stomachache.

Kids' antics are so funny because we work so hard to "raise them right" but they seem to have a sixth sense empowering them to know just how to drive us crazy. Despite this, most parents I know wouldn't trade those funny, crazy times for all the cruise ships in the Caribbean. If your kids are still at home, keep the following thoughts in mind:

The best thing that you can give your children, next to good habits, are good memories.

Children need models more than they need critics.

Childhood is like the old joke about a small town—one blink and it's gone.

Appreciate every moment with your kids. Don't wish their childhood away. One hundred years from now it will not matter what kind of car you drove, or what kind of house you lived in, or how many books you wrote, or what your clothes looked like; but the world may be a little better because you were important in the life of a child.

She Gave Her Own Birthday Party

Because I'm always urging people to put laughter into their lives, you can imagine how tickled I was when I got the following letter:

> Today is my birthday. Yesterday I attended a women's conference you did in San Bruno, California. I was so filled with joy afterwards I went to Mervyn's and put $100 on my charge card.
>
> You see, I am married to one of those very strange only children. He thinks so much of himself that I have to help him celebrate my birthday in the "proper" manner. So I bought myself some birthday presents. I also bought myself a cake and made myself some signs that state, "We love you. Happy Birthday, Mom!"
>
> You told us to look for ways to make joy happen. I'm having a wonderful day, thanks to me. In fact, this is about the best birthday I've had since I was with my mother last. I will be seeing her soon as I am going to be taking off for my homeland in about 24 hours. I'm the one who flies a lot. Thank you for all the laughter and the words of wisdom.
>
> P.S. I went for a walk today and saw the diamonds in the sidewalk. They were beautiful.

About a month later I got another letter from this same lady after she took her trip overseas to see her mom. When she came back, she found even more joy, but this time her family played a big part in it:

> I left for a two-week stay with my daughter, sister, and Mother the day after my birthday. This was the longest time I have ever been away from my family my entire married life. I had a good time being pampered, etc., by my mom.

When I returned here my eldest son, who was on his way out (in fact, he was literally driving away in a car and turned around when he saw me coming), opened the car door for me and gave me a very tender hug. He is 21 years old—I was blown away.

When I entered my home, they had made signs, "Welcome home, Mom. We missed you." The floor was clean, the rugs were recently vacuumed, the dishes done, as well as the wash. The wash was not folded but at least it was clean.

This was all done by my three sons ages 21, 16, and 15. Is this a miracle? And I didn't even pray for one. God really answers prayers that are not even uttered. . . .

Have a wonderful day. Remember that diamonds are a girl's best friend. Isn't it wonderful to have so many???

Laughter Lifts a Tired Spirit

A good laugh can lift your spirits when you're tired and a little cranky. Recently, my good friend, Lynda, and I were driving to Yucaipa, California, about ninety miles away, for a weekend conference at a Baptist church. I had gotten up feeling a little weary that morning and was thinking how much fun it would be to just have a weekend off for a change, when Lynda asked me, "Do you ever get tired of spreading your joy and sharing your story?"

"Well, yes, I sure do," I admitted. "Sometimes I think I can't go over the SAME story, the SAME events, the SAME details, ONE MORE TIME. In fact, I'm so tired of spreading joy I just wish I could stay home and never have to tell my story again."

As we turned off the freeway onto the road to Yucaipa, Lynda and I discussed what it was like to have the symptoms of burnout. I felt as if I had been experiencing just about ALL of them. Then, as we rounded a curve, a huge highway billboard loomed up on the right-hand side and on it were printed only three words in gigantic letters about twenty feet high:

SPREAD YOUR JOY!

In smaller letters near the bottom of the sign was the notation, "Paid for by First Baptist Church, Yucaipa"—the very place where I was going to speak! Talk about SOMEONE sending me a message! We both burst out laughing simultaneously and then drove on down the road to the church where we had one of the best conferences ever.

My joy was abundant that day and the results were 110 percent. Many women came forward for prayer, and several decisions were made to come to the Lord. Some might say the sign appeared when it did by pure coincidence; but isn't it strange how "coincidences" happen? Afterward, I realized again that in spreading my joy, God had restored ME. MY JOY WAS FULL! As soon as I had a moment to myself, I told God I was sorry for my petulant outburst and I thanked Him for His reminder that as we pour out ourselves for others we ourselves are renewed!

I found a little poem called "Boomerang" that sums up my "spread your joy!" experience perfectly:

> When a bit of sunshine hits ye,
> After passing of a cloud,
> When a fit of laughter gits ye,
> An' yer spine is feelin' proud.
> Don't fergit to up and fling it
> At a soul that's feelin' blue,
> For the minute that ye sling it,
> It's a boomerang to you![6]

Eight Ways to Put Laughter in Your Life

Dr. Paul McGhee, president of The Laughter Remedy, suggests eight ways to put more laughter in your life:

- Make a list of fun things you enjoy doing—and do them. Hang around positive people.

- Immerse yourself in humor. Watch cartoons or funny movies, spend Saturday night at a comedy club, your lunch hour at a costume shop, weekends with kids.

- Learn jokes—and tell them. Start with one and people will tell you their favorites.

- Focus on seeing and creating ambiguity, forming puns. Sometimes you see these in newspaper headlines ("Grandmother of Nine Shoots Hole in One") or in signs ("Use Stairs for Restroom").

- Look for humor in everyday situations. And if you overhear something funny, write it down so you can remember it and tell it to others.

- Just laugh—more often and more heartily. Work on great big belly laughs, not just chuckles.

- Learn to laugh at yourself in a kind way. Make a list of things you don't like about yourself, then just start poking fun at them, exaggerate them.

- Learn to find humor in difficult situations, in the midst of stress. This is when you really need it and when your sense of humor abandons you most often.[7]

That last suggestion by Dr. McGhee reminds me of a stressful situation I faced not long ago, when my sense of humor stayed intact, fortunately, even though my dignity suffered a little.

Happy Birthday on the Saw

While I try to make an effort to be dignified, I sometimes wind up in situations that are anything but. I grew up in a very musical family where my mom was a piano teacher, my dad played the violin and sang, and my sister played the vibraharp and piano. I played the piano accordion and sang too.

When I was about ten years old, my dad thought I should learn to play "the saw." Yes, I'm talking about an actual carpenter's saw.

If you bend it back and forth at just the right angle, you can get a screechy, whining sound out of it by using a violin bow—sort of like a sick cat howling on a fence.

Daddy asked one of the men in our church to come over to teach me this unusual "art." As I began to make progress, my father was thrilled because he thought it would be great for me to go along with him to play the saw when he did evangelistic speaking at jails or prisons. (I guess he thought the saw would be more portable than my heavy piano accordion and that the inmates would be so desperate for music they wouldn't mind listening to my amateur efforts.)

As I practiced on my saw, my mother served as my accompanist on the piano, which helped drown out some of the sour notes. After awhile, I could get through a few old songs, and even make them recognizable. My saw repertoire included "I Come to the Garden Alone" and "At the Cross, At the Cross, Where I First Saw the Light."

Mom thought my learning to play the saw was ridiculous, but she went along with the whole thing and pulled together a special outfit for me to wear and still look ladylike. In order to play the saw, you must hold it between your legs and a dress wouldn't work very well. In those days they didn't have slacks or pantsuits, so Mom made something like beach pajamas—today they'd probably be called culottes.

My saw-playing career didn't last long, but it did come back to haunt me years later. Not long ago, I went out to dinner with friends to celebrate the birthday of Mike, one of the young men in our group. As we were sitting in this lovely, conservative restaurant eating dinner, Mike reminded me that I had once told him I could play the saw and that I had promised I would play "Happy Birthday" on the saw for his next birthday!

Because it was Sunday night and I had just spoken at a local church, I had on a dress, and playing a saw was out of the question. Besides, I didn't have one handy so I thought I would get away scot-free. I placated him by saying that I surely would play it for him some other time, but he wasn't about to be put off. Then and there, he pulled out a carpenter's saw and a violin bow and insisted I keep my promise!

So there I sat in a restaurant booth, where we had to push the table away so I could get the saw between my legs, while I managed to screech out a few bars of "Happy Birthday" for the guest of honor.

We were all laughing and having fun when two men who had been in the church service that evening and had bought copies of my book came over to our table and asked me to sign their books. Terribly embarrassed, I quickly straightened my dress and tried to pretend that autographing books after playing the saw was nothing unusual at all, but I wonder what THEY thought!

I was just thankful no one had brought a camera and snapped a picture of me trying to play a saw while wearing a dress in a crowded restaurant. Later, on the way home, I admonished myself, *Barbara, that wasn't very mature!* But then I laughed out loud, because IT SURE WAS FUN!

A Joy Box Full of Sparkling Pinwheels

Back in chapter 1 I mentioned using a Joy Box to cope with the stresses of life. Lots of folks have taken me up on my idea over the years. Just about anything will do for a Joy Box. One lady wrote to describe using a lovely hat box covered with pictures of beautiful red apples. But perhaps the most common container is a plain old shoe box. It doesn't matter what the box is; it's what's inside that counts: cards, letters, curios, cartoons, pictures—anything to make you smile or laugh, particularly when the GLOOMEES attack.

One lady who lives in constant pain with joint disease and weekly migraine headaches admitted she loses joy when the pain makes it difficult to even want to be alive. She wrote:

> The last couple of months I have been "forgetting" to practice joy. . . . I know the Enemy wants me to spend as many days as possible with a big sour face muttering grumblings and complaints. I hope to smile as many days as possible despite the hurt and pain. And I know I get to *choose*

to smile and make an effort to surround myself with what is good and wonderful.

After I first read your book, I had so much fun gathering pleasure things for my Joy Box. I love shiny anythings and I found some sparkling, glittering, rainbow-ee pinwheels I purchased for my front yard. When my kids and husband asked why I was buying pinwheels for myself in the middle of winter, I just smiled and said, "Because Barbara said so!" (just kidding). Actually we had a talk about God's love and doing things that remind us of His many gifts. Sparkling pinwheels make me think of all the beautiful things we will see in heaven.

I started my first Joy Box after Larry disappeared. As I began sharing my story with folks, they started sending me contributions and soon I had several Joy Boxes. Eventually, my Joy Box grew into a twenty-by-sixty-foot JOY ROOM that today is filled with hundreds of signs, sayings, and novel gimmicks of every conceivable description. Everything in my Joy Room has one quality in common: it's bound to make someone smile or chuckle.

New contributions to my Joy Room come practically every week. In the last year or two, I've received more than twenty geranium hats from women who heard me speak about *Stick a Geranium in Your Hat and Be Happy*. These hats now adorn the walls of my Joy Room, but I do save one to put on my latest life-sized doll, who I call Miss Joybells. She's at least five feet tall, wears rolled-down stockings and granny glasses, and carries a purse containing real dentures, denture adhesive, and some corn pads. Oh yes, she also has a mole on her chin with a hair right in the center of it.

Miss Joybells has replaced Long Lena, another huge doll, as my traveling companion in the car, and she accompanies me on trips to conferences that are within driving distance of my home. I get a lot of weird looks from other motorists, but I don't mind. Sometimes I tell folks Miss Joybells is very helpful, particularly when I want to use the Diamond Lane, which, in California, is reserved for "commuter" cars with two or more passengers (just kidding, of course).

Although I love the feeling of a fireplace, we have no fireplace in our home now, and I have often missed it—until recently. To add to my joy collections, someone sent me a twenty-minute video of a roaring fire, complete with the crackling, popping sounds that only a fire can make. So now I just sit back in a nice easy chair and for twenty minutes I watch a roaring fire start up, burn merrily, and then diminish into glowing embers. I can almost SMELL the wood burning.

People often ask me, "How do you unwind after a busy day?" Now I tell them I not only use my bubble bath, but I can always "play my fireplace."

The Sound of Rain Refreshes My Soul

One other recent arrival in my Joy Room is what is called a "rain stick." It's a hollow tube about five feet long that contains cactus seeds. When you rotate it, the stick makes a perfect imitation of rain on the roof.

According to the instruction pamphlet, the rain stick is made from the fallen stalks of the normata cactus. Thorns from the cactus are pressed into the hollow staff so that when the stick is rotated the seeds fall on the thorns to create the sound of light showers or driving rain. The rain stick was used by the Diaguita Indians of Chile to call on the rain spirits. I'm not interested in contacting the rain spirits, but it is nice to tilt my rain stick at a 40 degree angle and thank the Lord for His showers of blessing.

While growing up in Michigan, I loved the sound of rain on the roof, but since living in Southern California (where it supposedly NEVER rains), I've missed that pleasure. So now I'm really happy, because I have my bubble bath, my fireplace, AND my rain sounds to comfort me. Whenever I listen to my rain stick, I think of a stanza from a poem written by my good friend, Betty Henry Taylor:

> I love to hear the sound of rain
>   splashing on my windowpane
>   or pounding on a roof of tin.
> 'Tis music to my ears.
> The sound of blessing from the Lord;
>   showers He has sent my way.
> Refreshing to my soul.[8]

On nights when I can't sleep, I wander out to my Joy Room to enjoy myself and pause to pray for people who've sent me certain items. The other night something stopped me and I had to laugh. I have this little mirror with a picture painted on it of a little boy furtively picking an apple off a tree, as if he hopes he won't get caught. Below the picture the sign says, "Look who God loves!"

As I looked into the mirror at the picture, of course I saw myself and then thought, *Why, yes, He DOES love me, even when I'm like the little boy and doing things I shouldn't.*

I went to bed, smiling as I thought of how God loves us all and He sends His enjoyment in every kind of package—even a piece of hollow cactus full of seeds that makes a sound like rain.

I'm sure you'll see why, then, I especially treasure a letter from a mom with an openly gay son who is a policeman in a large city. She wrote me recently to share her gloomees, but I love her P.S., which says:

> One last thought! Last night at midnight I was awakened to the sound of rain falling. What a wonderful sound to our drought-stricken land. As I lay there listening to the rain, it was like God saying to me, "I'm washing away some of your pain. I'm washing away your pain." Today I laughed—I actually was able to laugh! I can almost see the light.

Gloomee Busters

(Because this chapter is about fun and laughter, I've included some extra Gloomee Busters—just for fun, of course!)

REASONS TO SMILE

Every seven minutes of every day, someone in an aerobics class pulls a hamstring.

Really rich people are much more likely to drown in yacht accidents.

Mechanics' cars break down, too.

Thin people are not really happy.

□   □   □

Laughter for the Here-After!

An inexperienced preacher was conducting his first funeral. As solemnly as he knew how, while pointing to the body, he declared, "What we have here is only a shell. The nut is already gone."

Laughter cannot be buried. Consider these headstones:

Here lies Col. Brown.
Shot in battle by an enemy soldier.
"Well Done Thou Good and Faithful Servant"

Here lies Tom Stone
Drowned in the waters of the sea.
"By a Few Affectionate Friends"

Here lies Lucy Mann
(Unmarried)
She lived an old Maid
She died an old Mann

If you haven't purchased your headstone yet, you might be interested in this one. A local classified ad read, "For sale, one used headstone. Good buy for anyone named Murphy."[9]

LIFE IS AN ENDLESS STRUGGLE
FULL OF FRUSTRATIONS AND CHALLENGES
BUT EVENTUALLY YOU FIND A HAIRSTYLIST YOU LIKE!

Q: What do you get when you cross an insomniac, an agnostic, and a dyslexic?

A: A person who lies awake all night trying to decide if there really IS a doG.

□ □ □

Creative Ways to Handle Stress

1. Forget the diet center and send yourself a candy gram.
2. Put a bag on your head. Mark it "Closed for remodeling."
3. Brush your teeth vigorously with Cheez Whiz.
4. Pound your head repeatedly on a pile of lightly toasted Wonder Bread.
5. Find out what a frog in a blender really looks like.

□ □ □

A young lady went to heaven. Saint Peter met her and asked if she knew God's Son. She said, "Yes."

"Do you know His name?" Saint Peter inquired.

"Yes," the young woman said, "His name is Andy . . . You know, Andy walks with me, Andy talks with me, Andy tells me I am His own. . . ."

□ □ □

Every woman KNOWS that one special
way to drive a man WILD . . .
(Hide the TV remote control.)

DIFFERENT DEFINITIONS

HIGHBROW—A person who can listen to the William Tell Overture without thinking of the Lone Ranger.

MOONLIGHTER—A man who holds day and night jobs so he can drive from one to the other in a better car.

RINGLEADER—First one in the bathtub.

□ □ □

Examples of Unclear Writing

From actual letters received by a large city's welfare department:

1. I am writing the Welfare Department to say that my baby was born two years old. WHEN do I get my money?
2. Mrs. Jones has not had any clothes for a year and has been visited regularly by the clergy.
3. I cannot get sick pay. I have six children. Can you tell me why?
4. This is my eighth child. What are you going to do about it?
5. Please find for certain if my husband is dead. The man I am now living with can't eat or do anything till he knows.
6. I am very much annoyed to find you have branded my son illiterate. This is a dirty lie as I was married a week before he was born.
7. In answer to your letter, I have given birth to a boy weighing ten pounds. I hope this is satisfactory.
8. I am forwarding my marriage certificate and three children, one of which is a mistake as you can see.
9. I have no children yet as my husband is a truck driver and works day and night.
10. In accordance with your instructions, I have given birth to twins in the enclosed envelope.

Unsolved Mysteries of Anatomy

Where can a man buy a cap for his knee,
Or the key to a lock of his hair?
Is the crown of your head where jewels are found?
Who travels the bridge of your nose?
If you wanted to shingle the roof of your mouth
Would you use the nails in your toes?
Can you sit in the shade of the palm of your hand?
Or beat on the drum in your ear?
Can the calf of your leg eat the corn off your toe?
Then why not grow corn on the ear?
Can the crook in your elbow be sent to jail?
If so, what did he do?
How can you sharpen your shoulder blades?
I'll be darned if I know, do you?

There is a right time for everything: . . .
A time to cry;
A time to laugh. . . . (Ecc. 3:1, 4 TLB)

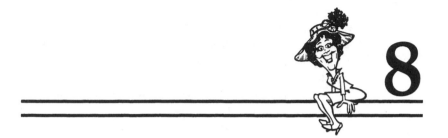

At Day's End, I Turn
All My Problems Over to God . . .
He's Going to Be Up Anyway

Thank You, dear God
For all You have given me,
For all You have taken away from me,
For all You have left me!

Sometimes when you try to run away from your problems, you only run smack into more. I can remember a stressful time when two of our boys were in their teens and giving us difficulties. Steven, in particular, had started running with a crowd we didn't approve of; he also wanted to leave school to join the Marines. Tim had a girlfriend we weren't too happy about either. After dinner one night, Bill and I left the boys at home watching TV while we went for a walk to sort things out.

We walked down to the park at the corner and, because it was a warm evening, we decided to sit on one of the benches located in a pleasant spot well off the street. As we sat there trying to sort through our problems, Bill began tying and untying his shoelaces, a nervous habit he engages in while thinking. (Bill wears out lots of shoelaces that way.)

We had laid out our alternatives and were realizing our options seemed rather limited when suddenly it seemed that Old Faithful had erupted on us. Actually, it was the park sprinkler system, which the automatic timer had activated at full force. We sprang to our feet, and with our shoes sinking deep into the wet grass, we dashed through the sprinklers to reach the safety of the sidewalk.

Soaking wet, we hurried home where we found all four of our boys still watching TV in the living room. They looked up to see their parents, clothes dripping, hair matted down and soggy, and they began roaring with laughter. Tim knew where we had gone and why, and he quipped, "Well, you've got it all solved now, eh? Were you baptized with the answer, or is it raining out right now?"

I had been laughing all the way home and continued laughing at Tim's remark. But Bill didn't laugh. With his melancholy disposition, what happened only dampened his spirits. But I learned something about problems. I was reminded that the best thing to do is lighten up, laugh at your misfortunes, and trust God a lot more.

So that's why the title of this chapter is really more than just facetious fun. Turning your problems over to the Lord is a very good idea that has been confirmed for me by one of my favorite theologians, eight-year-old Danny Dutton, who wrote the following "Essay on God."

> One of God's main jobs is making people. He makes these to put in place of the ones that die, so there will be enough people to take care of things here on earth. He doesn't make grownups. Just babies. I think because they are smaller and easier to make. That way He doesn't have to take up His valuable time teaching them to talk and walk. He can just leave that up to mothers and fathers. I think it works out pretty good.

God's second-most important job is listening to prayers. An awful lot of this goes on, because some people are like preachers, and pray other times besides bedtime. God doesn't have time to listen to the radio or TV on account of this. Because God hears everything, not only prayers, there must be a terrible lot of noise going on in His ears, unless He has thought of a way to turn it off.

God sees everything and hears everything and is everywhere. Which keeps Him pretty busy. So you shouldn't go wasting His time by going over your parents' heads and asking for something they said you couldn't have.

Atheists are people who don't believe in God. I don't think there are any in our town. At least there aren't any who come to church.

Jesus is God's Son. He used to do all the hard work, like walking on water and doing miracles and trying to teach people about God who didn't want to learn. They finally got tired of His preaching to them and they crucified Him. But He was good and kind like His Father, and He told His Father that they didn't know what they were doing and to forgive them, and God said O.K.

His Father appreciated everything He had done and all His hard work on earth, so He told Him He didn't have to go out on the road any more. He could stay in heaven. So He did. And now He helps His Father out by listening to prayers and seeing which things are important for God to take care of and which ones He can take care of Himself without having to bother God. Like a secretary, only more important, of course. You can pray anytime you want and They are sure to hear you because They've got it worked out so One of them is on duty all the time.

You should always go to Sunday school because it makes God happy, and if there's anybody you want to make happy, it's God. Don't skip Sunday school to do something you think will be more fun like going to the beach. That is wrong. And besides the sun doesn't come out at the beach until noon.

If you don't believe in God, besides being an Atheist, you will be very lonely, because your parents can't go everywhere with you, like to camp, but God can. It's good to know He is around when you're scared of the dark or when you can't

swim very good and you get thrown in real deep water by big
kids.

But you shouldn't just always think of what God can do for
you. I figure God put me here and He can take me back
anytime he pleases.

And that's why I believe in God.[1]

Do You Still Believe the Way You Used To?

Many older and more learned theologians have written a lot
about God, but I am not sure they have always matched the
wisdom in little Danny's words. I have no idea where Danny
Dutton's essay came from, or how long ago he wrote it. Danny
is probably a grown man by now, and I'd love to meet him. The
first thing I'd ask him is, "Do you still believe in God the way
you used to? Do you still trust Him with that childlike faith?"

Those are basic, bottom-line questions for all of us, and, although my mail is full of pain, it reflects the ability many folks
have to turn their problems over to God. Often it seems the
more problems folks have, the stronger their faith becomes. For
example, one lady wrote to say that she lost her father, then two
days later her mother died, and five days later her husband of
thirty-two years came in and told her that she should be getting
a lawyer because he was leaving her for another woman. She
added:

> By the grace of God my 16-year-old son and I are "making
> it." On top of all that, we lost our only cat! Your book, as I
> said before, really helped.

Another mother tells me she has always had stress. Married
at seventeen to an alcoholic husband, she had six children in ten
years but lost three of them through death. On the week of her
twenty-fifth wedding anniversary, she and her husband
planned to have a church wedding and rededicate themselves.
Just a few days before, however, he was in an explosion at work

and burned over 65 percent of his body. He survived and when things started to look up a little, she learned she had lupus.

Next, her daughter, who has three children, was divorced by her husband, who remarried just a few weeks later. Her latest news came from her son, who wrote a letter on his birthday thanking his parents for all their love, and then adding that he was gay. Her letter continues:

> I wrote and told our son that we loved him and would pray for him. My first inclination was to preach how wrong he was, but I stopped long enough to ask what Jesus would do. I was saved from much remorse. I'm still grieving but Satan no longer has power to taunt me over this. I have put on God's armor, Ephesians 6:13, but I am a war-torn, battle-scarred mom trying to hang in there. Please send me any information you can. . . .

A Spatula friend took along a copy of my book, *Splashes of Joy in the Cesspools of Life,* while waiting for her husband to be examined by the eye specialist for what he thought might be a very serious problem. She wrote about enduring the stressful moments as they waited for the doctor's verdict:

> I have to tell you as I looked at my big strapping hubby in that doctor's chair I prayed. I saw the chair as the palm of God's hand holding on to him!! I kept repeating, "I gift-wrap you and hand you to the Lord." My worries were erased and a feeling of peace was in that examining room!!!

Later, the doctor came in and told the woman there was no need for laser surgery on her husband's eye. There was some swelling, but the retina was intact and conventional therapy would do the job.

Everyone has different pain to deal with, and it's your attitude that makes the difference. That's what one wife wrote to me as she explained what had happened to her and her husband:

Presently, my husband and I own half of a convenience store/gas station. We're in the midst of a partner split and the realization that our partner misappropriated funds that were to be used for paying taxes, as well as the realization that all we've put into this business is owed to the IRS . . . BUT . . . the Lord has this situation in His hands and after all, it will come to pass!

Another sparkle came in the mail from a mom who had some good news to tell me about her son:

We're so proud (in the "humble" way) that our son is doing so well, out of drugs and alcohol and the gay life. He has a good job. . . . He lives alone. One thing I do know: we must love and care about our kids, no matter what. And pray and pray and God will do it! Life is sure "no bowl of cherries" but our hope is in the Lord. I just say, "Hang in there and love 'em the best we can."

Lord, I Believe, But I Need to Believe MORE

Letters like those above are a real sparkle for me because they help build MY faith. As I admitted earlier, I have an abundance of joy but I'm slim on faith. I know that doesn't make sense because most Bible teachers will tell you that joy comes out of faith. But I can identify with the lady who wrote to say:

The special thing I learned from you is that I can have joy but still be low on faith. I always thought faith had to be with joy. It caused me to feel guilty because my faith is not always strong.

And I also appreciate the mom who wrote to say:

Barbara, I've just finished reading two of your books back to back. I now feel like I have a full coat of armor on. However, I have located the nearest <u>dump</u> just in case.*

---

*When a drunk driver killed our son Tim I spent a lot of nights grieving at a nearby dump. See chapter 2.

Like the father of the paralytic boy, I know what it's like to tell God, "I do have faith; oh, help me to have *more!*" (Mark 9:24 TLB). I probably shouldn't admit it, but I even kind of like the old Moroccan proverb:

TRUST IN GOD,
BUT TIE YOUR CAMEL TIGHT.

And yet God has rewarded the little mustard seeds of faith I've planted by restoring my son to us after he had disowned his family and disappeared into the gay lifestyle. Today Larry and I are best friends, so it was very special for me this past Mother's Day when he came over and brought me a necklace that says, "FIRST RATE MOM."

A lot of folks receive jewelry that says "First Rate Grandma," or "First Rate Friend," but to receive "FIRST RATE MOM" from the boy who had disowned us, changed his name, and never wanted to SEE us again really has a special meaning. I will always treasure this little necklace because it stands in such contrast to a relationship that was broken for eleven years.

Maybe one reason Larry and I are good friends is that we both cope with needing stronger faith—at least on certain occasions. It seems that the longer you're a Christian, the harder it is to have faith because you have more opportunities to be disappointed, more prayers that appear to go "unanswered." I've often thought it's easier for new Christians to have faith because they haven't had time to become a little cynical yet. It reminds me of the bumper sticker that says:

IF YOU CAN REMAIN CALM,
YOU JUST DON'T HAVE ALL THE FACTS.

Don't Worry, Mom, the Keys Are Safe with Us!

Not too long ago Bill and I were invited to use a friend's condo for a couple of weeks on the island of Maui in Hawaii.

Larry and his friend, Tom, who was a new Christian, were going to come over for the second week to enjoy Maui with us. As that second week came to a close, Bill and I had a flight that left the day BEFORE the boys were to depart.

Playing my role of cautious mom to the hilt, I painstakingly instructed Larry about locking up the condo and being SURE not to lose the keys to the condo or to our rental car, which he was to turn in for us. The owners of the condo had told us if the key to any unit got lost, it would mean re-keying the whole complex at a cost of several hundred dollars.

After talking to Larry and stressing the importance of all this, I also tacked written instructions on the refrigerator to remind him to be sure to guard those keys with his life, and to put gas in the rental car before returning it.

Larry drove us to the airport to catch our plane home and on the way, I AGAIN reminded him to be careful about returning all the keys, locking up securely when he left the next day, returning the rental car with the gas tank filled. By now I had moved across the line from REMINDING to NAGGING, but Larry good-naturedly assured me he would take care of it and we flew back to California. The boys returned home a day later and we assumed all had gone well.

Several MONTHS after our Hawaiian vacation, I had occasion to borrow Larry's car. According to my usual custom, I opened the ashtray to put in all my loose change so Larry would have parking-meter money if he ever needed it. There inside the ash tray was a brand-new, shiny gold car key. I could tell the key wasn't to his car and I couldn't help but ask him what the new key was for. He looked rather sheepish, then laughed and told me what had happened.

Evidently, on the same day Bill and I had left, Larry and Tom drove the rental car up to a beautiful beach called Kapalua where snorkeling is terrific. You can swim way out into the bay, where the crystal clear water is filled with coral, shells, and beautiful fish. Larry locked up his wallet and clothes in the car and then put the keys to the car and the condo in the back pocket of his swim trunks.

Remembering all of my instructions, Larry buttoned the pocket of his swim trunks securely—he thought. For an hour or two, Larry and Tom had a terrific time, snorkeling about a mile out in the bay. Finally they decided to grab some lunch, so they swam back to shore. As Larry reached for the keys to the car (and the condo) he realized THE KEY RING WAS NOT IN HIS POCKET. The keys were gone!

Larry and Tom swam back out into the bay and for over an hour they searched almost hysterically, peering down into the water, trying to spot the keys on the ocean floor. Back and forth they swam, retracing all the places they thought they had been—but no keys.

Exhausted, they returned to the little shack on the beach where they had rented their snorkeling equipment.

"Has anyone turned in any lost keys?" Larry frantically asked the proprietor. He promptly pulled down a huge glass jar of car keys, obviously collected over many months from many similar tourist mishaps. But as he pointed to the jar he said, "I've got a whole jar full of lost keys, but none were turned in today."

Larry was desperate. Because his wallet was locked up in the car, he had no money to even make a telephone call to the car-rental agency to see if they could make him another car key. He finally hiked up to a hotel about a half a mile away and explained his situation. A kind hotel clerk let him use a phone to call the car-rental agency, which told him a spare key could be made but he would have to come and get it. That made no sense to Larry since he had NO WAY TO GET THERE. The car-rental agency suggested he could take a taxi to their office.

Larry reminded them he had no wallet; then he suggested, "Why don't you send me a duplicate key with a taxi cab driver? Then I can open the car, get my wallet, and pay the cab fare."

The car-rental agency said that would be acceptable, but it would take a couple of hours to have the duplicate key made and then have it driven over to him.

Larry paced up and down, waiting for the cab and wondering how in the world he could explain the loss of the condo key to the manager of the condominium complex. Meanwhile, Tom, a comparatively new Christian, just kept saying, "Hang on, Larry, just trust the Lord. Those keys will show up."

"Are you kidding?" Larry replied. "Don't you know that I lost them at least a mile out in the OCEAN? How would you expect we could ever get them back? My mom will just die when she finds out we have lost those keys to the condo, not to mention the car. And how will we get in the condo? I don't even know the owner's name, and it's a big place with lots of units—the manager won't know who we are."

Relax, All We Need Is a Miracle

Tom persisted in believing that miracles do happen and God would answer their prayers. But all Larry could say was, "Get REAL! Do you think some guardian angel is going to fly those keys back here from the bottom of the ocean? What if they really do have to re-key the whole place, just as my mom said they would? I'm telling you, this is big trouble and it's going to be expensive . . ."

Larry kept fretting about his loss, waiting for the cab to come with the key to the rental car. At that moment he would have agreed with the motto that says:

THINGS AREN'T AS BAD AS THEY SEEM . . .
THEY'RE WORSE!

The hours dragged by with frustrated, stressed-out Larry pacing in circles and confident Tom just "trusting the Lord." There was no money for lunch, no money to call anyone, no nothing—only their beach towels and Tom's firm conviction that God would answer their prayers to find the keys.

As time ticked slowly on, the boys waited near the rental shack on the beach, anxiously watching for the cab to come with the key to the rental car. Suddenly Larry heard a guy hollering, "Hey, aren't you the guy who lost your keys in the ocean this morning?"

Larry looked up and saw the proprietor of the rental shack leaning out his window, and shouting toward them. He ran quickly over to the office where the man dangled a set of keys— THE KEYS THAT LARRY HAD LOST OVER A MILE OUT IN THE OCEAN!

Larry was so amazed he could hardly talk. "How . . . how . . . how did you get THESE?"

"Well, some people who rented scuba diving gear found them on the ocean floor. They just now turned them in and I had a feeling they might be yours. They found them about a mile out from the beach."

Larry thanked the man profusely, took the keys, and went back over to where Tom was waiting. He admits he was tempted to tell Tom that a big fish had swallowed the keys, that a lady in a restaurant was eating the fish and had found them and . . .

On second thought, he decided against that kind of fish story and just held up the key ring. When Tom saw the keys, he smiled and said, "See? I knew the Lord would answer our prayers . . ."

Next Larry tried to call the car-rental agency to cancel the spare key, but they told him the cab was already on the way. The cab pulled up just a few minutes later and Larry paid for the key as well as the taxi—a total of $75.

The cost of getting the key (which he no longer needed) was one thing, but the bigger cost was the anxiety he had experienced all afternoon, worrying about what would happen. Meanwhile, Tom had kept calm. He waited for his miracle and it WAS, indeed, a miracle.

So that's why Larry kept that shiny new gold key in the ashtray of the car, just to remind him of that day when a guardian angel was looking over his shoulder and something he knew was lost forever had come back to him. Now when he gets in stressful situations—heavy traffic, for example—he just takes out that key and remembers it's far better to say a prayer, trust the Lord, and relax. It is a symbol of God's care for him.

When Hope Is Deferred, Pray Harder

Larry's car key adventure makes a good point about trusting in God's care, but at the same time, for many folks there are times when the keys AREN'T found, when the miracle DOESN'T happen. Actually, however, that's when we REALLY need to turn our problems over to God. That's when we need to pray EVEN MORE than we ever have before.

When Larry disappeared into the gay lifestyle and was gone for years with no word, I went through what I call a "hope-deferred" period. As King Solomon said, "Hope deferred makes the heart sick" (Prov. 13:12 TLB). I could have driven myself and everyone around me crazy if I thought each day was supposed to include a miracle. But day after day went by, and nothing seemed to happen. It took eleven years for our hopes to be realized and to experience the joy of having our son return home to ask forgiveness for the pain he had caused us. Then the rest of Proverbs 13:12 was ours: "when dreams come true at last, there is life and joy."

While living in a hope-deferred set of parentheses we have to realize that it often takes years before our prayers are answered, but that doesn't stop us from living expectantly through each day knowing God is still in control of it all. He will answer our prayers in His perfect timing. When our hope is deferred, we must remember:

GOD NEVER HAS TO SAY, "OOPS!"

Did you ever think of your life, with all the mistakes and sins of the past, as being much like the tangles in a ball of yarn? When hope is deferred, it's a comfort to know we can get up and face each day by putting ourselves and our loved ones in His hands, knowing that in His loving mercy He will untangle it all.

You could never hope to straighten out a mess you're facing, but you don't have to. If there is one message I have tried to communicate in this book, it is this:

PLACE YOUR CHILD IN GOD'S HANDS
AND RELEASE THE LOAD TO HIM.

John White is the author of many fine books, but perhaps his most heartfelt writing is *Parents in Pain* because Dr. White is a parent who knows what pain is like. When one of his sons wound up in jail, he wrote an article that contains many good points, including the disturbing thought that you must allow your children to face tragedy and even death by allowing them to live with the consequences of their own actions. White believes relinquishment means trusting God with your children, rather than relying on your own ability to manage their lives. Relinquishment means giving up your delusions about your own power to determine the destinies of your children.

Turning to the parable of the Prodigal Son, White observes that we must be to our children what God the Father is to each of us. We must let our children go and then never give up loving them. He writes:

> Hardest of all is to share the pain with the Father, to let our puddle of sorrow flow into His great ocean of woe. It is (in the case of our finite minds) to allow faith, hope, and love to go on living. This is what the father of the prodigal did.
>
> How do I know? Listen to what Jesus tells us:
>
> But while he was still a long way off, his father saw him and was filled with compassion for him; he ran to his son, threw his arms around him and kissed him (see Lk. 15:20).
>
> You don't identify your son when he is "still a long way off" unless you happen to be looking for him, staring at the horizon in hope. Either you give up trying, because the pain is too great, or else faith, hope and love refuse to die in you, and you go on looking, looking until you spot the prodigal in the distance. And then you run—run until you have him safe in your arms.
>
> That is how God is with us. He lets us choose. Then He swallows His pain and waits.
>
> Let's fall on our faces before Him. Let's ask Him to search our parental hearts and make them like His own.[2]

Only God Can Untangle Your Threads

John White's thoughts about the parable of the Prodigal Son remind me that God alone can untangle the threads of our lives. What a joy and comfort it can be for us to drop all of them into His hands and then LEAVE them there! A mother with a son in the gay lifestyle wrote:

> I have come in this past year to a better acceptance of my 24-year-old son and I would like to share this with you. It is a different kind of acceptance, perhaps based on my teaching of all kinds of physically and emotionally handicapped children and my work with their parents.
>
> I have come to accept homosexuality as a handicap. For the past four years, I was just angry that my son had chosen this path and only wanted him to CHANGE. I now feel that just as some physically handicapped people are able to conquer or rather rise above the handicap, so SOME homosexuals are able to. But many of the children I have worked with were also weak emotionally and just not able to handle their infirmities. As a teacher, I have worked around the problem to try to give the child as normal a life as possible. In time, I didn't even see the outward child but related to the humanness which is God-given to all.
>
> While I still often yearn for normal sexuality in my son, this is, in reality, a rejection of him. Because, like it or not, this is his present orientation. This must be a very difficult "place" for him to be and my role as his mother is not to make his life any harder. I no longer look for the miracle each time I'm with him, and I feel better when I do spend time with him. Perhaps these thoughts might be helpful to some other parents.

Note that this mom talks about her son's "present orientation." Isn't that true of all of us? We are all in some kind of present orientation, and we are all in a change process that means growing and becoming what God wants us to be. I especially like this mom's concept about learning how to enjoy pleasant times with her son and not constantly straining to see some sign of change. After all, only God can bring about any shift of behavior anyway. And, as she says, she might as well relax and enjoy the time they have together.

How to Pray for a Rebel

Another question I often get from folks who are struggling with a son, daughter, close relative, or friend involved in a self-destructive lifestyle, is:

How are we to pray about this? We pray and God doesn't seem to answer. We wonder if God even cares.

The following thoughts about prayer are adapted from a paper by my good friend, Bob Davies, of the Love in Action organization in San Rafael, California. If your loved one is in rebellion, remember:

- There is a natural law of cause and effect that all of us take for granted. This law means that every action we take has some kind of consequence. If our action is in agreement with the way God created us to live, we reap good results. If it is contrary to God's plan, the effects can be painful. This principle is so obvious, and yet so many times we actually work against it.

- In His love, God allows painful consequences to occur in a person's life as a result of his rebellion. Sometimes, it simply takes time until rebellious actions begin to bear sour fruit. We must be patient, and allow that time to pass. There is NOTHING that we can do to hurry this process, except to recognize what is happening and to allow the Lord to work.

- The built-in results of sinful actions are one of the strongest deterrents to continued sin. So don't pray that God will remove the consequences of your loved one's rebellion! And don't thwart God's purposes by removing them yourself. For example, the worst thing you can do for your wayward son (or daughter) is to send him all the money he wants when he has wasted his finances on weekend parties for all his gay friends.

• God may work in totally unexpected ways to bring an end to rebellion. Probably the way God will work in the situation is not any way that you have thought of. "For My thoughts are not your thoughts, neither are your way My ways," declares the Lord in Isaiah 55:8. We can only see a minute fraction of the whole situation; God sees all of it.

• Pray that God will work supernaturally, but be prepared! The weeks, months, even years that the person you are praying for is in rebellion may seem like forever. So pray for God's supernatural protection during your friend or relative's rebellion. God may still bring some hair-raising consequences into their life. Their health may suffer dreadfully. . . . But God is still at work—trust Him!

It is vitally important to realize that the final choice whether to serve God or self is up to the person involved in sin. God has given us a free will, and no one has ever been dragged into submission to the Lord against his will. You cannot make that choice for your child. To really grasp this principle will relieve you of much misunderstanding and frustration with God's ways.[3]

After I let go of Larry by praying "Whatever, Lord!" up there on that viaduct, God took me at my word and tested me to see if I really meant it. Letting go is one thing, but then you discover you have to keep turning it over to God in faith *every day*.

After Larry left a second time, I threw myself into my Spatula ministry with renewed energy. Folks would come up to me and ask, "And how is your family now?"

And I would answer, "Well, my two sons have not risen from the dead and my third son has disowned us, changed his name, and never wants to see us again. That doesn't sound like much of a victory, but two years ago when I said, 'Whatever, Lord!' I really meant it. So I'm still trusting God to bring our son back. God only gives the score on a life when the game is over, and the game ain't over *yet* with my kid."

Although my hope was deferred, I NEVER LOST HOPE. I clung to the belief that someday the values I had built into Larry would surface, and God would bring conviction to his heart. After eleven years that is just what happened.

During all those years, God was fine-tuning me for the ministry He has given me to do. While I was in that deferred-hope situation, I learned much about developing a "TURN-IT-OVER" attitude. And in His good timing, He brought us through to life and joy.

What Is a Turn-It-Over Attitude?

Recently a friend sent me a tape of a message preached by the Reverend Bruce Larson based on his best-selling book, *There's A Lot More to Health Than Not Being Sick* (Word, 1981). In his message Larson mentioned visiting the Menninger Foundation and asking members of its staff, "What is the single most important ingredient in your treatment here?"

The doctors answered, "We know it's hope. We don't know how it comes or how to give it to people, but we know that when people get hope, they get well."

"What does hope look like?" Larson asked next.

These skilled medical doctors told him they could tell almost immediately when patients suddenly turned the corner and realized they did not have to go on as they had before. As Larson put it in his message:

HOPE MEANS YOU ARE NO LONGER A PRISONER
OF YOUR TRACK RECORD.

I continually get letters from folks who have learned the meaning of hope. Their track record may sound depressing, but they know they are not prisoners. Instead, they are free. One mom put it this way:

> You came into my life when my 18-year-old son attempted suicide in November. I'm glad to report that he's doing fine. The Lord made it clear to me that this is not <u>who my son is</u> and that we must not let this spontaneous act define him. Everybody hits bottom, but it's what happens next that's really important. The Lord has shown me that I can be proud and thankful for the toughness he showed in healing, instead of focusing on the fact of what happened.
>
> I still have "panic attacks" but try to stand on raw faith and just decide to trust both him and the Lord.

Turning It Over Doesn't Mean You Quit Trying

In that same message, Larson went on to ask a provocative question: "Do you have the courage to be happy?"

I hear from so many folks who understand that a turn-it-over attitude doesn't mean you put your feet up and quit trying. Two of my favorite verses are Philippians 2:12–13:

The secret to success is to stay cool and calm on top and paddle like crazy underneath.

"Therefore . . . work out your own salvation with fear and trembling; for it is God who works in you both to will and to do for His good pleasure" (NKJV). That sums up a principle for living that is a sure-fire combination for success:

PRAY AS IF EVERYTHING DEPENDED ON GOD
AND WORK AS IF EVERYTHING DEPENDED ON YOU.

There is an old story that illustrates this principle very well. It seems that two frogs were playing on the rafters of a dairy farm one night and they fell into adjoining pails of cream. Both frogs scrambled for survival, but one fought longer and harder, and stayed the course.

When the farmer came in the next morning, he found one frog floating on the top of a pail of cream, dead; and the other frog standing on a cake of butter—exhausted, but happy to be alive.

Moral: When we let problems overwhelm us, when we stop jumping and hopping and scrambling for survival, we stop living. But when we hang in there and fight the good fight we end up on a cake of butter.

One mom whose gay son causes her all kinds of hurt is a beautiful illustration of this frog story. In a letter to me, she admitted that things haven't been so good lately. Although her son lives in the next block, she sees him seldom. For the past year, he has missed her birthday and Easter, although he did manage to send a Mother's Day card that arrived the following week.

But this mother hasn't let it get her down, as her letter described:

> I want to share something that the Lord led me to see in the Bible. So often, holidays are ruined for me because I want a family like other people have. Nonetheless there are a lot of caring people in my life: a wonderful young mother who lived here as a student many years ago and is like a daughter to me, and people from a Bible study who have become very close to me and many others. But, like David in 2 Samuel

18:33, I continued to grieve for the lost life of my son while I made my friends feel that no one was as important to me as he was.

Then God, like Joab did to David, made me see, as you said in your book, that the sin of one person was ruining my life. That made all the difference in my Mother's Day. I sent cards to all the first-time mothers I knew and to my young friends who care about me when it hurts. I accepted a dinner invitation, took lilacs and candy to my hostess, a lady in her eighties, and had a great day. It was the nicest Mother's Day in many years.

Hope Equals Endless Possibilities

According to Bruce Larson, hope also means being excited about your future because you believe God sets you free from your past mistakes. Hope has you saying, "I can't wait to get up in the morning." In fact, if you have the habit of turning all your problems over to God at day's end, you will be ready for whatever tomorrow may bring. As Larson puts it:

WHEN JESUS CHRIST IS THERE
LIFE HAS INFINITE POSSIBILITIES.

I'm big on optimism and thinking positively, but those aren't the real ingredients of hope. Hope comes out of knowing to whom you belong and knowing that He is in control.

When Tim was in college, he worked for one of the most prestigious mortuaries in Southern California. One of his chief duties was driving the grieving family to the grave site in a rose-colored limousine and, if they had no minister to preside, he would also conduct a brief service by reading some words of comfort from a prepared text.

One day I came home and found the limousine, with the familiar mortuary monogram on the side, parked in our driveway. Tim was supposed to be working, so I wondered what had

brought him home during that hour of the day. I went into the
house, and found him sitting forlornly at the kitchen table.
When he saw me, he jumped up, ran over, and hugged me
tightly.

I wondered what on earth had prompted all this attention,
but then Tim explained. He had been conducting a funeral service that morning and, as he read from his prepared text, he
looked down and saw the "loved one" in the casket. She looked
so much like me—same coloring and same appearance—that
he could hardly continue with the service. Even though he
knew it wasn't his mother, he still had a lump swelling up in his
throat.

As soon as the service was over, he dashed home to be sure
"Everything was okay." I'm not quite sure why this made such
an impression on Tim. He had been brought up in the church
and had made a decision for Christ while still a very young
child. He had been to many summer church camps and had
attended church all his life, but he always concerned us because
his faith just didn't seem real to him. He wasn't rebellious; he
was just sort of "flat" and never very excited about being a
Christian.

Perhaps seeing someone who looked like his mother lying in
a coffin caused Tim to stop and realize that death would touch
his own family someday—that life is fleeting and none of us
lasts forever.

It could well be that this unsettling experience helped prepare Tim for the encounter he would have later with a man
named Bill Pritchard, whose counsel helped him reach a new
level of spiritual understanding and commitment that he'd
never had before. A few months later, Tim went into training
with the sheriff's department, and part of that training included
spending time guarding prisoners at one of the "honor farms"
north of Los Angeles. One night he penned a letter to Bill
Pritchard, part of which said:

> This place reminds me of a Marine boot camp, and every
> officer is a drill instructor. You can't really sit down and talk

with these inmates, but I knew God would provide a way for me to witness to some of them. I got a couple of dozen booklets (*The Four Spiritual Laws*, etc.) and distributed them among the barracks. It gave me a good feeling when I walked into the barracks after reveille to see Hell's Angels and Black Panthers lying on their bunks reading these booklets. I could get fired for passing out literature, but it would be well worth it to know that another person received eternal life. . . .

Less than six months later, Tim's own life was snuffed out on the Alaska Highway. The bodies of Tim and his friend, Ron, were shipped home, and a few days later we held a memorial service that was attended by nearly a thousand people. We printed bright green bookmarks, about a thousand with Tim's picture and another thousand with Ron's picture, and beneath the photos was the poem "Safely Home," which says, in part:

> I am home in Heaven, dear ones;
>   All's so happy, all's so bright!
> There's perfect joy and beauty
>   In this everlasting light.
>
> All the pain and grief are over,
>   Every restless tossing passed;
> I am now at peace forever,
>   Safely home in Heaven at last.
> . . . .
> Then you must not grieve so sorely,
>   For I love you dearly still;
> Try to look beyond earth's shadows,
>   Pray to trust our Father's will.
>
> There is work still waiting for you,
>   So you must not idle stand;
> Do your work while life remaineth—
>   You shall rest in Jesus' land.

When that work is all complete,
He will gently call you home;
Oh, the rapture of the meeting!
Oh, the joy to see you come![4]

Why Tim had to die just when his own faith was at a new level is one of the secret things I'll have to leave with God, but even in his death he left many folks with new hope for their lives. Someone has said, "Hope is not the conviction that something will turn out well, but the certainty that something makes sense, regardless of how it turns out."

Ralph Waldo Emerson wrote:

One of the illusions of life is that the present hour is not the critical, decisive hour. Write it on your heart that every day is the best day of the year. He only is rich who owns the day, and no one owns the day who allows it to be invaded with worry, fret and anxiety. Finish every day and be done with it. You have done what you could.

And for the Christian I would add, "Trust God with what was undone or even done incorrectly. In His good time, He will make it right."

Gloomee Busters

The measure of success is
not whether you have
a tough problem
to deal with, but whether
it's the same problem
you had last year.
—John Foster Dulles

□ □ □

You are struggling . . .
   I see it,
      I feel it,
         I hurt for you.
But I must tell you, dear friend,
I believe with all my heart
   that you will emerge
      somehow wiser, stronger,
         and more aware.
Hold on to that thought,
   tuck it away in a
      corner of your heart
   until the hurt melts enough
      for the learning to have
         meaning.[5]

Worry Defined

Worry is the senseless process of using today to clutter up
tomorrow's opportunities with leftover problems from yesterday.

When someone
says,
"Life is hard,"
ask them,
"Compared to what?"

I believe the nicest and sweetest days are not those on
which anything very splendid or wonderful or exciting
happens, but just those that bring simple little pleasures,
following one another softly, like pearls slipping off a string.[6]

STEADFAST HEART

I've dreamed many dreams that never came true.
I've seen them vanish at dawn.
But I've realized enough of my dreams, thank God,
To make me want to dream on.

I've prayed many prayers when no answer came,
Though I waited patient and long,
But answers have come to enough of my prayers
To make me keep praying on.

I've trusted many a friend that failed,
And left me to weep alone,
But I've found enough of my friends true blue,
To make me keep trusting on.

I've sown many seed that fell by the way
For the birds to feed upon,
But I've held enough golden sheaves in my hands,
To make me keep sowing on.

I've drained the cup of disappointment and pain
And gone many days without song,
But I've sipped enough nectar from the roses of life
To make me want to live on.

—Source unknown

□   □   □

GOODNIGHT, DEAR GOD

The sun has gone down from the sky
    And peace of night is drawing nigh.
I pray, Dear God, my soul You'll keep
    While in Your loving arms I sleep.
Forgive the things I did today
    When from Your glorious path I'd stray.
And as I slumber through the night
    Please take my hand and hold it tight.
And when I awake to a bright new morn,
    Restored, refreshed, renewed, reborn,
I'll try again, Dear God, to be
    The person You would hope of me.

—Source unknown

□   □   □

I run in the path of your commands,
  for You have set my heart free.
                              (Ps. 119:32 NIV)

Always Take Your Rainbow with You!

After the darkness,
the daylight shines through
After the showers,
the rainbow's in view
After life's heartaches,
there comes from above
The peace and the comfort
of God's healing love.
—Kristone

Before closing the lid on the gloomees box, I want to share some final thoughts with you that I came across as I was straightening my Joy Room the other day. I ran across a little sign that says:

AMUSING GRACE . . .
HOW SWEET THE SOUND OF LAUGHTER.

The more I thought about that, the more I realized we need all the *amusing* grace we can get from God's amazing, inexhaustible supply. If you're like me, you've learned that some days you can be confident you will get through it, but on other days, you're back to square one. As somebody said,

> CONFIDENCE IS WHAT YOU HAVE
> WHEN YOU DON'T REALLY UNDERSTAND
> THE SITUATION.

The Case of the Missing Cotton Picker

Several years ago I received a call from a lady with a problem and I was "confident" I knew the answer—until I realized I didn't understand the problem!

This darling mother called me from Arizona, exasperated because her gay daughter had promised to come to their ranch and feed the animals and watch over the place while she and her husband were going to another ranch to pick cotton. Instead of minding the ranch for a few days as she had promised, the gay daughter wanted to go off with her lesbian friend, and the parents had no one who could take her place on such short notice. Furthermore, the mother said it was imperative that they take all nine of their cotton pickers to the other ranch to make sure the cotton got picked.

Well, it all sounded OBVIOUS to me. I told this mom that it would be simple to just leave one of the cotton pickers there to tend the ranch and use the other eight cotton pickers to do the job. Wouldn't this solve the problem rather easily?

Fortunately, the woman was gracious and, realizing I was not a farm girl, she patiently explained to me that cotton pickers are not PEOPLE; they are MACHINES that cost ninety thousand dollars apiece!

Oh well, win a few, lose a few! Having a sense of humor is a requisite for working in this ministry, or for just living in this zoo we call the world today. So I hope you'll keep yours in working order—your sense of humor, of course, not the zoo. There is no better way to keep your sense of humor than to remember that God's grace—His love, mercy, and help—is ALWAYS available.

Grace Is God—in the Flesh

Grace is one of those "theological" words that we say we believe in and even count on, but sometimes it's good to consider what grace really *does* mean in a world where the gloomees are always out to get you. As Lewis Smedes says, God's grace can make life all RIGHT despite the fact that everything is obviously all WRONG . . . Grace is the reality of God entering history—and our lives—to make things right at the very center:

> He came as a living Person called Jesus, talking and hurting and dying and coming to life again; His mission was to bring grace to the world, and so in deepest reality to make it All Right precisely when things are all wrong. Grace? It is shorthand for everything that God is and does for us in our tired and sinful broken lives.[1]

Grace does not stand for an escape mechanism, some kind of all-expense-paid trip to Disneyland because God knows we can't afford to go ourselves. Grace has nothing to do with Disneylands, Fantasy Islands, magical cures, or instant solutions. As Smedes says,

> Grace is rather an amazing power to look earthy reality full in the face, see its sad and tragic edges, feel its cruel cuts, join in the primeval chorus against its outrageous unfairness, and yet feel in your deepest being that it is good and right for you to be alive on God's good earth.[2]

You may have seen the acrostic on grace that puts it all in perspective:

> God's
> Riches
> At
> Christ's
> Expense

Jesus never used the word *grace*. God left that for Paul, but if you want to describe grace in one word it is *Jesus*.

Grace (Jesus) is the answer for our guilt and failure.

Grace (Jesus) is the strength we need to cope with life.

Grace (Jesus) is the promise that gives us the hope that keeps us going.

The Gloomees Thrive on Guilt

Most dangerous of all the gloomees that lie in wait to drag us down is guilt, that pervading feeling that we haven't measured up to our own standards, not to mention God's. Almost daily I hear from parents who are downhearted and guilt-ridden. Their children, usually grown adults themselves, have disappointed them and they don't understand what happened. For example:

> Our 17-year-old son just decided he couldn't go to high school here because (in his own words) ". . . the teachers hate me and you don't stick up for me and, and, and . . ." He went to live with my brother and his family in North Dakota. He is the baby and I am feeling like a failure. He has two older brothers. The 25-year-old moved out with our blessings in May, but now he is keeping company with a married woman and quit church.

Now, it would be easy to look at a situation like this one and say, "Oh, I see the problem—these parents were TOO STRICT." Or perhaps we could quickly surmise, "Yes, it's obvious what happened here—PERMISSIVENESS. They were far too lenient."

It's simple to see the answer to someone else's problem. We can wrap up our "solution" in a neat little package of slick answers and present it to them with smug assurance.

But when you're IN that hurting family, there are no slick answers. I pray with hurting parents and I hurt with them, as well. I feel their frustration and their pain. I speak and write for hurting parents who haven't found any Band-Aid solutions. Often they have sought help from the experts, the specialists, and the authorities, but they have found no answers that meet real needs.

They've heard all the cozy Christian phrases such as, "Just praise the Lord," or "You can give it all to Jesus." Please understand, there is nothing wrong with praising God or giving it all to Jesus, but it's all too easy to push pat answers on others without being sensitive to their problem. I have done it myself and I have learned to use extreme care in dealing with hurting folks. I am sure that sometimes I still miss the mark, but I can only ask forgiveness and throw myself at the mercy of God's grace.

When everything goes wrong and the bottom drops out, we are overwhelmed with a barrage of emotions: panic, frustration, anger, fear, and shame, all of which are just the beginning of the final death blow called guilt. You condemn yourself and then you begin to hate yourself as you watch your family spinning out of control. One guilt-burdened mom says it with words that are so gut-level honest they speak for many parents I know:

> It has only been a month since our son sat and defended homosexuality. He would never come right out and say he was involved—but my husband and I agree he might as well have. . . . Did we just think we were a happy family with normal problems? I ask myself. I cannot get past the guilt. I always loved my children—but I was too domineering, too outspoken—my husband says I am focusing only on my faults and magnifying them. . . . I don't see how mothers/ fathers (mostly mothers) get out from under the cloud of guilt—and why should we—if we have had anything to do with it? If mothers help cause this—then we deserve to suffer forever. I've read your books—I still don't know how you got away from the guilt enough to be happy. My heart is like lead in my chest.

How can this dear mom get rid of her lead-heavy load of guilt? She doesn't even have positive confirmation her son is a homosexual, yet she is condemning herself and wondering how I got free from guilt over my own son. When a parent feels this overwhelmed, there is only that one, positive answer: *God only knows*—and what God has to offer is His grace.

I can only hope this mother won't multiply her guilt feelings by lashing out at her son as I did at mine. I said many harsh things to Larry in the beginning; my words were sharp and cutting. I didn't listen to him as he tried to tell me what his hurts were. I just blasted him with a recital of my own feelings.

Our kids don't need our condemnation. What they do need is our encouragement to be open and honest with us. They need to know that, yes, we are hurt, and yes, we are disappointed, but we can honestly share these feelings without being destructive. Jesus met people right where they were, whatever their condition. He didn't show them sympathy. He didn't necessarily show them mercy. But He ALWAYS showed them grace.

Amazing Grace from the IRS

Not long ago I saw grace demonstrated in a most unlikely setting—the INTERNAL REVENUE SERVICE. Julia had a son in trouble, and in desperation she came to our Spatula support group for help. We became good friends and shortly thereafter she came to know Christ. Overnight we saw big changes in her life.

Then one hot summer day she called with the news that she was to be audited by the IRS! Tearfully she confessed to me that she had lied on her prior year's income tax return, saying she had given large amounts to an orphanage in Mexico. Now they were calling her in to a local IRS office to document her records. There was only one problem: this orphanage didn't even exist!

As we talked, she asked me to go with her when she was audited. What good could I possibly do except give moral support? I agreed to go, however, and when we got to the IRS office, we just sat in the car a moment and prayed together. I prayed that whoever we talked to would show MERCY. Julia was not expecting any kind of pardon, but a little mercy would be most welcome. She was truly repentant for what she had done. It had all happened before she had become a Christian, but now her past sins had caught up with her.

Julia's sweet prayer for forgiveness was touching. This was right where the rubber meets the road, no wobble room here. Julia definitely repented of that deception and wanted to make things right.

We walked into the IRS office and sat waiting until Julia's name was called. The income-tax examiner who would handle her case ushered us into a tiny cubicle. As I looked around, I noticed a fish sign on her calendar. Could it BE? Was this lady a Christian?

Julia had already decided to come clean and she didn't hesitate: "I wasn't a Christian last year, and when we filled out the tax form I lied. I put down that we gave money to this orphanage in Mexico. But that was all a lie because the orphanage is nonexistent, and I am truly sorry and I have asked God to forgive me. I felt heavy conviction about it even before I got your notice to come in and be audited, but I am here to tell the truth. Actually, all the deductions for contributions I claimed are false; I never gave anything to any charity last year."

Julia choked out her confession between tears, then continued to sob quietly.

The IRS examiner had listened without interrupting. Now she reached out, patted Julia on the shoulder, and said, "God forgives you for that. Now, let's see how we can work all this out . . ."

She began to go over Julia's income tax report for the prior year and carefully asked questions about other areas where there might be deductions. Her questions brought out some things Julia hadn't even thought were legitimate. Before we knew it, the woman had it all worked out. Julia did not owe a dime, even though the trumped-up deductions had all been removed from the tax report.

We both thanked the woman profusely. I gave her a hug and said, "I noticed the little fish sign on your calendar. We're Christians, too, and we're so glad God led us to you today."

Our IRS friend smiled, but maintained her official government decorum. She said she understood, but that she had another appointment soon and that our time was up. I think perhaps she would have liked to have talked longer, but she knew her supervisor could look in and wonder what all this hugging and crying was about.

Julia and I left the IRS offices rejoicing. We sat out in the car while Julia wept tears of joy for several minutes. I couldn't help but note the difference. Before we had gone in we had sat in the car, praying for MERCY, and now we were sitting there thanking the Lord that Julia had received GRACE.

The best part about Julia's story is not that she "got off" and didn't have to go to jail or pay some huge fine. The best part is what the lady said after Julia sincerely confessed what she had done wrong:

"God forgives you . . . now let's see how we can work all this out . . ."

Isn't that just like the Lord? When we come to Him in true repentance, asking for forgiveness, He says, *"Of course* I forgive you. Now let's see what we can do—*together."*

Grace Gives Us a Helping Hand

Before Christ gave grace its full meaning through His death on the cross, the Old Testament referred to grace with the Hebrew word *hen,* meaning ". . . the compassionate response of one who is able to help another person in need." Whenever we are unable to deal with life, we ask for help in one way or another. The Psalms can give us a great example of how this works as we see the psalmist crying out for help because of:

Distress—Psalm 4:1; 31:9
Agony—Psalm 6:2
Persecution by enemies—Psalm 19:13; 56:1
Loneliness and affliction—Psalm 25:16
Disaster—Psalm 57:1
The contempt of others—Psalm 123:3
Weakness and trouble—Psalm 41:1; 86:16
Sin itself—Psalm 51:1

All of the above are only a part of what theologians call the "human condition" that holds all of us in bondage. As Bible scholar Larry Richards put it:

> Only God can act to release us and enable us to overcome the foes within us and around us.
> But God is Who He is. He is compassionate and loving. We are confident that when we call on God, He will respond. He will act, not because we merit help, but because He recognizes our desperate need and love moves Him to exercise His power to meet our need. This indeed is grace![3]

The Mail Is Full of God's Grace

The postman continues to bring me stories of how people find themselves facing distress, disaster, loneliness, and all those other gloomees faced by the psalmist. But somehow God's grace sees them through. They find the strength to handle the situation. One mother wrote to say:

> I have two adopted sons, and the 20-year-old is having homosexual feelings. My husband and I are really appalled by the whole thing but we are trying to work with him and help him in every way we can. This is kind of like our worst nightmare come true.
> Our 15-year-old is going through a rebellion that is very scary. He has run away from home, broken nearly every window in our house, lived with friends for a short time and is now at home doing quite well, I think. We have taken him out of public school and I am now home schooling him, as he was failing everything in school and getting mixed up with the wrong crowd. We are working together and with the Lord to work out our family problems, but books like yours really help, it's great knowing what I am feeling is shared with others.

Sometimes grace can be found in the strangest places, even on a foggy highway. My friend, Evelyn Heinz, who is an author and poet, shared a fabulous episode of grace she had experienced. She faced a very difficult trip of 125 miles one way to visit her dying mother. The weather was supposed to be clear, but the night before it changed radically, and the next morning she had to start out in the rain and fog. Her letter continued:

> The night before, I read one meditation from a little book . . ."I am sending an angel ahead of you to guard you along the way. . . ." That verse eased my thoughts for the morning ride. To my surprise, my angel (angels) came in human form under a white Winnebago camper. God put him ahead of me to keep my speed down and I followed his camper through the fog. Then, before he turned, another angel in human form came ahead of me, this time in a black van with three initials on its out-of-state license, EMH. Barbara those are mine! Evelyn Marie Heinz! The fog was clearing, the van turned and the rest of the 60-some-odd miles were clear!
>
> My visit with my mother went very compassionately, the time moved too swiftly, but I felt the "JOY" of being with her. Hiding my tears, I held her hand and kissed her forehead and we exchanged "I love yous" before it came time for me to go. Her last words were, "Be careful on the drive home. I'll be praying for you!" I smiled and said, "Mom, I'll be praying for you too."

We Live from Hope to Hope

I've given away several copies of Lewis Smedes's fine book, *How Can It Be All Right When Everything Is All Wrong?* because I love how he helps his readers discover hope through the gift of grace. In his introduction, Smedes says he wrote this book for people who are still trying hard to believe in God even though a hundred voices inside are telling them to stop believing. He confesses that, at times, his faith has waned and that his words are filtered "through many years of believing against the grain."

Believing doesn't come easy for Smedes because many people he cares about hurt too much. People close to him have died of cancer "too soon," despite his fervent prayers to take away the pain. He's had friends whose marriages have turned into battlefields as their children have gone through all kinds of "mini-hells." Smedes admits, "God does not do many miracles for my crowd."

There are folks in the Spatula crowd who are short on miracles too. I received an eight-page letter from a mother who apparently just can't take any more:

> Why has my life been so awful? I accepted Christ when I was twelve. I have now so many hurts, so many injustices—Why? I would commit suicide, but God would condemn me to hell. I sometimes wonder if hell wouldn't be better than this life. Our finances are a wreck, my health is a wreck, I don't believe my husband really believes or comprehends my pain. I don't feel loved. God may say all those great things in our Bible, but He doesn't really carry them out to all. . . . I'm happy for you. You are one of the chosen ones—I'm not—I really am not a pessimist, just have become realistic.
>
> You don't have to pray for me, God has dealt all the blows I need. . . . I just don't know how much longer I can *continue to function.* Please don't promise happy futures for everyone who believes. It just doesn't happen. I'm afraid I don't fit anywhere.

This precious mother sounds like she can't be sure if life is passing her by or running her over. She says she believes I am one of the "chosen ones," but I am no more chosen than she is. I HAVE chosen to *trust in God's grace,* and THAT is what has brought me through the fiery trials. As Lewis Smedes puts it:

> Grace does come. . . . Grace happens to me when I feel a surge of honest joy that makes me glad to be alive in spite of valid reasons for feeling terrible. . . . Grace is the gift of feeling sure that our future, even our dying, is going to turn out more splendidly than we dare imagine. Grace is the feeling of hope.[4]

I have mentioned hope several times in this book because, when the gloomees close in *hope is really all we have.* As Jean Kerr put it,

> HOPE IS A FEELING YOU HAVE
> THAT THE FEELING YOU HAVE ISN'T PERMANENT.

As I was working on these final chapters, I received a letter from a mother whose words so nicely describe how grace is the feeling of hope:

> It seems our last ten years have sort of been one situation on top of another. In that time God has taught me a great deal. For one thing I learned to thank Him for "all things" and MEAN it (something I had tried to do, but never was quite able to carry off). He taught me what it means to really, truly, totally trust Him! I have always trusted Him, but never with the kind of trust I now have. He taught me that I can endure many things I would have never dreamed I could do without losing my sanity, and He showed me how to be happy while I was going through the trial.

This mother closes her letter with the assurance that she knows that God holds her hand and walks day by day through each circumstance with her. Then she adds a thought that we all need to burn into our hearts:

> FAITH NEVER KNOWS WHERE IT IS BEING LED,
> BUT IT LOVES THE ONE WHO IS LEADING.

God's Grace Paints the Rainbow

Have you ever thought of how a rainbow is a perfect picture of God's grace? Life's storms may buffet us, ripping apart our plans, and flooding us with multiplied problems, many of which are of our own making. But grace is God's promise that we will not be destroyed, just as a rainbow was His promise that He would never again send a flood to devastate the earth.[5]

Because rain is in such short supply in Southern California, we don't see many rainbows, but when one does appear, I try to take full advantage of its beautiful hues and colors. Phyllis Eger tells a lovely little story about how a phone call interrupted her dinner preparations as a neighbor told her to hurry outside to see the most beautiful rainbow in the eastern sky. She turned off her stove and dashed outside, and there it was—a double arc of lovely colors, pink, lavender, blue, and gold.

She quickly called her mother who lived on the other side of town to tell her about the rainbow, and her mother in turn passed the word to a neighbor. Other families saw them looking up at the sky and came out to see what was going on. Soon, more than a dozen people were appreciating that beautiful rainbow—all because one lady made a phone call. Eger observes:

> Why is it that bad news travels fast? We habitually keep one another updated on the latest burglaries, jet crashes and divorces. But how often do we tell a friend or neighbor about a nest of robins, a baby's first steps, a new kitten or an inspirational book we've read? It's the little things that add color and texture to our days, so why not share the Rainbow?[6]

Yes, why not, indeed? Share life's simple pleasures with others and always remember to share life's greatest pleasure—God's grace.

After the Storm—the Rainbow!

Do you remember the all-American family whose story of multiple tragedies became the first letter to be shared back in chapter 1? As I was preparing to ship this manuscript to the publisher, another letter from the same mother came in, not describing more tragedy, thank God, but with GOOD NEWS:

> In these—our glorious Christian lives—the "Paschal cycle" of dying and rising goes on and on. The trials ("dyings") we experienced from '86 through '91 are now giving way to some

wonderful risings. We have a grand new son-in-law. Our anorexic daughter grew into a beautiful young woman, valedictorian of her class with a four-year scholarship to a great university. We are grateful for the progress of modern psychiatry coupled with an expert knowledge of pharmacology. The depressed daughter has been helped. The alcohol-addicted son has gone to AA and by the grace of God has enjoyed, so far, six months of sobriety.

There's even more, but that's enough to confirm how all things work together for good for those who love God. (Romans 8, right?)

I guess the best thing is what I'll use to close. After my son's suicide, one of the recommendations on a list of "grieving techniques" was, "Ask God to give you a sign that your loved one is with Him." This was not my usual way of praying, but I felt led to ask for the resolution of an incredibly difficult situation. Last November (two years and one month after his death), the sign came bright and clear and the situation has been clearly <u>sustained by the grace of God!</u>

P.S. Thank God <u>a much brighter day</u> has dawned for us!

This joyful mom's letter is a special sparkle I just had to tuck in before closing this book. She knows from experience the wisdom in a cross-stitch that hangs on the wall of my Joy Room. It says:

> THE SOUL WOULD HAVE NO RAINBOWS
> IF THE EYES HAD NO TEARS.

One of my favorite poets is Joan Anglund, who does bits of gentle verse with lovely illustrations. One of her collections is called "Rainbow Love," and in it she reminds us that though the days may be dark and full of gloomees we can still "keep a Rainbow in our hearts." We can choose to stay under a cloud, or we can busy ourselves in finding our rainbow.

Yes, the rainbow is God's gift to us to remind us of His greater gift—His amazing grace. His grace is ALWAYS THERE to draw upon *when we remember to do so*. So, pack up your gloomees in that great big box, then sit on the lid and laugh and . . .

ALWAYS REMEMBER TO TAKE
YOUR RAINBOW WITH YOU.[7]

Discussion Guide

Because many readers use my books in Spatula groups and other sessions, I've included these questions to help you get your discussions started.

Introduction **If It's Free, It's Advice;**
If You Pay for It, It's Counseling;
If You Can Use Either One, It's a Miracle!

1. Why is it important to share your problems with others?

2. What has been the most difficult part of your problem to accept?

3. Where have you already looked for help and comfort? Which sources helped and which ones didn't?

Chapter 1 **We're All in This Together . . .**
You're Just in a Little Deeper

1. How has your current situation helped you look at your life from a new perspective? How have your priorities changed?

2. How can you look at your problem with a positive attitude? Can you find something to be happy about or thankful for without becoming a "Pollyanna" who hides from reality?

3. Look at different translations of Ps. 69:1–3 and see the different words used to symbolize David's problems. What

words would you use to symbolize your own problems? Now use symbolic words to describe your continued trust in God.

4. Ask yourself the questions Larry Crabb asks his seminar participants: Do you use God to solve your problems? Or do you use your problems to find God? Why is it better to use our problems to find God?

**Chapter 2   If You Can't Go Around It, Over It, or Through It,
                You Had Better Negotiate with It**

1. How has humor helped accelerate your trip through the grief process?

2. Which stage of grief are you in—shock, suffering, or recovery? Describe the progress you've made through the grief process, and how you see yourself a year from now.

3. How have others impeded or assisted you in moving through the grief process?

4. Now that you have "credentials," how will you help others who are hurting?

**Chapter 3   There's One Place You Can Always
                Find Me . . .
                At the Corner of Here and Now**

1. Can you see yourself as "desert-sweetened grapefruit"? In what way is your current situation bittersweet?

2. Describe your own experiences in some or all of the five steps of emotional pain:

    a. Churn
    b. Burn
    c. Yearn
    d. Learn
    e. Turn

3. Are you ever tormented by the "if onlys" or the "blame game"? How have you overcome those regrets or accusations?

4. Do you see Proverbs 22:6 in a new light now? How has your understanding of this verse changed?

Chapter 4   You're a WHAT?!?

1. On a scale of one to ten, where do you rate the problem of having a homosexual child? If you have a homosexual child, has this rating changed since you first learned of his or her homosexuality? What caused the change?

2. How have you "handled" your child's homosexuality: critically? acceptingly? harshly? lovingly? How would you do things differently if you could start over again after learning of his homosexuality?

3. How can you show unconditional love to your homosexual child without accepting his behavior?

4. Imagine Jesus scooping up a hurting child in His loving arms. Can you also imagine that this hurting child is a homosexual? How do you think the Lord would treat one of His followers who was homosexual?

Chapter 5   Life Is a Sexually Transmitted, Terminal Disease

1. Many AIDS victims, knowing they don't have long to live, often come to grips with who they are and what is going to happen to them. How would your life change if you suddenly learned you had only a short time to live?

2. How would Jesus respond to AIDS victims?

3. Many parents have trouble letting their homosexual children with AIDS come home for care and treatment. What would it say about you as a Christian if you allowed your homosexual child with AIDS to come home?

4. How can you refute the argument that AIDS is God's punishment on homosexuals?

Chapter 6   Where Do I Put My Hatred While I Say My Prayers?

1. What has caused you to feel anger or hatred as you've wrestled with your hurt?

2. What signs of depression have you experienced? What has helped you overcome these symptoms?

3. Have you been able to "let go"? If so, what helped you release your problem and turn it over to God? If not, what is keeping you from giving it up?

4. Look at 1 Cor. 10:13. How does this verse apply to you?

Chapter 7   Pack Up Your Gloomees in a Great Big Box, Then Sit on the Lid and Laugh!

1. What are some of your "Jell-O" memories?

2. How have laughter and humor helped ease your hurt? How has God taken painful episodes in your life and used them to infuse others with joy?

3. One of the suggestions in this chapter is to "learn to laugh at yourself." Think of three things you don't like about yourself, then poke fun at them and exaggerate them.

4. I found comfort in a bubble bath, my video fireplace, and the soothing sounds of my rain stick. What brings you comfort?

Chapter 8 **At Day's End, I Turn All of My Problems Over to God . . . He's Going to Be Up Anyway**

1. Do you still believe in God the way you used to? Have your trials increased or diminished your trust in God?

2. How does this Moroccan proverb apply to your life: "Trust in God but tie your camel tight"?

3. In what ways are you to your child as God is to you?

4. How has God worked in unexpected ways to help you deal with your problems?

P.S. **Always Take Your Rainbow with You!**

1. How can God's grace make life all RIGHT despite the fact that everything is obviously all WRONG?

2. If your child has disappointed you, how has that caused you to feel guilty? How can you overcome that guilt?

3. Look at your relationship with your child. How is it a condemning relationship? How is it an encouraging relationship?

4. What does a rainbow mean to you?

Endnotes

**Chapter 1   We're All in This Together . . .
You're Just in a Little Deeper**

1. Henry Asher, "Attorney's Large Family One That Stays Together," *New Orleans Times-Picayune* (10 June 1984).
2. Ashleigh Brilliant, Pot Shots No. 1753, © Ashleigh Brilliant Enterprises, 1980. Used by permission.
3. Margaret Clarkson, *Grace Grows Best in Winter* (Grand Rapids: Zondervan, 1972), 55.
4. Psalm 42:5 KJV.
5. Michael Malloy, *Christian Counseling Services Newsletter* (Spring 1992).
6. Ibid.
7. Robert Fulghum, *Uh-Oh* (New York: Villard Books, 1991), 6.

**Chapter 2   If You Can't Go Around It, Over It, or
Through It, You Had Better Negotiate with It**

1. Robin Williams, quoted in *The Fourth 637 Things Anybody Ever Said*, Robert Byrne, comp. (New York: Fawcett Crest, 1990).
2. Ashleigh Brilliant, Pot-Shot No. 1510, © Ashleigh Brilliant Enterprises, 1979. Used by permission.
3. From a card published by Morris Printing Company, 326 West Park, Waterloo, Iowa 50701. Used by permission.

4. Granger Westberg, *Good Grief,* copyright © 1962 Fortress Press. Reprinted by permission of Augsburg Fortress.

5. Westberg, *Good Grief,* 7.

6. Westberg, *Good Grief,* 13.

7. Gini Kopecky, "Have a Good Cry," *Redbook* (May 1992), 109.

8. Paul R. Van Gorder, *Daily Bread,* July 1988.

9. From a card printed by David M & Company, 6029 Etiwanda Avenue, Tarzana, California 91356, © 1986.

10. Westberg, *Good Grief,* 46.

Chapter 3   There's One Place You Can Always Find Me . . . At the Corner of Here and Now

1. Taken from the Dear Abby column by Abigail Van Buren. Copyright 1992 UNIVERSAL PRESS SYNDICATE. Reprinted with permission. All rights reserved.

2. Barbara Johnson, *Stick A Geranium in Your Hat and Be Happy* (Dallas: Word, 1990), 66–67.

3. Robert Fulghum, *Uh-Oh: Some Observations from Both Sides of the Refrigerator Door* (New York: Villard Books, 1991), 30.

4. Planet Greetings, Box 410, Fresh Meadows, N.Y. 11365.

5. Charles Swindoll, *You and Your Child* (Nashville: Thomas Nelson, 1977), 20.

6. Fritz Ridenour, *What Teen-Agers Wish Their Parents Knew About Kids* (Waco, Tex.: Word, 1982), 64.

7. This line is part of the dialogue between actresses Jessica Tandy and Cathy Bates in the movie *Fried Green Tomatoes.* Produced by 20th Century Fox, 1991.

8. Alan Francis, *Everything Men Know About Women* (Austin, Tex.: Newport House, 1990).

9. See Margaret Nelson, "Too Tough to Die," *People Weekly* (3 February 1992), 30. Later reports revealed that the surgery had been successful and the reattached arms were beginning to work (see Margaret Nelson and Karen S. Schneider, "Comeback Kid," *People Weekly* [25 May 1992], 44).

10. Psalm 107:35 RSV.

11. Source unknown.

12. © Recycled Paper Products, Inc. All rights reserved. Original design by John Richard Allen. Reprinted by permission.

13. Ashleigh Brilliant, Pot Shots No. 981, © Ashleigh Brilliant Enterprises, 1976. Used by permission.

Chapter 4   You're a WHAT?!?

1. "Most Gay Readers Glad About Orientation," Ann Landers, *San Gabriel Valley Tribune* (26 April 1992), D6. Permission granted by Ann Landers and Creators Syndicate.

2. Anita Worthen, "Guess Who's Coming to Dinner," *Love in Action* (1988).

3. Herbert Vander Lugt, "How to Love Unconditionally," *Discovery Digest* (July-August 1982): 48–51.

4. From a message presented by Stephen Arterburn in February 1991 at Biola College, La Mirada, California.

5. "From This Moment on . . . Love!" *Moment Ministries*, 235 E. Chestnut, Monrovia, California 91016.

6. Ashleigh Brilliant, Pot-Shots No. 1027, © Ashleigh Brilliant Enterprises, 1977. Used by permission.

7. Ashleigh Brilliant, Pot-Shots, No. 2212, Ashleigh Brilliant Enterprises © 1991. Used by permission.

Chapter 5   Life Is a Sexually Transmitted, Terminal Disease

1. A slogan of Love & Action, 3 Church Circle, Annapolis, Maryland 21401. Used by permission.

2. See Revelation 6:8.

3. Statistics on AIDS reported in "Straight Talk About HIV/AIDS," *Staying Current* 4, No. 2 (March/April 1992): 1.

This is the newsletter of AIDS Information Ministries, P.O. Box 136116, Fort Worth, Texas 76136.

4. Ibid., 2.

5. Harold Ivan Smith, "Christians! AIDS Victims Need Your Help," *Charisma* (September 1987), 38.

6. Philip Yancey, "Jogging Past the AIDS Clinic," *Christianity Today* (7 March 1986), 64.

7. Ibid.

8. Wayne E. Caldwell, "Moments with Readers," *Wesleyan Advocate* 149, No. 7 (July 1991).

9. Jerry Arterburn with his brother, Stephen Arterburn, *How Will I Tell My Mother?* (Nashville: Oliver Nelson, 1988), 126–27.

10. Ashleigh Brilliant, Pot-Shots No. 295, © Ashleigh Brilliant Enterprises, 1971. Used by permission.

Chapter 6   Where Do I Put My Hatred While I Say My Prayers?

1. Ashleigh Brilliant, Pot Shots No. 595, © Ashleigh Brilliant Enterprises, 1974. Used by permission.

2. Source unknown.

3. Carl Sherman, "Is It Just a Mood or Real Depression?" *Family Circle* (1 April 1992), 65.

4. Frank B. Minirth and Paul D. Meier, *Happiness Is a Choice* (Grand Rapids: Baker, 1978), 124–28.

5. Ibid., 125.

6. Bob Davies and Lori Torkelson. Reprinted with permission from "Love in Action," P. O.Box 2655, San Rafael, California 94912.

7. Lewis B. Smedes, *How Can It Be All Right When Everything Is All Wrong?* (New York: Pocket Books, a division of Simon and Schuster, 1982).

8. Ibid.

9. From the poem "Letting Go." Author unknown.

Chapter 7   Pack Up Your Gloomees in a Great Big Box, Then Sit on the Lid and Laugh!

1. Source unknown.
2. Included in *Poems That Touch the Heart*, A. L. Alexander, compiler, (New York: Doubleday, 1956), 304.
3. Diane Suchetka, "Laughter . . . Is the Best Medicine," *The Orange County Register* (10 March 1992), E-1.
4. Ibid., E-1, E-2.
5. See Charles Swindoll, *Living on the Ragged Edge* (Dallas: Word, 1985), 262. Swindoll thanks his friend, Dr. Ken Gangel, for the remark, "Have a blast while you last!"
6. Source unknown.
7. Dr. Paul McGhee, quoted in Diane Suchetka, "Laughter . . . Is the Best Medicine," *The Orange County Register* (10 March 1992), E-1.
8. Betty Henry Taylor, "Sound of Rain," *Opening Up Closets and Dumping Out Drawers* (New York: Chrysalis Publishing, 1991), 98. Used by permission.
9. George Goldtrap, *Laughter Works* newsletter, 3, no. 2 (Spring 1991).

Chapter 8   At Day's End, I Turn All of My Problems Over to God . . . He's Going to Be Up Anyway

1. Danny Dutton. Publishing source unknown.
2. John White, "Relinquishment of Adult Children," *Equipping the Saints* 5, No. 2 (Spring 1991).
3. Bob Davies, Love in Action, San Rafael, California.
4. Source unknown.
5. Source unknown.
6. From L. M. Montgomery, *Anne of Avonlea* (New York: New American Library, 1987).

P.S.   Always Take Your Rainbow with You!

1. Lewis B. Smedes, *How Can It Be All Right When Everything Is All Wrong?* (New York: Pocket Books, a division of Simon and Schuster, 1982), 17.
2. Ibid., 18.
3. Lawrence O. Richards, *Expository Dictionary of Bible Words* (Grand Rapids: Zondervan, 1985), 317.
4. Smedes, 11.
5. See Genesis 9:8–16.
6. Phyllis Eger, "Share the Rainbow," *Sunshine Magazine* (May 1989).
7. Adapted from poetry by Joan Walsh Anglund, "Rainbow Love," Determined Productions, P.O. Box 2150, San Francisco, California 94126.